EUROPEAN CORP.

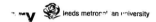
leeds metropolitan university

For decades, Europe has sought to become more financially integrated with the United States, and thus European legal institutions, regulatory, governance and accounting practices have faced pressures to adapt to international competitive markets. Against this backdrop, European corporate governance systems have been criticized as being less efficient than the Anglo-American market-based systems.

This textbook examines the unique dimensions and qualities of European corporate governance. Reforms of key institutions, the doctrine of shareholder value, and the seemingly irresistible growth of CEO power and reward are critically analyzed. The book brings out the richness of European corporate governance systems, as well as highlighting historical weaknesses that will require further work for a sustainable corporate governance environment in the future.

In light of the most severe financial crisis since the 1930s, this intelligent look at European corporate governance makes it a vital textbook for courses on corporate governance and a great supplementary textbook on a host of business, management and accounting courses.

Thomas Clarke is Director of the Centre for Corporate Governance and Professor of Management at UTS Sydney, Australia. He is also Visiting Professor at the University of Paris IX Dauphine, and at ESC-Lille, France, and the author of *Theories of Corporate Governance* and *International Corporate Governance*, both published by Routledge.

Jean-François Chanlat is Professor of Management and Director of the EMBA program at the University of Paris IX Dauphine, France. He is also Director of the Centre for Research on Management and Organization.

European Corporate Governance

Readings and perspectives

Edited by Thomas Clarke and
Jean-François Chanlat

Routledge
Taylor & Francis Group

LONDON AND NEW YORK

First published 2009 by Routledge
2 Park Square, Milton Park, Abingdon, Oxon OX14 4RN

Simultaneously published in the USA and Canada
by Routledge
270 Madison Ave, New York, NY 10016

Routledge is an imprint of the Taylor & Francis Group, an informa business

Typeset in by Saxon Graphics Ltd, Derby
Printed and bound in Great Britain by the MPG Books Group in the UK

British Library Cataloguing in Publication Data
A catalogue record for this book is available from the British Library

Library of Congress Cataloguing in Publication Data
European corporate governance: readings and perspectives / edited by Thomas Clarke and Jean-François Chanlat.
p. cm.
Includes bibliographical references and index.
1. Corporate governance--Europe. I. Clarke, Thomas, 1950- II. Chanlat, Jean-François, 1950-
HD2741.E895 2009
338.6094--dc22
2008054271

ISBN 10: 0-415-40533-5 (hbk)
ISBN 10: 0-415-40534-3 (pbk)
ISBN 10: 0-203-87589-3 (ebk)

ISBN 13: 978-0-415-40533-1 (hbk)
ISBN 13: 978-0-415-40534-8 (pbk)
ISBN 13: 978-0-203-87589-6 (ebk)

CONTENTS

FIGURES

TABLES

ACKNOWLEDGEMENTS

The authors and the publisher would like to thank the following publishers:

Blackwell for permission to reprint Kees van Kersbergen and Frans Van Warden, Governance as a Bridge Between Disciplines: Cross-disciplinary Inspiration Regarding Shifts in Governance and Problems of Governability, Accountability and Legitimacy, from *European Journal of Political Research*, 43, 143–171, 2000.

Sage for permission to reprint Josef Wieland, Corporate Governance, Values, Management and Standards: A European Perspective, from *Business and Society*, 44, 1, 74–93, 2005.

Blackwell for permission to reprint Andrea Melis, Corporate Governance in Italy, *Corporate Governance: An International Review*, 8, 4, 347–355, 2000.

Routledge for permission to reprint Richard Deeg, Remaking Italian Capitalism? The Politics of Corporate Governance Reform, from *West European Politics*, Routledge, 28, 3, 521–548, 2005.

Taylor and Francis for permission to reprint Francis Morin, A Transformation in the French Model of Shareholding and Management, from *Economy and Society*, 29, 1, 36–53, 2000.

Maney Publishing for permission to reprint Andrew Pendleton, How Far Does the United Kingdom have a Market-based System of Corporate Governance? A Review and Evaluation of Recent Developments, from *Competition and Change*, 9, 1, 107–127, 2005.

Routledge for permission to reprint Lucian Cernat, The Emerging European Corporate Governance Model: Anglo-Saxon, Continental, or Still the Century of Diversty?, from *Journal of European Public Policy*, 11, 1, 147–166, 2004.

Maney Publishing for permission to reprint Christel Lane, Changes in Corporate Governance of German Corporations: Convergence to the Anglo-American Model?, from *Competition and Change*, 7, 2–3, 79–100, 2003.

Edward Elgar for permission to reprint Michel Aglietta and Antoine Rebérioux, Convergence of Divergence? The Outlines of an Answer, in Michel Aglietta and Antoine Rebérioux, *Corporate Governance Adrift: A Critique of Shareholder Value*, Copyright 2005, pp. 60–74.

CEPS and the Centre for Transatlantic Relations for permission to reprint Karel Lannoo, A Transatlantic Financial Market?, in Daniel S. Hamilton and Joseph P. Quinlan, *Deep Integration: How Transatlantic Markets are Leading Globalisation*, Copyright 2005, pp. 122–131.

Bernard Colasse for his permission to reprint Bernard Colasse, International Accounting Harmonisation: The Resistible Rise of the IASC/IASB, from *Gérer et Comprendre*, 75, 30–40, 2004.

Blackwell for permission to reprint Joseph A. McCahery and Eric P.M. Vermeulen, Does the European Company Prevent the 'Delaware Effect'? from *European Law Journal*, 11, 6, 785–801, 2005.

Routledge for permission to reprint Alistair Howard, UK Corporate Governance: To What End a New Regulatory State? From *West European Politics*, 29, 3, 410–432, 2006.

Sage Publishing for permission to reprint Michel Goyer, Varieties of Institutional Investors and national Models of Capitalism: The Transformation of Corporate Governance in France and Germany, from *Politics and Society*, 34, 3, 399–430, 2006.

The American Economic Association for permission to reprint Luca Enriques and Paulo Volpin, Corporate Governance Reforms in Continental Europe, from *Journal of Economic Perspectives*, 21, 1, 117–140, 2007.

Routledge for permission to reprint Ulrich Jürgens, Yannick Lung, Guiseppe Volpato and Vincent Frigant, The Arrival of Shareholder Value in the European Auto Industry: A Case Study Comparison of Four Car Makers, from *Competition and Change*, Routledge, 6, 1, 61–80, 2002.

Edward Elgar for permission to reprint Michel Aglietta and Antoine Rébérioux, The Theory of the Firm and Shareholder Value in Aglietta and Rébérioux, from *Corporate Governance Adrift: A Critique of Shareholder Value*, Copyright 2005, pp. 32–48.

Maney Publishing for permission to reprint Sigurt Vitols, Negotiated Shareholder Value: The German Variant of an Anglo-American Practice, from *Competition and Change*, 8, 4, 357–574, 2004.

Carfax Publishing for permission to reprint Alexander Börsch, Globalisation, Shareholder Value, Restructuring: the (Non) Transformation of Siemens, *New Political Economy*, 9, 3, 365–388, 2004.

Ernie Englander and Allen Kaufman for permission to reprint Ernie Englander and Allen Kaufman, Executive Compensation, Political Economy, and Managerial Control: The Transformation of Managerial Incentive Structures and Ideology, 1950–2000, George Washington University SMPP Working Paper 03–01, p.34, 2004.

Maney Publishing for permission to reprint Robert Boyer, From Shareholder Value to CEO Power: the Paradox of the 1990s, *Competition and Change*, 9, 1, 7–47, 2005.

CONTRIBUTORS

Michel Aglietta, University of Paris X Nanterre, France

Alexander Börsch, Warwick Business School, UK

Robert Boyer, PSE and CEPREMAP–ENS, France

Jean-François Chanlat, University of Paris IX Dauphine, France

Lucian Cernat, United Nations Conference UNCTAD, Switzerland

Thomas Clarke, University of Technology, Sydney, Australia

Bernard Colasse, University of Paris IX Dauphine, France

Richard Deeg, Temple University, USA

Ernie Englander, George Washington University, USA

Luca Enriques, University of Bologna, Italy

Vincent Frigant, University of Montesquieu-Bordeaux IV, France

Michel Goyer, Warwick Business School, UK

Alistair Howard, Temple University, USA

Ulrich Jürgens, Social Science Research Center Berlin, Germany

Allen Kaufman, University of New Hampshire, USA

Christel Lane, University of Cambridge, UK

Karel Lannoo, Centre for European Policy Studies, Brussels

Yannick Lung, Université Montesquieu-Bordeaux IV, France

Joseph A. McCahery, University of Amsterdam, The Netherlands

Andrea Melis, Università degli Studi di Cagliari, Italy

François Morin, Université Toulouse, France

Andrew Pendleton, Manchester Metropolitan University Business School, UK

Antoine Rebérioux, University of Paris X Nanterre, France

Kees van Kersbergen, Vrije Universiteit, The Netherlands

Frans van Waarden, Utrecht University, The Netherlands

Erik P.M. Vermeulen, Tilburg University, The Netherlands

Sigurt Vitols, Social Science Research Center Berlin, Germany

Giuseppe Volpato, Ca' Foscari University of Venice, Italy

Paulo Volpin, London Business School, UK

Josef Wieland, University of Applied Sciences, Germany

INTRODUCTION: A NEW WORLD DISORDER? The Recurring Crises in Anglo-American Corporate Governance and the Increasing Impact on European Economies and Institutions

Thomas Clarke and Jean-François Chanlat

INTRODUCTION

The prolonged systemic crisis in international financial markets commencing in 2007/2008 was also a crisis in corporate governance and regulation. The most severe financial disaster since the Great Depression of the 1930s exposed the dangers of unregulated financial markets and nominal corporate governance. The crisis originated in Wall Street where de-regulation unleashed highly incentivized investment banks to flood world markets with toxic financial products. As a stunning series of banks and investment companies collapsed in the United States and then in Europe, a frightening dimension of the global economy became fully apparent: a new world disorder of violently volatile markets and deep financial insecurity. Advocating systemic change President Nicolas Sarkozy of France proclaimed, "The world came within a whisker of catastrophe. We can't run the risk of it happening again. Self-regulation as a way of solving all problems is finished. Laissez-faire is finished. The all-powerful market that always knows best is finished" (*Washington Post* September 28, 2008), as if presidential rhetoric alone could sweep away an enveloping, financially-driven political economy.

For decades Europe has actively sought deeper financial integration with the United States, reducing barriers to trade, and liberalizing markets, leading onwards towards globalization. Transatlantic integration is forging economic relations involving financial markets, services, manufacturing, pharmaceuticals, telecommunications and other industry sectors (CTR/CEPS 2005). However, for this effort at integrating markets and businesses to succeed, a supporting integration of institutions, regulation and corporate governance is required. European legal institutions, regulatory, governance and accounting practices face insistent pressures to adapt to the reality of international competitive markets. The European relationship-based corporate governance systems in particular are often criticized as being inherently less efficient than the Anglo-American market based systems.

This book seeks to challenge this contention by examining the unique dimensions and qualities of European corporate governance, exploring the different varieties of capitalism they manifest, and critically inquiring further into the ongoing debate on convergence or diversity of governance systems. A critique is offered of the reform and transformation of European corporate governance institutions, the increasing impact of the doctrine of shareholder value, and the apparently irresistible growth of CEO power and reward. The objective of the book is to demonstrate the richness of the variety of European corporate governance institutions, and to show how this variety contributes to the unique qualities of creativity and innovation in European industry, as well as to highlight specific historical and structural weaknesses of European systems that will require remedy if uniquely European governance systems are to remain viable, and European industry sustainable.

IMPLICATIONS OF THE 2008 WALL STREET FINANCIAL CRISIS

America's financial institutions have not managed risk; they have created it. (Joseph Stiglitz 2008a)

The apparent ascendancy of Anglo-American markets and governance institutions was profoundly questioned by the scale and contagion of the 2008 global financial crisis. The crisis was initiated by falling house prices and rising mortgage default rates in the highly inflated US housing market. A severe credit crisis developed through 2007 into 2008 as financial institutions became fearful of the potential scale of the subprime mortgages concealed in the securities they had bought. As a result banks refused to lend to each other because of increased counter-party risk that other banks might default. A solvency crisis ensued as banks were slow to admit to the great holes in their accounts which the subprime mortgages had caused (partly because they were themselves unaware of the seriousness of the problem), and the difficulty in raising capital to restore their balance sheets. As an increasing number of financial institutions collapsed in the US, UK, and Europe, successive government efforts to rescue individual institutions, and to offer general support for the financial system, did not succeed in restoring confidence as markets continued in free-fall, with stock exchanges across the world losing half their value (Figure I.1).

Financial insecurity rapidly became contagious internationally as fears of a global economic recession became widespread and stock markets around the world crashed. This financial crisis was larger in scale than any crisis since the 1930s Great Depression, involving losses conservatively estimated in October 2008 by the IMF as potentially $1,400 billion dollars, eclipsing earlier crises in Asia, Japan and the US (Figure 2). Martin Wolf was quick to realise the implications of the crisis, as he put it in the *Financial Times* (September 5, 2007):

We are living through the first crisis of the brave new world of securitised financial markets. It is too early to tell how economically important the upheaval will prove. But nobody can doubt its significance for the financial system. Its origins lie with credit expansion and financial innovations in the US itself. It cannot be blamed on 'crony capitalism' in peripheral economies, but rather on responsibility in the core of the world economy.

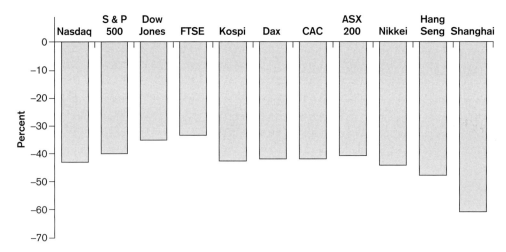

Source: Stock Exchanges

Figure I.1 **Collapsing stock exchanges in 2008 global financial crisis**

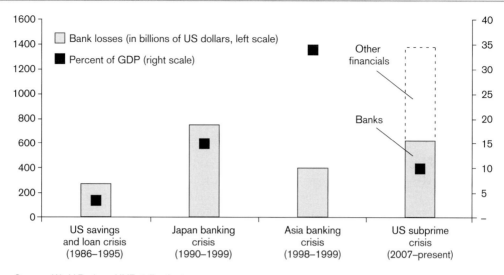

Sources: World Bank; and IMF staff estimates.
Note: US subprime costs represent staff estimates of losses on banks and other financial istitutions from Table 1.1. All costs are real in 2007 dollars. Asia includes Indonesia, Malaysia, Korea, the Philippines, and Thailand.
Source: IMF (2008:9)

Figure I.2 **Comparison of international financial crises**

Origins of the crisis

In the cyclical way markets work, the origins of the 2008 financial crisis may be found in the solutions to the previous market crisis. The US Federal Reserve under the sage Alan Greenspan responded to the collapse of confidence caused by the dot-com disaster and Enron failures in 2001/2002 by reducing US interest rates to 1 percent, their lowest in 45 years, flooding the market with cheap credit to jump-start the economy back into life. US business did recover faster than expected, but the cheap credit had washed into the financial services and housing sectors producing the largest speculative bubbles ever witnessed in the American economy (Fleckenstein 2008). The scene was set by the 1999 dismantling of the 1932 Glass-Steagall Act which had separated commercial banking from investment banking and insurance services, opening the way for a consolidation of the vastly expanding and increasingly competitive US financial services industry. Phillips (2008:5) describes this as a "burgeoning debt and credit complex":

Vendors of credit cards, issuers of mortgages and bonds, architects of asset-backed securities and structured investment vehicles—occupied the leading edge. The behemoth financial conglomerates, Citigroup, JP Morgan Chase et al., were

liberated in 1999 for the first time since the 1930s to marshal banking, insurance, securities, and real estate under a single, vaulting institutional roof.

In this newly emboldened finance sector the name of the game was *leverage* – the capacity to access vast amounts of credit cheaply to take over businesses and to do deals. Wall Street investment banks and hedge funds flourished with their new found access to cheap credit. Exotic financial instruments were devised and marketed internationally: futures, options and swaps evolved into collateralized debt obligations (CDOs), credit default swaps (CDSs), and many other acronyms, all of which packaged vast amounts of debt to be traded on the securities markets. Abandoning their traditional financial conservatism banks looked beyond taking deposits and lending to the new businesses of wealth management, and eagerly adopted new instruments and business models. As the IMF put it

Banking systems in the major countries have gone through a process of disintermediation—that is, a greater share of financial intermediation is now taking place through tradable securities (rather than bank loans and deposits)...Banks have increasingly moved financial risks (especially credit risks) off their balance sheets and into securities markets—for example, by pooling and converting assets into tradable securities and entering into interest rate swaps and other derivatives transactions—in response both to regulatory incentives such as capital requirements and to internal incentives to improve risk-adjusted returns on capital for shareholders and to be more competitive… Securitization makes the pricing and allocation of capital more efficient because changes in financial risks are reflected much more quickly in asset prices and flows than on bank balance sheets. The downside is that markets have become more volatile, and this volatility could pose a threat to financial stability.

(Hauster 2002:2)

Global derivatives markets

As the new financial instruments were developed and marketed, the securities markets grew massively in the 2000s dwarfing the growth of the real economy. For example, according to the Bank of International Settlements the global derivatives markets grew at the rate of 32 percent per annum from 1990, and the notional amount of derivatives reached 106 trillion dollars by 2002, 477 trillion dollars by 2006, and exceeded 531 trillion dollars by 2008 (though gross market value is a small fraction of this) (McKinsey and Company 2008:20). The supposed purpose of this increasingly massive exercise was to hedge risk and add liquidity to the financial system. Derivatives allow financial institutions and corporations to take greater and more complex risks such as issuing more mortgages and corporate debt, because they may protect debt holders against losses. Since derivatives contracts are widely traded, risk may be further limited, though this increases the number of parties exposed if defaults occur.

> Complex derivatives were at the heart of the credit market turmoil that rippled through financial markets in 2007, raising concerns about the financial players' abilities to manage risk as capital markets rapidly evolve. Unlike equities, debt securities and bank deposits, which represent financial claims against future earnings by households and companies, derivatives are risk-shifting agreements among financial market participants.

(McKinsey and Company 2008:20)

Because of this fundamental difference and indeterminacy McKinsey did not include derivatives in their calculation of the value of global financial assets, an indication of the ephemeral quality of derivatives.

Yet derivatives certainly have their defenders who claim that they make an essential contribution to international liquidity. A riveting analysis of the legacy of the former Chairman of the Federal Reserve in the *New York Times* detailed how Alan Greenspan defended derivatives markets as an innovation helping to develop and stabilize the international financial system, "Not only have individual financial institutions become less vulnerable to shocks from underlying risk factors, but also the financial system as a whole has become more resilient." Others were less sanguine, and both George Soros and Warren Buffett avoided investing in derivatives contracts because of their impenetrable complexity. Buffet described derivatives in 2003 as "financial weapons of mass destruction, carrying dangers that, while now latent, are potentially lethal," and pointed out that collateralized debt obligation contracts could stretch to 750,000 pages of impenetrable (and presumably unread) text (*New York Times* October 8, 2008).

Greenspan was skeptical about successive legislative efforts to regulate derivatives in the 1990s. Charles A. Bowsher, head of the General Accounting Office, commenting on a report to Congress identifying significant weaknesses in the regulatory oversight of derivatives, said in testimony to the House Sub-Committee on Telecommunications and Finance in 1994:

> The sudden failure or abrupt withdrawal from trading of any of these large US dealers could cause liquidity problems in the markets and could also pose risks to others, including federally insured banks and the financial system as a whole. In some cases intervention has and could result in a financial bailout paid for or guaranteed by taxpayers.

In his testimony at the time, Greenspan was reassuring. "Risks in financial markets, including derivatives markets, are being regulated by private parties. There is nothing involved in federal regulation per se which makes it superior to market regulation," though he did accept derivatives could amplify crises because they connect together financial institutions: "The very efficiency that is involved here means that if a crisis were to occur, that that crisis is transmitted at a far faster pace and with some greater virulence." When the Commodity Futures Trading Commission, the federal agency which regulates options and futures trading examined derivatives regulation in 1997, the head of the Commission, Brooksley E. Born said in testimony to Congress that such opaque trading might "threaten our regulated markets or, indeed, our economy without any federal agency knowing about it," but she was chastized for taking steps that would lead to a financial crisis by Treasury officials (*New York Times* October 8, 2008).

The explosive potential of derivatives was always present, as the implosion of the hedge fund Long Term Capital Management (LTCM) in 1998 revealed. With equity of $4.72 billion and debt of $124 billion LTCM had managed to secure off-balance sheet derivative positions of $1.29 trillion (mostly in interest rate swaps). The rescue of LTCM by a consortium of banks led by the Federal Reserve Bank of New York in order to maintain the integrity of the financial system, was a harbinger of how a decade later on massive systemic financial risk-taking would be rescued by governments after the event, rather than regulated by governments before the event.

The subprime mortgage debacle

The subprime mortgage phenomenon demonstrated how unconscionable risks could be taken on by investment banks, concealed in securities, and sold on to other financial institutions that had little idea of the risk they were assuming. Encouraged by a political climate in the United States that favored extending home ownership, by the rapid inflation in the US housing market, and by the ready availability of cheap credit, mortgage companies across the United Stages began extending house loans to people with little prospect of ever repaying them. While asset prices continued to rise this problem was concealed for individuals who could borrow more money using their increased house equity as collateral. Banks did not feel exposed due to the apparently endless increase in asset values backing their loans. From 2001 subprime mortgages increased from a small segment of the market, to hundreds of billions of dollars of mortgages by 2006 (Figure I.3).These mortgage contracts were sold on to larger financial institutions, who bundled them into securities in a manner that ultimately proved fatal for a significant part of the international financial system as Le Roy (2008) explains:

Securitisation becomes increasingly complicated when financial institutions choose to retain Mortgage Backed Securities (MBS), and re-securitise pools of MBS bonds into Collateralised Debt Obligations (CDOs). Securitisation becomes more complicated again when institutions create Special

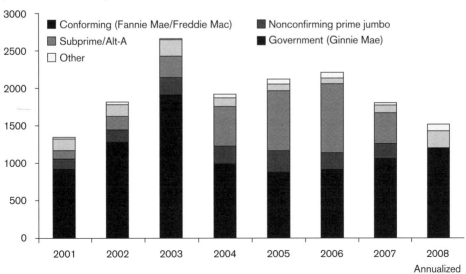

Mortgage Securitizations
(In billions of US dollars)

- Conforming (Fannie Mae/Freddie Mac)
- Nonconfirming prime jumbo
- Subprime/Alt-A
- Government (Ginnie Mae)
- Other

Sources: US Board of Governors of the Federal Reserve System; UK Office of National Statistics; European Central Bank; and inside MBS and ABS; IMF staff estimates.
Source: IMF (2008:68)

Figure I.3 **The growth of subprime mortgages in the United States**

Investment Vehicles (SIVs), off balance sheet entities which hold pools of MBSs and CDOs and issue short and medium term debt (rather than longer term debt like most CDOs) referred to as Asset Backed Commercial Paper (ABCP) (Rosen 2007; Schwarcz 2008). It is easy to see why securitisation is seen as a "shadow banking system", whereby off balance sheet entities and over the counter (OTC) credit instruments lie outside the reach of regulators and capital adequacy guidelines, making risk increasingly difficult to price, manage and quantify (Whalen 2008; Schwarcz 2008). The increasing complexity of securitisation and the change in lending practices to "originate to distribute" led to acute moral hazard, where each participant in the mortgage chain was trying to make continuously greater returns whilst assuming that they passed on all the associated risks to other participants (Lewis 2007; Ee and Xiong 2008). Financial innovation was meant to distribute risks evenly throughout the financial system, thus reducing the risk for the system as a whole, however increased risk tolerance, moral hazard and an insatiable thirst for return pushed all participants to borrow larger sums and to take increasingly bigger bets. The result was that whilst risk was dispersed for the individual players, it was amplified for the entire financial system (Lim 2008).

The financial system was exposed as the US housing bubble burst as house mortgage holders exhausted the teaser low rates that had enticed them into borrowing, and were confronted by much higher rates of repayment they could not afford. With non-recursive loans in the US, mortgagees could simply walk away from their debt, posting the keys back to the bank ('jingle mail') leaving properties in many inner urban areas to become derelict, as advancing foreclosures emptied whole neighborhoods in some cities. This surge in mortgage defaults and foreclosures was followed by a plunge in the prices of mortgage-backed securities. The subprime crisis unfolded as it became apparent that subprime mortgages had been mixed with other assets in CDOs, somehow given double A ratings by the ratings agencies, and marketed world-wide. Innovative securities, originally conceived to insulate against risk, had through misuse metastasized into the wide distribution of acutely dangerous and uncontrollable risks. Adrian Cadbury observed on this:

I suggest that there are two aspects of what went wrong. One was that in general risk was undervalued by the financial institutions. The second was that the banks simply did not know where their risks lay. Subprime mortgages were parcelled out by banks and sold through perhaps three or four levels of intermediary. When house prices fell people handed in their keys. The intermediaries found they were in the property business which they could not finance and in turn each level went bust. The banks found that they were ultimately responsible, a contingent liability they were unaware of and had not provided for. I think a sound rule is that if you do not understand the business you are getting into, don't!

(email communication, November 6, 2008)

The opaqueness and complexity of the financial instruments which served as a means to conceal the toxicity of the trillions of dollars of securities developed and sold by the investment banks returned to haunt them with the realization that no international financial institution fully understood how much of these subprime assets were buried in their portfolios, and with the growing possibility of counter-party failure, the credit markets seized up, and banks and other financial institutions began falling over as they announced huge write downs, not only in the US, but the UK, and throughout Europe (Table I.1). Instead of risk being hedged, it had become inter-connected and international, and unknown.

US FINANCIAL INSTITUTION FAILURES

As financial institutions, over-burdened with debt, desperately attempted to *deleverage* by selling assets, including the mortgage backed securities, the cruel 'paradox of deleveraging' was exposed: that the firesale of assets simply drives asset prices down, and left the banks in an even worse position. (Paul Volker, the former President of the US Federal Reserve, whom President Obama welcomed back as an economic adviser, referred to "the transient pleasures of extreme leverage.") Caught in these financial maneuvres, one of the largest Wall Street investment banks Bear Stearns failed in March 2008, and in a deal sponsored by the US Federal Reserve was sold to JPMorgan Chase. With the collapse of a string of venerable Wall Street institutions the US Treasury, Federal Reserve, and SEC were galvanized into action, and selectively nationalized those companies thought too vital to the US financial structure to allow to fail, arranged the

	Company	Country	(bn $US)
1	Citigroup	US	66.6
2	Wachovia	US	52.7
3	Merrill Lynch	US	54.6
4	Washington Mutual	US	45.6
5	UBS	Switzerland	44.2
6	HSBC	UK	27.4
7	Bank of America	US	21.2
8	JPMorgan Chase	US	18.8
9	Morgan Stanley	US	15.7
10	IKB Deutsche	Germany	14.7
11	Royal Bank of Scotland	UK	16.5
12	Lehman Brothers	US	18.2
13	AIG	US	16.8
14	Fannie Mae	US	12.7
15	Deutsche Bank	Germany	11.4
16	Ambac	US	10.3
17	Wells Fargo	US	10
18	MBIA Inc.	US	9.4
19	Barclays	UK	9.2
20	Crédit Agricole	France	8.6
21	Crédit Suisse	Switzerland	8.1
22	HBOS	UK	7.5
23	Canadian Imperial Bank of Commerce	Canada	7.1
24	Fortis	Belgium/Netherlands	6.9
25	Bayerische Landesbank	Germany	6.7
26	Freddie Mac	US	6.7
27	ING	Netherlands	6.5
28	Société Générale	France	6.4
29	Mizuho Financial Group	Japan	6.2
30	Dresdner Bank	Germany	5
31	Bear Sterns	US	3.4
32	WestLB	Germany	3.1
33	BNP Paribas	France	2.7
34	UniCredit	Italy	2.7
35	Lloyds TSB	UK	2.6
36	Nomura Holdings	Japan	2.5
37	DZ Bank	Germany	2
38	Natixis	France	2
39	Swiss Re	Switzerland	1.8
40	HSH Nordbank	Germany	1.7
41	LBBW	Germany	1.7
42	Commerzbank	Germany	1.2
43	Mitsubishi UFJ	Japan	1.2
44	Sumitomo	Japan	1.2
45	AXA	France	1.1
	Total Losses		**582.60**

Sources: Individual Banks; Central Banks.

Table I.1 **Subprime losses by international banks, October 2008**

sale of companies that could be salvaged, or allowed companies to collapse that were thought dispensable (Appendix, p.36).

In September 2008 in quick succession the two giant US mortgage corporations Fannie Mae (FNMA) and Freddie Mac (FHLMC) could not raise capital, and with $5 trillion in mortgage backed securities, the US government was forced to intervene assuming a 'conservatorship' of the agencies, investing $200 billion in preferred stock and credit. (This reversed policy, establishing these government-sponsored enterprises as private corporations in 1968 and 1970 respectively.) Within days AIG, one of the world's largest insurance companies, which was responsible for insuring many of the securities contracts of other financial institutions, was rescued by the Federal Reserve which offered a credit facility of $85 billion for a 79.9 percent equity stake (the largest government bail-out of a private company in US history, and bizarrely making the US government the major sponsor of Manchester United football club, who wore 'AIG' emblazoned on their shirts).

The investment bank Lehman Brothers was the only major institution allowed to become bankrupt, with Barclay's buying the investment arm after negotiations for Barclay's to acquire the whole firm stalled. The consequences of this fateful decision by Henry Paulson the US Treasurer (and formerly CEO of Goldman Sachs) not to rescue Lehman's reverberated painfully through the international financial system: as Lehman's derivative positions were unwound, inter-bank lending froze up, and confidence in the viability of financial institutions around the world suddenly collapsed. Merrill Lynch which had racked up $54 billion dollars in losses on asset backed securities was the third of the top five Wall Street investment banks to fail, and was sold to Bank of America for $50 billion. Washington Mutual the sixth largest bank in the US was declared bankrupt, and JPMorgan Chase bought the banking assets from the government. Wachovia, the fourth largest bank holding company, was the subject of a US$15 billion takeover from Wells Fargo contested by Citigroup.

Though this was the greatest series of government interventions in US financial markets in recent decades, the NYSE continued in free-fall, and the whole of the US banking sector appeared vulnerable. When selective assistance did not resolve the problem an enormous rescue operation offering up to $700 billion to buy up toxic securities from the financial institutions in order to restore credit markets was brought by the Bush administration to a Congress reluctant about rescuing Wall Street from its own folly. The Emergency Economic Stabilization Act 2008 authorized the US Treasurer Henry Paulson to spend up to $700 billion purchasing distressed assets, particularly mortgage-backed securities from the banks. The purpose of the act was to purchase the toxic assets, assuring the worth of the bank's remaining assets, and restoring the confidence of the market. Reflecting the widespread public opposition to the bail-out, the House of Representatives rejected the proposal, and the Dow Jones dropped 777 points—a 1.2 trillion dollars fall in market value. Criticism of the original Paulson proposals included objection to the idea that taxpayers should bail out Wall Street; the ambiguity of objectives and lack of oversight of the new agency responsible for buying assets, the prospect of over-paying for bad assets, giving the executives and investors in financial firms a windfall at taxpayers' expense; and a conviction that any purchase should be of preferred stock in the banks, avoiding the problem of valuing complex assets, and offering a greater degree of control and the possibility of a more significant return from the exercise (Stiglitz 2008b; Krugman 2008).

Finally a heavily amended proposal was eventually passed through Congress on October 3 2008 giving the Treasurer immediate access to $250 billion; following that a further $100 billion could be authorized by the President, with Congress confirming the last $350 billion. Transparency details were required for each transaction, also a set of oversight mechanisms involving a Financial Oversight Board, Congressional Oversight Panel, and Special Inspector General of the program. The Treasurer was required to obtain the right to purchase non-voting stock in companies that participated in the sale of assets giving the government an equity interest in the companies. The Treasury was required to maximize assistance to homeowners facing foreclosure. Finally companies participating in the scheme were prohibited from offering executives incentives to take excessive risks, or to offer golden parachutes to executives, and were given the right to clawback senior executive bonuses if they were later found to be based on inaccurate data. When stock markets opened the following Monday after the Act was passed, the Dow Jones was down 700 points, the FTSE down 7.9 percent, the Dax down 7.1 percent, and France's CAC 40 down 9 percent, revealing that markets were not

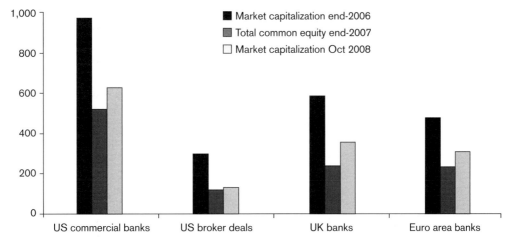

Source: Bloomberg L.P.
Note: US broker dealers include Lehman Brothers, Morgan Stanley, Goldman Sachs and Merrill Lynch. The other three categories, namely, US, UK and euro area banks include institutions that have retail banking businesses in their respective regions.

Figure I.4 **Market capitalization and equity book values of financial institutions 2006–8 (billions of US dollars)**

going to be easily reassured, and the financial crisis was becoming internationally contagious.

EUROPEAN FINANCIAL INSTITUTIONS FAILURES

All over Europe, as the contagion spread, the impact of the subprime crisis was wreaking havoc in financial institutions, threatening entire financial systems, and severely undermining the fragile unity of the European Union (Appendix). The scale of the crisis for European financial institutions, relative to the size of the sector, was becoming just as serious as for US financial institutions (Figure I.4). The first tremors of the crisis were felt in the UK, which rivals the US as the centre of the international financial system. Among the early casualties of the subprime crisis were Northern Rock, one of the largest mortgage lenders in the UK, which depended on the wholesale market for short-term credit. Northern Rock could not raise sufficient capital in September 2007, and after a run on the bank reminiscent of the 1920s, was effectively nationalized by the UK government trying desperately to contain an impending mass public financial panic. As the credit crisis worsened for institutions used to relying on the wholesale market and inter-bank lending, a liquidity crisis gripped the major British banks, while their share prices collapsed.

In September 2008 HBOS, the UK's largest mortgage lender was sold to Lloyds TSB as the government suspended the regulations limiting maximum market share of any one bank. Bradford and Bingley, another large mortgage provider, was nationalized by the government, with the sale of its savings arm to Abbey (owned by the Spanish Santander). As panic selling continued on the London Stock Exchange with HBOS and Bank of Scotland bank shares losing 40 percent of their value in a single day's trading, the UK government intervened with a £500 billion ($850) billion rescue package for eight of the largest UK banks intended to restore stability to the system. This package consisted of up to £50 billion in capital investment for the banks in exchange for preference shares, short-term loans up to £200 billion from the Bank of England, and loan guarantees for banks lending to each other of up to £250 billion. The offer of assistance was conditional on restraint in executive incentives and rewards and on dividend payments, and that banks must be able to lend to small businesses and home owners.

In other European countries the response to the crisis was largely managed on a national basis as financial institutions failed. Fortis, one of the world's largest banking, insurance and investment companies, was rescued by the Netherlands nationalizing its Dutch operations, and France's BNP Paribas buying its Belgian and Luxembourg operations. Dexia, the Belgian financial services company, was rescued by the French, Belgian, and Luxembourg governments. As the entire banking system of Iceland began to fail, the government invested €600 million for a 75 percent stake in Glitnir, the second largest bank. Finally in Germany the second largest property lender Hypo Real Estate received a €50 billion rescue coordinated by the government, including €20 billion from the Bundesbank. However the efforts of Nicolas Sarkozy as EU president to secure a coordinated response to the crisis in establishing a European fund to rescue failing banks did not meet with early success: unlike the national central banks, the European Central Bank was not a lender of last resort, simply acting as the Eurozone's monetary authority. Subsequently the announcement by Ireland and Greece, apparently followed by Germany, to guarantee all depositors' savings, led other countries, including Sweden and Denmark, to do the same—seeming to cast aside any sense of European unity in the effort to save national banking systems. Spain established its own bail-out package, and Germany and other European countries established similar provisions.

The market capitalization of the stock markets of the world had peaked at $62 trillion at the end of 2007, but by October 2008 they were in free fall, having lost 33 trillion dollars, over half of their value, in 12 months of unrelenting financial and corporate failures (Figure I.5). However in an unprecedented effort to provide a coordinated response, the central banks of the major industrial powers simultaneously lowered interest rates, as it became clear that a

systemic response was required to a systemic crisis. As the finance ministers of the G7 countries met in emergency session in Washington, Dominique Strauss-Kahn the head of the IMF insisted, "Intensifying solvency concerns about a number of the largest US-based and European financial institutions have pushed the global financial system to the brink of systemic meltdown." The G7 ministers announced a plan to free up the flow of credit, back efforts by banks to raise money and revive the mortgage market. The 15 Eurozone leaders agreed to meet again in Paris to attempt a common approach, with Angela Merkel the German Chancellor declaring "We must redirect the markets so that they serve the people, and [don't] ruin them" (*BBC*, October 12, 2008).

At the meeting of 15 Eurozone countries convened by President Sarkozy, the UK Prime Minister Gordon Brown was invited (the UK not being a member of the Eurozone) to explain the measures the UK government had adopted. There was agreement to implement a coordinated framework of action to take preference shares in banks and underwrite interbank lending. A few days later a meeting of all EU leaders confirmed support for this approach. Brown argued for a two stage process:

Stage one was to stabilise the financial system with liquidity, recapitalisation and trying to get

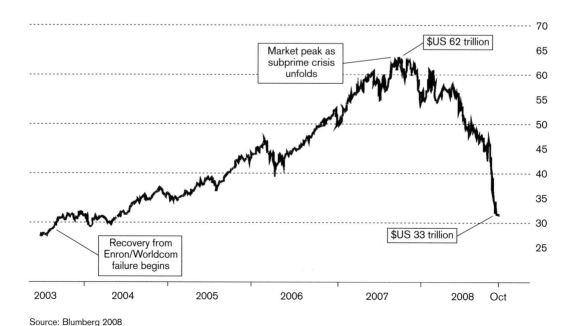

Source: Blumberg 2008

Figure I.5 World exchange market capitalization (US$ trillion)

funds moving for small businesses and consumers," he said. "Stage two is to make sure that the problems of the financial system, which started in America, do not recur." The target was to "root out irresponsibilities and excesses" in the system. "We need supervision and regulation where it has been lacking and where it is necessary, and international co-operation. We need an early warning system and proper co-ordination.

(*The Times* October 16, 2008)

The rescue package unveiled at this meeting committed the EU countries potentially to intervening with 1.8 trillion dollars, more than double the rescue package agreed by the US Congress.

The UK rescue package won wide acceptance among the financial community, and internationally, which led US officials to emphasize that their rescue package also allowed for the government to buy preference shares in the banks they assisted. This was a clause the Democrats in Congress had insisted on inserting into the emergency act, contrary to Paulson's original intention to simply purchase the toxic debt of the banks. At a crucial moment in the international financial crisis it was apparent that the US government was adjusting its own policy and following Europe's lead:

With his new initiative, Paulson appears to be conducting an about-face with regard to his government's previous policies and to be adopting an approach similar to that being used in Europe. Paulson's original plan envisioned primarily purchasing bad mortgages and other rotten debt in order to restore trust in the financial system. The Bush administration hadn't even considered the idea of government investments—Congress first addressed the issue in its revisions of the bailout package. According to the *Wall Street Journal*, the new plan largely replaces the former ideas, which failed to restore confidence, leading to dramatic decline of stock markets last week.

(*Spiegel Online* October 14, 2008)

The US government announced a $250 billion plan to purchase stakes in a wide variety of banks in an effort to return them to solvency, with major investments of $25 billion each in Bank of America, Citigroup, JPMorgan Chase, Wells Fargo, and $10 billion investments in Goldman Sachs and Morgan Stanley.

Europe and the US had come to adopt similar strategies to address the enveloping crisis, yet with different philosophies regarding the outcome. President Bush declared, "This is an essential short-term measure to ensure the viability of America's banking system. This is not intended to take over the free

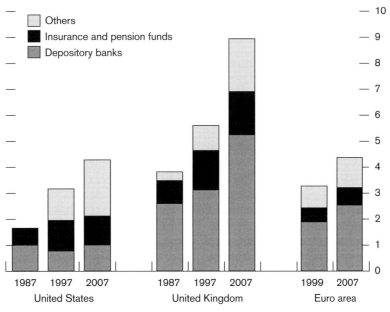

Sources: US Board of Governors of the Federal Reserve System; UK Office of National Statistics; European Central Bank; and IMF staff estimates (IMF 2008: 83).

Figure I.6 **Scale of financial assets in multiples of gross domestic product**

market, but to preserve it." The Treasury Secretary Henry Paulson said the lack of confidence in the financial system was a threat to the US economy, and argued that the government taking equity stakes was "objectionable to most Americans, including myself. We regret taking these actions, but we must to restore confidence in the financial system" (*BBC* October 14, 2008). In contrast the President of the European Union Nicolas Sarkozy insisted *"Cette crise est la crise de trop. Il faut refonder le système.... fonder un nouveau capitalisme sur des valeurs qui mettent la finance au service des entreprises et des citoyens et non l'inverse".* ("This crisis is one too many; the system has to be re-established...a new capitalism based on values that place finance in the service of businesses and citizens, and not the reverse") (*France Info* October 27, 2008).

THE FINANCIALIZATION OF THE GLOBAL ECONOMY

Directing markets was now a great deal more difficult since financial markets have become much larger, inter-connected and internationalized. A McKinsey survey illustrates how European capital markets are catching up with US markets (including equity securities, private debt securities, government debt securities, and bank deposits).

> The United States remains the world's largest and most liquid capital market, with $56 trillion in assets, or nearly one-third of the global total. But Europe's financial markets are approaching the scale of the US markets. Including the United Kingdom, Europe's financial markets reached $53 trillion in 2006—still less than the US total, but growing faster. Three quarters of the gain came from the deepening of Europe's equity and private debt markets. The eurozone's financial markets reached $37.6 trillion, the UK markets reached $10 trillion, and other Western European nations $5.6 trillion. Equally important, the euro is emerging as a rival to the dollar as the world's global reserve currency, reflecting in part the growing vibrancy and depth of Europe's financial markets. In mid-2007, the value of euro currency in circulation surpassed that of dollar notes in the world for the first time, and the euro has been the top choice in the issuance of bonds.
>
> (McKinsey and Company 2008:11–12)

Relative to gross domestic product the financial sector in all of the industrial countries grew considerably in the last two decades of financial de-regulation, innovation and globalization. The size of financial assets in both the US and UK had more than doubled in 20 years. The massive growth of the UK finance sector and also the sustained growth of the European finance sectors involved the adoption of similar financial innovation and exotic instruments as in the United States. British and European financial institutions had also succumbed to the temptations of high leverage (in some cases higher than the Wall Street investment banks), minimal risk management, and a fascination with the returns that new financial securities and speculative industries—most notably the property sector—might deliver. In the UK the financial sector became gargantuan, with assets around nine times GDP (Figure 6), a multiple more than double that of the US finance sector. A concentration on financial services was considered in the US and UK as an essential part of the new economy, and was associated with rapid market growth, high profits and very high salaries for a privileged few dealing in the most exotic financial securities. London basked in its developing reputation as the financial capital of the world, and when annual bonuses were paid in the finance sector, property prices in central London (already now among the highest in the world) jumped again (City of London 2008).

Fuelling the whole process of financialization were volcanic eruptions of debt. When Alan Greenspan became Chairman of the Federal Reserve in 1987 public and private debt in the US totaled $10.5 trillion, but after his departure in 2006 it had quadruped to $43 trillion.

> Debt in record quantities had been piled on top of the trillions still extant from previous binges of the eighties and nineties, so that by 2007 the nation's overseers watched a US economy in which public and private indebtedness was three times bigger than that year's gross national product. This ratio topped the prior record, set during the years after the stock market crash of 1929. However, in contrast to the 1920s and 1930s when manufacturing retained its overwhelming primacy despite the economy's temporary froth of stockmarket and ballyhoo, the eighties and nineties brought a much deeper transformation. Goods production lost the two-to-one edge in GDP it had enjoyed in the seventies. In 2005, on the cusp of Greenspan's

retirement, financial services—the new *ubercate-gory* spanning finance, insurance and real estate—far exceeded other sectors taking over one-fifth of GDP against manufacturing's gaunt, shrunken 12 percent. During the two previous decades (and only marginally stalled by the early 1990s economic bailouts) the baton of economic leadership had been passed.

(Phillips 2008:5)

A debate has continued for some time about the costs and benefits of the financialization of advanced industrial economies (Epstein 2005; Erturk *et al.* 2008; Froud and Johal 2008; Froud *et al.* 2006; Langley 2008; Martin 2002). Competing definitions of 'financialization' include:

- the ascendancy of 'shareholder value' as a mode of corporate governance (Aglietta and Rebérioux 2005);
- the growing dominance of capital market financial systems over bank-based financial systems;
- the increasing political and economic power of a particular class grouping: the *rentier* class for some (Hilferding 1985);
- the explosion of financial trading with a myriad of new financial instruments;
- the "pattern of accumulation in which profit making occurs increasingly through financial channels rather than through trade and commodity production' (Krippner 2005);
- the increasing role of financial motives, financial markets, financial actors and financial institutions in the operation of the domestic and international economies (Epstein 2005:3).

There were many critics of financialization, and the long progression of financial crises around the world served as a reminder that the system was neither self-regulating nor robust (Laeven and Valencia 2008). However few imagined that the international financial system might prove so willfully self-destructive as this 2008 crisis revealed. "You've seen the triumph of greed over integrity; the triumph of speculation over value creation; the triumph of the short term over long term sustainable growth" was the verdict of Australia's Prime Minister, Kevin Rudd (*The Australian* October 6, 2008). More forcefully still, the Archbishop of Canterbury Rowan Williams argued,

Trading the debts of others without accountability has been the motor of astronomical financial gain for many in recent years…The crisis exposes the element of basic unreality in the situation – the truth that almost unimaginable wealth has been generated by equally unimaginable levels of fiction, paper transactions with no concrete outcome beyond profit for traders. The biggest challenge in the present crisis is whether we can recover some sense of the connection between money and material reality – the production of specific things, the achievement of recognisable human goals that have something to do with a shared sense of what is good for the human community in the widest sense.

(*Spectator* September 27, 2008)

THE CORPORATE GOVERNANCE CAUSES OF THE CRISIS

The explanation of why investment banks and other financial institutions took such spectacular risks with extremely leveraged positions on many securities and derivatives, and the risk management, governance and ethical environment that allowed such conduct to take place is worth further analysis.

Masters of the Universe

Each financial boom is associated not only with reckless risk-taking and wildly inflated rewards, but an indulgent culture proclaiming the new Masters of the Universe. Tom Wolfe coined this phrase (based on a children's comic book) for financial *parvenus* in the middle of the 1987 boom in his book *The Bonfire of the Vanities*. (Oliver Stone's iconic movie *Wall Street* set in this period was supposed to be about crime and punishment on Wall Street, but Michael Douglas playing the ruthless takeover magnate Gordon Gekko, who won an Oscar for his "Greed is Good" speech, now cannot have breakfast in New York without being approached by young men saying it was seeing the movie that made them want to become Wall Street traders.) The hubris returned a decade later with the NASDAQ boom and the posturing of the executives of Enron, WorldCom and other companies who in strenuous self-promotion declared they were leading the best companies in the world, before they ran out of funds and then ran out of hype as they faced the courts. With the recovery of US financial markets after the Enron debacle, the explosion of financial innovation gave the world a new breed of Masters of the Universe in the derivatives dealers and hedge fund managers who manipulated trillions of dollars, while charging immense fees. This long financial boom of recent years saw the culture of financial excess permeate through swathes of the rich industrial countries as people were encouraged to live on debt with escalating mortgages and multiplying credit cards.

Symptomatic of the humiliating fall from assumed greatness was the end of Lehman Brothers, a 158-year-old Wall Street institution forced into bankruptcy by an incapacity to face reality. Lehman's had failed before in 1984, selling itself to American Express at a discount price (Auletta 1986). The Chairman at the time, Lewis L. Glucksman said, "We never made a culture where people were concerned with the firm and not just each other. We had a level of greed here and personal selfishness that was disgraceful" (*New York Times* January 19, 1986). Later Richard S. Fuld became Chief Executive returning Lehman back to being an independent bank in 1994. Lehman's was the fourth largest investment bank on Wall Street and was a self-proclaimed 'innovator in global finance.'

As the Wall Street investment banks stumbled, Fuld had dinner with Henry Paulson in April 2008 and came away thinking Lehman's had a "huge brand" with the US Treasury. The announcement of a first quarter 2008 loss of $2.8 million and a larger second quarter loss of $3.9 billion exposed the weaknesses in Lehman's position. As Fuld cast about for a white knight to invest in the firm in the US, Europe and among Asian sovereign wealth funds, Lehman's was publicly presenting a rosy view of its future. After the company collapsed three separate federal investigations began into the conduct of Lehman's in the final months, and Fuld was hauled in front of the US Congress House of Representatives oversight committee. Democratic congressman John Sarbanes referring to a June 2008 statement in which Fuld insisted the company's liquidity was strong said, "Either he has lost all perspective and is completely clueless or he is quite savvy and deceiving people" (*Financial Times, New York Times* October 6, 2008)

But nobody imagined the scale of the tragedy that befell Wall Street's leading investment banks. "Wall Street: RIP," pronounced *The New York Times* (September 28, 2008). "A world of big egos. A world where people love to roll the dice with borrowed money, of tightwire trading, propelled by computers... that world is largely coming to an end." Replacing the triumphal past was disillusion and disorientation: "Enthusiasm was gone from Wall Street yesterday, replaced by a febrile uncertainty and a foreboding that 2008 might turn into 1929" (*Times Online* October 1, 2008). No one had imagined this all could happen this quickly, or could anticipate when it might end. On November 18, 2008 Henry Paulson told Congress he was handing over to President-elect Barak Obama "A signficantly more stable banking system, where the failure of a systemically relevant institution is no longer a pressing concern rattling the markets." The following day the second largest bank in the United States Citigroup's shares went into free-fall, losing 20 percent of their value each day until the Treasury and Federal Reserve agreed a rescue package of over $300 billion.

De-regulation

Financial institutions are critical to the operation of any economy, and traditionally subject to a framework of firm regulation. However as the financialization of the US and international economy proceeded, paradoxically the regulatory touch lightened considerably. In the words of one US finance expert, in the years before the crisis

> We were developing a system of very large, highly levered, undercapitalized financial institutions – including the investment banks, some large money centre banks, the insurance companies with large derivative books and the government-sponsored entities…Regulators believe that all of these are too big to fail and would bail them out if necessary. The owners, employees and creditors of these institutions are rewarded when they succeed, but it is all of us—the taxpayers—who are left on the hook if they fail. This is called private profits and socialized risk. Heads I win. Tails, you lose. It is a reverse Robin Hood system.
>
> (Einhorn 2008a:16–17)

The abolition of the Glass-Steagall Act in 1999 paved the way for a regulatory loosening of the US financial system, enhanced in 2004 by a new SEC rule intended to reduce regulatory costs for broker-dealers that were part of consolidated supervised entities. Essentially this involved large broker-dealers using their own risk-management practices for regulatory purposes enabling a lowering of their capital requirements (the core capital which a bank is required to hold to support its risk-taking activities which normally includes share capital, share premium, and retained earnings). In addition the SEC amended the definition of net capital to include securities for which there was no ready market, and to include hybrid capital instruments and certain deferred tax assets, reducing the amount of capital required to engage in high risk activities. Finally the rule eased the calculations of counterparty risk, maximum potential exposures, margin lending, and allowed broker-dealers to assign their own credit ratings to unrated companies. Einhorn comments on this regulatory capitulation of the SEC

> Large broker-dealers convinced the regulators that the dealers could better measure their own risks, and with fancy math, they attempted to show that they could support more risk with less capital. I suspect that the SEC took the point of view that these were all large, well-capitalized institutions, with smart, sophisticated risk managers who had no incentive to try to fail. Consequently, they gave the industry the benefit of the doubt.
>
> (2008a:16)

Ratings agencies

As international financial markets have expanded, the role of the credit ratings agencies (CRAs) has proved critical. The International Organization of Securities Commissions (IOSCO) claims that

> CRAs assess the credit risk of corporate or government borrowers and issuers of fixed-income securities. CRAs attempt to make sense of the vast amount of information available regarding an issuer or borrower, its market and its economic circumstances in order to give investors and lenders a better understanding of the risks they face when lending to a particular borrower or when purchasing an issuer's fixed-income securities. A credit rating, typically, is a CRA's opinion of how likely an issuer is to repay, in a timely fashion, a particular debt or financial obligation, or its debts generally.
>
> (IOSCO 2003:1)

Yet the question asked by everybody when the financial crisis erupted was how could asset-backed securities containing subprime mortgages and other high-risk debt possibly be given AA credit ratings by Standard and Poor's or Moody's?

The answer was again that financial innovation had outpaced regulatory prowess. The ratings agencies instead of monitoring rigorously the growth of financial markets and instruments had become junior partners in this enterprise. Coffee (2006) in his critique of the failure of the gatekeeper professions in US corporate governance including auditors, corporate lawyers, and securities analysts, raises the following issues regarding rating agencies:

1 *Concentration*

    Given the immense capacity of the ratings agencies to influence the fortunes of financial institutions and instruments in terms of the public perception of risk, they have maintained a highly profitable duopoly with Standard and Poor's Ratings Services and Moody's Investor Services, only recently joined by Fitch Investor services for specialized submarkets. The SEC has supported this entrenched market position, reinforced by a reputational capital only now being challenged.

2 *Conflicts of interest*

    Traditionally the ratings agencies rated thousands of clients in the corporate debt business with little chance of being captured by single clients. However as the importance of the structured debt market grew, there were only a few investment banks active but the scale of the market grew exponentially. From the 1970s the ratings agencies business changed from their revenue coming from subscribers for their ratings services, to their revenue coming from the issuers of debt products, creating a context for capture by client's interests.

3 *Complex financial products*

    Rating corporate debt utilizing corporate financial history, audited financial statements, is less difficult than complex structured finance products issued by investment banks. Understanding the nature of the underlying assets and cash flows generated by these assets and the risks involved over time is a major undertaking. The ratings agencies deny any obligation to do due diligence on the portfolio backing structured finance products.

4 *Timing and relevance*

    Even if the ratings agencies were close in their original rating, they do not review how a debt product may change over time in different market conditions, and rating agencies were slow to downgrade subprime asset backed securities.

(Scott 2008: 23-24; Coffee 2006).

The ratings agencies believed in the investment banks of Wall Street, and in their risk controls, and assumed that "everything was hedged." Though the CRAs do have the power to review non-public information to assess the credit-worthiness of institutions and securities, they did not have the inclination, manpower or skills to do this thoroughly in all cases, and they did not get paid until they gave a rating.

> The market perceives the rating agencies to be doing much more than they actually do. The agencies themselves don't directly misinform the market, but they don't disabuse the market of misperceptions—often spread by the rated entities— that the agencies do more than they actually do. This creates a false sense of security, and in times of stress, this actually makes the problems worse. Had the credit rating agencies been doing a reasonable job of disciplining the investment banks— which unfortunately happen to bring the rating agencies lots of other business—then the banks may have been prevented from taking excess risk and the current crisis might have been averted.
>
> (Einhorn 2008a:13)

Risk management

Financial businesses' activities in rapidly changing markets are highly sensitive to variance, and it might be expected that as the financial services industries have grown inexorably and financial products become more complex, that the sophistication of risk management techniques will have developed in parallel. However, the reality is that innovation in financial products has far exceeded the capacity of risk management measurement and monitoring tools to gauge risk. The most widely employed risk management tool is value-at-risk (VaR), which measures how much a portfolio stands to make or lose in 99 percent of the days. But as Einhorn argues, this measure ignores what might happen at the moment of greatest risk:

> A risk manager's job is to worry about whether the bank is putting itself at risk in the unusual times— or, in statistical terms, in the tails of distribution. Yet, VaR ignores what happens in the

tails. It specifically cuts them off. A 99 percent VaR calculation does not evaluate what happens in the last 1 percent. This, in my view, makes VaR relatively useless as a risk management tool and potentially catastrophic when its use creates a false sense of security among senior managers and watchdogs. This is like an airbag that works all the time, except when you have a car accident. By ignoring the tails, VaR creates an incentive to take excessive but remote risks.

> (Einhorn 2008a:11)

Yet VaR was the tool international finance industries relied upon in transactions involving billions of dollars. For example UBS was the European bank with the largest losses from the crisis, involving the Swiss government and central bank providing an aid package of $59.2 billion to take risky debt securities from its balance sheet. In a report to shareholders published in April 2008 UBS laid bare the risk management failings that had led to such immense losses. (Though wealthy clients continued to desert the bank in droves, withdrawing $58 billion in the third quarter of 2008.) The report highlights in worrying detail the incomplete risk control methodologies, with market risk control (MRC) placing considerable reliance on VaR and stress limits to control the risks of the business, without implementing additional risk methodologies, or aggregating notional limits even when losses were made (UBS 2008:13):

1 Mortgage portfolio trades were certified by the UBS investment bank's quantitative risk control "But with the benefit of hindsight appears not have been subject to sufficiently robust stress testing. Further, the collateralized debt obligation desk did not carry out sufficient fundamental analysis as market conditions deteriorated" (UBS 2008: 30).

2 With regard to asset backed securities trading also there were incomplete risk control methodologies. "There was considerable reliance on AA/AAA ratings and sector concentration limits which did not take into account the fact that more than 95% of the asset backed securities trading portfolio was referencing US underlying assets (i.e. mortgage loans, auto loans, credit card debt, etc.)" (UBS 2008:32).

3 In fixed income there was a growth orientation: "The investment bank was focused on the maximization of revenue. There appears to have been

a lack of challenge on the risk and reward to business area plans within the investment bank at a senior level. UBS's review suggests an asymmetric focus in the investment bank senior management meetings on revenue and profit and loss, especially when compared to discussion of risk issues. Business-peer challenge was not a routine practice in those meetings...Inappropriate risk metrics were used in strategic planning and assessment. Investment Bank planning relied on VaR, which appears as the key risk parameter in the planning process. When the market dislocation unfolded, it became apparent that this risk measure methodology had not appropriately captured the risk inherent in the business having subprime exposures" (UBS 2008:34).

4 With regard to UBS group governance there was: "Failure to demand a holistic assessment. Whilst group senior management was alert to the general issues concerning the deteriorating US housing market, they did not demand a holistic presentation of UBS's exposure to securities referencing US real estate assets before July 2007, even though such an assessment may have been warranted earlier in view of the size of UBS's real estate assets" (UBS 2008:35).

5 The report concluded with reference to risk control that there was over-reliance on VaR and stress: "MRC relied on VaR and stress numbers, even though delinquency rates were increasing and origination standards were falling in the US mortgage market. It continued to do so throughout the build-up of significant positions in subprime assets that were only partially hedged. Presentations of MRC to UBS's senior governance bodies did not provide adequate granularity of subprime positions UBS held in its various businesses. No warnings were given to group senior management about the limitations of the presented numbers or the need to look at the broader contextual framework and the findings were not challenged with perseverance" (UBS 2008:39).

6 Finally the report condemned the lack of independence and healthy skepticism in UBS governance: "Fundamental analysis of the subprime market seems to have been generally based on the business view and less on MRC's independent assessment. In particular there is no indication that MRC was seeking views from other sources than business... Further, risk systems and infrastructure were not improved because of a

willingness by the risk function to support growth" (UBS 2008:40).

Incentivization

The final and most critical part of the explanation of why investment banks and other financial institutions took such extreme risks with highly leveraged positions in complex securities, neglecting risk management, governance principles, and often basic business ethics, was that *they were highly incentivized to do so.* Massively incentivized irresponsibility became the operating compensation norm in the financial community, as banks and fringe financial institutions chased the super profits available as global financial markets expanded exponentially.

> The management teams at the investment banks did exactly what they were incentivized to do: maximize employee compensation. Investment banks pay out 50 percent of revenues as compensation. So, more leverage means more revenues, which means more compensation. In good times, once they pay out the compensation, overhead and taxes, only a fraction of the incremental revenues falls to the bottom line for shareholders. The banks have done a wonderful job at public relations. Everyone knows about the 20 percent incentive fees in the hedge fund and private equity industry. Nobody talks about the investment banks' 50 percent compensation structures, which have no high-water mark and actually are exceeded in difficult times in order to retain talent.
>
> (Einhorn 2008a:11).

The report on the vast write-downs at UBS examines how the compensation structure directly generated the behaviour which caused the losses, as staff were motivated to utilize the low cost of funding to invest in subprime positions.

> Employee incentivization arrangements did not differentiate between returns generated by skill in creating additional returns versus returns made from exploiting UBS's comparatively low cost of funding in what were essentially carry trades... The relatively high yield attributable to subprime made this asset class an attractive long position for carry trades. Further, the UBS funding framework amplified the incentives to pursue

compensation through profitable carry trades. The compensation structure generally made little recognition of risk issues or adjustment for risk/other qualitative indicators (e.g. for group internal audit ratings, operational risk indicators, compliance issues etc.)

As a result there were insufficient incentives to protect the UBS franchise for the longer term.

It remains the case that bonus payments for successful and senior international business fixed income traders, including those in the businesses holding subprime positions, were significant. Essentially, bonuses were measured against gross revenue after personnel costs, with no formal account taken of the quality and sustainability of those earnings.

(UBS 2008:42).

REGULATION AND GOVERNANCE OF FINANCIAL INSTITUTIONS

While the accumulated cost of the global financial crisis was being realized the commitment to establish a new international financial regulatory framework increased. As the costs of all forms of intervention to alleviate the crisis by the US government ballooned out to $7.7 trillion (including credit discounts, credit extensions, securities lending, term auction facilities, portfolio funding, money market funding, TARP, assistance to specific institutions, economic stimulus packages, and homeowner assistance). The general market assistance and specific rescue packages for individual financial institutions amounted to almost $11 trillion worldwide by October 2008 (Table I.2). While these funds could be regarded as a temporary investment in the financial economy, with the hope of recouping much of the funds back at a later stage, this was an optimistic view when the crisis spread to other sectors of the economy. As the financial crisis impacted upon the real economy the fears of a prolonged recession grew, with US industrial production falling further than it had for over 30 years. For example, the US automotive industry became increasingly precarious and announced further major redundancies and looked for support from the federal government (including support from the assistance intended for financial institutions, since the automotive companies had also become finance companies).

Table I.2 Government support for global financial crisis, 2008

	US$
Europe	1.8 trillion
UK	856 billion
US	7.74 trillion
Sweden	205 billion
South Korea	130 billion
Australia	10.4 billion
Rest of the world	105.12 billion
Total	**10.93 trillion**

Source: Compiled from:
BBC Credit Crisis: World in Turmoil http://news.bbc.co.uk/2/hi/business/7654647.stm,
ABC News, Tuesday October 21, 2008: http://www.abc.net.au/
Reuters: http://www.reuters.com/article/forexNews/idUSTRE49J2GB20081020
IMF Global Financial Stability Report October 2008: http://www.imf.org/external/pubs/ft/gfsr/2008/02/index.htm

The International Labour Organization in Geneva estimated that up to 20 million people in the world would lose their employment as a consequence of the financial crisis, and that for the first time in a decade the global total of unemployed would be above 200 million (*Associated Press* October 21, 2008). The prospect of the whole world falling into recession at the same time became possible, something not witnessed since the 1930s.

There was a widespread sense that this regulatory failure of financial markets could not be allowed to occur again. Angela Merkel, the Chancellor of Germany, usually a stalwart ally of President Bush, derided the lack of regulation that, in her view, allowed the financial crisis to erupt in the United States and seep inexorably toward Europe. She reminded the German public that the United States and Britain rejected her proposals in 2007 for regulating international hedge funds and bond rating agencies. "It was said for a long time, 'Let the markets take care of themselves,'" Merkel commented. Now, she added, "even America and Britain are saying, 'Yes, we need more transparency, we need better standards.'" Germany's finance minister, Peer Steinbrueck, said that the "Anglo-Saxon" capitalist system had run its course and that "new rules of the road" are needed, including greater global regulation of capital markets *(Washington Post* September 28, 2008).

Gordon Brown and Nicolas Sarkozy called for a Bretton Woods agreement for the twenty-first century, aimed at rebuilding the international financial system. Though the economic summit meeting of leaders of the G20 countries was arranged for Washington in November 2008, it was clear George Bush would not be taking the lead in this initiative. Yet something of a sea-change was occurring in American domestic politics in response to the financial crisis and with the sweeping election to the US presidency of Barak Obama. The experience of Congress and the White House equivocating about a rescue package of buying securities had made a deeply unfavourable impression on the US public. The UK government had recognized the deeper problem of a lack of confidence in the banks themselves, which was resolved by governments becoming the investor of last resort and the guarantor of loans between banks, and it was the adoption of a similar strategy by the US government that finally staunched the panic on Wall Street. As Andrew Moravcsik, professor of politics and international affairs at Princeton University suggested, "Americans, especially conservatives, have a particular view of Europe as over-regulated, therefore suffering from weak growth and Euro-sclerosis. This could change that view and create more respect for the European view of regulation more generally" (*Australian Financial Review* October 20, 2008).

A problem in devising a new financial regulatory architecture was that Bretton Woods in 1944, though it established the International Monetary Fund and World Bank, was essentially dealing with national financial markets. Digital and interconnected global financial markets presented a much bigger challenge. A series of measures were proposed by Gordon Brown:

1 Improving risk disclosure by financial institutions was fundamental, together with stricter rules on bank liquidity and leveraging.
2 Ensuring banks take bigger stakes in any loans they pass on to others through securitization might constrain irresponsible innovations.
3 Establishing a central clearing house for complex derivatives could help to discipline their use.
4 Increased supervision and regulation might include new standards for off-balance sheet accounting, and supervision of the largest international banks and insurance companies.
5 Reforming executive compensation structures that encouraged excessive risk-taking, and

aligning reward with long-term value creation was another imperative.
6 Finally a capacity to police the potential for future dangers to the international economy, and the means of cooperation for future crises were important (*The Times* October 16, 2008).

These principles for reforming international financial market were broadly supported in Europe, and had public resonance in the United States where it was argued that the rapid expansion of unregulated financial institutions and instruments from hedge funds to credit default swaps should be contained by extending financial reserve requirements, limiting leveraging, and ensuring trading occurred on public exchanges (*Wall Street Journal* July 25, 2008; IPS 2008). With the international financial community still in a state of profound shock, and heavily dependent upon state aid, any protests about the dangers of over-regulation were muted. Adair Turner, head of the Financial Services Authority (FSA) in the UK (responsible for regulating financial institutions), commented,

> If a year and a half ago, the FSA had wanted higher capital adequacy, more information on liquidity, had said it was worried about the business models at Bradford & Bingley and Northern Rock, and had wanted to ask questions about remuneration, the fact is that we would have been strongly criticised for harming the competitiveness of the City of London, red tape, and over regulation. We are now in a different environment. We shouldn't regulate for its own sake, but over-regulation and red tape has been used as a polemical bludgeon. We have probably been over-deferential to that rhetoric.
>
> (*Guardian,* October 16, 2008)

However the question is, will the deference of regulators return when financial markets recover, and financial institutions and markets are free again to pursue their self-interest? An early indication of how entrenched the irresponsibility of the financial sector had become was the astonishing news that the surviving US financial institutions were preparing to pay 2008 end of year executive bonuses approximately equivalent to the billions of dollars of aid they had just received from Congress. While the US economy was collapsing around them, and the US public were becoming increasingly concerned how they might survive a severe recession, the executives of major banks seemed focused primarily on maintaining their bonuses. Horrified by so immediate a betrayal of the public intervention to assist the banks, Henry Waxman, the Chairman of the US Congress Committee on Oversight and Government Reform sent a letter to the CEOs of Bank of America, Bank of New York, Citigroup, Goldman Sachs, JPMorgan Chase, Merrill Lynch, Morgan Stanley, State Street Corp. and Wells Fargo:

> Earlier this month, the Treasury Department announced plans to invest $125bn of taxpayer funds in nine major banks, including yours, as an emergency measure to rebuild depleted capital. According to recent public filings, these nine banks have spent or reserved $108bn for employee compensation and bonuses in the first nine months of 2008, nearly the same amount as last year. Some experts have suggested that a significant percentage of this compensation could come in year-end bonuses and that the size of the bonuses will be significantly enhanced as a result of the infusion of taxpayer funds. According to one analyst, "Had it not been for the government's help in refinancing their debt they may not have had the cash to pay bonuses". Press accounts report that the size of the bonuses could exceed $6bn at some firms receiving federal assistance. While I understand the need to pay the salaries of employees, I question the appropriateness of depleting the capital that taxpayers just injected into the banks through the payment of billions of dollars in bonuses, especially after one of the financial industry's worst years on record. As one newspaper recently reported, "critics of investment banks have questioned why firms continue to siphon off billions of dollars of bank earnings into bonus pools rather than using the funds to shore up the capital position of the crisis-stricken institutions".
>
> (*Washington Post* October 29, 2008)

Waxman demanded data from the banks on the total compensation per employee from 2006 to 2008 broken down by salaries, bonuses (cash and equity), and other benefits; the number of employees who were paid over $500,000 in total compensation and how this was structured; the total compensation paid to the ten highest paid employees; and all policies on bonus payments.

Mikhail Gorbachev now president of the International Foundation for Socio-Economic and Political

Studies commented on this extreme inequality revealed by the financial crisis:

> The greed and irresponsibility of the few will affect all of us. No country, no sector of the economy, will escape this crisis. The economic model rooted in the early 1980s is falling apart. It was based on maximizing profit by abolishing regulation aimed at protecting the interests of society as a whole. For decades we have been told that all this benefits everyone: 'a rising tide lifts all boats.' Yet the statistics say that it didn't. The economic growth of recent decades—quite modest compared with the 1950s and 1960s—has disproportionately benefited the wealthiest members of society. The living standards of the middle class have stagnated, and the gap between the rich and poor has widened in the most economically advanced countries.
>
> (*New York Times,* October 18, 2008)

The G20 leaders meeting in London in April 2009 was goaded by Angela Merkel and Nicolas Sarkozy to go beyond the commitment to develop a coordinated stimulus package to relieve the impact of the financial crisis in world markets, and to robustly address the weaknesses in the international regulatory architecture. An action plan approved by the leaders to strengthen the regulation of the international financial system resolved:

- to establish a new Financial Stability Board (FSB) with a strengthened mandate, as a successor to the Financial Stability Forum (FSF), including all G20 countries, FSF members, Spain and the European Commission;
- that the FSB should collaborate with the IMF to provide early warning of macroeconomic and financial risks and the actions needed to address them;
- to reshape national regulatory systems so that national authorities are able to identify and take account of macro-prudential risks;
- to extend regulation and oversight to all systemically important financial institutions, instruments and markets. This will include, for the first time, systemically important hedge funds;
- to endorse and implement the FSF's tough new principles on pay and compensation and to support sustainable compensation schemes and the corporate social responsibility of all firms;

- to take action, once recovery is assured, to improve the quality, quantity and international consistency of capital in the banking system. In future, regulation must prevent excessive leverage and require buffers of resources to be built up in good times;
- to take action against non-cooperative jurisdictions, including tax havens, deploying sanctions to protect public finances and financial systems, with the end of the era of banking secrecy, and the publication by the OECD of the list of countries assessed by the Global Forum against the international standard for exchange of tax information;
- to call on the accounting standard setters to work urgently with supervisors and regulators to improve standards on valuation and provisioning and achieve a single set of high-quality global accounting standards; and
- to extend regulatory oversight and registration to Credit Rating Agencies to ensure they meet the international code of good practice, particularly to prevent unacceptable conflicts of interest.

PARALLEL OR COLLIDING UNIVERSES OF CORPORATE GOVERNANCE?

The international financial crisis exposed in high relief the different systems of corporate governance that exist in the United States and Europe. Just as the 2001 Enron era corporate excesses and collapses were centered in the US, the origin of the 2008 global financial crisis was in the irresponsible extremes of the securities industry of the investment banks of Wall Street. The US presided over the explosion of the global securities markets in the early 2000s, issuing over 75 percent of new securities: for example in 2006 of the world total of $4,138 billion of securitization issuance, the US contributed $3,256 billion (IFSL 2008:9). Though the financial institutions on both sides of the Atlantic succumbed to similar adventures with these high yielding exotic financial instruments and pursued leverage to dangerous levels, there were important differences in the way European leaders and regulators responded to the ensuing financial crisis compared to their American counterparts. The commitment to reform the international financial regulatory structure was much greater among Europeans, which reflected their different approach to regulation and governance. Underpinning this divergence in regulatory and governance systems, was a different conception of the logic of capitalism and the role of markets.

Varieties of capitalism/varieties of inequality

Different varieties of capitalism with different logics of political economy produce different levels of inequality. The Anglo-American variant of corporate governance in its US manifestation has afforded CEOs of large corporations inordinate power and wealth, with all of the consequences of this for inequality in the wider society (EPI 2008; Clarke 2007). Yet this is precisely the model of capitalism that is being propagated most vigorously in other regions of the world by executives themselves, large international corporations, institutional investors, and international agencies such as the OECD and IMF. This dynamic induced the international financial crisis, in which investment bank executives were massively incentivized to pursue vast securitization and leverage which hugely enriched themselves, but caused the collapse of financial institutions worldwide, and the violent instability of financial markets. The social and economic consequences of this reckless financial irresponsibility in terms of structural damage to international economies, unemployment and lost investment opportunities in sustainable and innovative industries were vastly undermining. There is a deep historical tendency in the Anglo-American model to instability and inequity (Galbraith 1993; MacAvoy and Millstein 2004) and the appropriateness of the rapid adoption of this model in other regimes is highly questionable (Mitchell 2001; Oman *et al.* 2005; McClintick 2006; Clarke and dela Rama 2006)

There is a developing literature comparing different models of capitalism from alternative analytical frameworks highlighting the nature and extent of diverse forms of capitalism, their relative strengths and weaknesses, and the prospects for institutional diversity when confronted with growing pressures for international economic integration (Deeg and Jackson 2006). The varieties of capitalism thesis elaborated by Hall and Soskice (2001) adopts a firm-centred approach focusing on the incentives for coordination; a wider typology of governance mechanisms in terms of social systems of production is offered by Hollingsworth and Boyer (1997); and a national business systems approach of Whitley (1999) examines the internal capacities of business firms. The varieties of capitalism literature have great resonance in the consideration of comparative corporate governance.

The question of whether economies will converge towards a common corporate Anglo-American governance system, or sustain the present diversity of institutions is one of the key issues facing countries in Europe, the Asia Pacific and throughout the rest of the world. Lower economic growth and higher unemployment in Europe, compared to the Anglo-American countries since the mid-1990s, undermined some of the confidence in Europe's social model (though by 2005 Germany had returned to its former position as the world's largest exporter). As Freeman (2000) has suggested there has been a series of ideal models of political economy associated with success over the decades:

- central planning of national projects in the New Deal period of the Great Depression in the 1930s in the United States;
- indicative planning of prestige projects as in the 1960s in France;
- co-determination and diversified quality production as in the 1970s in Germany;
- the New Economy of liquid investment markets as in the 1990s in the United States.

Each of these models has enjoyed a period of apparent ascendancy over other forms of political economy until superseded by an apparently more dynamic or productive system, and each is associated with a different institutional order. As Amble (2003:4) states,

> There is a considerable amount of theoretical and historical work that insists on the central role of institutions in economic dynamics. Institutions define incentives and constraints that will lead agents to invest in certain assets, acquire certain skills, cooperate, or be opportunistic. These individual decisions will affect macroeconomic growth performance. However, it is in general difficult unambiguously to relate one particular institutional form to "superior" economic performance when it comes to empirical testing. One reason could be that institutions do not affect economic decisions independently of each other. Interrelations between institutions are likely to lead to a complex of influences that are hard to analyse and whose empirical effects are difficult to unravel. Economic models are characterised precisely not by one but by many institutional forms that exert their effects in interaction.

Despite the pressures towards adopting Anglo-Saxon modes of corporate governance, the divergences in both the policy and practice of corporate governance in Europe have thus far resisted any move towards European standards. However with greater market integration and the developing influence of Anglo-American institutional investors, it is possible the market will play a greater role, and become an even more dominant force than it is presently. Yet debates on company law harmonization in the European Union have been held up by countries not wishing to see elements of their own systems of corporate governance disappear in the process. One explanation for this impasse is the *institutional complementarity thesis* which justifies the continuing diversity of systems, rejecting the 'one-best-way' strategy adopted by the 'convergence thesis.' Instead, a plurality of models is assumed, each corresponding to local circumstances, supported by a cluster of social norms and regulation, enabling balanced economic development. As Rebérioux, argues what is often presented as the practical economic inevitability of convergence, is in essence a profoundly ideological and political argument:

> Two competing theories behind forms of corporate governance can thus be discerned. In the first case, the US model – the predominance of widely held corporations controlled by their owners – is presented as optimal. If one adds a general law that institutions are evolving toward efficiency, then one obtains the convergence thesis: the European system is bound to change in the direction of the Anglo-Saxon one; it is only a matter of time. From a neo-institutionalist perspective, this process of convergence is seen as the result of rational micro-behaviour by individuals when crafting their governance structure (Williamson 1995)…Without delving further into a complex debate, it is worth noting that the micro-efficiency of shareholder value has not yet been proved, and probably never will be. The fundamental reason is that shareholder sovereignty is not an efficient arrangement, but rather a power relationship, that is a particular (societal) way to design a corporation…The *institutional complementarity thesis* provides a contrasting perspective on the continuing diversity of capitalist systems (Amble 2000). The core of this theoretical approach is a rejection of the 'one best way' strategy adopted by the convergence thesis in analysing institutions. Rather, a plurality of models is assumed, each corresponding to local circumstances. The focus should not

be upon a particular (isolated) institution, but on the cluster of social norms that underpin national regulation. This societal approach emphasises the systemic links between institutions that enable balanced economic development.

(2000:117-8)

Five fundamental institutional areas are recognized by Amble (2003:14) the interaction between which defines the political economy of the respective system:

- product–market competition
- wage labour nexus and labour market institutions
- financial intermediation sector and corporate governance
- social protection and the Welfare State
- education sector.

From the many potential types of market capitalism that may result from the inter-relations of the different arrangements in each of these institutional areas, Amble posits the existence of five types of capitalism each characterized by specific institutional forms and institutional complementarities:

- market-based model (Anglo-American)
- social-democratic model (North European)
- Continental European model
- Mediterranean model (South European)
- Asian model.

The diversity of corporate models is valuable and is rooted in societal characteristics that together shape the competitiveness of the different models. Though shareholder value may be gaining ground due to the influence of Anglo-Saxon institutional investors, and other new market impulses and intermediaries (including private equity and hedge funds), a stakeholder approach is closer to the reality of European social democracies, and the outcome of the confrontation between the two competing philosophies is highly uncertain. It is unlikely that imported Anglo-Saxon capital market-related features of corporate governance will work well with Continental labour-related aspects of corporate governance as represented in supervisory boards. It is likely any such European compromise would be more unstable than existing systems (Rebérioux 2000; Cernat 2004).

A more critical view is offered by Christel Lane (2003) who reviews the evidence on the German case and concludes that a new Anglo-American logic of corporate governance is diffusing beyond the major corporations of the DAX 30, and that this is not simply attributable to external constraints, but to powerful actors within the German economy including large banks and insurance companies. This is significant first because Germany has been the paradigm for the model of coordinated capitalism as distinct from competitive or liberal market capitalism. If the cohesive German system is in the process of fundamental change, then other continental European business systems are likely to be vulnerable. Second, Lane argues that it is wrong to assume that the adoption of the Anglo-American model is simply about changes in capital markets and corporate financing:

Because forms of corporate governance structure most other relationships within firms and even in society as a whole, they are inherently connected with a distribution of power and material welfare. They therefore decisively shape the logic of the whole political economy. Hence there is strong concern, particularly but not only on the part of labour, with the consequences of change for the distribution of surplus and control to various stakeholders in the firm, as well as the future viability of the production paradigm of diversified quality production.

Contrasting conceptions of corporate governance

Different understandings and practices of corporate governance begin with different interpretations of what corporate governance is: competing definitions range from the very narrow, concerned simply with the relationship of shareholders with managers, as in agency theory, to very expansive definitions involving all of the relationships in which enterprises are engaged. European interpretations of corporate governance tend towards more substantive definitions that recognize the wider implications of governance: "how corporations are *governed* – their ownership and control, the objectives they pursue, the rights they respect, the responsibilities they recognize, and how they distribute the value they create" (Clarke and dela Rama 2006:xix).

From this wider perspective, governance implies a large and more complex conception of how order, efficiency and equity is maintained:

While classical economics assumed markets to be spontaneous social orders that flourish best in the absence of any intervention, many political theorists and lawyers start from the opposite assumption. Following Hobbes, they assume that the natural societal condition is one of chaos, uncertainty and conflict. New institutional economics, economic sociology and comparative political economy brought these approaches together by emphasizing that markets are not spontaneous social orders, but have to be created and maintained by institutions. These provide, monitor and enforce rules of the game, which among other things fix property rights, back up contracts, protect competition, and reduce information asymmetries, risk and uncertainties. Societies have produced a variety of institutions to govern economic transactions, help reduce their costs and hence increase the likelihood of their occurrence (Van Kersbergen and Van Waarden 2004:143).

Corporate governance has competing definitions, but in Margaret Blair's estimation encompasses the "the whole set of legal, cultural, and institutional arrangements that determine what publicly traded corporations can do, who controls them, how that control is exercised, and how the risks and returns from the activities they undertake are allocated" (1995:3). These expansive dimensions of corporate governance were narrowly translated in the Anglo-American world in recent decades with the increasing ascendancy of financial markets and intellectual domination of agency theory into an almost obsessive concern for the problems of accountability and control involved in the dispersal of ownership of large listed corporations, and a rigid focus on the mechanisms that orientate managers towards delivering shareholder value (Dore 2000; Froud *et al.* 2000; Davis 2005). European perceptions of the role and significance of governance have changed in recent years towards the Anglo-American view, but often the change has proved partial with political leaders, regulators and business executives advocating the salience of shareholder value, while acknowledging the continuing legitimacy of stakeholder values.

Alternative corporate governance systems

Different approaches to the financing and governance of corporations in different regions of the world

have prevailed since the diverse origins of capitalism. The evolution of the corporate form can be traced from the family and closely held capitalism of the early nineteenth century, with the protection of ownership rights, through to the managerial capitalism of the early twentieth century, with further protection for listed corporations and limited liability, and finally the popular capitalism of the late twentieth century with protection of minority interests and mass ownership. However, different routes were followed in this evolution and different destinations reached in corporate practice, company law, and associated institutional development of Anglo-American, European, and Asian forms of corporate enterprise. In the Asian system of corporate governance stronger elements of family ownership survive intact, and in the European system more managerial forms have survived.

The result is two parallel universes of corporate governance: a dispersed ownership model characterized by strong and liquid securities markets, high disclosure standards, high market transparency, and where the market for corporate control is the ultimate disciplining mechanism; and second a concentrated ownership model characterized by controlling shareholders, weak securities markets, low transparency and disclosure standards and often a central monitoring role for large banks who have a stake in the company (Coffee 2002; Clarke 2005). Often colliding in recent years, the two parallel universes of corporate governance have been engaged in a recurring clash of institutional vigor and business values. The dispersed ownership (market-based, Anglo-American corporate governance systems) and the concentrated ownership (European and Asian relationship-based corporate governance systems) are described by a variety of names that reflect their different characteristics: including market systems and blockholder systems, rules-based and relationship-based systems, and market and bank-based systems. However the simplest characterization is that between outsider and insider-based systems.

Outsider systems are typified by dispersed ownership, a clear separation of ownership and control, lower debt/equity ratios, and sophisticated financial markets. In this system, there is less incentive for outsiders to participate in the control of the corporation, except insofar as they do so through the equity markets, and the severest sanction is hostile takeover. The interests of outside stakeholders are not formally represented, and investors themselves often have less interest in the strategic goals of the enterprise than in the short-term returns that are available. In contrast, *insider systems* are typified by highly concentrated ownership which is closely connected with the managerial control of the enterprise, and high debt/equity ratios, with a higher rate of bank credits due to the closer relationship with banks that are often represented on the board of major corporations along with other stakeholders including related firms and employees. Traditionally in these systems hostile takeovers rarely, if ever, occur and there is often a dense network of supportive relationships with related businesses that occasionally can develop into collusion. European countries exhibit a rich diversity in corporate governance practices, structures and participants that reflect differences in history, culture, financial traditions, ownership patterns, and legal systems. However, common understandings are emerging of the importance of corporate governance for developing modern corporations and growing economies. The biggest continuing difference between the market-based systems of the US and UK, and the relationship-based systems that predominate in many European countries, is that Europeans emphasize co-operative relationships and reaching consensus, whereas the Anglo-Saxon tradition emphasizes competition and market processes (Nestor and Thompson 2000).

With the move towards equity financing and broader share ownership in Europe in the 1990s and 2000s, it has seemed at times as if the shareholder value market-based system was inexorably advancing, but important elements of the European tradition have proved resilient and enduring. The European *insider* model relies on the representation of interests on the board of directors. More diverse groups of stakeholders are actively recognized including workers, customers, banks, other companies with close ties, local communities and national government. Stable investment and cross shareholdings mean the discipline of management by the securities market is not strong, and similarly the market for corporate control is weak. This is the continental European system with a supervisory board for oversight of management, banks playing an active role, inter-corporate shareholdings, and often close ties to political elites.

In most European countries (and indeed in most countries in the world) ownership and control are held by cohesive groups of insiders who have long-term stable relationships with the company (La Porta *et al.* 1999). Groups of insiders tend to know each other well

and have some connection with the company in addition to their investment, and are typically drawn from family interests, allied industrial concerns, banks and holding companies. Insider groups monitor management that often acts under their control. The agency problem of the outsider system is much less of a problem in this context (Nestor and Thompson 2000:9). Countries with insider systems tended not to have developed the institutionalization of wealth of the English speaking countries, and there were not pension funds, mutual funds and insurance companies of comparable scale and significance. Previously in place of this institutional investment, corporate finance was highly dependent upon banks with companies having high debt/equity ratios. Replacing the arm's-length relationship of equity markets, banks and other major investors often enjoyed complex and long-standing relationships with corporate boards. Consequently displacing the emphasis upon public disclosure of market-based systems, the insider system is based more on deeper but more selective exchange of information among insiders.

Insiders exercise control of a company either by majority ownership of voting shares, or by owning significant minority holdings and employing a combination of devices to augment their control over the company. Included among the devices to redistribute control are arranging corporate structures, shareholder agreements, discriminatory voting rights and procedures intended to reduce the participation of other minority investors. Pyramid structures enable people to dominate a company with only a small share of the total equity of the company. Multiple share classes can enable the insider group to have increased voting power. Shareholder agreements are means by which groups of shareholders who individually hold small amounts of equity, act in concert to constitute a working majority, or at least form the largest block of shareholders (Becht *et al.* 2005) Such agreements can give the participants preferential rights to acquire shares, and can cover issues such as how the chairman will be selected. In the past, many companies operating in this system have treated the AGM as a formal exercise tightly controlled by management with restrictions upon voting, and the possibility of participating in decisions circumscribed (Nestor and Thompson 2000:10).

Critiques of European corporate governance ownership practices and the impact upon equity and efficiency continue, with recurring evidence of the abuse of majority share ownership positions in some companies, and more serious evidence of pyramid structures and tunneling being used to extract the value from companies in inequitable ways by minority interests.

> The existing literature is split concerning the effect of ownership on performance. Bebchuk and Roe (1999) and Roe (2003) argue that what, at face value, appear to be inefficient ownership structures (whether dispersed or concentrated), are in fact efficient in the context of their institutional environment. Coffee (1999:3) argues that the current ownership arrangements are more a 'product of a path-dependent history than the "neutral" result of an inevitable evolution toward greater efficiency.' If this second proposition is correct, then the predominant ownership structure might not necessarily be the best performing one. This suspicion is confirmed by Thomsen *et al.* (2003) who pointed out that blockholders might destroy firm value when studying firms in the largest continental European countries.
>
> (Kirchmaier and Grant 2005)

Intense debate over the last decade concerning the globalization and convergence of corporate governance has focused on the relative merits of the different corporate governance systems, often with the assumption that the Anglo-American system with stronger security markets and higher levels of disclosure represents a more advanced and efficient mode of corporate finance and governance, and leading to the conclusion that inevitably there will be either an early, or more gradual, shift of the European and Asian systems of corporate governance towards the Anglo-American model (Hansmann and Kraakman 2001; McCahery *et al.* 2002; Hamilton and Quinlan 2005). However, the argument for inevitable convergence has tended to underestimate the extent of the different orientations and objectives of the alternative systems as well as the different institutional complementarities that have evolved. It has also failed to appreciate the significance of different cultures and conceptions of what a company is (Branson 2001; McDonnell 2002; Gordon and Roe 2004; Clarke 2004, 2007). In different regions of the world there are deeply embedded differences regarding business values and ways of doing things, and very different relationships with stakeholders.

There exist profoundly contrasting beliefs in the role of the market in the different systems, which influence the way the corporation is considered: simply as a bundle of tradable assets in the worst case scenario of the market-based system; but as a productive institution to be passed on to future generations in the best case of the insider governance system. As a result different measures of performance are applied, with the market-based system looking for short-term returns, and the European and Japanese systems having much longer-term horizons.

One of the main criticisms of Anglo-American market-based corporate governance has been that managers tend to be obsessed with quarterly performance measures and have an excessively short-termist perspective. Thus, Narayanan (1985), Shleifer and Vishny (1989), Porter (1992a,b) and Stein (1988, 1989), among others, have argued that USA managers are myopically 'short-termist' and pay too much attention to potential takeover threats. Porter, in particular, contrasts USA corporate governance with the governance in German and Japanese corporations, where the long-term involvement of investors, especially banks, allowed managers to invest for the long run while, at the same time, monitoring their performance.

(Becht *et al.* 2005:33–4)

Stakeholders and shareholders

The insistent focus of corporate governance in the Anglo-American market perception on boards, CEOs and shareholders, who are oriented almost obsessively towards short-term performance to satisfy financial markets, has not served the discipline—or corporations—very well. This approach not only narrows the dimensions of corporate governance to a restricted set of interests, but also as a result, it has a very limited view of the dilemmas involved in corporate governance, the interests served, or the people engaged in the enterprise and its success (Jurgens *et al.* 2000; Aguilera and Cuervo-Cazurra 2004; Deakin 2005).

Contemporary discussions of corporate governance have come to be dominated by the view that public corporations are little more than bundles of assets collectively owned by shareholders (principals) who hire directors and officers (agents) to manage those assets on their behalf. This principal–agent model, in turn, has given rise to two recurring themes in the literature: first, that the central economic problem addressed by corporation law is reducing 'agency costs' by keeping directors and managers faithful to shareholders' interests; and second, that the primary goal of the public corporation is—or ought to be—maximizing shareholders' wealth.

(Blair and Stout 1999:248)

In practice this approach to governance often has translated into companies either being driven simply by narrow financial goals to the exclusion of other concerns, or descending into self-interested managerialism by executives who have slipped the leash of shareholders' scrutiny.

This is not the form of management or corporate governance that has been widely practiced in Europe where a stakeholder approach to management and governance is deeply embedded in institutions and thinking. The ideal principles that underpin the stakeholder orientation in European approaches are outlined by Rienk Goodijk (2000) as:

- decision making in consultation
- a broad and responsible weight of interests
- countervailing power and competition of ideas
- a certain/minimum balance of power in relations
- an open dialogue and continuous feedback
- ability and power to learn, creating adaptability and flexibility
- not only short-term problem solving but also longer-term orientation
- durable commitment
- shared responsibility
- societal legitimacy
- visions and values, based on debate
- performance-measurement and ethical auditing.

Exercising these principles necessitates an active role and involvement of stakeholders. Stakeholders are able to participate in the decision-making, and hold the top management of the company accountable where strategic choices, investments, reorganizations, dividend policy, etc. are concerned (Rienk Goodijk 2000). Astonishing as this might appear to executives instilled with finance driven Anglo-American values, this consultative approach is part of the social democratic tradition of managers in North European economies, who have a deeper understanding of stakeholder engagements that complements, and if necessary, counterbalances market orientations.

Compounding inequality in market economies

As Lane (2003) emphasizes, different approaches in corporate governance produce different forms of political economy directly influencing the structure of power and inequality. For the last two decades the US has been portrayed as a great economic success with regeneration achieved by a new economy based on high technology goods, high value-added financial and professional service industries, and full employment. What is rarely considered is that behind the veneer of success is a society and economy blighted by increasing inequality, poverty and social malaise. Essentially the way the new economy has been managed in the US has left virtually *the whole* of the working population behind:

Two related points are central to understanding the income growth in America. First, the most recent business cycle—the 2000s—was unique: despite significant productivity growth in the overall economy, most families experienced stagnant or falling real incomes. The American workforce is working harder, smarter and more efficiently, yet failing to share fairly in the benefits of the growth they themselves are creating. In fact, with data going back to the mid-1940s, it appears that the real income of a typical, middle-income family (i.e. the median) was lower at the end of the 2000s cycle than at the beginning. This never happened before… In the 2000s the longest jobless recovery on record hurt families' earnings capacity, while increased inequality meant the growth that did occur bypassed the middle class. Second, this sharp rise of income inequality has meant the link between economic growth and broadly shared income gains is broken. The most comprehensive data on inequality reveal this stark imbalance. Data on income concentration going back to 1913 show that the top 1% of wage earners now hold 23% of total income, the highest inequality level in any year on record bar one: 1928. In the last few years alone, $400 billion of pretax income flowed from the bottom 95% of earners to the top 5%, a loss of $3,660 per household on average in the bottom 95%.

(2008:3)

The starkness of this inequality is manifest in the levels of pay now commanded by executives in the

United States. During the boom years of the 1990s there was rapid and sustained escalation of executive salaries in the US. However with the market crash of 2001 any adjustment downwards was a very temporary phenomenon before meteoric growth in executive reward returned in the mid-2000s. Included in remuneration is base salary, bonuses, benefits, long-term incentive plans, and profits from cashing out stock options. Despite efforts to link CEO compensation to performance, US CEOs in the S&P 500 continued to be hugely rewarded whether their companies performed well or not. Lucrative share option schemes continued to be extravagantly generous, and if the remuneration packages became more sophisticated, there were many devices available such as backdating utilized to ensure executives extracted the best possible reward from their options. Research by the Washington based Institute for Policy Studies indicates that the average remuneration of the ten highest paid US CEOs of public companies in 2006 was over $46 million. In contrast the ten highest paid European CEOs of public companies in 2006 received $17 million approximately (IPS 2007).

CEO salaries are only a part of wider structures of inequality that have become more extreme in recent years, and rewards for executives in the finance sector have become even more astronomically inflated, for example the hedge funds: James Simons, the Director of Renaissance Technologies, received $1.5 billion in compensation in 2006, Steven Cohen of SAC Capital received $1.2 billion, Kenneth Griffin of Citadel Investment Group also received $1.2 billion, T. Boone Pickens of BP Capital picked up $1.1 trillion, and George Soros earned a modest $950 million. While CEOs of corporations might be criticized for putting their self-interest before that of the companies they manage, the directors of fringe financial institutions appear to have manipulated and destabilized world markets to secure even greater personal reward (IPS 2007; Soros 2008).

Whatever loss occurs to shareholder funds due to excessive CEO salaries in US corporations and financial institutions the wider implications of this extravagance are more serious, in terms of how the corporations are managed, the objectives they pursue, and the consequences for the wider economy and community (IPS 2007; Clarke forthcoming).

Economies that begin to adopt Anglo-American market-oriented corporate governance approaches are not immune to the accompanying implications for levels of inequality. The out-of-control inflation in executive pay in the United States threatens to impact upon executive reward internationally. As Table I.3 reveals, though US CEO compensation across a sample of 350 large public companies remains more than double the reward of CEOs drawn from similar samples of public companies in other advanced industrial countries, the rate of growth of CEO compensation in many other countries in the last decade exceeds that of the United States. Acceptance of this economic model and the accompanying inequality is not inevitable either on equity or efficiency grounds:

> While the United States is a very rich country—currently second only to Norway in per capita income—it also has both the highest level of inequality and the highest level of poverty (including child poverty) of its peers. In other words, much less of the vast income of the United States is reaching the lower end of the income distribution. While it is true that many families in the United States are well-off, a great many are not, especially when compared to low- and moderate-income families in other advanced countries. Second, it is far from a foregone conclusion that economies that have strong welfare states and labor protections are also necessarily less productive, less employment-generating, and less "flexible" than the US economy. Many peer countries with strong unions, high minimum wages, generous social benefits, and high taxes have caught up with, and in many cases surpassed, US productivity while achieving low unemployment levels. Both Norway and the Netherlands, for example, have higher productivity than the United States and lower unemployment rates. It is an important point that so many peer countries have been successful and productive within very different economic models.
>
> (EPI 2008:358)

Strengths and weaknesses of different governance systems

As a consequence of the differences in corporate governance structure and objectives, and the unique business strategies that result, the different systems demonstrate unique strengths and weaknesses: essentially they are good at doing different things, and they all have weaknesses as well as strengths (Moerland 1995; Dore 2002). The Anglo-American

Country	CEO compensation ($ thousands)			Percent change 1988–2005	Ratio of CEO to worker pay, 2005*	Foreign pay relative to US pay, 2005 US =100	
	1988	2003	2005			CEO	Worker
Australia	180,760	737,162	707,747	292	15.6	33	82
Belgium	383,718	739,700	987,387	157	18	46	99
Canada	423,358	944,375	1,068,964	152	23.1	49	83
France	404,331	780,380	1,202,145	197	22.8	56	95
Germany	412,259	1,013,171	1,181,292	187	20.1	55	106
Italy	342,492	893,035	1,137,326	232	25.9	53	79
Japan	502,639	484,909	543,564	8	10.8	25	91
Netherlands	396,403	716,387	862,711	118	17.8	40	87
New Zealand	—	476,926	396,456	—	24.9	18	29
Spain	352,006	658, 039	697,691	98	17.2	32	73
Sweden	234,670	743,160	948,990	304	19.2	44	89
Switzerland	510,567	1,263,450	1,390,899	172	19.3	64	130
United Kingdom	453,485	881,047	1,184,936	161	31.8	55	67
United States	**805,490**	**2,386,762**	**2,164,952**	**169**	**39.0**	**100**	**100**
Non-US average	383,057	794,749	946,931	173	20.5	44	85

* Ratio of CEO compensation to the compensation of the manufacturing production workers
Source: Table 3.47 from Mishel Lawrence, Jared Bernstein and Sylvia Allegretto, *The State of Working America 2006–2007*, an EPI Economic Policy institute Book, Ithaca, N.Y. ILR Press, an imprint of Cornell University Press, 2007.

Table I.3 **International comparison of CEO pay trends, 1988–2005**

governance system supports a dynamic market orientation, with fluid capital which can quickly chase market opportunities wherever they occur. This agility and speed equipped the United States to capitalize on the new economy of electronics, software, media, financial and professional services: an industrial resurgence that reasserted the US global economic ascendancy. The downside of this system is the corollary of its strength: the inherent volatility, short termism and inadequate governance procedures that have often left US manufacturing industry stranded, and caused periodic stock market panics and recurrent crashes.

In marked contrast, European enterprise, as typified by the German governance system, traditionally has committed to a long-term industrial strategy supported by stable capital investment and robust governance procedures that build enduring relationships with key stakeholders (Cernat 2004; Lane 2003). This was the foundation of the German economic miracle which carried the country forward to becoming the leading exporter in the world of products renowned for their quality and reliability, including luxury

automobiles, precision instruments, chemicals, and electrical engineering. Again the weaknesses of the German system were the corollary of its strengths: the depth of relationships often leading to a lack of flexibility, that made it difficult to pursue initiatives for new businesses and industries while accumulating costs in established companies, resulting in high unemployment. The Latin variant of European corporate governance as practiced in France and Italy is highly network-oriented, with dominant holdings by the state, families, or industrial groups. Ownership concentration provides for stability and long-term horizons, with strong relationships with stakeholders. This governance system has allowed the Southern European countries to specialize in selected industries with notable success; for example in France, aerospace, rail and other industries have benefited from state involvement, and luxury goods derived from centuries of expertise have passed down through family firms. In Italy, fashion and design goods developed in long-standing networked supply chains, have brought high fashion and creative interior design to the world (Goyer 2001). However, in this system often weak governance accountability and frequent network and pyramid control diminishes the integrity of the equity market with the dominance of blockholder relationships precluding others from becoming involved.

Superiority of any one system of governance cannot be accepted, yet this is often implied in the official policies of international agencies such as the OECD, IMF and World Bank (O'Sullivan 2001; Lane 2004; Clarke 2007). Confidence and trust in the Anglo-American system after the market crashes of 1987, 2001, and 2008 cannot be assumed, even if recovery is managed quicker than expected (Lorsch *et al.* 2005). There is some connection in the pattern of these cyclical crises in American capitalism, and the resuscitation from one crisis can set in train the circumstances that lead to the next crisis, as occurred with the cheap debt used to recover from the crisis of 2001, that ultimately caused the much bigger crisis of 2008. There is a deep historical tendency in the Anglo-American model towards instability and inequity (Galbraith 1993; MacAvoy and Millstein 2004) and a certain inappropriateness in the rapid adoption of this model in other regimes (Mitchell 2001; Oman *et al.* 2005; McClintick 2006; Clarke and dela Rama 2006).

Cycles of crisis and regulation in corporate governance

All of the different corporate governance systems have experienced recurrent periods of crisis that have exposed their structural weaknesses. Just as the OECD, World Bank and IMF were increasingly confidently projecting the Anglo-American market-based outsider system of governance as the preeminent model from which all other countries might learn, the Enron disaster occurred. The corrosive greed that became an integral part of the incentive system in US corporate governance yielded a more sinister fruit in the protracted spate of corporate frauds and bankruptcies of 2001/2002 leading to the collapse of the Nasdaq and NYSE. The apparently dynamic, competitive and performance-oriented US economy of the 1990s degenerated over time as executives, faced with the necessity to demonstrate ever-increasing returns, resorted to illegal means to do so (Boyer 2005). Creative accounting and a sometimes criminal collusion between executives, auditors and analysts inflated a speculative bubble which finally burst, but

not before many executives had cashed in their options, leaving their own employees destitute and superannuation funds depleted around the world. Both the European and Asian forms of corporate governance have also experienced some acute difficulties. Though Europeans have not witnessed anything quite as catastrophic as the corporate collapses in the US, there have periodically been disasters, for example the Parmalat debacle which revealed a leading Italian listed company which had been used as personal property by its chief executive for many years. There are continuing doubts concerning the close network relationships that typify much of European enterprise.

The worldwide commitment towards improving standards of corporate governance has encompassed a succession of legislative changes to company law, most strikingly in the US with Sarbanes-Oxley, but progressive legal reform has occurred in almost all jurisdictions. This has been supported by the national corporate governance codes introduced in many countries. Reinforcing the effort to achieve substantial reform, the international agencies—especially the OECD, World Bank and Asian Development Bank—have maintained a constant drive towards the adoption of more *rules-based* corporate governance systems. This culminated in the publication of the OECD *Principles of Corporate Governance* in 1999, and revised in 2004 in the light of the post-Enron lessons. A growing number of corporate governance ratings agencies have monitored changes at both corporate and national levels. Yet *rules-based* corporate governance is often portrayed as the antithesis of *relationship-based* corporate governance (that is the systems of corporate governance that exist in Europe, Asia and throughout most of the rest of the world). The drive for reform of corporate governance, for greater accountability and transparency, should not be conflated with the simple adoption of Anglo-American practices in this way. (Often when this occurs a veneer of rules-based systems simply conceals the continuing practice of underlying traditional institutions and relationships.)

Experience suggests corporate governance crisis and reform is essentially cyclical (Clarke 2004,2007). Waves of corporate governance reform and increased regulation occur during periods of recession, corporate collapse and re-examination of the viability of regulatory systems. During long periods of expansion, active interest in governance diminishes, as companies and shareholders become again more concerned with the generation of wealth, than in its retention. This cyclical pattern of stock market booms encouraging and concealing corporate excesses undoubtedly will continue. When recession highlights corporate failings, statutory intervention invariably occurs. Avoiding mandatory restrictive over-regulation requires active market regulation – particularly in times of expansion. There will never be a 'perfect' system of corporate governance. Market systems are competitive and volatile and dynamic systems of governance will reflect this. But corporate governance is about risk-management. The drive to make corporate governance both improve corporate performance, and enhance corporate accountability will continue (Clarke 2007). However in Europe the drive to reform corporate governance is often conflated with the drive to establish more firmly Anglo-American governance policies and practices to the exclusion of traditional European approaches and values.

EUROPEAN CORPORATE GOVERNANCE REFORM

Europe has become very engaged in corporate governance reform and market reform in recent years. A series of policy initiatives commenced with the *Action Plan on Modernizing Company Law and Enhancing Corporate Governance in the EU* (2003) which gave the reasons for change as:

- the impact of recent financial scandals;
- the trend of European countries to engage in cross-border operations in the Internal Market;
- the integration of European capital markets;
- the rapid development of new information and communication technologies;
- the increase of Member States to the European Union.

The European Commission DG Internal Market stated:

Harmonization of the rules relating to company law and corporate governance, as well as to accounting and auditing, is essential for creating a Single Market for Financial Services and products. In the fields of company law and corporate governance, objectives include: providing equivalent protection for shareholders and other parties concerned with companies; ensuring freedom of establishment for companies throughout the EU; fostering efficiency and competitiveness of business; promoting cross-border cooperation between companies in different Member States; and stimulating discussions between Member States on the modernization of company law and corporate governance.

(IFC 2008:3)

The policy areas are covered in the Action Plan included:

- the reform and harmonization of corporate governance;
- the raising and maintenance of legal capital;
- regulating the operation of groups of companies;
- restructuring and takeovers of companies;
- new European company forms such as the European private company as well as other enterprise and foundation forms;
- the transparency of national legal forms of corporate governance.

Recognizing this extensive set of policies as a unified project Hopt argues:

The objectives of the Action Plan are twofold. The first goal is to strengthen shareholders' rights and the protection for employees, creditors, and other parties with which companies deal. This is meant mainly to create and maintain confidence in companies within the European Union. The second aim is closely interrelated with the first. The Commission intends to foster the efficiency and competitiveness of business, with special attention to some specific cross-border issues. The one cannot be reached without the other; they are two sides of the same coin.

(2005:3)

However, the long and controversial process of deliberation at every level of the European political apparatus that these proposals have engendered, and the bargaining and insistence on national interpretations of these policies as they have been implemented is not simply a result of the protective stance of national governments towards their own institutional traditions and practices, but a wider sense of unease about the ultimate destination of these reforms. "Popular resistance to Europeanization focuses on the perceived contradiction between market liberalism and social protection." (Leisink and Hyman (2005:279)

The central objective of European Commission policy was to "consolidate dynamically towards an integrated, open, inclusive, competitive and economically EU financial market" in order that "capital can circulate freely throughout the EU at the lowest possible cost" (*White Paper on Financial Services Policy (2005–2010)*. The provisions concerning corporate governance were largely directed to the same goal to enable the free movement of capital by facilitating the establishment of companies in other member countries with similar regulatory frameworks, offering legal certainty in intra-Community operations, strengthening shareholder rights to enable companies to raise capital at the lowest cost, and fostering efficiency and competitiveness of business. Similarly the vision laid out in the *Lisbon Strategy/2005 Community Lisbon Programme* "to become the most competitive and dynamic knowledge-based economy in the world capable of sustainable economic growth, with more and better jobs and greater social cohesion" was related closely to the "full integration of financial markets," contributing to raising output and employment "by allowing more efficient allocation of capital and creating better conditions for business finance."

The key areas for corporate governance reform included the following:

- Requirements for companies to publish corporate governance statements (usually involving 'comply or explain' statements relating to national corporate governance codes – or in the Dutch version, 'apply or explain');
- Creation of company board nomination, remuneration and audit committees, (composed of independent non-executive directors);
- Confirming directors' collective responsibility for company financial statements;
- Adopting structural flexibility by giving companies a choice between different board structures (as already adopted in Italy and France);
- Increasing sanctions for directors' malfeasance;
- Enhancing the freedom of shareholders to vote across countries;
- Examining shareholder control-enhancing mechanisms and the potential for abuse by pyramid groups.

All of these proposed measures encountered a degree of dissension among different national governments and their business elites, however it was the proposal on reforming shareholder control-enhancing mechanisms that together with the policy on takeover bids that provoked the greatest opposition. The EU *Takeover Bids Directive* (2007) acknowledged that takeovers "discipline management and stimulate competition" and that the aim of the European Commission was to "promote integration of European capital markets by creating favourable conditions for the emergence of a European market for corporate control." The European Corporate Governance Forum (ECGF) (2007:9) argued that:

> By making control over listed companies contestable, companies are enabled to restructure efficiently and to develop the optimal size and scope of activities in the light of EU and global markets. In addition, the mere existence of a market for corporate control (specifically, the threat of a takeover bid in the case of underperformance) has a disciplining effect on management.

This rationale was not as persuasive on the ground, and both national governments and companies continued to find ingenious ways to protect themselves from hostile takeover bids.

The issue of control-enhancing mechanisms remains the central dilemma of European corporate governance with continuous efforts to address the question of the proportionality between capital and control. This dilemma lies at the heart of the continuing effort of European countries to protect their industries from what they view as the danger of rapacious takeovers by overseas companies or hedge funds, and what overseas investors often interpret as the self-interest of inside block-holders who deny the rights of other shareholders. The "Proportionality Principle" as defined in the Report of the High Level Group of Company Law Experts of 2002 that prepared the way for the EU Action Plan was that:

> Proportionality between ultimate economic risk and control means that share capital which has an unlimited right to participate in the profits of the company or in the residue on liquidation, and only such share capital, should normally carry control rights, in proportion to the risk carried. The holders of these rights to the residual profits and assets of the company are best equipped to decide on the affairs of the company as the ultimate effects of their decisions will be borne by them.
>
> (Shearman and Sterling 2007:5)

There are many kinds of control-enhancing mechanisms (CEMs), and in one form or another they exist to a degree in all corporate governance systems. Some CEMs are employed to allow blockholders enhanced control by leveraging voting power such as pyramid structures (Figure I.7). Other forms of CEM may function as devices to lock-in control as with priority shares, voting rights ceilings, ownership ceilings and supermajority provisions. CEMs also may be part of legal structures adopted by companies such as partnerships limited by shares, or as part of privatizations with the state retaining the influence of golden shares, or may be incorporated in shareholder agreements. These mechanisms may be devised by companies as in multiple voting rights shares, or organized independently by shareholders as in voting pacts and pre-emption pacts. Survey evidence suggests that 44 percent of large European companies have one or more CEMs. Countries with the highest proportion of CEMs are France, Sweden, Spain, Hungary, and Belgium, all of which have a majority of companies with CEMs. As Figure 7 indicates the most common CEMs in large European companies are pyramid structures, multiple voting rights shares, and shareholder agreements (Shearman and Sterling 2007:6).

The ECGF (2008:6) argues that "Non-proportional systems do raise concerns in relation to board entrenchment, extraction of private benefits by the controlling shareholder, incontestability of control and ineffectiveness of corporate governance codes based on 'comply or explain' approaches." However, depending on the context in which they are utilized, control-enhancing mechanisms can have benefits as well as drawbacks. The literature is inconclusive on whether differentiated voting rights lead to lower performance, managerial entrenchment and impair firm value compared to one-share-one-vote companies. In Europe the distinction is more recognized between the interests of the shareholders and the interests of the company. Further empowering transient shareholders may be more in their interests than those of the company concerned:

The one-share-one-vote mandatory rule can further exacerbate the dark side of institutional shareholder activism, i.e. short-termism. Institutional shareholders have taken a greater advocacy role to support the rule (of one-share-one-vote) but just for their own interest rather than that of their fellow or minority shareholders. Combining the rule with the application of different derivative

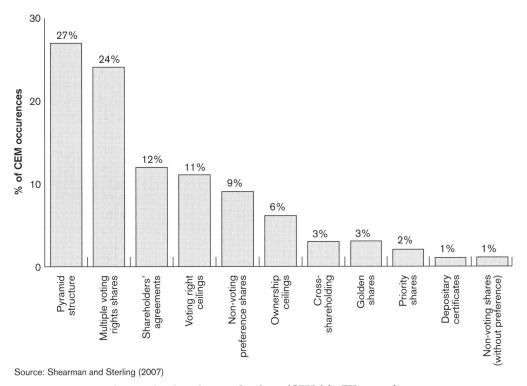

Source: Shearman and Sterling (2007)

Figure I.7 **Frequency of control-enhancing mechanisms (CEMs) in EU countries**

techniques such as stock lending, equity swaps, direct and indirect hedges, hedge funds particularly can retain formally more voting control as compared to cash flow rights. This will effectively allow them more voting shares as compared to cash flow ownership, and hence compromising long-term profitability for the sake of short-term payoffs. The one-share-one-vote mandatory rule combined with derivative techniques will allow hedge funds to destroy shareholder value through proxy fights for corporate control… The company can be either shielded from value-increasing takeovers or transferred to inefficient management. In both cases, the more stock prices slide and more shareholder value is destroyed, the more profits are made from hedge fund short positions.

(Khatchaturyan 2006a:1, 2006b)

When reference is made to "shareholder democracy" and sometimes "corporate democracy" with regard to the one-share-one-vote principle, not only should it be remembered that these votes will not always be used responsibly in the long-term interests of either shareholders or companies, but that this whole conception of shareholder democracy is often part of an exclusive claim for control rights to the company, which goes far beyond the rights of shareholders enshrined in law even in the Anglo-American legal system. That the myth of the shareholder prerogative has been disseminated so successfully in recent decades does not make it right either in law or practice (Blair and Stout 1999, 2001). Traditionally in all European forms of corporate governance the obligations of the company have been more widely interpreted, which has proved integral to social cohesion. As the ETUC has argued:

The Lisbon Agenda speaks out in favour of a "high road" strategy against a "low road" strategy for industrial restructuring and wealth creation. However, following the "high road" of a highly skilled, committed workforce and high productivity requires the acceptance by European companies of the broader notion of social quality, rather than just a narrow approach geared towards serving shareholder interests. In this connection companies need to respect and consider the interests and wishes of their employees very carefully in the interests of achieving a high level of economic performance. EU company law initiatives should therefore endorse the emergence

and evolution of a European model of corporate governance, fostering company boards' orientation towards long-term value creation, high-trust labour relations, workers' participation in companies' decision-making processes and societal responsibility. Not only shareholders, but also workers, other citizens and the community at large have an interest in good corporate governance. Accordingly, the European corporate governance framework should lay down proper institutional conditions for companies to promote long-term profitability and employment prospects, define mechanisms that prevent mismanagement and guarantee transparency and accountability with regard to investments and their returns.

(ETUC 2006a)

The ETUC goes on to emphasize that in 12 out of 28 EU and EEA member states (Sweden, Denmark, Czech Republic, Slovak Republic, Netherlands, Finland, Hungary, Austria, Germany, Slovenia, Luxembourg and Norway),

Workers have a mandatory, legally binding right to be represented in company boards and to influence management decisions in both state-owned and private companies. Co-determination in these countries is a fact, diverse in structure, but deeply rooted in different cultural and historically developed environments. Workers' participation seems to work well in both single and two-tier board environments, making a positive contribution to companies' performance. In other countries participation is the result of bargaining practices and also guarantees an influence on the strategic choices of companies.

In this context of employee rights and stakeholder interests being part of the institutional foundations of corporate governance in Europe, in the great surge of European reform "it should not be a deliberate aim or even a collateral effect of Community legislation that they be undermined or by-passed through optional corporate forms immune to employee participation" (ETUC 2006b).

CHALLENGES AHEAD

In preparing for the economic challenges ahead Europe is confronting two inescapable imperatives:

the first is the necessity to rejuvenate mature industries and to create new, innovative industries; the second—and much greater challenge—is to achieve sustainability in all economic activity (Benn and Dunphy 2006). It is difficult to imagine how economic reforms directed simply at developing the market mechanisms and shareholder value of the Anglo-American model could possibly contribute effectively to either of these challenges. Of course America is associated with the arrival of the New Economy based on information technology and financial services, but it is ironic that in both of these industries unrestrained speculation in the NASDAQ in the late 1990s, and in financial instruments in the 2000s has led to catastrophic crashes. (Interestingly Germany's brief flirtation with its Neuer Markt established in 1997 and modeled on the NASDAQ, was plagued with scandals and collapsed at the end of 2003.) When the sustainability challenge is contemplated, the United States has proved the greatest break not only on developing its own economy towards sustainability, but impeding the progress of the international effort to work towards sustainability and slow the pace of climate change. The dismal record of the US car industry in this regard, is demonstrable evidence of how a single-minded focus on stock price can ruin an industry.

Bill Lazonick has charted how throughout the long boom of the New Economy in the United States in the 1990s, rather than a general renewal of business enterprise leading to higher productivity and shareholder value, there were three different forces at work simultaneously:

> High stock yields reflected a combination of three distinct forces at work in the US corporate economy: a) *redistribution* of corporate revenues from labour incomes to capital incomes, especially by older corporations, through a combination of down-sizing of the labour force and increased distribution to shareholders in the form of dividends and stock repurchases; b) *innovation*, especially by newer technology companies, that boosted earnings per share; and c) *speculation* by stock market investors, encouraged, initially by stock price increases due to the combination of redistribution and innovation. An understanding of these three sources of an ebullient stock market is essential for a critical evaluation of the efficiency claims of the shareholder-value perspective.
>
> (2007:5)

By the mid-2000s, under sustained pressure from the stock market to perform, corporate America had returned to an emphasis on redistribution (something Jensen (1986) once referred to as disgorging the cash flow). Even the most established high technology companies such as Microsoft were forced to announce tens of billions of dollars in share buyback programmes in order to restore the companies, share price. This earnings game consisted of top executives and boards allocating profits to increased dividends and share buybacks, and receiving for themselves huge stock option awards, while weakening the firm's resources needed to innovate and compete (Lazonick 2007:41-2). If innovation is a gradual, cumulative and collective process, the social conditions of innovation require more careful nurturing than this. Europe has diverse traditions of industrial and business innovation that have proved more durable.

Responding to the urgent imperative to discover and apply sustainable approaches to economic activity will be a demanding challenge for all developed and developing countries in the coming years. At a national level the United States was left as the only advanced country in the world that did not sign the Kyoto agreement, and at a corporate level US corporations lost a major opportunity to translate their technological leadership into sustainable products and processes in the early 2000s. Though with a new Democratic President and Congress energetic efforts will be made to recover this opportunity, there is little indication the US stock market is far-sighted enough to support these endeavors. In contrast the European Union recognized that environmental sustainability and climate change required an integrated program of policies relating to European industry, and the promotion of sustainability in developing countries (Behrens 2008). The initiative to build a Global Climate Change Alliance in 2007, is aimed at practical cooperation between the EU and developing countries most vulnerable to climate change. Other aspects of EU policy including the common agricultural policy impact on the environment, and the commitment to building the infrastructure of the integration of the common market are open to question. Similarly with European companies, often they have been at the forefront of international business policy on sustainability, though their actions may not always have lived up to their declared intentions. However it is hard to see how a shift towards a more market-based investment and governance system would encourage the pursuit of sustainability in Europe.

REGIME CHANGE? THE TRANSFORMATION OF EUROPEAN CORPORATE GOVERNANCE

The readings in this collection examine in detail the question of whether the current transformation of corporate governance in Europe amounts to a *regime change* from the established relationship-based system. The implications for the future political economy of Europe involved in the changes in corporate governance taking place are explored in depth. Part One examines the dimensions of governance in the widest perspective. The structures of governance, processes of decision-making and forms of accountability have all been subject to extensive reformulation. The moral dimensions of economic transactions, and the integration of value creation and moral values are examined. The fundamental question of what is the corporation, and what are the objectives, and what are the appropriate structures to pursue those objectives of the corporation are addressed. Part Two explores the rich variety of capitalism that exists in Europe, and investigates the distinctive qualities of each system, and how each system is developing. The defining feature of European corporate governance is its institutional diversity. The governance systems of Italy, France, and the UK are analyzed. How European countries are pragmatically adopting elements of different governance systems, while retaining a distinctive national institutional identity is considered.

Part Three questions whether European countries will converge towards a common corporate governance system, or sustain the present diversity of institutions. Despite the pressures towards adopting Anglo-Saxon modes of corporate governance, the divergencies in both policy and practice of corporate governance in Europe thus far have resisted any move towards a universal application of pan-European standards. In Europe the obligations towards transparency and regulation of financial markets continue to develop, but national variations in corporate law remain largely intact. Critical to the pressures towards convergence in corporate governance are the vast growth in scale and increasing activity of international financial markets. Part Four examines how while absorbing the impact of international financial markets, and reorienting towards shareholder value conceptions of the firm, Europe has been engaged in the reform and transformation of corporate governance as part of the wider harmonization project. Lengthy deliberations involved in securing reforms have often left member countries with the freedom of choice they demanded on how to implement particular reforms.

Part Five isolates the doctrine of shareholder value as the sharpest point of advance of the Anglo-Saxon mode of corporate governance in Europe. The methods used to generate shareholder value, and the impact of an excessive focus on shareholder value are investigated. The problematic nature of the concept of shareholder value is considered, and the practical imperative of returning to a more holistic conception of the objectives of firms. Part Six assesses the implications of the power and reward attributed to the CEO in Anglo-American models of corporate governance. In contrast in Europe almost invariably there is a requirement for CEOs to work within an inclusive, and often social democratic normative order. How US executives have reformulated the functions of the board, and their own remuneration is examined, and what this means for the objectives pursued by the corporation. The paradox of how stock options and financial market incentives, which were introduced to discipline managers, have allowed them to enhance their power and reward is examined. The question of how CEO performance and reward could become inversely related, and how CEOs could become increasingly focused on financial markets is addressed, together with the consequences of this for business accountability and performance.

APPENDIX – TRANSATLANTIC CONTAGION: US AND EUROPEAN BANK FAILURES

September 2007			
1	Northern Rock	UK	Northern Rock faced a run on the bank, rescued by the British government loan of £26 billion and guarantees of £30 billion and was effectively nationalized in February 2008 ultimately extending £119 billion in support.

March 2008			
2	Bear Sterns	US	Federal Reserve of New York offered an emergency loan, but could not be saved. Bought by JPMorgan Chase in a deal sponsored by the US Federal Reserve, sold at $10 per share, far below 52-week highest price of $133 per share.
July 2008			
3	IndiMac	US	A commercial bank with $19 billion in deposits, on the brink of failure was taken over by the Federal Deposit Insurance Corporation.
September 2008			
	Fannie Mae and Freddie Mac	US	With combined losses of $14.9 billion and their ability to raise capital and debt threatened, the two agencies had outstanding more than $5 trillion in mortgage-backed securities (the national debt of the US is by comparison $9.5 trillion). The US government took the two mortgage agencies into 'conservatorship' with the Treasury contributing $US 200 billion in preferred stock and credit through 2009.
4	AIG	US	AIG was one of the world's largest insurance companies specializing in high margin corporate coverage. Its share price fell 95 percent to $1.25 from a 52 week high of $70, with the company reporting a $13.2 billion loss for the first six months of the year. The Federal Reserve offered a credit facility of up to $85 billion in exchange for warrants for a 79.9 percent equity stake, the largest government bailout of a private company in US history. Later this rescue package was increased to $150 billion, with the US Treasury purchasing $40 billion in preferred shares.
5	Lehman Brothers	US	With large positions in subprime mortgages it was declared bankrupt after US Federal Reserve refused bailout. Barclay's bought its investment banking arm for $1.75 billion.
6	Merrill Lynch	US	Bloomberg reported that Merrill Lynch had lost $51.8 billion in mortgage-backed securities. The firm was bought by Bank of America for $US 50 billion.
7	HBOS	UK	The UK's largest mortgage lender, it was bought by British rival Lloyds TSB for £12 billion.
8	Washington Mutual	US	After a 10-day $16.4 billion bank run it was declared bankrupt and placed in the receivership of the Federal Deposit Insurance Corporation; JPMorgan Chase bought the banking assets from US government. Before this it had been the sixth largest bank in the US (with assets of $327 billion). This was the largest bank failure in US history.
9	Bradford & Bingley	UK	Nationalized by British government; savings operations sold to Spain's Group Santander.
10	Fortis	Benelux	A banking, insurance and investment company, it was the twentieth largest business in the world by revenue. Dutch operations nationalized by Netherlands; Belgian and Luxemburg operations bought by France's BNP Paribas.

11	Dexia	Belgium	A financial services company which was bailed out by French, Belgian and Luxemburg governments with € 6.4 billion.

October 2008

12	Wachovia	US	With assets of $783 billion, the fourth largest bank holding company in the US. Reported an anticipated $8.9 billion loss for the second quarter of 2008. Subject of a $US 15 billion takeover offer from Wells Fargo, which is being contested by Citigroup.
13	Glitnir	Iceland	One of the three major commercial banks of Iceland, Icelandic government injects €600 million for 75 percent stake, as part of a rescue of the country's entire financial system. Shortly afterwards Kaupthing Edge part of Iceland's leading bank failed, and Landsbanki, the third bank failed, as Iceland's entire banking system collapsed and was taken over by the government. Since Icelandic banks held foreign assets worth 10 times the GDP of the country, there are concerns that the government is bankrupt as it urgently sought loans from the IMF and Russia.
14	Hypo Real Estate	Germany	The second largest commercial property lender in Germany, which includes Depfa property finance bank. German government leads a €50 billion bailout with the German banks contributing €30 billion and the Bundesbank €20 billion.
15	Preference shares in: Bank of America, Citigroup, JPMorgan, Wells Fargo, Goldman Sachs, Morgan Stanley, PNC, and 18 other banks	US	Following a series of individual rescue attempts, the US government resolves to offer general support to the failing financial system. The US Federal Treasurer Hank Paulson's package of US$720 billion to relieve financial institutions of subprime and other toxic assets. After a troubled passage through Congress reflecting the public's anger at 'bailing out Wall Street' conditions are attached regarding public oversight and executive pay. Subsequently followed the UK policy in purchasing preference shares of banks to rebuild the capital adequacy of large banks in the United States.
16	Preference shares in: Barclays, HBOS, Lloyds TSB, Nationwide, Royal Bank of Scotland, Abbey, Standard Chartered	UK	In response to collapsing bank share prices, and a rapidly weakening financial sector, the UK government determines on a major three part intervention: a £50 billion offer to buy preference shares to assist the major banks to rebuild their capital reserves; £200 billion of liquidity in short term loans to thaw the inter-bank lending markets; and a further £250 billion to underwrite lending between banks. Conditions include restraint on dividend policies, executive pay, and support for lending to small businesses and home buyers.
17	UBS	Switzerland	Swiss bank UBS AG told it expected to post net losses of 12 billion Swiss francs (US$12.1 billion) for the first quarter of 2008 and would seek 15 billion Swiss francs (US$15.1 billion) in new capital. UBS announced losses and writedowns of approximately US$19 billion on US real estate and related credit positions, Swiss government took an indirect SF 6 billion stake in UBS. Swiss national bank took $59 billion of UBS's illiquid US securities.

18	ING	Netherlands	ING one of the world's largest banks with 85 million customers worldwide, and with 385 billion euros in saving and current account deposits announces it expects to make a €500 million third quarter loss. The Dutch government makes a €10 billion cash injection for shares in the bank.
19	D.Carnegie & Co AB	Sweden	Sweden's largest publicly traded investment bank founded 200 years ago having lost 87 percent of its value, was seized by the Swedish government, accused of taking exceptional risks, to be sold off in parts.
20	Citigroup	US	Citigroup is unable to stem losses and markets become concerned. Citigroup's shares fall 23 percent on 19 November to their lowest since May 1995. CEO announces winding down off-balance sheet businesses and making 52,000 redundancies. The following day the shares fall a further 20 percent, and the day after another 20 percent. Realising only government rescue will save one of the world's largest banks, the Federal Reserve and Treasury agree Citigroup a "systemic risk" to allow $300 billion rescue.

BIBLIOGRAPHY

Amble, B. (2000) Institutional Complementarity and Diversity of Social Systems of Innovation and Production, *Review of International Political Economy*, 7(4) 645–687.

Amble, B. (2003) *The Diversity of Modern Capitalism*, Oxford: Oxford University Press.

Aglietta, M. and Berrebi, L. (2007) *Désordres Dans Le Capitalisme Mondiale*, Paris: Odile Jacob.

Aglietta, M. and Rebérioux, A. (2005) *Corporate Governance Adrift: A Critique of Shareholder Value*, Cheltenham: Edward Elgar.

Aguilera, R. and Cuervo-Cazurra, A. (2004) Codes of Governance Worldwide: What is the Trigger? *Organization Studies*, 25: 415–443.

Auletta, K. (1986) *Greed and Glory on Wall Street: The Fall of the House of Lehman*, New York: Random House.

Bebchuk, L.A. and M.J. Roe (1999) A Theory of Path Dependence in Corporate Ownership and Governance, *Stanford Law Review*, 52: 127–170.

Becht, M., Bolton, P. and Röell, A. (2005) Corporate Governance and Control, *Finance Working Paper 02/2002*, (Updated 2005). Brussels: European Corporate Governance Institute.

Behrens, A. (2008) Financial Impacts of Climate Change: An Overview of Climate Change-related Actions in the European Commission's Development Cooperation, CEPS Working Document No. 305/September, Brussels: Centre for European Policy Studies.

Beitel, K. (2008) The Subprime Debacle, *Monthly Review*, May.

Benn, S. and Dunphy, D. (2006) *Corporate Governance and Sustainability*, London and New York: Routledge.

Blair, M.M. (1995) *Ownership and Control: Rethinking Corporate Governance for the 21st Century*, Washington DC: Brookings Institute.

Blair, M. and Stout, L. (1999) A Team Production Theory of Corporate Law, *Virginia Law Review*, 85(2): 247–328.

Blair, M. and Stout, L. (2001) Director Accountability and the Mediating Role of the Corporate Board, *Washington University Law Quarterly*, 79: 403.

Boyer, R. (2005) From Shareholder Value to CEO Power: the Paradox of the 1990s. *Competition and Change*, 9(1): 7.

Branson, D. (2001) The Very Uncertain Prospects of "Global" Convergence in Corporate Governance, *Cornell International Law Journal*, 34: 321–362.

Centre for Transatlantic Relations/Centre for European Policy Studies, Washington D.C. (CTR/CEPS) (2005) *Deep Integration: How Transatlantic Markets are Leading Globalization*, John Hopkins University: CTR/CEPS.

Cernat, L. (2004) The Emerging European Corporate Governance Model: Anglo-Saxon, Continental or Still the Century of Diversity?, *Journal of European Public Policy*, 11 (1): 147–166.

Chesnais, F. (2008) Fin d'un cycle. Sur la portée et le cheminement de la crise financière. *Carré Rouge – La Brèche*, 1: 17-31, January.

City of London (2008) *The Global Financial Centres Index*, Guildhall: www.cityoflondon.gov.uk/economicresearch.

Clarke, T. (2004) *Theories of Corporate Governance*, London: Routledge.

Clarke, T. (2005) *Corporate Governance: Critical Perspectives in Business and Management: Volume 1: The Genesis of Corporate Governance, Volume 2: Anglo-American Corporate Governance, Volume 3: European Corporate Governance, Volume 4: Asian Corporate Governance, Volume 5: Contemporary Developments in Corporate Governance*, London: Routledge.

Clarke, T. (2007) *International Corporate Governance: A Comparative Approach*, London and New York: Routledge.

Clarke, T. (forthcoming) A Critique of the Anglo-American Model of Corporate Governance, *Economy and Society*.

Clarke, T. and dela Rama, M. (2006) *Corporate Governance and Globalisation*, London: Sage.

Coffee, J. C. (1999) The Future as History: The Prospects for Global Convergence in Corporate Governance and its Implications, *Columbia Law School Working Paper Series*.

Coffee, J.C. (2002) Convergence and its Critics: What are the Preconditions to the Separation of Ownership and Control? in McCahery, J.A., Moerland, P., Raaijmakers, T. and Renneboog, L. (eds.) *Corporate Governance Regimes: Convergence and Diversity*, Oxford: Oxford University Press.

Coffee, J. (2006) *Gatekeepers: The Professions and Corporate Governance*, Oxford: Oxford University Press.

Davis, G.F. (2005) New Directions in Corporate Governance. *Annual Review of Sociology* 31:143–162.

Deakin, S. (2005) The Coming Transformation of Shareholder Value, *Corporate Governance: An International Review*, 13(1): 11–18.

Deeg, R. and Jackson, G. (2006) Towards a More Dynamic Theory of Capitalist Variety, Research Papers, No. 40, King's College London, Department of Management, p. 49.

Dore, R. (2000) *Stock Market Capitalism: Welfare Capitalism*, Oxford: Oxford University Press.

Dore, R. (2002) Will Global Capitalism be Anglo-Saxon Capitalism? *Asian Business and Management*, 1(1): 9–18.

Economic Policy Insitute (EPI) (2008) *The State of Working America*, Washington: EPI.

Ee, K. and Xiong, K. (2008) Asia: A Perspective on the Subprime Crisis, International Monetary Fund, June 2008, Volume 45, Number 2, Last accessed 1 November 2008, http://www.imf.org/external/pubs/ft/fandd/2008/06/khor.htm.

Einhorn, D. (2008a) Private Profits and Socialized Risk, *Global Association of Risk Professionals Review*, June/July, 42: 10-18.

Einhorn, D. (2008b) *Fooling Some of the People All of the Time: A Long Short Story*, Hoboken, New Jersey: Wiley.

Epstein, G.A. (2005) *Financialization and the World Economy*, Northampton, MA: Edward Elgar.

Erturk, I., Froud, J., Johal, S., Leaver, A. and Williams, K. (eds.) (2008) *Financialization at Work: Key Texts and Commentary*, London: Routledge.

European Corporate Governance Forum (ECGF) (2007) *Working Group on Proportionality*, Brussels: ECGF.

European Corporate Governance Forum (ECGF) (2008) *Annual Report*, Brussels: ECGF.

European Trade Union Congress (ETUC) (2006a) ETUC Resolution Adopted at ETUC Executive Committee, Brussels 14/15 March 2006, Brussels: ETUC.

European Trade Union Congress (ETUC) (2006b) Executive Minutes, 18/19 Oct 2006, Brussels: ETUC.

European Union (EU) (2003) *Action Plan on Modernizing Company Law and Enhancing Corporate Governance in the EU*, Brussels: EU.

Fleckenstein, F. (2008) *Greenspan's Bubbles: The Age of Ignorance at the Federal Reserve*, New York: McGraw Hill.

Freeman, R. (2000) Single-peaked vs. Diversified Capitalism: The Relation between Economic Institutions and Outcomes, *NBER* Working Paper No. 7556.

Froud, J., Haslam, C., Johal, S. and Williams, K. (2000) Shareholder Value and Financialisation, *Economy and Society*, 29 (1): 80–110.

Froud, J. and Johal, S. (2008) Questioning Finance, *Competition and Change*, 12(2) June.

Froud, J., Johal, S., Leaver, A. and Williams, K. (2006) *Financialization and Strategy: Narrative and Numbers*, London: Routledge.

Galbraith, J.K. (1993) *A Short History of Financial Euphoria*, London: Penguin.

Goodijk, R. (2000) Corporate Governance and Workers' Participation, *Corporate Governance*, 8(4): 303–310.

Goodman, P. (2008) Taking a Hard New Look at the Greenspan Legacy, *New York Times*, October 8.

Gordon, J.N. and Roe, M.J. (2004) *Convergence and Persistence in Corporate Governance*, Cambridge: Cambridge University Press.

Goyer, M. (2001) Corporate Governance and the Innovation System in France 1985–2000, *Industry and Innovation*, 8(2): 135–158.

Greenspan, A. (2004) Risk and Uncertainty in Monetary Policy. American Economic Association, San Diego, California January 3, 2004, Federal Reserve Board. http://www.federalreserve.gov/BoardDocs/Speeches/2004/20040103/default.htm.

Hall, P. and Soskice, D. (2001) *Varieties of Capitalism*, New York: Oxford University Press.

Hamilton, D.S. and Quinlan, J.P. (2005) *Deep Integration: How Transatlantic Markets are Leading Globalisation*, Brussels: Centre for European Policy Studies/Center for Transatlantic Relations.

Hansmann, H. and Kraakman, R. (2001) The End of History for Corporate Law, *Georgetown Law Journal*, 89: 439.

Hauster, G. (2002) The Globalisation of Finance, *Finance and Development*,

Hilferding, R. (1985) *Finance Capital: Study of the Latest Phase of Capitalist Development*, London and New York: Routledge (original edition 1910).

Hollingsworth, J. Rogers and Boyer, R. (1997) *Contemporary Capitalism: The Embeddedness of Institutions*, Cambridge, UK; New York: Cambridge University Press.

Hopt, K.J. (2005) European Company Law and Corporate Governance: Where Does the Action Plan of the European Commission Lead? Law Working Paper 52/2005, Brussels: European Corporate Governance Institute.

International Finance Corporation (IFC) (2008) *The EU Approach to Corporate Governance*, Washington D.C.: International Finance Corporation/Global Corporate Governance Forum.

International Financial Services London (IFSL) (2008) *International Financial Markets in the UK*, London: IFSL.

Institute for Policy Studies (IPS) (2007) Executive Excess 2007, Washington D.C.: Institute for Policy Studies/United for a Fair Economy http://www.faireconomy.org/files/ExecutiveExcess2007.pdf.

Institute for Policy Studies (IPS) (2008) *A Sensible Plan for Recovery*, Washington: IPS October 15.

International Monetary Fund (IMF) (2002) The Globalization of Finance, *Finance and Development,* Washington: IMF 39, 1.

International Monetary Fund (IMF)(2008) *Global Financial Stability Report: Financial Stress and Deleveraging,* Washington: International Monetary Fund IMF.

IOSCO (2003) *IOSCO Statement of Principles Regarding the Activities of Credit Rating Agencies: A Statement of the Technical Committee of the International Organization of Securities Commissions,* Madrid: IOSCO.

Janszen, E. (2008) The Next Bubble: Priming the Markets for Tomorrow's Big Crash, *Harper's Magazine,* February, 39–45.

Jensen, M.C. (1986) Agency Costs of Free Cash Flow, Corporate Finance, and Takeovers. *The American Economic Review,* 76(2): 323–329.

Jurgens, U., Naumann, K. and Rupp, J. (2000) Shareholder Value in an Adverse Environment: The German Case, *Economy and Society,* 29(1): 54–79.

Khatchaturyan, A. (2006a) Trapped in Delusions: Democracy, Fairness and One-Share-One-Vote, *ECMI Commentary No. 11,* European Capital Markets Institute, 18 December.

Khatchaturyan, A. (2006b) The One-Share-One-Vote Controversy in the EU, *ECMI Paper No. 1,* European Capital Markets Institute, August 1, http://shop.ceps.eu/BookDetail.php?item_id=1364.

Kirchmaier, T. and Grant, J. (2005) Corporate Control in Europe, *Journal of Corporate Ownership and Control,* 2, 2.

Krippner, G.R. (2005) The Financialization of the American Economy, *Socio-Economic Review,* 3:173–208.

Krugman, P. (2008) Cash for Trash, *New York Times,* 21 September.

La Porta, R., Lopez-de-Silanes, F. and Shleifer, Al. (1999) Corporate Ownership Around the World, *Journal of Finance,* 54(2): 471–517.

Laeven, L. and Valencia, F. (2008) Systemic Banking Crises: A New Database, *IMF Working Paper,* WP/08/224, Washington D.C.: International Monetary Fund.

Lane, C. (2003) Changes in Corporate Governance of German Corporations: Convergence to the Anglo-American Model? *Competition and Change,*7(2): 79–100.

Lane, C. (2004) Globalization and the German model of capitalism – erosion or survival? *British Journal of Sociology,* 51 (2): 207–234.

Langley, P. (2008) *The Everyday Life of Global Finance: Saving and Borrowing in Anglo-America,* Oxford: Oxford University Press.

Lazonick, W. (2007) The US Stock Market and the Governance of Innovative Enterprise, *Industrial and Corporate Change 2007,* 16(6): 983–1035.

Leisink, P. and Hyman, R. (2005) The Dual Evolution of Europeanization and Varieties of Governance, *European Journal of Industrial Relations,* 11(3): 277–286.

Le Roy, P. (2008) *The Subprime Mortgage Crisis: Highlighting the Need for Better Corporate Governance,* University of Technology, Sydney.

Lewis, H., (2007) 'Moral hazard' helps shape mortgage mess, April 18, 2007, Last accessed 10 November 2008, http://www.bankrate.com/brm/news/mortgages/20070418_subprime_mortgage_morality_a1.asp?caret=3c.

Lim, M., (2008), Old Wine in a New Bottle: Subprime Mortgage Crisis—Causes and Consequences, *Working Paper No. 532,* The Levy Economics Institute, April.

Lockhart, D., (2008), The Subprime Crisis: Is It Contagious?, Federal Reserve Bank of Atlanta, 29 February 2008, Last accessed 10 November 2008, http://www.frbatlanta.org/invoke.cfm?objectid=65C8B587-5056-9F12-125B76D448344BEF&method=display.

Lorsch. J.W., Berlowitz, L. and Zelleke, A. (2005) *Restoring Trust in American Business,* Cambridge, MA: American Academy of Arts and Sciences.

McAvoy, P.W. and I.M. Millstein (2004) *The Recurrent Crisis In Corporate Governance,* Stanford: Stanford Business Books.

McCahery, J.A., Moerland, P., Raaijmakers, T. and Renneboog, L. (2002) *Corporate Governance Regimes: Convergence and Diversity.* Oxford, Oxford University Press.

McClintick, D. (2006) How Harvard Lost Russia, *Institutional Investor,* 40(1): 62–90.

McDonnell, B.H. (2002) Convergence in Corporate Governance – Possible, but not desirable, *Villanova Law Review,* 47(2): 341–386.

McKinsey and Company (2008) *Mapping Global Capital Markets,* Fourth Annual Report, San Francisco: McKinsey Global Institute.

Martin, R. (2002) *The Financialization of Daily Life,* Philadelphia, PA: Temple University Press.

Maximus, F. (2008), Consequences Of A Long, Deep Recession – Parts I, II, III. http://fabiusmaximus.wordpress.com/2008/06/18/consequences-1/ -2, -3. 18-20, June.

Mitchell, L.A. (2001) *Corporate Irresponsibility: America's Newest Export,* New Haven, CT: Yale University Press.

Moerland, P.W. (1995) Corporate Ownership and Control Structures: An International Comparison, *Review of Industrial Organization,* 10(4): 443–464.

Muolo, P. and Padilla, M. (2008) *Chain of Blame: How Wall Street Caused the Mortgage and Credit Crisis,* Hoboken, New Jersey: Wiley.

Narayanan, M.P. (1985) Managerial incentives for short-term results, *Journal of Finance* 40(5): 1469–1484.

Nestor, S. and Thompson, J.K. (2000) Corporate Governance Patterns in OECD Economies: Is Convergence Under Way? Discussion Paper, Paris: OECD.

Oman, C., Fries, S. and Buiter, W. (2005) Corporate Governance in Developing, Transition and Emerging-market Economies, *OECD Policy Insight No. 3,* Paris: OECD.

O'Sullivan, M.A. (2001) *Contests for Corporate Control: Corporate Governance and Economic Performance in the United States and Germany,* London: Oxford University Press.

Patel, B., (2008), Credit Crisis and Corporate Governance Implications: Guidance for Proxy Season and Insight into Best Practices, RiskMetrics Group, April 2008, Last accessed 1 Nov 2008 http://www.riskmetrics.com//system/files/private/CreditCrisisCorporateGovernance20080408.pdf.

Phillips, K. (2008) *Reckless Finance Bad Money: Reckless Finance, Failed Politics, and the Global Crisis of American Capitalism,* New York: Viking Books.

Porter, M.E. (1992a) Capital Disadvantage: America's failing Capital Investment System, *Harvard Business Review,* pp. 65–82.

Porter, M.E. (1992b) Capital Choices: Changing the Way America Invests in Industry, *Journal of Applied Corporate Finance*, 4.

Rebérioux, A. (2000) European Style of Corporate Governance at the Crossroads: The Role of Worker Involvement, *Journal of Common Market Studies*, 40 (1): 113–134.

Roe, M. (2003) *Political Determinants of Corporate Governance. Political Context, Corporate Impact*, Oxford: Oxford University Press.

Roe, M.J. (2005) The Inevitable Instability of American Corporate Governance, in J. Lorsch, L. Berlowitz and A. Zelleke, *Restoring Trust in American Business*, Cambridge: MIT Press.

Rosen, R. (2007) The Role of Securitization in Mortgage Lending, Chicago Fed, 11 October 2007, Last accessed 10 November 2008, http://www.chicagofed.org/publications/fedletter/cflnovember2007_244.pdf.

Schwarcz, S. (2008) Disclosure's Failure in the Subprime Mortgage Crisis, Research Paper Series, Research Paper No. 203, Duke Law School, March.

Scott, W.A. (2008) The Credit Crunch and the Law – A Commentary on Economic and Policy Issues, in R.P. Austin (ed.), *The Credit Crunch and the Law*, Monograph 5, Ross Parsons Centre of Commercial, Corporate and Taxation Law, University of Sydney.

Shearman and Sterling (2007) *Report on the Proportionality Principle in the European Union*, Paris: Shearman and Sterling/Brussels: Institutional Shareholder Services/Brussels: European Corporate Governance Institute.

Shiller, R. (2008) *The Subprime Solution: How Today's Global Financial Crisis Happened and What to Do About It*, Princeton, NJ: Princeton University Press.

Shleifer, A. and R.W. Vishny (1989) Equilibrium Short Horizons of Investors and Firms, *American Economic Review*, 80(2): 148–153.

Soros, G. (2008) *The New Paradigm for Financial Markets: The Credit Crisis of 2008 and What it Means*, New York: Public Affairs.

Stein, J.C. (1988), Takeover Threats and Managerial Myopia, *Journal of Political Economy*, 96: 61–80.

Stein, J.C. (1989) Efficient Capital Markets, Inefficient Firms: a Model of Myopic Corporate Behavior, *Quarterly Journal of Economics*, 104: 655–669.

Stiglitz, J. (2008a) Realign Wall Street's Interests, *Harpers Magazine*, November, 36-37.

Stiglitz, J. (2008b) Henry Paulson's Shell Game, *The Nation*, September 26.

Thomsen, S., Pedersen, T., Kvist, H. (2003) The Effect of Blockholder Ownership on Firm Value in Market and Control Based Governance Systems, *Copenhagen Business School Working Paper*.

UBS (2008) *Shareholder Report on UBS's Write Downs*, Zurich: UBS AG www.ubs.com/1/ShowMedia/investors/shareholderreport?contentId=140333&name=080418ShareholderReport.pdf.

Van Kersbergen, K. and Van Waarden, F. (2004) 'Governance' as a Bridge Between Disciplines, *European Journal of Political Research*, 43: 143–171.

Whalen, C. (2008) The Subprime Crisis—Cause, Effect and Consequences, Networks Financial Institute, Indiana State University, March.

Whitley, Richard (1999) *Divergent Capitalisms: The Social Structuring and Change of Business Systems*. Oxford: Oxford University Press.

PART ONE

Dimensions of Governance

INTRODUCTION TO PART ONE

Part One examines the dimensions of governance in the widest perspective. The recent transformation of European corporate governance is part of a wider restructuring of governance arrangements universally. This has encompassed changes in both the private and public sectors at local, regional, national and international levels. A replacement of traditional governance institutions by new forms of governance has transformed the management and control of social and economic institutions at every level. The structures of governance, processes of decision-making, and forms of accountability have all been subject to extensive reformulation in the interests of adapting to new social and economic demands. In this broad conception governance involves a "system of rule, as the purposive activities of any collectivity, that sustain mechanisms designed to ensure its safety, prosperity, coherence, stability and continuance" (Rosenau 2000:171).

In the first reading Kees Van Kersbergen and Frans Van Waarden discuss the concept of governance as a bridge allowing a cross-disciplinary consideration of issues of governability, accountability and legitimacy. The different aspects of the definition of governance they outline associates governance with legitimacy and efficiency. They recognize that increasingly the mechanisms delivering legitimacy and efficiency once identified with national governments are now often associated with international, regional or local collectivities. While internationalization continues, it remains clear that different regions, countries and localities manage successfully with different kinds of institutions and approaches to governance.

Good governance in the market sector refers to the system of ownership, direction and control of business corporations in the pursuit of the accountability and transparency that will attract investors and public respect. This consideration of the importance of good governance has progressed into new public sector management, often involving restructuring in the interests of better performance and customer satisfaction. A new frontier is in the governance of networks of public, private and community organizations. This mode of governance is self-organized and directed, and rooted in common trust and negotiated understandings. Networks can involve bringing together different levels of government across policy areas, finding multi-dimensional solutions to multi-dimensional problems.

Finally, in the market sector there is the morphing of hierarchical entities into an increasing emphasis on the cooperation of dense networks of firms whether in clusters of smaller enterprises, or in multiple strategic alliances (Hermens 2009). The question could be posed, "What is the relevance of individual corporate governance in an era of networked enterprises?" In fact, although the network has become the dominant organizational metaphor of the digital age, it remains an emergent form. Networks synthesize multiple experiences in informal and open social systems, and have demonstrated a remarkable capacity to coordinate complex activities. Networks have demonstrated a wide adaptability and have proved viable in facilitating creativity in knowledge development and innovation in a wide variety of industrial firms, public sector organizations, community groups, and international agencies. The many different types of dynamic knowledge network; their fluid form, and restless existence have compounded the difficulties of understanding the mysteries of network governance. Though networks have often been considered as antithetical to more traditional modes of organization including the bureaucracy, market and clan, it is interesting to consider how networks may coexist with other modes of organization (Josserand 2004:113). Much of the thinking on network governance concentrates on the more autonomous forms of network; however networks involved with more formal structures are probably as significant in their impact.

Even autonomous networks necessarily evolve governance frameworks around building relationships with prospective partners, establishing membership protocols, setting network objectives, specifying human and resource requirements, and codifying these understandings. Similarly many forms of network experience a life-cycle, a co-evolution of relations of knowledge, power and trust. Van Kersbergen and Van Waarden distil the essence of network modes of governance as relations between relatively autonomous but interdependent actors such as business firms, or public and private organizations, compared to more simplified structures of hierarchical control. Therefore in network governance the central processes are negotiation, accommodation, cooperation and alliances rather than command and control.

Van Kersbergen and Van Waarden go on to consider the implications of shifts in autonomous policy making and governance of nation states to transnational and supranational actors. Simultaneously there is also a shift of governance down to local agencies and community bodies. In the international economy both of these impulses are powerful with a pronounced shift towards multinational corporations operating in international markets, often regulated by international agencies, while at the same time often there are vibrant local economies with clusters of firms making important contributions. In this new and more complex and changing context traditional governance institutions often prove ineffective, and this has drawn attention to new sources of legitimacy, accountability and responsiveness.

Looking at how European corporate governance is responding to the new responsibilities it faces, Wieland focuses in upon the moral dimensions of economic transactions, and at integration of value creation and moral values. From this perspective formal compliance procedures cannot in themselves achieve improvements in corporate governance. Similarly a singular focus on shareholder value cannot displace the moral compass of the corporation. Hence Wieland offers an expansive definition of governance as the resources and capabilities of corporations, including moral resources, to accept responsibility for meeting the interests of all stakeholders. These principles have been reflected in the majority of European corporate governance codes surveyed, and often have deep historical and cultural resonances in different European countries. In essence what Wieland is arguing is that effective leadership, management and control of corporations is impossible without integrating the moral commitments and values which inform behaviour. Where governance systems of monitoring and compliances are unsupported by moral values and ethical cultures, disasters such as Enron, WorldCom and Arthur Andersen occur. When such dislocation of rules and values happens, not only are the rules circumvented but risks are concealed. Wieland emphasizes the importance of integrating corporate governance and business ethics and the relevance of this for strategic and operational decision-making processes.

This inevitably leads to fundamental questions of what is the corporation, what are the objectives of the corporation, who are the key economic actors, and what are the appropriate governance structures to pursue these objectives? Different theoretical approaches offer different answers to these key questions (Clarke 2004). Agency theory has a narrowly-focused, market-based utility-maximizing view of the corporate actors involved, and the governance structures that are required to allow owners to monitor and control managers. From the view of transaction cost economics the firm is a nexus of contracts that organize and regulate transactions of products and services, focusing on the hierarchical governance structures that decide the integrity of transactions, with the objective of the effective accomplishment of transactions. In contrast organization theory in its resource-based and competence-based approaches understands the corporation as a pool of human and organizational resources, where the purpose of governance is to coordinate these resources to achieve economic success.

There are similar important distinctions in approach among the great array of corporate governance codes that have been developed and applied across Europe in the last 20 years. Different codes represent different ideas on the objectives and orientations of the firm. Wieland distinguished three significant approaches of the European codes in their understanding of corporate governance:

■ *Maximization Model*
  Focusing on shareholder interests, this regards the firm largely from the viewpoint of agency theory as a vehicle for increasing shareholders' capital.
■ *Economizing Model*
  Adopting the view of transaction cost economics, the firm is regarded as an organizational vehicle for accomplishing economic transactions in an efficient way.

..

■ *Cooperation Model*

The firm is seen as a vehicle for coordinating the cooperation between possessors of internal and external resources to realize material and non-material benefits.

From his consideration of how different European codes manifest one or other of these three approaches, Wieland concludes that corporate governance codes that focus on the agency problem in a utility maximizing model are not open to the wider dimensions of business ethics beyond honoring contracts. In contrast the economizing and cooperation models do allow for the integration of moral and social responsibility into corporate governance and business decision making. This wider frame of reference of stakeholder-oriented codes enables economic calculation to be informed by questions of moral and social responsibility.

REFERENCES

Clarke, T. (2004) *Theories of Corporate Governance: The Philosophical Foundations of Corporate Governance*, London: Routledge.

Hermens, A. (2009) *The Governance of Strategic Alliances*, London: Routledge.

Josserand, E. (2004) *The Network Organization: The Experience of Leading French Multinationals*, Cheltenham: Edward Elgar.

Kooiman, J. (1993) *Modern Governance*, London: Sage.

Lazonick, W. (2001) Public and Corporate Governance: The Institutional Foundations of the Market Economy, *Economic Survey of Europe*, 2: 59–76.

Nooteboom, B. (2002) *Trust: Forms, Foundations, Functions, Failures and Figures*, Cheltenham: Edward Elgar.

Rhodes, R.A.W. (1997) *Understanding Governance*, Buckingham: Open University Press.

Rosenau, J.N. (2000) Change, Complexity and Governance in Globalising Space, in J. Pierre (ed.), *Debating Governance: Authority, Steering and Democracy*, Oxford: Oxford University Press.

von Tunzelmann, N. (2001) Historical Coevolution of Governance and Technology, *The Future of Innovation Studies*, Eindhoven University of Technology, The Netherlands, September 20–23.

1 "'Governance' as a Bridge Between Disciplines: Cross-disciplinary Inspiration Regarding Shifts in Governance and Problems of Governability, Accountability and Legitimacy"

from European Journal of Political Research (2004)

Kees van Kersbergen and Frans van Waarden

SUMMARY

Modern societies have in recent decades seen a destabilization of the traditional governing mechanisms and the advancement of new arrangements of governance. Conspicuously, this has occurred in the private, semi-private and public spheres, and has involved local, regional, national, transnational and global levels within these spheres. We have witnessed changes in the forms and mechanisms of governance by which institutional and organizational societal sectors and spheres are governed, as well as in the location of governance from where command, administration, management and control of societal institutions and spheres are conducted. We have also seen changes in governing capabilities (i.e., the extent to which societal institutions and spheres can, in fact, be steered), as well as in styles of governance (i.e., the processes of decision making and implementation, including the manner in which the organizations involved relate to each other). These shifts tend to have significant consequences for the governability, accountability, responsiveness and legitimacy of governance institutions. These developments have been generating a new and important research object for political science (including international relations).

One of the crucial features of these developments is that they concern a diversity of sectors. In order to get a thorough understanding of 'shifts in governance', political science needs, and is also likely to adopt, a much stronger multidisciplinary orientation embracing politics, law, public administration, economics and business administration, as well as sociology, geography and history.

INTRODUCTION

In recent decades, traditional governance mechanisms have started to become destabilized and new governance arrangements have emerged. Such shifts in governance have occurred in the private, semi-private and public spheres, and at (and in-between) the local, regional, national, transnational and global levels. Changes have taken place in the forms and mechanisms of governance, the location of governance, governing capacities and styles of governance. These changes have been the subject of a variety of literatures and disciplines, including political science, law, public administration, economics, business administration and sociology as well as geography and history. These literatures all give the term 'governance' different meanings. Nevertheless, the concept could function as a bridge between disciplines, and it might stimulate comparisons between rather different phenomena, which, when viewed under the more abstract perspective of governance, might be found to have something in common.

Political science has been studying such shifts in governance, but largely in ignorance of the increased use of the same concept in neighboring disciplines. In this article, we look over the fence to these other disciplines. Though we do not believe that the concept of 'governance' can in the near future become a common 'theory' shared between disciplines – the theoretical and methodological diversity is simply too great for that – it can become a vehicle for comparison and for mutual learning and theoretical inspiration.

We begin with a short review of the various meanings of the concept 'governance' in different literatures. A first commonality is empirical-analytical and descriptive: they all describe and analyse 'shifts in governance', albeit at different levels and in different sectors of society. Second, there is a common concern for the problems of governability, accountability and, hence, legitimacy associated with 'shifts in governance'. As such issues have traditionally been of central concern to political science, looking over the fence into other disciplines may enrich the political science research agenda. After all, many of the problems of legitimacy, accountability and legitimacy arise from shifts from traditional national political institutions to other levels, sectors and organizations of society that have been the subject of other disciplines. We therefore conclude by identifying some issues and questions for such a research agenda that could become part of a multidisciplinary one.

GOVERNANCE: A REVIEW OF LITERATURES

The study of governance has become a veritable growth industry. The Online Contents catalogue of journals, for instance, returned 24 hits of the term 'governance' in 1990, 510 hits in 1999 and 603 hits in 2000. The number of books in Dutch libraries carrying the term in their title was 23 in 1990, 154 in 1999 and 119 in 2000. However, there has been quite some theoretical and conceptual confusion. In what different meanings do we find the concept of 'governance' used? Hirst (2000) distinguished five versions of

'governance'. We follow him, but rearrange them and add a few uses derived from other authors (Rhodes 1997, 2000; Pierre & Peters 2000).

Good governance

The first prominent modern usage of 'governance' is in the field of economic development, where the World Bank and other international organizations have been stressing sound or good governance (see Janning 1997). Good economic governance belongs to the so-called 'second generation reforms', consisting of reducing wasteful public spending; investing in primary health, education and social protection; promoting the private sector by regulatory reform; reinforcing private banking; reforming the tax system; and creating greater transparency and accountability in government and corporate affairs (Rosenbaum & Shepherd 2000; Woods 2000; Philip 1999; Kiely 1998). This usage stresses the political, administrative and economic values of legitimacy and efficiency and, in the words of one theorist, therefore 'marries the new public management to the advocacy of liberal democracy' (Rhodes 2000: 57). However, good governance has also been promoted for advanced economies. Thus the OECD (Organization for Economic Cooperation and Development) has propagated good governance by comparing best practices in key areas such as public management, business–government relations and social policy.

Governing without government I: International relations

A second meaning of the concept stems from international relations theory and refers to the possibility of governing without government (Rosenau & Czempiel 1992), in the form of international or even global governance (Prakash & Hart 1999) and global democracy (Holden 2000; Murphy 2000; Sassen 2000; Ronit & Schneider 1999; Hewson & Sinclair 1999; Michie & Grieve Smith 1999). This literature has pointed to the possibility of policy cooperation between nation-states in an international system that *prima facie* is not conducive to such cooperation. The international system lacks a hierarchy, or – to put it differently – is characterized by an anarchy of competing, interdependent states that acknowledge no authority other than their own (see Lieshout 1995). Although states may cooperate in international organizations and regimes, these are 'cooperative acts to which authority may be attached but which can also be withdrawn if states so wish' (Rosenau 2000: 170).

However, theorists decreasingly perceive international politics solely as cooperation between independent states. Instead, international organizations, regimes and treaties are seen as new forms of international governance for dealing with typically transnational problems. Rosenau (2000: 171) defines governance as 'systems of rule, as the purposive activities of any collectivity, that sustain mechanisms designed to ensure its safety, prosperity, coherence, stability, and continuance'. These mechanisms, usually the core business of governments, are increasingly found in international collectivities.

Governance without government II: Self-organization

A third use of governance refers to self-organization of societies and communities, beyond the market and short of the state. Typical is the work of Elinor Ostrom (1990), who studied the capacity of communities in different places and times to manage common pool resources and prevent their depletion (a prime example is overfishing). Small local communities have done so without the help of a formal government through bottom–up self-government by associations, informal understandings, negotiations, regulations, trust relations and informal social control rather than state coercion. Ostrom's focus was on the conditions that facilitated such governance arrangements and made them effective, efficient and stable.

Economic governance (with and without the state): Markets and their institutions

A fourth usage is economic governance. This approach has developed in a variety of disciplines, including economic history (North & Thomas 1973; North 1990), institutional economics (Williamson 1975, 1985, 1996), economic sociology (Smelser & Swedberg 1994), comparative political economy (Hollingsworth & Boyer 1997; Crouch & Streeck 1997; Hall 1999), and labour relations and labour

economics (Soskice 1990; Brunetta & Dell'Aringa 1990; Streeck 1992; Teulings & Hartog 1999). They have all done so more or less in discussion with neoclassical mainstream economics.

While classical economics assumed markets to be spontaneous social orders that flourish best in the absence of any intervention, many political theorists and lawyers start from the opposite assumption. Following Hobbes, they assume that the natural societal condition is one of chaos, uncertainty and conflict. New institutional economics, economic sociology and comparative political economy brought these approaches together by emphasizing that markets are not spontaneous social orders, but have to be created and maintained by institutions. These provide, monitor and enforce rules of the game, which among other things fix property rights, back up contracts, protect competition, and reduce information asymmetries, risk and uncertainties.

Societies have produced a variety of institutions to govern economic transactions, help reduce their costs and hence increase the likelihood of their occurrence. Governments are only one source of such institutions. Others are contracts, commercial businesses, private sector hierarchies, voluntary associations, courts, clans and communities. In other words, 'governance' is a broader category than 'government'. Much of it takes place without direct state involvement, though the shadow of hierarchy may either incite private actors to create private governance institutions (to pre-empt state intervention) or back up private governance arrangements (e.g., courts enforcing contract law).

Comparative political economy has four conceptual approaches to economic governance: national policy styles literature (Van Waarden 1995), neo-corporatism, neo-institutionalism and the organization of production (Hall 1999). Recently new lines of research have been developed. Neo-corporatism has focused on sectoral governance (Hollingsworth & Boyer 1997). 'Flexible specialization' literature has focused on decentralization (Boyer & Saillard 2002; Jessop 2001), while neo-corporatism and neo-institutionalism have developed 'varieties of capitalism' literature emphasizing that countries may perform well with different sets of institutions, even in the face of internationalization (Crouch & Streeck 1997; Kitschelt *et al.* 1999; Coates 2000; Ebbinghaus & Manow 2001; Hall & Soskice 2001).

'Good governance' in the private sector: Corporate governance

The fifth usage is that of corporate governance – a watchword, according to Hirst (2000: 17), 'of those who wish to improve the accountability and transparency of the actions of management, but without fundamentally altering the basic structure of firms in which indifferent shareholders are the principal beneficiaries of the company'. As a generic concept, it refers to the system of direction and control of business corporations (Blair & Roe 1999; Cohen & Boyd 2000; Demirag 1998; Dine 2000; Hopt 1997; Keasey et al. 1999; Lannoo 1999; OECD 1999; O'Sullivan 2000; Sternberg 1998; Williams 1999). This usage is connected to the 'good governance' approach. Thus the OECD has established a set of (non-binding) principles of corporate governance that 'represent a common basis that OECD Member countries consider essential for the development of good governance practice' (see www.oecd.org/daf/ governance/ principles.htm). One idea is that governments can increase macroeconomic efficiency by promoting good corporate governance because investment possibilities increasingly come to depend upon it.

'Good governance' in the public sector: New public management

The sixth use of governance is found in the New Public Management (NPM) literature. While corporate governance brought 'good governance' practices to the business sector, new public management has endeavoured to introduce what it considered 'good governance' into public organizations. This has entailed, for the most part, bringing management concepts from private business into the public realm (e.g., performance measurement, customer and bottom line orientation, restructuring of incentives) as well as the conditions that would facilitate this, such as deregulation, outsourcing, tendering out and privatization (Hirst 2000: 18; Brudney et al. 2000; Lane 2000; Lynn 1998; Minogue et al. 1998; Pollitt & Bouckaert 2000). In their classic formulation, Osborne and Gaebler (1992) attempt to 'reinvent government' and distinguish 'steering' (policy decisions), of which a modern state needs more, from 'rowing' (service delivery) of which it needs less. They formulated principles for entrepreneurial government (Nagel 1997). Analytically and empirically, NPM focuses on the

similarities between public sector reforms in countries that are politically and economically very different. In all these reforms, the market is a model for public policy implementation. It will come as no surprise then that NPM is inspired by public choice, principal-agent theory and transaction cost economics (Kaboolian 1998).

Governance in and by networks I: In general

A seventh meaning of the term 'governance' is found in the burgeoning literature on governance through networks. There are many strands of this. A main distinction is between those that refer to networks of public and of private organizations, and of mixes of public and private ones. In all three literatures, networks are explicitly conceptualized as pluricentric forms of governance in contrast to multicentric (market) and unicentric or hierarchical forms (state, firm hierarchy). They are considered to be self-organizing, and to 'resist government steering, develop their own policies and mould their environments' (Rhodes 2000: 61). Furthermore, they are characterized by an exchange of resources and negotiations, and by game-like interactions 'rooted in trust and regulated by rules of the game negotiated and agreed by network participants' (Rhodes 2000: 61).

Networks of public policy organizations have been considered to be 'the analytical heart of the notion of governance in the study of public administration' (Rhodes 2000: 60). Yet, there are many versions of this literature, varying from early analyses of corporatist networks of interest groups (Schmitter 1974) via the state's (limited) capacity of societal steering (In't Veld 1991) and the actor-centred institutionalist (ACI) analysis of policy networks (Scharpf 1997; Mayntz & Scharpf 1995) to Castells's (1996) network society and the sociocybernetic analysis of public–private mixes of societal problem-solving (Kooiman 1993; Van Waarden 1992).

ACI, a more important recent contribution, combines rational choice theory and new institutionalism. It seeks to explain policies and policy outcomes from intentional actions of interdependent actors, acknowledging that these are shaped by their institutional settings. Self-organizing networks are such institutional settings. Unlike in anarchic fields, minimal, majoritarian and hierarchic institutions, negotiations are the typical mode of interaction. Scharpf uses the concept of 'network' to specify conditions that reduce transaction costs of negotiations. Network relationships 'reduce the risk of opportunism by two mechanisms, the longer "shadow of the future" and the higher visibility of transactions to relevant others' (Scharpf 1997: 137). Networks as informal institutional settings help overcome collective action problems.

Networks of private organizations are a sub-form of self-organization of society and, in particular, the economy. They have been studied by researchers in the fields of industrial economics, organization studies and political economy (for an overview, see Ebers 1999). Business firms may cooperate in networks to combine resources (knowledge, skills, market access, finance), to organize specific activities (e.g., innovation), to realize economies of scale and scope; but they may also play a role in economic governance (see above): reducing risk and uncertainty in transactions and markets, overcoming collective action problems, and regulating and ordering economic sectors. Examples are the development of technical standards, the provision of sectoral collective goods (e.g., training, basic research, collective insurance), price and wage setting, and channelling competition. Their advantage is that they tend to be more flexible than economic governance through hierarchies.

A third network form is that which combines both public and private organizations. Such networks have been studied, for instance, by the resource dependency approach (e.g., Alter & Hage 1993). It emphasizes that many public services are not exclusively delivered by government, but by networks of actors from the government, private and voluntary sectors. These networks coordinate and allocate resources, and are again an alternative to, not a hybrid form of, the market or the state.

Network governance II: Multilevel governance

The notion of 'multilevel governance', an eighth use of the term governance, has two origins. In international relations theory it was a modernization of the earlier 'regime' concept (Hasenclever et al. 1997; Verbeek 2001). Krasner (1983: 2) defined the latter as 'a set of implicit or explicit principles, norms, rules, and decision-making procedures around which actors' expectations converge in a given area of international relations'. 'Governance' is a related concept: it refers both to the power relations resulting from

such rules, as well as the substance of policies. 'Multilevel' refers to different government levels (e.g., European, national, sub-national), but also to the involvement of both public and private actors at these levels.

The other ancestor of multilevel governance is comparative European public policy analysis (Wallace & Wallace 1996; Peterson & Bomberg 1999; Richardson 1996; Marks et al. 1996a; Mazey 1996; Bulmer 1998; Hurrel & Menon 1996; Rhodes & Mazey 1995). It developed in response to state-centrism in European integration theory, which treats policy making in the European Union as a two-level game (Moravcsik 1993, 1998).

The state-centric or 'inter-governmentalist' school explains European integration – defined as policy coordination between nation-states – as a series of rational choices made by national leaders. Moravcsik (1998) explains the choices to 'pool and delegate' sovereignty to international institutions as efforts by governments to constrain and control one another and to enhance the credibility of commitments. Transnational institutions thus resolve incomplete contracting problems. One core assumption in this approach is that the state is a unitary and rational actor. This approach is criticized by multilevel theorists. They deny that nation-states are the exclusive connection between domestic politics and intergovernmental bargaining in the European Union (EU) and stress the importance of policy networks that are organized across policy areas and government levels (Marks et al. 1996b). Therefore, the multilevel governance literature is linked to the governance-as-network literature (Héritier 1999). In fact, a recent important study by Kohler-Koch and Eising (2000) prefers to speak of 'network governance' in the EU rather than multilevel governance. The core idea of network governance is that:

political actors consider problem-solving the essence of politics and that the setting of policy-making is defined by the existence of highly organised social sub-systems....The 'state' is vertically and horizontally segmented and its role has changed from authoritative allocation 'from above' to the role of 'activator'. Governing the EC [European Community] involves bringing together the relevant state and societal actors and building issue-specific constituencies. Thus, in these patterns of interaction, state actors and a multitude of interest organisations are involved in multilateral negotiations about the allocation of functionally specific 'values'. (Eising & Kohler-Koch 2000a: 5; emphasis in original)

European policy networks involve both public and private interests. It is assumed that actors in these networks are self-interested, but that they also have an interest in community-friendly behaviour.

Network governance III: Private – From hierarchies to networks

Network governance has also drawn the attention of disciplines that study the private sector, such as industrial economics, organizational studies and business administration, where a ninth use of the term 'governance' emerged. It has been noticed that in many economic sectors, a concentration phase was followed by a phase in which hierarchy was again replaced by a looser form of proto-organization: cooperation of smaller firms in networks. Existing large firms have felt compelled to concentrate again on 'core competencies' in order to rid themselves of activities and subsidiaries and to outsource these to other firms. They, as well as new, smaller start-up firms, have also felt a need for complementary resources – in particular, knowledge – leading them to engage in more or less enduring cooperative relations with a host of other firms, often leading to the formation of extensive, dense, complicated and more or less stable networks of customers and suppliers, and of competitors cooperating in certain activities (e.g., innovation, major projects) (see, e.g., Saxenian 1996).

Inter-firm cooperation can take many forms. Nooteboom (1999) distinguishes many of these on the basis of two dimensions: claims to profit and decision rights. The forms vary in degree of integration with one end of the continuum being contracting into the market and the other being merger into an integrated firm with centralized ownership and decision-making. In between the two are more or less centralized forms of organization connecting formally distinct firms through associations, industrial districts, consortia, franchises, equity joint ventures and so on.

Such relations have to be managed or 'governed'. They pose specific problems and risks, including loss of relation specific investments, free ridership, opportunism, hold up and blackmailing of the partner(s), and spillover. Firms and their supporting environ-

ment, including the government, have created institutions that help reduce the risks and uncertainties of such inter-firm relations, minimize transaction costs, enable or encourage trust, and facilitate choices within these dilemmas. Such 'governance' institutions include contracts, contract law, institutions for monitoring and enforcing contracts, and providing 'hostages' as security.

The nine approaches

The meaning of 'governance' in these nine approaches may differ, but most of them have some characteristics in common. First of all, the approach is pluricentric rather than unicentric. Second, networks, whether inter- or intraorganizational, play an important role. These networks organize relations between relatively autonomous, but interdependent, actors (e.g., business firms in a sector, public and private organizations, EU Member States). In these networks, hierarchy or monocratic leadership is less important, if not absent. The formal government may be involved, but not necessarily so, and if it is, it is merely one – albeit an important – actor among many others. Third, one finds an emphasis on processes of governing or functions as against the structures of government. These processes are relatively similar in the public and private sectors, and concern negotiation, accommodation, concertation, cooperation and alliance formation rather than the traditional processes of coercion, command and control. Fourth, the relations between actors pose specific risks and uncertainties, and different sectors have developed different institutions to reduce these in order to make cooperation possible or easier. Finally, many approaches are normative. They prescribe an ideal as well as an empirical reality. This holds in particular for the 'good governance', 'corporate governance', 'new public management' and 'multilevel governance' approaches.

These similarities might make it possible for the various literatures that use the concept of 'governance' to learn from each other. For instance, students of multilevel governance in the EU may learn from the organizational literature on economic governance through inter-firm networks by studying to what extent problems and risks are similar. Alternatively, institutions developed to govern inter-firm relations may also work for the governance of inter-organizational relations in the public sector. To advance interdisciplinary learning it is important to bring to light how 'shifts in governance' are perceived in the various literature. It is to this topic that we now turn.

SHIFTS IN GOVERNANCE

Each of the nine strands of literature that use the term 'governance' identify, hypothesize and discuss one or more crucial shifts in governance. To advance inter-disciplinary learning it is important to bring these shifts to light. Vertically, there are upward shifts from nation-states to international public institutions with supranational characteristics such as the EU, the WTO (World Trade Organization) or NAFTA (North American Free Trade Association). Controversies focus on the centrality of states in the international system and effects on their capacity for autonomous policy making. To what extent have EU Member States – as the classic international actors – had to make way for transnational and supranational actors? To what extent are policies decided at the European level? What policy-making capacity do nation-states still have? The formal and informal European policy-making institutions influence the capacity and auton-omy for policy making at the national level. On the one hand, European integration may enhance the capacity of national institutions to deal with the effects of economic internationalization. On the other hand, it may exert pressure on Member States to adapt to European rules and regulations, and thus may affect the national institutional framework of policy making (Moravcsik 1998; Sørensen 1999; Van Kersbergen et al. 1999, 2000; Green Cowles et al. 2001; Føllesdal & Koslowski 1998; Eriksen & Fossum 2000; Neyer 2000; Thomassen & Schmitt 1999b). Most attention has focused on shifts from national to international 'gov-ernments'. However, there is a comparable shift from national to supranational courts, such as the Euro-pean Court of Justice, the European Court of Human Rights, the International Court of Justice and the judi-cial agency of the WTO.

There is also a *downward vertical* shift from national and international to sub-national and regional levels. In part this is related to the internationalization shift: international bodies rely on local agencies to imple-ment and enforce their regulations, and therefore tend to strengthen them. In the economy, of course, there is a *vertical* shift from national to international governance as well: the increased importance of international markets, multinational corporations,

agencies that regulate international economic trans-actions; international standardization bodies such as those found in telecommunications, rating agencies such as Standard's and Poor's, merging stock exchanges that regulate financial capital mobility – all of which is further facilitated by the Internet, e-com-merce and the new economy.

Horizontally in the public sector there is a shift from governance by the executive and legislative powers to the judiciary. In many countries, and in particular also at the level of the European institutions (Stone Sweet 2000), the courts are assuming a more active role in rule interpretation, and as a result also in *de facto* rule formulation – often forced to do so by a more litigious population. That means that judges and courts increasingly occupy the seats of politicians and administrators and take – often reluctantly – political decisions. This seems to be part of a broader tendency of increasing juridification of social rela-tions. Informal relations are becoming increasingly formalized, and mutual expectations and agreements over reciprocal rights and duties fixed in more or less official 'contracts'. These have to be enforced, result-ing in more work and more influence for the courts.

The role of the judiciary in policy making is also increasing as more countries have introduced consti-tutional courts, constitutional review, administrative courts and administrative review. The body of admin-istrative law is quickly expanding. The process of European integration has promoted this tendency. It introduced the principle of judicial and constitutional review to countries like Britain and the Netherlands that did not have it previously. Furthermore, with the development of a European as well as a national body of law, the legal system has also become multilevel, increased in complexity, and created more opportu-nities for individuals and groups to get their way against the government. Tate and Vallinder (1997) have captured this tendency well in the title of their study: *The Global Expansion of Judicial Power*.

Another horizontal public shift is that from public to semi-public organizations and governance. Policy making, policy implementation, enforcement and control have become differentiated as separate func-tions. For reasons of efficiency and effectiveness in complex situations and political prudence or credibil-ity, some of these sub-tasks have been delegated to more autonomous semi-public organizations. An early example was the central bank, while more recent examples are the control agencies that regulate priva-tized sectors such as telecommunications, energy and the media. This trend is related to a broader horizontal shift in the public domain away from the three branches of government – for instance, from parliaments to semi-autonomous state agencies, from the European Commission to 'Comitology' (the system of committees created by, assisting and circumventing the European institutions), from statutory instruments to instruments under private law such as contracts or covenants between public and private actors, and from command and control to information management. Horizontal governance shifts from public to private organizations have gone even further. Public state agencies have been outsourcing more and more tasks to private business. In addition, formerly public organizations have been wholly or partially privatized, including gas and water utilities, telecommunications, highway management, harbour piloting, compulsory social insurance, health care, and even real public services such as prisons.

There are also horizontal shifts in private economic governance, such as those towards less coordination through the market and more through hierarchies – raising the degrees of concentration of markets – and through inter-firm networks. The increased importance of knowledge in the economy has made firms more interdependent, as many do not by themselves harbour all the knowledge and information needed for innovation. Knowledge has to be shared, but at the same time property rights have to be protected. Firms have to invest in knowledge, machinery and software, relevant only for relations with specific customers or suppliers, and so do employers and employees. This has increased the risks of poaching, hold up and opportunism, and consequently raised transaction costs, at least potentially. In order to reduce these risks and transaction costs, firms have merged or taken over relevant customers, suppliers or competitors. Internationalization has raised competition in many sectors to a regional (European) or world level and has increased it, also stimulating mergers and takeovers, as firms try to occupy important competitive positions in these larger international markets, even if only out of a fear of 'eating, in order to avoid being eaten'. In addition to these shifts from markets to hierarchies and networks, the literature refers also to changes from associations (trade associations, cartels) to large business firms, or from competitive markets to monopolistic or oligopolistic ones. And the corporate governance literature is concerned with the ongoing shift from shareholder to management control of business firms.

Finally, there are various kinds of mixed vertical–horizontal shifts – for instance, from national public standardization bodies to international private ones (an example is the telecommunications sector). Increasingly, governance decisions are made in complicated networks encompassing supranational, national and sub-national actors – public, semi-public and private.

With the changes in the location of policy and in rule production, the style of governance seems to change as well. In more complicated network structures, the traditional approaches of command and control and enforcement are less effective and efficient. New forms of governance come to replace them, such as negotiation and concertation and the management or manipulation of information in networks. These new reforms include, for instance, the comparison of information and of performance scores, exemplified in the increasing popularity of benchmarking and the comparison of best practices, first in the private and now also increasingly also in the public sector.

Several recent and ongoing trends seem to be redrawing the boundaries of the various societal spheres like those between the public and private and the political and economic. These trends are interlinked, sometimes mutually reinforcing, but at times also contradictory. They seem to be affecting the governance capacity of existing arrangements. Decision-making power is being shifted, and with that sources and relations of regulation, of providing social order. Again, such issues are the core business of political science, but by their nature can best be dealt with by adopting a multidisciplinary approach.

PROBLEMS OF GOVERNABILITY, ACCOUNTABILITY AND LEGITIMACY

Another central element the various literatures have in common is a concern with new problems of governability, accountability, responsiveness and legitimacy. The shifts in public and private governance have one major consequence in common: traditional institutions of checks and balances on power and accountability could become obsolete, or at the very least less effective. Such issues are of central importance to an interdisciplinary political science. In order to highlight the new forms in which problems of governability and accountability appear, let us first summarize how the classical political and economic institutions have been a response to these problems in the past.

Governability and accountability have developed hand in hand with the process of state formation, albeit not always at exactly the same pace. There was a need for both. Governability – the capacity to solve urgent societal problems – often required a certain centralization and concentration of political power. Basic examples are the protection of man against man – the problem of social order, of criminality, civil war and war – the protection of man against nature – the problem of material and economic survival – and the protection of nature against man – the problem of the environment.

At the same time, the historical process of modernization has led to a differentiation of society into semi-autonomous spheres, each providing solutions to different problems of survival. Thus separations have developed – for instance, between the public and the private, between politics and economics, between politics and administration, and between for-profit organizations and not-for-profit sectors. These different societal, political and economic spheres have all developed their own governance institutions: organizations that have become concentrations of power and are hence able to make binding decisions, ordering their segment of society: states, public administrations, large business firms and large interest associations. Each one of these, in turn, requires some minimal degree of centralization of power and decision making.

However, any concentration of power carries immediately the danger of arbitrariness, of abuse, corruption and advancing self-interest by those in control. Therefore, in the course of history, societies have not only centralized political and economic power in such organizations, but they have also gradually developed a system of checks and balances to control the exercise of power, prevent its abuse and arbitrary application, hold power holders accountable, and protect citizens, consumers and workers from them. It should be noted, however, that there is an inherent tension between the functional requisites of centralization and the containment of power. Not enough controls on power allow for abuse and arbitrariness, but too many checks and balances can reduce power too much and inhibit the capacity of organizations to act and to realize policies (i.e., their governability). Both affect their legitimacy. Institutions of power wielding can be legitimate in the eyes of citizens either because they 'work', 'perform', are able to 'deliver the goods' (output legitimacy); or because they result from decisions made according to procedures that include some minimal forms of accountability such as the rule of law, democracy, or political or economic competition (input legitimacy).

The primary control of economic and private organizations is through the *exit option*. Firms and associations are typically controlled by competition. The presence of alternative suppliers, clients, employers and employees provides the clients, suppliers, workers and employers with an exit option. In case of dissatisfaction they can turn to a competitor of the organization with which they have been dealing. This is a major check on the abuse of power. Political and other public organizations lack such competition. There is usually only one organization in a specific jurisdiction – one agency for distributing driver's licences or one police force. This is linked to the fact that they provide typical collective goods (and that is their legitimacy), which often require a monopoly in order to deal with collective action problems. Therefore, political organizations are controlled through institutions that channel a *voice option* for citizens. The principle of the rule of law, periodic democratic elections, the separation of powers, federalism, judicial review and administrative law all check the arbitrary use of political and administrative power, and provide citizens and users of state services with channels for redress and appeal. Much constitutional and administrative law is concerned with such institutions that control public monopolies. The tension between governability and accountability holds for institutions controlled through both voice and exit. Too many constitutional checks and balances may render political institutions incapable of governing (Lazare 1996); and too much competition may reduce the capacity of a business firm to govern privately (e.g., to innovate).

A consequence of the shifts in authority of and within governance mechanisms might be that traditional instruments for control of power may become less effective. For instance, it is questionable whether a minister effectively can still be held accountable by Parliament, the voters, the Court of Accounts or administrative courts for decisions that have shifted to European institutions, to semi-independent regulatory agencies or to only partially privatized formerly public organizations. One may ask whether a minister's formal responsibility for actions already taken by his civil servants (that he did not and could not have known about) are becoming more and more a strange legal fiction as the size and differentiation of the administration increases and as decisions are increasingly taken in networks of actors located at different levels of aggregation in both the public and private spheres. A national competition authority, applying national criteria for market power, may have lost effective control over the power of firms active in globalizing markets. It may be increasingly difficult for a supervisory board or the shareholders to hold the Chief Executive Officer (CEO) of a private firm responsible for decisions that have been taken by some minor subsidiary involved in a joint venture with others. The long list of CEOs replaced in the last years could be an indication that living up to such expectations of control becomes increasingly difficult for leading entrepreneurs.

In other words, the central question is whether the shifts in location of public, semi-public and private governance are threatening to make old established systems of accountability obsolete. The traditional separation of powers may be less suited to organizing accountability for these new forms of network governance. The same may hold for traditional competition policy or traditional principles of corporate governance. Where decision making becomes less transparent, it is less easily to locate *loci* of power, to identify where decisions are being taken and who is responsible. With that, legal certainty, legal equality and legal interest protection may become endangered.

Perhaps one could doubt that there is a problem of accountability at all or even welcome the loss of function of – in the light of the information and communication technology revolution – such 'archaic' institutions of representation as political parties and parliaments. So, what is the exact nature of the developments and does this actually pose a problem? Do the new actors or governance arrangements have legitimacy? Does the public trust them, the courts, the privatized companies, the independent regulatory agencies, the expert networks, the large business enterprises? What is the relationship between institutional controls and trust? How 'independent' are independent regulatory agencies such as the European Central Bank, and how 'independent' should we allow them to be? Who controls the controllers? What are the roads for public discourse on the performance of governance mechanisms, criticism, redress? These and similar questions have been of major concern to the various governance literatures. Let us take a closer look at some of them.

A major shift that has increased legitimacy problems, and that has received much attention, is the one from national to European governance, and in particular towards governance through European policy networks. This has been of major concern to multi-level governance theorists. They have made the distinction between input and output legitimacy. Input legitimacy implies that a political system and specific policies are legitimated by the rules-of-the-game and the processes by which they have come about. It stresses that 'a well functioning system of political representation is a precondition for a legitimate democratic political system' (Thomassen & Schmitt 1999b: 255). Output legitimacy implies that a political system and specific policies are legitimated by their success. This implies that governability is a precondition for legitimacy.

Scharpf (1999) has used this distinction first of all to explain the process of European integration. He argued that a decrease in problem-solving capacity of national political systems – a loss of output legitimacy – forced national governments to engage in European integration. However, he argued that this could not solve the problem of accountability and legitimacy in terms of input: the stronger the role of the non-accountable supranational institutions, the less legitimacy can be assured through the intergovernmental mechanism of national accountability. Yet it could not solve these problems in terms of output either. The complicated decision-making procedures of the EU lead regularly to stalemate, joint decision traps or asymmetries in output (economic integration at the cost of social protection). On important policy issues, consensus among democratically accountable governments is difficult, European action is blocked and solutions are again left to the national level. Furthermore Scharpf (2001: 14–15) observes that 'market making policies on which Europe can agree will damage the capacity of national governments to adopt those "market correcting" policies on which the Union cannot agree'.

Thomassen and Schmitt (1999a) are less pessimistic as regards input legitimacy. Whereas Scharpf argues that there is no European collective identity, let alone a single political constituency, they show that the requirements of the (moderate) responsive party model (e.g., a congruence of political agendas among representatives and represented) is not that far removed from what is typical at the national level with respect to cleavage structures and the left–right dimension of the political spectrum. In fact,'a truly European system of political representation involving transnational political parties competing for the votes of a single European electorate might be more feasible than is often suggested' (Thomassen & Schmitt 1999b: 257). It may be that there is no congruence between the agendas of European voters and representatives on strictly European issues (Thomassen & Schmitt 1999b: 258). However, this does not rule out the European responsible party model. A broad consensus among political elites (in contrast to opposite views among the electorate) may be enough for the development of an effective system of political representation in the EU. Still, in our view, various shifts in governance tend to cause a loss of responsiveness of traditional intermediary institutions and organizations, most notably political parties. This does add to the already considerable problems of responsiveness and hence – in this case, input – legitimacy.

Eising and Kohler-Koch (2000b) continued Scharpf's reasoning on the relation between lack of legitimacy and search for new forms of governance. They claim that the EU's frail democratic legitimacy favoured the emergence of EU network governance. 'The member states and the community institutions accept *consociation* as the central ordering principle in their relations, and regard *interest* as the constitutive basis of the EC system' (Eising & Kohler Koch 2000b: 269; emphasis in original; see also Gabel 1998). Network governance is supposed to increase both the governability (output legitimacy) and to involve more national actors in the process of European integration (input legitimacy). For them, network governance is the dependent variable and lack of legitimacy the independent variable, where most analysts have concentrated on the opposite causal relation (Haverland 1998; Van Kersbergen et al. 1999, 2000). And indeed, that opposite relation exists as well. Network governance – the solution – creates in turn new problems of legitimacy. Scharpf (2001: 14) points out that 'it is hard to see how informal networks of interest intermediation and anonymous expert committees could be considered satisfactory substitutes for the democratic accountability of representatives whose mandate is derived, directly or indirectly, from general elections based on the formal equality of all citizens'.

Other literatures have been concerned with problems of accountability and legitimacy as well. A major problem in the international relations literature on 'governing without government' has been the accountability deficit – that is, the fact that 'most collectivities in globalized space are not accountable for

their actions' (Rosenau 2000: 192), whether they be multinationals, nongovernmental organizations or international organizations. In international law, the so-called 'democratic entitlement thesis', which has gained in significance, is pushed beyond the human rights treaty system and hence is argued to have consequences for the relationship between democratic governance, accountability and international law (Fox & Roth 2000).

Critics have argued that the new public management may be detrimental to the representativeness of bureaucracies and democracy because it prioritizes performance over accountability to citizens. There is a problem with democratic accountability, not only because elected officials under NPM lose their top–down authority over public bureaucracies and managers, but also because it is difficult to maintain and increase the bottom–up control of all officials, including those employed on contracts as well as elected officials (Kelly 1998). Privatization and delegation to 'independent' regulatory agencies give citizens fewer chances to control such agencies through voice and there is often insufficient compensation for this through new exit options.

Similar concerns exist in the broader network literature. Rhodes (2000: 61) writes: 'Networks are not accountable to the state: they are self-organizing.' Studying developments in Britain, Rhodes (1994: 138–139) has introduced the phrase 'hollowing out the state' in order to summarize how privatization, the transfer of public services to agencies, the relocation of governmental functions to the EU and the restriction on bureaucratic discretion reduce and fragment government. Hollowing out has as its main victim accountability.

Accountability has been of concern to the corporate literature since its inception. The separation of ownership and control with the 'managerial revolution' early on led to concerns about, among other things, who was to control the managers and how the interests of shareholders (or, more broadly, stakeholders) should be protected. The problem has been exacerbated by the participation of firms in networks. Just as parliaments have more difficulty controlling governments bound up in networks of corporatist concertation or in interstate networks (agreements reached after difficult negotiations in these networks cannot easily be amended by parliaments), so shareholders cannot easily modify the results of painstaking inter-firm negotiations.

EMERGING ALTERNATIVES?

How might these new problems of governability, accountability and legitimacy be solved? This question is relevant both from a normative and empirical-analytical point of view, for new principles are already developing, both in empirical reality and as theoretical concepts. However, they do so in different spheres and are studied in different literatures. Can they really replace the old institutions of control with proven effectiveness over decades, if not centuries, like the rule of law, the separation of powers, judicial appeal or competition? Getting some familiarity with these other literatures embraced by the concept of 'governance' may inspire political scientists and students of public administration to develop new conceptions of control over the public institutions. Let us look at some such new conceptions.

The development of new levels (vertical) and arenas (horizontal) in public and private multilevel networks implies that these different levels and arenas form checks and balances for each other, just as federalism at the level of the nation-state has traditionally been a major check on central state power. However, can the 'public interest' be trusted with this new form of federalism, or will the different levels be more likely to represent rather particularistic interests? It seems that this is less a problem of accountability and more an issue of effectiveness of decision making (the joint decision-making trap of Scharpf).

An interesting idea, stemming from political science itself, is the concept of 'deliberative democracy' of Paul Hirst (1994). In essence, this suggests that policy networks be extended to include all the governed. 'Democracy in this sense,' says Hirst (2000: 27), 'is about government by information exchange and consent, where organized publics have the means to conduct a dialogue with government and thus hold it to account.' Government by consent dissolves the problem of accountability, so to speak. This requires large-scale institutional reform, the adoption of the so-called 'associative democratic model', which 'involves devolving as many of the functions of the state as possible to society (whilst retaining public funding) and democratizing as many as possible of the organizations in civil society' (Hirst 2000: 28).

Where formerly public organizations are privatized and where economic governance through markets or associations has shifted in the direction of governance through large firm hierarchies, other controls on economic power may be needed to complement the control through competition. Thus different combinations of competition and regulation may be required, and new kinds of referees and market superintendents. 'Sectoral' and 'sectoral-unspecific' regulators will have to protect a minimum level of competition and set the rules of the game in the competition between the large players. Such independent regulators have been created in recent years, but they are not without their problems. The issue of how independent they are – as well as can they be and should they be – from politics, but also from the sector they are to regulate, is not easily solved. In addition, new mechanisms need to be introduced to guard the guardians, to control the regulators. One can think of courts, interest associations, professions, peers, science and policy evaluation studies, or some 'ombudsman' for competition, all with their own advantages and drawbacks. In fact, in this context it is not even certain whether control of competition and setting the rules of the game in the marketplace have to come from state or semi-state agencies anyway. Perhaps economic governance mechanisms may play a role here, such as liability litigation, self-regulation by industry, the setting of terms by insurance companies, commercial certification and the reputation rating of organizations.

With the increase in knowledge-based policy making, many participants in the governance network have expert knowledge or have recourse to sources of information and knowledge. Many also specialize in the production of knowledge, such as government planning bureaus, universities, ministerial research organizations, consultants and accountants. Their knowledge production involves, among other things, policy evaluation and comparison, cost–benefit analysis, benchmarking and competition over standards. It is fed into policy-making arenas, including the public media, and confronts policy makers with policy consequences: real consequences of past policies and prospective ones of future policies. These new forms of technocracy pose serious problems of accountability. It is unclear who has enough counter-expertise to control the experts. Independence may be crucial for the objectivity of information and the neutrality of the providers, but how independent are government planning bureaus? The combination of accountancy and legal representation in large accountancy and law firms may very well reduce the credibility of the accountants.

New forms of technocracy may pose problems, but they also provide solutions. Other actors, for instance, are induced to produce counter-expertise and information. Examples are the publication of benchmarking studies on the performance of individual schools, hospitals and municipalities. Thus information exchange and disputation itself becomes part of the system of checks and balances within the network administration and the network economy. It works also as a mechanism for mutual learning, and functions both in private and public (media) arenas. In this way, networks may be producing their own system of mutual control. There are, however, still many problems related to this production and exchange of information that require investigation. For instance, it is complex to control the quality of information and the credibility of information providers and critics. It may or may not be desirable and possible to create a 'certification' system. Perhaps there are possibilities and conditions for 'peer review' among information producers (such as sociological researchers or accountants).

There seems to be an increased need for new forms of quality control over organizational agents. The professionalization of the staff of organizations and their growth in size has increased the information asymmetries between organizational leaders and workers. This holds for the public bureaucracy, but also for independent agencies and even commercial organizations. It may no longer be realistic to hold leaders responsible for all the deeds of their employees. The constitutional principle of ministerial responsibility may increasingly become a fiction, but are any alternatives being developed? Perhaps we may learn from principal-agency theory in economics, for instance by looking at how organizations compensate for such asymmetries and studying the possibilities of giving 'agents' more responsibilities, greater discretion and holding them directly accountable to the outside world. If they were not held to account to Parliament, then perhaps this could be a role for an institution specifically designed to evaluate the quality of the civil service and individual civil servants. Such solutions undoubtedly have pitfalls that need to be addressed in the light of possible alternatives, such as peer review among civil servants.

An important contribution to controlling the policies of both state agencies and private business comes from public interest associations, which have spontaneously developed from the bottom up in civil society. Examples are the various national and international associations of environmentalists and critical consumers. In addition, organizations have emerged

that control in general how efficiently government agencies spend their resources, similar to the ones already in existence in the private sector (e.g., rating agencies and accountants). They too produce critical knowledge and information: policy evaluations, benchmarking studies and other performance comparisons. In addition, they feed it into the various policy networks and policy communities in which they often participate. They also facilitate public democratic control by publishing their critical information and drawing political attention by public events, demonstrations or spectacular actions. The issue is whether such organizations are acquiring a more stable position within the formal system of political checks and balances. Perhaps they should be given such a position, although too much institutional integration may backfire and reduce their effectiveness and legitimacy among the general public as countervailing powers.

Recent years have seen a strong increase in the interest in business ethics, especially in the United States, as exemplified by the number of courses taught on the subject in major business schools and by the number of articles in the management literature devoted to it. Here ethics could have a role to play, as do appeals to norms and morals, in controlling the behaviour of powerful actors. Similar considerations may hold with regard to bringing such business ethics – if necessary through new public management – to public sector organizations.

The question is whether reliance on voluntary normative schemes is a real option. Training institutes may play a role in the socialization of expert and policy communities into specific 'professional' standards of behaviour (such as with the French *Grandes Ecoles*, or Westpoint for the United States Army Corps of Engineers). The effectiveness of the sanctions of 'naming' and 'shaming' is perhaps unstable, as it depends on the sensitivity of actors regarding their reputation. A reputation may or may not be important for functioning in economic and political arenas. More and more control systems are already relying on this, such as peer review in academia and in the professions, but can this be extended to the business world, and in which settings (e.g., large or small communities) is 'naming' and 'shaming' most effective?

From the sociological network literature (Knoke & Kuklinski 1982; Laumann & Knoke 1987) we know that actors who occupy a more central position in a network are more visible to others inside and outside the network, that information about their behaviour spreads more rapidly, that they are therefore more careful about maintaining a positive reputation, and that they are hence better able to resist temptations for opportunism, fraud or abuse of power. They also make a greater effort to be exemplary citizens. Thus larger and more visible firms care more about their reputation – for instance, regarding the environment or the treatment of their personnel (e.g., having a works council). This points to the importance of information spreading. It seems that new technologies – the internet, e-mail, telecommunications – offer opportunities for spreading information more rapidly, and hence for making 'naming' and 'shaming' more effective instruments for social, political and economic control. However, there is of course also another side to this coin, because these new technologies also pose the danger of overhasty, sloppy, arbitrary and unfair blemishing of reputations. Modern day equivalents of witch hunts are a real danger and some actors, especially the more visible ones, may need new legal protection to ensure fair treatment in the arenas of Internet and the global mass media. Issues such as whether it is acceptable to use information about an actor's personal life for the evaluation of his functional performance need to be settled.

science in its relation to the disciplines of law, public administration, economics, business administration, geography and sociology.

Description of shifts in governance

There is a need for a more precise understanding of what the new forms, locations and capacities of governance look like and how relevant they are in diverse areas and at different levels. There is no consensus on which set of phenomena can properly be grouped under the title 'governance', while at the same time the significance of the topic is well appreciated by most researchers. In addition, there is considerable debate on the issue of whether (and to what extent) we, in fact, observe 'shifts' in government or whether we rather witness a process of redefining 'governance' or symbolic changes. These issues, we propose, may be defined as the problem of empirical identification and this touches, among other things, on the issue of to what extent we are still capable of describing observable new empirical phenomena with the help of the traditional conceptual tools of political science in an analytically sensible manner.

CONCLUSION

Such control institutions could all be topics for both empirical and normative studies. Which new control institutions and mechanisms do we see emerging?

Our point is that it pays to look over the fence of political science, particularly to sectors or spheres studied by other disciplines, as many of the issues of governability, accountability, legitimacy and responsiveness arise here rather than in traditional political institutions. Yet such issues have momentous consequences for traditional institutions. How well do new control institutions and mechanisms perform? How well can they? Under what conditions? What changes would be useful in organizational structures, tasks and authority, and what resources are required for such instruments of control? And can solutions found in the private sector, in private networks, also be used in public networks?

By way of conclusion, we offer an ordering of these issues by identifying three main questions, or rather, clusters of interesting conceptual, theoretical and empirical problems and questions that are highly relevant for the theoretical advancement of political

Causes

There is a debate on what is driving the observed shifts in governance. This, we suggest, may be characterized as the problem of the identification of causality and, among other things, concerns the development or elaboration of theories that are capable of explicating causes and causal mechanisms connecting independent variables and shifts in governance as the dependent variable of interest. One important and unresolved question is whether observed shifts in governance are brought about by changes in the type of problems with which governments are confronted.

Consequences

There are also controversies over the issue of the outcomes of shifts in governance. This, we think, can best be characterized as the problem of the identification of effects and concerns the issue of the effects of shifts in governance on a wide variety of empirical phenomena and associated normative matters. We hold that for political scientists it is particularly important to focus on issues of governability, accountability and legitimacy. Note that here 'shifts in governance' is brought into the equation as an independent variable. A further relevant distinction is that between questions and possible answers that are empirical-analytical – that is, those that deal with the issues of what is already happening and why – and questions and possible answers that are normative-evaluative – that is, pertain to questions of what should be and what should not be done – perhaps not only measured by the standards of effectiveness, efficiency and legitimacy, but also by the criteria of justice and equality. Finally, the observed shifts in governance and their (hypothesized) causes seem to require a new, proactive effort of institutional reconstruction and constitutional engineering, that is to say it raises questions of political-institutional design in reaction to observed shifts or in anticipation of expected changes in governance.

REFERENCES

Alter, C. & Hage, J. (1993). *Organizations working together.* London: Sage.

Blair, M.M. & Roe, M.J. (1999). *Employees and corporate governance.* Washington, DC: Brookings Institution Press.

Boyer, R. & Saillard, Y. (2002). *Regulation theory: State of the art.* London/New York: Routledge.

Brudney, J.L., O'Toole Jr, L.J. & Rainey, H.G. (eds.) (2000). *Advancing public management: New developments in theory, methods and practice.* Washington, DC: Georgetown University Press.

Brunetta, R. & Dell'Aringa, C. (eds.) (1990). *Labour relations and economic performance.* Houndmills/London: Macmillan.

Bulmer, S. (1998). New institutionalism and the governance of the Single European Market. *Journal of European Public Policy* 5(3): 365–386.

Castells, M. (1996). *The rise of the network society.* Cambridge, MA: Blackwell.

Coates, D. (2000). *Models of capitalism: Growth and stagnation in the modern era.* Cambridge: Polity Press.

Cohen, S.S. & Boyd, G. (eds.) (2000). *Corporate governance and globalization: Long range planning issues.* Cheltenham: Edward Elgar.

Crouch, C. & Streeck, W. (1997). *Political economy of modern capitalism: Mapping convergence and diversity.* London: Sage.

Demirag, I.S. (ed.) (1998). *Corporate governance, accountability and pressures to perform: An international study.* Stamford, CT: JAI Press.

Dine, J. (2000). *The governance of corporate groups.* Cambridge: Cambridge University Press.

Ebbinghaus, B. & Manow, P. (eds.) (2001). *Comparing welfare capitalism: Social policy and political economy in Europe, Japan and the USA.* London: Routledge.

Ebers, M. (ed.) (1999). *The formation of inter-organizational networks.* Oxford: Oxford University Press.

Eising, R. & Kohler-Koch, B. (2000a). Introduction: Network governance in the European Union. In B. Kohler-Koch & R. Eising (eds.), *The transformation of governance in the European Union.* London/New York: Routledge.

Eising, R. & Kohler-Koch, B. (2000b). Governance in the European Union: A comparative assessment. in B. Kohler-Koch & R. Eising (eds.), *The transformation of governance in the European Union.* London/New York: Routledge.

Eriksen, E.O. & Fossum, J.E. (eds.) (2000). *Democracy in the European Union: Integration through deliberation?* London: Routledge.

Follesdal, A. & Koslowski, P. (eds.) (1998). *Democracy and the European Union.* Heidelberg: Springer.

Fox, G.H. & Roth, B.R. (eds.) (2000). *Democratic governance and international law.* Cambridge: Cambridge University Press.

Gabel, M.J. (1998). The endurance of supranational governance: A consociational interpretation of the European Union. *Comparative Politics* 30(4): 463–547.

Green Cowles, M., Caporaso, J. & Risse, T. (eds.) (2001). *Transforming Europe: Europeanization and domestic change.* Ithaca, NY/London: Cornell University Press.

Hall, P.A. (1999). The political economy of Europe in an era of interdependence, in H. Kitschelt et al. (eds.), *Continuity and change in contemporary capitalism.* Cambridge: Cambridge University Press.

Hall, P.A. & Soskice, D. (eds.) (2001). *Varieties of capitalism: The institutional foundations of comparative advantage.* Oxford: Oxford University Press.

Hasenclever, A., Mayer, P. & Rittberger, V. (1997). *Theories of international regimes.* Cambridge: Cambridge University Press.

Haverland, M. (1998). *National autonomy, European integration and the politics of packaging waste.* Utrecht: Thela Thesis.

Héritier, A. (1999). *Policy-making and diversity in Europe: Escaping deadlock.* Cambridge: Cambridge University Press.

Hewson, M. & Sinclair, T.J. (eds.) (1999). *Approaches to global governance theory.* Albany, NY: State University of New York Press.

Hirst, P. (1994). *Associative democracy: New forms of economic and social governance.* Cambridge: Polity Press.

Hirst, P. (2000). Democracy and governance. In J. Pierre (ed.), *Debating governance: Authority, steering and democracy.* Oxford: Oxford University Press.

Holden, B. (ed.) (2000). *Global democracy: Key debates.* London/New York: Routledge.

Hollingsworth, J.R. & Boyer, R. (eds.) (1997). *Contemporary capitalism: The embeddedness of institutions.* Cambridge: Cambridge University Press.

Hopt, K.J. (ed.) (1997). *Comparative corporate governance: The state of the art and emerging research.* Oxford: Clarendon Press.

Hurrell, A. & Menon, A. (1996). Politics like any other? Comparative politics, international relations and the study of the EU. *West European Politics* 19(2): 386–402.

In't Veld, R.J. (1991). *Autopoiesis and configuration theory: New approaches to societal steering.*Dordrecht: Kluwer.

Janning, J. (1997). *The state in a changing world: World development report.* Oxford: Oxford University Press.

Jessop, B. (ed.) (2001). *The Parisian regulation school.* Aldershot: Edward Elgar.

Kaboolian, L. (1998). The new public management: Challenging the boundaries of the management versus administration debate. *Public Administration Review* 58(3): 189–193.

Keasey, K., Thompson, S. & Wright, M. (eds.) (1999). *Corporate governance.*Cheltenham: Edward Elgar.

Kelly, R.M. (1998). An inclusive democratic polity, representative bureaucracies and the new public management. *Public Administration Review* 58(3): 201–208.

Kiely, R. (1998). Neoliberalism revised? A critical account of World Bank concepts of good governance and market friendly intervention. *Capital & Class* 64: 63–88.

Kitschelt, H. et al. (eds.) (1999). *Continuity and change in contemporary capitalism.* Cambridge: Cambridge University Press.

Knoke, D. & Kuklinski, J.H. (1982). *Network analysis.* Beverly Hills, CA: Sage.

Kohler-Koch, B. & Eising, R. (eds.) (2000). *The transformation of governance in the European Union.* London/New York: Routledge.

Kooiman, J. (ed.) (1993). *Modern governance: New government–society interactions.* London: Sage.

Krasner, S.D. (ed.) (1983). *International regimes.* Ithaca, NY: Cornell University Press.

Lane, J.-E. (2000). *New public management.* London: Routledge.

Lannoo, K. (1999). A European perspective on corporate governance. *Journal of Common Market Studies* 37(2): 269–294.

Laumann, E.O. & Knoke, D. (1987). *The organizational state: Social choice in national policy domains.* Madison, WI: University of Wisconsin Press.

Lazare, D. (1996). *The frozen republic: How the constitution is paralyzing democracy.* New York/San Diego, CA/London: Harcourt Brace.

Lieshout, R.H. (1995). *Between anarchy and hierarchy: A theory of international politics and foreign policy.* Aldershot: Edward Elgar.

Lynn Jr, L.E. (1998). The new public management: How to transform a theme into a legacy. *Public Administration Review* 58(3): 231–238.

Marks, G., Hooghe, L. & Blank, K. (1996a). European integration from the 1980s: State-centric versus multi-level governance. *Journal of Common Market Studies* 34(3): 341–378.

Marks, G. et al. (1996b). Competencies, cracks and conflicts: Regional mobilization in the European Union. in G. Marks et al. (eds.), *Governance in the European Union.* London: Sage.

Mayntz, R. & Scharpf, F.W. (eds.) (1995). *Steuerung und Selbstorganisation in staatsnahen Sektoren.* Frankfurt am Main: Campus.

Mazey, S. (1996). The development of the European idea: From sectoral integration to political union. in J. Richardson (ed.), *European Union: Power and policy-making.* London: Routledge.

Michie, J. & Grieve Smith, J. (eds.) (1999). *Global instability: The political economy of world economic governance.* London/New York: Routledge.

Minogue, M., Polidano, C. & Hulme, D. (eds.) (1998). *Beyond the new public management: Changing ideas and practices in governance.* Cheltenham: Edward Elgar.

Moravcsik, A. (1993). Introduction: Integrating international and domestic theories of international bargaining. In P.B. Evans, H.K. Jacobson & R.D. Putnam (eds.), *Double-edged diplomacy: International bargaining and domestic politics.* Berkeley, CA: University of California Press.

Moravcsik, A. (1998). *The choice for Europe: Social purpose and state power from Messina to Maastricht.* London: University of California Press.

Murphy, C.N. (2000). Global governance: Poorly done and poorly understood. *International Affairs* 76(4): 189–203.

Nagel, J.H. (1997). Radically reinventing government: Editor's introduction. *Journal of Policy Analysis and Management* 16(3): 349–356.

Neyer, J. (2000). Justifying comitology: The promise of deliberation. In K. Neunreither & A. Wiener (eds.), *European integration after Amsterdam: Institutional dynamics and prospects for democracy.* Oxford: Oxford University Press.

Nooteboom, B. (1999). *Inter-firm alliances: Analysis and design.* London: Routledge.

North, D.C. (1990). *Institutions, institutional change and economic performance.* Cambridge: Cambridge University Press.

North, D.C. & Thomas, R.P. (1973). *The rise of the Western world: A new economic history.* Cambridge: Cambridge University Press.

OECD (1999). *OECD principles of corporate governance.* Paris: OECD.

Osborne, D. & Gaebler, T. (1992). *Reinventing government: How the entrepreneurial spirit is transforming the public sector.* Reading, MA: Addison-Wesley.

Ostrom, E. (1990). *Governing the commons:The evolution of institutions for collective action.* Cambridge: Cambridge University Press.

O'Sullivan, M. (2000). *Contests for corporate control: Corporate governance and economic performance in the United States and Germany.* Oxford: Oxford University Press.

Peterson, J. & Bomberg, E. (1999). *Decision-making in the European Union.* Basingstoke: Macmillan/New York: St Martin's Press.

Philip, G. (1999). The dilemmas of good governance: A Latin American perspective. *Government and Opposition* 34(2): 226–242.

Pierre, J. & Peters, B.G. (2000). *Governance, politics and the state.* Houndmills: MacMillan.

Pollitt, C. & Bouckaert, G. (2000). *Public management reform: A comparative analysis.* Oxford: Oxford University Press.

Prakash, A. & Hart, J.A. (eds.) (1999). *Globalization and governance.* London/New York: Routledge.

Rhodes, R.A.W. (1994). The hollowing out of the state: The changing nature of the public service in Britain. *Political Quarterly* 65(2): 138–151.

Rhodes, R.A.W. (1997). *Understanding governance: Policy networks, governance, reflexivity and accountability.* Buckingham: Open University Press.

Rhodes, R.A.W. (2000). Governance and public administration, in J. Pierre (ed.), *Debating governance: Authority, steering and democracy.* Oxford: Oxford University Press.

Rhodes, C. & Mazey, S. (1995). Introduction: Integration in theoretical perspective. In C. Rhodes & S. Mazey (eds.), *The state of the European Union. Vol. 3: Building a European polity?* Harlow: Longman/Boulder, CO: Lynne Rienner.

Richardson, J. (1996). Policy-making in the EU. In J. Richardson (ed.), *European Union: Power and policy-making.* London: Routledge.

Ronit, K. & Schneider, V. (1999). Global governance through private organizations. *Governance* 12(3): 243–266.

Rosenau, J.N. (2000). Change, complexity and governance in globalizing space. In J. Pierre (ed.), *Debating governance: Authority, steering and democracy.* Oxford: Oxford University Press.

Rosenau, J.N. & Czempiel, E.-O. (eds.) (1992). *Governance without government: Order and change in world politics.* Cambridge: Cambridge University Press.

Rosenbaum, A. & Shepherd, A. (2000). IASIA Symposium on governance, responsibility and social enhancement: Governance, good government and poverty reduction. *International Review of Administrative Sciences* 66(2): 269–284.

Sassen, S. (2000). Territory and territoriality in the global economy. *International Sociology* 15(2): 372–393.

Saxenian, A. (1996). *Regional advantage: Culture and competition in Silicon Valley and Route 128.* Cambridge, MA: Harvard University Press.

Scharpf, F.W. (1997). *Games real actors play: Actor-centered institutionalism in policy research.* Boulder, CO: Westview Press.

Scharpf, F.W. (1999). *Governing in Europe: Effective and democratic?* Oxford: Oxford University Press.

Scharpf, F.W. (2001). Notes towards a theory of multilevel governing in Europe. *Scandinavian Political Studies* 24(1): 1–26. Schmitter, P.C. (1974). Still the century of corporatism? *Review of Politics* 36(1): 85–131.

Smelser, N.J. & Swedberg, R. (eds.) (1994). *The handbook of economic sociology.* Princeton, NJ: Princeton University Press.

Sørensen, G. (1999). Sovereignty: Change and continuity in a fundamental institution. *Political Studies* 47(3): 590–604.

Soskice, D. (1990).Wage determination:The changing role of institutions in advanced industrialized countries. *Oxford Review of Economic Policy* 6(4): 36–61.

Sternberg, E. (1998). *Corporate governance: Accountability in the marketplace.* London: Institute of Economic Affairs.

Stone Sweet, A. (2000). *Governing with judges: Constitutional politics in Europe.* Oxford: Oxford University Press.

Streeck, W. (1992). *Social institutions and economic performance: Studies of industrial relations in advanced capitalist economies.* London/Newbury Park, CA: Sage.

Tate, C.N. & Vallinder, T. (eds.) (1997). *The global expansion of judicial power.* New York: New York University Press.

Teulings, C. & Hartog, J. (1999). *Corporatism and competition: An international comparison of labor market structures and their impact on wage formation.* Cambridge: Cambridge University Press.

Thomassen, J. & Schmitt, H. (1999a). Issue congruence. In H. Schmitt & J. Thomassen (eds.), *Political representation and legitimacy in the European Union.* Oxford: Oxford University Press.

Thomassen, J. & Schmitt, H. (1999b). In conclusion: Political representation and legitimacy in the European Union. In H. Schmitt & J. Thomassen (eds.), *Political representation and legitimacy in the European Union.* Oxford: Oxford University Press.

Van Kersbergen, K., Lieshout, R.H. & Lock, G. (eds.) (1999). *Expansion and fragmentation: Internationalization, political change and the transformation of the nation state.* Amsterdam: Amsterdam University Press.

Van Kersbergen, K., Lieshout, R.H. & Verbeek, B. (2000). Institutional change in the emerging European polity. In O. Van Heffen, W.J.M. Kickert & J.J.A. Thomassen (eds.), *Governance in modern societies: Effects, change and formation of government institutions.* Dordrecht: Kluwer.

Van Waarden, F. (1992). Dimension and types of policy networks. *European Journal of Political Research* 21(1–2): 29–59.

Van Waarden, F. (1995). Persistence of national policy styles: A study of their institutional foundations. In B. Unger & F. Van Waarden (eds.), *Convergence or diversity? Internationalization and economic policy response.* Aldershot: Avebury.

Verbeek, B. (2001). De sturende overheid in het perspectief van internationalisering en Europeanisering. In R. Torenvlied & J. Hakfoort (eds.), *De staat buitenspel? Overheidssturing en nieuwe instituties.* Amsterdam: Boom.

Wallace, H. & Wallace, W. (eds.) (1996). *Policy-making in the European Union*, 3rd edn. Oxford: Oxford University Press.

Williams, A. (1999). *Who will guard the guardians? Corporate governance in the millennium.* Chalford: Management Books.

Williamson, O.E. (1975). *Markets and hierarchies: Analysis and anti-trust implications: A study in the economics of internal organization.* New York: Free Press.

Williamson, O.E. (1985). *The economic institutions of capitalism: Firms, markets, relational contracting.* London: Macmillan.

Williamson, O.E. (1996). *The mechanisms of governance.* New York/Oxford: Oxford University Press.

Woods, N. (2000). The challenge of good governance for the IMF and the World Bank themselves. *World Development* 28(5): 823–842.

2 "Corporate Governance, Values Management, and Standards: A European Perspective"

from Business and Society (2005)

Josef Wieland

SUMMARY

This chapter brings forward the argument that the practical implementation of a corporate governance code cannot be realized by a compliance program alone. Its relevance in everyday business is determined by the moral values of the company culture. In this context, *governance* is defined as a company's resources and capabilities, including the moral resources, to take on responsibility for all its stakeholders. A critical discussion of the agency theory, transaction cost theory, and organization theory shows that such an approach is possible only when a company is not perceived as a maximizing machine for shareholders' interests but as an economic form of cooperation of internal and external resources and stakeholders. An empiric study on 22 European corporate governance codes shows that the predominant majority of European codes orientate themselves to stakeholders and the company. The discussion of the empirical data reveals six basic principles that determine all European corporate governance codes: shareholder rights, transparency, voting rights, regulation of remuneration, design of organizational structures, and corporate social responsibility.

CORPORATE GOVERNANCE AND BUSINESS ETHICS

For some years now, the question of how to implement and operationalize moral values, convictions, and intentions in firms has received increasing attention in the business and corporate ethics literature. The main issue is to develop management systems capable of integrating the moral dimension of economic transactions and questions of value into firms' strategies, policies, and procedures. The challenge for such management systems is to achieve this in a sustained way, and to carry the moral dimensions and questions of values down to the level of typical decisions taken in everyday business. In Germany, this discussion has unfolded under the label *values management*, emphasizing the link between value creation and moral values. It parallels the manifold endeavors on the European level to secure the credibility and verifiability of value management systems, as well as their documentation and reporting structures, by imposing standards or guidelines and assurance processes to evaluate those.[1] In Germany, the main standard is the ValuesManagementSystem[ZfW] developed by the Zentrum für Wirtschaftsethik (Center for Business Ethics).[2] It has been developed based on a decade of practical experience and cooperation with leading German firms, ranging from small-and-medium enterprises (SMEs) to multinationals. The German standard aims at sustainable management by integrating its economic, moral, legal, and political dimensions. Governance structures that implement such an approach are comprehensive and integrative in nature and are part of corporate strategy (Wieland, 2003). No consensus has yet been reached on the question who should verify or enforce such programs—the firms themselves, nongovernmental organizations (NGOs), or state regulation. Self-enforcement and third-party enforcement thus appear as two opposed alternatives. I want to propose a different perspective on the matter: It is conceivable that third-party enforcement could be an expression of self-governance. Third-party enforcement could be based on a voluntary decision on the part of the firm (Wieland, 2003).

The endeavor of developing standards for individual and collective action is not at all confined to the relationship between economics and ethics. We also find such endeavors in the many disciplines that lie at the interface between economics, law, and politics (Brunsson & Jacobsson, 2000). Certainly, the globalization of economic activity and the lack of regulation and institutions that address it are among the drivers of such endeavors. The global movement for the creation of corporate governance codes can serve as an example. On one hand, there was a drive toward homogenizing rules and transparency for international investors. On the other hand, the uninterrupted series of recent scandals, capricious behavior on the part of top management, and the gaps and weaknesses of conventional risk management that correspond to such behavior have certainly also driven that movement. The starting point of the corporate governance discussion has, therefore, always been the compliance aspect of business ethics. It has always, however, been interpreted from a legal point of view. Rarely have actors adopted a values orientation when implementing it.

In what follows, I argue that efforts of standardization need to be synchronized in both areas, and finally be integrated. From the perspective of the corporate governance movement, the central insight is that effective and efficient leadership, management, and control of the firm will be impossible without integrating moral attitudes and requirements with behavior. From the perspective of business ethics, it is important, in my view, to acknowledge that such a comprehensive understanding of corporate governance actually means to consider the objective of values management a strategic management task and thus

anchor it on the top management level. From such a perspective, increasing the importance that business ethics has in all corporate processes and structures would then be decisive. I also argue that a discussion of high relevance to the social sciences is connected to the topic of corporate governance, that is, the discussion of the question of the objective and purpose of firms as organizations in market economies. From the perspective of business ethics, such a discussion only makes sense if an adequate notion of corporate governance is available. For this reason, in what follows I also review the European research frontier on this issue.

For this purpose, I propose a definition of governance that aims to be integrative: I define *corporate governance* as leadership, management, and control of a firm by formal and informal, public and private rules. The governance matrix (Figure 2.1) formalizes such an understanding of comprehensive corporate governance as institutionalization and organization of formal and informal, private and public rules.

The leadership element covers codified guidelines in firms as well as informal leadership standards and the function of managers to serve as role models. The management aspect covers the formal decision mechanisms of a firm as well as the informal values of its corporate culture. Firm-specific control, finally, covers audits and other assurance processes, as well as the exclusion of risks by moral individual conduct. The public formal rules I consider here are of the type of the Sarbanes-Oxley Act in the United States, the German laws on the control and transparency (KonTraG), and on the transparency and publicity (TransPuG) of transactions or the widely diffused type of "comply-or-explain" regulation contained in many governance codes that directly influence the corporate governance of a firm. Public informal rules include such things as the impact of a national or regional culture on social or ecological responsibility of firms, or on how to deal with corruption.

Adopting such a comprehensive interpretation of corporate governance leads to the conviction that any efficient and effective governance structure needs

	Formal Rules	Informal rules
Public	Sarbanes-Oxley Act Comply-or-explain	Economic culture Tradition, mores, conventions
Private	Corporate governance code Values management system	Corporate culture Corporate values

Figure 2.1 **Governance matrix and management of rules**

to serve two functions: to constrain and to enable. Corporate governance cannot be interpreted solely as constraint of behavior (e.g., as limitation of exposure to risk). It should also be understood as enabler of behavior (e.g., in so-called grey zones) for managing transactions with integrity (on this distinction, see Wieland 2001a). A crucial objective of the notion of governance I propose here is to realize both functions in everyday business conduct.

It is obvious and beyond dispute that no broad agreement with such a definition of corporate governance exists in many countries and regions. The Anglo-Saxon countries and Switzerland, for instance, emphasize management control and the defensive aspects of monitoring. The Danish or Dutch, on the other hand, interpret corporate governance as effective stakeholder management. From such a perspective, monitoring and management control also have an important role to play. They are, however, embedded in a conception of the firm that sees it as a part of the society at large, and that takes the interests of different stakeholders into consideration. I develop these issues in further detail below. At this point, I just want to emphasize once more that only a comprehensive and integrative understanding of corporate governance is capable of providing a link between questions of business and corporate ethics, and the strategic and operative management of firms. At the same time, only the process of understanding corporate governance in a comprehensive and integrative way creates the conditions that enable the governance structure as a whole to be effective, including its public and private rules of compliance. Public and private, formal and informal rules form a network. The network linkages support the individual components and increase their effectiveness. This indeed appears to be the lesson from the recent scandals: firms such as WorldCom, Enron, and Arthur Andersen all had formally implemented brilliant systems of corporate governance and compliance—they just did not live according to those, especially top management did not do so. There are two problems with corporate governance that are not backed by a corporate culture suited to it, and with formal rules not backed by the mobilization of informal values that support the enforcement of the formal rules. First, their effectiveness is limited. Second, they can also serve to disguise risks. They can lead to the impression that means for risk prevention would be available within the firm. I discussed this in detail elsewhere (Wieland & Fürst, 2004).

There are additional important arguments for coupling questions of corporate governance with those of business ethics in the way proposed here, bundling them into the ethics of governance (for this research program, see Wieland, 2001b).

First: Questions of corporate governance relate to all processes taking place in firms. They arise on the strategic and the operative level of management and span all hierarchical levels. Moreover, the decision to codify a corporate governance code is a top management decision. Coupling questions of corporate governance with those of business ethics will help to strengthen the endeavor to pursue an applicable and practically relevant approach to business ethics within firms. It will add to import and importance.

Second: Corporate governance provides an interface between the legal and moral aspects of transactions, between the notion of compliance and corporate culture, and between the process of implementation and that of enforcement of systems of ethics management or value management. Such an interface is provided precisely when and if corporate governance is conceived as a self-enforcement process, conditioned by a comply-or-explain rule. Such a process is an instance of structural coupling, which is characteristic for the governance of modern societies.

Third: Finally, it is important to note an aspect often rather neglected in the corporate governance discussion. The discussion in all countries includes the question on what the goals and tasks of firms in a global economy should be. Should they be purely economic, or also include social goals and tasks? This question leads to a discussion of the definition and raison d'être of firms from an economic perspective, and from the perspective of the society. That discussion carries normative baggage and aims at providing legitimation. The answer I arrive at is therefore of the utmost importance for the further theoretical and practical development of business ethics.

In what follows, I focus on the third aspect. My aim is to identify the European perspective at present, and sketch out what it could be in the future.

DIVERSITY OF CORPORATE GOVERNANCE

The term *corporate governance* is used on a global scale. Nevertheless, interpretations of what it means are not at all homogenous. Divergences relate to the term *corporation* and *governance*. On the definition and raison d'être of corporations and on the interpretation of the term governance, large differences in opinion prevail. The causes of those divergences in interpretation are to be found in theories and in the cultural background. The next paragraph is dedicated to explain this in more depth.

The notion of corporate governance is much less sharply defined than one might expect at first glance. In fact, many different interpretations exist of what is a corporation (firm) and which types of transactions the systems of leadership, management, and control—that is, the governance system—should be focused on. What is the objective of a firm, what are its aims? Who are its relevant actors? What do the relevant governance structures need to look like to achieve the purposes chosen? What is the role of the firm as an economic organization situated within the context of society? It is not difficult to see that all those questions and the answers that will be given have a crucial impact on the positioning of a firm in terms of ethics. For the moment, it seems to make sense to make an attempt to assemble a theoretical framework for dealing with those differences, to facilitate their understanding and to estimate their consequences.

Based on the theoretical findings of the institutionalist theory of the firm and the new economics of organization (Kroszner, 1996), three theories of corporate governance can be distinguished: (a) agency theory, (b) transaction cost theory, and (c) organization theory (see Figure 2.2).

Agency theory

Agency theory is focused on the problems relating to the separation of ownership and control. The personal separation of owners and managers, and the legal separation of ownership rights and decision rights, lead to the core problem of agency theory: the conflict of different utility functions and interests between owners and managers in a firm.

The assumption shared by all economists is that managers, similar to all other economic actors, strictly maximize their own utility. Furthermore, economists also share the assumption that managers' interest does not need to converge with the owner's interest. Under such assumptions, adequate governance structures are required for allowing owners to monitor and control managers (Jensen & Meckling, 1976; cf. Berle & Means, 1932/1991; Shleifer & Vishny, 1997). The point of reference of this model of corporate governance is the market. Its competitive mechanisms, however, fail where they encounter the limits posed by incomplete contracts and insurmountable information asymmetries. Precisely that is the meaning of Jensen and Meckling's (1976, p. 310) term *residual loss*, which refers to the difference between a pure market solution and an agency solution.

These three aspects are of fundamental importance for any corporate governance system: the fact that actors who are in relations with the firm have different objectives; the incompleteness of the contracts of which the business cooperation is made, and which comes to the surface in its everyday practice; and finally, the problem of asymmetric and incomplete information, which can concern any team member or stakeholder. Against this backdrop, it is clear why governance structures can be understood as instruments for "structuring, monitoring, and bonding a set of contracts among agents with conflicting interests" (Fama & Jensen, 1983, p. 304).

Theory	Focus	Governance Regimes	Reference
Agency theory	Ownership or control	Control, monitoring, performance-based compensation	Market
Transaction cost theory	Allocation of governance to distinct transactions	Informal and formal rules, structures	Hierarchy
Organizational theory	Rights or responsibilities of stakeholders	Organizational resources, competences	Strategic management

Figure 2.2 **Theoretical diversity of corporate governance**

At the present moment, principal-agency theory dominates the theoretical discussion of corporate governance. I show in the following that this is not true for the practical discussion of the respective national corporate governance codes—in particular, if one considers them from a European perspective. In terms of the matrix presented in Figure 2.1, agency theory focuses exclusively on the problems in the left-hand column.

Transaction cost theory

Contrary to agency theory, transaction cost economics uses the term governance explicitly and at a point that is decisive from a theoretical perspective. From a transaction-cost-economics vantage point, the firm is a comparatively efficient hierarchical structure that serves for accomplishing contractual relations. The firm is a nexus of contracts that organize and regulate transactions of products and services. The central problem of transaction cost economics is, therefore, to explain the carrying out of economic transactions by the efficiency of the chosen governance structures that have been tailored to carry out the transactions at hand. Oliver E. Williamson, the founder of transaction cost economics, defined governance structure as follows: "A governance structure is thus usefully thought of as an institutional framework in which the integrity of a transaction or related set of transactions, is decided." (Williamson, 1996, p. 11). For Williamson, governance regimes consist of formal and informal structures and rules that enable carrying out economic transactions in an economic manner. Transaction-cost economics focus on hierarchical governance structures—such as firms and other organizations—as alternative to the market as governance structure. The corporate governance problem of transaction-cost economics is, therefore, not the protection of ownership rights of shareholders, rather the effective and efficient accomplishment of transactions by firms in their cultural and political environment (Williamson, 1996, pp. 322–324). From such a vantage point, law and contracts are considered governance structures, just like corporate culture and the moral atmosphere of an economic transaction (Wieland, 1996; Williamson, 1996). Transaction-cost economics, therefore, refer to all four quadrants of the comprehensive corporate governance approach presented in Figure 2.1.

Organization theory

The most interesting contributions of organization theory for our topic here are the resource-based view and the competence-based view. Where economic organizations are understood as a pool of human and organizational resources, capabilities or competences, the objective of the governance regime is to generate, combine, and activate such resources to attain a competitive advantage. Daily, Dalton, and Canella (2003), for instance, wrote, "We define governance as a determination of the broad uses to which organizational resources will be deployed and the resolutions of conflicts among the myriad participants in organizations" (p. 371). For Aoki (2001), corporate governance refers to "the structure of rights and responsibilities among the parties with a stake in the firm" (p. 11). The point of reference of organization theory is neither market nor hierarchy. Rather, strategic management of resources and competences within and by means of an organization are the points of reference. Accordingly, for transaction-cost economics and organization theory, the firm is considered fundamentally different from market solutions. In this regard, both are in contrast to agency theory. The consequences for the notion of stakeholder are important. In the pure market model, stakeholders are reduced to being the counterpart to shareholders. They are not part of the economic problem. In the other two approaches, exactly the opposite is the case. There, shareholders are just one type of stakeholder, even though the most important one.

THE EMPIRICS OF CORPORATE GOVERNANCE

In the following, I refer to the results of an empirical analysis on corporate governance codes of 21 states that I carried out. Some of these only have one code, such as Hungary. Others have several documents, such as Great Britain. Some are purely technical, others more political in character. They are edited by economic and political organizations. All those are covered in the empirical analysis (see Appendix for detail).

Several distinctions have been proposed for building taxonomies of the European corporate governance regimes. Basically, there is a distinction between the   shareholder-value   and   stakeholder-value approach. Others proposed a distinction between market or blockholder system (McCahery [with Bratton], 2002), or between shareholder, stakeholder, and enterprise interest approaches (Wymeersch, 2002; cf. Becht, Bolton, & Roell, 2002). As opposed to these proposals, from the perspective of the ethics of governance that I propose, and in the light of the empirical results, it is important to start by acknowledging that different ideas on the meaning and the objectives of the firm are attributed to each code. From a pure shareholder perspective, usually built on the theoretical foundation of agency theory, a firm is a vehicle for increasing the capital invested by the owners. I call this the maximization model. From a transaction-cost-economics perspective, the firm is a formal or informal organization structure that can accomplish economic transactions in an economizing way. I call this the economizing model of the firm. The organization theory perspective sees the firm in the context of cooperation between owners of internal and external resources to realize pecuniary and nonpecuniary income from their resources. I call this the cooperation model of the firm.

These three different perspectives, based on different theoretical foundations, are mirrored in the European corporate governance codes. The *Swiss Code of Best Practice for Corporate Governance* for instance, refers exclusively to agency theory and the maximization model: "Corporate Governance is the sum total of the principles focussed on the interest of shareholders" (p. 6). To the contrary, the French code, Viénot (Association Française de la Gestion Financière, 1998), the basis for the French system of corporate governance, says

> In Anglo-American countries, the emphasis in this area is on enhancing share value, whereas in continental Europe and particularly in France it tends to be on the company's interest. … The interest of the company may be understood as the overriding claim of the company considered as a separate economic agent pursuing its own objectives which

are distinct from those of shareholders, employees, creditors including the internal revenue authorities, suppliers and customers. It nonetheless represents the common interest, which is for the company to remain in business and prosper. The committee thus believes that directors should at all times be concerned solely to promote the interests of the company. (I.1.)

Here, the firm as a distinct organizational form is the point of reference. It is conceived as consisting of independent objectives and interests, which corporate governance structures are supposed to realize. These independent objectives and interests need to be distinguished from those of their members and stakeholders. Here, we meet a classic example of a firm-oriented corporate governance perspective. It corresponds to what I call the economizing model. Finally, as an example for the cooperation model, I would like to cite the *Dutch Corporate Governance Code* of 2003. Point 3 of its preamble states, "The code is based on the principle accepted in the Netherlands that a company is a long-term form of cooperation between the various parts involved" (n.p.).

If we align the European corporate governance codes according to the models distinguished above, the huge diversity of codes in Europe becomes apparent very clearly (see Figure 3).

As Figure 3 shows, most European corporate governance codes do not refer to agency theory and its focus on shareholder interest. Rather, they focus either on the conflict of interests between shareholder and stakeholder, or the conflict of interests between the firm as a legal and moral actor in itself and the stakeholders (including shareholders, which might be identified as the crucial stakeholders). In a certain sense, the latter category is a theoretical challenge for conventional stakeholder theory. The reason is that conventional stakeholder theory does not have an explicit, theoretically based notion of the organization. Therefore, it is just the inverse of agency theory. The crucial point, though, is that the distinction

Perspective	Shareholder Value		Stakeholder Value	
Focus	Shareholder Management	Shareholder Stakeholder		Corporation Stakeholder
Countries	Switzerland, Czechoslovakia, Portugal, Sweden, Finland, Great Britain, Ireland	Denmark, Netherlands, Spain, Lithuania, Poland, Romania, Slovakia		Austria, Belgium, Germany, France, Italy, Hungary, Russia, Turkey
Entries	7	7		8

Figure 2.3 **Concepts of shareholder vs. stakeholder**

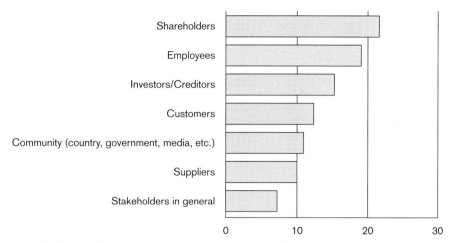

Figure 2.4 **Stakeholders in European corporate governance codes**

between organization or stakeholder (including shareholder) is indispensable for those who want to understand firms not just as organizations of the economy but also as organizations of society—as forms of social cooperation. Precisely that is the declared intention of stakeholder theory. My diagnosis is that the lack of a notion of organization could well be at the root of the unsatisfactory analysis of the stakeholder problem. Further research is needed on the issue. It should perhaps not go unnoticed that stakeholder approaches and approaches focused on the firm do, of course, mention the paramount importance of shareholder interest—while approaches focused exclusively on shareholders do not mention stakeholders and their interest at all.

STAKEHOLDERS AND VALUES IN CODES

If we investigate the diversity of European corporate governance codes a little more in depth, we find further differences that are of importance for the corporate ethics discussion. Of particular interest in this context is the question that stakeholders are acknowledged and identified as having an interest in the firm (see Figure 2.4). This particularly depends on the committees responsible for issuing the corporate governance codes, that is, on the fact whether they are appointed by government departments, stock exchange bodies, or professional bodies. In addition, the stakeholder engagement in reality depends on law and the common national practice. Moreover, most codes follow the recommendations of the according OECD principles.[3]

As mentioned, the Swiss corporate governance code is the only one that exclusively identifies shareholders as stakeholders. The Dutch code, to the contrary, identifies shareholders, employees, whistleblowers, investors, suppliers, customers, government, and the civil society. In most of the European corporate governance codes, shareholders, customers, employees, suppliers, and creditors constitute the core of stakeholders. Depending on the function of the particular code, some of these stakeholders are then dropped or others added.

An especially telling example is the Russian corporate governance code "Corporate Governance is a term that encompasses a variety of activities connected with the management of companies. Corporate Governance affects the performance of economic entities and their ability to attract the capital required for economic growth" (p. 3)[4]. The Russian standard, therefore, belongs to the firm-oriented standards. It mentions the interests of all shareholders (thus, private and public shareholders), the benefit of the Russian economy as a whole and high ethical standards. However, no other stakeholders are identified. This is probably an expression, in cryptic form, of the orientation toward the state that Russian firms have. Coded as respect of the law and the social morale, it refers back to the socialist tradition.

A further differentiation of corporate governance codes shows up via an analysis of the values mentioned in the corporate governance codes (Figure 2.5).

Shareholder-oriented codes emphasize the interests of owners, problems of incomplete information, transparency, accountability, performance-based

Stakeholder-Related Issues	
Issue	Entries
Code of ethics, ethical standards	11
Cooperation, codetermination, partnership	10
Reports, dialogue, communication	7
Wealth, prosperity, jobs	6
Environmental protection	6
Social responsibility	5
	45

Figure 2.5 **Issues in European corporate governance codes**

remuneration, and sustained financial solidity. Stakeholder-oriented codes, on the other hand, have a wider frame of reference, as Figure 5 shows. In addition to the points emphasized by shareholder-oriented codes, the relevance of ethical standards for management, the importance of cooperation and partnership in the firm, the importance of reporting, communication, and dialogue are highlighted; they also put the interest in social welfare, prosperity, the creation of jobs, as well as taking social and ecological responsibility at par with shareholders'profit interests. A similar differentiation can also be identified in the respective control regimes (Figure 2.6).

Shareholder-oriented codes work by control through the market (market for managers, capital market, incentive systems) and the organization of the firm (relations of voting rights, legal responsibilities, reporting system, board structure). For stakeholder approaches, on the other hand, imposing morally sensible standards, reporting systems, and internal and external assurance systems are the important working mechanisms.

A synoptic summary of the fundamental principles of European corporate governance codes confirms this impression. Such a synoptic summary of a comprehensive and complete corporate governance code of European enterprises is available from the study "Corporate Governance Principles for Listed Companies", carried out by the European Corporate Governance Service (ECGS) in 2003 and 2004.[6]

From the analysis, we can see that a so-called typical European benchmark code deals with questions relating to the board of directors (e.g., board structure, board size, role of chairperson, director training) and to shareholder rights (e.g., equitable treatment, controlling shareholders, anti-takeover devices; see Figure 2.7). Furthermore, aspects of transparency and reporting and audit systems of transparency (e.g., transparency, auditing process, reporting structures, internal control), and instruments for the adjusting interests (e.g., company constitution, shareholder resolutions, extraordinary general meetings) are also important. The imposition of a remuneration policy for managers (e.g., framework, incentives, pensions, contractual terms) and of guidelines for the area of corporate social responsibility (e.g., environment, social standards, human rights) complete the picture.

CONCLUSION

In conclusion, we can now recognize the following: corporate governance codes that focus exclusively on the agency problem and pursue the maximization model offer no entry points whatsoever for a dimension of business ethics that goes beyond the honoring of contracts on the part of the managers. Corporate governance codes, on the other hand, which pursue the economizing or cooperation model, directly and immediately lead to the integration of questions of moral and social responsibility of firms and their engagement in terms of corporate citizenship. Most of the European states follow one of the latter two models. This assessment appears to be a good foundation for a practically applicable and theoretically

Shareholder Perspective	Stakeholder Perspective
■ voting	■ internal or external assurance
■ market (manager, capital)	■ internal and external whistleblowing
■ liability	■ reporting systems
■ reporting	■ standards (VMS[ZfW], SA 8000, AA, Q-RES, …)[5]
■ boards	
■ incentives	

Figure 2.6 **Regimes of control**

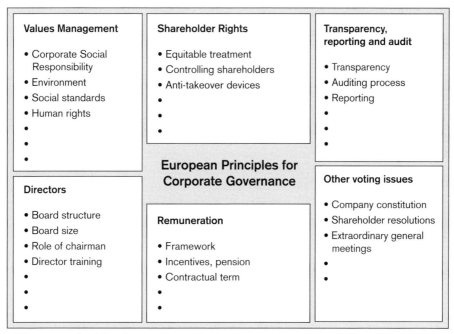

Values Management

- Corporate Social Responsibility
- Environment
- Social standards
- Human rights
- •
- •
- •

Shareholder Rights

- Equitable treatment
- Controlling shareholders
- Anti-takeover devices
- •
- •

Transparency, reporting and audit

- Transparency
- Auditing process
- Reporting
- •
- •
- •

European Principles for Corporate Governance

Directors

- Board structure
- Board size
- Role of chairman
- Director training
- •
- •
- •

Remuneration

- Framework
- Incentives, pension
- Contractual term
- •
- •

Other voting issues

- Company constitution
- Shareholder resolutions
- Extraordinary general meetings
- •
- •

Figure 2.7 **European principles for corporate governance**

interesting discussion of the notion of corporate governance. After all, the discussion of a European approach to corporate governance has not at all come to a conclusion but has just begun. Despite all historical differences, a tendency for codes to converge can now be discerned. Take for instance the idea of corporate governance as a process of self-governance of firms. Adopting such an idea implies that the role of the state should be contained within the framework set by a comply-or-explain rule. It cannot, moreover, escape the observer that in codes such as the German one, Anglo-Saxon influences are attaining an increasing weight, such as when shareholder interests are emphasized more. At the same time, the Sarbanes-Oxley Act in the United States that is of international importance because of its trans-territorial impact explicitly demands moral standards and value management systems for risk prevention (Wieland & Fürst, 2004). In this context, The EU Commission's corporate governance action plan of May 21, 2003 is notable as well; it is based on the preparatory work of the Winter reports (Winter, 2002). Although this action plan negates the establishment of a standardized European Corporate Governance Code, it stipulates requirements that are

to be implemented according to the national perspective of each member state. And in the context of the Global Compact, the Financial Sector Initiative of European Banks' "Who cares wins. Connecting financial markets to a changing world" is of eminent importance as well.[7] It contains detailed "Recommendations by the financial industry to better integrate environmental, social and governance issues in analysis, asset management and securities brokerage" (p. 1) and is endorsed by major banks such as AXA Group, Banco do Brasil, CNP Assurances, Crédit Suisse Group, Deutsche Bank, Goldman Sachs, HSBC, ISIS Asset Management, KLP Insurance, Morgan Stanley, UBS, Westpac, and others.

We can take these examples as instances of reciprocal learning processes that have clarified that a modern economic and moral focus on corporate governance does not necessarily need to end up in the inadequate and not very fruitful reductionism of agency theory. Nowadays, the economic and business ethics literature contains theoretical approaches that integrate economic calculation and the pursuit of social responsibility by framing it as an allocation problem of economic resources, to be solved with the help of organizations.

Appendix
European Corporate Governance Codes

United Kingdom:	*Cadbury Report* (Financial Reporting Council and London Stock Exchange)
	Greenbury Report (Confederation of British Industry Committee
	Hampel Report
	Hermes Statement on International Voting Principles (Hermes Investment Management Ltd.)
	Code of Good Practice (Association of Unit Trusts and Investment Funds)
	The Hermes Principles (Hermes Investment Management Ltd.)
	Combined Code on Corporate Governance (The Financial Reporting Council)
Switzerland:	*Swiss Code of Best Practice for Corporate Governance* (Economie Suisse)
	Richtlinien Corporate Governance der Schweizer Börse (RLCGSWX)
France:	*Vienot 1* (French employers' association CNPF and private business association AFEP)
	Vienot 2 (Committee on Corporate Governance MEDEF and AFEP)
Netherlands:	The *Dutch Corporate Governance Code* (Corporate Governance Committee)
Russia:	*Russian Corporate Governance Code*
Affix:	European Corporate Governance Codes

Western and Middle Europe:

Austria:	*Austrian Code of Corporate Governance* (Austrian Group on Corporate Governance in Austria)
Belgium:	*Merged Code* (Brussels Stock Exchange BXS and Finance Commission)
	Recommendation from the Federation of Belgian Companies *Directors Charta* (Belgian Directors Foundation)
France:	*Vienot 1* (French employers' association CNPF and private business association AFEP)
	Vienot 2 (Committee on Corporate Governance MEDEF and AFEP)
	Recommendations on Corporate Governance (Commission on Corporate Governance AFG-ASFFI)
	Promoting Better Corporate Governance in Listed Companies (MEDEF and AFEP)
	The *Corporate Governance of Listed Corporations* (MEDEF and AFEP)
Germany:	*German Code of Corporate Governance* (Berlin Initiative Group)
	Corporate Governance Rules for Quoted German Companies (German Panel on Corporate Governance)
	Baums Commission Report (German Government Panel on Corporate Governance)
	German Corporate Governance Code (Government Commission German Corporate Governance Code)
Netherlands:	*The Dutch Corporate Governance Code* (Corporate Governance Committee)
Switzerland:	*Swiss Code of Best Practice for Corporate Governance* (Economie Suisse)
	Richtlinien Corporate Governance der Schweizer Börse (RLCGSWX)

South Europe:

Italy:	*Preda Report* (Committee for the Corporate Governance of Listed Companies)
	Corporate Governance Code (Committee for the Corporate Governance of Listed Companies)
Portugal:	*Recommendations on Corporate Governance*
Spain:	*The Corporate Governance of Listed Companies* (The Olivencia Commission)
	The Aldama Report (Aldama Special Commission)
Turkey:	*TÜSIAD Corporate Governance Code of Best Practice:* Composition and Functioning of the Board of Directors (Corporate Governance Association of Turkey)

North Europe:

Denmark:	*Guidelines on Good Management of a Listed Company* (Danish Shareholders' Association)
	Recommendations for Good Corporate Governance in Denmark (Norby Committee)
Finland:	*Corporate Governance Code for Public Limited Companies* (Central Chamber of Commerce and Confederation of Finnish Industry and Employers)
	Ministry of Trade & Industry Guidelines (Finnish Ministry of Industry and Trade)

Ireland: *Corporate Governance, Share Option and Other Incentive Schemes* (Irish Association of Investment Managers)

Sweden: *Corporate Governance Policy* (Swedish Shareholders' Association)
                  The NBK Rules (Naringslivets Borskommitte)

United Kingdom: *Cadbury Report* (Financial Reporting Council and London Stock Exchange)
                  Greenbury Report (Confederation of British Industry Committee)
                  Hampel Report
                  Hermes Statement on International Voting Principles (Hermes Investment Management Ltd.)
                  Code of Good Practice (Association of Unit Trusts and Investment Funds)
                  The Hermes Principles (Hermes Investment Management Ltd.)
                  The Combined Code on Corporate Governance (The Financial Reporting Council)

East Europe:

Czech Republic: *Revised Corporate Governance Code* (Czech Securities Commission)

Hungary: *Corporate Governance Recommendations* (Budapest Stock Exchange Company Limited by Shares)

Lithuania: *The Corporate Governance Code for Companies Listed on the National Stock Exchange of Lithuania* (National Stock Exchange of Lithuania)

Poland: *Best Practices in Public Companies in 2002* (Best Practices Committee at the Corporate Governance Forum)
                  The Corporate Governance Code for Polish Listed Companies (Polish Corporate Governance Forum)

Romania: *Corporate Governance Code in Romania* (Corporate Governance Initiative for economic democracy in Romania)

Russia: *Russian Corporate Governance Code*

Slovakia: *Corporate Governance Code* (Financial Market Authority and others)

NOTES

1. For details, see http://europa.eu.int/comm/ employment_social/soc-dial/csr/ greenpaper.htm
2. For details, see www.dnwe.de/2/content/bb_01.htm
3. Compare to www.oecd.org/document/49/0,2340,en_2 649_34813_31530865_1_1_ 1_1,00.html
4. For details, see www.cipe.org/pdf/programs/corp_ gov/RusCGCodedraft.pdf
5. The VMSZfW can be downloaded from www.dnwe. de/2/content/bb_01.htm. The other codes can be found on the following Web sites: www.cepaa.org/ SA8000/SA8000.htm; www.account ability.org.uk, and www.qres.it
6. The report can be ordered from ECGS at www.ecgs. net/publications.htm
7. The report can be downloaded from www.wbcsd.org/ web/projects/sl/ whocareswins.pdf

REFERENCES

Aoki, M. (2001). *Information, corporate governance and institutional diversity: Competitiveness in Japan, the USA and the transnational economies*. Oxford, UK: Oxford University Press.

Association Française de la Gestion Financière. (1998). *Rapport Viènot II: Gouvernement d'enterprise et intérêts des actionnaires*. France: Author.

Becht, M., Bolton, P., & Roell, A. (2002, December). *Corporate governance and control* (National Bureau of Economic Research [NBER] Working Paper No. 9371). Available at http://papers.ssrn.com/so13/papers. cfm?abstract_id=343461

Berle, A., & Means, G. (1991). *The modern corporation and private property*. New York & New Brunswick, NJ: Transaction Publishers. (Original work published 1932)

Brunsson, N., & Jacobsson, B. (2000). *A world of standards*. Oxford, UK: Oxford University Press.

Daily, C. M., Dalton, D. R., & Cannella, A. A. (2003). Corporate governance: Decades of dialogue and data. *Academy of Management Review*, 28(3), 371.

European Corporate Governance Service Ltd. (n.d.). *Corporate governance principles for listed companies*. Available at www.ecgs.org

EU Commission. (2003, May 21). *Modernisierung des Gesellschaftsrechts und Verbesserung der Corporate Governance in der Europäischen Union* [Modernization of corporate law and enhancement of corporate governance in the EC]. Brussels, Belgium: Author.

Fama, E. F., & Jensen, M. C. (1983, June). Separation of ownership and control. *Journal of Law and Economics*, 26, 304.

Jensen, M. C., & Meckling, W. (1976). Theory of the firm: Managerial behavior, agency costs and ownership structure. *Journal of Financial Economics*, 3(4), 305–360.

Kroszner, R. S. (1996). *The economic nature of the firm: A reader*. New York: Cambridge University Press.

McCahery, J. A., with W. W. Bratton. (2002). Comparative corporate governance and barriers to global cross reference. In J. A. McCahery & L. D. R. Renneboog (Eds.), *Corporate governance regimes: Convergence and diversity* (pp. 23–55). New York *et al.*: Oxford University Press.

Shleifer, A., & Vishny, R. W. (1997). A survey of corporate governance. *Journal of Finance, 52*(2), 737-783.

Wieland, J. (1996). *Ökonomische organisation, allokation und status* [Economic organization, allocation, and status]. Tübingen, Germany: Mohr (Siebeck).

Wieland, J. (2000). Corporate governance und unternehmensethik [Corporate governance and corporate ethics]. In J. Mittelstrass (Ed.), *Die Zukunft des Wissens* (pp. 430–441). Berlin, Germany: Akademie Verlag.

Wieland, J. (2001a). *Die moralische Verantwortung kollektiver Akteure*. Heidelberg, Germany: Physica.

Wieland, J. (2001b). The ethics of governance. *Business Ethics Quarterly, 11*(1), 73-87.

Wieland, J. (2003). *Standards and audits for ethics management systems: The European perspective*. Heidelberg, Germany: Springer-Verlag.

Wieland, J. (2004). *Ethik der Governance* [The ethics of governance] (3rd ed.). Marburg, Germany: Metropolis.

Wieland, J., & Fürst, M. (2004). Moral als element der good corporate governance in banken [Morals as an element of good corporate governance for banks]. In A. Wagner & Chr. Seidel (Eds.), *Ethik in der Bankenpraxis* (pp. 21–43). Frankfurt am Main, Germany: Bankakademie Verlag.

Williamson, O. E. (1996). *The mechanisms of governance*. New York *et al.*: Oxford University Press.

Winter, J. (2002). *Report of the high level group of company law experts on a modern regulatory framework for company law in Europe*. Brussels, Belgium: EU Commission.

Wymeersch, E. (2002). Convergence or divergence in corporate governance patterns in western Europe? In J. McCahery (Ed.), *Corporate governance regimes: Convergence and diversity* (pp. 230–250). New York: Oxford University Press.

PART TWO

Varieties of Capitalism: Latin, Germanic and Anglo-American Systems

INTRODUCTION TO PART TWO

Part Two explores the rich variety of capitalism that exists in Europe, and investigates the distinctive qualities of each system and how it is developing. The defining feature of European corporate governance is its institutional diversity. However, if two broad regional variations are identified, the Latin forms of corporate governance existing in Southern Europe, and the Germanic systems predominating in Northern Europe, in recent years both variations have come under increasing pressure to assume elements of the Anglo-American market-based approach to corporate governance. An analysis of corporate governance in Italy reveals one of the least reconstructed systems among the advanced industrial countries. Italian corporate governance is characterized by a poor capital market, and traditionally at least, almost non-existent market for corporate control, with banks that have a stake in corporate financing but play a minor part in governance. This leaves the field open for major active investors or blockholders, to monitor senior management, with minority shareholders likely to be ignored.

Andrea Melis suggests that unlike the US system summarized by Roe as "strong managers, weak owners," in Italy the reality is almost the reverse with "weak managers, strong blockholders, and unprotected minority shareholders." Since Italian company law has supported the certainty of majority control rather than the representation of minority interests, there has been little incentive for small investors to become involved in the stock market. Similarly Italian managers tend to be committed to the interests of majority blockholders rather than shareholders in general. These legal and managerial preferences can be explained by the very high concentration of ownership in Italy with the main shareholder owning on average 48 percent of the total shares in non-financial listed companies in the mid-1990s. This direct ownership is further leveraged by the use of pyramid structures to further concentrate control with complex shareholding structures. The existence of a powerful blockholder allows the effective monitoring of management. However if the Anglo-American system is typified by concerns regarding the abuse of executive power, the Italian system of governance is typified by the potential abuse of power by blockholders. Some sectors of Italian industry such as fashion, design, textiles, footwear and ceramics have succeeded in becoming world leaders based on a networked, family-based mode of ownership and control that has allowed skill formation through many generations. Yet the bankruptcy of Parmalat in 2003 has exposed a similar disregard for accounting conventions as witnessed in the US, and focused attention on some of the manifest weaknesses in the Italian system of corporate governance.

The recent changes in the finance and corporate governance systems of Italy are examined further by Richard Deeg, who explores the political and economic dynamics of change. In explaining institutional change he draws on three perspectives: a legal origins/quality of corporate governance approach; a varieties of capitalism approach; and a coalitional approach. Each of these explanations offers some insights to the processes of change in Italy, but also possesses limitations. With reference to the view that if legal changes occur then market changes will follow, he shows how the relevant corporate laws have changed but without the changes in behavior and growth of markets that might have been anticipated. The varieties of capitalism approach suggests the interdependency and complementarity of institutions, yet there is evidence that in Italy liberalizing corporate governance reforms has not been accompanied by commensurate changes in labour market reforms to maintain system coherence. Finally, from the coalitional viewpoint a reform coalition in favor of greater transparency in corporate governance may have succeeded in securing significant institutional change in Italy, meeting the standards demanded by European Union regulators and investors. Yet the blockholding coalitions have effectively evaded these reforms, and sustained their insider control. Regulators and the judiciary remain ill-equipped to enforce the new regime, leaving Italy with its unique coalition framework, with the state retaining a degree of strategic influence, appearing in form, though less in substance, to conform with the new more competitive European corporate and financial requirements.

In France the corporate governance system was dominated traditionally by cross-shareholdings, what Morin calls a "financial networked economy", that is the State and a pattern of cross-shareholding between large companies created a tight and largely closed network of financially linked companies. In recent times, inspired by the US shareholder value model, the French investment system is transforming towards a "financial market economy," eroding the system of cross-shareholdings and replacing this with equity provided through the stock market. These changes have been hastened by the influence of the large Anglo-Saxon institutional investors in the ownership structure of the largest French firms, without any equivalent French institutional investors able to mobilize long-term investment funds. In turn the institutional investors have made their own demands on what should be the primary objective of corporations. In the past in France corporate finance was not determined through the capital market, but governed by groups of leading actors organized in interlocking networks of corporate alliances. This allowed the state and leading companies to impose their own logic upon corporate strategies and economic growth. The new logic of the French system is increasingly provided by the capital markets, in which Anglo-American financial institutions and institutional investors have the greatest influence. This means corporate management is no longer free to pursue restructuring according to their own objectives, protected from the possibility of external aggressors in the capital market. With foreign investors now significantly larger than any surviving company cross-shareholdings, French executives have to dance to a different tune.

The nature and investment strategies of the institutional investors themselves have changed over time. The switch from defined benefit pension schemes where the employers bear the risk, and pension fund trustees can follow long-term and prudent investment policies, to defined contribution pension schemes where the employee bears the risk, have changed pension fund investment strategies towards higher risk strategies with more explicit attempts to target equities and portfolios that will outperform the market. In turn this more aggressive investment strategy places corporate management under growing pressure to deliver value. This is defined as *shareholder value* that is potentially transferable at some stage to shareholders themselves. Now the largest French corporations are increasingly subject to Anglo-Saxon management techniques and return-on-investment measures. Among the demands now made upon French managers are developing a concentration in core businesses to reduce costs; breaking up conglomerates and outsourcing non strategic activities; and buying back shares when the company has accumulated cash but is not able to find sufficiently profitable investments to deliver adequate returns going forward. The argument is that these strategies all contribute to the profitability and efficiency of leaner and fitter firms, but in reality important strategic possibilities and the commitment to sustained, long-term growth is often closed off by these often inherently short-term corporate objectives. In summary corporate governance in France is in a state of transformation in which the discourse of financial performance is becoming dominant relative to any industrial logic as managers are encouraged to pursue shareholder value above all else.

In governance terms the UK traditionally has been regarded as the original source of the market-based Anglo-American approach. In a nineteenth-century economic empire that preceded the twentieth-century economic hegemony of the United States, Britain delivered to large parts of the world international trade and commerce and the common law that regulated this. In more recent times, as London continued to rival New York as a center for global financial markets, UK corporate governance reforms have influenced the codes of practice developed in many countries, and impacted upon market and institutional developments internationally. UK influence internationally has not been as universal as the American emphasis on agency theory and shareholder value, but it has provided significant financial and legal weight in support of the Anglo-American approach to governance and accountability. In this way the UK has often stood apart from the rest of Europe, and appeared closer in terms of market institutions, corporate governance and strategic objectives to the United States. However Pendleton questions whether the UK actually does fit very closely the market-based view of governance, and suggests a web of social relationships between investors and managers runs parallel to, and often displaces market-based forms of discipline. From this view the UK system of corporate governance demonstrates characteristics of a relationship-based or network system, together with elements of a market-based system. This suggests the distinctions between the relational and market forms of governance are more complex and ambiguous than often assumed, and that the processes of convergence may be multi-directional rather than a uniform adoption of Anglo-American market-based elements by the relationship-based approaches of Europe, the Asia-Pacific, and much of the rest of the world.

From this perspective the dichotomous division of La Porta *et al.* (1999; 2000), Rajan and Zingales (2003) and other authorities between market-based systems of governance and other systems of governance based on relationships between firms, investors and stakeholders does not allow sufficiently for the diversity of governance forms that exist in practice. Pendleton refers to the evidence that the insider, network-based category of relationship governance puts together a diverse group of governance systems, for example Rhenish corporate governance differs substantially from Latin models, and Japanese corporate governance is substantially different from other Asian countries. Furthermore, national systems of governance continue to display profound differences, and the outcome of pressures to globalize generates hybrid rather than homogenous models.

If the power of larger and more liquid equity markets has dissolved some of the strength of the networks in the relationship model, it is also the case that the increasing governance activity of major investors in the UK has to some degree replaced a transactional market model with stronger relationships. Further evidence Pendleton cites that the UK is far from being a paradigmatic market-based system of corporate governance is that if coalitions of large shareholders are considered, ownership concentration and influence in UK companies is far greater than usually assumed; second if the listed company sector as a whole is considered and not just the largest companies, then concentration of ownership increases to higher levels still. Though less prevalent than in the rest of Europe, it remains the case that family ownership is important in smaller quoted companies in the UK. Furthermore institutional investment in the UK is becoming more highly concentrated, and is now dominating the shareholder base in the FTSE 100 companies, contrary to the market model of highly dispersed ownership. Relationship investing is becoming a significant part of the approach to corporate governance in the UK therefore, bringing the UK model a little closer to European modes of governance.

In other European countries there are indications of the pragmatic adoption of elements of different governance systems while retaining a distinctive national institutional identity. For example, the forces of globalization have also impacted on segmented capital markets in Northern Europe, where companies are being drawn towards adopting the structures of Anglo-American corporate governance to secure access to lower costs of capital. As Oxelheim and Randoy's (2003) study of firms headquartered in Norway and Sweden reveals, it is possible to "import" Anglo-American directors as an indication of openness to foreign investors and a commitment to corporate transparency, bringing stiffer monitoring of the company. In the Netherlands the system of corporate governance represents a unique combination of the characteristics of the market-based Anglo-Saxon regime, and the bank-based Continental-European system. However, a two-tier board system is prevalent with the principle of co-option of the supervisory board. Van Ees, Postma and Sterken's (2003) research indicates that the small management boards perform effectively, but with the larger supervisory boards there is a negative impact in the size of the board. They conclude management may have too much influence over the selection of the supervisory boards, and that Dutch shareholders have no real influence over the size and composition of supervisory boards. European corporate governance remains generally in a state of flux and transformation, with distinctive approaches to development and reform, with the continuance of a wide diversity of institutions and approaches and the emergence of a range of hybrid forms. The future path of development of European corporate governance institutions is difficult to determine, and it is likely that impulses towards convergence will co-exist with enduring commitments towards distinctiveness and diversity.

BIBLIOGRAPHY

Aguilera, R. and Jackson, G. (2003) The Cross-national Diversity of Corporate Governance: Dimensions and Determinants, *Academy of Management Review*, 28(3): 447–465.
Clarke, T. (2007) *International Corporate Governance: A Comparative Approach:* London: Routledge.

Della Sala, V. (2004) The Italian Model of Capitalism: On the Road Between Globalization and Europeanization? *Journal of European Public Policy*, 11 (6): 1041–1057.

Hall, P. and Soskice, D. (2001) *Varieties of Capitalism*, New York: Oxford University Press.

La Porta, R., Lopez-de-Silanes, F. and Shleifer, A. (1999) Corporate Ownership Around the World, *Journal of Finance*, 54: 471–517.

La Porta, R., Lopez-de-Silanes, F., Shleifer, A. and Vishny, R. (2000) Investor Protection and Corporate Governance. *Journal of Financial Economics*, 58(1): 3–27.

Moerland, P.W. (1995) Corporate Ownership and Control Structures: An International Comparison, *Review of Industrial Organization*, 10(4): 443–464.

Morin, F. (2000) A Transformation in the French Model of Shareholding and Management, *Economy and Society*, 29 (1): 36–53.

Oxelheim, L. and Randoy, T. (2003) The Impact of Foreign Board Membership on Firm Value, *Journal of Banking and Finance*, 27: 2369–2392.

Rajan, R. and Zingales, L. (2003) Financial Systems, Industrial Structure, and Growth, *Oxford Review of Economic Policy*, 17: 467–482.

van Ees, H., Postma, T. and Sterken, E. (2003) Board Characteristics and Corporate Performance in the Netherlands, *Eastern Economic Journal*, 29(1): 41–58.

3 "Corporate Governance in Italy"

from Corporate Governance (2000)

Andrea Melis

SUMMARY

This chapter has analysed the Italian prevailing corporate governance system in terms of issues such as ownership and control structures, structure and functioning of the boards, executive remuneration and evaluation, the mission of the companies, the role of banks and market for corporate control. The issues determined by the presence of the blockholder have been analysed as well as the changes that derive from the Draghi reform. The Italian system of corporate governance seems to be effectively summarised by the expression 'weak managers, strong blockholders and unprotected minority shareholders', paraphrasing Roe's (1994) sentence.

INTRODUCTION

Today's developed economies are dominated by two main basic corporate governance systems: the relationship-based corporate system and the market-oriented corporate system (Franks, Mayer, 1992; Moerland, 1995). Regarding EU countries, the former may then be distinguished in two main sub-groups: the Latin and the Germanic systems (De Jong, 1997; Melis, 1999a). The Italian corporate governance system belongs to the Latin sub-group, although it has its own individual features, and does not fit completely into the international standard models.

The main purpose of this chapter is to analyse the Italian corporate governance system. The characteristics of the ownership and control structure will be described, in order to offer a clear view of the Italian reality. Our attention is focused on the structure of the board and the following relationships: executive-non executive directors, directors–shareholders and majority–minority shareholders. The roles of the market for corporate control and the banks are analysed in order to underline the specificity of the Italian system. In contrast to the other European systems, neither the market nor the banks have a relevant influence on the Italian corporate governance system (Bianco, Casavola, 1996).

HISTORICAL BACKGROUND

In Italy, the problems of corporate governance have usually been discussed concerning State-owned companies. However, in recent years, mainly due to the process of privatisation and EU integration, the issues related to corporate governance in public companies have increased their relevance among scholars and policy makers (e.g. Barca, 1995; Bianco, Casavola, 1996; Bianchi *et al.*, 1997; Molteni, 1997).

Italian company law has probably favoured excessively certainty of control at the expense of shareholders' protection (Bianchi *et al.*, 1997). For this reason, many potential small investors have avoided investing in the stock exchange in the past.

Empirical evidence shows that the great majority of Italian senior managers believe that the main objective for their companies is to maximise value for the shareholders (Melis, 1999b). However, this fact should not be a source of misunderstanding. In fact, the expression "shareholders' value maximisation" does not represent the same concept in Italy as in the Anglo-American corporate model. In order to understand the exact meaning of 'shareholder' given by the Italian senior management, it has to be considered the average ownership structure, which is characterised by the relevant presence of blockholders. When senior managers claim that they run the company in order to maximise the value for the shareholders, they probably should say "to maximise the value for the blockholder".[1] This may happen at the expense of the minority shareholders' interests.

For this reason, both CONSOB[2] (1995) and Bank of Italy (1996) have stressed the importance of a reform that would have reorganised the entire corporate governance system in Italy. The consequent debate has led to a new law for listed companies: the so-called Draghi reform,[3] in force since July 1998.

The Draghi reform regulates financial markets and corporate governance in listed companies. The aim of the reform is to "strength investors' protection and minority shareholders", by regulating listed companies on issues such as shareholders' agreements, internal controls, minority shareholders' rights and public bids.

The Draghi reform differs from the previous codes on corporate governance (e.g. Cadbury, 1992; Vienot, 1995, etc.) for two main reasons:

- it is not merely a code of practice, but is legally binding for all the listed companies;
- it does not cover any topics regarding the board of directors.

OWNERSHIP AND THE MARKET FOR CORPORATE CONTROL

Ownership and control structure

The ownership structure of the Italian non-financial listed companies is characterised by a high level of concentration. CONSOB (1996) reports that the largest shareholder owns, on average, 48 percent. The identity of owners reveals that families, coalitions and other companies have a major role. Financial institutions hold a very limited amount of shares. The State plays an important role in some important companies, but is likely to lose its relevance due to the on-going process of privatisation.

The great majority of the companies' control structure is characterised by the dominance of a main shareholder (Bianchi *et al.*, 1997), who acts as blockholder.

Blockholders tend to have a major control over management not only because of their high level of direct ownership, but also due to some devices, such as pyramidal groups, the issue of non-voting shares and shareholders' agreements. Cross-shareholdings are rarely important because of the limit imposed by Italian company law.

Pyramidal groups have been defined as "a cascade of companies which can exert control through a complicated shareholding structure at a minimum cost" (Kendall, Sheridan, 1992: 68–69). In these groups, the holding company controls (directly or indirectly) the majority of voting rights of the companies which belong to the group and its ultimate control is either by a single entrepreneur, or a family or a coalition. This device is generally used to maximise the ratio between the amount of resources controlled and the own capital invested to maintain the control. The structure of these groups is usually quite complex. Despite the rules of ownership disclosure, their exact control structure is difficult to trace, especially at an international level.

Market capitalisation	Individuals	Foreign	State	Non-financial companies	Banks	Insurance	Mutual funds	Other financial	Total
5 percentile	9,00	17,02	0,00	38,98	6,36	0,07	0,44	1,35	73,22
10 percentile	19,14	15,19	0,00	23,81	11,14	3,52	0,44	0,00	74,58
25 percentile	6,00	11,15	0,00	46,68	12,18	0,47	0,47	2,16	79,11
50 percentile	5,22	9,44	0,60	43,90	8,06	1,13	1,46	1,94	72,41
75 percentile	3,39	10,55	5,87	38,17	8,04	2,88	0,85	0,42	69,26
90 percentile	2,74	4,05	0,70	34,31	10,22	5,61	0,53	0,19	58,35
95 percentile	0,00	1,77	1,38	26,74	17,68	1,05	0,20	0,62	49,44
> 95 percentile	0,00	0,43	16,42	17,22	10,40	5,66	0,00	0,77	50,90
Total	5,01	9,29	2,62	38,08	9,57	2,37	0,76	1,09	68,50

Source: Consob (1996), in Bianchi *et al.* (1997), *Ownership, pyramidal groups and separation between ownership and control in Italy,* Appendix, table 32.

Table 3.1 **Average ownership concentration of listed companies by type of investor**

Market capitalisation	Largest stake	2nd	3rd	4–10th
5 percentile	50,53	14,18	4,19	4,20
10 percentile	46,33	10,31	6,59	9,29
25 percentile	53,27	8,90	4,92	10,87
50 percentile	47,57	11,98	5,09	6,54
75 percentile	50,09	10,1	3,52	6,12
90 percentile	42,42	9,36	2,95	3,54
95 percentile	37,02	7,00	3,17	2,23
> 95 percentile	48,63	2,55	2,03	2,31
Total	48,02	10,14	4,12	6,13

Source: Consob (1996), in Bianchi *et al.* (1997), *Ownership, pyramidal groups and separation between ownership and control in Italy*, Appendix, table 22.

Table 3.2 **Average ownership concentration of listed companies**

The issue of non-voting shares is largely diffused among the Italian companies (Barca, 1993) with the only limitation in the total par value not higher than the total par value of voting shares. With this mechanism, the management has an alternative source for corporate funding, which is risk-free for the control of the company, since it has no voting right.

Shareholders' agreements are a fundamental device especially at the highest level of the control chains. The Draghi reform has modified their regulation, in order to weaken their power as a mechanism to maintain control of the company by a coalition of blockholders. The length of the agreement between the shareholders cannot be longer than three years, after which it has to be re-negotiated. The partners are now given the right to withdraw from the agreement in case of public bids. This right may weaken this mechanism since it seems to foster the possibility of takeovers, at least in theory. In fact, it is not predictable how it will work since not only have shareholders' agreements always been contracts but also implicit contracts, i.e. a sort of gentlemen's agreement among some of the most important Italian coalitions.

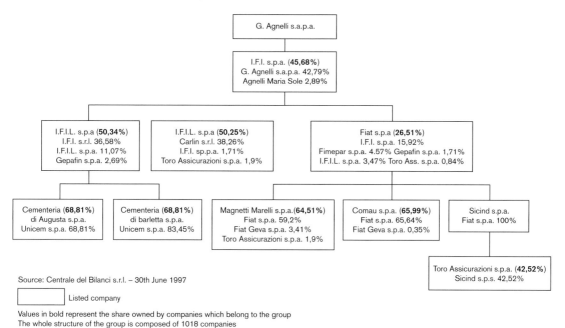

Source: Centrale del Bilanci s.r.l. – 30th June 1997

☐ Listed company

Values in bold represent the share owned by companies which belong to the group
The whole structure of the group is composed of 1018 companies
G. Agnelli s.a.p.a. is a partnership

Figure 3.1 **A simplified company structure of Fiat group**

By the previous devices, it is possible to create a separation between ownership and control, so that blockholders may control huge amounts of capital by owning a relatively small share. CONSOB (1996) reports an average separation (capital under control/capital owned) of 2.8. The data are probably under-estimated because of the difficulty in identifying the ultimate controlling agents when the control chain ends with a company (Bianchi *et al.*, 1997).

Market orientation and the role of the market for corporate control

The capital market orientation of the companies and the role of the market for corporate control are key features to understand the institutional framework of a corporate governance system. The Italian system is characterised by a limited role of the stock market. However, if the role assumed by the stock market may appear as an anomaly to Anglo-American eyes, in this respect the Italian case is not too different from other continental European countries, such as Germany and, especially, France (Pagano *et al.*, 1998).

The stock exchange does not play a highly relevant role, even in listed companies. Self-financing and bank debts are the main sources for corporate funding. The issue of new shares, with or without shareholders'

stock option, has a minor relevance (Melis, 1999b). This choice of corporate funding leads to a financial structure which is characterised by one of the lowest levels of equity compared to debts and assets among the OECD large economies (Guatri, Vicari, 1994). This financial structure seems to be effective in order to allow senior management to help the blockholder to keep the control of the company since potentially dangerous (for the blockholder) investors are not allowed to have a relevant stake in the company. Empirical evidence seems to confirm this strategy. Despite the fact that the main factor that influences the choice of corporate funding is its cost, the importance of 'political' reasons has to be stressed as well (Melis, 1999b). It is not rare that the senior management prefers a certain source of corporate finance in order to prevent any potential threat against the control of the company.

The market for corporate control does not have an important relevance and hostile takeovers are rare.[4] When mergers and acquisitions occur, they are basically friendly and through either the mediation of a main merchant bank (e.g. Mediobanca) or a private agreement between coalitions or families. The sales of a majority stake are normally arranged at prices implying a very large premium on stock market prices (Caprio, Floreani, 1996). Zingales (1994) reports an average premium of 82 percent associated with the voting rights of shares on the Milan stock market. This

Country	Market capitalisation* in ECU mn	No. of listed companies**		
		Domestic	Foreign	Total
France	813.323	782	179	961
Germany	996.830	739	2766	3505
Italy	465.100	239	4	243
UK	1,886.765	2407	521	2928

Source: * Federation Internationale Des Bourses De Valeurs (FIBV); ** Federation of European Stock Exchanges (FESE), November 1998.

Table 3.3 **Listed companies by country and their total market value**

1. Giovanni Agnelli & C. S.a.p.a	8.86	7. Ligresti Salvatore	4.83
2. Compart S.p.a. (1)	4.35	8. Berlusconi Silvio	3.66
3. Benetton	1.46	9. Bulgari S.p.a. (1)	1.80
4. Pirelli	1.95	10. De Benedetti Carlo	10.33
5. Radici Pesenti Rosalia	4.15	11. Pininfarina Sergio	5.93
6. Tanzi Calisto	1.68	12. Bosatelli Domenico	1.39

Source: Consob (1996). (1) The head of the Group is the coalition controlling the company.

Table 3.4 **Degree of separation of ownership and control among non-financial groups**

large premium may be interpreted as evidence of significant benefits of private control that arise at the expense of the minority shareholders (Shleifer, Vishny, 1997).

The Draghi reform has modified the regulation of public bids. For example, the bidder will have to offer a public bid for the total amount of shares if he or she owns more than 30 percent of the shares. The aim of this regulation is to give the minority shareholders of a target company the opportunity to gain the same economic advantage as the majority shareholder. However, this change on the mandatory public bid might be ineffective, because it could reduce the possibilities of takeover either making it too expensive for the public bidder or encouraging the exclusion of potential target companies from listing on the stock exchange.

THE ROLE OF THE BANKS AND OTHER FINANCIAL INSTITUTIONS

Banks usually play a minor part in corporate governance in Italy. Although they have a relevant stake in corporate external financing, feeble bank–firm relations jeopardise the role of the banks (Ferri, Pesaresi, 1996). Despite the similar framework of 'universal bank', the Italian system is not characterised by a main bank relationship as is the German system. The practice of multiple loans is widespread. This multilateral relationship may be considered to be efficient in order to spread the risk, but also reduces the incentives for the banks to have a stake and monitor corporate management, since it never happens that a bank has a large share in a single firm. Even when, and it is not rare, banks provide long-term capital to companies, they are neither involved in the corporate strategies' formulation and implementation, nor considered as a partner for corporate strategies by the management, and rarely have their representatives on the board of the companies.

Being involved in the management of companies is not considered to be the objective of banks (De Polis, 1997). For this reason, banks do usually not influence management strategies, as long as companies are able to refund their debts. This is the main objective of most of the Italian banks. However, a bank may influence management indirectly, by recalling its credits.

An important exception to this behaviour is Mediobanca. This bank, linked through a web of inter-

corporate shareholdings to some of main Italian families, has had a relevant corporate governance role guaranteeing the stability and growth of the largest private groups and has often acted to pursue major corporate rescue plans (De Cecco, Ferri, 1996).

The other financial institutions usually play a marginal role (Bianchi *et al.*, 1997); however, things are changing rapidly and they are developing and are also starting to have an active role in some shareholders' meetings. A good example has recently been given by foreign institutional investors, during the successful fight to remove the management of Olivetti Spa.

WEAK MANAGERS, STRONG BLOCKHOLDERS AND UNPROTECTED MINORITY SHAREHOLDERS

Italian mainstream literature (e.g. Saraceno, 1964; Coda, 1967; Onida, 1968; Zanda, 1974) analyses the issue of the separation between ownership and control mostly according to a non-sectional managerial perspective, arguing that managers pursue the interests of shareholders, i.e. the separation between manager and shareholder does not produce relevant agency costs. The prevailing ownership and control structure reduces the potential agency problems between senior management and shareholders, because the blockholder is an active investor, able to reduce the information asymmetry and has the incentive to monitor effectively and influence senior management according to its interests.

Stonehill and Dullum (1990) note that the ownership structure in Europe leads to a choice of corporate objectives consistent with the corporate maximisation model. However, survival of the firm with a fair remuneration for the shareholders is chosen as the main objective only by a small minority of Italian senior managers (Melis, 1999b). This fact seems to confirm the weakness of managers in relation to the strength of the blockholders, since this goal may be considered as an optimal managerial objective (it may maximise managerial interests), while it does not maximise shareholders' interest.

However, the agency problem is not totally eliminated, but simply shifted towards the relationship between different types of shareholders.

Conflicts of interests arise both between shareholders with full voting rights and shareholders with no voting rights, who are interested in the guaranteed dividend, as well as between blockholders and minority shareholders with no possibility of monitoring the management. Because of the reality of the market for corporate control, minority shareholders cannot even count on outside managerial discipline mechanisms. Consequently they often found themselves in the difficult situation of the impossibility of having their interests effectively safeguarded. Minority shareholders often cannot have any significant role in corporate governance, they are not guaranteed enough by the intervention of courts, because the device of fiduciary duties is largely unavailable and derivative suits are ineffective (Giudici, Paleari, 1998).

The Draghi reform fosters the rights of the minority shareholders: shareholders representing at least 10 percent (or the lower percentage established by the by-laws) of the equity issued may convene a shareholder meeting. Moreover, shareholders, entered in the register of shareholders for at least six months, representing at least 5 percent of issued equity may bring a company action for liability against the directors, the members of the board of statutory auditors or general managers, even if the company is in liquidation. Company's by-laws may lower the threshold.

Corporate governance is still seen by senior management as a private issue (Molteni, 1997). There is little evidence of the presence of any corporate governance committee and only a few companies (e.g. Fiat) have a plan to set it up in the close future. Most companies have no intention to set up a committee within five years (Melis, 1999b). This evidence seems to confirm the argument of Molteni (1997), who notes that senior management believes that there are already too many laws and regulations to be willing to set up new rules for the structure of a board and the corporate governance of a company.

THE STRUCTURE OF THE BOARDS

The Italian listed companies are characterised by a particular board structure composed by a board of directors (Consiglio di Amministrazione) and a board of statutory auditors (Collegio sindacale), both appointed by the shareholders' meeting.

The Draghi reform has not made any changes to the structure of the board of directors. Relating to the composition of boards of directors, non-executive directors (NEDs) generally represent the majority of the board. Directors, both executive and non-

executive, are proposed by the chairperson or by the blockholder and appointed by the shareholders' meeting, which is under the control of the blockholder. The duration of their appointment is usually predetermined and lasts three years.

NEDs usually have the duty to control the executive directors and support them in the formulation and implementation of the corporate strategies. NEDs are sometimes involved in the decision on CEO remuneration. Empirical evidence shows that the research and selection of the executive directors is not a task which NEDs are involved in (Melis, 1999b). Executive directors are usually researched and selected by the blockholder.

Interlocking directorship is a common reality among listed companies, especially within the same pyramidal group, and acts either as a substitute or as an integration of the ownership links in order to let the blockholder maintain control of the group.

Separation between Chairperson and CEO usually characterises the structure of the board. This separation tends to be considered as crucial to allow the board independence (Cadbury, 1992). Despite respect for this condition, Italian senior management can hardly be considered as independent for two main reasons:

- the division of roles between the Chairperson and the CEO is not clear enough;
- the great influence that the blockholder has on the management. The board of directors often simply ratifies the decisions taken by the blockholder (Brunetti, 1997).

NEDs often find difficult to verify the information given by the executive directors. They do have the access to the sources of information, however the act of verifying the information tends to be perceived as being against the implicit rules within the board (Molteni, 1997).

The board of directors is rarely characterised by the presence of organs such as an audit committee, remuneration committee and nomination committee. Sometimes there is the presence of an executive committee which absorbs most of the key functions of the board of the directors, giving the rest of the board the duty to ratify what is decided in the executive committee (Molteni, 1997). The presence of an executive committee with such a degree of power may offer a basis on which to develop a two-tier board structure.

The Draghi reform has modified the role and the functioning of the board of statutory auditors. This board is to be composed of at least three members, with minimum one (at least two, if the board is composed of more than three members) representative of the minority shareholders. At least two members of the board have the power to call the shareholders' meeting when they believe it necessary because of a senior management's decision. Before the Draghi reform, its main duty was to monitor the board of directors to safeguard corporate property (concerning accounting issues), but it had no voice in the strategic decisions. The Draghi reform has solved the previous problem of potential overlapping of the role of the board of statutory auditors with the external auditor, since monitoring of the accounting issues is given to the external auditor. The board of statutory auditors is now given the duty of supervising the executive directors, with a duty similar to the NEDs. However, now the potential risk of overlapping is between the board of statutory auditors and the NEDs. In fact, the board of statutory auditors has partially remained 'non-political' (i.e. not involved in strategic issues), but has also become closer to the German supervisory board. In this perspective it may be interpreted as the presence of the minority shareholders' representatives in the board. The Italian corporate governance system seems to have changed its character, becoming something a sort of 'half-way house' between a unitary board system and a two-tier board system.

EXECUTIVE REMUNERATION AND EVALUATION

The executive evaluation is mostly conducted by the board of directors with a non-structured procedure. The control structure allows the flow of information and does not always need a structured and constant method to effectively evaluate the executive directors. The evaluation is based on criteria such as the degree of achievement of the objectives stated in the year plan and a comparison with the industry results, rather than the share value on the stock market.

Executive remuneration is usually either decided by the shareholders' meeting or the management board. However, cases where both the board of directors and the shareholders' meeting have a joint decision-making process are not exceptional (Melis, 1999b). The remuneration committee is not a common tool.

Due to the lack of disclosure about executive remuneration (before Consob regulation in 1998, annual accounts have usually reported only the total compensation paid to the executive directors altogether), there is a lack of information about this issue.

Empirical evidence reports that the executive compensation is characterised by the limited use of long-term incentives (Brunello *et al.*, 1997). The fixed amount represents most of the remuneration, which may be integrated either with bonus (more often) or with stock option (rarely). The use of pension funds is exceptional, at least among non-financial companies, because of a 'generous' State pension system (Melis, 1999b).

The role of stock options seems limited by the inefficiency of the Italian stock exchange market, with the consequent poor reliability of stock returns as a measure of managerial performance. However, it seems that the relevance of share plans may increase in coming years. A 1998 survey by Studio Ambrosetti shows that 49 percent of listed companies have stock option plans for the next years.

Sometimes, executive remuneration is strictly linked to corporate profits. In fact, a small amount of executive directors of non-financial listed companies receive a percentage of corporate profit as compensation (Melis, 1999b). Linking executive remuneration to corporate profit may seem to be dangerous for the shareholders, since executive directors might manipulate profit in order to pursue their own interests. However, it must be taken into consideration that all the companies that use this mechanism are characterised by the presence of a blockholder, who monitors senior management effectively in the calculation of the corporate profit.

FINAL REMARKS

This paper has analysed the key features of the corporate governance in Italy. The Italian system is characterised by a poor capital market orientation and a virtually non-existent market for corporate control. Although banks have a relevant stake in corporate external financing, they play a minor part in corporate governance. The ownership and control structure is characterised by the presence of a blockholder, an active investor, able to monitor the senior management effectively. Due to this structure, minority shareholders are likely to be the victims of the blockholder.

While in Anglo-American corporate governance systems there is great concern about the potential abuse of executive power, in Italy the concern should be for the potential abuse of power from the blockholder. If "strong managers, weak owners" (Roe, 1994) summarises the issues of corporate governance in the USA, the expression 'weak managers, strong blockholders and unprotected minority shareholders' may effectively summarise the Italian reality. Undoubtedly, the minority shareholders' rights are fostered by the Draghi reform, however the question is to what extent the law will let minority shareholders have a real stake and be effectively active in corporate governance, weakening the power of the blockholders.

Further research should also analyse how the possible developments of board structure, taking into consideration the evolution of the board of statutory auditors and the presence of the executive committee as potential pressures could move towards a two-tier board structure.

NOTES

1. A good example of this behaviour is given by the Comit Spa case. Regarding this case, Zingales (1999) notes that the previous management has been dismissed because it preferred the offer from Unicredito Spa to the one of Banca Intesa Spa. The new senior management has accepted the second offer. However, regarding shareholders' value maximisation, the Banca Intesa's tender bid is not any better than UniCredito's hostile bid. However it may better pursue the strategic interest of control of the blockholder.
2. The body that specifically controls the securities markets, which is, to some extent, modelled on the SEC of the USA.
3. Law: Decreto Legislativo 24 febbraio 1998, n. 58.
4. The hostile takeover of Telecom Italia Spa. by Olivetti group may be considered as exceptional, due to the particular (according to the Italian standards) ownership structure of the target company.

REFERENCES

Banca d'Italia (1996), *Considerazioni finali del Governatore*, Roma

Barca F. (1993), *Allocazione e riallocazione della proprietà e del controllo delle imprese: ostacoli, intermediari e regole*, Temi di discussione, N. 194, Roma: Banca d'Italia

Barca F. (1995), *On corporate governance in Italy: issues, facts and agenda*, FEEM working paper 10.96.

Bianchi M., Bianco M., Enriques L. (1997), *Ownership, pyramidal groups and separation between ownership and control in Italy*, Brussels: European Corporate Governance Network

Bianco M. and P. Casavola (1996), *Corporate governance in Italia: alcuni jatti e problemi aperti*, Rivista delle Società, N.41

Brunello G., Graziano C., Parigi B. (1997), *Executive compensation and firm performance in Italy*, FEEM working paper 50.97

Brunetti G. (1997), *Il funzionamento del Consiglio di Amministrazione nella realtà italiana: problemi e prospettive sulla base di alcune evidenze empiriche*, in Molteni (1997), *I sistemi di corporate governance nelle grandi imprese italiane*, Milano: EGEA

Cadbury Report (1992), *The financial aspects of corporate governance*, London: Gee

Caprio L. and A. Floreani (1996), *Transjer of control of listed companies in Italy: an empirical analysis*, FEEM working paper 8.96

Coda V. (1967), *Proprietà, lavoro e potere di governo dell'impresa*, Milano: Giuffré

CONSOB (1995), *Relazione per l'anno 1995*

De Cecco M. and G. Ferri (1996), *Le banche d'affari in Italia*, Bologna: Il Mulino

De Jong H. (1997), *The governance structure and performance of large European corporations*, Journal of Management and Governance, Vol. 1, Fall

De Polis S. (1997), *La vigilanza creditizia nel sistema di corporate governance*, Banche e Banchieri, N. 1

Ferri G. and N. Pesaresi (1996), *The missing link: banking and non banking financial institutions in Italian corporate governance*, FEEM Working paper 4.96

Franks J. and C. Mayer (1992), *Corporate control: a synthesis of the international evidence*, IFA working paper 165-92, LBS

Giudici G. and S. Paleari (1998), *Income shifting in Italian business groups and some governance implications*, Journal of Management and Governance, Vol. 1, Issue 2

Guatri L. and S. Vicari (1994), *Sistemi d'impresa e capitalismi a confronto. Creazione di valore in diversi contesti*, Milano: EGEA

Il Sole 24 Ore (1998), *Remunerazioni. La febbre delle stock option*, 7th September

Kendall N. and T. Sheridan (1992), *Corporate governance. An action plan for profitability and business success*, Pitman

Melis A. (1999a), *Corporate governance. Un'analisi empirica della realtà italiana in un'ottica europea*, Torino: Giappichelli

Melis A. (1999b), *Corporate governance. Le imprese non finanziarie quotate alla Borsa Valori di Milano*, Auditing, N. 36

Moerland P. (1995), *Corporate ownership and control structures: an international comparison*, Review of Industrial Organization, N. 10

Molteni M. (1997), *I sistemi di corporate governance nelle grandi imprese italiane*, Milano: EGEA

Onida P. (1968), *Economia d'azienda*, Torino: UTET

Pagano M., Panetta F., Zingales L. (1998), *Why do companies go public? An empirical analysis*, Journal of Finance, Vol. 53, N. 1, February

Roe M. (1994), *Strong managers, weak owners: The political roots of American corporate finance*, Princeton: Princeton University Press

Saraceno P. (1964), *La produzione industriale*, Venezia: L.U.E.

Shleifer A. and R. Vishny (1997), *A survey of corporate governance*, in Journal of Finance, Vol. 52, June

Stonehill A. and K. Dullum (1990), *Corporate wealth maximisation, takeovers and the market for corporate control*, Nationalokonomisk Tidsskrift

Vienot Rapport (1995), *Le conseil d'aministration des societés cotées*, CNPF-ETP

Zanda G. (1974), *La grande impresa. Caratteristiche strutturali e di comportamento*, Milano: Giuffré

Zingales L. (1994), *The value of the voting right: a study of the Milan Stock Exchange experience*, The Review of Financial Studies, N. 7

Zingales L. (1999), *I soci Comit e l'offerta di Intesa*, Corriere della Sera, 4th July

T
W
O

4 "Remaking Italian Capitalism? The Politics of Corporate Governance Reform"

from West European Politics (2005)

Richard Deeg

SUMMARY

This chapter addresses the issue of how to explain institutional change in national political economies. Within an actor-centred institutionalist theoretical framework, it explores the utility of a coalitional explanation for changes in the financial and corporate governance systems of Italy. Finance and corporate governance are useful foci for understanding change and the evolutionary direction of national political economies as a whole because, first, national and European reformers have focused a great deal of their energy on transforming financial market structures and corporate governance and, second, the regulation of finance and corporate governance is increasingly important as a means for states to exert influence over their economies. The chapter finds considerable change in Italian capitalism as a result of successful elite reformers, party system changes, and the emergence of a reform coalition. However, change is limited and Italy retains a distinctive model of capitalism.

It is no surprise that Italy, like other European nations, has undergone substantial change in its political economy over the last two decades. However, it is by now well documented and accepted that change varies considerably across national cases, both in the extent and in the direction of change, thus muting more simplistic arguments that globalisation is leading to convergence. It also means that we require more nuanced explanations of change that address the political dynamics of change, that is, explanations that go beyond economic determinism. This article examines the changes in the financial and corporate governance systems of Italy in order to explore such political dynamics, evaluate alternative political and economic forces for change, and illuminate paths and barriers to change.

Finance and corporate governance are a useful focus for understanding the dynamics of change and the evolutionary direction of national political economies as a whole.[1] First, national and European reformers intent on 'modernising' national political economies have focused a great deal of their energy on transforming financial market structures and corporate governance rules. This is so because these institutions and systems are at the core of each national economy and changing them has ripple or knock-on effects throughout. Second, the regulation and control over financial and corporate governance systems is increasingly important as means for states to exert influence over their economies. This concern is particularly the case for Eurozone countries which no longer have independent monetary policies and are significantly constrained in their fiscal policies. Together with a substantial reduction in direct firm ownership, states must increasingly rely on the regulation of markets to steer them toward politically-desired outcomes.

Examining the Italian case provides us with further insights into these dynamics but also throws light on some intriguing puzzles present not only in Italy but many other European countries as well. For instance, why do workers not oppose neo-liberal financial market and corporate reform agendas when such reforms can be expected to raise job insecurity? Why do left-wing parties turn out to be major proponents of neo-liberal reforms? What made reforms possible in the first place, especially in Italy – a country notorious for its inability to reform? Finally, how do we explain continued divergence across national political economies even as they undergo (many of the same) institutional changes?

The most common explanation of change is the globalisation or external shock arguments of a generally deterministic nature. But it is now widely recognised that international capital mobility and the demands of institutional investors for greater transparency in corporate finances do not, in themselves, produce convergence across national systems of corporate governance, even if there is a general trend toward transparency and an emphasis on shareholder value (Guillén 2000). On the one hand, external pressures for reform appear actually to play a much greater role in Italy than elsewhere in shifting the institutions of corporate governance and interests/preferences of political and economic actors toward a more transparent system. In this sense Italy conforms to the more popular conception of globalisation's power. Though, in reality, the most pressure emanated from the process of European capital market integration, EMU and the need for Italy to conform with EU Directives. On the other hand, the march of 'shareholder capitalism' and transparent corporate governance in Italy appears to lag behind that of most other advanced economies, thus affirming that the power of globalisation – and even Europeanisation – is more limited than often assumed.

In explaining institutional change in finance and corporate governance, one could draw on three distinct approaches: a legal origins/quality of corporate law approach, a varieties of capitalism approach, and a coalitional approach. In the legal approach, the expansion of securities markets and separation of ownership and control (dispersed ownership) are contingent upon the quality of the legal context and regulation. In other words, from this perspective securities markets in Italy are weak because the legal framework and the courts' capacity to support private contract enforcement between (dispersed) owners and managers (e.g., laws regarding disclosure, liability standards, and private enforcement incentives) are weak and regulatory enforcement is also weak. Thus the risks for small investors are high and the incentive is to hold large blocks of shares in order to have direct influence over management. Further, it is argued that civil law countries are generally characterised by a dearth of the requisite legislation while common law countries do (and therefore have much stronger equity markets: La Porta et al. 2000). Thus, if countries get the laws 'right', markets will expand. The problem with this approach is that there are countries with 'good' law but still concentrated ownership and weak securities markets, and 'good' law does not in itself eliminate other incentives for concentrated ownership (Roe 2003: 160). In Italy, as we shall see, much of the relevant corporate law has been changed yet actual behaviour and the growth of markets have not followed suit to the degree one might predict from this perspective.

A 'varieties of capitalism' approach argues that the structure of the financial and corporate governance system is connected to the broader model of production employed in the economy and the role of labour in firms (Hall and Soskice 2001). Key institutions of the economy are interdependent or complementary. Thus institutional change will either ripple throughout the system, or not happen at all because the material interests of actors in the existing system prevent them from adopting any sort of radical institutional change. With regard to corporate governance, two broad models are conceived: in one, concentrated ownership of firms complements a comparatively tightly regulated labour market and a strong role for labour in firm management in order to support skill-based production and long-term management; in the other model dispersed ownership combines with flexible labour markets to support managerial autonomy and a focus on profit maximisation. The problem with this approach is that it predicts a high level of institutional stability and the Italian case exhibits too much change simply to argue that these are modest institutional modifications. Moreover, it predicts that where there is significant corporate governance reform there should also be commensurate and complementary changes in industrial relations in order to retain systemic coherence. But in Italy liberalising corporate governance reforms have not been matched by a similar level of labour market reforms (much like in Germany; see Höpner 2001).

A third approach is a coalitional approach and there are two variants highlighted here. The first is that of Mark Roe (2003), who argues that countries with a politically dominant 'social democratic' coalition will exhibit concentrated ownership, weak securities markets and a corporate governance system favourable to 'insiders' (large owners, management and labour). The reason is that when labour is protected – through institutions like co-determination and employment protection laws – owners want to hold large blocks of shares in order to counter the pressure on management from workers to stabilise employment, focus on growth rather than profitability and avoid high risk investments. Such management behaviour constitutes 'agency costs' (i.e., extent to which management deviates from profit- or wealth-maximising behaviour which is what owners want) which is best controlled through concentrated ownership. This approach suggests that changing formal laws and regulations to promote securities markets, 'good corporate governance', etc. will have limited impact so long as the social democratic coalition dominates. Real change is more likely to arise from an increase in market competition for firms which forces managers to focus more on profitability in order to ensure firm survival. This suggests that firms in sectors more exposed to international competition will press for (or in the case of workers, tolerate) changes in the financial system and corporate governance that enhance firm profits and thus their viability.

A second variant of the coalitional approach highlights the full range of coalitions that can feasibly emerge among owners, managers, and workers (Höpner 2002; Cioffi, 2003; Gourevitch and Shinn 2003). At least three kinds of coalition among these groups are possible. Depending upon which coalition arises, actors will seek different finance and corporate governance systems through lobbying but also through party system allies. A 'class conflict' coalition pits owners and management against labour. An 'insider–outsider' coalition pits labour and management against owners. An 'accountability' or 'transparency' coalition pits owners and labour against management. Gourevitch and Shinn (2003) highlight a fourth possibility; namely a 'corporatist coalition' among managers, workers and blockholding owners against minority shareholders. As a political framework, this approach also emphasises the important role of political processes and political institutions – especially the legislative and regulatory – in shaping the outcome of political struggles among groups.

Following this coalitional approach, in Italy (outside of the state sector) a corporatist coalition came to predominance in the postwar period. Large private Italian firms were almost all controlled by a relatively small number of blockholders who were quite often

families. In such enterprises family members were also typically involved in firm management, thus blurring any hard distinction between owners and managers. Relations with organised labour most typically followed a conflictual pattern, suggesting a class-conflict coalition dominated. However, through legislation and collective bargaining labour attained a very high level of job protection by the 1970s.[2] Thus it is more accurate to argue that a corporatist coalition prevailed (at least since the 1970s) because labour had strong incentives to align itself with management and blockholders on issues of corporate governance. This coalition preferred – and enjoyed – a financial and corporate governance regime that favoured 'insiders' at the expense of minority shareholders.

The second variant of coalition theory predicts a shift in the corporate governance system will occur when a transparency coalition becomes sufficiently powerful to counter or supplant the corporatist coalition. One likely source of such a shift is a change in workers' political preferences. In short, when (and if) workers begin to hold a substantial amount of their wealth in securities instruments (which is likely to happen when they rely on private pension assets) they will begin to pursue their material interests as investors over their material interests as workers. Workers might also support a transparency coalition if they come to see a corporate governance system that makes firms transparent, managers accountable, and protects the interests of small shareholders as enhancing job security (in effect by reducing the chance of mismanagement).

On the whole, the coalitional approach appears to be the most useful of these three for explaining the character and extent of institutional change in Italy. All three approaches, however, exhibit a strong tendency to see the state as merely an arena in which social actors pursue their preferences. The Italian case to be presented suggests we must also examine the state as a potentially independent actor that can shape outcomes. Thus the coalitional approach is augmented by bringing the state into the analysis. More broadly, the approach taken in this paper is an actor-centred institutionalist approach that highlights the interplay of actors' shifting preferences and strategic interaction within the constraints of existing institutions, while allowing that actors can also change those institutions (see Scharpf 1997; Aguilera and Jackson 2003).

In more empirical terms, in Italy the emergence and strength of the transparency coalition is conditioned by three factors: first, the rise of a reformist elite within key state institutions that enabled them to pursue a liberalising reform agenda; second, the shift in preferences among key domestic social groups – both firms and workers (unions) – conditioned, among other things, by the imperatives of European integration (and market competition); and, third, the transformation of the party system and political parties in the wake of the Christian Democratic party's collapse which made the emergence of a reform-oriented centre-left political coalition possible.

Consistent with the coalitional framework, from the early 1990s onwards, a growing transparency coalition has succeeded in engineering considerable institutional changes in Italy. On paper, at least, Italy now has a 'modern' system of corporate governance that generally meets (in some cases exceeds) the standards of transparency demanded by many foreign (read EU) regulators and investors and academic advocates of 'good corporate governance'. In practice, however, the old blockholding coalition has resisted many of these reforms and found ways to evade or turn them to their advantage in sustaining blockholding and insider (family) control. The influence of transparency-oriented reforms has also been limited by the ability of this coalition to inhibit reforms that would strengthen regulators and by other institutional weaknesses in Italy – notably a judicial system ill-equipped to help enforce the new regulatory regime.[3] Ironically, corporate governance in Italy has become a good deal more transparent and responsive to small investors, yet the fundamental organisation of capital (i.e., ownership) has changed little; it remains so far a blockholder system.

THE POSTWAR ITALIAN SYSTEM

To a certain degree, postwar Italian capitalism can actually be divided into three models of economic coordination and control (i.e., corporate governance subsystems). The first is the state-dominated model. From the early 1930s onward the Italian state controlled a substantial portion of industrial capital – notably through its holding company, IRI. The state was especially prominent in energy, steel, chemicals, and banking. The second model is that of unlisted small and medium-sized (overwhelmingly family-owned and -managed) firms. Indeed, the Italian economy distinguishes itself from other advanced industrial economies by the high proportion of output accounted for by such firms, many of which are organised in industrial districts.

The third model was that of large, private firms. Such firms are relatively few in number, though they are quite significant in terms of the overall economy. Many of them, despite their large size, are family-controlled (e.g, Fiat by the Agnellis).[4] Most of these firms were part of intricate inter-firm networks cemented by alliances and strategic shareholdings which created controlling blocks. Shareholders' pacts (including anti-takeover ones) were common. In the course of the 1970s and 1980s large-scale family capitalism evolved into family-owned holding companies which used pyramidal structures, non-voting shares, and other techniques to control a large number of firms with only minor equity holdings. Boards were dominated by insiders – family members, allies and former managers, and other large owners. Italian law demanded – and got – little transparency in firm affairs or equality of treatment between majority and minority shareholders. Pulling many of the strings in this system from the 1960s onwards was Mediobanca, the Milan-based investment bank headed since its early postwar founding by Enrico Cuccia. Until his death in 2000, Cuccia was the principal dealmaker (and breaker) in the secretive world of large private Italian capitalism; in this case all roads led to Milan. The cluster of firms centred around Mediobanca was often referred to as the 'Northern Galaxy'.

The Italian banking system was divided mostly among three types of banks; commercial, savings (and other public banks) and cooperative banks. But for all three the central hallmark of the Italian postwar financial system was the heavy presence of the state. Public ownership was extensive; first through the Treasury that controlled several of the largest banks, and second through communal governments that controlled the extensive savings bank sector.[5] Public banks accounted for the large majority of banking sector assets, deposits, and loans (Aiello *et al.* 2000: 28). Many banks were highly politicised in terms of board appointments and credit decisions and are often viewed by public authorities as having a public interest rather than market function. Restrictive regulation and segmentation of the financial system severely restrained competition ('The Transformation …', 1997). The banking system was very decentralised, leaving Italy with relatively small, localised banks in international terms.

By international standards, debt finance by non-financial firms has been comparatively high while equity finance was low (OECD 1995: 70–71).[6] A very high percentage of external debt is to banks (but also from other firms),[7] and a very high percentage of bank debt by firms is short-term (OECD 1995: 72; Zattoni 1999).[8] This is due largely to the fact that only special credit institutes were allowed to do medium- and long-term lending, and their lending decisions were largely made by political and administrative bodies and directed toward state-owned firms (Amatori and Colli 2000: 12). SMEs often faced credit shortages, a high cost of borrowing, and heavy reliance on annually renewed overdraft facilities on current accounts (de Cecco 1994; Ferri and Mesorri 2000). As a result, few ordinary banks had the expertise to do long-term lending. Aside from smaller firms in industrial districts (and those connected to Mediobanca), banks and firms generally did not have close, long-term relations typical of 'bank-based' systems such as Germany. Until the mid-1990s the very large bond market was overwhelmingly dominated by government debt and Italian retail investors put a very large portion of their savings into these (Guiso and Jappelli 2000). Thus retail investors, including the broad middle classes, had little material interest in the regulation of securities markets and corporate governance.

The finance and corporate governance system of the large firm private sector fits an 'insider' model: It was a system of corporate control dominated by private, informal arrangements and norms of reciprocity. Private firms, especially family-owned, sought to minimise state interference (Segreto 1997). Reflecting this logic, share ownership in Italy is highly concentrated. In the early 1990s, the top five largest shareholders in a large firm held, on average, 87 percent of its shares; more than half of listed firms were majority controlled by a single owner (OECD 1995: 60–61). The stock market itself was, not surprisingly, very narrow with just a relatively small number of firms accounting for most of its capitalisation and turnover. With the notable exception of Mediobanca, since the 1930s banks have not had equity stakes in non-financial firms and therefore do not perform a monitoring role in corporate governance. This situation was due in part to the relatively small size of banks compared with the large non-financial firms and by tight restrictions on commercial banks holding equity and sitting on boards of non-financial firms. Thus, most big companies faced little external control/monitoring from either banks or the stock

market. There was also therefore no market for corporate control in Italy, since relatively few companies were listed and control over those was usually firmly in the hands of a family or a group of core, allied shareholders.

THE ROAD TO REFORM

At first blush it appears that major changes in the Italian financial and corporate governance systems began in the 1980s. No longer able to sufficiently self-finance or borrow, large firms turned to the equity market. Aided in part by a new law on investment trusts in 1984, the number of listed firms soared from 138 at the beginning of the decade to 217 by its end, while market capitalisation rose from about 6 to 14 percent of GDP (Amatori and Colli 2000: 12; Aguilera 2001: 17–18). But rather than expanding the market, most of the newly listed companies were spin-offs from the large industrial holding groups. This enabled them to raise new capital while retaining ultimate control over these firms through pyramidal or cascading shareholdings (and the generous use of non-voting shares). Thus even in 1987 the nine largest industrial holding groups (mostly family-controlled) accounted for nearly all of the market's capitalisation (Amatori and Colli 2000: 14). Not only did these groups control much larger numbers of firms, they were also linked to each other through interlocking directorates, cross-shareholdings, and financial alliances. A key architect and orchestrator of this strategy was Mediobanca. While formally controlled by the three largest (and state-owned) banks in Italy, Mediobanca called its own shots.[9] Indeed, Cuccia engineered a partial privatisation of the bank in the late 1980s that enabled the private industrial groups of the Northern Galaxy to take stakes in it and seats on its board, thus further tightening the bonds among them. The institutional linkages among these firms were augmented by voting syndicates that protected them from hostile takeover and entrenched incumbent management and major owners (and trounced minority shareholder rights: Amatori and Colli 2000: 19–21). Thus Italy entered the 1990s with its traditional model intact.

The current transformation of the Italian financial and corporate governance systems, therefore, really begins in the early 1990s. There were both internal and external pressures for change. Internally, the state's finances were in a shambles due to massive public debt. Huge losses by state-owned firms added both to the debt and the declining legitimacy of state ownership. The Lira was pummelled out of the EMS in 1992 and forced to devalue. The economy was in recession. The bribery scandal and demise of the Christian Democratic party in 1992/93 added further impetus for major change, since the DC had long been a supporter of the corporate governance system favoured by the blockholder coalition and, more generally, of family-oriented capitalism (Roe 2003). Externally, the Single Market was nearing completion and Italian firms, especially banks, were unprepared for an integrated market and faced with rising (or soon to be) competitive pressures. The Maastricht Treaty and its implications for stricter government finances added further pressure on Italy to get its house in order.

Thus, at the beginning of the decade Italian reformers – primarily in the Bank of Italy and the Treasury – set out to overhaul Italian capitalism through privatisation and the modernisation of the financial system, including the expansion of the stock market and the dispersion of corporate ownership in Italy (Amatori and Colli 2000: 24–6). Similar to France, in Italy the main actors cultivating institutional change in the early years were in the state: there was little social basis for a broad 'transparency coalition' at this time. Most reformers were associated with the Socialist Party of Italy or other centre-left parties. Key among them were Giuliano Amato, a top Treasury official in the late 1980s and Treasury Minister under the last Christian-Democratic-led government of Giulio Andreotti (July 1989–June 1992), twice Prime Minister (June 1992 to April 1993 and April 2000 to June 2001), head of the Italy's antitrust authority in the mid-1990s, and again Treasury Minister under Massimo D'Alema's second government; Romano Prodi, head of IRI during much of the 1980s and part of the early 1990s, later Prime Minister (May 1996–October 1998), who played a key role in privatisation of state assets and oversaw the most significant corporate governance reform in 1998; Mario Draghi, Director General of the Italian Treasury from 1991 to 2001 and privatisation commissioner from 1993 until 2001; Antonio Fazio, Governor of the Bank of Italy since 1993; Carlo Azeglio Ciampi, Governor of the Bank of Italy from 1979 to 1993, Treasury and Economics Minister during the Prodi government and President of Italy since May 1999.

While in the early reform years of the 1990s the Christian Democrats were still powerful, reformists used their positions to begin a long-term process of transformation. The political independence gained by the Bank of Italy during the 1980s, for instance, enabled it to pursue a tighter monetary policy that, in turn, increased pressure for further reforms in state finances and privatisation.[10] External pressures gave reformers the legitimacy and political backing to take the first measures. The general discrediting of political parties following the bribery scandals further enhanced executive autonomy, especially over the budget (Felsen 2000). The collapse of the Christian Democratic party also paved the way for the first true centre-left governments in postwar Italian history, starting with the Prodi government in May 1996 and ending with Silvio Berlusconi's return to power in June 2001. It was during this period of centre-left government that the most far-reaching corporate governance reforms were enacted by a stronger though not dominant transparency coalition.

A key first move in the reformer's strategy for promoting major change was to create new private sector actors – notably privatised state banks – who would be committed to the reform agenda and strengthen their budding transparency coalition: Reformers knew that building a new business elite (who were managers but not owners) would be indispensable to overcoming entrenched interests. Thus Mario Draghi and Antonio Fazio came to be, in many respects, key actors because of their tremendous influence over the privatisation process and banking sector throughout the 1990s. These two used the privatisation and merger process to carefully construct new shareholder arrangements and large commercial banks conducive to a more open, transparent form of capitalism. And while they did not always accomplish their specific objectives, their long tenure in office put them in a position to pursue steadfastly, and with frequent success, their broader goals.

Sustained regulatory change and a programme for systematic reform of the Italian financial system began in 1990 with the Amato law (since it was sponsored by Amato as Treasury Minister). The Amato law, heavily shaped by EC Directives, was promoted by the Bank of Italy and supported by most Italian banks. One of its most important elements was the conversion of all banks to joint-stock corporations. This paved the way for public banks (about 80 banks, mostly savings banks) to be privatised and thereby open up the banking industry to consolidation (though most public banks remained under local government control through the vehicle of foundations which held the newly-issued shares).[11] It was clearly passed in anticipation of financial market integration in Europe and the fear that large foreign banks would overrun much smaller Italian banks unless the latter consolidated extensively (Bank of Italy 1995: 174). Even so, there was considerable resistance in the parliament to the law, since most banks were connected to one or more political parties and board seats were used as patronage spoils. During the parliamentary debates the Communist party strongly opposed any privatisation, and while the Christian Democrats took no formal position, they were generally opposed to the privatisation of savings banks. The Socialists took the middle ground, supporting privatisation of savings banks but not the large, national public banks. Only the small Republican and Liberal parties backed privatisation unequivocally (Lane 1990). Since bank mergers threatened the parties, the government limited the flotation of public sector bank shares to 49 percent of equity.[12] The 49 percent limit was also reportedly motivated by a desire to keep large banks from falling under the control of the Northern Galaxy; the law permitted exceptions to this rule but only with the direct consent of parliament, the cabinet, and the Bank of Italy (Simonian 1990).

In the first few years following enactment of the law there was relatively little consolidation and only a few flotations of bank shares, despite concerted efforts by Ciampi, then Governor of the Bank of Italy, to bring them about. One reason for this reflected market incentives; namely, Italy was relatively underbanked and thus banks focused their energies not on mergers but on expanding their branch networks. The other reason was that any merger constituted a potentially serious threat to the material interests of the parties. The one major merger in this early period involved three Roman banks (creating Banca di Roma, now Capitalia), all of which were tied to the Andreotti wing of the Christian Democratic party (Lane 1992; 'Italian Banking' 1992).

In 1992, during the first Amato government (June 1992–April 1993), the state laid the groundwork for the privatisation of other state-owned firms with the transformation of all state holdings into stock companies held by the Treasury. The privatisation programme was driven forward by several goals, including the improvement of the state's fiscal crisis, enhanced efficiency of the firms, increased industrial competition and the enlargement of the stock market. Despite strong initial criticism and opposition, the programme moved forward under the leadership of

Mario Draghi, head of the privatisation commission from 1993 onwards, and Romano Prodi, once again head of IRI during 1993 and 1994. The process was further shaped by a 1994 law that was crucial in setting more specific rules for the allocation of shares and corporate governance. In this law the government aimed for broader share ownership in privatised firms by limiting any single shareholder to no more than 5 percent of equity, while at the same time attempting to retain strategic influence through golden shares, the creation of *noyeux durs*, and the right of the Treasury to veto mergers or takeovers. The law was partly a response to criticism of early privatisations that they appeared to favour the Northern Galaxy. Under this framework and the guidance of the reformers, the Italian Treasury proceeded on the largest privatisation programme in the world during the1990s, raising about €90 billion between 1992 and 1999 (the largest flotation was Telecom Italia which raised nearly €20 billion in 1997: Amatori and Colli, 2000: 25–6).

Another major reform step in the early 1990s was the comprehensive Banking law passed in 1993. Like the Amato law, it was heavily shaped by the need to transpose EC directives into Italian law, including the bank passport provisions, which significantly increased access of foreign financial institutions to Italy. This sweeping reform bill also reflected the desire among Italian financial officials to create a mixed (or universal) banking system resembling that of Germany with its close, long-term relations between banks and firms (Cesarini 1994). Towards this end, the law ended decades of enforced market segmentation by permitting ordinary banks to issue bonds and extend medium- and long-term credit. The law also empowered banks to acquire stakes in non-financial firms. Notably, the Italian banking industry as a whole did not embrace many of these changes initially, especially those intended to stimulate securities markets (Onado 1996: 100). The Treasury and Bank of Italy, in contrast, welcomed the political opening created by the EU to modernise the Italian financial sector.

The mid-1990s turned out to be a crucial watershed in the transformation of Italy's financial and corporate governance systems. One reason is that the reformers were now not only strategically placed in key institutional positions, but they were also firmly (relatively speaking) in control of the government, especially during Prodi's centre-left (Olive Tree coalition) government. Indeed, the rise of the centre-left to power and five years of continuous rule (May 1996 to June 2001) were arguably indispensable preconditions to wide-ranging reforms in corporate governance and Italian capitalism more generally (see also Cioffi and Höpner 2004). The remaking of the Left and a new alliance with more reform minded unions provided the broader political coalition reformers needed to enact more sweeping change.

In the wake of the 'twin collapses' – Communism and Italian Christian Democracy – the Italian Left underwent a significant ideological shift. Jettisoning Marxist baggage, the Left revived older Italian writers and ideas about liberal socialism. Echoing left-libertarianism elsewhere in Europe, the Italian Left placed the goal of promoting individual freedom and social justice at the heart of its political agenda. Indeed, the Left has gone so far as to recast itself as the true force of liberalism in Italian politics while the Right practises a 'phoney liberalism' – espousing liberalism while in practice upholding monopolism in the polity and economy. In economic policy terms, this meant attacking the traditional oligarchism of Italian capitalism and replacing it with a competitive and modern liberal market order. For the 'new' left, 'modernisation', 'normalisation', 'Europeanisation', and 'liberalism' were now the core leitmotifs. In the vanguard of this new left were the Democrats of the Left (Democratici della Sinistra, DS) – the core of the Olive Tree coalition – led by Massimo D'Alema (Favretto 2002).

The transformation of the party system helped bring about a transformation of the Italian labour unions as well. In an effort to reduce their waning influence, in the early 1990s the main union confederations, especially the CGIL, changed their general strategy from one of confrontation with employers to one of cooperation with employers and the state. The Amato Accord of 1992 formalised this broader transformation by strengthening the unions in collective bargaining and shopfloor representation in works councils (RSUs). In exchange the union federations agreed to end wage indexation (*scale mobile*) and pursue wage moderation, thus aiding the state in its new commitment to fiscal austerity and reforms and aiding employers in their efforts to restore competitiveness in an increasingly integrated European market (Locke and Baccaro 1999: 257). Employers reciprocated by taking a generally more cooperative approach to labour. In the revival of neo-corporatism the unions had decided to support general reform efforts and espouse moderation and responsibility as opposed to class conflict (Locke and Baccaro 1999:

223). Thus the unions became an important partner of the centre-left reform coalition in power in the second half of the 1990s. The outcome was that unions were willing to engage in political exchange which meant yielding on reform demands in order to pursue broader, long-term goals.

With regard to corporate governance, unions obviously tolerated reforms that could potentially weaken employer's commitments to maintain employment. In this sense they lent important support to the transparency coalition. On the other hand, unions stood fast against reforms to Italy's strong employment protection laws that would make labour-shedding easier, thus counteracting such a scenario. With legal protection against unilateral labour-shedding, a more cooperative relationship between management and labour meant that unions could negotiate employment reductions in firms when competitive conditions warranted such (which is increasingly the case: Jackson 2003). Moreover, under tripartism there was a broad commitment among the partners to increasing general employment through other means (such as reducing payroll taxes).[13] In Germany, unions took a similar approach; tolerating corporate governance reforms (even actively supporting some) while vigorously resisting major labour market reforms (Höpner 2001). This combination suggests that labour can benefit from increased transparency in corporate governance, since it gives labour more information with which to negotiate with management. On the other hand, it suggests there is a limit to which labour will support the transformation of corporate governance. But a combination of more rights for shareholders and protection for labour is apparently more compatible than is often presumed (see Jackson 2003).

With a relatively solid transparency coalition in power, Italian reformers were able to respond to strong external pressures in the mid-1990s. At this time, European capital market integration, and thus competition among financial service providers and markets, was heating up (The EU's Investment Services Directive came into effect in 1996). Along with this development Italy was desperately struggling to qualify for EMU. This was such a powerful and widespread goal among Italians, including the unions, that the traditionally quarrelsome parties more or less adopted a 'ceasefire' in order to give the Prodi government the leeway to make the policy changes and reforms seen as essential to accomplishing it – most notably a willingness to swallow fiscal austerity, wage moderation, and unpopular welfare state reforms

('Romano Prodi' 1998; D'Aquino 1997; Locke and Baccaro 1999: 228). Thus for the first two years of the first Olive Tree government reformers such as Prodi, Ciampi, Fazio and Draghi had a relatively free hand.

One of the most significant knock-on effects of austerity and tighter monetary policy was a steady and dramatic decline in interest rates. This, in turn, greatly reduced the attractiveness of state bonds to Italian investors and increased the attractiveness of buying shares in the market – and most of the new liquidity came from privatised state firms. The flotation of Telecom Italia in late 1997 was a national event and served as the entrée for many Italians into the stock market. Thus privatisation became the central driving force of the stock market's expansion in the late 1990s when Italians, like most of the rest of the industrialised world, caught stock market fever. Adding to the momentum, in late 1997 the Italian Stock Exchange (Borsa Italiana) was privatised; sold mostly to Italian securities firms and banks. The Borsa, in turn, became a vocal proponent of further securities market reform and development (along with CONSOB, the securities market regulator, and the Treasury).

The single most important development in corporate governance reform came in 1998, however, when the Treasury succeeded in guiding the passage of the Uniform Code for the Governance of Capital Markets (aka Draghi law).[14] This was the most sweeping reform of corporate law and corporate governance since the 1930s. The process began in mid-1997 when the Prodi government formed a commission led by Mario Draghi. The commission's charge was to overhaul and 'modernise' Italian corporate law and governance (and bring it in line with EU Directives). The commission's work was highly controversial and faced considerable opposition from the 'blockholder coalition' and parties of the Right and (ex-Communist) Left that still opposed privatisation (Blitz 1997). But the reformist 'transparency coalition' had political momentum and, frustrated by the persistence of concentrated control over Italian firms (even newly privatised ones), seized the opportunity to push its agenda forward.

The overall goal of the law was to make a significant push toward further modernisation and development of the equity market through greater transparency, wider ownership and protection of small investors. It was a massive, omnibus law that aggregated, reformulated and renewed virtually all civil and criminal rules pertaining to capital markets, securities management, institutional investors, brokerage services,

public offerings and rules for listed joint stock corporations. Among the key reforms of the law were: lowering to 2 percent the threshold at which equity holdings must be made public and reported to Consob; the obligation to make public shareholder and syndicate agreements; lowering the percentage of capital required to exercise 'minority rights'; enabling banks and institutional investors to solicit and vote proxies at shareholder meetings; strict regulation of insider trading; limits on cross-shareholdings; banning the use of anti-takeover pacts between shareholder syndicates; and takeover regulation more favourable to small investors ('Italy' 1998). Accompanying the Draghi law were tax changes designed to provide strong incentives for firms to issue new equity and make initial public offerings (Betts 1997).

The measures regarding takeovers were particularly hard fought within the parliament between supporters of the blockholder and the transparency coalitions. The blockholder coalition supported a rule that, in end-effect, would likely entrench existing blockholders. However, in a major defeat for the blockholding coalition, the parliament supported instead a more minority-shareholder-friendly 30 percent takeover threshold. This measure brought Italy in line with British and French rules and was intended to make it more difficult for shareholder alliances to control firms with less than 51 percent of equity (Blitz 1998).

However, the Draghi law was not a complete loss for blockholder interests. The first comprehensive regulation of tender offers had been adopted in 1992 and introduced a rule of 'absolute passivity', i.e., management could do nothing to thwart a takeover bid once launched. The regulation was adopted in anticipation of large-scale privatisation and the hope to use this as a mechanism to create more widely held firms and some kind of market for control. The rule met surprisingly little resistance at the time, probably because hostile takeovers had henceforth been rare and no one thought this situation was likely to change. By the time of the Draghi commission, however, the picture had changed dramatically. Under pressure from many large firms, the takeover regulations were amended to allow management to adopt takeover defences after a bid was launched (but only with shareholder approval). Management can now adopt a wide range of anti-takeover defences prior to bids, though some measures also require shareholder approval. Thus, for firms with concentrated ownership and a solid shareholder alliance or family control, the takeover rules give them plenty of opportunity to protect themselves (Portolano 2000).

As part of its efforts to increase corporate accountability to shareholders, the Draghi law also made important changes governing the role of auditors. One key rule was that seats on the internal audit boards of listed firms could henceforth only be occupied by external accountants. More importantly, though, the Draghi law shifted all official certification of listed firm accounts to external statutory auditors. And despite intense lobbying from the major accounting firms, the parliament upheld a fairly strict ban on the provision of management consulting services to firms by auditing companies. It also maintained mandatory rotation of the auditing firm for listed firms.[15] Subsequent efforts by the accounting firms to alter these last two rules have repeatedly failed.

Consob, the stock market regulator, was given considerable formal power to carry out the Draghi agenda. To carry the corporate governance reform momentum forward, the Treasury created a committee named the 'Italian Financial Centre' to promote and coordinate further initiatives on the development of the market (Draghi 1998). The 1998 law was followed by the creation of a self-conduct code for good corporate governance (Codice Preda) in 1999 drafted by university, business, and government representatives. This code covered both listed and unlisted firms and works on a 'comply or disclose' basis. As elsewhere, the booming domestic stock market in the late 1990s eased the way for additional efforts to further the long-term development of securities markets. Thus, in 1999 the Borsa opened its own high-tech exchange, the Nuovo Mercato, and in 2001 a new exchange (STAR) for 'old economy' SMEs.

The return of Silvio Berlusconi – himself a practitioner of old-style Italian corporate practices – and centre-right government in June 2001 was an important test of the staying power of the reforms adopted under centre-left rule. Forebodingly, not long after coming to power the parliament initiated a review of the Draghi law. Reformers hoped to use this occasion as an opportunity to tighten corporate governance rules. To the extent parliament may have had any counter-reform inclinations, these were blunted by the Enron scandal which played in Italy – as elsewhere – into the hands of minority shareholder-oriented reforms (Galbraith 2002). In the end, the review ultimately led to a mixture of results. On the one hand, the Berlusconi government adopted measures that formally favour transparency and minority

shareholders. Thus a 2002 Corporate Crime Reform Act required firms to demonstrate sufficient internal controls to prevent fraud and made boards responsible for criminal acts committed by employees. In early 2003 parliament approved further corporate governance reforms that transformed several features of the voluntary code into statutory law. Most notably it gave firms more autonomy to structure their own internal governance through the ability to choose either the traditional Italian single-board model with an internal (and presumably independent) board of statutory auditors, the Anglo-Saxon one-board model, or a German-style two-tier board system ('Corporate law reform …' 2003: 10).

On the other hand, the centre-right government pushed for changes that undermine the reformist agenda. One significant setback was the government's partial decriminalisation of false accounting and reduction of the statute of limitations from 4.5 to 3 years. Berlusconi's government also eliminated the estate tax, a move that will strengthen family capitalism (Moretti 2003). Not surprisingly, the Parmalat scandal in late 2003 put considerable pressure on the government to strengthen corporate regulation. The government did rush to pass pending reforms of its antiquated bankruptcy laws, thus making it possible for Parmalat to attempt a reorganisation like US-style chapter 11 (Gumbel 2004). But in general the Berlusconi government has been less reformist than the preceding centre-left coalition, including corporate governance, or at least it has failed to achieve many of the reforms it claimed to seek.

THE FRUITS OF REFORM?

A decade and more of reform brought substantial change to the Italian financial and corporate governance systems. But what does this all add up to? The capitalisation of the main exchange soared from 18.6 percent of GDP in 1995 to 70.2 percent of GDP at the end of 2000.[16] While much of this rise was due to share price appreciation, a significant amount of new equity was also issued during this time (mostly from privatisations).[17] Italian retail investors clearly also found much greater enthusiasm for investing in stocks. Though, as everywhere, that enthusiasm has been dampened (at least temporarily) by the end of the boom.[18] In Italy, as elsewhere, institutional investors have also become more important.[19] The growth of institutional investors is widely viewed as prerequisite to the sustained development of equity markets and, more broadly, to an equity culture based on transparency in capital markets and corporate governance. Though despite their growth, institutional investors' share of financial assets in Italy remains well behind that of their counterparts elsewhere.[20] In formal legal terms, Italy is now seen as having corporate governance rules largely in line with those elsewhere in Europe. In other words, the formal institutional prerequisites for a shift to a more transparent, shareholder value-oriented and open system of capitalism appear to be largely in place. In practice many new business leaders – and even some leaders of Northern Galaxy firms such as Gilberto Benetton and Marco Tronchetti Provera (who controls Pirelli and Telecom Italia) – publicly profess their commitment to this new style of capitalism (Kapner 2003a).

Thus, if the quality of law thesis is correct, we should see a significant expansion of the stock market and a clear trend toward the separation of ownership and control (i.e., dispersion of ownership). While there is some evidence for this development, a more in-depth examination reveals less change than might appear to be the case. First, there appears to be little change in firm financing patterns (Deeg and Perez 2000). Second, the efforts to expand the stock market had mixed success. The total number of firms listed on the main exchange increased only slightly during the 1990s (from 225 firms in 1987 to 237 at the end of 2001: www.borsaitalia.it). As elsewhere, the internet/telecoms mania helped push up the Nuovo Mercato and stimulate excitement among Italians for stock trading. But the bursting of the bubble dramatically slowed new listings on the exchange and its capitalisation has plummeted. There has been some increase in ownership transparency, but insufficient evidence to suggest that the intricate networks of shareholdings linking large private Italian firms have changed all that much. Concentration of ownership of the market as a whole declined in the late 1990s due to privatisations, but quickly returned to previous levels. Moreover, control over major Italian firms is still in the hands of other large Italian firms and families: Some 60 percent of Italian listed firms still have a single controlling shareholder who owns, on average, 42 percent of equity but controls the firm through a pyramidal chain (O'Brian 2002a). In 2002 only 32 of 275 listed firms were not controlled by a majority shareholder or group.[21] The use of pyramids and shareholder agreements to control firms remains steady, thus ensuring that insider control over firms remains high (Amatori and Colli 2000: 37–8; Aguilera 2001: 14).

There is, as yet, no open market for control over firms (Aguilera 2001: 13). Even though Olivetti managed to take over Telecom Italia in a hostile bid during 1999 in accordance with the new institutional framework – which many interpreted as a sign that Italian capitalism had definitely changed – it actually occurred in a thoroughly Italian fashion: Olivetti used an elaborate pyramidal holding structure to gain control of Telecom while owning just 3.2 percent of its shares (Amatori and Colli 2000: 49; McCann, 2000: 57)! Further demonstrating the vitality of the old system, two years later Pirelli, under the leadership of Marco Tronchetti Provera and backed by Benetton, Intesa and UniCredito, took control of Olivetti (and indirectly Telecom Italia) using complex investment vehicles and cascading holdings that short-changed small investors and was viewed as destroying shareholder value ('Keeping it in the Family' 2001; Webster 2001). Through pyramids the Provera family investment firm, with €100 million of equity, reportedly controls a string of companies worth some €160 billion (Kapner 2003a).

Furthermore, the new corporate governance code and transparency rules are still eschewed by the majority of listed Italian firms and Consob is widely viewed as a toothless tiger, unable to enforce the new rules of corporate governance (*Financial Times*, 5 April 2001; Onado 1998: 404). Consob is poorly staffed and funded, cannot impose fines, investigate insider trading or bring criminal charges on its own (McHugh 2004). At times Consob was also perhaps unwilling to enforce the rules (Kapner 2002). This defect also points to another weakness in the new corporate governance regime, namely the weak legal system that might otherwise help enforce the new rules. Court challenges have been rare so far in Italy. The Draghi takeover rules have yet to be tested in court, for example (Kapner 2003b). Minority shareholders cannot sue directors unless they own 5 percent or more of the company (McHugh 2004). Class-action lawsuits (and contingency fees) are not permitted in Italy and there are no established procedures in civil law to help investors recover money lost through corporate malfeasance (Delaney 2004). And even if such complaints made it into court, most judges are not well prepared to handle corporate law cases. The many lawsuits growing out of the 2004 Parmalat scandal, however, will probably provide a good test of the legal system's ability to protect minority shareholders. Thus there is also evidence to support the quality of law argument (see also Roe 2002). However, the evidence as a whole suggests that formal legal provisions and enforcement institutions are most likely necessary but alone insufficient to bring about dramatic growth in markets.

One of the key predictions of some coalition theorists is that the more workers hold their assets in securities, the more they will begin to demand legal changes and the like that protect minority shareholders (which, in turn, should facilitate further expansion of the market). This move would also bolster a socio-political transparency coalition. In Italy we do see a significant shift in household assets beginning in the late 1990s out of government bonds and into securities (primarily via mutual funds). By the end of 2002 Italy had developed the second largest mutual fund market in Europe. However, most funds and the majority of assets under management are controlled by Italian banks. And Italian fund managers rarely take issue with company management, i.e., make little effort to monitor and influence management (and neither do the banks themselves) (OECD 2003; Brunello *et al.* 2003). This situation appears to be so for two reasons: First, voting in shareholders' meetings is cumbersome and costly, thus acting as a disincentive for minority shareholders to participate. Second, and perhaps more important, banks have a conflict of interest since they conduct considerable business (e.g. lending) with the corporate clients in which their funds also invest ('Fund management in Italy' 2003). Thus banks and their mutual funds do not have an unambiguous interest in controlling firm managers in the interest of minority shareholders. Moreover, the shift in worker assets toward securities may be limited in the future by the very small role of private (defined-contribution) pension funds in Italy (they represented only 3.5 percent of total household financial assets in 1998: Guiso and Jappelli 2000: 46). In countries with large stock markets such pension funds are a significant source of investment capital in the market but also a basis for changing workers' interest toward corporate governance reform (Gourevitch and Shinn 2003; Jackson and Vitols 2001).

This brings us back to the banks which, in many ways, have been at the centre of the reformer's campaign to remake Italian capitalism. Since the Amato law in 1990, the banking system itself has undergone radical change. The most significant change is the greatly reduced role of the state; in 1992 public sector banks controlled 70 percent of bank industry assets.

By the end of 1999 this was down to 12 percent (Bank of Italy 2000: 190), though many banks now considered private, including some larger ones, are still controlled by foundations which, in turn, are controlled by communal governments.[22] Nonetheless, even banks with significant public ownership are rapidly changing as commercial organisations. Since the late 1990s virtually all banks (including savings and cooperative banks) have responded to increased competition by radically restructuring their operations and organisations, innovating new products, cutting costs, and making efficiency and profitability primary objectives.

During the second half of the 1990s there was much merger activity among Italian banks and substantial concentration in the industry. The process of consolidation occurred rapidly and was guided to a significant degree by the Bank of Italy which prevented several mergers not to its liking – and steadfastly defended Italian banks from foreign control (Wilson 2002). Indeed, in some respects the process of bank consolidation was characterised far more by traditional Italian methods of building complex interfirm alliances than by the use of market mechanisms (McCann 2000: 59). It was also, not surprisingly, shaped by competitive party dynamics as mergers among banks affiliated with the Right tended to beget mergers among banks affiliated with the Left, since no side wanted the other to dominate banking markets. In mid-2002 the Bank announced that it considered the consolidation of banks on the national level essentially complete; the four largest banking groups – IntesaBCI, Sanpaolo-IMI, Unicredito, and Capitalia (formerly Banca di Roma) – now control about half of the sector's business.[23]

The banks, as hoped for by Fazio, Draghi and other key reformers, greatly aided their campaign for transformation. Alessandro Profumo, head of UniCredito, is perhaps the most visible and active leader among the big banks in promoting a more transparent and shareholder-oriented system of capitalism. Yet at the same time their development and actions have not always supported a continued evolution to a new system. The story of Mediobanca provides an excellent illustration of the banks' role and both what has changed in Italy and what has not.

Well into the 1990s, Mediobanca was still the kingmaker of Italian private capitalism. But Mediobanca's power rested on its own network of key shareholders and allies (such as Fiat, Olivetti and Pirelli) and, as it turned out, on the lack of domestic competition.

During the late 1990s Mediobanca's position eroded as foreign investment banks made significant strides in gaining the business of major Italian firms, especially for cross-border deals. But more damaging for Mediobanca, in the wave of privatisations during the 1990s the Treasury gave significant business to foreign investment banks. The Treasury feared that too much business for Mediobanca would strengthen the banks' influence rather than open up the Italian system as it intended. With this opening, foreign investment banks soon came to dominate the domestic mergers and acquisitions market, as well as debt and equity issues (*The Economist*, 1 June 2001). As Mediobanca's star waned the 'gravitational pull' holding the Northern Galaxy together weakened and a process of reshuffling alliances among member firms (and several newly privatised firms) began. For example, in July 2001, Fiat, together with three Italian banks and EdF (a large French energy firm) launched a hostile bid for Montedison, a firm under Mediobanca's control since the 1960s. With this move the long-running Fiat-Mediobanca alliance appeared to be over.

In recent years Mediobanca has been engaged in a power struggle with its own major shareholders who were fighting among themselves over what to do with the bank (and grabbing some of the bank's key assets for themselves). Mediobanca's two most important shareholders – Capitalia and UniCredito – have also become competitors. Capitalia, for example, bolstered its own investment banking unit during 2002 by bringing in other large, influential Italian firms as shareholders (and allies), thus mimicking Mediobanca's own model of influence ('Capitalia …', 2002). At the same time, IntesaBCI, Italy's largest bank and formerly supported by Mediobanca, announced a link-up with Lazard Italia – the nation's leader in M&A advising – in order to strengthen its own investment banking market power within Italy (O'Brian 2002b). The struggle between the battered but still powerful Mediobanca and its own shareholders came to a climax in early 2003 when a group led by Unicredito and acting with the blessing of the Bank of Italy (and the acquiescence of Berlusconi), accumulated a 20 percent stake in Generali, Italy's largest insurance company.[24] Because of the financial interlock between Mediobanca and Generali, this stake allowed the investors to bring it under their control by ousting the long-time head of Mediobanca, Vincenzo Maranghi.

This last anecdote reflects the contradictory nature of changes in Italy. On the one hand, the methods used by Unicredito and its allies to assert their control over Mediobanca very much conformed to the old system: shares in Generali were bought at a high price (i.e., not shareholder-friendly) and now several of the 'new' large banks are firmly in control of Mediobanca and its empire. More generally, these banks have become increasingly involved in the old insider corporate networks by taking equity stakes and making large loans to the same clients. For example, Unicredito and Banca Intesa are large lenders to Telecom Italia and Pirelli, in which they also have significant equity stakes.

On the other hand, Unicredito and its allies justified their actions as necessary to overcome the blockage Mediobanca represented to a more shareholder-oriented capitalism in Italy and say they will reduce their holdings (Kapner 2003a). While it may be tempting to conclude, as many have, that the ouster of Maranghi (and death of Giovanni Agnelli in early 2003) and the rise of new challengers to Mediobanca are further proof that the Northern Galaxy is beginning to collapse, at this point it still seems equally plausible that the assaults on Mediobanca spell not an end to the old system but more a realignment of who owns whom and who is allied with whom (and with some foreign firms now becoming minor players in the game too). The available evidence suggests that the Northern Galaxy may be weakening but it is far from gone. And while a few new 'mini-galaxies' may be forming, this does not indicate the triumph of markets as mechanisms for corporate monitoring or executing changes in corporate control (see also McCann 2000).

CONCLUSION: ITALY BETWEEN TWO WORLDS?

So, what kind of capitalism is Italy now? Italy never did fit well within the standard typologies of capitalist systems. It was clearly not an example of Anglo-Saxon capitalism. In some ways it was more akin to the German blockholder/insider system of ownership but also quite different in that it lacked the major banks of Germany and the Italian state had a far greater role in the economy. But neither was Italy squarely in the statist camp, such as France, since in Italy private, family-dominated firms – large and small – have long played a huge role in the economy alongside the state-controlled sector.

The widespread privatisation of state firms suggests that the statist portion of the Italian economy is slowly passing into history. Yet, like the French state, it continues to attempt to steer the direction of change by retaining – and deploying – strategic levers of influence such as golden shares. More importantly, for the first half of the 1990s the transparency coalition was a fairly shallow coalition in social terms, i.e., workers were not yet 'investors' with an interest in corporate transparency, and minority shareholder protections and non-blockholding owners were very weak politically. Thus in this period reform can be fairly described as an elite project, driven in good part by external pressures to conform with EU directives, to qualify for EMU, and to be competitive in a rapidly integrating European financial and corporate space. The long tenure and institutional autonomy of reformist elites were important factors in explaining their ability to pass through a number of reforms in this period, despite much turmoil in the party system. In sum, Italy is in some ways arguably shifting from a (partially) state-led to a 'state-enhanced' model as in France (on France see Schmidt 2003) and the coalition framework advanced here should be amended to account for an autonomous state role in change.

Italy still has a huge family capitalism sector and this is equally true for large, private firms which are supposed to form the core of a modernised, internationally competitive sector. So far it seems that the present model for large firms in Italy could best be described as 'market-enhanced' blockholder capitalism: In this present system firms (i.e., management and block owners) are somewhat more constrained by codified rules designed to encourage transparent transactions within the market and more rights for minority shareholders (for a similar argument regarding Germany see Vitols 2003). Yet blockholders still dominate the system and it continues to operate on more or less the same logic as before. This, then, begs the question; has Italian capitalism been transformed? The evidence in this article suggests an affirmative but qualified answer; the transformation is limited largely to the substantially reduced role of the state in the economy while the private sector model of capitalism so far shows more continuity than change.

The obvious remaining question is, of course, which direction is Italy likely to follow in the future? On the one side, there are numerous forces working in favour of continued evolution toward a more market-oriented model. The lack of macro-policy autonomy will, as for other Eurozone members, continue to pressure Italy to carry out major reforms, including labour, finance, and corporate governance, in order to restore the economy to a solid growth path. Most

importantly, the privatisation, corporate reform, and fiscal and monetary policies undertaken in the 1990s together produced an important economic structural shift. Namely, the rapid decline of interest rates produced a huge shift in the asset allocation of average Italians from government bonds into securities (primarily via mutual funds). In accordance with the predictions of the coalitional framework, this arguably led to a major shift in the interest and preferences of workers regarding corporate governance policies (Gourevitch and Shinn 2003). Now, rather than just being wage earners, they were also rapidly becoming small investors with a growing interest in corporate transparency and minority shareholder protection. Thus, in the second half of the 1990s the transparency coalition deepened considerably beyond the elites who pushed it forward in the first part of the decade. It should be little surprise, then, that from the Draghi law in 1998 forward we find continued support for corporate governance reform (even after the centre-right returned to power). While it cannot be established that workers as voters voted in a conscious fashion in the 1996 elections for corporate governance reform per se, their strong support for the centre-left, which ran on an economically liberal campaign, can be taken as broad voter support for the 'modernisation' or transformation of the Italian system (including corporate governance). Partly a product of the reformers' early efforts, a small group of business leaders emerged to support this transparency coalition as well.

That said, it is also clear that the blockholding coalition is still quite strong and large segments of the working classes still have an economic interest in maintaining many aspects of the old system (especially blockholding which prevents takeovers). It is also very unclear how much the cultural norms (informal institutions) shaping the Italian political economy have changed. While many new corporate leaders – notably the heads of the four largest banks – advocate for more transparency in corporate governance and shareholder value, they are still a minority and even many of their actions are often more consistent with the old system. Thus, despite many formal legal and regulatory changes promoting corporate transparency and the role of securities markets, large Italian firms have not gone nearly as far as many of their European counterparts toward 'shareholder value' practices (see also Amatori and Colli 2000).

The growth of markets and dispersion of corporate ownership in Italy is slowed by the fact that the interests and preferences of workers, managers and blockholding owners do not clearly line up in favour of either the old, opaque system or a newer, transparent system. Future developments will depend importantly on whether workers-as-investors' assets continue to shift into securities. Private pensions – often the carriers of corporate governance reform – are only slowly emerging in Italy. So far institutional investors in Italy have not been particularly strong supporters of transparency and minority shareholders because of conflicts of interest. Thus the future impact of transparency-oriented reforms in Italy will also depend much on whether truly independent institutional investors become active shareholders pressing for real openness and management accountability.

We also know that political and policy outcomes are not simply a matter of shifting preferences: the political system itself heavily conditions these. Up to the 1990s, Italy's consensus-oriented and fragmented party and political systems generally hindered reform. During the 1990s, three key political institutional changes facilitated Italy's ability to respond to pressures for change with notable success in reform; these include party system changes, particularly the end of DC dominance and the transformation of the Left, change in industrial relations and the reformist orientation of unions, and measures to strengthen the autonomy of the executive, Treasury and Bank of Italy. The new electoral system is encouraging a slow consolidation of left and right blocs. Such a development is likely to marginalise more radical policy prescriptions while encouraging coalitional stability, centrist policies and more meaningful policy alternatives between Left and Right (especially if the DS continues to pursue a liberal-socialist agenda; see also Newell 2000). These are factors likely to favour future reform. Nonetheless, in Italy actual practice deviates considerably from the new corporate governance rules, and state capacity and willingness to enforce them is uneven. In this sense change in corporate governance reflects a broader and traditional pattern in Italian politics and policy making.

ACKNOWLEDGEMENTS

The author wishes to acknowledge the helpful comments of Roberto Tamborini, Nicholas Ziegler, and the anonymous reviewers for their helpful comments on earlier drafts.

NOTES

1. Corporate governance refers to the system of rules determining the respective rights and obligations of key stakeholders within firms, namely owners, management and workers.
2. It is this fact that allows Roe (2003) to consider Italy a country that had a social democratic political coalition in place, even though the centre-right dominated Italian politics until the early 1990s.
3. The fact that formal legal changes have not induced the outcomes predicted by the legal quality approach weakens its claims; but on the other hand there is also evidence to support it since aspects of corporate law are still inadequate according to the theory, and courts and regulators are weak. Roe (2003: 83–6) acknowledges this but argues that the law approach is still insufficient by itself.
4. In the early 1990s, 50.8 percent of all private firm assets were held by families; this compared to 27 percent in France, 16.9 percent in Germany and 13.3 percent in the UK (Cobham *et al.* 1999: 327).
5. The Treasury, through IRI, controlled the only banks authorised to do business throughout the nation (Banche di Interesse Nazionale); three of the most important such banks were Banca Commerciale Italiana, Credito Italiano, and Banco di Roma (Aiello *et al.* 2000: 28).
6. This characterisation has been recently challenged in a study which found that Italian firms, in addition to using more bank financing, actually use more equity finance than their Anglo-Saxon counterparts (and smaller firms use equity more than larger firms). Though much of this equity is not raised on the formal exchange, but rather from family and friends. Thus the authors conclude that Italy does not fit into either the bank-based model of Japan or the high self-finance Anglo model, and it forms, along with France, a distinct Mediterranean model (Cobham *et al.* 1999).
7. In 1995, 81 percent of lending to firms in Italy was done by banks; compared with 77 percent in Germany, 73 percent in France, 56 percent in UK, and 22 percent in the US (Thomas 1998).
8. In 1992, 84.7 percent of bank loans were short-term (less than 18 months (Cesarini 1994: 32–6). However, it was also common practice among banks to repeatedly renew short-term credits without loans being earmarked for specific uses in firms, thus to some extent overcoming the lack of long-term financing.
9. The three major state-owned banks controlling Mediobanca (which also supplied it with funds at preferential rates) were Banca Commerciale Italiano, Credito Italiano, and Banca di Roma (McCann 2000). These were the three major universal banks of Italy between the late nineteenth century and their takeover by the state in the early 1930s. They were major shareholders in a significant number of large Italian firms during this period. Thus the transformation of Mediobanca beginning in the 1960s into a major force in private Italian capitalism is in some sense a revival of the banking system's function during the prior era.

10. The Governor of the bank is 'the sole institutional official not directly appointed by the government and whose term of office is indefinite' (Graham 1993).
11. The law contained term-limited tax incentives to encourage major restructuring and mergers. As of late 2001 only nine foundations had withdrawn completely from their banks and about one-quarter of foundations continued to own at least 50 percent of their bank (*The Economist*, 27 October 2001, 70).
12. The transfer of bank shares to government-controlled foundations also ensured continuity of political influence over banks (Coyle 1991).
13. In 1996, for example, an employment pact was signed.
14. Testo Unico delle disposizioni in materiali di mercati finanziari, Legislative Decree 24/02/98 No. 58. The Law came into effect on 1 July 1998.
15. After three years the chief auditing partner must be rotated; after nine years a new auditing firm must be hired. In non-listed firms internal audit boards have in many cases been allowed to certify accounts (Galbraith 2002).
16. It slid back to 48.5 percent of GDP by the end of 2001 as a result of share price declines (www.borsaitalia.it).
17. In 1999, for example, 82 percent of new equity raised on the exchange was through privatisations (Bank of Italy 2000: 178).
18. Equities and investment fund units rose from 38 percent of household assets in 1996 to 51 percent at the end of 1999 – though, again, much of this rise was due to share price appreciation (Bank of Italy 2000: 137) – but dropped to 36 percent by mid-2002 (Betts 2002).
19. From 1990 to 1997 the value of financial assets held by institutional investors rose from 13.4 percent to 53.2 percent of GDP (Aguilera 2001: 22). The vast majority of Italian mutual funds and fund assets are controlled by banks (Amatori and Colli 2000: 36).
20. Assets under management as a proportion of household assets rose from 9.8 percent in 1990 to 34.1 percent in 1999; but at the end of 1998, equities still represented only 19 percent of total institutional assets, leaving Italy well behind the US and UK. Moreover, only about 5 percent of assets under management are pension funds and without further pension reform this is likely to change only slowly (Bank of Italy 2000: 153–57).
21. ('Fund management in Italy' 2003). And of the 100 largest firms, over 40 are controlled by a single family (Moretti, 2003).
22. Most of the major commercial banks count banking foundations – there were 89 in 2002 – among their significant owners. Since the mid-1990s market reformers have made repeated efforts – with some success – to reduce the role of the foundations in the banking sector (Aiello *et al.* 2000: 31–7). The foundations are run by local governments but also by representatives of civil groups. They are required by law to spend their income on social and cultural projects (Lane 2002).
23. The number of banks declined from 1,108 (of which 708 were cooperatives) in 1991 to 830 (474 cooperatives) by the end of 2001 (Bank of Italy 2001).
24. Profumo, head of UniCredito, met with both Fazio as head of the Bank of Italy and Berlusconi in advance of the shareholders' meeting in which Maranghi was ousted (Kapner 2003c).

REFERENCES

Aguilera, Ruth V. (2001). 'Institutional Pressures Shaping Shareholder Value Capitalism and Corporate Governance in Italy and Spain', paper presented at Conference on Shareholder Value Capitalism and Globalization, Bad Homburg, Germany.

Aguilera, Ruth V., and Gregory Jackson (2003). 'The Cross-National Diversity of Corporate Governance: Dimensions and Determinants', *Academy of Management Review*, 28:3, 447–66.

Aiello, Francesco *et al.* (2000). 'Ownership Structure, Behavior and Performance of the Italian Banking Industry', unpublished paper, University of Calabria.

Amatori, Franco, and Andrea Colli (2000). 'Corporate Governance: The Italian Story', unpublished paper, Bocconi University.

Bank of Italy (1995). 'Annual Report for 1995'. Rome: Bank of Italy.

Bank of Italy (2000). 'Annual Report for 2000'. Rome: Bank of Italy.

Bank of Italy (2002). 'Governor Alludes to Merger of MPS with BNL', *The Banker*, 1 July.

Barber, Tony. (2004). 'Italian Reforms join a Legislative Logjam as Coalition Parties Bicker', *Financial Times*, 30 January.

Bebchuk, Lucian Arye, and Mark J. Roe (1999). 'A Theory of Path Dependence in Corporate Ownership and Governance', *Stanford Law Review*, 52, 127–70.

Betts, Paul (1997). 'The Bourse: Market "Half the Size it Should Be"', *Financial Times*, 10 December.

Betts, Paul (2002). '"BOTs" Revert to Old Habits', *Financial Times*, 12 August.

Blitz, James (1997). 'The Driving Force behind Privatization', *Financial Times*, 10 December.

Blitz, James (1998). 'Italian Takeover Reforms take Shape', *Financial Times*, 12 February.

Brunello, Giorgio *et al.* (2003). 'CEO Turnover in Insider-Dominated Boards: The Italian Case', *Journal of Banking and Finance*, 27, 1027–51.

'Capitalia Throws Down the Gauntlet'. (2002). *European Banker*, 9 August.

Cesarini, F. (1994). 'The Relationship Between Banks and Firms in Italy: A Banker's View', *Review of Economic Conditions in Italy*, 48, 29–50.

Cioffi, John (2003). 'Expansive Retrenchment: The Regulatory Politics of Corporate Governance Reform and the Foundations of Finance Capitalism'. German Studies Association, New Orleans.

Cioffi, John, and Martin Höpner (2004). 'The Political Paradox of Finance Capitalism: Interests, Preferences, and Center-Left Party Politics in Corporate Governance Reform'. Conference of Europeanists, Chicago.

Cobham, David, Cosci and Mattesini (1999). 'The Italian Financial System: Neither Bank Based nor Market Based', *The Manchester School*, 67:3, 325–45.

T W O

'Corporate Law Reform in Italy offers Flexibility to Choose Board Structure' (2003). *The Accountant*, July, 10.

Coyle, Diane (1991). 'The Restructuring of Italy's Banking System has been Triggered by the Amato Law. Will it go Far Enough?', *Investors Chronicle*, 29 November.

D'Aquino, Niccolo (1997). 'Italy Prepares for EMU', *Europe*, July/August.

de Cecco, Marcello (1994). 'The Italian Banking System at a Historic Turning Point', *Review of Economic Conditions in Italy*, 48, 51–67.

Deeg, Richard, and Sofia Perez (2000). 'International Capital Mobility and Domestic Institutions: Corporate Finance and Governance in Four European Cases', *Governance: An International Journal of Policy and Administration*, 13:2, 119–53.

Delaney, Sarah (2004). 'Parmalat Spurs Call for Reform in Business', *Washington Post*, 20 January.

Draghi, Mario (1998). 'Corporate Governance and Competitiveness', *Review of Economic Conditions in Italy*, 52, 341–57.

Favretto, Ilaria (2002). 'The Italian Left in Search of Ideas: The Rediscovery of the Political Ideas of the Action Party', *Journal of Modern Italian Studies*, 7:3, 392–415.

Felsen, David (2000). 'Changes to the Italian Budgetary Regime: Reforms of Law no. 94/1997', in David Hine and Salvatore Vassallo (eds.), *Italian Politics: A Review, Volume 14*. Oxford: Berghahn Books, 157–73.

Ferri, Giovanni, and Marcello Mesorri (2000). 'Bank–Firm Relationships and Allocative Efficiency in Northeastern and Central Italy and in the South', *Journal of Banking and Finance*, 24, 1067–95.

'Fund Management in Italy: Dependency Culture' (2003). *The Economist*, 2 July.

Galbraith, Robert (2002). 'Disappointment and Dissatisfaction in Italy', *The Accountant*, September.

Gourevitch, Peter, and James Shinn (2003). 'Explaining Corporate Governance: The Role of Politics', unpublished manuscript.

Graham, Robert (1993). 'Respect for the Elderly', *Financial Times* (London edn.), 10 December.

Guillén, Mauro F. (2000). 'Corporate Governance and Globalization: Is there Convergence across Countries?', *Advances in International Comparative Management*, 13, 175–204.

Guiso, Luigi, and Tullio Jappelli (2000). 'Household Portfolios in Italy'. Centro Studi in Economia e Finanza, Salerno, Working Paper no. 43.

Gumbel, Peter (2004). 'Italy: Land of Bilk and Money', *Fortune*, 26 January.

Hall, Peter A., and David Soskice (2001). *Varieties of Capitalism*. Oxford: Oxford University Press.

Höpner, Martin (2001). 'Corporate Governance in Transition: Ten Empirical Findings on Shareholder Value and Industrial Relations in Germany'. Max Planck Institute for the Study of Societies, Cologne, Discussion Paper 01/4.

Höpner, Martin (2002). 'European Corporate Governance Reform and the German Party Paradox', unpublished paper, Max Planck Institute for the Study of Societies.

'Italian Banking: Half a Renaissance' (1991). *The Economist*, 21 March.

'Italy: The Italian Uniform Code for the Governance of Capital Markets' (1998). Business Briefing – Studio Legale Sutti, 5 October.

Jackson, Gregory (2003). 'Toward a Comparative Perspective on Corporate Governance and Labour Management'. RIETI Discussion Paper Series 04-E-023.

Jackson, Gregory, and Sigurt Vitols (2001). 'Between Financial Commitment, Market Liquidity and Corporate Governance: Occupational Pensions in Britain, Germany, Japan and the USA', in Bernhard Ebbinghaus and Philip Manow (eds.), *Comparing Welfare Capitalism: Social Policy and Political Economy in Europe, Japan, and the USA*. London: Routledge.

Kapner, Fred (2002). ' Investors Aghast at Fondiaria Imbroglio', *Financial Times*, 22 March.

Kapner, Fred (2003a). 'An Emerging Generation of Leaders is Promising to Sweep Away Secrecy and Cronyism', *Financial Times*, 7 April.

Kapner, Fred (2003b). 'All Roads Lead to Reform', *Financial Times*, 3 April.

Kapner, Fred (2003c). 'Rivals Step Up Their Efforts to Oust Maranghi', *Financial Times*, 5 March.

'Keeping it in the Family' (2001). *Financial Times*, 31 July.

Lane, David (1990). 'Italy: Year of Profound Structural Change', *Financial Times*, 19 November.

Lane, David (1992). 'Italy: Losers, 2; Winners; 1', *The Banker*, 1 August.

Lane, David (2001). 'Italy – A Year to Forget', *The Banker*, 1 June.

La Porta, Rafael, Florencio Lopez de Silanes and Andrei Shleifer (2000). 'Investor Protection and Corporate Governance', *Journal of Financial Economics*, 58:3.

Locke, Richard and Lucio Baccaro (1999). 'The Resurgence of Italian Unions?', in Andrew Martin and George Ross (eds.), *The Brave New World of European Labor*. Oxford: Berghahn Books, 217–68.

McCann, Dermot (2000). 'The "Anglo-American" Model, Privatization and the Transformation of Private Capitalism in Italy', *Modern Italy*, 5:1, 47–61

McHugh, David (2001). 'Parmalat Case raises Questions about Corporate Regulation in Italy's "Family Capitalism"', *Associated Press*, 1 January.

Moretti, John (2003). 'After the Death of Agnelli, Family Business as Usual', *Italy Weekly*, 31 January.

Newell, James L. (2000). *Parties and Democracy in Italy*. Aldershot: Ashgate.

O'Brian, Heather (2002a). 'Fewer Shareholders Control More Italian Companies', *Daily Deal*, 8 April.

O'Brian, Heather (2002b). 'IntesaBCI, Lazard Link in Italy', *Daily Deal*, 10 September.

Onado, Marco (1996). 'The Italian Financial System and the Challenges of the Investment Services Directive', *Review of Economic Conditions in Italy*, 50, 89–103.

OECD (Organization for Economic Cooperation and Development) (1995). *OECD Economic Survey: Italy 1994–95*. Washington, DC: OECD.

OECD (2003). 'Assessment and Recommendations: Italy', *OECD Economic Surveys*. Washington, DC: OECD.

Portolano, Alessandro (2000). 'The Decision to Adopt Defensive Tactics in Italy', *International Review of Law and Economics*, 20, 425–52.

Pradhan, M. (1995). 'Privatization and the Development of Financial Markets in Italy', *Finance and Development*, 32:4, 9–20.

Roe, Mark (2003). *Political Determinants of Corporate Governance: Political Context, Corporate Impact.* Oxford: Oxford University Press.

'Romano Prodi: Italy's Would-be Record-Breaker' (1998). *The Economist*, 10 October.

Scharpf, Fritz (1997). *Games Real Actors Play: Actor-Centered Institutionalism in Policy Research. Boulder*, CO: Westview.

Schmidt, Vivien (2003). 'French Capitalism Transformed, yet still a Third Variety of Capitalism', *Economy and Society*, 32:4, 526–54.

Segreto, Luciano (1997). 'Models of Control in Italian Capitalism from the Mixed Banks to Mediobanca, 1894–1993', *Business and Economic History*, 26:2, 649–61.

Simonian, Haig (1990). 'Parliamentary Helmsman – Profile; Maurizio Sacconi, Under Secretary in the Treasury', *Financial Times*, 19 November.

Thomas, G. (1998). 'EMU a Panacea for Corporate Issuance', *Corporate Finance*, May.

'The Transformation of Financial Markets' (1997). *Review of Economic Conditions in Italy*, 51.

Vitols, Sigurt (2003). 'Negotiated Shareholder Value: The German Version of an Anglo-American Practice', Discussion Paper of the Social Science Research Centre, Berlin, SP II 2003 – 25.

Webster, Philip (2001). 'Pirelli Takeover of Olivetti Destroys Value, Prompts Concern on Debt'. AFX Europe, 31 July.

Wilson, Ted (2002). 'Middle Layer Hots Up in Italy', *Acquisitions Monthly*, 31 May.

Zattoni, Alessandro (1999). 'The Structure of Corporate Groups: The Italian Case', *Corporate Governance: An International Review*, 7:1, 38–48.

T
W
O

5 "A Transformation in the French Model of Shareholding and Management"

from Economy and Society (2000)

François Morin

SUMMARY

This chapter explores the French model of shareholding and management, identifying a significant transformation in the pattern of shareholding in the largest companies. In earlier configurations of ownership, first the State and then the system of cross-shareholdings were at the centre of French capitalism; the new pattern of shareholding operates under a different logic and motivation. In effect, France has undergone rapid change from a 'financial network economy' to a 'financial market economy'. This new pattern of shareholding has not only broken the traditional system of cross-shareholding, but it has also facilitated the arrival of foreign institutional investors who bring with them new techniques and demands on corporate management.

INTRODUCTION

As the twenty-first century approaches, the French economy is facing a triple challenge: to become successfully integrated in a globalized world economy, to manage the transition to the single European currency successfully and finally to achieve the balance between employment and growth. It is likely that major new legislation will soon be working towards the attainment of these objectives: the law relating to the 35-hour working week, social security reform and, in particular, reform relating to how pensions are financed. This chapter relates these prospects and questions to the French model of shareholding and management and considers the question of whether the model is in the process of change because the French economy is being opened up on an international basis.

Our analysis can give a precise answer to this question: the shareholding model of the largest French groups is today rapidly disintegrating. In previous configurations, first the State and then subsequently cross-shareholdings were at the centre of capitalist relations; by way of contrast, the new share-holding relationship which is now evolving complies with norms which are entirely different from the previous model. Directly inspired by the American 'shareholder value' model, the largest French groups are going through a managerial revolution, whose consequences are only now beginning to become apparent, most noticeably in the new way in which the French stock exchange operates. This chapter aims to illustrate this revolution, which has already started, and to specify its effects on the strategic behaviour of the largest companies.

In summarizing the most general features of this 'break', we start from the notion that the French economy is in the process of undergoing an extremely rapid transition from a 'financial network economy' towards a 'financial market economy'. Until now its financial macro-circuits had been mainly governed by groups of actors organized in large systems of inter-corporate alliances, not by the workings of the capital market. This financial network economy is currently in the process of rapidly acquiring a new logic, that of a financial market economy. In this respect, the French economy is beginning to operate in the same way as the American and British economies and is distancing itself from the German and Japanese models of capitalism which had, to some extent, previously motivated its shareholding system. The extent to which US and British norms have penetrated the system is impressive and total. This infiltration is demonstrated by the currently massive presence of North American investors in the capital of French firms. In this respect it should be noted that France is the only country alongside the US and Britain to offer such a large opening to foreign investors. Neither Germany nor Japan, for example, is in a similar situation. As a result of this, in France more than elsewhere, there is an absence of shareholder commitment, which puts French firms at a certain competitive disadvantage.

In analysing this transformation, our chapter aims to relate and synthesize evidence from different sources about several developments, all of which have very different origins.[1] In this context, we shall try to clarify the development path which French capitalism is currently taking. The current path has three key features: first, it will, in the long term, put an end to the cross-shareholdings system; second, it promotes the entrance of new investors, especially foreign institutional investors; third, the new investors bring with them new norms of company management. This chapter will consider each of these new developments in turn.

THE DECLINE OF CROSS-SHAREHOLDINGS

In France, relations between firms have been historically organized along the lines of a financial network, whose dominant features are interlocking share-holdings and a controlling role for managers. This model, whose characteristics were specifically reinforced in 1986 with the withdrawal of state influence from control of economic activities, now seems to be becoming increasingly fragile.

In principle, the cross-shareholdings system is essentially governed by the control and self-protection mechanisms of the leading management teams. Its main fault is that it immobilizes capital stocks in circular interlocking stakes, so creating a fictitious capital that cannot be called up by the concern. In the case of companies that are integrated into financial network business relations, a typical shareholding profile can be established by describing the matrix of cross-shareholdings which structure the shareholding base of a company as well as the interventions of players, such as the Caisse des Dépôts et Consignations, which plays a particular role in stabilizing the shareholding base of French companies.

It can thus be seen that on average the interlocking stakes, held by the network 'hard cores' through small groups of companies, directly accounted for no more than 20.5 percent of the capital of the companies in 1997, whereas the average had exceeded 30 percent at the start of the 1990s. To this percentage, we can legitimately add the share holdings of employees, some 2.77 percent, which constitute frozen savings tied up in a concern whose management is in practice widely influenced by the company's managers. Even after adding this stake, the controlling interest in firms included in the cross-shareholdings system on average accounts for no more than 23.3 percent of shares. Moreover, this percentage tends to decline markedly as one shifts from the centre of the system of holdings by the principal French institutions. For example, the committed shareholding group in Elf accounts for a lower percentage of around 17 percent and in Alcatel the committed shareholding group accounts for no more than about 15 percent. Overall, this type of shareholding has a relatively reduced base in relation to the growing presence of foreign investors in the majority of quoted companies.

However, an examination of recent data on the shareholding structure of the largest groups qualifies any vision of a French capitalism that is totally exposed to the powerful forces of liberalization. Interlocking shareholdings continue to have a role, even if they have recently declined in number. In their two forms – insider control via interlocking shareholdings within a group and cross-shareholdings via cross-shareholdings between two groups – these quite specific financial relations continue to articulate the configuration of the French financial network. Insider control, even if it is no longer a source of voting rights at the shareholders' annual general meeting, continues to function, providing corresponding shares are assigned between friendly organizations. Such 'parked up' shares account for significant proportions in some parent companies: 6.4 percent at Elf; 5.2 percent at Société Générale; 5.5 percent at AXA–UAP; and 10 percent at Paribas. They can be explained only by the protective function they have for the management teams.

French financial core concern	Shareholding structure
Network cross-holdings	20.52%
Employees	2.77%
French mutual funds (OPCVM)	7.17%
Insurance companies (non-network)	6.32%
State capital	5.86%
Mutual societies sector	2.62%

Source: from Sisife-Lerep database on cross-shareholdings and share ownership, University of Toulouse, LEREPS

Table 5.1 **Shareholding profile of a firm in the French financial network (September 1997)**

Cross-shareholdings, on the other hand, are a source of actual voting rights, even if the cross-share-holding makes part of the capital of firms connected in this way fictitious. Their *raison d'être* is again their protective function. The following are amongst the best known of these arrangements between major companies: Société Générale with Alcatel; Alcatel with Générale des Eaux; Havas with Canal Plus; Paribas with AXA–UAP; BNP with AXA–UAP; Suez-Lyonnaise with Saint Gobain; Saint Gobain with Générale des Eaux.

The mode of organizing financial relations is moving away from interlocking and concentrated ownership structures and towards less complex, mar-ket-oriented structures, closer to the US and British models. The financially net-worked organization does, of course, still exist, as we have seen but, on current trends, we are moving away from this model which has had its day and this shift has implications for the way in which a company is run.

The logic of the old system was to sustain a system of protecting concerns and management teams which some considered useful because it allowed firms or groups to carry out internal restructuring. According to many of the company bosses we interviewed, the old network system, where companies believe they are protected from external aggression, is seriously defective because it loses sight of the main object of capital investment, which is to maximize financial return. They add that the low return on invested capital in France (which is another feature of the French model) is definitely a consequence of this situation.

Having said that, should financially networked economies be condemned at a general level as an infe-rior system of holding or managing capital? We do not think so. In networked economies, it is the banking and financing organizations, and not the markets, which play a key role in restructuring measures and their financing. Thus they create the possibility of long-term

regulation. It could also be argued that financially net-worked economies spread the financial shocks associ-ated with systemic risk. We do not believe this. By its very nature, systemic risk is independent of the model of capitalism although it is expressed in different ways in each model. In the financially networked economies, the spread of crises is slow, smooth and increases financial interconnection. In the financial market econ-omies, their spread is brutally manifest in the form of financial bubbles which, when they burst, do not affect just one specific market (acting as circuit breaker), but affect all the monetary and financial markets because of the increasing extent to which they are now interconnected.

DISINTEGRATION AND THE NEW FOREIGN INVESTORS

The start of the current major break can be dated fairly precisely. With the AXA–UAP merger in December 1996, the French financial network reached the culmination of a trajectory which had started thirty years earlier. The new AXA–UAP group now concentrates financial holdings on a massive scale and has a capacity to co-ordinate activities never previously attained. At present it has all the means to enable it to be the key actor and central fulcrum of the French financial network: its ramifications along the major poles of this network are really numerous and powerful. French capital still has the choice of whether to develop along the lines of a Japanese model or, alternatively, a more Germanic one.

But the new group is not accepting its traditional responsibility and choosing this option. In a break with tradition, the management team of the new group is deliberately neglecting its power of co-ordi-nating and regulating economic activities. Only some investments will still be regarded as truly strategic: as

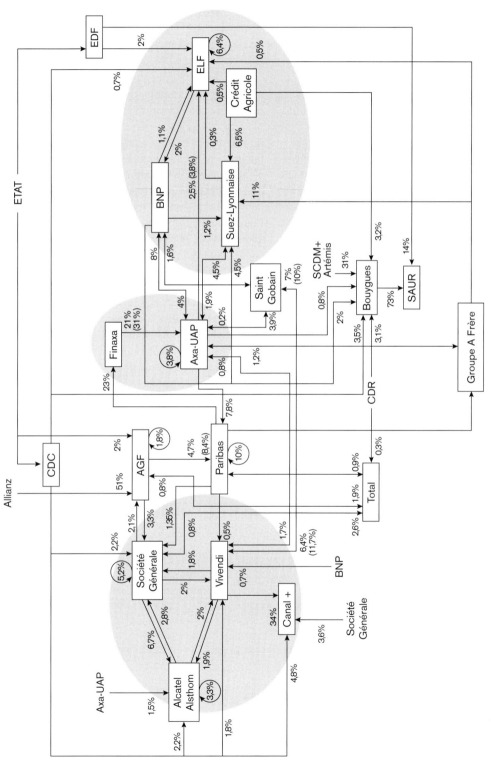

Figure 5.1 **The French financial core (December 1998)**

in the case of the link with Paribas, for example, or that with BNP. The remaining shareholdings will from now on go into the portfolio of group activities to be managed financially according to Anglo-Saxon profitability norms. Clearly, AXA is totally separating its positions on asset management from its strategic choices and, from this point onwards, its aim is to become one of the world leaders in asset management.

The takeover of AGF perfectly illustrates the new stance of the largest asset-management company in France. By acting jointly with the small, central group of shareholders in the company coming under attack, AXA–UAP was in a position to organize an adequate counter-attack; instead, AXA–UAP gave the Allianz group a huge opportunity to seize control of the second largest French insurance group. Either acting jointly with other parties or even acting on its own, AXA–UAP could surely have raised the 60 billion francs needed for counterattack when, at the time of the transaction, its assets amounted to 3,500 billion francs.

This spectacular and symptomatic result actually expresses a more general tendency: the increasing role of foreign investors in the Paris Stock Exchange. Their presence has increased only in the last few years, due to several factors: a more open regulatory system, the arrival of the single market, in anticipation of the single European currency, and, more generally, the current globalization of monetary and financial markets. Today, according to the Bank of France, the share of foreign ownership is impressive: between 1985 and 1997, foreign owners have increased their share of stock exchange capitalization from 10 percent to 35 percent.

The Bank of France is now undertaking statistical analysis of the presence of foreign investors in the capital of quoted companies. Its results, which so far relate to 60 percent of the companies, show that foreign investors hold nearly 35 percent of the capitalization of the Paris stock market. The figure does depend on the methods used to measure foreign shareholdings and the method used in the Sallustro report does give much lower figures. But the Bank of France figure is the one often used when trying to appreciate, in a global way, the impact of foreign capital invested on the Parisian market. According to the 1997 data, the level of foreign capital penetration on the French market has reached average levels which are clearly higher than in comparable countries. As Table 5.2 shows, even if we make the comparison with the UK and USA, it is the Paris Stock Exchange that is, a priori, the most open and the most receptive to foreign investors.[2] We shall return a little later to the consequences of this French peculiarity.

Within the past couple of years, the dominant and highly significant trend has been towards the

France	Great Britain	Japan	United States
35%	9%	11%	6%

Source: Gestionnaires de marchés

Table 5.2 **Share of capital held by foreign investors on various stock exchanges (in 1997)**

French companies	Percentage of capital held by foreign investors	Percentage held by foreign mutual funds
Alcatel	40	19.81
AGF	42	8.61
AXA–UAP	37	7.42
BNP	35	14.56
Elf	51	12.11
Générale des Eaux	42	10.13
Paribus	38	8.94
Société Générale	45	11.31
Suez Lyonnaise	39	8.64

Source: Sisife-Lerep, database on cross-shareholdings and share ownership, University of Toulouse, LEREPS

Table 5.3 **Foreign shareholdings in French companies within the cross-shareholding system (end of 1997)**

purchase of increasing stakes in French firms by North American pension funds (or by those who manage such funds for third-party accounts). The rising share of foreign owners should obviously be related to the gradual freeing of the French system of cross-shareholding. The large American pension fund companies buy up blocks of shares held by previously committed owners; the blocs most notably include those of AXA–UAP and also those of Elf, Société Générale, etc. This trend is so strong that more than 50 percent of the capital of many companies belonging to the elite CAC 40 group of companies is now held by foreign investors.

Table 5.3 establishes the point that it is the foreign investors who now dominate. Their holdings are, in every case, larger than those of cross-shareholders; and this conclusion remains true even if the shares held by French mutual funds are added to the average value of domestic cross-shareholdings because that would increase the value of French national holdings only to some 30.94 percent. But there is also another element that must be taken into consideration. The capital share held by just one group of foreign investors, the foreign mutual funds, already represents on average more than 50 percent of the value of the shares held by the system of interlocking shareholders. In some cases, such as Alcatel, the foreign mutual funds alone hold a greater proportion of the capital than is controlled by the group of committed shareholders.

At this stage of the argument and with the aim of understanding the long-term implications of these changes, it is appropriate to make a clear distinction between two kinds of fund management.

■ Pension funds were initially invested in the United States and the rest of the world under a system of *direct management* where the fund assumes the risk on a defined benefit (or DB basis). In, for example, the older kind of British pension fund typically set up by large firms, the pension is guaranteed by the firm in relation to final income. The pension payments are financed out of employer and employee contributions into the fund with the employer providing 'top ups' or taking contribution holidays according to the balance between assets and liabilities. This typically results in prudent direct management of one employer's fund around the principles of diversified portfolios which distribute financial investments in a balanced way between the elements that make up the market indices. In

addition, such investors ask firms to respect codes of corporate governance on the understanding that failure to comply may result in the withdrawal of the investments. This first form of direct management still mobilizes sizeable resources and manifests itself in France through the investments of a group such as Calpers which has significant holdings in all of the CAC 40 companies.

■ Driven by financial deregulation in America, new actors, *the third-party account managers*, have come to the fore since the mid-1980s, and in a much more marked way since the start of the 1990s. These managers run already mutualized savings on a defined contributions (DC) basis, without bearing the risk. The risk is assumed directly by the contributors who get no more and no less than the accumulated value of what they have paid into the fund. Extremely lively competition between account managers manifests itself in the search for the highest possible financial returns at the same time as management of these funds is more aggressive and focused in terms of shareholder presence. This structural information on how the DC funds delegate management provides an essential key to their behaviour in the market. It leads funds, such as Fidelity or Templeton, to pursue policies which involve higher profitability-risk pairings. Given the terms and conditions of their own third-party activity, it is essential that the companies in which they are involved achieve financial performances.

Table 5.4 provides some indication of the relative importance of two of the new third-party managers, Fidelity and Templeton, for the share registers of some major French companies. Fidelity is engaged simultaneously in portfolio diversification and targeted investment in specific companies with value potential; the targeted investment policy accounts for investments within Total since December 1996 and in Alcatel since March 1997. Practically all of Templeton's investments are targeted; and this specifically accounts for its investments in Elf since February 1997 and in BNP since April 1997 (see the impact of these funds on the French financial core as shown in Figure 5.1).

Foreign mutual funds have a growing weight in the share registers of the principal French firms. In exerting their influence on French management, they do not hesitate about joint action within and between groups. Internally, a group like Fidelity can

French groups	Foreign mutual funds	Of which:		
		CALPERS (DB funds)	Fidelity	Templeton (DC funds)
AGF	8	0.20	0.09	0.20
Alcatel–Alsthom	20	0.30	10.40	1.90
AXA–UAP	7	0.36	0.26	1.06
BNP	15	0.24	0.15	4.90
Bouygues	5	0.21	0.05	0
Canal Plus	8	0.20	1.31	0
Elf	12	0.26	0.43	2.10
Générale des Eaux	10	0.41	0.07	0
Havas	4	0.21	0.04	0
Paribas	9	0.21	0.18	0
Saint Gobain	9	0.36	0.06	0.17
Société Générale	11	0.39	0.68	0
Suez–Lyonnaise	7	0.53	0.13	0.50
Total (Group)	15	0.33	5.14	1.50

Source: Sisife-Lerep database on cross-shareholdings and share ownership, University of Toulouse, LEREPS

Table 5.4 **Shareholding by foreign mutual funds in French firms (September 1997): percentage of capital held**

intervene, for example, by means of twenty-four bearer funds in Total's capital. These bearer funds can operate as a unitary bloc, especially in votes at the annual meetings of shareholders. Externally, if in their view minority interests are threatened, different funds do not hesitate to combine forces. This has recently been seen in the case of Eramet where, although the French state was a majority shareholder, it had to yield in the face of a joint action by several pension funds.

The result of this dual process is obvious. The directly managed American pension funds such as Calpers or TIAA CREF, just like the third-party account managers of funds such as Fidelity, Templeton and Capital Group, not only have a strong presence in share registers but have become the leading shareholders in French firms. As 'active' shareholders they will henceforth make their voices heard as they are in a strong position to influence the firms' management methods and strategic choices. The entry of international investors thus does more than rearrange the financial macro-circuits because such changes also have primary impacts on corporate behaviour. In developing this point in the next section, we propose to concentrate on how the new management principles, introduced by the new investors, establish new constraints on firms.

THE NEW MANAGEMENT NORMS

Whatever their nature and regardless of differences in strategic behaviour, institutional investors share certain fundamental characteristics which result in a precise requirement of increasing *shareholder value* which is potentially transferable to the shareholders. The economic value realized by the concern must, as a matter of priority, be applied to benefit the shareholders as they are considered to be the stakeholders who incur the greatest risk. It was in this context that the idea of respecting principles of *corporate governance* appeared as an increasingly strong requirement, first in the United States at the beginning of the 1990s, then in Great Britain.

Once enunciated by the public pension funds (for example, Calpers' Charter of Corporate Governance), all institutional investors have subsequently adopted the principles. Further, these principles have been applied quickly because they seemed to be absent from certain financial markets, including, until very recently, the French market.

The speed of this development has been such that it is now a verifiable fact: the largest French firms are subject to Anglo-Saxon management and return on capital norms. We have been able to verify that this diktat regarding norms is being observed throughout the CAC 40 companies. At this level, it involves a considerable upheaval while the consequences have yet to become clearly apparent.

Consultation with the regulatory authorities, in particular the COB (French equivalent of the Securities and Exchange Commission (SEC)) confirms this result; at the same time, the authorities want to be reassuring. According to COB executives, the new foreign investors are lacking in vision and industrial or strategic objectives and are therefore not a threat to French capitalism. On the other hand, they are trying to diversify their portfolios, and the reasons behind their presence are basically financial. Until recently, the French economic situation attracted them with appealing priccs and a stock exchange which seemed to be looking for capital.

The discussions we had with company bosses enable us to reveal the new environment of the French firm: that of *shareholder value*. We have collected and compiled the various 'norms' of the model through what we have chosen to call the 'precepts' of shareholder value that are imposed on company bosses. Reading these principles is not a mere presentation device. Some company directors are totally convinced of the efficacy of and absolute need for these norms. Others are developing a critical, perhaps even ironic view, while recognizing that there is at present no escaping them. We have simply endeavoured to render the company bosses' double stance by means of a restrained tone.

Understanding the investor's criteria

Most company bosses admit that they often find it difficult to understand precisely what motivates the institutional investor's decision.

■ There are, of course, geographical and sector-specific criteria. Thus, in the Morgan Stanley Index (MSCI), France obtains a 5 or 6 percent share of the allocation of assets (whereas Australia obtains 1 percent). With the introduction of the Euro this geographic grid will disappear. The effect of this will be to increase the competition between firms to profit from investors' transfers.

In a more general way, portfolio diversification management is primarily targeted at the economic policy of a country (and soon of Europe), while, for their part, the focused investment management teams target concerns in the same industrial sector. If, for example, the French economy achieves poor macro-economic results, this mediocre performance means that, *ipso facto*, France will be given a lower weighting in the geographic grid and as a result the securities in question will fall.

Seen from this viewpoint, the arrival of the Euro and the European indices will create a new arrangement whose most obvious feature is that the market will straight away become European. In this new context, it is likely that the sector-specific indices will assume an increased importance.

Beyond these points of reference, it is apparently difficult for the company bosses to understand the criteria at work in the decision behind the investment. The following firm-level considerations are often cited:

■ The clarity of the decision-making context and of the decision-making process itself.
■ The search for 'hidden value' (some say 'nuggets').
■ Confidence in the management, which is assessed as a matter of credibility.

Some company bosses have noticed a new trend, where the fund companies would, as a criterion for investment, consider whether the firm had a credible medium- and long-term strategic project.[3] For their part, this new approach by pension funds does not imply that their investments will be held for a longer period, because behind the new criterion is the idea that share prices reflect expectations and are the means by which the investor sees far ahead.

Seeking the (temporary) presence of investors

Every company manager tries to attract the investor in a universal, global game. But, it is essential that, once on the share register, an institutional investor must not leave after just a few months. Although it is difficult to set precise limits in this regard, it does however seem that, in the vast majority of cases, on average, pension funds retain their holdings in French firms for between two and four years. They can remain for slightly less, sometimes the figure of eighteen months is cited for Fidelity investments; or for slightly longer as when a five-year period was also cited. These are thus neither long-term nor very short-term investments. (It is therefore difficult to talk about short-termism in relation to these investors.)

Another rule would be that the bigger the pension fund the bigger the investment and the longer the period of holding: the big fund investors do not churn their holdings quickly and speculatively. They follow a traditional investment strategy, whereby investments are rotated every two or three years and the added value from the investments is regularly externalized. As a general rule, when US and British investors sell, they sell everything. When that happens, the company bosses reassure themselves by noting that a new investor can quickly replace the one they have lost.

In the eyes of many company bosses, the debate on short-termism and long-termism seems, in these circumstances, to be too black and white. It is true that, on the one hand, the investments are of a rather short-term nature, but, on the other hand, the decision to invest is increasingly based on the long-term visions of company strategy. This balanced view also does away with another debate, the one on the notion of the firm that traditionally opposes the stakeholder approach and the shareholder approach. If you consider that shareholders' interests must be defined in the long term, then this of necessity incorporates parameters that relate just as much to the environment of the firm as to employee relations.

For all that, company bosses are not unaware of the existence of certain very short-term investors, also described as raiders or arbitrage investors, who are in the habit of making very short-term investments (of only a few months) in the concerns. Several names have been in the news recently. 'Pure' investors such as the American Wyser Pratte group (in Strafor Facom) and Asher Edelman (in the Louvre company) have been mentioned repeatedly as Hedge Funds that can harm the concerns in which they have taken shareholdings.

Communicating continuously

All the companies we met take part in road shows, which usually take place twice a year (mainly in London, Boston, New York, Sydney). All company bosses attend on these occasions for the presentation of the half-yearly and annual results, knowing that (even if these occasions are a little like religious services) they will meet investors and analysts. In between doing the rounds, teams are set up to listen constantly to institutional investors.

It is different in the case of 'one on one' meetings. Here it is a question of working meetings where the fund managers visit the concerns and meet senior managers. Fidelity states that it made 24,500 visits in the USA and 6,500 in Europe in 1996. This type of meeting shows that the fund managers pay constant attention to management and that they carry out forms of evaluation that go way beyond the traditional criteria used as well as research from publicly available information. In this context at least, investors do seem to want a presence in, and knowledge of, the companies that goes beyond what is required to implement the policy of managing a diversified portfolio.

In the various contacts and meetings, there was clearly an initial learning period as mutual incomprehension was gradually eliminated on both sides. On the one hand, the company bosses had to learn how to adapt to the demands of *shareholder value*, particularly when copying the Anglo-Saxon financial model. On the other hand, the French social model (especially social rights) had to be explained to the investors in order to make it easier for them to accept. The same work had to be carried out to explain the logic behind financial networks.

In this sense, some people spoke of 'shared pedagogy'. French companies are now used to seeing astute, professional and technically adept fund managers. But in the eyes of such investors, a concern acquires credibility and legitimacy only if its directors know how to say yes *and* no. For example, they must know how to understand the difference between:

■ reasonable demands which preserve the medium- and long-term value,
■ and demands that lead to the destruction of the short-term value. (There do not have to be redundancies when a concern carries out research and development work.)

Explaining company strategy

Directors must be able to articulate an intelligible strategy. Investors expect major decisions to be taken only after careful examination of value, and understanding of that practice called 'management for value'. If these essentials are not understood, investors will sell.

The crux is the ability to elucidate and explain strategy. Institutional investors insist on clarity: just one core business, for example. If the company develops several businesses, it is vital that the market value of the whole must be at least as large as the capital value of the parts corresponding to each business, since, generally speaking, investors do not like conglomerates. Why? Because each represents distinct projects which require adequate management capacity. In relation to this particular point, many company bosses acknowledge that the investors are not necessarily wrong. This is also probably why investors prefer what they call 'focused' management.

In this context, conglomerate approaches are understood to be very difficult to defend. The only way they can be justified is by proving the economic efficacy of each area of activity.

These investors thus play an important role through the questions they ask management and, most importantly, through their own vision of the strategy. Just how far can it go? In France, company bosses confide that they are still free to respond and choose, which is no longer the case in Great Britain. The case of Barclays was cited many times. Barclays felt it had no choice but to break up the company in a way that, finally, proved to be disastrous for the British bank. (The division of Imperial Chemical Industries (ICI) was also cited, as was Rhone Poulenc Rorer.)

From the same point of view, in the eyes of US and British investors, cross-shareholdings at first appeared to be unjustifiable protection measures. But there is also a second argument: why fix considerable amounts of liquid assets in activities which are not your own? The Americans and British thus have a very poor view of networked cross-shareholding. To their mind, it is unhealthy because the firm is caught in business relations that are not really justified. The acceptability of this system is thus very limited and it is only accepted inasmuch as firms undertake fairly specifically to unwind cross-shareholdings.

Conforming to the dominant strategic model

All these elements converge strongly towards a fairly precise representation of the ideal strategic model. Investors clearly want companies to be simple objects with as few component parts as possible; it is not the firm's role to arbitrate between the different sectors of the market. Above all, they do not want companies to carry out their own role of institutional investor.

Due to increasing involvement in the United States, these investors are now forced to play an active role with regard to enterprises. They cannot remain inert.

As a result, they are increasingly led to clarify their concept of enterprise strategy. The latter can be summarized in three basic ways:

- supporting concentration of ownership in each business area and defence of the 'core business' (aligning assets with business cost reduction);
- breaking up conglomerates as well as externalizing activities which are not directly strategic;
- buying back shares when liquid assets are not allocated to sufficiently profitable projects (this is a function of the economic investment calculation).

Many directors admit that it is impossible to escape the demands made by the US and British investors.

But their demands are sometimes contradictory. For example, how can you concentrate on one activity without making acquisitions, which is often the only way possible? Now US and British investors are hostile to acquisition transactions, as they always weaken the concern involved. What is more, the effect of an acquisition on company structure lasts three or four years and this period very often corresponds to the time horizon of financial investment.

Submitting to the imperative of profitability

The debate with the US and British investors centres on the rate of financial return which the shareholders are entitled to expect of the firm. Return on equity (ROE) is generally calculated taking into consideration two parameters: the yield of government stocks on the one hand and a risk premium related to the activity or sector. One of the new indicators used today by international investors to gauge firms' financial performance is EVA™/MVA.[4] Using this technique, when determining the EVA™ the investor estimates *ex ante* the concern's available cash flow. This is done by fixing the difference between the net result after tax and the flow of liquidity necessary for the return on invested capital.

It should be remembered that the basic principle behind the investors' investment policies is to increase the economic and financial value transferred indirectly to their clients. As all funds invested by fund managers belong to clients and are managed under contract, investment managers must secure a return in line with that which clients are theoretically entitled to demand.

At the risk of being schematic, one can put forward the idea that the presence of pension funds on a company share register is ultimately motivated by the aim of making the invested funds yield a profit. The investment is required to comply with a profitability projection that in most cases turns out to be on average 15 percent per annum.

Joining the debate on shareholder value

Many company bosses have told us that we are today entering a period of intellectual revolution as far as company management is concerned. The necessity of making a profit clearly has repercussions for internal organization. Above all it is essential to make the objectives of financial profitability credible and to develop a discourse about financial performance. In this context, the fundamental attraction for the investor continues to be the return. But, for all that, the discourse on value should not be forgotten. It continues to be equally essential in sectors where there will be only a few operators.

The pension funds do not intervene in operational matters. The debate on shareholder value has only a single aim: to encourage company bosses to create value. It is this necessity that explains the logic behind the debate on corporate governance and the institutional bodies which go with it, particularly with regard to how they are composed: the boards of directors, independent administrators, payment and audit committees.

In the investors' opinion, the involvement of the directors is essential. They aim to encourage the managers to strive for value above all else by means of payment incentives linked to the performance achieved by the firms. The mechanism of payment by stock option – a system which in this context makes it possible to reconcile the interests of top managers and those of the shareholders – thus seems to be one of the vectors which these investors would like to see applied. The company directors are thus being asked to show their payment systems to the investors periodically.

Finally, the general feeling among the company bosses has softened somewhat with regard to the penetration by pension funds. Many think that it is not necessary to paint a diabolical picture of this movement, which is a way of modernizing the French capitalist system. The latter must take note of the shareholders' role and their requirements, and learn to live under their constant pressure to create value. Other French company bosses do not hesitate to express their feeling of helplessness in the face of the increasingly world-wide application of the idea of shareholder value. Yet others are more critical and denounce this veritable overweening verbosity, which they still have to learn all the same. But all acknowledge that it has now become impossible not to apply the precepts that arise from it.

CONCLUSION

The French system of ownership and management of equity is confronted by three problems: the very marked presence of Anglo-Saxon institutional investors in the ownership structures of the largest firms; an absence of national investors who are able to mobilize long-term savings; and a system of retirement which depends on the distribution of funds. These problems are exacerbated by the desire of the French government to reform retirement pensions around a new social compromise, whereby state pensions to individuals are to be supplemented by private pensions. The experience of Anglo-Saxon nations with pension schemes is relevant to such policy change, although the institutional context is different.

Under defined contribution (DC) schemes the significant feature is that it is employees who bear the risk, with no guarantees on rates of return or payouts. The responsibility of pension scheme trustees is to select fund managers on the basis of their past performance; the obligation here is that of the selection of managers, not their results. For the fund managers who operate in this fragmented industry, this creates a highly competitive situation where, in order to win business, they must demonstrate superior results. This encourages fund managers to pursue higher risk-return strategies with more explicit attempts to target equities and portfolios which will allow them to outperform the market. With this dual mechanism of hedging the risks, from the liabilities side onto the employee-pensioner and from the assets side onto the companies, the defined contribution pension fund manager represents a new type of institutionalized capitalism. By virtue of their weight and power relations, these new financial intermediaries are becoming the true masters of the financial valorization of capital and of how it should be allocated. Through introducing new norms about how firms operate, the fund managers are part of a new model of institutional capitalism which searches for shareholder value that can be transferred without the funds themselves taking any significant risk.

In contrast, under defined benefit (DB) pension schemes, whether state or privately funded, it is the employer who bears the financial risk of the under-performance of the funds. In assuming the obligation of results, trustees are likely to adopt a different approach to the selection of fund managers, leading to longer-term and more prudent investment policies. Not only are bonds very important in their portfolios, but their approach to equities is also intended to mini-mize the specific risk attached to each share or to each market in which the fund is exposed. In this way the investment funds are fully diversified. Although DB fund managers may be authors of corporate gov-ernance charters and may play an important role in the development of company management tech-niques, they are unlikely to make their presence felt by aggressive approaches to share buying.

There are thus advantages to both employees and industry of DB-oriented fund management (in con-trast to DC schemes). Hence it is important that policy makers distinguish between the different groups of financial investors and not assume that all will behave in the same way or that all will have the same consequences.

NOTES

This chapter is an abridged and updated summary of the first chapter of our report: 'Le modèle Français de détention et de gestion du capital: analyse, prospective et compara-isons internationales' (The French model of ownership and management: analysis, outlook and international comparisons), presented to the French Minister for the Economy, Finance and Industry in June 1998 and published by Editions de Bercy in September 1998.

1   One of our sources is interviews with about forty subjects with very different points of view: bosses of French companies, trade unionists and representatives from several government bodies. These interviews were held between 1 February and 15 March 1998. The company bosses were selected on the basis of two fundamental criteria: first, they belonged to a company quoted on the Paris Stock Exchange; second, the company was a French financially networked company which was involved in cross-shareholding networks. National and international databases provided a second source of information. The databases used were: DAFSA, MacCarthy, Dealer's Book, Spectrum, Lerep-Sisife. These enabled us to gather shareholding information on the largest French and foreign groups. Above all, they

helped us to grasp the significance of allowing institutional investors to buy shares in the largest firms.

2   One such example of this extremely rapid advance of foreign investors is given by developments at Société Générale where the share of foreign investors increased from 34.6 percent of the capital at the close of 1996 to 46 percent at the close of 1997.

3   In connection with this argument, one company boss explained rather testily that, in the road shows, the questions asked by investors such as Templeton or Fidelity are much the same as those asked of the CGT or CFDT.

4   EVA is a trademark of Stern Stewart.

REFERENCES

Bissara, P. (1997) 'L'identification des actionnaires des sociétés cotées' (under the chairmanship of), report to ANSA (Association Nationale des Sociétés Par Actions).

Blaine, M. (1995) 'Comparative contractual governance', in G. Boyd (ed.) *Competitive and Co-operative Macro-management: The Challenges of Structural Interdependence*, London: Elgar, pp. 67–106.

Camus, P. (1998) 'Assurer l'avenir de la place financière de Paris dans la perspective de la monnaie unique: les attentes des émetteurs' (under the chairmanship of), report of the working group to Europlace.

COB (1998) 'Les critères d'investissements des grands gestionnaires de fonds internationaux dans les entreprises françaises', 15 March.

Colin, M. (1996) 'Gouvernement d'entreprise, concurrence et performance', *Revue Economique* 27.

Davis, E. (1991) 'International diversification of institutional investors', *Bank of England, Discussion Papers Technical Series* no. 44.

—— (1995) *Pension Funds: Retirement-income Security, and Capital Markets: An International Perspective*, Oxford: Clarendon Press.

Dobbins, R., Witt, S. and Fielding, J. (1994) *Portfolio Theory and Investment Management*, 2nd edn, Oxford: Blackwell.

El Mekkaoui, N. (1996) 'Le cadre réglementaire et le comportement financier des fonds de pension dans les pays de l'OCDE', *Cahiers du Cerdo* 6, Université de Paris-IX Dauphine, Paris.

Elg, U. and Johansson, U. (1993) 'The institutions of industrial governance', *International Studies of Management & Organization* 23(1): 29–46.

Esambert, B. (1998) 'Le rachat par les sociétés de leurs propres actions' (under the chairmanship of), working group report to COB.

Farnetti, R. and Warde, I. (1997) 'Le modèle anglo-saxon en question', *Economica*, Paris.

Franks, J. and Mayer, C. (1996) 'Hostile takeovers and the correction of managerial failure', *Journal of Financial Economics* 40: 163–81.

French, K. and Poterba, J. (1991) 'Investor diversification and international equity markets', *American Economic Review* 81: 222–6.

Goldstein, M., Folkerts-Landau, D., Garber, P., Rojas-Suarez, L. and Spencer, M. (1993) 'International capital markets', part 1 in 'Exchange Rate Management and International Capital Flows', IMF, *World Economic and Financial Survey*, Washington.

Loulmet, L. (1998) 'L'évolution maitrisée du gouvernement d'entreprise au Japon face à la déreglementation financière et aux investisseurs institutionnels', *Revue d'Economie Financière* 49 (September): 173–87.

Métais, J. (1993) 'Un système financier international plus efficace?', in *L'Epargne*, under the direction of P. Artus, C. Bismut and D. Plihon, *Economica*, pp. 273–94.

Morin, F. (1996) 'Privatisation et dévolution des pouvoirs: le modèle français du gouvernement d'entreprise', *Revue Economique* 47(6): 1253–68.

—— (1998) 'Le modèle français de détention et de gestion du capital: analyse, prospective et comparaisons internationales', *Editions de Bercy*, Paris.

Pébereau, M. (1995) 'Le capitalisme français du XXI siècle' (under the chairmanship of), report to the Institut de l'Entreprise, April.

Punam, C. (1994) 'Are institutional investors an important source of portfolio investment in emerging markets?', Banque mondiale, *Working Paper*, no. 1243, January.

Rivaud-Danset, D. (1995) 'Les fonds de pensions anglo-saxons et les marchés financiers', in Montchrétien (ed.) *Rapport Moral sur l'argent dans le monde* Paris: AEF (Association d'Economie Financiére), pp. 119–20.

Sisife-Lerep database on cross shareholdings and share ownership, University of Toulouse, LEREPS.

6 "How Far Does the United Kingdom have a Market-based System of Corporate Governance? A Review and Evaluation of Recent Developments in the United Kingdom"

from Competition and Change (2005)

Andrew Pendleton

SUMMARY

This chapter questions the extent to which UK corporate governance fits the stereotypical market model. It is argued that the UK system displays features that sit uneasily with an emphasis on markets as the primary form of governance. A web of social relationships between investors and managers complements and to some extent substitutes for market-based discipline. Thus the United Kingdom possesses characteristics of relationship or network systems as well as those of market systems. Furthermore, it is argued that, contrary to the usual inferences from an apparently dispersed structure of ownership in the United Kingdom, investors are able to exert strong control of managers. This arises from a similarity of interests between investors, and involves some explicit forms of investor co-ordination. The chapter concludes with some observations on the utility of the two-systems model.

A two-systems view of the world dominates the comparative corporate governance literature. In this view, there are Anglo-American countries, reliant on arm's-length, market-based forms of governance, and relationship-based countries, where governance is exercised through large block holdings and 'insider' forms of monitoring (Rajan and Zingales 2003). Of late, there has been considerable debate about this distinction. One strand of research has questioned whether there is a single non-market model, whilst another has examined the extent to which relationship-based systems have evolved towards market-based systems. However, it has been assumed by most that Anglo-American countries continue to embody the main characteristics of market-based systems. This chapter questions whether this is the case by critically examining the extent to which the United Kingdom fits the stereo-typical model. It is argued that in some respects the United Kingdom is an exemplar of the market model but in others it displays features that sit uneasily with an emphasis on markets as the primary form of governance. A web of social relationships between investors and managers accompanies and increasingly substitutes for market-based discipline. There is considerable evidence of direct relationship-type contact between major investors and company managers, supplemented by various forms of institutional co-ordination amongst investors. Thus the United Kingdom may be seen as possessing characteristics of relationship or network systems as well as those of market systems. This raises the larger question as to whether the United Kingdom is converging to a relationship model or indeed whether a two-systems model is an appropriate way to carve up the corporate governance world.

The chapter therefore mounts an interpretation of the UK system of corporate governance which questions much of the conventional wisdom. It utilizes secondary evidence drawn from a wide variety of studies and sources, supplemented by some new interview-based data collected from a small number of investor trade associations and investors. Two interrelated aspects of the two-systems distinction are examined: structures of ownership, and market-based forms of shareholder discipline. The extent to which the United Kingdom fits the market model is considered for each of these. The chapter goes on to discuss non-market forms of corporate governance. It is argued that, contrary to the usual inferences from a dispersed structure of ownership, institutional investors are able to exert control over managers. Influence is mobilized through a variety of non-market, relational mechanisms. Occasionally, shareholder control is more explicit and directive. Investors' capacity to exert control over managers arises from a similarity of interests between investors (cf. Scott 1997) and the presence of institutions that co-ordinate their interests and activities. Finally, the conclusion raises some more general issues about convergence, co-ordination and the two-systems model. It is suggested that comparing market versus relational processes can be a useful way to analyse corporate governance, even though the distinctions between the two are blurred and complex. The danger resides in packaging these processes into simple, stereotypical models of national systems.

THE TWO-SYSTEMS PERSPECTIVE

In the corporate governance, political economy and business systems literature an enduring and widespread perspective has been a two-systems view of the world. The comparative corporate governance literature has persistently distinguished between market based systems of governance (typically the United States, the United Kingdom, Canada, Australia, New Zealand and Ireland) and other systems characterized by governance by relationships between firms and other actors (e.g. Hoskisson *et al.* 2004; Rajan and Zingales 2003). In some accounts the distinction is typified as between 'insider' and 'outsider' forms of governance (Franks and Mayer 1997; Mayer 1997). Insiders are large bloc holders, families and cross-owners, whilst outsiders are arm's-length institutional investors. Other observers contrast market governance with network-based governance (e.g. Moerland 1995). Some literatures widen the distinction to include inter-firm relationships and labour relations systems, and contrast liberal market economies with co-ordinated market economies (see Gospel and Pendleton 2003, 2004; Soskice 1999; Hall and Soskice 2001). In many cases the empirical basis of the distinction is just four countries: the United States and United Kingdom on the one hand and Germany and Japan on the other (as in Prowse 1995).

Moerland provides a succinct comparison of the two systems:

> Market-oriented systems are characterized by well developed financial markets, large-scale presence of open corporations with widely dispersed share ownership, and active markets for corporate control. Network-oriented systems are characterized by closely held corporations, group membership of corporations, and substantial involvement of universal banks in financing and controlling corporate firms. (1995: 448)

These structural features of finance and ownership systems are said to underpin distinct governance systems. Taking as a starting point the distinction between ownership and control identified by Berle and Means in the 1930s (1932), the wide dispersion of share ownership in the Anglo-Saxon model is seen to discourage active involvement of shareholders in governance, thereby giving managers considerable discretion to indulge in empire building and other self-interested behaviour (Rajan and Zingales 2003: 475). Investor passivity in governance increases the power of directors and company managements (Goergen and Renneboog 2001: 280). In these circumstances the main means by which equity owners can make their presence felt is by 'exit' rather than 'voice' (Hirschman 1972). Managerial discretion is therefore regulated by a market for corporate control and the attendant threat that incumbent managers may be replaced by new owners (Manne 1965). By contrast, the closer alignment of ownership, finance and control in countries like Germany and Japan is said to facilitate much closer and more informed monitoring by owners. Governance therefore takes a relationship-based or network-based form. Owners can be seen as insiders, with access to privileged information about the firm and a deep stake in its future. Investors have more direct power over managers but the lack of market-based competition in the supply of finance means that owners and investors are also locked in to a much greater extent than in market-based systems. It is therefore argued by some that this encourages long-term or 'patient' perspectives on the part of investors, in contrast to pressures towards short-termism in the Anglo-Saxon system (e.g. Hutton 1995). It also means that investors are more supportive of firms in distress (Hoshi *et al.* 1990).

Of late, this distinction has received a certain amount of critical conceptual and empirical scrutiny. A widespread criticism is that the relational/insider/network category lumps together a diverse group of governance and business systems in which the differences may be more important than the similarities (Allen 2004; Jackson 2004). Thus Rhenish corporate governance differs substantially from that in the Mediterranean or Latin countries such as France, Italy and Spain (see Goyer and Hancke 2004; Trento 2004; Aguilera 2004), and it may be appropriate to distinguish between Rhenish and Latin models (Weimar and Pape 1999). Japanese governance may be distinguished from that in other Asian countries (Whitley 1999). A second issue concerns the trajectory of corporate governance systems. An important stream of research in the last ten years has considered whether systems of corporate governance are converging. For the most part, this scrutiny has considered whether relational/insider/network countries are converging towards the market model, and has concentrated especially on Germany (Jackson *et al.* 2004; Vitols 2002; Lane 2003) and Japan (Araki 2004). Some have argued strongly that convergence is occurring (Hansmann and Kraakman 2000) whilst others argue that path-dependence means that national systems continue to display marked differences (Whitley 1999) or that the interplay of path-dependence and 'globalizing' pressures are generating hybrid models (Jackson 2004).

One issue which has not received so much attention is whether changes may be occurring in countries in the market category that take them away from the market model. This is perhaps not surprising, given that some of the most striking developments in comparative corporate governance in the last ten years have involved the development of more liquid equity markets in mainland Europe. However, there has been a series of notable developments in countries like the United Kingdom which raise the question as to whether a simple transactional model captures the complexity of corporate governance. For instance, a series of codes of conduct regulating corporate behaviour have been introduced, supplemented recently by 'soft' legislation requiring AGM votes on executive remuneration. There has been mounting pressure on major investors to take a more active role in the formal aspects of corporate governance, such as participation in AGMs. Some institutional investors such as Hermes have clearly championed the activist cause. It seems appropriate, therefore, to evaluate how far the market model provides an accurate portrayal of the current UK system of governance. In the next section the empirical evidence for assigning the United Kingdom to the market model is reviewed, alongside recent developments and their significance. Two dimensions of the market–relationship comparison structure the exposition: structures of ownership and the market for corporate control.

THE STRUCTURE OF OWNERSHIP OF UK LISTED FIRMS

The main basis for the argument that the United Kingdom has an 'outsider' or 'market'-based form of governance is the structure and composition of equity ownership. As is well known, a larger number of large UK firms are listed than in other European countries. For instance, in 2003 2,311 domestic firms were listed on the London Stock Exchange, compared with 684 in Germany (World Federation of Exchanges 2004). Total market capitalization of firms listed on the London-based markets was just over double that of Deutsche Börse in 2003 (ibid.). About 80 percent of the largest 700 companies in the United Kingdom are quoted (Franks and Mayer 1997).

The stylized facts of ownership structure in market systems are these: ownership is dispersed in market systems such that no single shareholder has control. This is especially so in the United Kingdom, where institutional investors have been the dominant investors for some years, and own a greater proportion of corporate equities than in any other of the market-

Investor type	% of total equity owned
Rest of the world	32.3
of which:	
North America	(31)
Europe	(36)
Asia	(22)
Insurance companies	17.3
Pension funds	16.1
Individuals	14.9
Unit trusts	2.0
Investment trusts	2.3
Other financial institutions	11.1
Charities	1.2
Private non-financial companies	0.7
Banks	2.2

Source: National Statistics (2003).

Table 6.1 **Beneficial ownership of UK shares in 2003**[1]

based systems (Table 1). These institutional investors (insurance companies, pension funds, unit trusts, investment trusts and other non-bank financial institutions) own just below 50 percent of equities. Overseas equity investment (32 percent of UK equities by value) is dominated by institutional investors, especially US-based ones (Golding 2001). Individuals own just under 15 percent of shares directly: this contrasts with the United States, where individual ownership continues to be considerably higher. A key point about dispersed institutional ownership is that institutional shareholders are motivated primarily or exclusively by financial returns rather than any 'private' benefits of control such as social status.

By contrast, ownership is far more concentrated in relationship or insider systems, with a single dominant or majority owner in many cases. In some systems, such as in the Latin countries, State or family owners are especially important. In other systems, banks play an important role: in Germany banks have been especially important as suppliers of credit, owners of shares and controllers of the voting rights of shares deposited with them (by households). Cross-ownership by other industrial firms is also very important. In Germany banks own about 13 percent and non-financial companies own just under 30 percent of Germany companies (see Jackson *et al.* 2004: 101). By contrast, the ownership stakes of these two groups in the United

Kingdom are negligible. The structure and concentration of ownership are such that, in countries like Germany, ultimate ownership often takes a pyramidal form. In countries such as Italy these pyramids are especially complex and often result in opaque control arrangements (see Trento 2004).

The relative dispersion of ownership in the United Kingdom has clearly emerged from a series of surveys and analyses of corporate ownership. Franks and Mayer (1997) found that just 16 percent of UK firms had a single shareholder owning 25 percent or more of the equity, compared with 79 percent in France and 95 percent in Germany. More recently, La Porta *et al.* (1999: 492–93) (using data for 1995) find that, using 20 percent ownership as a cut-off point, 100 percent of the largest twenty UK corporations based on market capitalization are widely held (the highest of the twenty-eight countries in their survey). Even when the cut-off point is reduced to 10 percent, the United Kingdom retains its position as the most widely held economy, with 90 percent of the top twenty firms being widely held. A comprehensive survey of nearly all listed firms in 1997 by Faccio and Lang (2002) found that 63 percent are widely held, i.e. there is no controlling owner with 20 percent of equity. This is considerably higher than other European countries (other than Ireland) in their study.

The United Kingdom, therefore, appears to be a paradigmatic case of the market/outsider system. However, there are a number of important qualifications that need to be made to this picture, and these have an important bearing on the nature of corporate control in the United Kingdom. These are: (1) UK firms are substantially owned by a small number of investors; (2) medium-size listed firms often have concentrated ownership by a single dominant owner; (3) institutional investment has become increasingly concentrated, so that a relatively small number of institutional investors dominate corporate ownership. These issues are dealt with in turn.

1. The focus on a single dominant owner in much of the literature diverts attention from the broader structure of ownership overall. A notable feature of UK ownership is that large shareholders other than the largest shareholder also hold substantial ownership stakes. Mayer (2000) finds that the second and third bloc holders hold 7.3 percent and 5.2 percent respectively. Even beyond the tenth largest bloc holding the mean voting bloc is greater than 3 percent. Franks and Mayer (1997) note that small coalitions of investors can now control 30 percent (the critical

point for mounting take-overs under the City Take-over Code). This contrasts with Germany, where other large owners besides the dominant owner tend to own much smaller proportions of total equity: thus there tends to be high ownership dispersion alongside a dominant owner(s). Even in mid-1970s' Britain, when ownership was more dispersed than today, Scott (1997: 90) found that the twenty largest share-holders owned substantial proportions of companies: in 60 percent of companies the twenty largest share-holders owned between 20 percent and 30 percent of the equity. By the early 1990s Prowse found that the mean stake owned by the five largest investors in a sample of eighty-five large manufacturing firms was 21 percent (1995).

The argument is therefore that ownership is concen-trated in a small group of investors rather than in a single owner. Scott (1997) refers to this ownership pattern as a 'constellation of interests'. If this group of owners has similar interests, or even co-ordinates its activities, the implications for control may be similar to where there is a single dominant owner. Thus the focus in much of the mainstream corporate governance lit-erature on the single largest bloc holder as a measure of control may be misplaced. Key empirical issues are whether the identity of owners is such that a 'constella-tion of interests' may be said to be present, and whether these owners combine together to exert explicit control. We return to this important question later.

2. The prevailing picture of dispersed ownership in the United Kingdom tends to be derived from the larger firms in the listed sector, and does not always fully capture the structure of ownership in the listed sector as a whole. Recent evidence indicates that, further down the exchange, ownership patterns are rather different. Looking at medium-size firms, La Porta *et al.* find that 40 percent have a family owner with a 20 percent stake, the same as in Germany. Sixty percent, however, are nevertheless widely held according to this definition, and this remains consid-erably greater than in relationship/insider countries. However, when the cut-off point is lowered to 10 percent a very different picture emerges. Only 10 percent of the UK firms are widely held, the same figure as for Germany. By contrast, 50 percent of US and 40 percent of Canadian medium-size firms are widely held. Sixty percent of UK firms have a domi-nant family owner, higher than comparable German and French firms. Other research indicates that other forms of insider ownership, such as directors' hold-ings, are important, especially in recent IPOs (Goergen

and Renneboog 2001). Faccio and Lang (2002) find that nearly a quarter of UK firms have a controlling family shareholder at the 20 percent level. Though this is substantially lower than in many other Euro-pean countries, it nevertheless indicates that there is some diversity in structures and characteristics of ownership in the UK listed sector. The continuing importance of family ownership in smaller quoted companies fits with the picture presented earlier by Chandler of the persistence of family ownership in the United Kingdom, as compared with the earlier devel-opment of managerially controlled firms and profes-sional management hierarchies in the United States (Chandler and Daems 1980).

3. UK institutional investment is becoming more highly concentrated as the larger institutions increase market share and as financial institutions merge or are taken over. For instance, the fifteen largest pension fund management firms have 71 percent of the pension fund market (HM Treasury 2001: 77). In turn the eighteen largest pension funds hold over half of total pension fund assets. Gaved (1998) found that half the UK equities in the UK stock market are owned by just fifty financial institutions, and that these institutions dominate the shareholder base of the FTSE 100. In fact the top ten institutional inves-tors own over a quarter of the UK market (Gaved 1998). Thus, even with portfolio diversification, it is inevitable that a relatively small number of major institutions are coming to own an increasing propor-tion of the equity of large UK listed companies. The tendency to concentration of ownership, both of individual firms and of the market as a whole, is assisted by the long-term decline in the number of listed firms, coupled with the aversion of many funds and institutions to smaller stocks because of liquid-ity problems and proportionally high transaction costs (see Golding 2001).

The portrayal of the United Kingdom as an exem-plar of dispersed ownership therefore needs to be qualified. Whilst the United Kingdom clearly has dis-persed ownership if the focus is a single dominant owner, this dispersion is less evident if other signifi-cant shareholders are brought into the equation. It is also apparent that ownership dispersion is most evident in the largest companies, and ownership structures can be rather different in other parts of the listed sector. When the focus is the investors them-selves, it is clear that the UK equity market is becom-ing more concentrated. This has important implications for the separation of ownership and control. If the ownership of firms is dominated by a small number of investors, with similar interests, then investors may be able to exert significant levels of control of management even though they may eschew direct involvement ('micro-management') in managerial decisions.

THE MARKET FOR CORPORATE CONTROL

An important aspect of the portrayal of market systems is that dispersed ownership leads to outsider forms of governance. It is generally argued, typically in a principal/agent framework, that market-based or 'outsider' forms of discipline are the principal forms of control available to owners (supplemented by legal protection of minority investors, as outlined by La Porta *et al.* 1998). The 'market for corporate control' (Manne 1965), whereby managers of under-performing firms may be replaced after a change of ownership, is a central element of the market paradigm. Central to this view of the importance of the take-over is the 'efficient capital market' hypothesis: the stock market is seen as capable of processing all available information about the value of a company's equity (Deakin and Slinger 1997: 127). Other observers have pointed to the managerial labour market as an additional control on management behaviour (Fama 1980; Stiglitz 1985).

A preference for market-based or outsider forms of control is said to derive from a number of sources. There is clearly a free-rider problem facing any investors choosing to take an activist or relational form of monitoring: they bear all the costs but share the gains. Furthermore, the structure of institutional investment in the United Kingdom is such that the controllers of equity stakes (pension fund managers, etc.) – what Gaved (1998: 22) terms the *de facto* operational owners – bear the costs of non-market intervention but the real or beneficial owners (pension funds) take the gains (see Short and Keasey 1997). Added to this, 'operational owners' such as fund managers face competitive pressures (and from their own shareholders) to deliver short-term returns because their performance is actively monitored (on a quarterly basis, in the case of funds), and this is said to encourage 'quick' market-based activity rather than 'patient' relationship building with firms (*ibid.*) Interventionist governance is also discouraged by conflicts of interest: pension fund managers derive business (investment bank services

as well as pension fund management) from firms, and are said to be wary of actions that might invite displeasure from potential clients. A further disincentive still to relationship forms of governance is legal regulation of 'insider trading'.

Dispersion of ownership, coupled with the structure of incentives described above, is said to underpin a market-based, 'outsider' form of discipline. The starkest example of market-based discipline is the take-over. Pagano and Volpin (2001) find that the United Kingdom had a higher level of mergers and acquisitions (M&A) activity per head of population than any other OECD country in the period 1990–97: 32.52 M&A deals per million population, compared with 23.73 in the United States, 10.11 in France, 9.03 in Germany and 0.48 in Japan (p. 46). Between 1993 and 1996 there were 283 agreed bids in the UK listed sector plus fifty-five contested bids (Deakin *et al.* 2002a: 17). The latter is of special significance, as it is the hostile take-over bid which is seen as a key device for shareholders to discipline managers in market-based systems. Franks and Mayer (1997) show that the number of hostile take-overs in countries like the United Kingdom far exceeds that in countries like Germany. Traditionally, Germany has had a low level of merger activity, with almost all mergers and acquisitions taking a friendly form, and driven by industrial rather than governance logic (Hopner and Jackson 2001: 15).

Although take-overs are a more prevalent feature of governance in countries like the United Kingdom, doubt has been cast on their efficacy as a discipline device. (1) They are an expensive way to discipline poorly performing managements, owing to the cost of surmounting management defences (i.e. meeting take-over premiums) and the transaction costs of changing ownership (Prowse 1995; Franks and Mayer 1997). Offers in excess of expected returns may signal that the bidder has information that the target firm will perform better than expected, thus providing an incentive for shareholders to retain their shares (unless very substantial premiums are offered) (Stiglitz 1985). As result, take-overs may be 'only important in correcting the most egregious cases of managerial laziness or incompetence' (Prowse 1995: 66), and may lack credibility for much of the time as a source of discipline (given that take-over activity also tends to be cyclical in incidence).

(2) Franks and Mayer (2000) have shown that the take-over market and hostile take-overs are not significantly related to poor performance. The majority

of hostile take-overs are not of poorly performing firms. Further, most take-overs in the United Kingdom are friendly rather than hostile: over 80 percent of take-overs in 1991–95 were agreed rather than contested (Deakin and Slinger 1997: 418). The majority of take-overs are motivated by concern to secure economies of scale or to expand the share of the product market (Froud *et al.* 2000) rather than to exert discipline. The use of mergers and take-overs as a growth strategy by firms, rather than as a governance device by investors, fits into a long tradition in the United Kingdom of growth by merger and acquisition (see Franks *et al.* 2004).

Although the presence of a large listed sector, coupled with a favourable regulatory environment, clearly facilitates restructuring activity, it should not be assumed that ownership is highly fluid. Indeed, large institutional shareholdings appear to be becoming more long-term. Gaved (1998) shows that the top ten shareholders in twenty of the largest listed UK companies changed their net ownership by very little over a two-year period (from 23.1 to 21.9 percent). Eighty-seven out of 200 holdings increased in size, and 112 decreased. The amount of buying and selling was almost evenly balanced, so that the average holding changed only from 2.3 percent in 1994 to 2.2 percent in 1996 (Gaved 1998: 28). Growth in long-term shareholding by major institutions is driven by a number of factors, including market concentration, lack of liquidity and the growth of 'passive' investing or indexing. The use of indexing strategies means that market activity is driven by the need to make periodic but often relatively small-scale adjustments to bring holdings in particular companies back into line with the index. A fund manager put it thus:

> The fact is that it's just not easy to get out at the top. Not for the bigger funds. For the likes of us that's definitely the case in the sense that if we have millions of pounds in a company and we start selling we are selling against ourselves, the share price will drop instantly and we don't do ourselves any favours, so we can't do it, and if we did do it it's a very long-drawn-out process. It takes weeks to offload the stock.

Given that market-based systems of corporate governance rely on trading to discipline managers, it would be anticipated that trading volumes in countries such as the United Kingdom would be relatively high. However, the evidence does not bear this out.

As Table 2 shows, in 2000–02 the average annual turnover ratio in the United Kingdom was 76 percent, similar to France and Japan but significantly lower than Germany and especially the United States. Trading velocity is just under three times smaller than in the United States.

UK trading volumes are, however, increasing. They rose from 37 percent of market capitalization in 1996 to 84 percent in 2002, the growth being more or less linear over the period. The absolute value of share trades increased in the same period from £741 billion to £1,876 billion, with the number of 'bargains' increasing from 11 million to 46 million (www.londonstockexchange.com). A notable feature of this growth is that the average size of share trades is falling, from £67,000 in 1996 to £40,000 in 2003. A number of distinct developments lie behind these figures. One is the growth in trading activity by individuals, taking advantage of Internet-based trading accounts (London Stock Exchange 2000). This accounts for the steep rise in the number of trades and the decline in their average size. The activities of hedge funds, of increasing importance in many economies, are also pushing up trading volumes. At the same time, trading activity by foreign investors (especially US-based investors) accounts for a substantial share of the rise in total trading value (London Stock Exchange 2000).

The evidence reported in this section suggests that the structure of ownership in the United Kingdom may increasingly be taking a dual form. On the one hand, a significant component of domestic institutional investment appears to be increasingly taking a long-term form. Insurance firms in particular emphasize the importance of long-term relationships with their investee companies. On the other hand, there has been a steep growth in hedge fund and speculative activity, which takes a very short-term market-oriented nature.

Country	Year			Annual average, 2000–02
	2000	2001	2002	
France	74	85	92	84
Germany	79	125	132	112
Japan	70	68	81	73
UK	67	78	84	76
US	201	201	210	204

Source: World Bank Development Indicators database.

Table 6.2 **Trading value as a proportion of market capitalization, 2000–2002**[2]

To this can be added the activities of overseas investors, who, for various reasons, may lack the capacity or inclination to engage in relationship-style investing. Of course, there has always been a diversity of investment approaches among investors. Charkham (1994a), for instance, draws attention to Type A and Type B investors: one holds stocks for the long term, the other seeks to maximize returns via active trading. What is notable in the current context is that divergent approaches to shareholding map on to divergent approaches to control and governance. Many of the largest domestic institutional investors accompany long-term holdings with relationship forms of governance and an active interest in the investee companies, whilst the more speculative investor groups rely solely or primarily on the market to generate short-term returns. This is not to say that investors necessarily restrict themselves to one form of activity. Holland (1995: 41) found that institutions classify their investments into three components: 'relationship' investment, where large stakes are held for the long term; 'stable stakeholder', where there is a long-term stake but some regular trading at the margin; and 'trader', where the orientation is short-term, transient and arm's-length. Institutions may therefore have a variety of approaches to governance. In the next section we consider the forms of relationship governance that characterize relationships between firms and their major institutional investors.

NEW FORMS OF GOVERNANCE

The combination of increasingly concentrated and stable ownership among some institutional investors has important implications for corporate governance and the separation of ownership and control. These are considered with reference to relationships between firms and investors, and to forms of co-ordination between investors. The evidence indicates that relational activity is a central component of governance activity, and that the relative dispersion of ownership is counteracted by co-ordination among major investors.

The private governance of public companies

A series of studies from the mid-1990s onwards has established that the institutional investment community is active in monitoring firms, with much of this process revolving around private meetings between companies and fund managers. These meetings facilitate private voluntary disclosure of information by companies to supplement that found in public releases of information. Holland has described how 'close financial institution–company links revolve around co-operative stable relationships, with regular meetings and other channels for two-way flows of information, and feedback mechanisms after meetings. These relationships are comparable in many ways to close [commercial] bank–corporate relations' (1995: 19). These meetings are viewed by fund managers as their most important source of information on companies. The information exchanged at these meetings is also seen as higher-quality than that made available publicly. Furthermore, they are seen as one of the most effective means by which investors can influence company managements (Barker 1998; Holland 1998a). This 'hidden world of informal monitoring' (Black and Coffee, 1994) substitutes for monitoring activity in public arena, such as the annual general meeting, which is seen by investors as far less effective (Holland 1998a). Thus investor quiescence in AGMs and a disinterest in voting should not be viewed as proof that investors in UK firms prefer to rely primarily on 'outsider', transactional forms of governance rather than 'insider', relational means.

The evidence indicates that firms meet their main investors once or twice a year, typically around formal financial announcements, supplemented occasionally by ad hoc meetings (Barker 1998; Holland 1998a; Hendry et al. 1997). Investors monitor around 250–300 firms in this way each year. These firms tend to be those in which a substantial stake is held: governance is more passive, or dominated by an outsider approach, where the stake is smaller. From a company point of view, the most important function of these meetings is to maintain and improve corporate financing capability and to defend against the possibility of take-overs (Hill 1995; Holland 1998a). For investors, the meetings enable them to assess the quality of management and the viability of business strategies. For both sides, it is clear that building trust and confidence in each other is a central aspect of this process. In other words, it is about building a sustainable relationship (see Hendry et al. 1997; Holland 1995, 1998a; Barker, 1998). Such a relationship is one in which there will be 'no surprises' (a common mantra in respondents' comments).

A critical question is whether these relationships exist simply for the exchange of information or whether they permit the mobilization of influence. In other words, do they generate active governance processes? The evidence indicates that they do, though the exercise of control often takes an implicit or 'non-decision' form. Hence, even taking into account the concern of the parties not to publicize the content of these relationships, it can be difficult to assess who has control. From the company point of view, there is some evidence that managers aspire to present the company in a light that helps to maintain the loyalty of preferred types of investor (see Deakin *et al.* 2002b). Roberts *et al.* (2004) emphasize the exercise of implicit influence via managers' perceived need to present themselves and their company in a light that will impress fund managers. Company managers adopt the views and language of investors – primarily that of 'shareholder value' – to win the approval of such shareholders. The discipline of governance is therefore realized by anticipation of what investors will want.

Investors' interests focus on three aspects of corporate activity: the basis of financial results and projected results, corporate strategy, and the capacity of top managers to realize that strategy and achieve projected financial outcomes (Hill 1995; Hendry *et al.* 1997; Holland, 1998a, b). Where managers propose a major change in corporate strategy, 'soundings' of major investors are generally undertaken. If investors are strongly critical of management proposals, they may be abandoned (Hill 1995). In this way, investors guide the business by setting parameters to management decisions. Within these parameters, however, there is a strong and shared ideology that investors should not 'micro-manage'. Thus managers have considerable autonomy in day-to-day management and the implementation of business strategy. This helps to explain why many large firms emphasize 'shareholder value' but may also display diversity in how they go about achieving it. Investors exercise control through setting the parameters of management decision making, supplemented by gentle 'nudges' to keep managers on course. Meanwhile, managers attempt to anticipate what shareholders want because it is in their career and remuneration interests to do so.

On occasion, the exercise of influence and governance by institutional investors may be far more explicit. These circumstances include a breakdown of relations between a company and its major investors, dramatic and unforeseen changes to the company and its prospects, and occasions where the company seeks help from its investors. When these situations occur, core investors may provide 'strong advice' to the management, with the presumption that such advice will be heeded. Where it is not, investors may take their dispute into the open by leaking to the press or mounting a challenge at the AGM. In either case the aim is to exercise governance by 'naming and shaming'. A non-executive director interviewed by Hill succinctly describes the type of processes at work:

First they [major investors] can use their influence by taking the chairman or perhaps another non-executive quietly to one side and telling him they're not happy with the way things are going – that's usually enough, but if it doesn't work they have to go and start threatening the management, that unless you do something we propose to take some sort of action. Not something you see happening frequently, but it happens quietly, and more often than you read in the press. (Hill 1995: 259).

In serious cases of management malpractice or incompetence, investors may seek the replacement of the management. For instance, in the Marconi debacle in 2001 major investors secured the resignation of the chief executive within a couple of days of the news that the company's order book had been grossly inflated. The crime: breach of trust. In extreme cases, it is speculated (though hard evidence is difficult to obtain) that core investors may stimulate takeover bids via their influence with other investee companies (Holland 1998b).

These governance processes are similar in many respects to those found in economies characterized as relationship systems. They are not new processes as such but they seem to have changed in form and become more important in recent years. Prior to reforms of the stock market in the mid-1980s, intermediaries were more important in the transmission of information between firms and major investors. Now, with the creation of US-style investment banks, fund managers have taken on more direct involvement, with 'sell-side analysts' declining in importance, at least in this respect (Golding 2001; Barker 1998). At the same time, this form of governance has become more important, because growing concentration of ownership has reduced the costs of monitoring and has functioned to lock in major investors (Parkinson 1993: 163).

Investor co-ordination and control

To argue that a group of investors exercise control requires demonstration that they consciously act in concert or, less strongly, that they explicitly share some common interests which lead them to act in very similar ways, even if formal or explicit co-ordination is absent. An argument for the weaker form of co-ordination has been advanced by John Scott (1997: 48–51). He argues that firms in countries like the United Kingdom are owned by a 'constellation of interests' – investors with similar interests and objectives – that lead them to act in broadly similar ways, even though they lack formal co-ordination and collective organization. Even though these investors compete with each other, the similarity of objectives means that there is a common if unco-ordinated pursuit of similar goals. These goals are typically those of 'shareholder value' in the UK case. Growing concentration of ownership in recent years, coupled with concentration of institutional investment, appears to enhance these 'constellations of interests'.

There is also evidence for the stronger version of the argument, that investors engage in co-ordinated activity. Institutional investors have created institutions that enable them to mobilize influence over corporations, even though they are usually reluctant to collaborate directly in the governance of particular firms. However, on some occasions major investors do combine together to directly influence the management of firms.

As evidence of institutional co-ordination, the major institutional investor groups each have trade associations (Association of British Insurers, National Association of Pension Funds, Investment Management Association, etc.), which in turn have an overall industry co-ordinating body (the Institutional Shareholder Committee). The recently reissued statement of principles by the Institutional Shareholders' Committee – *The Responsibilities of Institutional Shareholders and Agents* – provides for collective regulation by outlining the grounds and forms of governance intervention. The grounds for intervention include concern about company strategy, performance, restructuring activity, internal controls, remuneration, corporate social responsibility, etc. Intervention may take the form of meetings with management, co-ordinated activity with other investors, and AGM resolutions. The various codes of practice – the City Code on Take-overs, the Combined Code, etc. – can all be seen as consequences of the mobilization of collective interest by institutional shareholders and finance professionals (Deakin *et al.* 2002a).

Investor association bodies play an explicit and active role in corporate governance practice as well as establishing a floor of core principles of governance and intervention. For instance, both the ABI and NAPF operate a monitoring service on AGM resolutions, especially concerning directors' pay and directors' independence. The ABI service is an advisory one but the NAPF makes voting recommendations to its members. However, the ABI takes an activist role 'behind the scenes' by mobilizing significant investors when a company appears to be non-compliant and is unresponsive in initial discussions with ABI personnel. Typically a 'special committee' of four or five institutional investors is brought together to exert pressure on offending firms. A trade association representative described his role (when discussing executive remuneration) as follows:

> I look through the scheme in draft form. My role is to consult our members, representing their views in discussions with advisers and the company. My job is to seek clarification and improved terms. We have meetings when the balance of discussion requires it or requires face to face negotiations. Involving our members adds weight ... Our general approach is to go for quiet non-publicity.

There is also evidence that institutions share information among themselves via informal networks. Holland (1998a) notes that institutions are prepared to share information on management qualities, personalities and performance records, though not information on their assessment of company strategy and their valuation of the company. As another trade association representative put it:

> I think most individuals in the corporate governance circle know each other so I would not be surprised to find an e-mail ... which might say 'Have you seen the draft proposals that such-and-such company wishes to introduce in a new share incentive scheme? I have reservations concerning points 1, 6, and 8. Does anyone have similar feelings?' That type of informal approach or informal exchange of information goes on. A corporate governance specialist in the fund management arm of a leading insurance firm talked about similar processes, and the network created by

people in other insurance firms and pension fund managers: I think the individual firms are taking more of an interest (in governance) and individual firms have got other means of networking with each other (besides the trade associations) ... Now we all come together in a forum of our own and those that are interested get together so those that are likely to vote against management [of investee companies] are the ones that meet to exchange views. We're a much more cohesive group ... if we don't like something we tend to take a robust view.

Before the forum was established:

we knew of each other and we all did the same thing but we were doing it in isolation and every so often we would ring each other and say, 'Did you see that? What do you think of this?' and I think that feeling that we could be a lot more powerful if we were getting together ... so we formed this group and we went out and spoke to all these other investment managers and anybody interested.

Finally, small groups of institutional investors occasionally form coalitions to intervene in specific companies. This typically occurs when an investee company is in distress (see Black and Coffee 1994). Solomon and Solomon (1999: 293) found that 84 percent of unit trust managers had formed coalitions with other institutions in these circumstances. The convention is that the largest single shareholder or the most substantially 'over-weighted' institution (i.e. where the share of the company is greater than its share of the market as a whole) takes the lead in forming the coalition. Several courses of actions are open to the coalition in attempting to influence management. The first is to send signals and messages via the media registering concern about the company. The second is to meet the management of the company to explore how the company proposes to address the concerns raised by the coalition. These meetings occur privately (though often with considerable advance publicity in the press) and may take a 'gentlemanly' form such as a private dinner in the City. Such coalitions, in the words of Black and Coffee (1994: 2052), are 'an out of the ordinary event – neither extraordinary nor frequent'.

So it is not just the case that institutional investors share common interests, as in the 'weak' form of the 'constellation of interests' argument. There are tiers of co-ordinated activity, involving active trade associations and federations, as well as *ad hoc* and informal networks and alliances. These institutions have given rise over the years to a web of rules and conventions that govern corporate actions, and provide mechanisms and opportunities for investor interventions. These include the well publicized codes of conduct on board composition and executive remuneration (now consolidated in the Combined Code), and codes of practice operated by individual trade associations such as the ABI. These are increasingly supplemented by codes of practice operated by individual institutional investors. Intervention in governance on particular issues may involve trade associations directly, groups of investors marshalled by investors, self-selected groups of investors, and individual investment firms. As yet, though, we know little about configurations of investor activity and co-ordination or of the determinants of the nature of this activity. We don't know why trade associations may take the lead on one issue but not on another. Regulation of insider trading and the provisions of the Takeover Code will place limits on the extent of co-ordination and intervention, but how these parameters affect practices and processes of co-ordination is not clear. Further research is needed to delineate such activities more precisely, though it is not likely to be easy. Much of this activity is secret and behind the scenes, reflecting long-standing traditions in the City.

CONCLUSION

Social relationships between listed firms and institutional investors, and within the investment community itself, are clearly very important components of contemporary corporate governance in the United Kingdom. The evidence suggests that firm–investor relationships in particular have become more important in the last twenty years or so, with firms and their top managers now devoting considerable resources to 'investor relations'. Much of the time of chief executives and finance directors is spent managing relationships with major shareholders (see Pye 2001). Relationship forms of governance have become more important because of an amalgam of interrelated developments, including concentration of investment funds and fund managers, a decline in liquidity, and the diffusion of indexing investment strategies. As liquidity diminishes, relationships become a more compelling form of governance (Rajan and Zingales 2003): active governance is a response to the risks associated with illiquidity. Another response is to seek new, liquid investments: the entry of insurance companies and pension fund managers into speculative forms of investment activity, such as hedging, has occurred alongside relational governance of companies that form core investments.

Although relationship governance is increasing in importance, social relationships between these actors are by no means new. In particular, the financial community in the City of London has long been characterized by a 'clubby' and inward-looking culture, with a tight and complex web of social ties between and among individuals and financial firms (see Augar 2000; Kynaston 2001). As for firm–investor relations, a recent historical exploration by Franks *et al.* (2004) has demonstrated the critical importance of 'trust' from the turn of the twentieth century onwards. Contrary to the implications of the La Porta *et al.* thesis, trust functioned in lieu of formal investor protection and enabled dispersed ownership to develop in the first half of the twentieth century. Other material has emphasized the traditional preference for private, quiet and behind-the-scenes relationships between firms and investors (Black and Coffee 1994), in contrast to a more overt and explicit approach in the United States. This cultural, and path-dependent, aspect of UK corporate governance has tended to be obscured by a number of factors in recent years, including the deregulatory shock of Big Bang in the 1980s, episodic bouts of take-over activity and the appeal of the two-systems model to academics interested in corporate governance.

This raises the question of the merits of a two-systems conceptualization of corporate governance. Division of the world into two systems, one based on impersonal market transactions and the other on relationships, always ran the risk of simplifying complex social and economic systems, and obscuring characteristics that do not readily fit with the model. As Rajan and Zingales (2003) show, elements of both approaches may be found within national economies: some sectors may be characterized by relational forms of finance and governance whilst others may adhere more closely to the market model. However, deeper criticisms can be made of the conceptualizations of the two systems. An institutionalist critique would argue that markets are rarely purely transactional. In the real world markets are governed by socially determined norms and regulations, and are populated by actors who create and follow these social conventions (Aguilera and Jackson 2003). A good case in point is the City of London which, prior to 'Big Bang', had a complex social division of functions governed by an amalgam of formal and informal regulation. Ironically, since 'Big Bang', the adoption of IT-based trading activity, and the development of speculative forms of investment activity, equity transactions may have become more impersonal. However, as this chapter has shown, transaction-based governance is increasingly supplemented by relation-ships between investment institutions and companies, and between institutions. Indeed it could be argued, in a context of long-term and fairly stable investments, that equity transactions serve as an instrument and signal in the 'playing out' of relationships, alongside other market activity, such as managerial labour markets. So, in addition to an inevitable social dimension to markets, UK corporate governance is characterized by a distinct set of social relationships between key actors in which market transactions may be just one of several instruments.

So is the two-system model worth keeping? To some extent, an answer to this question depends on what is happening in other national systems that are usually ascribed to the market camp (the United States, Australia, Canada, Ireland, etc.). Recent work in the United States has also cast some doubt on a 'simple' market characterization of that national system (e.g. Pound 1993). However, as yet there is not a sufficient body of compelling evidence from across this range of economies to make an informed judgement on this issue. Another answer is provided by the convergence literature, which argues that European economies are converging to market models, and very occasionally that market systems are also converging towards relational systems (e.g. Thomsen 2004). A strand within this literature suggests that the interaction of pressures emanating from market systems (e.g. US foreign investment) with path-dependent national governance traditions leads to the creation of hybrids (e.g. Jackson 2004). The description of the contemporary UK system presented here certainly suggests a hybrid: the United Kingdom has elements of market and relational systems of governance.

The implication of this literature is that the two-systems model can be a useful analytical starting point even if it is unlikely to manifest itself in a straightforward way in the real world. However, the logic of our argument is that reference to distinct and varied market and relational processes is preferable to bundling these into a single characterization for each country. In each national system there is likely to be a complex amalgam of market and relational dimensions to governance whose richness may be lost if they are compressed into a simple stereotype. For instance, it is clear that the United Kingdom has more dispersed ownership than many European economies (despite the qualifications registered earlier) but that does not mean, as is often argued, that UK institutional investors are unable to exert relational forms of governance.

This leads us to a final point concerning control and power in corporate governance.The UK system presents us with a paradox in this respect. For the most part, large listed companies in the United Kingdom stress their obligations to shareholders over and above those to other stakeholders, and the language of 'shareholder value' is an ingrained part of corporate discourse (Froud *et al.* 2000). Yet why should firms be so beholden to their shareholders, given the relative dispersion of ownership? The answer in the conventional wisdom is the market for corporate control. Yet take-over activity is cyclical and episodic, and the evidence suggests that it is a poor instrument for correcting managerial failure (Franks *et al.* 2004). The answer provided here is the co-ordination of institutional investors via various institutions and networks.

Scott's notion of a 'constellation of interests' is useful for considering the mobilizationof influence by institutional investors. Hitherto this concept has been criticized on thegrounds that similarity of interests does not equate with purposive co-ordination, and that evidence of such co-ordination is rather scant (Wright and Chiplin 1999). In this chapter, drawing on both primary and secondary data, we have shown that institutional investors engage in co-ordinated governance activity in a variety of ways. These include active trade associations, codes of conduct, informal networks and occasionally coalitions. These networks are facilitated by the geographical concentration of domestic investment management activity in the City of London, and the social and labour market ties between key actors. The traditional quiescence of institutional investors at AGMs should therefore not be misinterpreted: such investors had other means of exerting influence. Furthermore, whilst codes of conduct have become increasingly important in the last fifteen years, they should be viewed as a manifestation of a broader phenomenon.

Co-ordination of governance activity by institutional investors sits oddly with thetwo-systems model in other respects than those mentioned above. It is worth recalling that the 'varieties of capitalism' literature contrasts liberal market economies (e.g. the United Kingdom) with co-ordinated market economies. In general, UK industrial firms indeed display low co-ordination, as Hall and Soskice point out (2001). Employers' associations, for instance, have been in decline for many years, in part due to the pressures exerted on firms by strong shareholders. Yet the institutional investors themselves display strong forms of co-ordinated activity: there is a dense network of ties between them, and various institutions have been created. How this has come about, and how it operates, needs further investigation. This would provide a useful contribution to further examination of the role of co-ordinated, relational activity in corporate governance.

ACKNOWLEDGEMENTS

Data were collected during a study in 2001–02 of the regulation of employee share plans and executive remuneration, financed by the European Foundation for the Improvement of Living and Working Conditions.

NOTES

1 Computed using information from HM Treasury (2001) and pension fund assets in National Statistics (2000).
2 Assets under management by European hedge fund managers grew by over 170 percent between 2003 and 2004, from US$125 billion to US$216 billion. About a quarter of assets in management are invested in European equities. Seventy percent of European hedge fund assets are operated by UK-based managers. (Source: www.eurohedge.com.) It is not possible to identify precisely the total value of equity trading by hedge fund managers, as such activity is not currently reportable.

REFERENCES

Aguilera, R. (2004) Corporate governance and employment relations: Spain in the context of Western Europe, in H. Gospel and A. Pendleton (eds) *Corporate Governance and Labour Management. An International Comparison* (Oxford, Oxford University Press).

Aguilera, R., and Jackson, G. (2003) The cross-national diversity of corporate governance: dimensions and determinants, *Academy of Management Review* 28, pp. 447–65.

Allen, M. (2004) The varieties of capitalism paradigm: not enough variety? *Socio-economic Review* 2, pp. 87–108.

Araki, T. (2004) Corporate governance, labour and employment relations in Japan: the future of the stakeholder model, in H. Gospel and A. Pendleton (eds) *Corporate Governance and Labour Management. An International Comparison* (Oxford, Oxford University Press).

Augar, P. (2000) *The Death of Gentlemanly Capitalism* (London, Penguin Books).

Barker, R. (1998) The market for information: evidence from finance directors, analysts, and fundmanagers, *Accounting and Business Research* 29, pp. 3–20.

Berle, A. A., and Means, G. (1932) *The Modern Corporation and Private Property* (New York, Macmillan).

Black, B., and Coffee, J. (1994) Hail Britannia: institutional investor behavior under limited regulation, *Michigan Law Review* 92, pp. 1997–2087.

Chandler, A., and Daems, H. (1980) *Managerial Hierarchies. Comparative Perspectives on the Rise of the Modern Industrial Enterprise* (Cambridge MA, Harvard University Press).

Charkham, J. (1994a) *Keeping Good Company* (Oxford, Oxford University Press).

Charkham, J. (1994b) A larger role for institutional investors, in N. Dimsdale and M. Prevezer (eds) *Capital Markets and Corporate Governance* (Oxford, Clarendon Press).

Deakin, S., and Slinger, G. (1997) Hostile take-overs, corporate law, and the theory of the firm. *Journal of Law and Society* 24, pp. 124–51.

Deakin, S., Hobbs, R., Nash, D., and Slinger, G. (2002a) Implicit contracts, take-overs, and corporate governance: in the shadow of the City code, Centre for Business Research Working Paper 254 (Cambridge, ESRC).

Deakin, S., Hobbs, R., Konzelmann, S., and Wilkinson, F. (2002b) Partnership, ownership and control: the impact of corporate governance on employment relations, *Employee Relations* 24, pp. 335–52.

Faccio, M., and Lang, L. (2002) The ultimate ownership of Western European corporations, *Journal of Financial Economics* 65, pp. 365–95.

Fama, E. (1980) Agency problems and the theory of the firm, *Journal of Political Economy* 88, pp. 288–307.

Franks, J., and Mayer, C. (1997) Corporate ownership and control in the UK, Germany and France, in D. Chew (ed.) *Studies in International Corporate Finance and Governance Systems* (New York, Oxford University Press).

Franks, J., and Mayer, C. (2000) Governance as a Source of Discipline, paper prepared for the Company Law Review Committee E on Corporate Governance, www.dti.gov.uk.

Franks, J., Mayer, C., and Rossi, S. (2004) Ownership. Evolution and Regulation, unpublished paper (London Business School).

Froud, J., Haslam, C., Johal, S., and Williams, K. (2000) Restructuring for shareholder value and its implications for labour, *Cambridge Journal of Economics* 24, pp. 771–97.

Gaved, M. (1998) *Institutional Investors and Corporate Governance. Proposal for a Code of Disclosure*, Issue Paper 3 (London, Foundation for Business Responsibilities).

Goergen, M., and Renneboog, L. (2001) Strong managers and passive institutional investors in the United Kingdom, in F. Barca and M. Becht (eds) *The Control of Corporate Europe* (Oxford, Oxford University Press).

Golding, T. (2001) *The City. Inside the Great Expectation Machine* (London, Financial Times/PrenticeHall).

Gospel, H. (1992) *Markets, Firms, and the Management of Labour in Modern Britain* (Cambridge, Cambridge University Press).

Gospel, H., and Pendleton, A. (2003) Finance, corporate governance, and the management of labour: a conceptual and comparative analysis, *British Journal of Industrial Relations* 41, pp. 557–82.

Gospel, H., and Pendleton, A. (2004) Corporate governance and labour management: an international comparison, in H. Gospel and A. Pendleton (eds) *Corporate Governance and Labour Management. An International Comparison* (Oxford, Oxford University Press).

Goyer, M., and Hancke, B. (2004) Labour in French corporate governance: the missing link, in H. Gospel and A. Pendleton (eds) *Corporate Governance and Labour Management. An International Comparison* (Oxford, Oxford University Press).

Hall, P., and Soskice, D. (2001) An introduction to varieties of capitalism, in P. Hall and D. Soskice (eds) *Varieties of Capitalism* (Oxford, Oxford University Press).

Hansmann, H., and Kraakman, R. (2000) The End of History for Corporate Law, Yale International Center for Finance Working Paper 00-09 (New Haven CT, ICF).

Hendry, C., Woodward, S., Harvey-Cooke, J., and Gaved, M. (1997) *Investors' Views of People Management* (London: Institute of Personnel and Development).

Hill, S. (1995) The social organization of boards of directors, *British Journal of Sociology* 46, pp. 245–78.

Hirschman, A. (1972) *Exit, Voice, and Loyalty. Response to Decline in Firms, Organizations, and States* (Cambridge MA, Harvard University Press).

HM Treasury (2001) *Institutional Investment in the UK. A Review* (London, HM Treasury).

Holland, J. (1995) *The Corporate Governance Role of Financial Institutions in their Investee Companies*, Research Report 46 (London, Chartered Association of Certified Accountants).

Holland, J. (1998a) Private disclosure and financial reporting, *Accounting and Business Research* 28, pp. 255–69.

Holland, J. (1998b) Influence and intervention by financial institutions in their investee companies, *Corporate Governance* 6, pp. 249–64.

Höpner, M. and Jackson, G. (2001) *An Emerging Market for Corporate Control? The Mannesmann Takeover and German Corporate Governance*, Discussion Paper 01/4 (Cologne, Max Planck Institute).

Hoshi, T., Kashyap, A. and Scharfstein, D. (1990) The role of banks in reducing the cost of financial distress in Japan, *Journal of Financial Economics* 27, pp. 67–88.

Hoskisson, R., Yiu, D. and Kim, H. (2004) Corporate governance systems: effects of capital and labor market congruency on corporate innovation and global competitiveness, *Journal of High Technology Management Research* 15, pp. 293–315.

Hutton, W. (1995) *The State We're In* (London, Vintage).

Jackson, G. (2004) Towards a comparative perspective on corporate governance and labour management: enterprise coalitions and national trajectories, in H. Gospel and A. Pendleton (eds) *Corporate Governance and Labour Management. An International Comparison* (Oxford, Oxford University Press).

Jackson, G., Höpner, M. and Kurdelbusch, A. (2004) Corporate governance and employees in Germany: changing linkages, complementarities, and tensions, in H. Gospel and A. Pendleton (eds) *Corporate Governance and Labour Management. An International Comparison* (Oxford, Oxford University Press).

Kynaston, D. (2001) *The City of London* IV, A Club No More, 1945–2000 (London, Chatto and Windus).

Lane, C. (2003) Changes in corporate governance of German corporations: convergence to the Anglo-American model? *Competition and Change* 7, pp. 79–100.

La Porta, R., Lopez de Silanes, F. and Vishny, R. (1998) Law and finance, *Journal of Political Economy* 106, pp. 1113–55.

La Porta, R., Lopez de Silanes, F. and Shleifer, A. (1999) Corporate ownership around the world, *Journal of Finance* 54, pp. 471–517.

Lazonick, W., and O'Sullivan, M. (2000) Maximising shareholder value: a new ideology for corporate governance, *Economy and Society* 29, pp. 13–35.

London Stock Exchange (2000) *Survey of London Stock Exchange Transactions* (London, London Stock Exchange).

Manne, H. (1965) Mergers and the market for corporate control, *Journal of Political Economy* 3, pp. 110–20.

Mayer, C. (1997) Corporate governance, competition, and performance, *Journal of Law and Society* 24, pp. 152–76.

Mayer, C. (2000) Institutions in the New Europe. The Transformation of Corporate Organization, presented at the first Saint-Gobain Foundation for Economics conference 'What do we Know about Institutions in the New Europe?' Paris, November.

Moerland, P. (1995) Alternative disciplinary mechanisms in difference corporate systems, *Journal of Economic Behaviour and Organization* 26, pp. 17–34.

National Statistics (2004) *Share Ownership. A Report on the Ownership of Shares at 31st December 2003* (London, Office for National Statistics).

Pagano, M., and Volpin, P. (2001) The Political Economy of Corporate Governance, Centre for Economic Policy Research Discussion Paper 2682 (London: CEPR).

Parkinson, J. (1993) *Corporate Power and Responsibility. Issues in the Theory of Company Law* (Oxford, Clarendon Press).

Pound, J. (1993) The rise of the political model of corporate governance and control, *New York University* Law Review 68, pp. 1003–71.

Prowse, S. (1995) Corporate governance in an international perspective: a survey of corporate control mechanisms among large firms in the US, UK, Japan and Germany, *Financial Markets, Institutions and Instruments* 4, pp. 1–63.

Pye, A. (2001) Corporate boards, investors, and their relationships: accounts of accountability and corporate governing in action, *Corporate Governance* 9, pp. 186–95.

Rajan, R. and Zingales, L. (2003) Financial systems, industrial structure, and growth, *Oxford Review of Economic Policy* 17, pp. 467–82.

Roberts, J., Sanderson, P., Barker, R. and Hendry, J. (2004) In the Mirror of the Market. The Disciplinary Effects of Company/Fund Manager Meetings, unpublished paper, University of Cambridge.

Scott, J. (1997) *Corporate Business and Capitalist Classes* (Oxford, Oxford University Press).

Short, H. and Keasey, K. (1997) Institutional shareholders and corporate governance in the United Kingdom, in K. Keasey, S. Thompson and M. Wright (eds) *Corporate Governance. Economic and Financial Issues* (Oxford, Oxford University Press).

Solomon, A. and Solomon, J. (1999) Empirical evidence of long-termism and shareholder activism in UK unit trusts, *Corporate Governance* 7, pp. 288–300.

Soskice, D. (1999) Divergent production regimes: co-ordinated and unco-ordinated market economies in the 1980s and 1990s, in H. Kitschelt, P. Lange, G. Marks and J. Stephens (eds) *Continuity and Change in Contemporary Capitalism* (Cambridge: Cambridge University Press).

Stiglitz (1985) Credit markets and control capital, *Journal of Money, Credit and Banking*, 17, pp. 133–152.

Thomsen, S. (2004) Convergence of corporate governance systems to European and Anglo-American standards, in A. Grandori (ed.) *Corporate Governance and Firm Organization* (Oxford, Oxford University Press).

Trento, S. (2004) Corporate governance and industrial relations in Italy, in H. Gospel and A. Pendleton (eds) *Corporate Governance and Labour Management. An International Comparison* (Oxford, Oxford University Press).

Vitols, S. (2002) Shareholder value, management culture and production regimes in the transformation of the Germany chemical-pharmaceutical industry, *Competition & Change* 6, pp. 309–25.

Weimar, J., and Pape, J. (1999) A taxonomy of systems of corporate governance, *Corporate Governance* 17, pp. 152–66.

Whitley, R. (1999) *Divergent Capitalisms. The Social Structuring and Change of Business Systems* (Oxford, Oxford University Press), 2003.

World Federation of Exchanges (2003) Annual statistics, Paris: World Federation of Exchanges.

Wright, M., and Chiplin, B. (1999) Corporate governance and control: beyond managerialism and Marxism, *Human Relations* 52, pp. 1189–204.

TWO

PART THREE

Convergence or Diversity of Governance Systems?

INTRODUCTION TO PART THREE

The question of whether the countries of Europe will converge towards a common corporate governance system, or sustain the present diversity of institutions is one of the key issues facing the continent. Despite the pressures towards adopting Anglo-Saxon modes of corporate governance, the divergences in both the policy and practice of corporate governance in Europe have thus far resisted any move towards the universal application of pan-European standards. With greater financial market integration, the developing influence of institutional investors and privatization, it is likely that the market will play a greater role. However, debates on company law harmonization in the European Union have been held up by countries not wishing to see elements of their own systems of corporate governance disappear in the harmonization process. This impasse in policy integration reflects the continuing vigor of a variety of institutional approaches in Europe. The institutional complementarity thesis explains the continuing diversity of systems, in contrast to the one-best-way strategy adopted by the convergence thesis. Instead, a plurality of models is recognized, each corresponding to local circumstances, supported by a cluster of social norms and regulation, enabling balanced economic development. Antoine Rebérioux (2000) argues that the diversity of corporate models is valuable and is rooted in societal characteristics that together shape the competitiveness of the different models. Though shareholder value may be gaining ground due to the influence of Anglo-Saxon institutional investors, a stakeholder approach is closer to the reality of European social democracies, and the outcome of the confrontation between the two competing philosophies is highly uncertain.

According to Lucian Cernat the convergence process towards Anglo-Saxon "best practices" is driven by the interrelated forces of liberalized international financial markets which make it difficult to resist their shareholder orientation, and the European Union's project to promote harmonization towards important features of the Anglo-Saxon system of capital markets. Paradoxically, the Europeanization project with regard to labor relations has the objective of developing the Continental model of worker representation in corporate governance. Cernat suggests the two central categories of corporate governance mechanisms are capital-related and labor-related, and that in Europe these two policies are essentially engaging in a contest, the outcome of which will determine the future direction of development of corporate governance in Europe. The capital-related characteristics include ownership structure, disclosure, voting, and the role of institutional investors. The labor-related characteristics include the stakeholding position of labor, employee involvement, participatory management and codetermination.

Clearly, the Anglo-Saxon and European approaches to corporate governance differ in their conception of the role of capital and the role of labor. The Anglo-Saxon conception of the corporation is based on a fiduciary relationship between the shareholders and managers. In this view self-interest acting in decentralized markets can function in a self-regulating way, reinforcing profit orientation with a set of institutions to ensure effective monitoring and performance. In contrast, in the European continental tradition the company has an identity independent of the shareholders, and this influences the rights of shareholders, the duties of the board and the position of labor and other stakeholders. Thus if the underlying principle of the Anglo-Saxon conception of the company is the shareholder theory of the firm, the underlying principle of the European corporate governance system is the stakeholder theory of the firm. Cernat contends that it is unlikely that imported Anglo-Saxon capital-related features of corporate governance will work well with Continental labor-related aspects of corporate governance as represented in supervisory boards. It is likely that any such European compromise would be more unstable than existing systems.

Further investigation of the forces for convergence or divergence of the "two principal and opposing systems of corporate governance" is conducted by Michel Aglietta and Antoine Rebérioux. They highlight the contrast between the two systems in that the US system considers the firm as an object of property rights, in which the interests of the shareholders are served by the medium of the depth and liquidity of share markets which reward and discipline corporations for performance. The continental European model, on the contrary, is founded on a partnerial interpretation of the firm in which management is protected from the share market by large, stable blockholdings and employee support. Though they acknowledge the increasing salience of share markets in Europe, and the increasing influence of overseas institutional investors, they do not believe this represents a fundamental impetus in the direction of convergence towards the market-based model, and undermining of the essential characteristics of the European approach.

In Europe the obligations towards transparency and regulation of financial markets continues to develop, but national variations in corporate law remain largely intact. The further consolidation of workers' rights to participate in the affairs of European companies represents, in their view, a significant brake on the process of convergence. The implications of this are revealed in the negotiations regarding the regulation of corporate takeovers in Europe, which represents an intersection of securities law, corporate law and labor law. In considering the corporate law directive on takeovers, the European Parliament was confronted by two opposing conceptions of the company from a liberal market perspective as "belonging" to the shareholders, and the continental conception of the company as a community. When adopted in 2003 by the European Parliament the takeover directive left considerable choice for member countries on whether managers facing takeovers should be able to take defensive measures, and whether multiple voting rights could be used to resist hostile takeovers. Furthermore, the rights of worker representatives to be consulted during takeovers were strengthened, implying some continued legitimacy of the community conception of the corporation in Europe.

Focusing on developments in German corporations, Christel Lane examines the process of erosion of the differences between "coordinated market economies" most notably the Germany economy, and "liberal market economies" of the US and UK. The underlying logic of German political economy, which delivered sustained economic success, was a network of control involving concentrated ownership, retained earnings in firms, cross-ownership between non-financial firms, professional managers and involved employees.

The strategies that developed from this were aimed at long-term growth, skill development and diversified quality production, rather than short-term high returns on investment. A pessimistic view is offered by Christel Lane who reviews the evidence on the German case and concludes that a new Anglo-American logic of corporate governance is diffusing beyond the major corporations of the DAX 30, and that this is not simply attributable to external constraints, but to powerful actors within the German economy including large banks and insurance companies. This is significant first because Germany has been the paradigm for the model of co-ordinated capitalism as distinct from competitive or liberal market capitalism. If the cohesive German system is in the process of fundamental change, then other continental European business systems are likely to be vulnerable. Second, Lane argues that it is wrong to assume the adoption of the Anglo-American model is simply about changes in capital markets and corporate financing. Corporate governance is directly associated with the distribution of power and material reward, and changes in governance orientation will directly impact on the position of employees as important stakeholders of the firm, entitled to a fair share of the surplus and a role in decision making in areas that affect their well-being. Equally the position of other stakeholders may be undermined if the viability of diversified quality production is eroded by a relentless pursuit of what are assumed to be shareholders' interests.

Critical to the pressures towards convergence in corporate governance are the vast growth in scale and increasing activity of international financial markets. The opportunities (and dangers) of developing a transatlantic financial market are examined by Karel Lanoo. Though the European and US financial systems still retain fundamental differences, the amount of transatlantic financial integration is advancing. Europe has a highly developed banking market, and a less developed bond and equity markets, while the US has strong equity and bond markets, and a less developed banking market. Competition between banks in the US stimulated the innovation of disintermediation and securitization of loans. As banks fully disintermediated and securitized their loan books, relationship banking disappeared, displaced by deep and highly liquid money and capital markets.

Meanwhile a rapid internationalization of portfolio investment was taking place, with EU investors' ownership of US equities increasing from $144 billion in 1990, to reach $2,631 billion in 2000. US ownership of

European equities in the same period increased from $141 billion to $1,937 billion, with the emergence of a more securitized and disintermediated financial system attracting US firms to the European market. This further encouraged discussions on making equivalent regulatory and financial reporting standards, to reduce transaction costs.

During this period European and US corporations were learning more about each others' investment and governance systems, with 235 European Union companies acquiring listings in the US by 2005, and 140 US companies listed on the London, Deutsche and Euronext exchanges. Lanoo outlines some of the problems of excessive regulatory cooperation at the international level leaving little room for innovation in securities regulation. However the risks of transatlantic securities integration were revealed in a very dramatic way in the fall-out from the subprime credit market in the US in 2007/2008, as European banks that had acquired hundreds of billions of dollars' worth of securitized debt obligations found them to be toxic financial products making huge holes in their accounts, causing a spate of bank failures and, in the case of UBS and many other major established European banks, long-term damage.

International accounting harmonization, another component in the convergence process, is critically examined by Bernard Colasse. He charts how behind the bureaucratic maneuvres involved in developing the international standards, the issues at stake involved the manner of governance of major companies and control over their access to international financial markets. As the International Accounting Standards Committee (IASC) negotiated a path between the International Federation of Accountants, and the International Organization of Securities Commissions, IASC sought the normative legitimacy that would lead to the acceptance of the new standards in the US and European markets. In the course of this process the conceptual framework, whereby the sole responsibility of a company was to report to its shareholders, was adopted to win the support of the American financial markets and regulators. This provoked Jacques Chirac, the President of France, to write to Romano Prodi, the President of the European Commission, that the international accounting standards ran the risk of an increasing financialization of the French economy, and the imposition of short-term methods upon business management. The European Accounting Regulation Committee refused to accept two of the standards on financial instruments, though the effectiveness of any resistance in the longer term remains to be seen.

BIBLIOGRAPHY

Aguilera, R. and Jackson, G. (2003) The cross-national diversity of corporate governance: dimensions and determinants, *Academy of Management Review*, 28 (3): 447–465.

Amable, B. (2000) Institutional Complementarity and Diversity of Social Systems of Innovation and Production, *Review of International Political Economy*, 7, (4): 645–687.

Bebchuk, L.A. and Roe, M.J. (2004) A Theory of Path Dependence in Corporate Governance and Ownership, in J. Gordon and M. Roe (eds.), *Convergence and Persistence of Corporate Governance Systems*, Chicago, IL: University of Chicago Press.

Beyer, J. and Hassel, A. (2002) The Effects of Convergence: Internationalization and the Changing Distribution of Net Value Added in Large German Firms, *Economy and Society*, 31(3): 309–332.

Bratton, W. and J. McCahery (2002) *Comparative Corporate Governance and Barriers to Global Cross Reference in Corporate Governance Regimes: Convergence and Diversity*, Oxford: Oxford University Press pp. 23–55.

Cioffi, J.W. (2000) Governing Globalization? The State, Law, and Structural Change in Corporate Governance, *Journal of Law and Society*, 27(4): 572–600.

Gordon, J.N. and M.J. Roe (2004) *Convergence and Persistence in Corporate Governance*, Cambridge: Cambridge University Press.

Lannoo, K. (2007) MiFID and Reg NMS A test-case for 'substituted compliance'? ECMI Policy Brief No. 8, July 2007, 1–7.

Maher, M. and Andersson, T. (2000) Corporate Governance: Effects on Firm Performance and Economic Growth, in L.J. Renneboog *et al.* (eds.) *Convergence and Diversity of Corporate Governance Regimes and Capital Markets*, Oxford: Oxford University Press.

O'Sullivan, M.A. (2001) *Contests for Corporate Control: Corporate Governance and Economic Performance in the United States and Germany*, London: Oxford University Press.

Rebérioux, A. (2000) European Style of Corporate Governance at the Crossroads: The Role of Worker Involvement, *Journal of Common Market Studies*, 40(1): 113–134.

7 "The Emerging European Corporate Governance Model: Anglo-Saxon, Continental, or Still the Century of Diversity?"

from Journal of European Public Policy (2004)

Lucian Cernat*

SUMMARY

During recent years the European Commission has been active in creating a 'level playing-field' for European companies through the creation of a harmonized regulatory framework. The Europeanization of national corporate governance models was seen as an important part in this endeavour. However, the likely policy consequences are far from clear and the direction of corporate governance convergence in Europe is still a matter of debate. One key question is whether national governance models across Europe will converge as a result of the European regulatory framework and, if so, what the shape of the European corporate governance model will be. This chapter advances the view that, owing to EU decision-making procedures and the diversity of national corporate governance models across Europe, it is difficult to ensure that the European project of governance convergence is underpinned by a dominant coalition promoting a well-articulated corporate governance model.

INTRODUCTION

A significant body of recent comparative corporate governance literature has been concerned with the question of whether there is a national corporate governance system that performs best in terms of competitive advantage.[1] This question arises in the wake of the globalization of the international economy, a surge in cross-border mergers and acquisitions, and various regulatory attempts to reform existing national corporate governance systems. The globalization of the economy and the Europeanization process advanced in the 1990s have renewed interest in the debate on the persistence of national specificities with regard to corporate governance and their convergence towards a harmonized model.[2] The claim that one set of institutions should prevail over another is based on several underlying assumptions. An extensive range of studies have addressed these questions in recent years identifying national variations across corporate governance arrangements and their impact on the international economic competitiveness of different national capitalist institutional arrangements.[3] This fact is exacerbated by globalization, which is expected to spare only the most fit kind of capitalism. Thus, it has been argued that corporate governance represents not only a crucial difference among varieties of capitalism but also a major factor determining their economic performance.

Despite this trend towards convergence, across Europe significant differences remain in terms of ownership structure and market for corporate control. Wymeersch (1994) identifies two broad types of corporate governance in Europe: a company-based system and an enterprise-based system. This classification parallels the shareholder versus stakeholder distinction. While this dual approach may exaggerate the difference among various European corporate governance systems, it nevertheless seems well suited to reflect the significant regulatory and social aspects of corporate governance across Europe.

In the UK, for instance, hostile takeovers through raids on the stock market play an important role. In the European Union (EU), the UK is generally viewed as the economy most similar to the US, and the reforms enacted by the Thatcher, Major and Blair governments have brought the UK even closer to the American model. In contrast, Germany had virtually no hostile takeovers before the Vodafone deal. A similar systemic aversion to hostile takeovers can be found in different degrees in other Continental European states (De Jong 1989).

Empirically, the different experiences in Europe both in terms of types of capitalism and economic performance give full legitimacy to the research question as to whether capitalist institutions (markets, hierarchies, networks, various state and private actors) can be related to various economic outcomes. Second, a crucial question in the European context is whether the EU has a coherent institutional project with regard to corporate governance and industrial relations. As economics itself finds it increasingly difficult to account for cross-national variations in institutional variety and economic performance, a more encompassing approach based on institutional political economy theories may hold the key to our understanding of European integration.

To the extent that this is happening, the convergence process towards Anglo-Saxon 'best practices' is driven by two interrelated forces. First, a liberalized financial market that is beyond any individual state or supranational institution makes it increasingly difficult to reconcile the *Hausbank*-style of Continental blockholders with the shareholder approach of financial markets. Second, the Europeanization project aims to promote harmonization towards several capital-related features of the Anglo-Saxon system.

In contrast, with regard to labour-related issues, the same Europeanization project aims to produce a Continental-oriented model of corporate governance. Change in the national corporate governance regime would then have to be explained as a consequence of a *dynamic interaction* between the specific political selectivities of national and supranational institutional constraints and opportunities, adding to the effects of interdependence between national systems competitively embedded in an encompassing common market.[4]

Thus, the interesting question regarding corporate convergence at European level is, what are the major characteristics of the emerging Europeanization project? The options are either a hybrid model combining 'best' with 'second-best' practices from Anglo-Saxon and Continental corporate governance models, or convergence towards one of the two models. The following sections investigate these issues further. After a short description of the main two types of corporate governance influencing the emerging European model, three distinct European legislative initiatives aimed at reshaping the corporate governance structures across Europe are examined in order to identify the influence of EU decision-making procedures on the degree and direction of convergence.

The remainder of the paper is organized as follows. Section 2 introduces the main features of the Anglo-Saxon and Continental models of corporate governance, the two models that shape current attempts at promoting a European model of corporate governance. Section 3 analyses the consequences of decision-making procedures in the EU on the direction of corporate governance convergence at the EU level by focusing on three specific legislative initiatives: the European Works Council Directive, the European Company Statute Directive and the 13th Takeover Directive. The conclusions with regard to the convergence debate over the Europeanization of corporate governance are presented in section 4.

2. MODELS OF CORPORATE GOVERNANCE

In the models of corporate governance literature one can organize the variety of variables and concepts used to describe the complexity of corporate governance mechanisms into two main categories: *capital-related* and *labour-related*. The capital-related aspects contain, among others, variables like ownership structure, corporate voting, the identity of owners, and the role of institutional owners.

The labour-related aspects refer mainly to the stakeholding position of labour in corporate governance. Here one could mention employee involvement schemes, participatory management, co-determination, etc.[5] Table 1 summarizes the various aspects of corporate governance, according to the proposed dichotomy. Based on this organizing principle, the next section further explores the concepts mentioned above and other key aspects of each corporate governance model.

2.1 The Anglo-Saxon model of corporate governance

In the Anglo-Saxon tradition, the corporate concept is based on a fiduciary relationship between shareholders and managers. Based on the concept of market capitalism, the Anglo-Saxon system is founded on the belief that self-interest and decentralized markets can function in a self-regulating, balanced manner. It comes as no surprise that these institutional settings are based on and reinforce profit-oriented behaviour and a struggle for material success by individual entrepreneurs and managers. This short-term, profit-oriented behaviour and individualism are combined with a set of appropriate institutions to enhance their effectiveness in the Anglo-Saxon model.[7] In the continental tradition, the company has an independent will, i.e. in theory what is good for the corporations might not be good for their shareholders. These differences penetrate to company law particulars such as shareholder rights, the role of statutory capital and the responsibility of the board, to mention a few.

Capital-related aspects
With regard to capital-related features of corporate governance, the Anglo-Saxon countries are known to offer well-developed mechanisms. Anglo-Saxon corporate governance systems are characterized by dispersed equity holding and a broad delegation to management of corporate responsibilities. In the UK and US, not only are there few large shareholders but the second, third and smaller shareholdings are not appreciably smaller than the largest. This gives rise to the possibility of effective control through coalitions but not by individual shareholders (Becht and Mayer 2001; Blair 1995). Although ownership and control are separate, minority shareholders enjoy protection

Aspects	Anglo-Saxon	Continental
Labour-related		
Co-operation between social partners	Conflictual or minimal contact	Extensive at national level
Labour organizations	Fragmented and weak	Strong, centralized unions
Labour market flexibility	Poor internal flexibility; high external flexibility	High internal flexibility; lower external flexibility
Employee influence	Limited	Extensive through works councils and co-determination[6]
Capital-related		
Ownership structure	Widely dispersed ownership; dividends prioritized	Banks and other corporations are major shareholders; dividends less prioritized
Role of banks	Banks play a minimal role in corporate ownership	Important both in corporate finance and control
Family-controlled firms	General separation of equity holding and management	Family ownership important only for small- and medium-sized enterprises
Management boards	One-tier board	Two-tier boards; executive and supervisory responsibility separate
Market for corporate control	Hostile takeovers are the 'correction mechanism' for management failure	Takeovers restricted
Role of stock exchange	Strong role in corporate finance	Reduced

Source: Adapted from Rhodes and van Apeldoorn (1997: 174–5).

Table 7.1 **Anglo-Saxon vs. Continental corporate governance: capital- and labour-related aspects**

owing to the not solely legal infrastructure, and to highly developed capital markets in the market-oriented system.

Probably the most distinctive capital-related aspect in relation to the two systems is the structure of corporate ownership. As seen in Table 7.2, in 1990 in the US (the textbook example for the Anglo-Saxon capitalist model) individual shareholders accounted for 50 percent of the total outstanding shares owned.[8]

This differs markedly from countries with Continental capitalism. The same sharp differences in ownership structure are present with respect to the other two major non-financial shareholders: banks and enterprises. From the ownership structure it follows that the Anglo-Saxon corporate governance system is one where share ownership is widely dispersed and shareholder influence on management is weak. In this system a well-functioning stock market is vital for dissatisfied shareholders to be able to sell their shares. In order to work, the system needs to protect the individual shareholder by strict regulations on corporations regarding information disclosure and insider trading.[9]

Still more striking than differences in average sizes of share blocks is the complete distribution of the largest shareholdings. Table 7.3 provides a more detailed breakdown of ranges for the largest ultimate voting block in listed industrial companies for various countries. It is noticeable that, whereas in the USA over 50 percent of companies have a largest shareholder who holds less than 5 percent of the shares, in Austria and Germany there are virtually no such companies. In some Continental European countries there is a fairly uniform distribution of the largest voting blocks (Germany, Netherlands), with a clear tendency towards ownership concentration.[10] In others, the ownership distribution is peaked. For instance, in Austria 54 percent of the companies in the sample have a large shareholder controlling between 50 and 75 percent of the voting rights. In contrast, in the UK and US there is a strong 'market bias' towards dispersed control.

Labour-related aspects

With regard to the role played by labour in shaping US policy-making, most authors agree that the influence of trade unions is much less in the Anglo-Saxon model when compared with the European model.[11] Organized labour in the US is characterized by a relatively high level of heterogeneity and fragmentation at national level. The Anglo-Saxon system also has a low and declining rate of unionization; see Pryor (1996). In contrast with European and developmental capitalism, the labour market in Anglo-Saxon capitalism suffers from poor internal flexibility owing to a fragmented training system and poor skills (Rhodes and van Apeldoorn 1997: 174). These negative features are partially balanced by higher mobility (both across professional groups and geographically) and by more flexible wages than those characterizing the European model.

Shareholder	US	Germany
Individuals	50.2	17
Banks	n.a.	10
Enterprises (cross-ownership)	14.1	42

Sources: US Federal Reserve Flow of Funds; Deutsche Bundesbank Annual Report.

Table 7.2 **Major non-financial shareholders of stocks (percentages), 1990**

Share of the largest shareholder	Continental countries			Anglo-Saxon
	Austria (%)	Germany (%)	Netherlands (%)	USA (NYSE) (%)
0–5	0	1.1	10.2	52.8
5–10	0	1.9	11.7	21.1
10–25	14	14.5	13.9	20.9
25–50	18	18.3	24.8	3.5
50–75	54	25.5	19.7	1.5
75–90	8	17.5	6.6	0.2
90–95	6	5.7	5.1	0
95–100	0	15.6	8.0	0

Source: Barca and Becht (2001).

Table 7.3 **Ownership concentration: percentage of companies and the share of their largest shareholders (various years)**

As can be seen in Figure 7.1, the Anglo-Saxon model of corporate governance does not allow for labour to participate in strategic management decisions. On the decision-making side, America's best firms have delegated more decisions to workers through employee involvement programmes and team decision-making than ever before. In the mid-1990s, over half of Americans reported that they worked in firms with employee involvement committees; and one-third of workers said that they were members of employee involvement committees of some sort (Freeman and Rogers 1999). However, this participation is restricted to operation management and has no equivalent at strategic management level.

Moreover, in the Anglo-Saxon world employee participation often has just a financial aspect. In contrast to many Continental countries, a major component of the US economic model is the growth of shared capitalism, including a diverse set of mechanisms for worker participation in production decisions and the financial stake of their firm and of capitalism more broadly. A large share of the US workforce receives compensation related to company performance in a variety of schemes. Dube and Freeman (2000) found that approximately 25 percent of the US workforce had a stake in their firm through some form of ownership. This includes working in a firm with an employee stock ownership plan (ESOP) or receiving a stock option through an employee stock option plan that involves most of the workforce, or through purchase of stocks in a firm that offers discounts on purchases.

2.2 The Continental model of corporate governance

The situation in Continental Europe is rather different. The underlying principle on which the Continental corporate governance system is based is embodied in the stakeholder theory of the firm.[12] The Continental capitalist model considers not only the interests of shareholders but also input from the relevant stakeholders (see Figure 7.2). Often, the most important stakeholders who take an active part in strategic decision-making at corporate level are employees, through trade union representation and/or works councils.[13]

Unlike the Anglo-Saxon model, many Continental European countries provide for a two-tier board: the executive board of directors and the supervisory board. The supervisory board is formed according to different procedures across Europe, but in many cases employees have the right to appoint or recommend several members to the supervisory board.

From the schematic relationships depicted in Figure 7.2 it can be seen that, unlike the Anglo-Saxon system, Continental corporate governance allows for multiple channels to deal with the shareholder-manager agency problem and ensure insider supervision.

Capital-related aspects
Unlike the Anglo-Saxon system, the Continental model is based on the prominent role of banks and on extensive cross-ownership links in corporate finance and control (see Table 7.2). It is common for banks in this model to own significant proportions of shares in their portfolios as a way of controlling their major

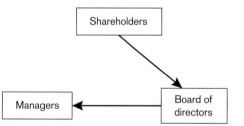

Figure 7.1 The Anglo-Saxon model of corporate decision-making

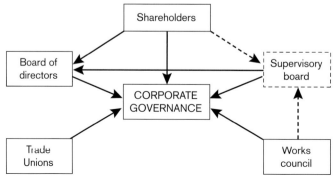

Figure 7.2 **The Continental model of corporate governance**

clients' economic activities. Bank representatives are also often found on the boards of directors of the companies to which they offered large loans. These organizational features and close banking–enterprise interaction create a more secure economic environment that allows firms to seek higher profits in the long term, as opposed to the short-term view imposed by stock markets on Anglo-Saxon companies (Albert 1993; Smyser 1992). Furthermore, banks are allowed to conduct business in all branches of banking (universal banking), while Anglo-Saxon countries strictly separate certain banking activities (Albert 1993). Both features make banks more attractive than stock markets for companies in Continental Europe wishing to raise capital for new investment.

Not only banks but also other shareholders and interested parties have a direct or indirect influence on corporate management. Since the number of freely traded shares is limited and dividends are less prioritized than in the Anglo-Saxon system, shareholders do not face the classic Hirshmanian choice of 'voice or exit'. Less fluid stock markets make exit more costly, and therefore shareholders have a strong incentive to gain a powerful 'voice' in the management of the firm by acquiring a sufficiently large share stock to enable them to monitor the managers and reduce the relative costs of this operation.[14] The same reluctance towards stock markets renders takeovers (especially hostile takeovers) more difficult in Continental capitalism.[15]

Labour-related aspects

The role of labour in the Continental corporate governance model is important not only at macro level but also at firm level through workers' councils and the principle of co-determination, although the latter is not found throughout Europe as a whole. There are well-established and institutionalized business–labour forms of co-operation and information exchange, whether in supervisory boards or at a more decentralized level in works councils.[16] Naturally, the board of directors bears the final responsibility for any decision taken and its effect on company performance. However, the board enters into consultation with workers and the supervisory board before any important decision is taken. Furthermore, certain Continental countries have links in place between the supervisory board and the works council.[17]

With regard to many strategic corporate decisions, Continental-based companies often involve works councils at an early stage. In such cases, better coordination and agreement between works councils and trade unions can strengthen the employees' position in mergers, acquisitions and corporate reorganization. In the German corporate model (and to a large extent in the Netherlands and other Western European countries) works councils are engaged in consultation and participation in the corporate decision-making process, while trade unions are mostly concerned with working conditions and wage bargaining.[18]

However, co-determination may also create disadvantages. If workers become too influential they may pursue opportunistic objectives. It may also slow down decision-making within firms by requiring lengthy procedures before decisions can be taken (Hopt 1994). Moreover, co-determination may reduce the flexibility of employment across firms and industries. Often employers have to consult the works council not only on the social consequences of important economic decisions, but on the economic and financial consequences as well, even though works councils have not been given a say in how the company profits should be distributed.[19]

Despite these institutionalized links between workers and management in the Continental model,

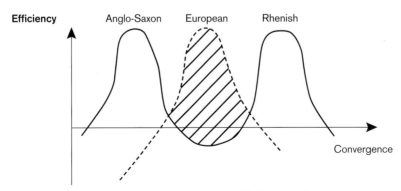

Figure 7.3 **The Europeanization of corporate governance: efficiency and convergence**

corporate governance and industrial relations are far from being a non-conflictual environment. The board of directors maintains its dominant position and sometimes acts in isolation from stakeholders. Even worker participation in corporate governance is at times characterized by a lack of co-ordination between trade unions and works councils.[20]

3. EUROPEAN DIVERSITY: IS THERE AN EMERGING EUROPEAN CORPORATE GOVERNANCE MODEL?

The diverse forms of corporate governance found across Europe and the long-standing attempts to promote a pan-European corporate governance regime are the object of two competing theories. The first – the convergence thesis – sees the landscape of efficient corporate governance as single-peaked. Depending on which features are taken to be more important, opinions are divided as to whether the Anglo-Saxon or the Continental model is the fittest to survive regime competition. The second view considers the landscape of efficient corporate governance as multi-peaked (as depicted in Figure 7.3) and advances two rather different hypotheses. The first considers cross-fertilization to be possible and therefore allows for natural convergence towards a hybrid model, based on 'best practices' borrowed from each other (the dotted line in Figure 7.3). The second hypothesis argues that corporate governance is a complex construct, based on a variety of systemic links among its elements. Consequently, the systemic view discards the feasibility of cross-fertilization on the grounds of high transition costs. Any attempts at convergence, either through cross-fertilization or survival of the fittest, will incur systemic costs for the existing model and therefore will be rejected.

Given these divergent views with regard to changes in corporate governance, the current process of the Europeanization of corporate governance raises several questions. These questions concern the extent to which policy convergence is taking place in the EU and, if so, the path and model where convergence occurs. Are we witnessing the harmonization of the various national corporate governance models along the lines of the Anglo-Saxon system? Or is the European model of corporate governance shaped more like the Continental model? Second, if there is an emergent European capitalist model, is it likely to be more or less efficient than at the starting point?

The following sections will discuss these points by briefly presenting EU attempts at harmonization of national systems of corporate governance. The main capital-related corporate governance issues dealt with at European level are scattered among the thirteen EU company law directives put forward over the years by the Commission. The subject matter of these capital-related directives ranged from the formation and registration of public companies (1st Directive of 1968) to disclosure requirements (11th Directive of 1989), cross-border mergers or disclosure of voting power.[21]

In many instances these directives contained proposals to reform labour-related corporate governance aspects. For example, the 5th Directive concerning the structure and management of public limited companies, first drafted in 1972 and subsequently revised in 1983 and 1989, called for among other things worker participation in company decision-making through a two-tier board and a works council or collective agreement. In parallel, the European Community promoted several proposals aimed at harmonization of labour-related aspects of corporate governance. Another earlier attempt to reform labour-related corporate governance aspects was the Vredeling Directive (1980). This was followed by several attempts to introduce a European Works Council Directive and worker involvement provisions in the proposed European Company Statute (Danis and Hoffman 1995).

Thus, from a cursory look at the specific actions taken towards the Europeanization of corporate governance, it seems that the model of corporate governance promoted at the European level is a mixture of Anglo-Saxon and Continental elements. Several aspects of corporate governance promoted at the European level were inspired by the Continental model of corporate governance and its various forms of employee information, consultation and participatory arrangements.[22]

The main question relates to the likely impact of such a hybrid corporate governance model. Rather than tackling the question directly, in the following text attention is paid to the decision-making process in order to understand the underlying EU institutional factors that encourage the adoption of a hybrid model of corporate governance. Based on the capital/labour distinction between aspects of corporate governance and the examination of the European Works Council Directive, the European Company Statute Regulation and Directive, and the 13th Takeover Directive, several considerations will be taken into account on the direction and pace of corporate governance change at EU level.

3.1 The EWC Directive

The European Works Council (EWC) Directive was enacted in 1994, with the main objective of establishing appropriate mechanisms at EU level for informing and consulting employees in Community undertakings (European Council 1994). However, despite the pioneering work contained in the Vredeling Directive and various amendments proposed by the Economic and Social Council and the trade unions, the EWC Directive does not contain any reference to participation. Yet, the EWC was thought to provide labour with a major institutional device to counteract the potential adverse effects of global capital.[23] Although many other factors influenced the non-inclusion of worker participation in the directive, its limited scope was significantly influenced by the decision-making procedure used.

The EWC Directive found much support in the Maastricht Protocol on Social Policy which was applicable to only eleven EU countries, owing to the opt-out granted to the UK. Stemming from the Protocol's Article 2(2), the decision-making procedure for the EWC Directive is the co-operation procedure, as mentioned in ex-Article 189c. Unanimity voting used to be the prevalent decision-making procedure prior to the Single European Act and the Maastricht Treaty. Subsequently, qualified majority voting (QMV) was extended to most Common Market decisions. Moreover, under the 'flexibility' provisions added by the Amsterdam Treaty, 'multi-speed Europe' had been formalized when allowing for a group of EU members to establish 'closer integration' (Nugent 1999: 166, 353).

Under this procedure, the European Parliament, although lacking veto power from the co-decision procedure, is still a significant actor. If the European Parliament rejects the Council's common position, the Council needs unanimity to pass its original common position. The same unanimity is required if the European Parliament amends the Council's common position but the amendments are rejected by the Commission. Therefore, the European Parliament enjoys to a certain degree the role of a 'conditional agenda-setter', whenever it rejects or amends the Council's common position.

Under Article 189c's co-operation procedure, the Council votes by QMV. Under the consultation and co-operation procedures, the Commission does not have an unconditional agenda-setting power and the Council can adopt a different proposal unanimously. What follows depends on the preferences of the European Parliament with regard to the EWC common position. Based on the political stance of the European Parliament, normally a common position reached by the Council under the QMV would be preferable to the status quo (no EWC) and therefore the European Parliament should vote on the common position without any amendment because, if the European Parliament decides to amend the Council's position or reject it, the fallback position in the Council is unanimity. Or, given the divergence of opinions between EU member states on the EWC, it is obvious that the Council's common position under unanimity, if any, would be less favourable for the EWC than under the QMV procedure. This new outcome makes the European Parliament worse off than the position under QMV and therefore it should be expected that the European Parliament would vote unconditionally for the Council's initial common position. Therefore, the application of Article 189c's co-operation procedure is more favourable for the adoption of corporate governance rules which include Continental-style elements.

3.2 The European Company Statute Directive (ECSD)

The ECSD draft has been at a negotiating impasse at EU level for over thirty years. After long discussions and lobbying from various interest groups,[24] on 15 December 2000, as instructed by the Nice European Council, the Committee of Permanent Representatives (COREPER) met to examine the texts of the directive on employee involvement within the European company and the regulation on the statute for a European company. Following tenuous negotiations, the Council significantly amended the Commission draft and changed the legal basis for decision-making from Article 100a (requiring co-decision) to Article 308 Treaty of the European Communities (TEC). Article 308 provides for unanimity in the Council and consultation of the European Parliament. By changing the legal basis, the Council ensured that neither the Commission (the original drafter of the decision) nor the European Parliament's potential amendments would put serious strain on the prevailing domestic institutions of the least integrationist member.

Unlike the case of the EWC, the use of Article 308's decision-making procedure eliminated the European Parliament's role as a 'conditional agenda-setter' and limited the political game to the European Commission's attempt to promote European integration by skilfully designing package deals that would facilitate compromise and unanimity in the Council.

Had the decision-making procedure been based on QMV and co-decision, the results would have been slightly different. Under co-decision, the European Parliament basically has a veto power over the Council's agreed position. As the European Parliament is generally in favour of more worker involvement in the case of the ECSD, the content of the ECSD would have been more similar to the pattern of corporate governance found in Continental Europe.

3.3 The 13th Takeover Directive

One of the regulations that aim to introduce more elements of the Anglo-Saxon model of corporate governance across Europe is the 13th Directive concerning takeover bids. The directive has as its main objective the harmonization of minority shareholders' protection throughout the EU, through the mandatory bid rule (MBR).[25]

On the most controversial part of the directive, the MBR, the 13th Directive imposes minimum requirements and the result will most likely be a minimum level of corporate governance harmonization. Although defensive measures are forbidden unless approved at the shareholders' meeting, they still exist in countries with large blockholders.[26] Another expected effect of the proposed directive will be to prevent the board of the target company from taking defensive measures. Another controversial aspect of the directive was the MBR threshold, owing to different set-ups which member states have in their national regulations. The Takeover Directive has, like many other cases of corporate governance harmonization, several contentious points. National preferences with regard to the MBR in the Council are difficult to harmonize, given the differences in ownership structure and blockholding across Europe. The decision-making procedure used was, as in most cases of the internal market, the co-decision procedure.

An interesting fact is the European Parliament's attempt to use the 13th Directive to upgrade the right of employee participation in the case of a takeover bid. Out of the fifteen amendments adopted by the EU after its second reading of the proposed 13th Directive, five concerned the introduction of worker participatory rights in the takeover process (European Council 2000a). Furthermore, the European Parliament tried to strengthen the anti-takeover devices already permitted by the proposal, signalling its implicit preference for a Continental model of corporate governance.

This strong preference for the Continental model places the European Parliament closer to the status quo than the median voter. This creates a situation where the European Parliament can credibly use its veto power, allowed under the co-decision procedure. The result of this veto power is a gradual adoption by the Council of European Parliament amendments (European Council 2000b). Moreover, after the European Parliament's first reading, several of its amendments had already been included by the Commission, not only those related to more precise wording and definitions but also those extending to the workforce the principle of disclosure to shareholders and providing workers with prompt information once a takeover bid is made public.

The historical development of the 13th Directive indicates that member states have been unable to reach an agreement on the directive which imposes strict rules regarding takeovers. After almost two decades and many amendments which diluted the initial European Community proposal, one must conclude that most of the issues will be left to the member states and dealt with at national level.

To the extent that the 13th European Directive aims to offer better protection to minority shareholders, it contributes towards the Europeanization of different national corporate governance structures along the lines of the Anglo-Saxon system. Should this harmonization happen, the private benefits of control currently enjoyed by large blockholders would decrease. As La Porta *et al.* (1999) suggest, the persistence of family- and bank-controlled companies in many European countries was due to lack of appropriate protection for minority shareholders and strong anti-takeover devices.[27] Once stronger minority shareholder protection is in place and takeovers are permitted, one would expect a more dispersed ownership in Continental states, and subsequently an orientation towards the Anglo-Saxon model. All these effects are promoted by, and expected to result from, the implementation of the 13th Directive.

Although the stated aim of the proposed 13th Directive is to upgrade the Continental corporate governance model to the Anglo-Saxon level of protection for minority shareholders, the directive is unlikely to promote an overall convergence towards the Anglo-Saxon model of corporate governance. The simple reason for this is that the minimum bid requirement is unlikely to produce the intended effects of stimulating cross-border mergers and acquisitions thought to be the main vehicle of eliminating concentrated ownership in Continental Europe. First, the introduction of the minimum bid requirement will actually increase the price of a takeover and will act as an extra 'poison pill', reducing a bidder's incentive to make a bid. Second, and more importantly, despite Article 8(1)(a) provisions forbidding any defensive measures once the bid has been made public (unless with prior approval from the shareholders), the directive allows target companies to seek friendly takeovers ('white knights') as a defensive measure against hostile takeovers (Article 9(1)(a)).

4. CONCLUSIONS

Many argue that globalization and Europeanization will lead to a convergence of national corporate governance varieties towards a harmonized model. This chapter has identified two major constraints at EU level against this trend. First, differences in the two models of corporate governance that influence the direction of Europeanization still exist and are rather difficult to reconcile. Second, decision-making at EU level is poorly equipped to advance a coherent model or a hybrid based on 'best practices'. Therefore, at least in the short term, the future of corporate governance in Europe is likely to remain multiple-peaked with large differences in key aspects among EU members.

The evidence presented here suggests that regulatory deficiencies are likely to have two kinds of effect. First, it is unlikely that Anglo-Saxon capital-related features of European corporate governance will work well with Continental labour-related aspects of corporate governance. Second, the incomplete level of harmonization achieved after more than thirty years

of attempts by the European Commission towards Europeanization of national corporate governance systems will add further strain on a pan-European hybrid model of corporate governance.

Therefore, the European project can hardly advance and enhance the efficiency of European companies without addressing the internal fracture of the model. Although employee participation is promoted in the European model of corporate governance, its interaction with shareholder capitalism is not without friction. The current wave of mergers and acquisitions promoting a shareholder approach to corporate governance as well as the increased importance of arm's length financing will put significant pressure on long-standing relationships with employees and participatory management. Given the EU regulatory framework described, there is a good chance that the European model of corporate governance will be more problematic than the Anglo-Saxon and Continental models.

What can be inferred from the above analysis is that, given the diversity of national corporate governance models across Europe and the persistence of various EU multiple decision-making procedures, it is difficult to ensure that the European project of governance convergence is underpinned by a dominant coalition promoting an articulated corporate governance model.

However, one can categorize the various decision-making procedures in accordance with their optimal impact on the adoption of a higher degree of harmonization. Table 7.4 offers a bi-dimensional matrix, grouping the voting procedures offering the highest level of policy harmonization along the lines of corporate governance models (Anglo-Saxon and Continental) and issues (capital- and labour-related).

As presented in Table 7.4, and stripped to its essentials, the options facing the Europeanization of corporate governance can be summed up in three basic propositions. First, to promote a high degree of harmonization across countries towards a best-practice hybrid model, co-decision and QMV should be used for both labour- and capital-related aspects of corporate governance. Second, if a high degree of harmonization towards the Anglo-Saxon system is the

	Anglo-Saxon model	Continental model
Labour-related issues	Consultation/Unanimity	Co-decision/QMV
Capital-related issues	Co-decision/QMV	Consultation/Unanimity

Table 7.4 **The corporate governance–EU decision-making matrix**

objective, consultation and unanimity should be used for labour-related issues and co-decision and QMV for capital-related aspects of corporate governance. Lastly, if the Continental model of corporate governance is the blueprint for the emerging European model, co-decision and QMV should be used for labour-related issues and consultation and unanimity for capital-related aspects of corporate governance.

NOTES

* The author would like to thank the participants of the EPRU Jean Monnet seminar 'Theorizing Multi-level Governance' (University of Manchester) for their useful comments. The financial support of ACE-PHARE Project No. P97–9238-S for this research is gratefully acknowledged. The views expressed herein are those of the author and do not necessarily reflect the views of the EU or the United Nations.

1   For general surveys of various facets of convergence, see Coffee (1998); Moerland (1995); Prowse (1995). For more specific studies, see for instance Berglof (1997); Shleifer and Vishny (1997).

2   With regard to the great diversity of national corporate governance across Europe, a good collection of country studies can be found in Isaksson and Skog (1994).

3   For an extensive review of this literature, see for instance Mayer (1997).

4   One argument found in the literature surveyed states that national institutional contexts have a significant impact on corporate governance regimes. It is also claimed that different models of capitalism (understood as specific institutional arrangements regulating the macro-societal space) are a determinant factor on the type of corporate governance found at national level (Scott 1997).

5   This difference is blurred to some extent by the transformation of labour into owners. However, unless employee financial participation is significant, worker identity does not become completely diluted into a shareholder identity.

6   The German co-determination system gives the employees of a company controlling rights without them owning any of the shares of the company. Thus, in many cases 50 percent of the supervisory board members are appointed in this way but the capital side has the casting vote.

7   For a classical description of the main Anglo-Saxon best practices, see for instance the Cadbury Report (1992).

8   The US and the UK governance systems are broadly similar (liberal market/ competitive; shareholder dominant) but starkly different when compared to the continental European variants. With regard to hostile takeovers, for instance, Franks and Mayer (1996) report a total of eighty (successful and unsuccessful) hostile bids in the UK for 1985–86, and eighty-five (successful and unsuccessful) hostile bids in the US in 1984–86. In Continental Europe the figures are much more modest.

9   In addition, the Anglo-Saxon system has a well-established anti-trust law and authorities to preclude the formation of anti-competitive cartels through mergers and acquisitions or cross-ownership.

10   However, it would be wrong merely to contrast Continental European with Anglo-American control. There is a marked variation within Europe, ranging from a 'private control bias' in Germany to a modest market bias in the Netherlands and Spain.

11   The comparison is more difficult with the developmental state because of the latter's state authoritarianism combined with extensive corporate welfare schemes and workers' active role at shop-floor level.

12   On the concept of stakeholder capitalism, the meaning of 'stakeholding' and various refinements of the concepts (stakeholder state, the stakeholder society, stakeholder company, stakeholder economy), see Kelly *et al.* (1997); Hutton (1999).

13   The dotted arrows and lines symbolize the national differences in these institutional arrangements across Continental Europe. In France, for instance, the Supervisory Board does not exist.

14   Dittus and Prowse (1996: 24) bring evidence in support of this argument. Germany has the highest share concentration ratio (42 percent) compared with the US (25 percent) and Japan (33 percent).

15   Prowse (1995) reports that market capitalization corresponds to 51 percent of GDP in the US, 90 percent in the UK, 71 percent in Japan, and only 29 percent in Germany. Adjusted for crossholdings, the figures are 48 percent in the US, 81 percent in the UK, 37 percent in Japan, and 14 percent in Germany.

16   The 'Nordic model' of workforce participation, which is based on national industrial agreements, differs from the German model based on 'rigid' legislation (Streeck 1997: 19)

17   In Germany, for instance, works councils have the right to appoint up to half the number of representatives on the supervisory board. In the Netherlands, works councils can only recommend and oppose supervisory board membership.

18   One should distinguish between two aspects of employee participation: (i) operational employee participation mechanisms (operational meetings, quality circles, self-guided teams, etc.) aimed at improving the work process and overall enterprise competitiveness (direct participation); (ii) employee participation in strategic management decisions at corporate level, through workers' representatives, aimed at ensuring that workers' interests are taken into account in any major decision, including mergers and acquisitions.

19   See Bolt and Peters (1997) on the Dutch co-determination system and the role of works councils.

20   In certain Continental countries, both unionized and non-unionized workers participate in works councils. Often there is competition between works councils and trade unions for legitimacy in negotiations with the management over working conditions and employment.

21 See the Large Holdings Directive (88/627/EEC). The Directive is also referred to as the 'Transparency Directive' or the 'Anti-Raider Directive'.

22 Clear instances when the EU tried to harmonize national corporate governance systems along Continental lines were the European Works Council Directive and the directive with regard to worker involvement in a European company.

23 On the negative effects on labour of free movement of capital and multinational corporate (MNC) activity in Europe, see the Hoover case, when production was shifted from Dijon to Glasgow, and Renault's Vilvoorde incident. In both cases, EU legislation did little to avoid MNC relocation in search of cheap and more flexible labour within Europe.

24 European interest groups manifested their preferences early in the drafting process. Since the Commission presented its first proposal for a European Company Statute in June 1970, the Union of Industrial and Employers' Confederation of Europe (UNICE) has repeatedly expressed concern that the creation of a European company could present problems for European companies. The existence of an optional legal form of this type would facilitate cross-border mergers and foster industrial co-operation in Europe, and is therefore an important element of the internal market.

25 The mandatory bid rule (MBR) requires that anyone who secures a certain amount of voting rights to give him control over a company must offer to buy the rest of the shares. Through the MBR, minority shareholders should be protected by having the choice of selling their shares when a new person acquires control over the company.

26 The most extreme case is the Netherlands where defensive mechanisms are still largely permitted.

27 Based on a survey of corporate ownership structures in twenty-seven countries, La Porta *et al.* (1998) found that countries with poor shareholder protection have more concentrated shareholding and vice versa.

REFERENCES

Albert, M. (1993) *Capitalism vs. Capitalism*, New York: Four Wall Eight Window.

Barca, F. and Becht, M. (eds) (2001) *The Control of Corporate Europe*, Oxford: Oxford University Press.

Becht, M. and Mayer, C. (2001) 'The control of corporate Europe', in F. Barca and M. Becht (eds), *The Control of Corporate Europe*, Oxford: Oxford University Press.

Berglof, E. (1997) 'A note on the typology of financial systems', in K.J. Hopt and E. Wymeersch (eds), *Comparative Corporate Governance: Essays and Materials*, Berlin: Walter de Gruyter, pp. 151–64.

Blair, M.M. (1995) *Ownership and Control: Rethinking Corporate Governance for the Twenty-First Century*, Washington, DC: Brookings Institution.

Bolt, W. and Peters, H.M. (1997) 'Corporate governance in the Netherlands', Research Memorandum De Nederlandsche Bank WO&E No. 493, February.

Cadbury Committee (1992) *Report of the Committee on the Financial Aspects of Corporate Governance*, London: Gee.

Coffee, J.C. (1998) 'The future as history: prospects for global convergence in corporate governance and its implications', Working Paper No. 144, The Centre for Law and Economics Studies, Columbia University School of Law.

Danis, J.J. and Hoffman, R. (1995) 'From the Vredeling Directive to the European Works Council Directive: some historical remarks', *Transfer* 1(2): 180–7.

De Jong, H.W. (1989) 'The takeover market in Europe: control structures and the performance of large companies compared', *Review of Industrial Organization* 6: 1–18.

Dittus, P. and Prowse, S. (1996) 'Corporate control in central Europe and Russia: should banks own shares?', in R. Frydman, C. Gray and A. Rapaczynski (eds), *Corporate Governance in Central Europe and Russia*, Vol. 1, Budapest: CEU Press, pp. 20–67.

Dube, A. and Freeman, R.B. (2000) 'Shared compensation systems and decision-making in the US job market'. Paper presented at Commission for Labour Cooperation, North American Seminar on Incomes and Productivity, 24–25 February.

European Council (1994) 'Council Directive 94/45 EC of 22 September 1994 on the establishment of a European Works Council or a procedure in Community-scale undertakings and Community-scale groups of undertakings for purposes of informing and consulting employees', *Official Journal* L 254, 30, pp. 64–72.

European Council (2000a) 'Amended proposal for a Council Regulation on the Statute for a European Company – guidelines for political agreement', Council of the European Union 14717/00, Brussels, 18 December.

European Council (2000b) 'Proposal for a Directive of the European Parliament and of the Council on company law concerning takeover bids', Council of the European Union 14044/00, Brussels, 22 December.

Franks, J.R. and Mayer, C. (1996) 'Hostile takeovers and the correction of managerial failure', *Journal of Financial Economics* 40(1): pp. 163–81.

Freeman, R. and Rogers, J. (1999) *What Workers Want*, Ithaca: Cornell University Press.

Hopt, K.J. (1994) 'Labour representation on corporate boards: impact and problems for corporate governance and economic integration in Europe', *International Review of Law and Economics* 14: 203–14.

Hutton, W. (1999) *The Stakeholding Society: Writings on Politics and Economics*, Oxford: Blackwell Publishers.

Isaksson, M. and Skog, R. (eds) (1994) *Aspects of Corporate Governance*, Corporate Governance Forum, Stockholm: Juristförlaget.

Kelly, G., Kelly, D. and Gamble, A. (eds) (1997) *Stakeholder Capitalism*, New York: St Martin's Press.

La Porta, R., Lopez-de-Silanes, N. and Shleifer, A. (1999) 'Corporate ownership around the world', *Journal of Finance* 54: 471–510.

Mayer, C. (1997) 'Corporate governance, competition and performance', *Journal of Law and Society* 24: 152–76.

Moerland, P.W. (1995) 'Alternative disciplinary mechanisms in different corporate systems', *Journal of Economic Behaviour and Organization* 26(1): 17–34.

Nugent, N. (1999) *The Government and Politics of the European Union*, London: Macmillan Press.

Prowse, S. (1995) 'Corporate governance in an international perspective; a survey of corporate control mechanisms among large firms in the US, UK, Japan, and Germany', *Financial Markets and Institutions* 1: 1–63.

Pryor, F. (1996) *Economic Evolution and Structure: The Impact of Complexity on the US Economic System*, Cambridge: Cambridge University Press.

Rhodes, M. and van Apeldoorn, B. (1997) 'Capitalism versus capitalism in Western Europe', in M. Rhodes, P. Heywood and V. Wright (eds), *Developments in Western European Politics*, New York: St Martin's Press, pp. 171–89.

Scott, J. (1997) *Corporate Business and Capitalist Classes*, Oxford: Oxford University Press.

Shleifer, A. and Vishny, R.W. (1997) 'A survey of corporate governance', *The Journal of Finance*, LII: 737–83.

Smyser, W.R. (1992) *The Economy of United Germany*, New York: St Martin's Press.

Streeck, W. (1997) 'Citizenship under regime competition: the case of the European Works Councils', MPIfG Working Paper 97/3.

Wymeersch, E. (1994) 'Elements of comparative corporate governance in western Europe', in M. Isaksson and R. Skog (eds), *Aspects of Corporate Governance*, Corporate Governance Forum, Stockholm: Juristförlaget.

8 "Changes in Corporate Governance of German Corporations: Convergence to the Anglo-American Model?"

from *Competition and Change* (2003)

Christel Lane

SUMMARY

This chapter examines the many changes which have transformed the German system of corporate governance during the last seven odd years. It concludes that it is in the process of converging towards the Anglo-American system and that this has fundamentally affected the way strategic decisions are made in firms. Large, internationally oriented companies are particularly affected. But the notion of shareholder value and its many behavioural effects are gradually spreading also to other parts of the economy. Consequently, the distinctive logic, which had underpinned the German variety of capitalism during most of the post-war period, is eroding. This transformation is affecting also labour and industrial relations in negative ways. The argument is empirically substantiated with data about recent trends in capital markets, banks and firms.

The chapter theoretically examines institutional change, focusing on the notions of system logic and institutional complementarity. It examines both external sources of change and internal powerful actors who promote the process of transformation. The notion of hybridisation of the German business system is examined but is rejected in favour of a trend towards convergence. Convergence is not seen as a functional necessity, nor is it viewed as inevitable.

I INTRODUCTION

After the collapse of state socialism in 1990, the focus of debate in the social sciences came to rest on differences within the capitalist world between different models of capitalist organisation. Just ten years on, the debate has shifted further, and there are now being voiced both triumphant claims and fears that one model of capitalism – that of competitive or liberal market capitalism – is displacing all others. The fundamental and long-established differences between what has come to be known as organised or co-ordinated market economies and competitive or liberal market economies are said to be in the process of erosion.

This new debate has focused on changes in capital markets, corporate financing and their implications for corporate governance – institutions widely held to be cornerstones of models of capitalism (O'Sullivan 2000; Deeg 2001). Corporate governance may be loosely defined as all those rules and arrangements structuring the exercise of control over company assets and the pattern of interaction between different stakeholders within the firm. Because forms of corporate governance are inherently connected with the allocation of power and resources and with a distribution of surplus they structure most other relationships within firms and the wider political economy, shaping its whole logic. Hence, there is strong concern, particularly but not only on the part of labour, with the consequences of any processes of change for the redistribution of surplus and control to various stakeholders in the firm.

Transformation of corporate governance in recent years has been most pronounced in coordinated market economies, and the impetus for and advocacy of change have come chiefly from the US (O'Sullivan 2000) and also from the UK. As Germany long has been portrayed as the paradigm case of coordinated capitalism (Deeg 2001), with many built-in institutional obstacles to erosion, debate around the German case is of particular interest. If the hitherto very cohesive German system can be shown to be in the process of fundamental change, then other continental European business systems also are vulnerable.

The processes of change which can be empirically observed have initiated a fresh debate on institutional transformation and how it might best be conceptualised. In particular, it is being debated whether the changes in corporate governance signal radical system transformation and a process of convergence, or whether they can be absorbed into the existing institutions of a coordinated market economy by processes of institutional adaptation and/or conversion (Thelen 2000). Four positions may be distinguished in this debate: an argument for system transformation and convergence; claims for system persistence, albeit with partial adjustment of the old model; and third, a diagnosis of the emergence of a hybrid model of capitalism. Partly overlapping with the third is a fourth position which posits functional conversion for one important institutional constellation within the German model.

This chapter seeks to further clarify the extent and exact nature of current transformations in the German system of corporate governance and political economy, as well as identify sources of change. I shall make the deeply contentious claim that convergence is, indeed, beginning to occur. Convergence has been variously defined, and in this paper it means one-sided adaptation of the 'coordinated market economy' model to that of the 'liberal market economy'. It is being recognised that existing German institutions will mediate the impact of the 'liberal market economy' model. Hence it is not being envisaged that convergence will result in the creation of a German model, identical in all its features to Anglo-American capitalism. Nevertheless, the transformation of the underlying system logic is viewed as initiating fundamental and far-reaching changes in all institutional sub-systems.

My argument is not based on the functionalist assumption that convergence is occurring because 'liberal market' economies have shown themselves to perform in a superior way and that imitation by the less efficient is compelling. As Mary O'Sullivan has shown, historical analysis of the evolution of systems of corporate governance and their impact on performance casts serious doubts on such claims. Hence I make no assumption that convergence is desirable and inevitable. On the contrary, it will be shown that convergence is connected with far-reaching consequences which will be highly negative for at least one important stakeholder – labour. I shall suggest that it is reversible, if there is sufficient political will.

The chapter offers both an in-depth theoretical analysis and empirical substantiation of institutional change. To this purpose, it will provide first, a discussion of institutional change in general and convergence, in particular and, second, an outline and evaluation of changes in the German system of corporate governance, placing them in their broader institutional context.

Change in patterns of corporate governance is a highly complex process, going far beyond changes in regulation of the capital market and the adoption of new company codes of good practice. A convincing evaluation of the degree and nature of transformation has to go further and deal with its multiple real consequences for various stakeholders at the level of the firm. It cannot rely on the protestations of managers that they continue to have the interest of labour at heart but, instead, has to examine managerial behaviour, instigated by changes in corporate governance. Such a study has to deal with any fundamental changes in company strategy and structure and with the new configuration of intra-firm relations initiated by them.

Evidence for such an in-depth assessment will be drawn from my own study of German companies in one important industry – chemicals/pharmaceuticals and from a range of secondary sources. Among the latter, I owe a particular debt to the excellent study by Steffen Becker (1999). (The industry is one of the most important in terms of its contribution to GDP and to R&D activity, and it also is a major employer).

The chapter is structured as follows. Section II outlines the theoretical framework adopted. It presents a brief outline of two models of corporate governance found in the literature. This is followed by a more sustained conceptualisation of the nature of institutional reproduction and change, with a special focus on the notions of institutional logic, coherence/complementarity and hybridisation. Section III, the empirical core of the chapter, first introduces a brief historical sketch of the German model of corporate governance up to the mid-1990s to enable an assessment of change. This will be followed in section III.2 by an analysis of the changes in formal and informal institutional arrangements at the levels of both the financial system and of the firm. It evaluates the consequences of change for various corporate stakeholders, as well as their opportunities to influence the direction of change or mediate its impact. Section III.3 dwells on persistence of institutional arrangements at both levels and enduring divergence of the German model from the Anglo-American one. Section III.4 considers the balance of persistence and change and then critically examines claims about hybridisation of the German business system. In section III.5, it is concluded that the concept of convergence more aptly characterises emergent tendencies of change and that we may expect acceleration of the transformation process in the coming decades. The Conclusion debates the import of the findings offered in part III for the debate on convergence versus divergence, in the context of the theoretical understanding of institutional change detailed in section II. Finally, the chapter draws out the consequences of convergence for the German variety of capitalism and the role of labour within it.

II THEORETICAL CONSIDERATIONS

II.1 Approaches to corporate governance

There are two major approaches to corporate governance. The first approach, current in mainstream economics, is only concerned with the relationship between financiers of firms – mainly shareholders and banks (principals) – and their agents (managers) and with formal and informal rules and procedures structuring it. The key goal of corporate governance here is to ensure a maximum return to investors. The development of a market for corporate control, through the threat of takeover, both structures the ex ante incentives of managers to fulfil this goal, as well as disciplining managers if they are under-performing or diverting too large a share of net value to themselves. The second approach, more common outside economics, is the stakeholder approach which focuses on the entire network of formal and informal relations

which determines how control is exercised within corporations and how the risks and returns are distributed between the various stakeholders. In addition to owners of capital and managers, employees are the most prominent. The principle embodied in this form of corporate governance is that companies should be required to serve a number of groups, rather than treat the interests of shareholders as overriding all others. The interests of labour here are foremost, and both their right to an equitable share of surplus and their entitlement to industrial participation are emphasised (e.g. Streeck 2001).

These two systems of corporate governance then may be mapped onto two different modes of exerting control (Mayer 2000). The first is equated with outsider and arms' length control, connected with dispersed share ownership and the prevalence of institutional investors. The second notion, dwelling on the whole network of control, occurs when share ownership is more concentrated and owners of significant portions of ownership are able to exercise insider control. Concentrated holdings may be held by family owners, banks or other non-financial firms.

In both types of systems, managerial performance is monitored and poorly performing managers are disciplined, but the way in which these two types of control are exercised differs decisively between outsider and insider control. In the insider system, control is exercised through board membership and legal rights of appointment and dismissal. It is said to be more direct and active, whereas in the outsider system control is indirect and exerted through the market for corporate control and the threat of takeover. Whereas the insider system is associated with management goals of stability and growth and longer-term returns to significant owners, the outsider system implies the goals of liquidity of capital markets and of opportunities for short-term maximisation of returns on capital invested.

This chapter starts by adopting the second notion of corporate governance which has been prevalent in Germany until the mid-1990s. I then proceed to investigate whether and to what degree it is giving way to the first type in current debates on this topic.

II.2 Analysis of institutional persistence and change

Theoretical analyses of varieties of capitalism conducted during the last decade or so have differed in the degree to which they have systematically considered institutional change. Works published during the 1990s, such as Whitley 1992 and 1999, Lane 1995; Hollingsworth and Boyer 1997, Berger and Dore 1997, Kitschelt et al 1999, and even Hall and Soskice 2001, have predominantly focused on institutional reproduction or persistence. In this, they have been influenced both by the notion of what constitutes system transformation and by an emphasis on system coherence (Whitley 1992 and Lane 1995) or interlocking complementarity of institutional ensembles (Hall and Soskice 2001). Institutional complementarity is said to exist when the presence or absence of one institution affects the efficiency of the other (Hall and Soskice 2001: 16), and the link between institutional complexes is specific incentive structures. These are seen to inhibit radical or fundamental socio-economic change and instead promote institutional reproduction.

Both the notions of institutional coherence and of institutional complementarity are derived from the assumption that there is an institutional logic expressed in concrete practices and organisational arrangements which influences what social roles, relationships and strategies are conceivable, efficacious and legitimate (Biggart and Guillen 1999: 725). Additionally, organising logics are held to be 'repositories of distinctive capabilities that allow firms … to pursue some activities in the global economy more successfully than others' (Biggart and Guillen 1999). The relationships and roles researched in the empirical part of their paper centres on relationships of control and identifies the categories of actors favoured by them in a number of political economies. Biggart and Guillen's sociological institutionalism views institutional logics as sense-making constructs and focuses on taken-for granted organisational arrangements. Hall and Soskice 2001, in contrast, committed to a 'rational actor' institutionalist perspective, are concerned above all with incentive structures and efficiency goals. Both these approaches, envisaging a system logic, internal coherence/complementarity and system reproduction have suggested that underlying logics are changed only with great difficulty and have therefore implied that only extreme external shocks are able to effect system transformation. Although change is not ruled out entirely, 'within system' incremental change has been theoretically privileged.

More recently, in the face of empirically observable, wide-ranging change in core institutional arrangements, analysts have begun to question three interconnected assumptions of the above approaches: 1. That system change necessarily has to be of the radical big-bang nature: 2. that it can be brought about only by external shocks (Mahoney 2001; Deeg 2001; Thelen 2000); and 3. whether institutional complementarity really is as strong as believed by the earlier approaches, or whether discrete institutions may change independently from the rest (Thelen 2000; Lane 2000; Becker 2001; Deeg 2001; Hoepner 2001; Vitols, 2001; Streeck 2001; Beyer and Hassel 2002; Morgan and Kubo 2002). These writers implicitly or explicitly dwell instead on more evolutionary and cumulative change. They place great importance also on the influence of internal actors in bringing about radical change. Most important, they do not assume system coherence but posit hybridisation of systems, or identify buffers which prevent change in one part of the system, affecting other parts (Morgan and Kubo 2001). Although these recent critics have elaborated a much more sophisticated and valid notion of institutional change they do not go far enough and mistake a temporary phenomenon for the final outcome. Hence they are unable to do full justice to an understanding of processes of change currently observable in coordinated market economies.

This chapter will further explore some of the assumptions underlying both sets of arguments and, in doing so, adopt an institutionalist approach, combining elements of the 'rational actor' and the more sociological variant of New Institutionalism. It will agree with more recent analysts that transformation can result from cumulative change and that a consideration of internal actors is vital when trying to understand the process of change. I also accept their claim that institutional ensembles may change independently from each other and that, for a short time, systems may contain opposed logics. At the same time, I agree with Biggart and Guillen 1999; Whitley (1999) and Hall and Soskice (2001) that there is an inherent strain for system coherence or complementarity, based on an underlying institutional logic, which cannot be disrupted in the longer run if the system is to prosper. In contrast to the second set of analysts, the chapter therefore concludes that hybridisation can only be unstable and temporary. Top managers cannot make strategic decisions based on a market logic in one arena and resort to an opposed logic in another arena of decision-making. Instead, it will be argued that, in the longer term, we must expect either a return to the old path or the adoption of a new one. As adoption of an entirely new path rarely occurs, convergence to the currently hegemonic Anglo-American model is the more likely outcome. I will provide evidence that the general movement is towards convergence, as well as a careful specification of what the concept does and does not entail.

Two further issues need to be dealt with. First, how does one know whether institutional innovation, resulting from evolutionary and cumulative change, is within-system or bounded change or whether it has led to the adoption of a new path and a more fundamental system change? How does one distinguish one type of change from another? System change has occurred when a new logic has replaced the old one, i.e. when it is accepted by most influential actors in the political economy. It is being assumed that the system of corporate governance, which defines relations of control within firms, as well as pinpointing the main stakeholders, is crucial to the definition of the institutional logic linking all parts of the system.

Second, how does system change differ from hybridisation? Hybridisation usually implies that complementarity no longer exists and that different parts of the system are dominated by different logics. Thus, to illustrate, the logic of the liberal market economy may be accepted by actors in the capital market and in large listed firms, but not by unlisted large companies or by small and medium-sized firms and their banks (Deeg 2001). Or, alternatively, the new logic may dictate strategy in product markets but not in firm-internal systems of co-determination (Hoepner and Jackson 2001).

To sum up this section, it has been argued that transformation of core institutional arrangements of the German political economy has been more striking than reproduction and that it is necessary to arrive at a theoretical understanding of this momentous process. It has been suggested that hybridisation generally is an unstable temporary phenomenon. If a cumulative change in a central institution, i.e. the financial system, has fundamentally changed the logic which governs relations within that system, and is supported by powerful actors both within firms and the political system, hybridisation does not usually endure. The power and/or legitimacy of internal champions of change will lead to a spill-over into other parts of the system, even into those more remote from the stock market. Complementarity eventually will be restored. Hybridisation, however, may be more enduring if it is supported by some powerful internal actors and effective buffers between

different spheres of the economy are erected (see Morgan and Kubo 2002 on Japan). These theoretical claims will be substantiated in the empirical part of this paper focusing on contemporary changes in the system of corporate governance (Part III.2 to III.4). First, though, a short description of the German system of corporate governance during the post-war period and up to the middle 1990s will be outlined. This will identify the institutional logic and coherence of that system, as well as provide a base line against which more recent transformation may be assessed.

III REVIEW OF EMPIRICAL EVIDENCE

III.1 Historical sketch of the German financial system and form of corporate governance

Throughout the post-war period, until the mid-1990s, the German financial system and mode of corporate governance showed a high degree of stability, distinguishing it, for example, from the French system (Morin 2000). It has often been described as being diametrically opposed to the system of outsider control, prevalent in Britain (Lane 1992 and 1995; Mayer 2000; Heinze 2001) and in the US (O'Sullivan 2000).

Among sources of capital for German firms, retained earnings has been the most significant, leaving firms highly autonomous (Deutsche Bundesbank 1997: 37, quoted by Becker, p. 31). Bank debt was low, and issuing of shares through listing on the stock market was common only among a small proportion of the largest firms. Due to a number of reasons, the stock market remained underdeveloped and insignificant both for domestic and foreign investors. Hence stock market capitalisation has been low in comparison with Britain, the US and even Japan. Thus, during the period of 1982 to 1991, stock market capitalisation stood at only 20 percent of GDP, compared with 75 percent in the UK (Mayer 2000: 1). Ownership in German firms has been relatively concentrated, and family ownership is still significant even in some very large firms. Cross ownership of non-financial firms has been more pronounced and interlocking directorships have been highly developed (Windolf 2002). For all these reasons, hostile take-over was almost unknown. Although historically banks have been important insiders in German firms, occupying a high proportion of seats on supervisory boards, their ownership stakes during recent decades have not been high. Their importance as insider controllers has been upheld primarily by their ability to cast proxy votes on behalf of the many smaller investors whose shares they administer. Important rights of control have been vested in the supervisory board, which is independent from the management board and on which seats are held in varying proportions by representatives of owners and of employees. Relatively effective employee co-determination has been a distinctive feature of the system of governance.

Such a system of corporate governance has implications for a wider range of stakeholders. Hence top managers in this system are said to be less autonomous than their British counterparts (Vitols *et al.* 1997), being more accountable to both large owners, banks, employees and even the local community. Decision-making is more consensus-oriented and may even be described as more collective.

There has, however, been a relatively low constraint to deliver very high returns to shareholders, and instead stability of the firm, market growth, together with adequate profits, have been management goals. Managers usually made their career in a given industry and advanced to top positions within the internal labour market. These circumstances have enabled managers to pursue strategies, oriented towards longer-term returns, and this orientation has shaped the German practice of skill development and the production paradigm of diversified quality production. Employees possess legally guaranteed rights of control, and they have exercised them to safeguard their skills, their employment security and an equitable distribution of surplus between various stakeholders. The pay gap between top managerial staff and other employees has been far less pronounced than, for example, in Britain and the USA (Crouch and Streeck 1997). The other side of the coin is that financial control of organisational subunits has been relatively lax, financial transparency of companies low, and small investors have had no means to safeguard adequate returns on their investment.

The underlying logic, informing all parts of the German political economy, has been shaped by a network type of control, aiming for stability and growth, rather than short-term high returns on investment. This network has included employees as important stakeholders in the firm, entitled to a fair share of surplus and to co-decision-making in areas directly affecting their current and future well-being.

III.2 Recent institutional changes in the German capital market and system of corporate governance

III.2.1 Sources of change

This network system of corporate governance has begun to change during the second half of the 1990s. The external impetus for change has come from three main sources. There usually is considerable interdependence between them, but each source of change also can be effective in isolation. Many analyses of changes in the German model of capitalism have focused only on the transformation of the capital markets (e.g. Heinze 2001) or deny the marked interaction in the influence on firms of internationalised capital and goods markets (e.g. Beyer and Hassel 2002: 12). Only a consideration of all three sources and a recognition of their mutually reinforcing impact, however, is able to capture the full force for change.

The first source of change has been liberalisation of international capital markets and the greater readiness of hitherto 'national' capital to seek out the most profitable opportunities for both accessing and investing capital wherever this may be in the world. This has entailed the modernisation of capital markets in continental Europe and the spread of the Anglo-American model of organising them, as well as the greater participation of firms from coordinated market economies in the stock markets of liberal market economies. The impact of the US/UK model of organising capital markets has entailed an introduction of new actors to those markets – foreign investment funds – and has established enhanced legitimacy for and wide acceptance of their primary goal – improved shareholder value. This, in turn, has put pressures on listed firms to restructure their operations in line with fund managers' expectations, particularly to increase financial transparency. A prominent aspect of this is a demand for reduction of product diversity and for concentration on what is considered core business. Failure to de-diversify is sanctioned by the so-called conglomerate discount on the share prices of non-compliant firms. Greater pressure for enhanced profits and dividends has forced managers to turn previously integrated organisational sub-units into independent profit centres. Capital market actors thus clearly have introduced the logic of the market into firms and have been able to influence managers' strategic decision-making.

Intensified competition in product markets has been the second source of change. Greater competitive pressure has made it important to attain sufficient size and market influence to prevail against international competitors and thus has exerted pressure for capital concentration, through merger and acquisition. This, in turn, may precipitate listing on stock markets. (An example is the Merck KGaA pharmaceutical company which, although in majority family ownership, listed a proportion of its shares in 1996.) Competitiveness on international markets also has been shaped by product innovation. The much increased speed of innovation and the greatly enhanced cost of research and development to achieve it, have created further pressures for capital concentration and reliance on the stock market to achieve it.

A third source of change in corporate governance has been the development of new cultural and/or ideological orientations, shaped by three processes of cultural diffusion. Here the reference is to the concept of shareholder value and associated motivations, cognitions and scenarios for action. These have been widely propagated by consultancy firms which often are of Anglo-American origin. They also have been absorbed through participation in new programmes of management education, particularly the MBA, and, last, during extended spells of direct exposure to Anglo-American business environments when managing German subsidiaries in these two countries. The management practice of measuring performance through application of precise financial indicators, fundamental to the concept of shareholder value, has become widely adopted by and legitimate among higher German managers (Becker 2001). They are regarded as modern management approaches, the adoption of which enhances managerial reputation.

All these external pressures, it will be shown below, have not simply been imposed on unwilling financial and non-financial firms. Core and powerful economic actors have begun to identify their own interests with those of capital market actors and to actively promote internal change. Political actors have given them important legislative support and have not stepped in to prevent hostile take-over, as became evident in the recent takeover of Mannesmann by Vodafone. (For details, see Hoepner and Jackson 2001.) However, the current and previous social democratic governments have been sending out conflicting messages. The new Takeover Law, in force since 1 January 2002, permits the target management to put in place anti-takeover defences, provided these have either received support from 75 percent of shareholders or

have been authorised in advance by the supervisory board (Deakin *et al.* 2002). The government also has adopted a very pro-labour stance on the issue of labour market reform, insisting that reforms can only be introduced in a consensual manner. There is as yet no indication as to how these conflicting stances are to be reconciled.

III.2.2 Changes in capital markets

Wide-ranging changes in German capital markets have been effected by both important market actors and by government changes in legislation. A long list of changes from the mid 1990s onwards (for an exhaustive list, see Hoepner 2001) by 1998 had led to the modernisation of the organisation and regulation of the German stock market and to the establishment of a centralised capital market on the US/UK model. Particularly significant steps were: the weakening of the regional decentralisation of stock markets and the creation of a unified market in Frankfurt, to become the privatised Deutsche Boerse; the creation, in 1994, of a federal authority for market supervision; the establishment of legal rules and conventions, creating greater transparency in firm structures and actions; safeguarding of the rights of minority owners; the removal of hurdles to hostile takeover; the creation of the initially successful Neuer Markt for smaller, technology-intensive firms, which caused a wider diffusion and acceptance of the market principle both among smaller firms and small German investors; and some curtailment of banks' influence on company supervisory boards through some limitation of the rule on proxy voting and the number of chairmanships individual bankers can hold.

Other government legislation fuelled the expansion and influence of the stock market on firms. Among these were the authorisation of stock options as part of managers' reward package, in order to realign incentives; the legalisation of share buy-back; the introduction of a semi-voluntary company code to encourage greater transparency and accountability of firms to investors.

The most far-reaching piece of legislation, however, passed in 2000 and implemented in 2002, is the exemption from tax payments of gains from sales of blocks of shares, previously tied up in cross holdings. It is expected that this law, encouraging investors' withdrawal from long-term share-holdings in underperforming companies, will unravel the German system of cross shareholding. It is likely to dissolve the large block holdings and destroy the network character of corporate control. This, in turn, will constrain companies to become more reliant on stock markets. The greater dispersion of holdings then will provide investment opportunities for outsiders, thus making firms more vulnerable to takeovers. As non-financial firms are the most significant owners of other non-financial firms this would knock out the basis of the current German system of insider control and put into question the long-termism that patient capital has permitted.

All these measures also have changed the role of banks, both in capital markets and within firms. Banks have begun to recognise that their business in large firms had been diminishing (Becker 2001; Deeg 2001) and, simultaneously, that more money could be made in underwriting and the lucrative market for company buying and selling. Deutsche Bank has led the way in transforming itself and entering investment banking on the Anglo-American model, and several other banks have since followed this move. Banks' partial disengagement from insider control is evident in their reduced representation on company supervisory boards (Luetz 2000) and, more dramatically from a significant surrender of chairmanships. Thus, between 1992 and 1999, banks' share of chairmanships fell from 44 to 23 percent in the largest forty companies (Hoepner 2001). They now have slightly less control over proxy votes (Deeg 2001). Together, these developments indicate their reduced willingness and capacity for insider monitoring. Deutsche Bank and Allianz – between them the most significant owners of large listed companies – have made it clear that they intend to restructure their holdings in accordance with profit levels (Heinze 2001). Many banks already put greater emphasis on short- and middle-term increases in share values of the companies in their ownership portfolio (Becker 2001: 316).

III.2.3 Changes within firms

The number of companies listed on the stock market has increased very slightly as has listing on foreign markets, and the proportion of shares owned by foreign institutional investors increased from 4 percent in 1990 to 13 percent in 1998 (Deeg 2001: 27, footnote 39). Also the degree of dispersion of share ownership has risen slightly. Those companies already quoted undertook a number of changes, significantly affecting corporate governance, organisational structures and strategies and the relations with other stakeholders. However, the number listed has remained small and of those quoted, only a minority

– around 10 percent – significantly changed their ownership structure and became exposed to takeover (Heinze 2001). A market for corporate control, it is widely agreed, has not yet developed. But the market is nevertheless shaping many managers' expectations and interests, and external monitoring of listed companies is prevalent. Together, these are sufficient to have exerted a significant effect on internal strategic decision-making. Many companies not exposed to shareholder pressures have adopted elements of the notion of shareholder value to legitimate restructuring and a greater performance orientation. Even firms still in substantial or total family ownership, such as Boehringer Ingelheim and Merck KGaA, now work with financial indicators and targets, as well as using managerial incentives, normally found only in listed and/or widely held companies.

Hence the influence of the stock market on managerial attitudes, goals and strategies of chemical/pharmaceutical companies has been pervasive, affecting both listed and unlisted internationally oriented companies. Although there is little evidence that investment funds are exerting strong direct external control over managers, the indirect influence of the stock market, via the movement of share prices, has been considerable. The listed companies are now more subject to external monitoring and have responded to such monitoring to varying degrees. This is evident not only in a greater cultivation of investor relations, the adoption of international accounting standards and the issuing of quarterly reports (Beyer and Hassel 2001). It is additionally expressed in more fundamental changes of strategy and structure, relating to enterprise goals, such as mode of growth, selection of product portfolio, incentive structures and systems of payment (Becker 2001; Hoepner 2001). The following examples from one industry will illustrate what I believe to be a more general trend.

As firm size is becoming more crucial to survival in global markets, more firms have had to dilute owner control and become listed to raise the additional capital needed for expansion (e.g. Merck KGaA and Fresenius) or to swap shares in mergers. Concern with the movement of company share price then motivates managers to introduce various strategy changes, welcomed and rewarded by capital market actors. Some or all of the following changes in strategy have been implemented by companies in the chemical/pharmaceutical industry: introduction of sometimes ambitious targets for growth in turnover and profits (most large companies in the industry); changes in organisational structure to enable better control of performance by both top managements and capital market actors, as well as to facilitate listing of organisational sub-units (Hoechst, Bayer and Fresenius); introduction of share options or equivalent schemes to align managerial incentives with those of investors (all major companies in the industry); introduction of reward systems for employees, tied to the company's or business unit's performance (all large companies in the industry); some reduction of product diversity to enhance transparency and a greater shift to the more profitable pharmaceuticals segment (executed most consequentially by Hoechst/Aventis and more hesitantly by most of the other companies) (Company Annual Reports 2001/02; Becker 2001).

Unlisted firms and those still substantially under family control have responded to a lesser degree. But they nevertheless have been compelled to make partial adjustments as they operate in the same competitive environment as the companies exposed to stock market control. Some also have found it convenient to refer to shareholder value notions to push through measures to enhance employee performance or to justify restructuring and job cutting. Thus Boehringer Ingelheim, still wholly family-owned, nevertheless has introduced changes in organisational structure which force managers to take more responsibility for their unit's performance and has introduced 'shareholder value' indicators for purposes of internal control. Additionally, the company has introduced a functional equivalent to a share option scheme, in order to attract and retain high calibre top managers (Becker 2001: 299). Merck KGaA, although over 70 percent family-owned, has introduced share options for the same reason (ibid.: 310).

Many of the younger managers, often with US training or experience, in any case are less committed to the German company structure and culture. Financial and business specialists are now more likely to be selected for promotion to management boards (Hoepner 2001; Baecker 2001), necessarily causing partial displacement of the traditionally strongly entrenched production-oriented engineers. (The radical restructuring of Hoechst, for example, in line with shareholder demands, was master-minded by just such a financial specialist – Juergen Dormann.) Career patterns of higher managers also are becoming more similar to those of their Anglo-American counterparts, as evidenced in the dramatic decline in

the average time in post during the 1990s (Hoepner 2001) – a feature more conducive to adopting a strong stance on raising short-term profitability. More generally, the new generation of German top managers recognises the importance of financial indicators and targets as bases for strategic decision-making (Becker 2001: 274). In sum, important aspects of managerial strategies have been decisively shaped by changes in corporate governance, even if there is still resistance on some aspects and different firms have adapted at different speeds and to different degrees.

All these changes in strategy, structure and reward systems have impacted on employees and on organised labour, i.e. company co-determination systems and industrial relations at industry level. Negative repercussions for employee stakeholders have been various. The famed German employment security has been eroded in some large shareholder value companies. Selling off or closing of sub-units and large-scale job cutting have become prevalent. Such firms now spend a higher share of net value generated on dividends and a lower proportion on labour (Beyer and Hassel 2002: 15, reporting on a survey of the 59 largest German companies). They have not reduced spending on labour but have cut the level of employment and thus have intensified labour for remaining employees (ibid.). In 'shareholder value' companies, a greater proportion of employees' pay is now variable (Kurdelbusch 2001), creating further insecurity, as well as undermining labour solidarity. Company-wide representation and the solidarity it affords have been weakened by linking pay more strongly to performance of individual company sub-units. A much increased focus by employees on the profitability and survival of their employing company also has made employee representatives less willing to cooperate with unions to achieve wider industry goals (Hoepner 2001: 27). At the same time, labour has not been fundamentally opposed to the imposition of shareholder value, and it has even seen some of the new developments, such as greater company financial transparency, as being very much in its own interest (ibid.). Hence organised labour, particularly at the company level, appears to be coopted into a more neo-liberal model.

III.3 Persistence of the German model

The story told so far has provided a one-sided picture. Many features of the old system of corporate governance persist, and convergence to and divergence from the Anglo-American model exist side by side in a complex mixture. An assessment of the degree of persistence has to bear in mind, however, that German companies have only achieved financial internationalisation since the late 1990s.

The most glaring example of persistence of the old financial system is that German firms have not been rushing to become listed, and the German stock market, in comparative perspective, remains strongly undercapitalised. Hence only the large flagship companies, and not all of those, are subject to stock market pressure, and family ownership of even very large companies persists. Companies become listed much later in their life cycle and at a much higher size threshold than in the UK (Mayer 2000: 1). Individual shareholding, although increased, remains low by international standards and thus retards the development of a shareholder psychology. Recent adverse developments in the capital markets, particularly the collapse of the Neuer Markt, have called forth a renewed scepticism about financial markets.

Among listed companies, ownership concentration, sustained often by cross ownership of shares, remains significant. Average size of voting blocks of nearly 50 percent may be opposed to blocks of less than ten percent for UK companies (Mayer 2000: 2). This continues to obstruct the development of an outsider system of control and of a market for corporate control. The influence of foreign investment funds – the most insistent claimants for shareholder value – has been significant in only a small proportion of cases – about ten percent of large listed companies.

Also there has been no change in company law, and the system of codetermination is still intact. Employee stakeholders still retain some degree of influence, if not control, within the enterprise, even if intensified competition often makes it difficult to voice their demands. The two-tier board, designed for insider control, also remains in place.

III.4 Balance of change and persistence: hybridisation?

The discussion under III.2 has shown that the German system of corporate governance has experienced far-reaching change in its underlying logic, indicating significant convergence with the Anglo American system. But, at the same time, it shows stubborn resistance to change on some central features of corporate governance. Most analysts nevertheless agree that the German financial system of corporate governance has converged to the Anglo-American model, but they do not wish to go as far as positing convergence for the whole political economy or variety of capitalism. Instead, these analysts are suggesting that other institutional configurations are persisting or merely are adapting in incremental ways. Hence these scholars prefer to conceptualise current transformations as a process of hybridisation (Deeg 2001; Vitols 2001 ; Streeck 2001; Beyer and Hassel 2002) or, more obscurely, posit the occurrence of hybrid convergence (Hoepner 2001). Such conclusions capture important aspects of the process of institutional transformation at the beginning of the 21st century. One important variant of the hybridisation thesis is that radical transformation in one institutional configuration calls forth adaptive functional conversion in other parts of the political economy. Such conversion, according to Thelen (2000: 105), occurs when exogenous shocks empower new actors who harness existing organisational forms in the service of new ends. Diagnoses of hybridisation have taken different forms, and three different arguments in support of hybridisation will be examined critically in the following. They will be analysed both for their internal theoretical coherence and for their plausibility in the light of empirical developments.

For some of these authors, advocacy of hybridisation is based on the belief that the great internal diversity of the German economy creates highly diverse contingencies for firms and hence, despite some common pressures, precludes convergent development (Deeg 2001; Vitols 2001; Becker 2001). The focus is particularly on diversity in terms of sector, size and type of firm, as well as degree of exposure to global pressures. A second argument advanced against convergence points to diversity in managerial perceptions, cognitive focal points and evaluations of contingent circumstances, regarded as at least in part endogenous to the institutions which govern managerial actors' rationality. This, in turn, is deemed to preserve diversity in strategy and hence in forms of corporate governance and other institutional constellations (Becker 2001). A third variant of the hybridisation thesis is that the system of codetermination and democratic participation of labour is both so well entrenched and of such centrality to the German production paradigm of diversified quality production that management will find a way to combine the logic of the capital market with the logic of an employee stakeholder system (Hoepner 2001; Hoepner and Jackson 2001; Streeck 2001; Beyer and Hassel 2002). Evoking Thelen's (2000) concept of functional conversion, it is being suggested (Hoepner 2001) that institutionalised practices of co-determination have become transformed, in order to re-establish complementarity with the system of corporate governance. In the process, they have changed from being an institutional structure to negotiate on issues of a 'class' type to one mainly supporting the company goal of enhanced efficiency.

How persuasive are these various hybridisation theses? Becker (2001) and Vitols (2001), in support of the first hybridisation thesis, cite the differing product strategies, organisational forms and cultures of large companies even in the same industry – chemical/ pharmaceutical – and contrast what they see as the highly divergent paths taken by Hoechst/Aventis, Bayer and BASF. This argument about diversity between firms, in my view, underestimates the pressure for isomorphic adaptation which emanates from the business press and the example of the large flagship companies. Additionally, it wrongly suggests that transformation of the German political economy could only occur if all economic actors were to adopt the 'shareholder value' model to the same degree.

A close analysis of recent developments of the three chemical/pharmaceutical giants, however, shows that Hoechst was merely the first to choose a strategy of de-diversification and radical organisational and legal restructuring in 1996/97. Bayer and BASF, although originally much more wedded to the retention of a diverse product portfolio and a traditional integrated organisational structure, have begun to embark on a similar, albeit still less radical path. Bayer retains chemicals for the time being, but the proportion of pharmaceuticals in the portfolio is being systematically increased. In 2002, the company began to restructure itself into a holding company, with legally independent subsidiaries – a pattern highly reminiscent of the Hoechst model. The push to proceed in this way clearly came from the capital market. According to the company's web site, this new structure gives greater transparency for internal resource allocation, for the capital market and for stockholders (Bayer web site, 13.8.2002). It may well be a preparation for the planned acquisition of pharmaceutical companies, to further increase the focus on this business area, favoured by the capital market. Both Bayer and Hoechst/Aventis, on Hoepner's index of shareholder value orientation, are ranked

very highly, and Bayer even tops Hoechst/Aventis in the ranking list. It is only in the area of gaining focus on core competences that Bayer has moved more slowly. BASF, too, has sought to gain more focus, albeit in a different direction from Hoechst. In 2000, it shed its business in pharmaceuticals to concentrate on chemicals. (Its subsidiary Knoll, which had the largest part of the pharmaceutical operations, was sold to Abbott Laboratories.) Thus, the three companies have not adopted identical strategies, but they are clearly changing in the same direction, albeit at different speeds.

Most other large German chemical/pharmaceutical companies have been engaged in strategic and organisational adjustments oriented towards capital market actors. Some have engaged in organisational restructuring affording greater internal and external transparency, others have down-graded geographical divisions (Landesgesellschaften) in favour of product-based business units. All have become more performance-oriented and have set relatively high profit targets to signal to capital market actors that they are concerned to raise shareholder value. According to Becker (2001), 'in all enterprises, there occurred during the 1990s, an upgrading of financial controlling, closely allied to centralisation of strategic management and the granting of operational independence to operative units, all allied to the use of performance indicators and targets as bases for decision-making (ibid.: 273–74). It is only in the area of greater focus on core competences that most German chemical-pharmaceutical companies have stalled and are holding on to a more diversified product portfolio for reasons of risk distribution.

Nor is diversity as pronounced when we move to other industries or descend in the size scale of firms. Although the pharmaceutical industry is among the most highly internationalised ones, there now exists hardly any industry sheltered from competitive pressures in international markets for capital and goods and services. Even industries with a low export propensity are exposed to international pressures from inward investors and, if listed, are not immune from takeover. The studies by Hoepner (2001) and Zugehoer (2001) well illustrate that the shareholder value orientation is prevalent also in other industries.

Furthermore, competitive pressures affect both large and medium-sized firms, albeit to different degrees. Firms in both size classes have to find funds to increase their size or to increase investment in R&D, in order to stay ahead in the international competitive race. Nor are smaller firms totally exempt from pressures as large firms have to pass on cost pressures to their smaller suppliers. The existence, until recently, of the Neuer Markt, too, has familiarised smaller firms with market practices and values. Pressures on non-commercial savings banks to become more profit-oriented, too, in the longer run will force them to pass these on to their SME clients, especially after the planned demise of the privileges currently still enjoyed by savings banks (Lane and Quack 2000).

Turning to the second argument, managers do indeed differ in the extent to which they acknowledge and accept the new pressures for greater transparency and shareholder value. But their perceptions, interests and motivations have been changing, together with the changing institutions and business culture. They are increasingly being shaped by the ideology of shareholder value. Associated goals and practices, such as monitoring profitability with numerical targets, are not seen in ideological terms, but as being part of modern management practice, likely to raise reputation. Hence some managers have embraced the new ideology with alacrity as, for example, the chief executive of Hoechst; others have done so more partially (the previous CEO of Bayer) or more reluctantly (the previous CEO of Merck) when the adverse consequences of non-compliance for stock price became obvious. In 2000, the Aventis share surpassed that of Bayer in value by nearly 100 percent although Bayer had been, if anything, more profitable than Aventis/Hoechst during most of the 1990s. But it was being punished by the so-called conglomerate discount, whereas Hoechst/Aventis was rewarded for conforming to all demands of capital market actors (Becker 2001: 137-140, 145). Merck's chief executive – a member of one of the owning families – publicly railed against stock market actors' demands and tried to pursue a strategy of maximum stability of earnings for the owning families. Merck's share price, despite good overall performance, consequently did poorly. This chief executive has now been replaced by a more compliant professional manager, and the share price has risen accordingly (ibid.). The new pressures for enhanced performance and more transparent organisation, exerted on managers of large listed companies, have to be passed on to both their subordinates and their business partners and thus gradually will diffuse throughout the economy.

The claim by Hoepner and Jackson (2001) that 'shareholder value and co-determination do get along fine' exemplifies one position among the third set of arguments for hybridisation. The authors are referring to the fact that many works councils have undergone functional conversion and are now seeing their main function as supporting management goals of enhancing efficiency and competitiveness (ibid.). The argument by Hoepner and Jackson (2001) that this institution is persisting, despite the changed logic of the system of corporate governance, does not convince. The goals of co-determination, it is true, therefore are no longer in opposition to those of corporate governance, but the reverse relation does not hold. Adherence to the shareholder value principle by management means putting investors first, and many of the activities undertaken to satisfy investors go counter to employees' interests, as already detailed in section III.2. What persists is only an institutional shell, emptied of all the old ideological content which allowed bodies of codetermination to execute checks on and provide a counterweight to the power of capital. The collapse of any real chances for co-determination and its substitution with a co-management stance would be better described by the term 'loss of function', than by the grand label of 'functional conversion'.

Up to now, the system of co-determination and the stakeholder company have, indeed, been deeply entrenched in contemporary German political culture, and it has appeared unlikely that any government would change the co-determination laws. But it now appears that the institution is no longer sacrosanct. The Commission which drafted the new corporate governance code is planning to introduce a new measure, designed to weaken the system of co-determination. This would permit companies which have more than half their employees overseas to opt out of being bound by co-determination (*Financial Times*, 8. November 2002: 9). Many of the big companies already have achieved or could easily achieve this 'overseas' employment target.

Even if such legal change were not to occur, the institution of co-determination already has been weakened from within. There no longer exists a link between the incentive structure underpinning corporate governance and that shaping industrial and labour relations. If the whole logic of the system of corporate governance has left or is in the process of leaving the path of stakeholder capitalism, then the continued existence of an empty institutional shell will not stand in the way of convergence.

A stronger argument in favour of a hybrid outsider/insider system of control is advanced by Streeck (2001) and Beyer and Hassel (2002). Echoing the view of Biggart and Guillen (19991) that a certain system logic 'breeds' certain capabilities, conducive to cultivation of particular market niches, they rightly point to the indispensability to the German production paradigm of high levels of human capital development and consensual decision-making. They further strengthen their claims by pointing to empirical evidence that, to date, wage levels have not fallen and commitment to a high-skill economy has not noticeably weakened.

Beyer and Hassel (2002) further claim that investors have not shown themselves opposed to the expensive training system and may recognise that this system enables German firms to deliver higher value. They therefore conclude that institutional investors might be willing to forego short-term profit maximisation in favour of longer-term gains. Beyer and Hassel (2002) thus are citing the arguments of 'enlightened shareholder value' and refer to the professed willingness of some fund managers to support the 'high road' to simultaneous gain both for shareholders and other stakeholders. But unfortunately, at the time of writing, these professed enlightened goals hardly have been put to the test. Research done in the UK on implicit contracts in the negotiation of takeover conditions established that, though legal and regulatory provisions permit directors to temper the pursuit of shareholders' interests with those of employees, in a situation of conflict of interests shareholders' short-term financial interests usually prevailed over those of employees (Deakin *et al.* 2002: 14, 24).

Furthermore, although many managers and policy makers will no doubt wish to preserve the venerable paradigm of 'diversified quality production', powerful constraints for profit maximisation will make this a much more problematic endeavour than is recognised by Beyer and Hassel (2002). Their argument attributes more subtle behaviour to investors than is possible in an arms' length market environment where resources usually flow to producers who are likely to guarantee the highest returns. Furthermore, their assumption that patience by stock holders will necessarily be rewarded by higher future yields from German producers is dubious. Although diversified quality production has served the German economy well it has never delivered above average returns of the magnitude which, for example, has induced

venture capitalists to take a long-term perspective in high-technology sectors. Nor is there evidence that the government would intervene to shore up the expensive German system of human resources development.

The various points made above seriously question whether the various theses on hybridisation and/or functional conversion will continue to be useful for the analysis of developmental trends in the German variety of capitalism. The next section therefore will pose the case for convergence. To do so, I will identify the underlying pressures which will eventually destabilise the hybrid system and initiate more complete convergence, as well as pinpoint the developments which already indicate such a progressive trend.

III.5 Pressures for system convergence

As pointed out by Deeg (2001), the changes in the capital market now are so well established that they have become irreversible. They have created a new logic for corporate governance which will prove compelling in the longer run. This is all the more the case because these changes have been accepted and promoted by powerful internal actors – German commercial banks and the insurance company Allianz. The gains from the switch to outsider control have amply compensated the large commercial banks for the progressive attenuation of insider control, and their interests now are firmly aligned with a stock market oriented economy (Becker 2001).

Their enduringly powerful position in the German political economy makes it most likely that these financial institutions have been instrumental in nudging the Schroeder government towards support for system change. This has been evident in the reluctance to intervene to save Mannesmann from takeover (Heinze 2001). But more important, the introduction of the so-called Eichel law, which encourages the unravelling of the system of cross shareholding by non-financial companies, has been passed without much debate. As the law only took effect in 2002, nothing definite can be said on its impact at this moment in time. But it appears highly likely that the vast opportunities for gain, entailed by withdrawing poorly performing ownership stakes for utilisation in more lucrative investments, will be seized by both financial and non-financial firms. Indeed, both Deutsche Bank and Allianz already have signalled their intention to follow this course of action (Heinze 2001). Such a development would further transform the system of corporate governance, leading to de-concentration of capital holdings, much increased stock market listing, new openings for foreign investment funds and hence to a market for corporate control. This would deal the death knell to the old-entrenched German system of cross shareholding and the system of insider control it has been upholding.

Pressures for convergence have come not only from capital market actors, but the ideology and practice of shareholder value also have been more or less enthusiastically embraced by a significant group of company managers – those making strategic decisions in internationalised firms. Their positive stance towards the concept of shareholder value has been brought about by changes both in business culture and by new powerful incentive structures. Processes of cultural diffusion have wrought changes in what is considered legitimate business behaviour and what serves to enhance managerial reputation. Changes in incentive structures mean that strategic managers' interests are better served by a transformation of the German model of corporate governance.

Although this transformation is not in the longer-run interest of labour, in the short run employees have not necessarily been averse to the new model as share ownership has been made widely available to employees at all levels of the firm (Becker 2001; Hoepner 2001). This might at least partly explain the low degree of opposition from labour against the change in corporate governance introduced. The growing conflict between the goals of company-based industrial relations actors and unionists (Hoepner 2001), together with a pronounced weakening of organised labour during the last decade or so, also explains wide-spread acquiescence.

Another powerful impetus for convergence, discussed in detail by O'Sullivan (2000) and hence not covered in this paper, comes from the crisis of the German pensions system and the increased likelihood of developing private schemes ensuring higher liquidity of funds. Such a development would boost the importance of pension funds as prominent stock market actors on the Anglo-American model and enlarge the German stock market.

Last, pressures for convergence have existed for only a relatively short period of time, gaining momentum only during the late 1990s. If they have been able to unleash fundamental change in so many areas in this short time span we must expect that many hith-erto persistent features of the German variety of capitalism will be swept away during the coming decade.

IV CONCLUSIONS

The preceding theoretical analysis and empirical description of changes in the German model of corporate governance since the mid-1990s has considered both the nature and the outcomes of change. It has attempted to make evident the complexity of the change process and has explored the conditions which have to be fulfilled in order to diagnose either system reproduction or system convergence. There has been a particular focus on how to conceptualise the role which the notions of institutional logic and of institutional coherence or complementarity play in our understanding of change, and the discussion also has problematised the notion of hybridisation.

I have explored whether the outcome or direction of change in the German case can best be conceptualised as persistence of the model of coordinated market capitalism, as imminent convergence to the model of 'liberal market' capitalism, or whether the current state of affairs is best typified as a hybrid model, incorporating elements from both varieties of capitalism.

The virtual consensus of previous analyses of the transformations in Germany has been that, despite much persistence of traditional 'coordinated market' features, change in the core area of corporate governance has been fundamental and that a new logic is in the process of establishing itself. Change has proceeded too far and is supported by too many powerful 'within system' actors to be reversible. However, in contrast to previous analysts, this paper has concluded that the typification of this process of change as hybridisation is unhelpful. It can at most depict a temporary unstable stage of development. The new logic of corporate governance is beginning to feed through into other sections of the economy – beyond the larger listed and highly internationalised firms – and to other institutional sub-systems, particularly to labour relations and utilisation and development of human resources. In this way, it eventually will lead to convergence with the Anglo-American model. Further development in the direction of convergence is not simply attributed to external constraints, but is shown to be receiving support from powerful actors within the German economy, particularly from large banks and insurance companies and from many of the large internationally oriented and listed German companies, but also from some politicians. Such internal support is explained in terms of change in both cultural orientations and incentive structures of these actors. Evidence in support of an emergent tendency towards convergence is drawn from an analysis of managerial behaviour in the vital area of strategic decision-making.

The chapter has *not* argued that the German variety of capitalism already has converged towards the Anglo-American type. It has merely identified a developmental tendency and predicts an intensification of this tendency in the coming decades. My focus on convergence has not been based on any functionalist assumption of a necessity to imitate the most successful economic model but on the belief that it would be dangerous to underestimate or ignore such tendencies. An important precipitating event here will be the implementation of the Eichel law and the likely dissolution of the cross-shareholding system which has been at the very heart of the German variety of capitalism for more than a century. Such convergence will not entail the copying of all details of the model of liberal market capitalism, but the embracing of the underlying logic of shareholder value nevertheless will have a powerful transformative impact on all relations within and between firms. A system of corporate governance does not have a determining impact but also depends to some degree on the values of those most centrally involved in its implementation and on the nature of the environment in which they have to operate (Deakin *et al.* 2001). This implies that shareholder value might be implemented in a manner more congruent with German institutionalised practices. Such implementation will, however, fall short of hybridisation and would be better described as a softening of the hard edges of the 'liberal market' model.

Occurrence of convergence to liberal market capitalism is not merely of theoretical interest. It will have far-reaching practical consequences, to the detriment of employees and organised labour, as well as increasing the level of social inequality in German society. It is, therefore, important to ask whether there are any powerful or influential supporters within Germany of the *status quo* who might be able to erect buffers between the capital market and labour and industrial relations.

Here the arguments of Hoepner (2001) and Beyer and Hassel (2002) carry particular weight. They point out that the production paradigm of diversified quality production is indispensable to German international competitiveness and that it is premised on cooperative labour relations. The latter involves the continuation of active participation by labour in shaping company strategy and adherence to the high-wage/high skill model. The question thus becomes whether the proven importance of viewing labour as a stakeholder would result in the adoption of a model which can satisfy both international investors and labour.

Hoepner (2001) and Beyer and Hassel (2002) plead for the evolution of a new stable system, combining two different logics which may nevertheless establish complementarity. I am, however, sceptical of the claim that the combination of two opposed logics can result in the establishment of complementarity and a stable system. My pessimism about evolving a new complementarity is based on two arguments. First, even the German managers who would like to preserve the old system and its values may either succumb to the powerful incentives of the 'shareholder value' idea and become seduced by the new opportunities for material enrichment they offer. Or they will be constrained to implement the shareholder value concept, even if they do not welcome it. Last, functional conversion of the institutions of co-determination is not likely to save them as meaningful industrial relations entities. Although the structures may persist, their rationale will be changed fundamentally. They will no longer be an avenue through which labour may exert a significant amount of insider control – the feature which has long endowed the German variety of capitalism with its distinctive character. Although the legal shell may remain in place for a while, the new capital market regulations and their pressures on top managers to conform to investors' demands will transform co-determination mechanisms from encouraging labour participation in strategic decision-making to merely endorsing such management decisions.

But the future is never as closed as my pessimistic prognosis makes it appear, and events may occur to halt or reverse the convergence process. Given the strength of cultural values and social institutional embeddedness of the 'Rhine' model, there may yet emerge a coalition of industrial managers, representatives of labour and politicians working for a new, as yet inchoate compromise solution. The present government owes its re-election to union support, and both cautious labour market reform and the 2002 Takeover Law are indicative of a stance trying to protect the old system.

At the present time, however, the emergence of such a macro level coalition cannot be detected – political leaders still send out mixed messages and confusing signals. At the micro level, continually shifting shorter-term alliances between investors, managers and labour are more notable (Hoepner 2001: 27).

Alternatively, powerful external shocks and a sea change in the international business environment could reverse the convergence process. The 'Enron' syndrome has dented the faith in the US system of corporate governance, but it has not completely undermined it. The passing of the Sarbanes-Oxley Act, moreover, has already begun to restore investor confidence. The only chance for a halting or reversal of the convergence process lies in a strong de-legitimation of the Anglo-American system of corporate governance. This might come about through the occurrence of deep world economic recession and the inability of the US economy to find a way out of it.

REFERENCES

Becker, S. 2001, *Einfluss und Grenzen des Shareholder Value. Strategie- und Strukturwandel deutscher Grossunternehmen der chemischen und pharmazeutischen Industrie.* Frankfurt a. Main/Peter Lang.

Berger, S. and Dore, R. eds. 1997, *National Diversity and Global Capitalism.* Oxford: OUP.

Beyer, J. and Hassel , A. 2002, 'The market for corporate control and financial internationalisation of German firms', *Economy and Society,* 31.

Biggart, N.W. and Guillen, M. F. 1999, 'Developing difference: social organization and the rise of the auto industries of South Korea, Taiwan, Spain, Argentina', *American Sociological Review,* 64, 5: 722–747.

Crouch, C. and Streeck, W. (eds) 1997, *Political Economy of Modern Capitalism. Mapping convergence and diversity.* London: Sage.

Deakin, S. Hobbs, R., Konzelmann, S. and Wilkinson, F. 2001, 'Partnership, Ownership and Control: the Impact of Corporate Governance on Employment Relations'. ESRC Centre for Business Research Working Paper 200.

Deakin, S., Hobbs, R., Nash, D. and Slinger, G. 2002, 'Implicit contracts, takeovers, and corporate governance: in the shadow of the city code'. ESRC Centre for Business Research, University of Cambridge Working Paper 254.

Deeg, R. 2001, 'Institutional change and the uses and limits of path dependency: the case of German finance'. 01/06. Unpublished paper, posted on web site www.mpli-fg-Koeln.mpg.de.

Hall, P. and Soskice, D. 2001, *Varieties of Capitalism,* Oxford: OUP.

Heinze, T. 2001, 'Transformation des Deutschen Unternehmenskontroll-Systems?' *Koelner Zeitschrift f. Soziologie und Sozialpsychologie,* 53, 4: 641–674.

Hoepner, M. 2001, 'Corporate governance in transition: ten empirical findings on shareholder value and industrial relations.' Discussion Paper 01/5, Max-Planck-Institut f. Gesellschaftsforschung, Cologne.

Hoepner, M. and Jackson, G. 2001, An emergent market for corporate control? The Mannesmann takeover and German corporate governance. MPIfG Discussion Paper 01/4, Cologne: MPIf.G.

Hoepner, M. and Jackson, G. 2002, 'Das deutsche System der Corporate Governance zwischen Persistenz und Konvergenz'. Replik auf den Beitrag von Thomas Heinze in Heft 4/2001 der KZfSS. Koelner Zeitschrift f. Soziologie und Sozialpsychologie, 54, 2: 362–368.

Hollingsworth, J.R. and Boyer, R. (eds) 1997, *Contemporary Capitalism. The embeddedness of institutions.* Cambridge: Cambridge University Press.

Kitschelt, H., Lange, P., Marks, G. and Stephens, J. (eds) 1999, *Continuity and Change in Contemporary Capitalism.* Cambridge: Cambridge University Press.

Kurdelbusch, A. 2001, 'The upswing of variable pay in Germany – evidence and explanations'. Unpublished paper. Max-Planck-Institut f. Gesellschaftsforschung. Cologne.

Lane, C. 1992, 'European business systems: Britain and Germany compared', R. Whitley (ed.), *European Business Systems. Firms and Markets in their National Contexts.* London: Sage.

Lane, C. 1995, *Industry and Society in Europe. Stability and Change in Britain, Germany and France.* Aldershot: Edward Elgar.

Lane, C. and Quack, S. 2001, How banks construct and manage risk. A sociological study of small firm lending in Britain and Germany. Working Paper 217, Centre for Business Research, University of Cambridge.

Mayer, C. 2000, 'Corporate Governance in the UK'. *Hume Papers on Public Policy,* 8, 1, 2000: 1–9.

Morgan, G. and Kubo, I. 2002, 'Beyond path dependency? Constructing new models for institutional change: the case of capital markets in Japan'. Paper presented at the 18th EGOS Colloquium, Barcelona, July 2002.

Morin, F. 2000, 'A transformation in the French model of shareholding and management, *Economy and Society,* 29, 1: 36–53.

O'Sullivan, M.A. 2000, *Contests for Corporate Control. Corporate governance and economic performance in the United States and Germany.* Oxford: Oxford University Press.

Streeck, W. 2001, 'The transformation of corporate organization in Europe: an overview'. MPIfG Working Paper 01/8, December 2001. MPIfG/Cologne/Germany.

Thelen, K. 2000, 'Timing and temporality in the analysis of institutional evolution and change', *Studies in American Political Development,* 14, 1: 101–108.

Vitols, S., Casper, S. Soskice, D. and Woolcock, S. 1997, *Corporate governance in large British and German companies.* London: Anglo-German Foundation.

Vitols, S. 2001, 'Viele Wege nach Rom? BASF, Bayer und Hoechst'. Unpublished paper. Wissenschaftszentrum Berlin/Germany.

Whitley, R. 1992, *European Business Systems. Firms and markets in national context.* London: Sage.

Whitley, R. 1999, *Divergent Capitalisms. The Social Structuring and Change of Business Systems.* Oxford: Oxford University Press.

Windolf, P. 2000, *Corporate Networks in Europe and the United States.* Oxford: Oxford University Press.

Zugehoer, R. 2001, 'Capital market, codetermination and corporate restructuring. A comparative study of Siemens and Veba'. Paper presented at the 13th Annual Meeting of the Society for the Advancement of Socio-Economics, Amsterdam, 28 June–1 July.

9 "Convergence or Divergence? The Outlines of an Answer"

from Corporate Governance Adrift: A Critique of Shareholder Value (2005)

Michel Aglietta and Antoine Rebérioux

We [...] have two principal and opposing systems of corporate governance. The US system considers the firm to be the object of property rights; the submission of this object to the interests of the shareholders is achieved in the first place by the depth and liquidity of stock markets. The continental European model, on the contrary, is founded on a holistic or partnerial vision of the firm; company management is partially protected from the stock market by the stability of large blockholdings and by employee participation.

The thesis of convergence, with its underlying apologetic vision of shareholder value, sees in current developments a gradual abandonment of continental specificities in favour of an alignment with US standards. Besides the development within business circles of a rhetoric focused on the creation of value for shareholders, there are three empirical elements underpinning this thesis. Taken together, these factors are said to be contributing to a shift in the centre of gravity of the continental model of governance, away from 'inside' control towards 'outside' control.

- The first and most obvious factor is the significant increase in the weight of stock markets, in terms of both the traditional indicator of stock market capitalization as a proportion of GDP, and the daily volume of exchanges carried out in the different stock markets;
- Following this movement, banks are investing more in capital markets to the detriment of their traditional role as both lender and controlling shareholder;

- Lastly, US and British institutional investors (pension and mutual funds) have steadily asserted their presence in the capital markets, to the point where, today, these institutional investors are the second most important shareholders in France. The penetration of foreign investors in the capital of German companies also appears to have accelerated since the second half of the 1990s (Gehrke, 2002).

In the first analysis, these developments do indeed represent a weakening of the characteristic traits of the continental model, but they are insufficient to justify any affirmation of convergence towards the US model. It is difficult, for example, to grasp the impact of market liquidity on the exercise of power within companies without examining the performance of the takeover market. Likewise, the weight of institutional investors in equity capital is not enough to assert that these investors are running the companies. We now present an overall appraisal of the thesis of convergence, concentrating on the transformations that affect the structures of ownership and the legal environment. The current movement appears to us to be much more complex than that announced by the 'end of history' thesis.[1]

FINANCIAL MARKET LAW AS A FACTOR OF CONVERGENCE

Parallel to the very favourable development of capital markets, financial market law is the domain which has undoubtedly drawn closest to US standards.

First, obligations in terms of the disclosure of information and financial transparency have greatly increased. The European Union has been a driving force behind this increase. The 1988 directive on financial transparency, aiming to develop information about the identity of shareholders, gave impetus to this movement, even though its transposition into national law took time: Germany only became compliant in 1994. The 2001/34/EC directive, which strengthens publicity norms and standardizes information connected with share issues with the creation of a unique prospectus, also constitutes an important step in the transformation of European capital markets. In this field, France has appeared as a model, with two major texts: the 1989 law relating to the security and transparency of the capital market, and the 1996 financial activity modernization law.

Second, there is a tendency towards the centralization of market authorities, along the lines of the SEC. The German case is particularly striking: in 1994, the second law for the promotion of capital markets instituted a federal market authority, the *Bundesaufsichtsamt für den Wertpapierhandel* (BAWe), thus breaking with the fragmentation of German stock market authorities. Centralization was further strengthened in April 2002 with the FinDAG law, which replaced the BAWe by the BAFin (*Bundesanstalt für Finanzdienstleistungsaufsicht*), a body of which the prerogatives exceed even those of the SEC. In France, the law on 'new economic regulations' (NRE), passed in May 2001, gave more powers to the COB, while the Financial Security Act, passed in July 2003, took a further step forward with the creation of the Financial Markets Authority (AMF), a merger of the COB and the Financial Markets Council (CMF, created in 1996). In the field of financial market law, the signs of convergence are therefore evident: the transparency of information given to shareholders as a whole has progressed greatly, while the role of market authorities continues to grow.

CORPORATE LAW AND CONTROLLING INTERESTS: OVERALL STABILITY

In corporate law, on the contrary, it is impossible to draw such a clear conclusion. Certain signs of convergence can be observed. Most notably, the risk of litigation, characteristic of the US model, is tending to increase as the accountability of managers and directors and the possibility of bringing legal actions against them grow: the NRE law in France (Frison-Roche, 2002) and, to a lesser extent, the KonTrag law in Germany, passed in 1998, both move in this direction. As for the protection of minority shareholders and the stability of blockholdings, it is difficult to make a final judgement. Certain measures favouring these blocks are losing ground: in Germany, the KonTrag law has forbidden multiple voting rights and voting caps and has restricted the banks' use of their voting rights. However, the most recent studies (Barca and Becht, 2002; Becht and Mayer, 2002; Faccio and Lang, 2000; Boutillier *et al.*, 2002) show that these devices, which are constituent of the contintental European model at the same time as they reveal national specificities, remain widespread. For example, it appears that voting caps are on the increase in France (Magnier, 2002). The existence of blockholdings remains the situation of reference in various continental European countries, despite the increase in market liquidity. The massive presence of US and UK institutional investors in the capital of European companies does not call this observation into question: essentially, these investors have taken their place in the 'float' of company equity, in other words outside the structures and controlling interests (Boutillier *et al.*, 2002). Furthermore, given the size of the blocks they possess individually (rarely exceeding 2 or 3 percent), the ability and desire of these investors to impose their views in a foreign context is doubtful.

WORKER INVOLVEMENT: AFFIRMING THE EUROPEAN MODEL

The existence of forms of 'negotiated involvement' in Germany and France has already been mentioned in the sections on the German and French models of governance. This participation, which can be found in various forms throughout continental Europe, constitutes an original, specifically European model of corporate governance. It is possible, at the present time, to observe a movement of consolidation of the rights of employees to participate in the affairs of their company, not only on a national level[2] but also, and above all, on the level of the European Union. This movement is putting a brake on the process of convergence of the European model towards the US model.

The adoption, in September 1994, of directive 94/45/EC on European works councils can be interpreted as the first step in this process. Since it came into force in 1996, companies of 1000 employees ore more, with a minimum of 150 workers in at least two member states, must have established a 'European' works council, representative of the international composition of the workforce of the firm and endowed with information and consultation rights. While there were only about 30 such structures in the European Union in 1994, and about 400 in 1999, today there are nearly 800, out of a total of a little more than 1800 companies concerned. The directive appears to have succeeded in developing what used to be a minority practice, by imposing employee representatives as legitimate partners. Its success can also be appreciated in terms of the spreading effects it has provoked. Thus, even before the UK signed the Maastricht social protocol, within the framework of which the directive had been adopted, a large number of British multinational companies had established European works councils through voluntary agreements (more than 150 in 1999), exceeding even the most optimistic predictions (Jobert, 2000, p. 161). This phenomenon also seems to have influenced non-transnational companies, which have adopted information and consultation bodies after observing these practices within firms subject to directive 94/45 (Streeck, 2001).

This movement of consolidation of a European model of governance through legislative action, based on the 'negotiated involvement' of employees, accelerated significantly with two EU legislative advances following the Nice summit (December 2000).

The first step forward was the adoption, in October 2001, of regulation 2157/2001 relating to the status of European Company Statutes and of directive 2001/86/EC, which completed this statute in terms of worker involvement. A European company (EC) is a moral person possessing an original, specifically EU status. It must be registered in one of the member states of the European Union, with the obligation of establishing its central administration in that state. We shall see the importance of this point later. An EC cannot be created *ex nihilo*, but through one of three different paths: (a) the conversion of a national company possessing subsidiaries in another member state for at least two years; (b) the merger of companies from at least two different member states; and (c) the formation of a holding company by companies established in at least two member states.

The diversity of European practices with regard to employee participation (information, consultation and co-determination) has represented an obstacle to the adoption of a European partnerial structure for more than 30 years. In particular, the question of board-level participation (supervisory boards or boards of directors) has crystallized these conflicts, with certain countries fearing the import of this practice (Spain, the UK and Ireland), and others seeing in this statute the means to avoid strong national requirements in this domain (Germany). The *tour de force* of this directive was to overcome these disputes, thanks to an original legal technique, which, however, also added to the complexity of the text. Box 9.1 presents the main points of this directive.

This text, while preserving national differences, clearly moves towards a strengthening of employees' rights in terms of governance (Bordogna and Guarriello, 2003): not only do the rights accorded in the field of information/consultation go further than those provided for by the directive 94/45 on European works councils, but the rights of employees previously covered by board-level participation have, essentially, been preserved. This latter requirement is to guard against the use of the directive to weaken labour rights. Moreover, spread or contamination effects, depending on how one judges them, are to be expected from the installation of companies with a strong participative structure in countries where this form of governance does not exist. We have already remarked on the occurrence of such effects concerning the directive on European works councils. These processes of diffusion are hard to contain in the present case, as an EC cannot be registered in one country and transfer its central administration to another. It is precisely to avoid this 'shock wave' that Spain obtained the right not to transpose the fall-back provision for board-level participation in the case of a merger (Moreau, 2001, p. 975); consequently, no company that falls under this measure can register in Spain (see Box 9.1). We can therefore expect this text to lead to a certain generalization of worker participation on boards throughout Europe.

The adoption of directive 2002/14/EC, establishing a general framework relating to information and consultation of employees throughout the Union, in March 2002, represented the second step forward in the consolidation of employees' rights in Europe. This directive is to be applied, depending on the choice of the member states, to all companies with more than 20 or more than 50 employees. Three types of subjects must be covered: economic and strategic questions (solely in the form of information), employment

Box 9.1   Worker involvement in the European company (Directive 2001/86/EC)

The provisions for worker involvement in European companies (EC), drawn from the recommendations of the Davignon Report, are the object of a separate directive – as the regulation is a form relatively unsuited to questions of labour law. This directive does not directly define the conditions of employee involvement – given the differences between member states on this question, that would have been impossible – but establishes a protocol of negotiation between employers and worker representatives of the future entity on the forms of participation that will be implemented. Thus the directive requires the constitution of a Special Negotiating Body (SNB), representative of the international composition of the labour force, entrusted with leading these negotiations with the employers to a fruitful conclusion. In addition to the conditions or negotiation (parties involved and agenda), the directive sets fall-back statutory provisions on information/consultation and on board-level participation. These reference provisions can be applied if the parties so wish, and must be applied if agreement cannot be reached in the negotiations. The provisions of this model, relatively favourable to employees, have the aim of encouraging management to come to an agreement. The protection of acquisitions in the matter of board-level participation was one of the main stakes in this text. Thus the agreement reached must not, when an EC is created through conversion of a national company, result in a lower level of participation (number of representatives sitting on the board) than in the previous situation. In the case of creation of an EC by merger or holding (see above), a lower level is possible if and only if it is accepted by a two-thirds majority of the SNP, representing at least two-thirds of the total workforce. This point was introduced to avoid, for example, an EC resulting from the merger of a big company not practising participation with a small German firm, being required to introduce co-determination.

The directive distinguishes clearly between fall-back provisions (obligatory in the event of unsuccessful negotiations) relating to information/consultation and those relating to board-level participation (in an annex to the directive). The former provide for the establishment of a representative body, closely modelled on the SNB, endowed with information and consultation rights slightly higher than those possessed by European works councils, in accordance with the directive 94/45. As for the measures concerning staff representation on governing bodies, these depend on the way in which the EC was formed:

(a) In the case of *conversion*, the measures previously in force continue to apply.

(b) In the case of *merger*, the EC will have the level of representation (in the proportion of seats) of the merging company the most advanced in the matter. However, this obligation only applies if at least 25 percent of the workforce were previously covered by board-level participation. This fall-back provision relating to board-level participation in the case of merger presents one particularity: it is not obligatory, but *optional*, in the sense that a member state can choose, when the directive is being transposed into national law, not to accept it. In this case, no company created out of a merger and concerned by this measure (i.e. with more than 25 percent of the workforce previously involved in this form of co-determination) can register in this country, nor can it establish its head office there. This option had to be introduced to obtain agreement from the Spanish, who were the last obstacle to adoption of the directive. Spanish employers feared spread effects resulting from the installation of companies with board-level participation on Spanish soil.

(c) Lastly, in the case of creation of an EC by *holding*, the EC will possess the highest level of representation from among the companies at the origin of the EC, if and only if 50 percent of the workforce was previously concerned by the participation. Contrary to the previous case, this measure is not optional.

Sources: Moreau (2001); Goetschy (2002); *Journal officiel* (2001).

evolution within the company and the organization of work. The changes are particularly significant for Ireland and the UK which, apart from directive 98/59 and 77/187, had no regulations in this field. The directive does not specify particular conditions within this general framework, but defines a protocol for negotiation of these measures. Here again, fall-back provisions are set out in case negotiations fail. This text completes Union legislation on information/consultation, composed, at the national level, of directives 98/59 (collective layoffs) and 77/187 (establishment transfers), and, on a supranational level, of directive 94/45 on European works councils.

Labour law therefore represents an even greater thorn in the side of the convergence thesis than corporate law.

THE REGULATION OF TAKEOVERS: CHAOTIC DEVELOPMENT

The question of exchange offers and takeover bids[3] – at the intersection of financial market law, corporate law and labour law – crystallizes the oppositions running not only through Europe, but also through each country, concerning the way in which companies should be considered. The questions of managerial accountability and the nature of the firm arise forcefully at the time of takeover offers (Deakin and Slinger, 1997). For agency theorists, these operations represent the ultimate weapon of small shareholders against management [...]. Yet in the United States, most states adopted anti-takeover measures at the beginning of the 1990s. The repeal of these measures, alleged to reduce the stock market valuation of companies, is one of the traditional demands in the activism of institutional investors.

In Europe, the history of the thirteenth directive, concerning takeovers, does not correspond to the predictions of the convergence thesis (see Box 9.2).[4] This history is a good illustration of the two opposing conceptions of the nature of the firm present within the Union. According to the liberal economic conception, the firm 'belongs' to the shareholders. This is the conception underlying the proposition of the directive in its initial version. The continental conception, on the contrary, seeks to implement the idea of the company as a community. There are two ways to do that. First, management could be authorized to act in the name of a greater interest (the corporate

interest). Second, the employees could be integrated into decision-making processes. That would mean partially merging the corporation, as a moral person, and the firm, as a productive entity. In fact, the text voted on by the European Parliament on 16 December 2003, leaves considerable freedom to member states in their choice of the rules that are to apply to companies within their jurisdiction. In this respect, the text constitutes a certain setback for the advocates of the creation of an active and integrated takeover market into the European Union.

Within national jurisdictions, the construction of legal frameworks to regulate takeover bids has revealed similar tensions – to such an extent that it is difficult to observe any alignment with the standards of the outsider model. Thus France, since the end of the 1980s, has adopted a series of measures that have considerably improved the functioning of the takeover market. The year 2001 was marked by particularly effervescent legal activity, with no less than four successive reforms, the most important of which was part of the law on the 'new economic regulations' (NRE). Current developments do not all go in the same direction. The NRE law established the obligation for the company making the takeover offer to inform and consult the works council of the targeted firm about its industrial projects; if it does not, the voting rights acquired during the operation will be cancelled. This text, which increases the number of measures, does not come out clearly in favour of either a pro-shareholder vision or a more institutional vision of the firm. It can also be observed that the recent generalization of voting caps and multiple voting rights is tending to seize up the takeover market. For Becht and Mayer (2002), the growth in anti-takeover devices is a specifically European phenomenon.

In Germany, we can observe a strengthening in anti-takeover devices. One week after the rejection of the thirteenth European directive in July 2001 – partly ascribable to German MEPs – the *Bundestag* adopted a law on takeover bids. The text, initially very close the proposition of the directive, was heavily modified, to such an extent that its final contents appear to combine opposites. As in article 5 of the European directive, a takeover offer becomes obligatory when a shareholder exceeds a threshold of 30 percent of voting rights. In addition, the principle of neutrality is validated, preventing the directors (*Vorstand*) from taking defensive measures once the takeover bid has been launched. At the same time, however, the law

Box 9.2 The eventful history of the thirteenth takeover bid directive

On 4 July 2001, the European Parliament rejected the proposition of a corporate law directive on takeover offers, with 273 votes for and 273 votes against. Formulated by the Commission as early as 1985, this directive has had an eventful history. The objective of this text was to facilitate the restructuring of companies in Europe, the idea being to harmonize the takeover market within the Union. After a series of closely argued negotiations between the Commission, the Parliament and the Council, the text was structured around three articles.

■ Article 5 provided for the obligation to make a takeover bid once a certain level of voting rights had been acquired (with each member state free to choose this threshold). This measure aimed to prevent takeovers without the agreement of minority shareholders, in other words by the gradual and discreet purchase of shares in a company. The price of the bid (referred to as an 'equitable price') was not defined in the directive.

■ Article 6 obliged the company targeted by the takeover bid to inform employee representatives of the conditions of the operation, once this had been made public by the bidder.

■ Article 9 prevented, according to the principle of 'neutrality', the managers and the board of the targeted company from interfering with the free choice of the shareholders. For example, it should be impossible for the board of directors to take defensive measures once a takeover operation has been started, without submitting them to the general meeting for approval.

The last two articles were the subject of debates which led to rejection of the text. With regard to article 6, many members of Parliament considered that the measures proposed in favour of employees were highly insufficient and should go beyond a simple procedure of information. It was article 9 that proved to cause the biggest problems: the principle of neutrality – the heart of the directive – derives straight from the doctrine of shareholder sovereignty. According to this article, only the shareholders have the right to decide the fate of the company in the event of a takeover bid, despite the fact that such an operation has major consequences for the future of the firm: the restructuring that generally follows such operations bears witness to this. According to article 9, management cannot use corporate interests or the interests of the firm as grounds to oppose a takeover, a measure which goes against the holistic vision of the firm.

In response to this failure, the Commission nominated a group of experts in corporate law, chaired by law professor Jaap Winter. This group was entrusted with the task of producing a report on the drafting of a new directive to harmonize the law concerning takeovers. This report, delivered in January 2002, shaped the drafting of a second directive project; the most controversial elements of the first text were kept. Notably, article 9, setting forth the principle of neutrality, was not changed. It was in fact reinforced by article 11, forbidding the use, during general meetings convened to decide on the adoption of defensive measures, of devices to restrict voting rights, as well as the use of double and multiple voting rights: this article prevents management from taking advantage of mechanisms that could be used to adopt anti-takeover measures undemocratically, thus bypassing the principle of neutrality. Moreover, although one article (article 13) was added concerning the information of employees, it only refers back to labour law directives already in existence. This is a way of leaving workers out of the debate, all the more so since managers cannot intervene to take worker interests into account (in accordance with article 9). This raises the question of the usefulness of consultation of the employees by the managers, if these latter subsequently have no power to intervene.

After many negotiations, the second directive project was finally adopted on 16 December 2003, by the European Parliament (321 votes for, 219 against and 9 abstentions), accompanied by numerous amendments which considerably reduce the impact of the text. Among these amendments, three are particularly important:

■ Article 9 is optional: each member of the Union can decide, when the directive is transposed into national law, to keep this article or to drop it. In addition, each state can authorize a company within its national jurisdiction not to respect article 9, if this company is targeted for a takeover by a company that is not subject to this article ('reciprocity' clause).

- Article 11 is also optional: nothing obliges a member state to restrict the use of double and multiple voting rights during hostile takeover operations.
- Lastly, obligations in the field of information/consultation have been strengthened. The worker representatives of the targeted company and of the assailing company must be consulted for the procedure to be considered legitimate.

These optional clauses are shifting the focus of debates to national borders. Although it is still too early to appreciate fully the impact of this text, the fact that articles 9 and 11 are not obligatory clearly deprives this directive of some of its substance. The perspective of a unified takeover market in Europe – a factor of competitiveness and modernity according to the champions of shareholder value – has been, if not definitively dismissed, then at least postponed. On the other hand, the fact that article 9 has been conserved (its abandonment being optional) is a relative failure for the advocates of a holistic or partnerial vision of the firm.

increases the possibility for managers to adopt anti-takeover measures *in advance*. This point is decisive, certainly more so than the acceptance of the principle of neutrality: hostile takeovers can thus be effectively slowed down. The position of employees has been improved considerably. First, the role of the supervisory board, on which worker representatives sit in accordance with co-determination laws, is increased during these operations. Second, both the assailing firm and the target firm are required to inform and consult the works council (*Betriebsrat*) of the latter.

Taken as a whole, recent developments in the legal framework covering hostile takeovers, and in particular the failure to introduce a specifically European takeover market, are incompatible with the thesis of convergence. The continental European treatment of this issue is certainly changing. However, rather than strictly imitating US standards, the changes taking place in Europe are the result of the confrontation between European specificities and capital market requirements.

CONCLUSION

We are now in a position to present an overall appraisal of the thesis of convergence. Table 1 summarizes the main points of convergence, resistance or divergence of the continental European model of corporate governance. The developments related in this table illustrate a movement of considerable complexity. The diagnosis of a one-dimensional movement, such as that put forward by the thesis of convergence, is proved to be erroneous. It is possible to break down recent developments in the following manner.

- Financial market law constitutes a strong factor of convergence, both in content and form. In terms of content, the strengthening of the transparency of European capital markets is a movement towards the affirmation of shareholder power. In terms of form, the centralization of capital market regulatory authorities, with the creation of the AMF in France and the BAFin in Germany, tends to reproduce the US model, embodied in the SEC. Equally, from an institutional point of view, even if we stray somewhat from financial market law towards corporate law, the growth in the risk of litigation in Germany and France brings them closer to the US system.
- Corporate law, at least the branch dealing with measures of control, displays a certain inertia. Germany, where the KonTrag law abolished double voting rights and voting caps, represents an exception in this respect.
- Lastly, labour law is a factor of resistance, even of divergence. Directives on European works councils, the information and consultation of workers on a national level, and worker involvement in the European Company all strengthen the European model of governance, founded on 'negotiated involvement'. The symbolic dimension of these directives, particularly the directive on employee involvement within European companies, should not be underestimated. By reminding European players, notably managers, of the foundations of

the conception of the firm which prevails in Europe, this directive is capable of favouring European integration and social cohesion.

It therefore appears that convergence becomes ever stronger as we draw closer to the financial sphere, the spearhead of globalization. On the contrary, the institutions connected with labour relations, in other words the way in which internal company relations are conceived of and codified, act as a brake on convergence towards the US model or, alternatively, are no longer a factor of inertia, but a factor of divergence. Corporate law, which occupies a position in between these two spheres (financial and labour) is globally the most stable (Cioffi and Cohen, 2000). Lastly, the regulation of takeover bids, at the intersection of financial market law, corporate law and labour law, is marked by the contradictory evolutions specific to each of these corpora. It is therefore very difficult to pass a definitive judgement on the direction taken.

There is, however, one element which makes a significant contribution to the destabilization of the European model: the ideological domination of the Anglo-American world. The rise to power of US and British investment funds, the liberalization of European capital markets, and so on, are accompanied by the spread of a discourse or culture that is globally favourable to shareholder value. This redefinition of the conceptions underlying entrepreneurial activity, described by Boltanski and Chiapello (1999) as the 'advent of a new conception of the firm', constitutes one of the facets of shareholder power. There are several factors behind this domination, including the superiority of US expertise in accounting [...], the power of US audit firms (the Big Four), the attractiveness of the US university systems and the country's macroeconomic performances of the last decade. The consequences are clear: national and international codes of good conduct are, to a large extent, champions of shareholder value and the agency model is omnipresent in scientific publications on

Domains	Main changes	Degree of convergence
Financial market law	Improvement of financial transparency: ++ ■ EU: directives of 1988 and 2001 ■ France: 1996 law on the modernization of financial activities	++
	Centralization of market authorities: ++ ■ Germany: BAWe (1998) followed by BAFin (FinDAG law, 2002) ■ France: AMF (financial security law, 2003)	
Corporate law	Rise in risk of litigation: + ■ France: NRE law (2001) ■ Germany: KonTrag law (1998)	+
	Blockholdings: 0 ■ France and Europe: stability and blockholdings ■ Germany: KonTrag law forbidding multiple voting rights and voting caps	0/+
Takeovers	XIIIth European directive: 0 France: NRE law: 0 Germany: law of 2001: –	0
Labour law	Directive on European works councils (1994) Directive on information/consultation of employees (2002) Directive on employee participation in European Companies (2002)	– –

Note: The '+' sign signifies that this field of governance contributes significantly to the convergence of the European model towards US standards. The '0' sign indicates stability. The '–' sign represents affirmation or divergence of the European model

Table 9.1 **Principal transformations of the continental European model of governance**

corporate governance. On the scale of the European Union, the British influence reveals this disequilibrium: despite the fact that only two (the UK and Ireland) of the 15 EU countries (prior to 2004 enlargement to 25 countries) give no credence to the partnerial vision of the firm, this vision has failed to become established – as evinced by the Thirteenth Directive on takeovers, and the two Winter reports, the first on takeovers (see above), the second on corporate law [...].

The 'end of history' thesis of corporate governance, besides the fact that it adheres blindly to the doctrine of shareholder value, is the product of a faulty interpretation of globalization, according to which the model that appears to have dominated during a given period (the US model of the second half of the 1990s) is imposing itself on an international scale. On the contrary, we have demonstrated that globalization involves a process of confrontation of supra-national phenomena (in this case the integration of financial markets) with more local, continental, national or regional regulations. In this respect, the convergence of the European model of governance is far from established: although certain elements are indeed moving closer to the US model, factors of resistance, or even of divergence are equally identifiable – particularly in the field of labour relations.

NOTES

1   For a similar conclusion in relation to the British case, see Armour *et al.* (2003).
2   Germany, for example, strengthened the co-determination powers of the works council (*Betriebsrat*) in a law passed in 2001.
3   These operations can be carried out either using liquidities (takeover bids) or shares (exchange offers).
4   For a detailed analysis of the history and contents of this directive, see Beffa *et al.* (2003).

REFERENCES

Armour, J.S., Deaking, S. and Konzelmann, S. (2003) Shareholder Primacy and the Direction of UK Corporate Governance, University of Cambridge, ESRC Centre for Business Research, Working Paper 266.

Becht, M. and Mayer, C. (2002) Introduction, in, F. Barca and M. Becht (eds) *The Control of Corporate Europe*, Oxford: Oxford University Press, pp. 1–45.

Beffa, J-L., Langenlach, L. and Touffut, J-P. (2003) How to Interpret the Takeover Bid Directive, *Prisme*, 1, Saint-Gobain Centre for Economic Studies, September.

Boltanski, L. and Chiapello, E. (1999) *Le Nouvel Esprit du Capitalisme*, Paris: Gallimard.

Bordogna, L. and Guarriello, F. (2003) *Aver Voce in Capitolo: Societa Europea e Paticipazione dei Lavoro Nell'Impressa*, Rome: Edizioni Laboro.

Cioffi, J. and Cohen, S. (2000) The State, Law and Corporate Governance: The Advantage of Forwardness, in S. Cohen and B. Gavin (eds) *Corporate Governance and Globalisation: Long Range Planning Issues*, Cheltenham, UK and Northampton, MA: Edward Elgar, pp. 307–49.

Deakin, S. and Slinger, G. (1997) Hostile Takeovers, Corporate Law, and the Theory of the Firm, *Journal of Law and Society*, 24, 124–51.

Frison-Roche, M-A., (2002) Le Droit Français des Sociétés Entre Corporate Governance et Culture de March, in D. Plihon and J-P. Ponssard (eds) *Le Montée en Puissance des Fonds D'Investissement : Quals Enjeux Pour les Enterprises*, Paris: Les Etudes de la Documentation Francais, pp. 77–91.

Gehrke, I. (2002) Valeur Actionnariale: le Rattrapage de l'Allemagne, in D. Plihon and J-P. Ponssard (eds) *Le Montée en Puissance des Fonds D'Investissement : Quels Enjeux Pour les Enterprises*, Paris: Les Etudes de la Documentation Français, pp. 147–62.

Goetschy, J. (2002) EU Social Policy and Developments in Worker Involvement Arrangements From Multi-Level Governance to Company Level Worker Participation, in M. Gold (ed.) *Industrial Democracy in Europe*, Cheltenham, UK and Northampton, MA: Edward Elgar.

Jobert, A. (2000) *Les Espaces de la Negociation Collective, Branches et Territoires*, Toulouse: Octares.

Journal Officiel (2001) Journal Officiel des Communautes Européennes, Directive 2001/86/CE du Conseil, L294, 10 October, pp. 22–32.

Moreau, M. (2001) L'Implication des Travailleurs dans la Société Européenne, Droit Social, November 967–76.

Streeck, W. (2001) The Transformation of Corporate Organisations in Europe : An Overview, in J-P. Touffut (ed.) *Institutions, Innovation and Growth: Selected Economic Papers*, The Saint-Gobain Centre for Economic Studies, Cheltenham, UK and Northampton, MA: Edward Elgar, pp. 4–44.

10 "A Transatlantic Financial Market?" [1]

From Daniel S. Hamilton and Joseph P. Quinlan,

Deep Integration: How Transatlantic Markets are

Leading Globalisation (2005)

Karel Lannoo

Back in the early days of the European Single Market, a "reciprocity" provision in the second banking directive caused much uproar in transatlantic relations. According to this clause, the EU could ask trading partners to grant access to their markets in a manner that was reciprocal to the one obtained for third countries in the EU. It was claimed that the European Union was becoming a "fortress" and that the United States would never accept being forced to change its regulatory structure. Although the provision has never actually been applied, it took more than 10 years before officials started to have regular discussions on coming to more equivalence in regulatory regimes on both sides. This dialogue culminated in an agreement on April 22, 2005 between the US Securities and Exchange Commission (SEC) and the European Commission on equivalence of accounting standards.

Yet equivalent standards also have some drawbacks. First, financial markets on both sides are fundamentally different in structure, meaning that it is not easy to find issues that are of comparable importance. Moreover, EU financial markets are still largely fragmented and consolidated at the national level, meaning that the benefits of the Single Market still have not been realized within the EU. Second, the process may be seen as a way to reduce regulatory competition, which could limit the benefits of equivalence.

A BANK-BASED VERSUS MARKET-BASED FINANCIAL SYSTEM

The EU and US financial systems continue to differ fundamentally. In comparing the size of bank, bond and equity markets in the US and the EU, it is striking to note that a highly developed banking market and a (much) less-developed bond and equity market characterize the EU, while the opposite is true for the US (see Figure 10.1). This asymmetry between the two systems largely results from regulatory differences, in particular the universal banking system in Europe and the segmentation of the US financial system by the 1933 Glass-Steagall Act, which separates commercial banking from investment banking. In addition, the 1933 Securities Act laid the basis for the market-based financial system in the US as we know it today.

The segmentation of the US financial industry stimulated tough competition between intermediaries. It provided the environment in which capital market financing, specialization and innovation emerged, creating the most competitive industry worldwide. As noted by Chief Economist at the European Investment Bank, Alfred Steinherr, "In no other industry has the United States been as resolutely superior as in the financial industry. (...) All significant innovations have come out of the US financial system." [2]

Competition between commercial banks, investment banks and brokers in the US stimulated a

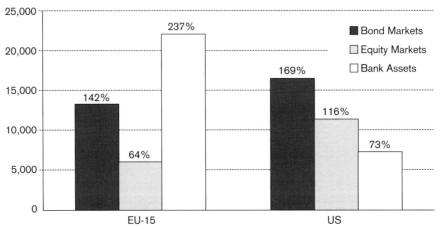

Figure 10.1 **Amounts of bonds outstanding, total domestic stock market capitalization and bank assets, end 2003 (in billions of euros and as a percentage of GDP)**

process of disintermediation and securitization. Caps on short-term bank deposits led to the emergence of higher-yielding money market mutual funds. Banks responded by transforming liabilities into negotiable certificates of deposits, on which interest could be paid without restrictions. In order to obtain a share of the profitable loan market, investment banks stimulated corporations to securitize their loans. As a result, the balance sheets of banks became fully disintermediated and securitized and relationship banking disappeared. The growth of a deep and liquid money and capital market had deprived relationship banking of its implicit insurance value and made valuations more important. The key principle of transparency, which underlies US financial, securities and accounting law, emerged.

In Europe, the universal banking system has remained dominant, having been taken as the model in the EU's 1992 program of financial market liberalization. There was no incentive for banks to securitize debt and capital markets remained underdeveloped. Furthermore, the regulatory framework for direct issues on capital markets left much to be desired and differed from one member state to another. For example, until recently corporate bonds were discouraged in Germany through very strict emission criteria, including the obligation to issue the bonds only in the domestic currency of the local market, with unfavorable tax treatment. Governments wished to keep close control of the local debt securities market to ease public finance.

So far, there has been no real break in the structure of the EU financial system. Bank assets to GDP have continued to grow and stood at 237 percent of GDP in 2003, but there has been a pronounced growth of debt securities markets in the EU, which increased from 84 percent of GDP in 1992 to 142 percent in 2003. The creation of the euro has allowed Europe's capital markets to deepen, accounting for 31 percent of the global financial stock in 2003, up from 28 percent in 1999. This compares to 37 percent for the US, whose share declined from 40 percent in 1999.[3]

The realization that the EU would not fully capture the benefits of economic and monetary union, but also that its financial system was missing out on innovative investments led to the adoption of the Financial Services Action Plan (FSAP) in 1999 and the reform of its system of financial lawmaking and supervisory cooperation as discussed in the 2001 'Lamfalussy' report. By mid-2004, a new regulatory framework was in place for the issuance of securities on capital markets (Prospectus Directive, 2003/71/EC), market disclosure (Transparency Directive, 2004/109/EC), tackling insider trading and market manipulation (Market Abuse Directive, 2003/6/EC) and promoting fair trade and the best execution of securities transactions (Markets in Financial Instruments Directive, 2004/39/EC). The effects of these directives should allow a more market-based system to develop.

EU–US DIALOGUE ON FINANCIAL MARKETS REGULATION

The success of the EU in reforming its financial regulatory and supervisory structure led to the start of a regular dialogue with the US, which could be considered a model for other areas of transatlantic or bilateral trade cooperation. Although the direct motive was the impact of the EU's Conglomerates Directive (2002/87/EC) on US firms, it has become a permanent feature, focusing on a broader set of financial market issues and involving the EU Commission and Lamfalussy Committees on the one side and the US Treasury, the SEC and Federal Reserve Board on the other. The aim is to improve understanding and identify potential conflicts in regulatory approaches on both sides of the Atlantic and to discuss issues of mutual interest.[4] As noted by EU Commissioner for the Internal Market and Services Charlie McGreevy in New York on 20 May 2005, "The goal must be mutual recognition of equivalence. You can also call it the home-country principle. If you agree to accept each other's system as equivalent then duplicative requirements disappear. You can then operate in the other country under the rules of your country."[5] Hallmarks so far have been the agreements on the equivalence of rules for auditor oversight and accounting standards, but difficult issues remain on the agenda, such as the implementation of the Basel Accord and the direct access to EU exchanges by the US market.

The background to the start of the regulatory dialogue was the exponential growth of transatlantic portfolio investment in the second half of the last decade. Purchases of US equities by EU investors grew from $144 billion in 1990 to reach $2,631 billion in 2000. At the same time, US investors also stepped up their diversification into EU equities, rising from $141 billion in 1990 to reach $1,937 billion in 2000.[6] This trend was mainly driven by institutional investors. Moreover, the emergence of a more securitized and disintermediated financial system increased the attractiveness of the EU market for US firms.[7]

Until a few years ago, the EU was not considered a credible partner for discussions on financial regulatory and supervisory matters. Progress toward the adoption of the FSAP, however, changed things. Still, US regulators were hardly interested in discussing some form of equivalence with other countries. It strictly applied the principle of territoriality and considered its financial regulatory system superior.[8] Then the corporate scandals of Enron and others altered things further. Serious flaws had been revealed in the US securities supervisory system and its accounting standards were no longer held to be superior. At the same time, because of the scandals, new laws such as the Sarbanes-Oxley Act (2002) were adopted, creating severe problems at the transatlantic level.

The issue regarding auditor oversight results from the passage of the Sarbanes-Oxley Act in the US, which created the Public Company Accounting Oversight Board (PCAOB), and required all audit firms to be registered with the PCAOB, including EU-based audit firms with US-listed clients. A declaration of intent on the equivalence of rules for auditor oversight, reached between the European Commission and the US PCAOB in March 2004,[9] would lift the requirement for EU-based audit firms. It stipulates, however, that EU member states create auditor oversight authorities, which are not yet present in all member states, and agree on the European Union's draft 8th Company Law Directive on the statutory audit, as a precondition.[10]

The agreement on equivalence between International Financial Reporting Standards (IFRS) and US Generally Accepted Accounting Principles (GAAP), reached between the European Commission and the US SEC on April 22, 2005, probably has the most far-reaching implications. It would effectively allow companies to use one single accounting standard in the EU and US. So far, the US has always required firms to reconvert their accounts to the US GAAP when listing on US capital markets, whereas the EU requires listed firms and issuers to report in IAS or the equivalent from 2005 onwards. The agreement allows US firms to continue to issue bonds on EU capital markets in the US GAAP, whereas the SEC will eliminate the need for companies using the IFRS to reconcile to US GAAP standards possibly as soon as 2007, but no later than 2009.[11]

The transatlantic dialogue has also proliferated to the supervisory side, where the Committee of European Securities Regulators and the US SEC announced a cooperation agreement on June 4, 2004 covering increased communication about regulatory risks in each other's securities markets and the promotion of regulatory convergence in the future. This move was followed by a cooperation initiative with the US Commodities and Futures Trading Commission on October 21, 2004. The same form of extended cooperation is happening in the areas of banking and insurance, with the Committee of European Banking Supervisors and the Committee of European Insurance and Occupational Pensions Supervisors.

Other issues still on the agenda are the latest capital adequacy rules resulting from the new Basel Accord and the direct access of EU exchanges to the US market. Whereas the EU would leave all EU-licensed banks the choice of which approach to follow for the measurement of their minimum level of regulatory capital, US regulators would allow only the advanced internal ratings-based approach of the new Basel Accord to some 20 internationally active banks and apply the old Basel I framework to all the other banks. This action would seriously distort the playing field for EU banks in the US market, while US banks would have the full range of choices in the EU. The justification of the US supervisors that these internationally active banks control 99 percent of the foreign assets in the US banking system does not take into account the significant stake EU banks have in the US banking system. In addition, it will also hamper integrated risk-management and supervisory reporting within these groups, with all the negative consequences this may entail.

A similar distortion applies with regard to trading on regulated stock markets. Whereas US-regulated stock markets are directly accessible for EU licensed brokers, the same is not the case for EU regulated markets in the US. American authorities argue that the level of investor protection in the EU stock market is not equivalent to what is in place in the US. From the EU perspective, this is seen as a protectionist measure. While all major EU stock exchanges operate a screen-based trading system, the major US stock exchange, the New York Stock Exchange (NYSE), maintains a floor-based trading structure. Having direct access to the EU-regulated market would allow US brokers to trade directly on EU stock markets, thereby not only reducing the listings of EU firms on the NYSE, but also threatening the antiquated trading structure of the world's largest exchange.[12]

BENEFITS OF A TRANSATLANTIC MARKET

Although the agreements reached in the context of the transatlantic agenda clearly have benefits, how to quantify these is not evident. Some studies have been undertaken on the specific aspects of the transatlantic financial market, but an overall figure would be almost impossible to distill. Moreover, as an integrated financial market does not yet exist at the EU level, how could the benefits of a transatlantic market be measured?

As regards the integration of securities markets, Steil has estimated that full transatlantic integration may lead to a 9 percent reduction of the cost of capital for listed companies. This study is based on the assumption that greater competition between the more efficient, automated trading structures on the EU side and the more competitive brokerage industry in the US would reduce transaction costs by 60 percent. This cost reduction would also lead to an increase in trading volume of almost 50 percent.[13] On top of that, a fully integrated capital market would also do away with the duplicate costs and fees companies incur through listing on multiple markets. By mid-2005, there were 235 EU companies with listings in the US, whereas there were 140 US companies with listings on the London Stock Exchange, Deutsche Börse and Euronext.

A much more important reduction in the cost of the capital and regulatory burden would accrue from the agreement on the equivalence of accounting standards, although no studies have been carried out on the aggregate benefit of this equivalence, as far as we are aware. This exercise would certainly be a complex undertaking, as many elements need to be taken into account. First, there are costs for European companies of converting their accounts to the US GAAP, as a condition for listing on the US capital market (the US GAAP is accepted in most EU markets), of which individual figures exist. Second, there is the advantage of having mutually accepted accounting languages, which means that analysts on both sides will trust firms' financial statements, leading to higher investment across the Atlantic (and certainly in the EU). Third, the agreement does away with the cost of the confusion and the lack of credibility caused by converting accounts to another language, often depressing the stock price. An example is Deutsche Bank's shift to the US GAAP in 2002, which led to net profit distortions in the US GAAP of minus 88 percent for 2001 to plus 220 percent in 2000 because of differences in the tax treatment of the disposal of industrial holdings.[14] Analysts therefore considered the changeover a strategic mistake.

At a more general level, stronger market integration could be an important incentive to stimulate the competitiveness of the EU financial services industry, which is lagging behind its American counterpart in performance. Return on assets in the EU banking industry stood at about 0.4 percent in 2003, compared with 1.4 percent in the United States, a performance that has stabilized at these levels for the last few years.[15] The strong productivity growth observed in the US in the second half of the 1990s can largely be attributed to a limited number of services that use information and communications technology intensively, including certain financial services. Hence, there is a need to stimulate EU financial market integration.[16] Segmented markets at the retail level in the EU, such as in mortgage lending or investment funds prevent firms from exploiting economies of scale and increasing their overall performance, which ultimately increases costs for the end-users of financial services.

Would transatlantic dialogue therefore only have beneficial effects? Not necessarily: the danger is not imaginary that it may lead to over-regulation – that the one side may hope the other will follow its standards, even if circumstances or needs may be different. Examples are the implementation of the new Basel Accord in the United States or the impact of the Sarbanes-Oxley Act on corporate governance regulation in the European Union. In these two cases, circumstances are different and do not require full equivalence, although there are clearly pressures from both sides respectively to level up the host-country model to the one presently applicable at home.

Within certain bounds, competition between regulatory regimes can be healthy – something that is also noticeable in the EU. Nevertheless, a high degree of international cooperation between regulators replicates the dangers of excessive regulatory intervention at the national level: an (unaccountable) regulatory leviathan with monopoly authority, which does not need to pay great attention to the quality of regulation, and an opaque entity subject to capture by special interest groups. Not only does this scenario have the ability to reduce welfare by excluding some economic options that free market competition would have enabled market participants to choose from, but it also removes the freedom to choose in the first place, a value from which economic actors may derive some utility. In addition, excessive regulatory cooperation at the international level outside the contours of a clearly defined legal framework effectively amounts to a lack of democratic legitimacy.

Two forces – one public, one private – can explain why excessive regulatory convergence leaves little room for innovation in securities market regulation. To begin with, a common standard or regulatory regime enjoying a monopoly need not pay much attention to upstart rivals, so there is little incentive for regulators to improve their regime or to introduce better standards when they cooperate closely at the international level. In addition, there is an inherent risk in 'benevolent planners' choosing what they believe to be the most appropriate market structure,

because they may impose the wrong market structure and respond inadequately to changes in demand or to the introduction of new technologies, which may warrant a need to radically alter the market structure.[17]

With regard to private forces, as the incumbent standard is challenged on efficiency grounds, pioneers with low switching costs may migrate to the new standard, undermining the entrenched standard in the process. Yet, firms with high switching costs owing to scale effects will be loathe to part from the old standard. They may deliberately stifle innovation to maintain a certain market infrastructure that is advantageous to them. Such behavior can explain why outdated trading systems such as that employed by the NYSE are still in existence.[18]

NOTES

1. This chapter builds upon earlier work by the author. For a more extensive discussion of ongoing EU financial market regulation issues and references, see K. Lannoo and J.-P. Casey, *Financial Regulation and Supervision beyond 2005*, CEPS Task Force Report, CEPS, Brussels, February 2005. For US-EU issues, see M. Draghi and R. Pozen, *US-EU regulatory convergence: Capital market issues*, John M. Olin Discussion Paper Series No. 444, Harvard Law School, Cambridge, MA, 2003; and also E. Posner, "Market power without a single market: The new transatlantic relations in financial services", mimeo, George Washington University, Washington DC, June 2004.

2. A. Steinherr, *Derivatives, the Wild Beast of Finance*, New York: John Wiley & Sons Inc., 1998, p. 29.

3. McKinsey Global Institute, *Global Financial Stock Database*, 2005.

4. See the *Joint Report to leaders at the EU–US Summit on 25–26 June by participants in the Financial Markets Regulatory Dialogue*, for the June summit held at Dromoland Castle, Ireland (retrieved from http://europa.eu.int/comm/internal_market/finances/docs/general/eu-us-dialogue-report_en.pdf); both of the parties at the meeting agreed to "intensify" their cooperation.

5. See "The integration of Europe's financial markets and international cooperation" by C. McCreevy, Concluding Remarks at the Euro Conference in New York on April 20, 2005. There is no full agreement on the terminology. While the EU uses the phrase 'mutual recognition', US authorities prefer 'equivalence', which may be more correct, as supervisory accountability remains at the federal level. See also the testimony of Alexander Schaub, Director-General of the European Commission DG on the Internal Market, before the US House of Representatives Committee on Financial Services, May 13, 2004.

6. B. Steil, *Building a Transatlantic Securities Market*, International Securities Markets Association, Zurich, 2002, pp. 17–23.

7. See the testimony of Marc Lackritz, President of the Securities Industry Association, at a Congressional hearing of the Committee on Financial Services on May 22, 2002, who stated, "Our very largest members engaging in global business receive about 20 percent of their net revenues from Europe. And I might add that is about two times more than the net revenues that we receive from Asia. And we employ about 35,000 Europeans in the business."

8. Evidence of this attitude was revealed by former Chairman of the SEC Arthur Levitt in a *Financial Times* article, *in tempore non suspectu*, concerning the International Accounting Standards (IAS). He argued that the US GAAP (Generally Accepted Accounting Principles) was "the most transparent and comprehensive disclosure regime in the world" and that the US should never recognize IAS as equivalent. See A. Levitt, "The world according to GAAP: Global capital markets cannot work without uniform, high-quality financial reporting standards", *Financial Times*, May 2, 2001.

9. This declaration of intent was made public by European Commissioner Frits Bolkestein and US PCAOB Chairman William McDonough in Brussels on March 25, 2004.

10. See the Proposal for a Directive of the European Parliament and of the Council on statutory audit of annual accounts and consolidated accounts and amending Council Directives 78/660/EEC and 83/349/EEC, COM(2004) 0177 final of March 15, 2004.

11. See D.T. Nicolaisen, "A Securities Regulator Looks at Convergence", *Northwestern University Journal of International Law and Business*, April 2005.

12. J. Board *et al.* for example do not expect substantial benefits from introducing EU screens in the US – see *Distortion or distraction: US restrictions on EU exchange trading screens*, Corporation of London, City Research Series, No. 3, 2004.

13. Steil, op. cit., pp. 28–30.

14. See *Financial Times*, September 10, 2002.

15. See the *Global Financial Stability Report*, International Monetary Fund, Washington, DC, April 2005.

16. Annex I of the European Commission's recent *Green Paper on Financial Services Policy (2005–2010)*, (COM(2005) 177, Brussels, May 3, 2005) reiterates the economic benefits of financial integration – on which studies had been published in 2002 showing the impact on the lower cost of capital and increase in GDP growth.

17. See L. Harris, *Trading and Exchanges*, Oxford: Oxford University Press, 2003.

18. Ibid.

11 "International Accounting Harmonisation: The Resistible Rise of the IASC/IASB"[1]

From Gérer et Comprendre (2004)

Bernard Colasse

On 16th July 2003, the European Accounting Regulation Committee (ARC) voted unanimously in favour of the Commission's Draft Regulation adopting all the standards of the *International Accounting Standard Board* (IASB[2]) with the exception of standards 32 and 39 on financial instruments.[3] Moreover, ARC decided that in future, standards should be discussed and validated one by one and not "en bloc".

ARC's rejection of two of the thirty-four standards together with its position regarding the examination of future IASB standards caused quite a stir amongst accounting professionals because it threatened to compromise the application of IASB standards by the European Union's 7,000 or so listed groups, scheduled to take effect from 1st January 2005. Prior to this, IASB standards had been thought of as an indivisible set and could only be adopted "en bloc".

ARC's decisions also caused ripples in business circles and even in public opinion. The big, non-specialist daily newspapers,[4] not usually particularly interested in accounting matters, wrote about them fairly extensively.

So why such interest in an accounting event, which after all, is of very minor importance compared to all the problems and disturbances the world now faces?

Let us attempt an answer.

The event, despite appearances to the contrary, was not strictly confined to accounting and realisation suddenly dawned that it was not, and that in fact, behind international accounting harmonisation, the issue at stake was the governance of major companies and control over their access to international financial markets. It therefore began to make sense outside the world of accounting since it raised questions on the new means of regulation being set up at international level, on the position of new private players such as the IASC/IASB in the context of globalisation, on the power and legitimacy of these players, on the nature of the relationships being created between the latter and governments or intergovernmental organisations, and also on the relationships being instituted between the United States and the rest of the world.

All this points to a need to examine the case of this mysterious organisation, the IASB, up until then, totally unknown to the general public and which was, in its relationship with the European Union, at the origin of this new awareness. The aim of the following chapter is to attempt such an examination.

We will begin by retracing the organisation's origins as a means of defining its identity as an international player. We will then deal with its relationship with the European Union.

THE IASC/IASB: A POWERLESS ORGANISATION IN SEARCH OF SUPPORT

The history of the IASC/IASB[5] is that of an organisation with no coercive power (Walton, 2001) that embarked on a strategic search for the support which would give it the power it lacked to achieve its objective and realise its ambitions. This search for support was undertaken with limited resources, at least in the beginning, and was based mainly on a rhetoric of competence, impartiality and independence.

A powerless organisation

The organisation that was to become the IASC was the brainchild of Henry Benson, a partner in the London firm of Coopers & Lybrand.

Henry Benson wanted to create an organisation that would draw up standards that could be adopted by countries around the world so that national reference systems would gradually converge. The term used to describe this convergence process was "harmonisation". Harmonisation is different from standardisation in that the aim of the latter is the application of identical standards within a given geographical space and uniformity of accounting practices within this space. Harmonisation, on the other hand, is intended to allow a variety of practices and aims simply to establish equivalency between them. In principal, it is less restrictive than standardisation. That said, it may be considered as an attenuated form of standardisation and a first step towards it (Colasse, 2000), as is demonstrated in the history of the IASC, moreover.

Henry Benson persuaded the *Institute of Chartered Accountants of England and Wales* (ICAEW), of which he had been the President, that it should invite professional accountancy organisations from various countries to participate in the creation of this new body. Professional organisations in nine countries (Germany, Australia, Canada, the United States, France, Japan, Mexico, the Netherlands, and the United Kingdom and Ireland (the latter two considered as one country) adopted the idea and in 1973, participated in the creation of the *International Accounting Standards Committee* whose first President was Henry Benson himself. From 1974, new members joined the founders: Belgium, India, Pakistan, New Zealand and Zimbabwe.

At this stage, it should be emphasised that the idea for the IASC came from a partner in a big practice, that we owe its creation to an initiative on the part of the British profession, and that the founding members were professional bodies from nine rich countries (with the exception of Mexico) with different accounting traditions. In greatly simplified terms, it can be said that the nine founding countries were divided between the Anglo-Saxon system of reference

(Australia, Canada, the United States, the United Kingdom, etc.) and the reference system for Continental Europe (Germany, France, etc.), with a predominance of countries whose accounting tradition tended towards the Anglo-Saxon, a situation that was reinforced in 1974 with the arrival of five former British colonies as members. As we will see, the various original characteristics of the IASC were to influence its strategy and future.

As an international body that was professional in origin, the IASC was not able to impose its standards within the countries in which its members were developing their activities. Members agreed simply to promote its standards in their respective countries. In countries where the power to set standards was not the province of the profession, the application of IASC standards was only possible where they did not run counter to national standards. This was the case in France, represented within the IASC by the *Ordre des Experts-Comptables* and the *Compagnie Nationale des Commissaires aux comptes,* organisations that did not, and still do not have the power to set standards, since such power belongs to an assembly, the *Conseil National de la Comptabilité*,[6] whose members represent the various parties concerned by accounting matters.

Support from IFAC

Aware that its power in most countries was simply a power of influence, the IASC set about elaborating standards that were open enough not to clash head-on with national accounting regulations. Moreover, some of these standards were devised as a result of gaps in these regulations which provided an arena for the IASC to demonstrate its competence; in matters of consolidated accounts, for example, at a time when their regulation was non-existent in very many countries. In the absence of French regulations on consolidated accounts, therefore, several French groups, under pressure from the *Commission des Opérations de Bourse* (COB) to draw up this type of account, preferred to abide by IASC standards rather than American standards, which contributed to building up the IASC's reputation for competence.

The IASC's work received its first consecration in 1982 when the *International Federation of Accountants* (IFAC) recognised it as a global accounting standard setter. IFAC, founded in 1977, brought together professional audit organisations from sixty or so countries and devoted its activities to the promotion of international audit standards and to the training of auditors.

IFAC's support was doubly advantageous for the IASC:

- on the one hand it considerably extended its power of influence in the world;
- on the other, it allowed it to include developing countries in its activities and to lose its image of being a club for rich countries (IFAC decided to shoulder the cost of 10 participations in the Board's activities for one developing country and to offer others the means of participating from a distance).

Thanks to IFAC, the IASC strengthened its international position, but in the long run it remained an organisation with no power and towards the middle of the 1980s, it ran into difficulties. Questions began to be raised as to its real usefulness.

These difficulties were linked to a greater or lesser degree to the moves towards European standardisation undertaken in the 1970s which were marked by the publication and gradual implementation in member states of the Fourth (1978) and Seventh (1985) directives. The Fourth Directive dealt with the objectives, presentation and content of the annual accounts of joint-stock companies. Although strongly inspired by the continental system of reference, it placed great importance on certain Anglo-Saxon principles such as that of the highly pragmatic "true and fair view". The Seventh Directive dealt with group accounts and was more heavily imprinted with the stamp of the Anglo-Saxon reference system, notably through the principle of "substance over form", i.e. the pre-eminence of the economic reality of operations over their strictly legal status.

These Directives were the fruit of a sort of normative compromise between the Anglo-Saxon reference system, defended by the United Kingdom, and the continental reference system, backed by Germany and France. Their content was introduced into the legislation of the member states over varying lengths of time. Faced with their implementation, and above all that of group accounts – its favoured sphere of action – the IASC lost hope of seeing its standards applied in Europe. For a time even, to ensure its survival, it was forced to reorient its strategy and play the role of standard-setter for developing countries, although its standards, mainly intended for big companies, were not really suitable for them. The IASC

needed a new lease of life.

This new lease of life came in the shape of the International Organization of Securities Commissions (IOSCO).[7]

Support from IOSCO

IOSCO federates all the controlling authorities of the national financial markets at global level, including the powerful American Securities and Exchange Commission (SEC) and the *Commission des Opérations de Bourse* (COB) – the French Stock Exchange Commission. It belongs to "a COB club" (Perier, 1995) and like the IASC/IASB its only power lies in influence, but since the SEC is amongst its members, this is considerable. In particular, IOSCO works to identify and promote standards intended to facilitate the development of international operations concerning financial instruments and accounting standards.

The IASC found itself more or less in competition with IOSCO and if the latter had drawn up its own standards, it would have been marginalised. So at the end of the 1980s, moves were made by the general secretary of the IASC to ensure that it became IOSCO's standards supplier, thus acquiring strong normative legitimacy in the face of the financial markets, in particularly the American markets. These initiatives bore fruit and IOSCO let it be understood that it would probably adopt these standards after they had been revised.

At the same time, the IASC reoriented this task and equipped itself with what is generally known as a conceptual framework.

This new direction was defined in a Declaration of Intent (Exposure Draft (E32)) entitled, *Comparability of Financial Statements* and published in 1989. The Declaration of Intent stated that the revised standards, as well as future standards, would no longer include options but would indicate a preferential, or "benchmark" treatment, and a second, merely tolerated "allowed treatment" for each problem. This tightening up of standards gave them a more coercive character and met the requirements of the financial markets yet at the same time, increased the risk that they would run counter to national regulations.

The IASC's conceptual framework,[8] entitled *Framework for the Preparation and Presentation of Financial Statements,* was also published in 1989. It was a summary of the conceptual framework adopted at the beginning of the 1980s by the *Financial Accounting*

Standards Board (FASB), the American standard setting body. In particular, Paragraph 10 contains the same affirmation of the primacy of investors over other users of accounting information:

> Although all the needs for information of the (various) users cannot be met by financial statements, there are needs which are common to all. Because investors are providers of risk capital to the enterprise, financial statements that meet their needs will also meet most of the general financial needs of other users.

In other words, what is good for investors is good for everybody. Implicitly, following FASB's lead, the IASB adhered to the Friedmanian idea of corporate responsibility whereby a company's sole responsibility is economic and the only accounts it need render are to its shareholders. Even though this is questionable to say the least, this allegiance to the conceptual framework of FASB and therefore to shareholder-oriented accounting, could not but satisfy IOSCO, largely dominated as it was, by the Americans.

So to meet the requirements of IOSCO and in an attempt to become its standards supplier, the IASC confirmed the Anglo-Saxon orientation of its work. Over and above IOSCO, this meant attracting the good graces of the Securities and Exchange Commission (SEC) and the American financial markets. SEC declared, moreover, that it was ready to recognise IASC's standards relative to cash-flow statements and consolidated accounts, which were very close to the FASB's corresponding standards.

Collaboration between the IASC and IOSCO was initiated at the beginning of the 1990s but paradoxically, IOSCO took its time recognising IASC's standards. In 1994, its technical committee, led by the President of the French organisation, COB, announced that it was ready to accept its standard on cash-flow statements and that it considered 14 other standards to be of the quality required by IOSCO, but that the remaining standards would have to be improved and new standards would have to be drawn up.

The reasons for what might seem like a turnaround on the part of IOSCO and a partial failure for the IASC are many and various but it would appear that the principle issue at stake in the elaboration of international accounting standards was, and doubtless will remain, access for non-American companies to the American financial markets. Yet in the 1990s, certain non-American companies were beginning to apply

the US GAAP[9] in order to be listed in the United States. So it is possible that the Americans thought it was no longer necessary to follow IOSCO's strategy of backing IASC standards (Walton, 2001) and that everyone would eventually have to to apply the American standards.

This setback did not discourage the IASC, however. Contact was maintained with IOSCO and in 1995, during IOSCO's annual congress held in Paris, the Presidents of IASC and of IOSCO's technical committee announced a new programme for the IASC that was expected to end in 1999 and which would lead to the approval of the IASC's standards by IOSCO. IOSCO's renewed backing can perhaps be explained by the hostility of certain of its members to the adoption of the US GAAP by their country's companies. For these members, IASC standards, even though they were technically similar, constituted a political alternative to the American standards.

In the end, the IASC was able to take advantage of the dissension within IOSCO itself and of the hostility of certain of its members to the American standards. So IOSCO eventually adopted IASC standards. However, this does not necessarily mean they will be applied in its members' countries. Just like the IASC, IOSCO is, in fact, an international organisation governed by private law and its powers are no greater than IASC's.

The situation of the European Union is quite different. It is an inter-governmental organisation capable of imposing its decisions on its members, hence its interest in the IASC since it can give it the coercive force it lacks.

But before dealing with its relationship with Europe, a few words on the rhetoric used by the IASC/IASB to legitimise and obtain the support it needs to extend and increase its power and achieve its objectives.

A rhetoric of competence, independence and impartiality

Rhetoric is the art of persuasion, by deed or by word. Lacking other means to obtain and retain the support it needs to achieve its objective of harmonisation, the IASC/IASB has, throughout its existence, developed a rhetoric of competence, impartiality and independence. This rhetoric is illustrated by its conceptual framework, its procedure for elaborating standards (the *due process*) and the recent reform of its structures.

By giving itself a conceptual framework in 1989 to guide its work, the IASC/IASB affirmed its theoretical competence on the one hand, and on the other, its wish to provide its work of elaborating standards with a "scientific" basis. This affirmation has only been partly validated, which is what gives it a rhetorical character. The IASC/IASB's conceptual framework is far from constituting a coherent accounting theory, if indeed such a theory is possible. Moreover, many of its standards contain elements that contradict its conceptual framework. This is quite simply because a standard-setting body, if it wants its standards to be applied, must necessarily take into account current practices and these may well be out of kilter with standards directly deduced from a pre-established theoretical framework, and also because it cannot ignore either the many economic consequences (Zeff, 1978), or the social consequences of the standards it publishes. The fact remains that a conceptual framework can create the illusion of a scientific approach and become a source of legitimacy that is all the more useful since there are no others (Peasnell, 1982).

Through its due process,[10] the IASC/IASB hoped to get all the stakeholders to participate in the elaboration of its standards, thus demonstrating its impartiality. Here again, rhetoric has its place. Indeed, the IASB can only be persuaded to effect change if the priority given to investors in its conceptual framework is not challenged. Moreover, only stakeholders with the financial resources and/or the necessary technical competence can really intervene in the due process and hope to have the Board's ear; other stakeholders are merely passive spectators in the potential negotiation between the IASC/IASB and more powerful stakeholders. Although as yet unproven, it might seem that in the context of the due process, the direct or indirect influence of the "big four" on the work of the IASC/IASB is significant. They have, in fact, the doctrinal and financial resources needed for effective participation and lobbying.

In the last analysis, the IASC/IASB can only be recognised by the organisations whose support it solicits if it is seen to be independent. This is doubtless the reason behind the structural reform[11] carried out in 2001 which freed it from the sole tutelage of the accounting profession[12] whilst allowing it to keep its distance from the national standard-setters. Its structure is a copy of that of FASB. The IASC thus became a foundation whose nineteen members, the trustees, represent the various parties directly concerned by the harmonisation of international accounting standards. The Trustees appoint the fourteen members of the IASB. Once appointed by the trustees, the fourteen members of the Board are supposed to act quite independently.

But who is independent? One is always the result of one's history (training, experience, social class etc.). Ten of the fourteen members of the Board are from an Anglo-Saxon environment and familiar with the accounting model that prevails there. Without in any way doubting their integrity, questions might well be asked as to their independence from this model.

Finally, even if an organisation such as the IASB can be independent, its independence raises the question of its legitimacy: to whom is it accountable? Who assesses it? There is a sort of paradox in the fact that an organisation that elaborates standards for the rendering of accounts is accountable to no-one!

To finish with its rhetoric, it is worth noting that the IASC/IASB has merely borrowed the instruments of the rhetoric of competence, independence and impartiality from FASB and is simply applying this rhetoric at international level.

THE IASC/IASB'S RELATIONSHIP WITH EUROPE

Relations between the IASC/IASB and Europe, and more precisely with the European Economic Community, which has since become the European Union, have always been characterised by a great deal of ambiguity.

A highly ambiguous relationship

Firstly, let us remember, with reference to the brief history of the IASC we have given, that it was founded at a time when Europe was embarking on a programme the aim of which was to harmonise the accounting regulations of the various member states. Was this a coincidence? Some do not think so and take the view that on the contrary, its creation, in accordance with the wishes of the big international practices and the British professional body, was to block the European initiative. It did not succeed however, and Europe, as mentioned above, armed itself with accounting directives that bore witness to a sort of normative compromise between the Anglo-Saxon and Continental reference systems. This explains the difficulties experienced by the IASC in the mid-1980s; it lost (though only temporarily as history was to show), the CEE states as places where its standards could be applied.

Fortunately (for the IASC), European accounting harmonisation was to meet a sticky end in the 1990s. Faced with the requirements of booming financial markets, the national regulations resulting from the Fourth and Seventh Directives quickly became obsolete and modernising them, a priority. The heavy legal machinery of the Directives prevented them from being modernised rapidly, however.

Some recommended the creation of a European standardisation body – a European Accounting Standards Board (EASB) – as a counterpart to the powerful American FASB. But the European Commission proved more interested in the single currency than in accounting harmonisation and let time slip away. An increasing number of European groups therefore fell back on either IASC standards or American standards. The IASC was then able to present its standards as an alternative to the American standards, offering its services to the Commission and trying to appropriate the power of standardising the Union.

In 2000, the Commission responded to its offers and defined the new European strategy for accounting harmonisation and its new relationship with the IASC, a relationship that can be qualified as one of delegation or sub-contracting. In a statement issued on 13th June 2000 in its capacity as an executive body of the Union, it recommended the application of IASC standards by listed European groups by January 1st 2005 at the latest.

A European regulation dated 19th July 2002 confirmed this strategy with the proviso that the IASC/IASB's standards would only be applied if they were in the Community's interests, which implied that there would need to be an approval mechanism.

At the centre of this approval mechanism was a specially created organisation, the European Accounting Regulation Committee (ARC), made up of representatives of the various member states in the Union. This organisation, despite its name, was not a technical standardisation organisation (the EASB did not progress beyond the planning stage), but a political organisation.

Each time the European Commission had to accept or reject one of the IASC/IASB's standards, it had to consult ARC. The latter announced its decisions after a qualified majority vote. When ARC accepted the standard, the Commission took the necessary measures to see that the standard was applied.

Moreover, in evaluating IASC/IASB standards, the Commission benefited from the help and expertise of a technical committee created in June 2001 on the initiative of the private sector and given the name European Financial Reporting Advisory Group (EFRAG). First and foremost, this technical committee supervised the process of elaborating the standards that were to be submitted to the European Commission and it could therefore intervene with the IASB whenever it deemed necessary.

This was the adoption mechanism that was tested for the first time in July 2003. For ARC, it was a question of pronouncing on the set of IASC/IASB standards to be applied on 1st January 2005 by the Union's listed groups, with the proviso that their accounts could not, according to the IASC/IASB, be declared in conformity with its reference system unless all its standards had been applied. The rejection of two standards out of a proposed thirty-four therefore appeared as an important obstacle to the application of the IASC/IASB's reference system, which explains the stupefaction of the business community and members of the IASC Board. So what were the reasons for this rejection?

The rejection of standards 32 and 39: from the technical "booing and hissing" of the banks and insurance companies to...

Standards 32 and 39 concern financial instruments and suggest that these be estimated at their fair value, that is to say market value. The recourse to fair value seems logical, moreover, when, in accordance with the conceptual framework of the IASC/IASB, it is a question of producing information for investors. But the application of the criteria of fair value has many drawbacks and raises awkward technical problems. These problems and drawbacks have been the subject of numerous articles by accountancy professionals and academics[13] which members of the Board seem to have ignored.

The main drawback to fair value, when it is set by the market (which supposes that it exists), is its extreme volatility, which can lead to a high degree of instability in the performances of companies measured in accounting terms.

Moreover, when it is not set by the market, it has to be calculated with the help of a model, with a risk of misadjustment. This risk of misadjustment, known as model misadjustment can have many causes: the underlying hypotheses may not have been satisfied, implementation may be defective, the parametering may be incorrect, and finally the model may lack robustness or stability. To these involuntary causes can be added voluntary causes… Directors may be tempted to manipulate the model to their advantage and to practise "creative" or "high risk"[14] accounting for the investor. Small modifications to the parameters can produce big variations in the calculated value.

The sectors most sensitive to the drawbacks of fair value were banks and insurance companies. The central banks reacted first; the Federal Reserve Board in April 2000 and the Basel Committee in May 2000. Although qualified, their conclusions were clear: standard 39 is not suitable for bank balance sheets and its application would be an obstacle to monitoring the sector.

The reaction of the presidents of the big European banks, although more technical, was more pointed. In a letter dated November 2002, they questioned the content of standards 32 and 39.

In the same way, the big European insurance companies demonstrated their hostility to standards 32 and 39. The insurance sector is an extremely specific sector. Most of its liabilities and the commitments made regarding its clients are not negotiable on the markets. Fair value estimation would presuppose the use of models based on various choices and in particular, on the choice of a discount rate. Such choices, which can have considerable consequences on the value of liabilities, are very difficult to make. The IASC has doubtless not properly understood the specificity of a sector, which, especially in continental Europe, stands apart from the financial markets to some extent. There are many mutual insurance companies in France in particular.

Moreover, bankers and insurers, over and above their reaction to the technical content of the standards, also questioned the IASB's consultation practice, emphasised it limits and thereby demonstrated the rhetorical nature of its procedure for elaborating standards (the due process mentioned above) calculated on that of the FASB. In defence of the IASB, it can nevertheless be said that EFRAG did not quite play the game as expected.

The debate they engendered took a more political turn with the intervention of the President of the French Republic. This intervention was to draw the attention of public opinion to the harmonisation of international accounting standards and to debates that had remained confined to an extremely limited circle of specialists.

… the political reaction

On 4th July 2003, Jacques Chirac sent a letter to the President of the European Commission, the Italian Romano Prodi, to alert him to the fact that,

> certain accounting standards in the process of being adopted in the European Union run the risk of leading to an increased financiarisation [*sic*] of our economy and to business management methods that favour the short-term too much.

For the first time, a leading French politician intervened directly in a debate on accounting and took accounting outside the professional circles to which it had been confined. It is possible that this intervention influenced the decision taken by ARC on 16th July 2003. Jacques Chirac's arguments are obviously not technical points and place the debate on a political level. They concern the governance of companies by investors, that is to say by the financial markets. The limits of this type of governance have been demonstrated by several cases, beginning with Enron.

What the French President also calls into question is not just IASB standards but no less than the conceptual framework from which they have been deduced, that is to say, an Anglo-Saxon conceptual framework that places the interests of shareholders over what the lawyers call social interest. Moreover, without establishing a link between the two, one cannot but be struck by the fact that his reaction came against a background of tension between "old Europe"[15] and the United States over the Iraq war. And it so happens that "old Europe" advocates a different accounting model from the Anglo-Saxon model and that rather late in the day, it wishes to defend it.

To sum up, this rejection by the European Union's Accounting Regulation Committee of its standards 32 and 39 is a good way of analysing the problems and contradictions with which the IASC/IASB has been confronted almost since its creation and which it has always managed to overcome.

As an international organisation governed by private law, it has no coercive power that would enable it to enforce the application of the standards it issues. It is therefore having to constantly prove its legitimacy and seek out the support of more powerful organisations. It has been supported in various ways by IFAC, IOSCO and the European Union. The backing of IFAC enabled it to extend the potential field of application of its standards, that of IOSCO gave it its legitimacy in the face of the financial markets (although its standards were not recognised by SEC), and that of the European Union indirectly gave it the power to impose its standards within Europe.

As an organisation that has drawn its normative legitimacy from the Anglo-Saxon world and aims its standards at the production of information intended for investors, it has found, as a sub-contractor, the means of coercive action in a Europe divided between two models of governance and the two accounting reference systems associated with them, the Anglo-Saxon shareholder model and the Continental partner model, hence its difficulties in fully satisfying the requirements of its European prime contractor. Linked to Jacques Chirac's statement, the rejection of standards 32 and 39 seems like opposition, by the supporters of the Continental model, to a reference system that differs too greatly from this model.

A case of organisational resilience

However, the organisation has always been able to face the various crises it has experienced with a great deal of skill, showing a rare capacity for survival and constituting a real case of organisational resilience. It is a fair bet that it will very quickly amend the two litigious standards. Moreover, on 17th December 2003, it made public new versions of standards 32 and 39.[16] It cannot allow itself to enter into a conflict with the European Union which might result in the postponement of the application of its standards in its member states. Still less can it take the risk of a rupture since this would deprive it of its means of action. But afterwards? Will it go as far as revising its conceptual framework, taking the risk of moving away from the American model, of disappointing IOSCO and losing the possibility that its standards may one day be recognised by the American financial markets? Probably not, and all the more so since it has just embarked on a collaboration with FASB.[17] Is it not secretly banking on the fact that, in the context of globalisation, the Anglo-Saxon model, the American[18] model to be more precise, will sooner or later

win out over the Continental model? In view of the power of the American financial markets, such a bet obviously makes some sense: Europe's inferiority in accounting is also the result of the relative weakness of its financial markets (Véron, 2003). Finally, the IASB may hope that the amendments made to its standards 32 and 39 will satisfy for once and for all the European Accounting Regulation Committee (whose delightful unanimity will surely be extremely temporary, given its composition) and it will not have to revise its conceptual framework.

The strength of the weak

Once again, the IASC/IASB will doubtless succeed in overcoming the obstacle. This obviously raises the question of what drives this type of organisation, which finds itself face to face with seemingly much more powerful organisations; what the strength of the weak is, in fact. The quality of a management team particularly skilled in steering a delicate course? Its successive presidents have proved highly pugnacious, and not least the current incumbent. The inertia of the big governmental and inter-governmental organisations, too restricted by their procedures? The weight of European bureaucracy doubtless counts for something in the success of the IASC/IASB. The latent conflicts that develop between the big international organisations and offer it strategic opportunities? The interests of IOSCO and the European Union do not converge. The European Union's lack of ambition? As in many other fields, this is obvious. Its fear of internal conflicts? Sub-contracting harmonisation is a sure way to externalise a potential conflict over accounting matters between the United Kingdom on the one hand and on the other, France and Germany.

The strength of the weak often resides in the indecision and weakness of the strong and in the way they cancel each other out. Which is perhaps what makes the resistible rise of the IASC/IASB, irresistible.

Notes

1   This article was published in *Gérer et Comprendre*, March 2004, no.75, pp. 30–40.
2   Since 2001, the IASB has been the operational arm of the IASC, a body created in 1973, and has taken over its work in elaborating international standards. In this

chapter, the acronyms IASC, IASB or IASC/IASB are used as appropriate.

3 ARC's opinion was confirmed by the Commission's Regulation no.1725/2003 of 29th September 2003. This regulation ratifies all IASC/IASB's standards with the exception of standards 32 and 39, and states in its preamble that these two standards should be radically modified.

4 Not only *Le Monde* and *Le Figaro*, but also *Libération*, which in its 17th July 2003 edition, devoted two articles to the event, written by Grégoire Biseau and Jean Quatremer and titled respectively, in true Libération style, *"L'Europe donne sa leçon de comptabilité: Europe gives a lecture on accounting"* and *"Un pataquès nommé 'IAS 32' and 'IAS 39': A muddle named 'IAS 32' and 'IAS 39'"*.

5 The factual information in this article is taken from: www.iasplus.com.

6 The CNC is currently made up of fifty-eight members and includes not only representatives of the public authorities and the accounting profession but also representatives of companies from all sectors and, unique in the world, representatives of unions representing employees.

7 The corresponding francophone acronym and title of IOSCO: *Organisation Internationale des Commissions de Valeurs mobilières* (OICV) are rarely used.

8 A conceptual framework can be defined as a coherent set of objectives, principles and concepts, intended to be used as a theoretical system of reference by a standard-setter which can, as it were, deduce its standards from it and practice deductive standardisation as opposed to standardisation resulting from the most generally accepted practices.

9 The various standards that must be respected by listed American companies are grouped together under the designation, *Generally Accepted Accounting Principles* (GAAP); these standards are currently drawn up by the FASB.

10 The elaboration of a standard is achieved according to a ritual procedure that includes the publication of preliminary documents and, in particular, an exposure-draft. The preparation of these documents is the subject of many discussions and their publication is accompanied by calls for comments. The procedure is a way of organising lobbying.

11 The new "constitution" of the IASC/IASB is presented on its site: www.iasb.org.uk.

12 However, five of the nineteen trustees are appointed by IFAC and two of the trustees appointed by IFAC must *"normally be senior partners/executives from prominent accounting firms"* (the "big four "?).

13 See for example (in French): Casta J.-F. and Colasse B. (2001), *La juste valeur: enjeux techniques et politiques – Fair Value: the technical and political implications*

14 The expression "high risk accounting" was used in the report of the American Senate on Enron to describe the company's accounting practices.

15 Expression used by George Bush to describe the European countries opposed to the use of force against Iraq.

16 At the date this chapter was sent to the editor, 14th January 2004, ARC had not yet pronounced on the new versions.

17 The IASB and FASB decided in October 2002 ("Norwalk Agreement") to coordinate their work programmes in the future. In November of the same year they also adopted a "programme of short-term convergence", the object of which was to resolve a certain number of differences between their respective standards. All this obviously only went to increase the Anglo-Saxon influence on the IASB.

18 To a journalist from *Le Monde* who said to him, "but it's the American model you are imposing on Europe with the IAS standards…", the vice-president of the IASB did not hesitate to reply with somewhat undiplomatic candour, "it's not a question of model! Since the United States is ahead of us in accounting research, it would seem wise to let Europe benefit from it". Interview published in *Le Monde*, 31st October 2003 under the title "Plaidoyer pour les future règles comtables, très contestées – In defence of the hotly disputed future accounting regulations".

BIBLIOGRAPHY

Aïdan, P. (2001), *Droit des marchés financiers: Réflexions sur les sources*, Editions Banque.

Cohen, E. (2001), *L'ordre économique mondial: Essai sur les autorités de régulation*, Fayard.

Colasse, B. (2000), Harmonisation comptable internationale, dans: *Encyclopédie de comptabilité, contrôle de gestion et audit*, Economica, pp. 757–769.

Colasse, B. (2002), Le défi de la mondialisation comptable, dans: Kalika M., *Les défis du management*, Editions Liaisons, pp. 139–150.

Heem, G. et Aonzo, P.(2003), La normalisation comptable internationale: ses acteurs, sa légitimité, ses enjeux, *Revue d'économie financière*, no.71, pp. 33–61.

Mistral, J. (2003), Rendre compte fidèlement de la réalité de l'entreprise, dans: *Les normes comptables et le monde post-Enron*, La documentation française, pp. 7–55.

Peasnell, K.V. (1982, aut.), The function of a conceptual framework for corporate financial reporting, *Accounting and business research*, pp. 243–256.

Véron, N. (2003), Normalisation comptable internationale: une gouvernance en devenir, dans: *Les normes comptables et le monde post-Enron*, La documentation française, pp. 123–132.

Wallace, R. S. O. (1990), Survival Strategies of a Global Organization: the Case of the International Accounting Standards Committee, *Accounting Horizons*, June, pp. 1–22.

Walton, P. (2001), *La comptabilité anglo-saxonne*, La Découverte.

Zeff, S.A. (1978, Dec), The rise of "economic consequences", *The Journal of Accountancy*, pp. 56–63.

THREE

PART FOUR

The Reform and Transformation of European Corporate Governance Institutions

INTRODUCTION TO PART FOUR

While absorbing the impact of international financial markets, and reorientating towards shareholder value conceptions of the firm, Europe has been engaged in the reform and transformation of corporate governance involved in the wider harmonization project of the European Union towards the member economies. The lengthy deliberations involved in securing reforms that have often left member countries with the freedom of choice they demanded on whether to implement particular aspects of reforms or not, suggests that if the convergence process of the European countries themselves is difficult to negotiate, then transatlantic convergence may be not possible to arrange, at least with regard to critical institutional and legal areas.

One long-standing initiative is the introduction of the European Company (Societas Europea, SE). Joseph McCahery and Erik Vermeulen indicate that though initially the intention was to secure a uniform set of rules across the European Union, eventually a more flexible approach was adopted towards national laws, creating the possibility of firms engaging in regulatory arbitrage (the choice by companies to locate investments or other economic activity based on the regulatory environment of the jurisdiction, and the effort by legal authorities to enhance the attractiveness of regulation relative to other states to encourage business to make this choice). In effect the strategy of the European Commission to introduce an EU-level company statute to compete with national business forms, was blocked by member states that viewed the EU proposal itself as a means to escape stricter national company law. The intention of member states was to prevent a "European Delaware" (the state in the US that has monopolized the lion's share of large corporate registrations, and effectively become the centre of US company law activity). The degree of discretion insisted upon by member states suggests a determination to protect their own company law.

In many ways the UK has been at the forefront of corporate governance reform, not only in Europe, but often influencing developments in governance reform led by the World Bank, OECD and other international agencies. However Alistair Howard argues that despite the institutional innovation initiated in the UK this largely occurred within existing structures of control. Though the possibility of moving towards a more stakeholder oriented governance system was debated for some years in the UK, substantial legal and policy changes did not materialize. The state in the UK has experienced a series of decentralizing restructuring exercises in a long-wave of neo-liberalism in the 1980s and early 1990s, followed by the new public management and rhetoric for the Third Way of the Blair and later Brown governments. From another perspective it can be argued that in the UK largely self-regulatory systems have been replaced by state-organized regulation as in the creation of the Financial Services Authority in 2000 with a wide brief to supervise the finance sector.

Reviewing the progress of corporate governance reform in the UK Howard suggests that through the shocks of successive cycles of corporate failure both in the UK in the early 1990s, and in the US in the early 2000s, though regulation was extended in most areas it was substantively contained to ensure that business and investor interests were not challenged. With reference to issues such as board reform, transparency and executive pay, though new reforms were an advance over private self-regulation, a balance was maintained between private, market and public authority that business found comfortable. When the deliberations of the Company Law Review (1998–2002) attempted a comprehensive reconsideration of the objectives of companies and the role of stakeholders, the changes resulting in the law were significant but did not represent the fundamentally new approach, transforming UK corporate governance towards a more European direction for which many critics had argued. When executive pay continued apparently out of control in the UK, it was conceded that shareholders should have an advisory vote on company executive remuneration reports, but left boards free to make whatever response they thought appropriate. On social and environmental responsibility, though the interpretation of directors' duties was widened, the duty to report on these matters in an Operating and Financial Review was abandoned in favor of weaker European legislation.

The different trajectories in the transformation of corporate governance in France and Germany are examined by Michel Goyer. According to the varieties of capitalism thesis, superior economic performance and competitive advantage develops from patterns of institutional complementarity that encourage distinctive firm competencies. Goyer contends that changes in France and Germany can better be understood as a process of functional conversion where institutions can be directed to new purposes, while apparently maintaining formal institutional stability. Access to patient capital traditionally constituted an important foundation of the coordinated market economies of Europe compared to liberal market economies that are based on shorter-term risk capital. Both the French and German coordinated market economy systems of corporate governance were characterized by high debt to equity ratios, meaning bank finance was more important than shares as a source of external funding. Ownership was highly concentrated in Germany through cross-shareholding among companies, banks' own direct shareholdings, and family ownership, while in France in addition to these major shareholders, the state often had an involvement in leading companies. Finally, the market for corporate control was very limited in both countries, which further enhanced stability and longer-term horizons.

However, with financial deregulation and the growth in the scale and international activity of the institutional investors, together with the increasing significance of equity markets across all regions, firms in the coordinated market economies are becoming increasingly dependent on equity finance. Goyer argues that firm-level institutional arrangements account for the different ability of French and German firms to attract funds from large Anglo-American institutional investors. Mutual investment funds and hedge funds tend to possess shorter-term investment strategies, fitting the corporate decision-making process in France well. The French firm-level institutions are characterized by the capacity of the CEO and top managers to reorganize the enterprise at will, allowing new strategies to deliver value in the short term. However the short term strategies of mutual and hedge funds do not fit well with the enterprise organization of German firms, which involve negotiation of changes between management and employees of new strategies in response to external pressures. In contrast pension funds with commitments to longer-term horizons are investing more extensively in Germany, and provide a stabilizing force for the workplace organization of German companies.

With corporate governance institutions, policy and practice subject to a continuous, if gradual and piecemeal, process of transformation in Europe it could be argued the system is in a "state of permanent reform" (Noack and Zetzsche 2005). A comprehensive survey of the reforms undertaken in France, Germany and Italy is offered by Luca Enriques and Paolo Volpin. However, first the basic question has to be addressed – what is the purpose of reform? In the Anglo-American world the fundamental problem of corporate governance is assumed to be the conflict of interest between dispersed shareholders and controlling managers, and the purpose of corporate governance reform is to alleviate this conflict by monitoring and regulating the performance of managers more effectively. The fundamental problem of corporate governance in Europe and throughout much of the rest of the world is thought to be the presence of dominant shareholders who exercise effective control often through pyramids, shareholder agreements, or dual classes of shares, resulting in the neglect of minority shareholders. Therefore the path of reform might be expected to be different in Europe compared to Anglo-American jurisdictions, since in Europe dominant shareholders already have the capacity to discipline management. It is the misalignment of the interests of majority and minority shareholders that requires resolution.

The concentration of ownership in France, Germany and Italy is detailed by Enriques and Volpin, as is the use of pyramidal forms (defined as an ownership structure in which the controlling shareholder exercises control of one company through ownership of at least one other listed company), with examples from leading European companies. A high proportion of ownership concentration is due to the presence of family-controlled companies. While family-controlled companies may be better managed in terms of their investment and innovation, this does not mean they are better governed. Family control may prevent management abuses, but the resources of the company may still be used disproportionately to benefit the family. When a dominant shareholder has untrammelled control, various forms of self-dealing can occur, including tunneling, where firm value is passed up the pyramid of ownership from where the dominant shareholder has a smaller share of the cash flow rights, to companies further up the pyramid where the dominant shareholder has a greater share of the cash flow rights. Other ways value can be transferred from the company include related party transactions, allocation of assets and liabilities, and excessive director compensation.

The forces actually driving corporate reform in Europe include the effort to make European capital markets more attractive to international investors; the desire to create a common regulatory framework in Europe; and the response to the series of corporate failures that have occurred both in the US and in Europe. France, Germany and Italy have attempted substantial corporate governance reform to strengthen internal governance, empower shareholders, enhance disclosure and improve enforcement, with attention to empowering minority shareholders and disclosure. Yet Enriques and Volpin conclude that too little has been done to resolve the problem of related party transactions. More generally, since the thrust of the European reforms has largely been structured in response to scandals that have occurred in the US, and the resulting reforms in corporation and securities law there, the relevance of this legislation could be questioned in terms of its appropriateness to deal with uniquely European issues. It is possible European policy makers may have adopted these reforms to be seen to be engaged in the reform process, without confronting the major problem of controlling majority shareholders in the European system of corporate governance.

BIBLIOGRAPHY

Armour, J., Deakin, S. and Konzelmann, S.J. (2003) Shareholder Primacy and the Trajectory of UK Corporate Governance, *British Journal of Industrial Relations*. 41(3): 531–55.

Deakin, S. (2001) Regulatory Competition Versus Harmonization in European Company Law, in D.C. Esty and D. Geradin (eds.), *Regulatory Competition and Economic Integration*, Oxford: Clarendon Press.

Enriques, L. (2004) Silence is Golden: The European Company Statue as a Catalyst for Company Law Arbitrage, *Journal of Corporate Law Studies*. 77: 77–95.

Gilson, R. (2003) Globalising Corporate Governance: Convergence of Form or Function, *American Journal of Comparative Law*, 49 (2): 329–57.

Gourevitch, P. and Shinn, J. (2005) *Political Power and Corporate Control: The New Global Politics of Corporate Governance*, Princeton, NJ: Princeton University Press.

Hopt, K.J. and Wymeersch, E. (2003) *Capital Markets and Company Law in Europe*, Oxford: Oxford University Press.

Morck, R., Wolfenzon, D. and Yeung, B. (2005) Corporate Governance, Economic Entrenchment and Growth, *Journal of Economic Perspectives*, 43(3): 655–720.

Noack, U. and Zetzsche, D.A. (2005) Corporate Reform in Germany: The Second Decade, *European Business Law Review*, 16(5): 1033–64.

Streek, W. and Thelen, K. (2005) *Beyond Continuity: Institutional Change in Advanced Political Economies*, New York: Oxford University Press.

Williams, C.A. and Conley, J.M. (2005) An Emerging Third Way? The Erosion of the Anglo-American Shareholder Construct, *Cornell International Law Journal*, 38(2): 493–551.

12 "Does the European Company Prevent the 'Delaware Effect'?"

from European Law Journal (2005)

Joseph A. McCahery and Erik P. M. Vermeulen

SUMMARY

This chapter analyses the history of EU company law and locates a stable 'non-competitive equilibrium'. This equilibrium follows from Member States that founded the EU unwilling to give up their lawmaking authority regarding company law issues. From the outset, Member States were determined to prevent the 'Delaware effect'. Since then, stability has ruled. The agenda-setting in EU company law has changed little during the existence of the EU. Operative incentives, market structure and regulatory results have been more constant than dynamic, even as the recent enactment of the European Company has triggered discussion about competitive lawmaking in Europe.

I INTRODUCTION

For well over four decades, the European Commission (EC) has been locked in a battle with Member States over the introduction of a new legal form, the European Company (Societas Europaea, SE). Although the EC initially assumed that this business form would provide a complete set of uniform rules without reference to national law, the EC eventually embraced a significantly more flexible approach in respect of national law in order to reach agreement on default provisions for employee involvement and the choice of board structure. Indeed, in October 2001 the European Council and Parliament approved a Regulation that has a limited number of provisions, which deal with the formation of a European Company, its governance structure, employee involvement and its real

seat, and approved a Directive that regulates employee involvement. The initial sceptical reaction to the passage of the new legislation is entirely consistent with the repeated and troublesome attempts to secure an agreement on the new company form. Thus, since the adoption of the Regulation, critics charge that the legislation falls short of what is needed for entrepreneurs. Some find, moreover, that the absence of uniform rules will bring few benefits in comparison to national business forms. Importantly, cumbersome provisions are likely to deter managers from pursuing cross-border mergers unless they produce significantly large countervailing benefits.[1] Lastly, although the adoption of the employee participation provisions offers employees with protection from opportunistic transfers, these arrangements—which are complex and time-consuming—provide businesses with little incentive to deviate from the status quo of national company law forms. These observations raise questions whether the European Company Statute is a sufficiently attractive tool for larger firms to engage in forum shopping activities.

It is therefore surprising that many company law scholars view the new Regulation with a mixture of expectation and scepticism, arguing that, in the context of agreed employee involvement, the new company law form could stimulate regulatory competition.[2] A common view attempts to explain that the ultimate appeal of the new company law vehicle, compared to other national-level company law forms, is a result, if anything, of absence of legal rules on shares, financing and legal capital. Proponents argue that the renvoi technique, used by the European Company Statute, creates the possibility for some firms to choose their place of central administration according to the law of the Member State that offers the most attractive benefits.[3]

In this chapter, we suggest that the European Company Statute could very well rekindle the interest in and discussions on competitive lawmaking within the EU. To the extent that the Regulation allows for reincorporation without liquidation of the old firm, firms may have incentives to migrate to Member States that they prefer. At the same time, the Statute's incompleteness and the significant differences in the national legislations may, we recognise, give rise to firms engaging in regulatory arbitrage.[4] There are a number of reasons, however, to believe that the legislation is unlikely to pose a competitive threat to Member States. First, as tax scholars have noted, the Statute does not contain tax provisions, leaving it up to national laws, international tax treaties and other European regulation's to sort out the problem of taxation.[5] Second, the European Company will be taxed, in absence of a consolidated common tax based on the possibility of offsetting losses in different Member States, in the Member State where its head office is located on the basis of its worldwide taxation, leading in the cases of branches to double taxation. Third, even if lawmakers eventually eliminate the tax obstacles to the use of the European Company Statute, it is unlikely, because of legal uncertainty, that firms will move from existing business statutes which continue to give them significant cost advantages. In addition to the arguments given above, we believe that the some Member States, particularly Germany, have substantial incentives to discourage other governments from agreeing to EU-legal tax rules that would encourage cross-border reorganisations. In particular, our analysis may provide an explanation for the regulatory strategy of limiting the mobility of companies within the EU.

Accordingly, this chapter focuses on the evolution of company law at the EU and Member State level and explores how the adoption of the Regulation regarding the European Company affects this development.[6] Its emphasis is on elucidating lawmaking processes, and not on comparing legal rules and doctrines. The aim therefore is to explain and assess the process by which company law evolves, rather than to evaluate the content of the law in several jurisdictions. This article seeks to explain which groups are responsible—in some important respects—for influencing the agenda for the reform of company law, and which considerations have been instrumental in constraining the emergence of a European Delaware.

It is particularly tempting to compare the lawmaking process in Europe with the development of company law statutes in the United States. There are two reasons that make the European Union and the United States suitable candidates for a comparative study. First, like the United States, the European Union can be viewed as a federation in which the individual countries retain considerable sovereignty, while at the same time allocating important prerogatives to a supranational government.[7] Second, because US firms of all sizes have long been operating throughout the nationwide market without severe constraints regarding company law, the federal system has set a benchmark for the European Union.[8] Viewed in this context, the emulation of the US approach regarding the evolution of company law seems logical. The development of legal rules in the United States—as a result of competition between jurisdictions—does appear to have essential lessons for Europe as it embarks on the modernisation of company law in general. In the evolving pattern of EU company law, the European Commission and the European Court of Justice have until recently consistently avoided intervention in the national legislation of Member States that have limited cross-border mobility of firms. The decision not to intervene has reinforced the Member States' strategy of avoiding taking steps to create a market for corporate charters, which could ultimately displace the lawmaking autonomy of the Member States.[9]

Even though the threat of competition continues to be a defining feature of the market for closely held firms and holding companies, the possibility of free choice for publicly listed firms is thwarted because of tax and other national law barriers, which have been reinforced by harmonising company law rules by Directives. The combination of the real seat doctrine along with exit taxes proved capable of creating a stable, long-run non-competitive equilibrium. With the core company law agenda defined by Member States, the role of Brussels was merely to protect the cooperative agreement between Member States—by limiting incentives for the emergence of a European Delaware—and to protect the public interest. Since its inception, the cooperative equilibrium has remained stable and largely intact, as a result of learning and adaptive changes made by the Member States and the European Commission. But, as demonstrated in the USA, the breakdown of a highly stable equilibrium could occur rapidly.[10] While it is difficult to foresee with certitude the conditions that could lead to the breakdown of an equilibrium strategy in the EU, it is argued, nevertheless, that the stability of the equilibrium depends crucially on the continued ability of Member States to protect their present legal system against possible competitive pressures from other Member States. Indeed, a close examination of the European Company Statute confirms our view that the legislation is unlikely to facilitate firm mobility in the EU. Thus, we presume that the defects in the legislation simply reflect the core characteristics of the EU company law régime.

This chapter is divided into five sections. Section II turns to examine the US market-based system for corporate charters. A notable feature of the EU is that it tends to look to the operation of Delaware and the charter market with suspicion. In the USA, a growing number of commentators have argued that the charter market is suboptimal because Delaware faces little competition from the other states. The absence of competition in the charter market calls into question the description of Delaware, as emblematic of a particular form of market-based lawmaking, used by EU regulators to justify policies to reinforce the cooperative arrangement between Member States and prevent the 'Delaware-effect'.[11]

Section III recounts the evolution of the EU company law harmonisation programme from 1957 through the recent enactment of the European Company Statute. This account shows that the aim of the EU was to limit the right of establishment of pseudo-foreign companies and create barriers to the introduction of charter competition.[12] This discussion goes on to describe the emergence of a non-intervention approach of EU lawmaking, excluding federal level regulators from disrupting state-level accords between interested parties that are reflected in company law legislation. In this view, it is not surprising that an early strategy of the European Commission to introduce a truly EU-level company statute, to compete against the national level business forms, was systematically blocked by the Member States who viewed an EU company form as a means to escape stricter national company law legislation. The compromise legislation, however, fails to offer a truly 'pan-European' business form, presenting an opportunity for firms to reincorporate to a more beneficial legal system. Section IV considers the evidence on whether the status quo in EU company law is indirectly challenged by the recent enactment of the European Company. Section V offers a brief conclusion.

II THE DELAWARE EFFECT

The US legal system traditionally views company law in general as a local matter reserved to the states' governments.[13] Consequently, the corporation statutes of some states may differ appreciably from those of most other states on many critical matters. Once US business owners decide to incorporate, they must select an attractive state of incorporation. Under traditional conflict-of-law rules,[14] courts will respect this choice even if the corporation in question has no other contact with the chosen state. The corporate laws of the incorporating state govern the basic rights and duties of a corporation and its participants.

At the end of the nineteenth century, New Jersey and Delaware, concerned about incorporation decisions, adopted modernised general incorporation statutes.[15] Eventually, Delaware's statute made it the leading incorporation state in the United States since the 1920s,[16] presently serving as the state of incorporation for nearly half of the corporations listed on the New York Stock Exchange and more than half of all Fortune 500 firms.[17] In addition, Delaware is also the leading destination for firms that opt to reincorporate. Clearly, Delaware's value to incorporating firms is more than an up-to-date statute. The possibility of other states rapidly free-riding on the efforts and resources of the Delaware legislature by copying its statute would entail Delaware's lead being exhausted in a very short period of time.[18] For instance, the less-easily replicated judicial expertise and other enduring advantages, such as a well-developed corporate case law, learning and network benefits, herd behaviour,[19] and the superiority of Delaware's specialised chancery court, arguably preserve Delaware's leading position over time.[20]

Delaware's corporate law plays a key role in the evolution of companies in the United States, because Delaware law provides an alternative set of rules that serve firms and their legal advisers across the country. Consequently, many commentators have dealt with the vexed question of whether the choice of Delaware's corporate law eventually leads to value maximisation. In other words, is regulatory competition better described as a 'race to the bottom' or as a 'race to the top'?

Some commentators continue to point to possible shortcomings of the competitive process that ensue from the divergence between the interests of managers and public shareholders.[21] In their view, the development of state anti-takeover legislation perfectly exemplifies the shortcomings of regulatory competition. Because of the ability of firms' management to capture state legislation, states (including Delaware) have developed anti-takeover statutes and judicial decisions permitting the use of defensive tactics that are overly protective of incumbent managers at the expense of shareholders.[22] If the possibility of shareholder exit by tender to a hostile offeror is severely threatened, market mechanisms cannot adequately align the interests of managers and shareholders. By providing a constant and credible risk of hostile acquisitions, the takeover market creates a powerful incentive for managers to restrain from managerial self-dealing. Assuming that the 'market-for-corporate-control' is economically efficient in that it increases firm value, regulatory competition has serious implications for the race-to-the-top thesis. Consequently, according to this argument, mandatory federal rules should at least ensure that the market for corporate control remains active, robust, and competitive.[23]

It is doubtful, however, that US company laws will be placed under federal jurisdiction in the near future. Although it is conventional wisdom among US scholars that regulatory competition produces a race to the top with respect to some areas of corporate law,[24] it certainly has its flaws. First, states do not pursue regulatory competition solely by offering rules that meet their clients' needs. High-powered interest groups within a particular state induce the competitive process because of considerable tangible benefits. It has been argued that Delaware's corporation law is devised to maximise the amount of work performed by lawyers who are members of the Delaware Bar.[25] By providing standards and ambiguous default rules rather than rules that are clear in application, Delaware law enhances the amount of litigation in the state.[26] Delaware lawmakers thereby respond to the lobbying efforts of in-state lawyers who are able to capture a considerable share of the incorporating revenues, due to litigation-increasing standards.

Furthermore, since Delaware can rely on its dominant position in the market for incorporations, it could allow itself to prevent the emergence of optimal legal rules that would prevail in a perfectly competitive market.[27] Lastly, recent empirical research indicates that regulatory competition in the context of corporate law is imperfect as not only the product quality, but also the location of the 'seller' plays a pivotal role.[28] It appears that since firms display a marked home preference with respect to company law rules, states are more successful at retaining in-state firms than attracting out-of-state business formations.[29]

Thus, Delaware closely resembles a monopolistic 'seller' possessing market power and competitive advantages that other jurisdictions cannot replicate.[30] The increasing return mechanisms act as substantial barriers to other states wishing to enter the market for out-of-state business formations. Since the radical change in company lawmaking in the late nineteenth century, the Delaware equilibrium has ruled. Delaware has played and still plays a pivotal role as the national lawmaker in the USA, protecting itself from other states and federal interference by responding to interest group pressures.[31] It follows from this discussion that regulatory competition may not automatically yield an efficient outcome. Its legal product, however, is arguably superior to what a centralised régime would produce.[32]

III THE EUROPEAN 'NON-COMPETITION' STRATEGY

The Treaty of Rome (1957) between France, West Germany, Italy, Belgium, the Netherlands, and Luxembourg established the European Common Market. The Treaty provided for the right of establishment for foreign corporations to establish branches in another Member State, without being subject to more restrictive company law provisions of the host state.[33] At the time, the real seat theory, which provides that the laws of the host state are applied if the actual centre of the corporation's activities has moved to the host state, was still dominant although many feared it was losing ground since the Netherlands had recently abandoned the doctrine. Furthermore, Article 293 (ex 220) of the Treaty,[34] which invited the Member States, for instance, to enter into negotiations regarding the 1968 Brussels Convention on the Mutual Recognition of Companies and Legal Entities, would have abandoned the real seat theory in favour of the incorporation doctrine.[35] Recall that the real seat doctrine was developed in opposition to the opportunistic conduct of island jurisdictions attempting to lure foot-loose firms at the expense of higher cost jurisdictions. Drawing on the concepts of evolutionary game theory, we see that, prior to the twentieth century, Belgium played a non-cooperative game vis-à-vis France, which enabled French managers to change their state of incorporation. The threat of losing firms to foreign jurisdictions provided the impetus for the introduction of the real seat doctrine in Europe.[36]

In these circumstances, the Treaty would have arguably enhanced the introduction of a market for corporate charters for companies. The reaction to this was split. The founding Member States, such as France and West Germany who feared the consequences of an outbreak of a so-called 'race-to-the-bottom' reacted in the 1960s by binding existing members and new entrants to accept the harmonisation of their company laws. More specifically, France was concerned that the Netherlands, which had a flexible company law code, would be able to attract a large number of pseudo-corporations.[37] The European Commission's preferred solution to this problem was the top–down harmonisation of national company laws. Under this strategy, the Member States entered into a cooperative game in which the parties agreed, in exchange for political benefits or rents, to desist from opportunism in exchange for membership in the Community.[38] From this discussion, it should be clear that the small number of Member States could negotiate and enforce a political agreement that protected their domestic national stock, which produced both fiscal and political benefits for these governments. It should be clear that the combined effect of these benefits outweighed the value of the payoffs of competitive lawmaking.

During the 1970s a number of countries also entered the EU for similar reasons of political stability and economic integration. Even though the new entrants, Denmark, Ireland and the United Kingdom, endorsed the incorporation régime,[39] which could easily have reinforced the possibility of the out-migration of domestic companies, the cooperative equilibrium was sufficiently stable to neutralise this tendency. The cooperative agreement also included another element. The Member States would only agree to the harmonisation of their national laws if this could be achieved without the alteration of the core components of company law.[40] This confirms the expectation that Member States would also respect each other's lawmaking autonomy.

The first generation directives restated,[41] in effect, the content of the Member States' national laws.[42] Rigid and complete 'top–down' harmonisation was high on the agenda. The mandatory rules, such as minimum capital requirements and disclosure rules, constituted part of the initial wave of harmonised rules.[43] The array of mandatory legal capital rules,

however, seemed to benefit domestic interest groups.[44] Incumbent management may have influenced the EU legislature to supply provisions that limit dividend payments and share repurchases so as to obtain more leeway to reinvest firm's profits. Accountants, who play a pivotal role in the required valuation, also had a substantial interest in exerting influence on the legislative outcome.

With the introduction of England and other Member States, the second wave of directives was arguably more flexible, granting states options to comply with the terms of the directives.[45] Given the diversity of legal régimes, the optional approach ensured that the directives did not interfere with the core elements of Member States' national company law rules and hence respected the cooperative agreement.

The rigid approach of the first and second generation directives quickly showed its limitations. The harmonisation of core areas of company law, such as the structure and responsibility of the board of directors, cross-border mergers, representation of employees and bankruptcy procedures, proved to be predictably slow and ineffective.[46] The fundamental disagreements among Member States with regard to important issues, such as employee participation and the reluctance of Member States to implement the harmonised rules,[47] shows the difficulty with touching the autonomy of member state law. For instance, Member States regularly vetoed directive proposals under Article 100 EC (now Article 94), unless a politically acceptable consensus would be achieved.[48]

It was clear early, given the legislative setbacks involving the first and second generation directives, that the European Commission would be unable to remove the most intractable barriers to economic integration. While the EU continued to pursue its harmonisation strategy, policymakers within the Commission set out to design a more independent agenda on the basis of Article 308 (ex 235).[49] To this end, the EC introduced the Regulation of the European Economic Interest Grouping (EEIG), which made it possible for firms from different Member States to develop certain joint activities without having to merge or to set up a jointly owned subsidiary.[50] The first genuine European business form came into existence because it was not detrimental to national doctrines and usages and hardly competed against national business forms.[51] In reality, the EEIG's restricted objectives and references to national law have resulted in a rather unpopular business form.[52]

In 1970 the Commission also proposed the introduction of the European Company. This legal business form was designed to allow firms operating in two or more Member States the option to employ a genuine European business form, meaning that they will be able to move registered offices from one country to another without needing to dissolve the company in the first member state and to formally establish it in the second one. The strong resistance of Member States to adopt the legislation, until recently, reflected their continued preference to retain legislative autonomy and control over core areas of company law.[53]

Thus, the early phases of the harmonisation process, with its root-and-branch approach, reached its inevitable terminus point with the failure of the Fifth, Ninth and Thirteenth Directives, and a new direction was required to achieve the aims of European economic integration.[54]

After the *Cassis de Dijon* judgment, and with the Commission's 1985 White Paper as accepted in a Council Resolution of the same year, the EU tried to respond to calls for greater flexibility.[55] Minimum harmonisation and mutual recognition formed the so-called 'new approach' to harmonisation.[56] The following year, the Single European Act (SEA) attempted to resolve possible veto blockages at Council level by providing for a consultation procedure and qualified majority voting.[57] With the second enlargement,[58] the EU adopted a new model of integration based on centralised federalism,[59] which gave the European Commission increased agenda-setting power. Between 1986 and 1992, the EU adopted the two third-generation directives, concerning the disclosure of branches and formation of single member companies, which were marginal to domestic company law arrangements.[60]

Despite greater flexibility under the 'new approach', imposed standards remain fairly high. Market regulation proves inadequate to market evolutions. Lacking solid foundations for legitimacy, the European Union remains a forum for Member States eager to impose or defend their own legislative products, and hence their own regulatory policies and legal doctrines.[61] EU ordering continues to be subject to consensus, and to compromise lawmaking.[62] Fragmentation and the lack of a general concept on the part of Brussels may be suggested as a best-case scenario. The harmonisation process cannot be explained on efficiency grounds only, but should be viewed as a response to pressures from several interest groups wanting to protect the existing legal framework and frustrate competitive lawmaking.[63]

A new stage in the evolution of federalism was characterised by the development of the subsidiarity principle, which Member States embraced in the 1992 Maastricht Treaty on the European Union.[64] With regard to areas that are not of the exclusive competence of the European Union,[65] the subsidiarity principle embodied in Article 5 of the Treaty commands the decision to locate competence at EU level or at Member-State level. Rather than listing the competencies of the Union and Member States, the subsidiarity principle provides for an efficiency test to determine competencies and, more crucially, to constrain the Commission's executive power.[66] Recently, though, the Commission responded by proposing a new approach in governance and regulation at the EU level that would reinforce the principle of subsidiarity, but at the same time strengthen the role of the European Commission as a political driving force.[67]

The European Commission, building on the principle of subsidiarity and proportionality, has introduced a new type of directive, based on general principles. Despite the further flexibilisation of directives (moving from the provision of certain minimum standards to a framework model for directives), promulgating directives remained much like running the gauntlet.[68] For instance, the collapse in 2001 of the Thirteenth Directive, on takeovers, exemplifies the deeply rooted conflict between some Member States over the direction and pace of the directives.[69]

At the national level, there are noticeably few incentives for lawmakers to modify regulatory design or reform inefficient rules because of legislative inertia and special interest.[70] Very generally, the differences in the normative arrangements between the continental and common law systems partly explain the deeply rooted conflict between the Member States over the direction and pace of the harmonisation programme. These insights provide key clues as to why only a relatively small number of EU-level initiatives have been heralded as major breakthroughs in the field of company law.

IV THE EUROPEAN COMPANY: CHALLENGING THE STRATEGY?

We noted earlier that the EU has, after more than thirty years of negotiation and bickering, finally created a truly genuine European business form: the

SE. The SE statute, which entered into force in October 2004, gives firms operating in two or more Member States the option to form a European company.[71] According to this view, a menu of European business forms could create a legal framework that helps firms to set up and develop at a European level, to create an economic environment through which firms can reach their full development in the internal market, and, more crucially, to promote cooperation between firms located in different regions of the European Union.

The EU initially pursued an exhaustive and comprehensive legislative measure for the creation of a European Company based on the German Aktiengesellschaft. The aim was to create uniform legislation for the internal governance without reference to national company laws. Although this approach should have been possible, it was ultimately shelved in the 1980s, when the European Community replaced the draft with framework legislation that referred extensively to national legislation. It took until the mid-1990s, when a group of experts, chaired by former Commission President Etienne Davignon, produced a report outlining a compromise solution regarding labour participation.[72] By December 2000, the political difficulties surrounding labour codetermination and board structure were resolved when the Council adopted the legislative measures governing the European Company.

The statute provides a number of means through which legal persons or corporate bodies may form a European Company.[73] Besides formation requirements, the Statute stipulates that the internal governance of the European Company will be regulated by national law of the place of its registration. In effect, the legislation allows firms to select either a one- or two-tier board.[74] Lastly, there are a number of provisions, set forth in the Directive on Involvement of Employees, which detail the level of employee involvement in a company.[75] A special negotiation procedure for worker participation must be followed upon the creation of a European Company.[76] The Directive distinguishes between information and consultation, on the one hand, and participation, on the other hand. The employee representatives should be informed about material decisions and given the opportunity to influence the deliberation and decision-making process. In many cases, the employees' representatives are permitted to consent on the composition of the supervisory board (two-tier board) or board of management (one-tier board).

Despite the relative absence of mandatory rules, the Regulation—which could hold out cost-saving benefits for some European firms—has some other legal difficulties that should play an important role in determining whether companies are likely to adopt the form. First, many European lawyers have expressed scepticism about whether the new legislative measures will lead to significant changes in corporate practice.[77] For example, the proposed statute excludes a large number of areas relevant to businesses operating in two states, all of which continue to be governed by national legislation.[78] Nevertheless, some argue that it is relatively easy to employ the European Company as a migration tool, especially when it is formed by merger.[79] However, the multiple layers of regulation, i.e., the statute itself, the laws implementing the European Company at a national level, national laws of the Member States, and the European Company's constituent documents, which govern the European Company are likely to lead to uncertainty, thereby decreasing rather than increasing the European Company's attractiveness. Second, the failure of the European Statute to address the problem of taxation will clearly undermine the number of firms incorporating as European companies.[80] The argument for the attractiveness of the European Company is premised on the ability of a European Company to transfer its registered office to another Member State. Although there is reason to expect that strong market pressures may lead some companies to reincorporate in jurisdictions with more hospitable company law régimes, we expect that the absence of a specific tax régime, particularly with regard to cross-border real seat transfers, will be a significant impediment to its use by a majority of firms.[81] Third, some companies may also be deterred by the complexity of the process of setting up a European Company. Again, the need to enter into negotiations with employee representatives will likely lead to a bottleneck.[82] Many firms may be uncomfortable with the idea of worker involvement in the re-incorporation process. Even if the difficulties with worker involvement are surmounted, there will be additional costs with employee participation. Accordingly, even if a class of firms would have sufficient incentives to convert to the European Company form, we are sceptical that there are sufficient cost savings to encourage managers to adopt this legal business form.

It is certainly the case that Member States could take steps to make the SE more attractive by adopting clear and effective provisions of laws that specifically implement EU measures relating to European Companies and, by doing so, provide the beneficial conditions for regulatory competition. However, although the first European Companies may already be formed, there are no signals that the Member States have actually engaged in competition-based lawmaking in connection with the European Company or public corporations.[83]

In addition, we are sceptical as to whether the European Company will eventually become an attractive vehicle for company law shopping within the European Union.[84] Even though many investors recognise the shortcomings of the Regulation described earlier, there is little evidence of business lobbying to make the SE a more attractive business law form. Yet, in contrast to the SE, investors have been responsive to the recent wave of corporate governance proposals advanced in the wake of the Enron and Parmalat scandals. Expanding business involvement in this area threatens to leave the laws governing the SE as a legislative backwater, which could deter policymakers from undertaking any new reforms.[85]

That is not to say that policymakers should disregard the European Company. Rather, Member States should arguably be on their guard against other jurisdictions trying to undermine their attractiveness by coming to the fore with a set of rules that are more ideally suited to public corporations. This issue becomes more pressing now that, in the new era of corporate accountability, regulatory groups and governing organisations have either adopted or modified existing corporate governance legislation and codes, which often establish mandatory goals and guidelines for the effective governance of publicly traded corporations.[86] Even though the European Company compromise offers a rigid and unattractive system,[87] the possibility of forum shopping, through cross-border mergers, could provide far-sighted policymakers with sufficient incentives to modernise national company law legislation, thereby eroding cumbersome and intrusive national laws.[88]

Yet if such pressures exist, there are few lawmakers, at least for now, that are willing to implement such reforms. Rather, in terms of incentives, policymakers have little incentive to take decisions that would give rise to greater flexibility and increased competition between jurisdictions. In fact, policymakers have recently suggested linking the European Company Statute to a European corporate governance code, which could provide a more efficient way to induce convergence of best-practice norms within the EU.[89] Indeed, if national lawmakers were to shift to this strategy, we expect two possible outcomes: (1) through linkage the Member States' codes would be left untouched and thereby divergence would be respected;[90] and (2) the prospect of regulatory competition by means of the European Company would be substantially diminished. Thus, the proposed linkage approach to the European Company Statute would serve to reinforce the non-competitive equilibrium within EU company law, a result that many lawmakers would appear to support.

V CONCLUSION

This chapter has pointed out that the potential for the Member States to engage in competitive lawmaking is limited. On this basis, we argued that Member States, upon entrance to the EU, entered into a long-term non-competition agreement regarding company lawmaking, thereby preventing the 'Delaware effect'.

Section II explained the Delaware effect, clarifying that Delaware does not currently engage in regulatory competition with the other US states. As a result of a series of historical coincidences, Delaware can rely on its dominant position in the market for companies. Delaware closely resembles a monopolistic lawmaker possessing market power and 'competitive' advantages that other states cannot replicate, which act as substantial barriers to other states wishing to enter the market for out-of-state companies.

In the EU, the harmonisation programme for publicly held companies set in place mechanisms that protected the lawmaking autonomy of Member States. Since these firms were most likely to engage in cross-border activities, re-incorporation strategies could put pressure on domestic lawmakers to conform to their peer jurisdictions. We have argued that Member States are unwilling, given their long tradition of independence, to relinquish their lawmaking autonomy in this area. All steps taken by Member States point in the same direction: to avoid a 'European Delaware'. The commitment of Member States to respect the cooperative lawmaking equilibrium is reflected in the following observations: (1) the first and second generation company law directives restated the dominant legal practices in the Member States; (2) the third and fourth generation directives became less detailed and precise leaving the important issues to the member state's discretion; (3) federal intervention through supranational provisions for truly European company forms faced severe objections and has, until now, not been very successful. Our analysis questions whether the compromise legislation regarding the European Company could actually serve to cause irritation to the non-competitive equilibrium by opening the door to regulatory arbitrage and eventually competitive lawmaking. Even though many commentators cast doubt about the beneficial aspects of opting-into the European Company, we should, nevertheless, not rule out the possibility of firms making use of this structure to circumvent costly national company law rules.[91] For this to become viable, however, the European Union must first introduce an EU-wide tax régime for the European Company, and also bring about a common EU corporate tax base.[92] We suspect, however, that there are few political incentives for lawmakers to pass legislation that might serve to disrupt the EU's non-competitive equilibrium in company law.

NOTES

1   See S. Lombardo and P. Pasotti, 'The Societas Europaea: A Network Economic Approach', (2004) 1 *European Company and Financial Law Review* 169 (summarising criticisms).

2   See J. Rickford, *The European Company, Developing a Community Law of Corporations* (Intersentia, 2003), at 140–141 (assessing the competitive effects of the European Company Statute).

3   See, e.g., L. Enriques, 'Silence is Golden: The European Company Statute as a Catalyst for Company Law Arbitrage', (2004) 77 *Journal of Corporate Law Studies* 77–95; J. Armour, 'Who Should Make Corporate Law? EU Legislation versus Regulatory Competition', (forthcoming) *Current Legal Problems*.

4   Regulatory arbitrage is the choice by firms to locate investment or other economic activity based on the regulatory environment of jurisdictions. See S. Woolcock, 'Competition among Rules in the Single European Market', in W. W. Bratton, J. A. McCahery, S. Picciotto and C. Scott (eds), *International Regulatory Competition and Coordination, Perspectives on Economic Regulation in Europe and the United States* (Clarendon Press, 1996), at 298; cf. Enriques, *op. cit.* note 3 *supra*.

5   See P. Conci, 'The Tax Treatment of the Creation of a SE', (2004) 44 *European Taxation* 15.

6   Council Regulation 2157/2001/EC, OJ L 294/1 2001. The Regulation is available at: <http://www.europa.eu.int/eur-lex/en/index.html>. See also, the Council Directive 2001/86/ECOJ L 294/22 2001 (supplementing the statute for a European Company with regard to the involvement of employees). The Directive is available at: <http://www.europa.eu.int/eur-lex/en/index.html>.

7   In contrast to the United States, the European Union is not a super state. However, it is more than just a free-trade area. It is an arrangement of countries, of which the shape and purpose have been adapted to changing circumstances with remarkable ingenuity. Cf. H.W. Micklitz and S. Weatherill, *European Economic Law* (Ashgate, 1997), at 1–3 (arguing that unlike the USA, the EU is not a federation of states, but a 'market without a State').

8   Cf. N. Moussis, 'Small and Medium Enterprises in the Internal Market', (1992) 17 *European Law Review* 483 ('[t]he new enterprise policy of the Community has three broad objectives: to create a legal framework which lends itself to the setting up and development of enterprises in the Community; to create an economic environment which will help enterprises reach their full development in the internal market; and to promote cooperation between enterprises situated in different regions of the Community').

9   See J.A. McCahery and E.P.M. Vermeulen, 'The Changing Landscape of European Company Law', (2004) TILEC Discussion Paper no. 023.

10   See W.W. Bratton and J.A. McCahery, 'The Equilibrium Content of Corporate Federalism', (2004) ECGI Working Paper no. 23. (explaining the factors that contributed to the introduction of the competition charters at the beginning of the twentieth century).

11   In this chapter, we assess the prospects for a single jurisdiction dictating the developments in the area of company law in the EU. As we discuss in the next section, Delaware plays this role in the context of the US state system of company lawmaking. However, we do not consider whether Delaware has a suboptimal impact on the quality of legal rules.

12   Pseudo-foreign corporations are firms that are incorporated in one state but conduct a significant amount of their business in another state.

13   See L.A. Bebchuk, 'Federalism and the Corporation: The Desirable Limits on State Competition in Corporate Law', (1992) 105 *Harvard Law Review* 1435, at 1438 (noting that even though federal law governs some important issues, including insider trading, disclosure and the making of tender offers, much of the law regulating a corporation's affairs stems from its state of incorporation). See also P. Leleux, 'Corporation Law in the United States and in the E.E.C., Some Comments on the Present Situation and the Future Prospects', (1968) 6 *Common Market Law Review* 133 (comparing the European and the US situation).

14   See L.E. Ribstein, 'The Evolving Partnership', (2001) 26 *Journal of Corporation Law*, 819–854.

15   With its 1888 corporation statute and the 1896 revision, New Jersey was the first state to enter the competition. Delaware joined New Jersey in 1899.

16   See, L.A. Bebchuk, 'Federalism and the Corporation: The Desirable Limits on State Competition in Corporate Law', (1992) 105 *Harvard Law Review* 1435 at 1443 ('[a]fter restrictive amendments to its corporation law were made in 1913, New Jersey lost the leading role to Delaware, whose corporation law was at the time a close copy of New Jersey's original statute').

17 See R. Romano, *The Genius of American Corporate Law* (The American Enterprise Institute Press, 1993), at 6–12. See also J.E. Fisch, 'The Peculiar Role of the Delaware Courts in the Competition of Corporate Charters', (2000) 68 *University of Cincinnati Law Review* 1061, at 1061 ('incorporations bring Delaware approximately $440 million per year in franchise taxes and related fees').

18 One should distinguish this process from legal transplantation, emulation or imitation. The latter occurs when laws are changed in the absence of pressures on the legislature in economic and political markets. See J-M. Sun and J. Pelkmans, 'Regulatory Competition in the Single Market', (1994) Centre for European Policy Studies (CEPS) Working Document no. 84.; Woolcock *op. cit.* note 4 supra, at 297–298.

19 See J.C. Coffee, 'The Future as History: The Prospects for Global Convergence in Corporate Governance and Its Implications', (1999) 93 *Northwestern University Law Review* 641, at 703) (arguing that corporations may prefer to locate in a popular jurisdiction of incorporation for reasons that are simply based on its popularity, not the inherent superiority of its law). 'Herd behavior loosely refers to a situation in which people imitate the actions of others and in so doing ignore, to some extent, their own information and judgments regarding the merits of their decisions'. See M. Kahan and M. Klausner, 'Path Dependence in Corporate Contracting: Increasing returns, Herd Behavior and Cognitive Biases', (1996) 74 *Washington University Law Quarterly* 347, at 355.

20 See, e.g. Fisch *op. cit.* note 17 supra, at 1063; M. Kahan and E. Kamar, 'Price Discrimination in the Market for Corporate Law', (2001) 86 *Cornell Law Review* 1205, at 1212–1214; R. Romano, 'Law as Product. Some Pieces of the Incorporation Puzzle', (1985) 1 *Journal of Law, Economics and Organization* 225–283.

21 See L.A. Bebchuk, 'Federalism and the Corporation: The Desirable Limits on State Competition in Corporate Law', (1992) 105 *Harvard Law Review* 1435; L. Bebchuk, A. Cohen and A. Ferrell, 'Does the Evidence Favor State Competition in Corporate Law?', (2002) 90 *California Law Review* 1775.

22 See W.W. Bratton and J.A. McCahery, 'Regulatory Competition, Regulatory Capture, and Corporate Self-Regulation', (1995) 73 *North Carolina Law Review* 1861, at 1887–1889.

23 See Bebchuk, *op. cit.* note 21 supra, at 1435; L.A. Bebchuk and A. Ferrell, 'Federalism and Corporate Law: The Race to Protect Managers from Takeovers', (1999) 99 *Columbia Law Review* 1168.

24 See Bebchuk and Ferrell, *op. cit.* note 23 supra, at 1171.

25 See J.R. Macey and G.P. Miller, 'Toward an Interest-Group Theory of Delaware Corporate Law', (1987) 65 *Texas Law Review* 469, at 491–498.

26 See Bratton and McCahery *op. cit.* note 22 supra at 1887–1888; Kahan and Kamar, *op. cit.* note 20 supra, at 1217.

27 See Kahan and Kamar, *op. cit.* note 20 supra, at 1252.

28 See Bebchuk, Cohen and Ferrell, *op. cit.* note 21 supra, at 1775.

29 See L.A. Bebchuk and A. Cohen, 'Firms' Decisions Where to Incorporate', (2003) 46 *Journal of Law and Economics* 383.

30 See L.A. Bebchuk and A. Hamdani, 'Optimal Defaults for Corporate Law Evolution', (2002) 96 *Northwestern University Law Review* 489.

31 See S. Tucker, 'Delaware Move Over Investor Powers', *Financial Times* 15 December 2004.

32 See Bratton and McCahery, *op. cit.* note 10 supra.

33 See Leleux *op. cit.* note 13 supra, at 133; R.M. Buxbaum and K.J. Hopt, 'Legal Harmonization and the Business Enterprise', *Corporate and Capital Market Law Harmonization Policy in Europe and the United States* (Volume 4) (Walter de Gruyter, 1988) (explaining that the freedom of establishment guaranteed by the Treaty proscribes use of the real seat theory).

34 The Treaty of Amsterdam renumbered the articles of the Treaty.

35 Article 293 (ex 220) of the Treaty provides that 'Member States shall, so far as necessary, enter into negotiations with each other with a view to securing for the benefits of their nationals: 'the mutual recognition of companies or firms within the meaning of the second paragraph of Article 48 (ex 58), the retention of legal personality in the event of their seat from one country to another, and the possibility of mergers between companies or firms governed by the laws of different countries'. So far, there has been one attempt to meet the obligation of Article 293: the 1968 Brussels Convention on the Mutual Recognition of Companies and Legal Entities. As early as 1956, the Hague Conference on Private International Law drafted a treaty on the mutual recognition of the legal personality of companies. Both attempts failed. See S. F.G. Rammeloo, *Corporations in Private International Law, A European Perspective* (Oxford University Press, 2001), at 24–37.

36 See D. Charny, 'Competition among Jurisdictions in Formulating Corporate Law Rules: An American Perspective on the 'Race to the Bottom' in the European Communities', (1991) 32 *Harvard International Law Journal* 423, at 428.

37 The European Commission established, in 1960s, the first expert committee to analyse the effects of different capital income taxation policies of the Member States. The Netherlands and Luxembourg, which had an interest in developing their thriving capital markets, successfully impeded the harmonisation of capital taxation to protect their successful policy of opening their borders. Cf. K. Holzinger, 'Tax Competition and Tax Co-operation in the EU: The Case of Savings Taxation', (2003) EUI Working Paper, RSC no. 07, European Forum Series.

38 See C. Timmermans, 'Harmonization in the Future of Company Law in Europe', in K.J. Hopt and E. Wymeersch (eds), *Capital Markets and Company Law* (Oxford University Press, 2003) 623–637, at 628). Political rather than economic rents were considered more valuable to Member States given their concern for political stability and economic integration, Cf. R.P. Inman and D.L. Rubinfeld, 'Subsidiarity and the European Union', in P. Newman (ed.), *The New Palgrave Dictionary of Economics*

and the Law, vol. 3 (Macmillan Reference Limited, 1998), at 548.

39 Under the incorporation régime, the company is not governed by the laws of the state of state where the actual centre of the companies are, but by the laws of the state incorporation.

40 See Charny, *op. cit.* note 36 *supra*.

41 See Ch. Villiers, *European Company Law—Towards Democracy?* (Ashgate, 1998) at 28–51 (distinguishes four generations of directives: the first generation emphasised uniformity and prescription; the second generation supplied a set of options that essentially represent the predominant approach in the Member States; the third generation explicitly left issues to the Member States; and the fourth generation took the process even further by adopting only a framework model).

42 See W.J. Carney, 'The Political Economy of Competition for Corporate Charters', (1997) 26 *Journal of Legal Studies* 303, at 318 (arguing that the first generation directives are likely to be representative of the dominant legal practices in the Member States because their adoption required unanimous consent of the Member States; B.R. Cheffins, *Company Law: Theory, Structure, and Operation* (Clarendon Press, 1997) at 448: 'the EU has typically done little more than superimpose a series of measures on domestic regulations already in place'; H. Halbhuber, 'National Doctrinal Structures and European Company Law', (2001) 38 *Common Market Law Review* 1385 at 1406: '[t]he directives do not purport to deal with crucial issues like fiduciary duties, exit, expulsion and redemption, transfer of shares etc.'.

43 The first generation directives include the First and Second Company Law Directives. First Council Directive [1968] OJ Spec Ed (I) (disclosure of corporate data); Second Council Directive [1977] OJ 26/1 (protection of capital).

44 See Carney, *op. cit.* note 42 *supra*, at 324; L. Enriques and J.R. Macey, 'Creditors versus Capital Formation: The Case against the European Legal Capital Rules', (2001) 86 *Cornell Law Review* 1165, at 1202–1203.

45 The second generation directives include the Third [1978] OJ L295/36 and Sixth Council Directives [1982] OJ L378/47 on Mergers and Split-Offs, Fourth [1978] OJ L222/11, Seventh [1983] OJ L193/1 and Eight Council Directives [1984] OJ L126/20 on Annual and Consolidated Accounts and the Qualification of Accountants.

46 See Woolcock, *op. cit.* note 4 *supra*, at 292. In the words of the Commission, 'relying on a strategy based totally on harmonization would be over-regulatory, would take a long time to implement, would be inflexible and could stifle innovation', (COM(85) 310 final, at 18.

47 See J. Wouters, 'European Company Law: Quo Vadis?', (2000) 37 *Common Market Law Review* 257, at 275. Germany's reluctance to implement Council Directive (EEC) 90/605 of 8 November 1990, extending the Fourth and Seventh Directive to partnerships and limited partnerships with corporate general partners, perfectly exemplifies this trend. These hybrid business forms were not within the original scope of the Fourth and Seventh Directive. See Fourth Council Directive [1978] OJ L

222/11 (single accounts); Seventh Council Directive [1983] OJ L193/1 (consolidated accounts). While some jurisdictions applied these Directives voluntarily to hybrid 'limited liability vehicles', like the Netherlands, the Commission took the view that it would run counter to the spirit and aims of the Fourth and Seventh Directive to allow these vehicles not to be subject to Community rules. The limited partnership with a corporate general partner (GmbH & Co KG) is particularly popular in Germany. Although the German government agreed on further extension of the directives after the European lawmakers announced further exemptions available to SMEs, it deferred implementing the amendment. Only after the Court of Justice's judgment in Case C-272/97 *Commission v Germany* did the German government change the law according to the amending directive. See V. Edwards, *EC Company Law* (Clarendon Press, 1999) at 124.

48 See R.P. Inman and D.L. Rubinfeld, 'Subsidiarity and the European Union', in P. Newman (ed.), *The New Palgrave Dictionary of Economics and the Law*, vol. 3 (Macmillan Reference Limited, 1998), at 548 (describing the initial steps toward the economic union as decentralised federalism).

49 Article 308 (ex 235) specifies two preconditions for unification: (1) action by the Community should prove necessary to attain; (2) the powers provided in the Treaty are insufficient. See Buxbaum and Hopt, *op. cit.* note 33 *supra*, at 210–212.

50 The EEIG is adopted in 1985 (Council Reg (EEC) 2137/85 on the European Economic Interest Grouping (EEIG) [1985] OJ L 199/1). The EEIG creates a European legislative framework that provides existing firms with an easy and accessible vehicle for restructuring across frontiers.

51 Cf. S. Grundmann, 'Europäisches Handelsrecht—vom Handelsrecht des laissez faire im Kodex des 19. Jahrhunderts zum Handelsrecht der sozialen Verantwortung', (1999) 28 *Zeitschrift für Unternehmens- und Gesellschaftsrecht* 635, at 645 fn. 36.

52 The EEIG is a mirror image of the French Groupement d'Interêt Economique, which has proved to be a popular business in the French business community. However, the Groupement d'Interêt Economique appears to owe its existence to limitation of the French partnership form. See M. Lutter, *Europäisches Unternehmensrecht, Grundlagen, Stand und Entwicklung nebst Texten und Materialien zur Rechtsangleichung* (Walter de Gruyter, 1996), at 67 (arguing that from a German perspective, the promulgation of the EEIG is a mistake). See also J. Wouters, 'European Company Law: Quo Vadis?', (2000) 37 *Common Market Law Review* 257, at 261.

53 At the outset of the EU, the Member States understood that, given the 'Delaware effect' in the US, the consequences of competitive pressures would be detrimental to their own national lawmaking powers and immediately took steps to insulate the (horizontal) threat by establishing a federal type institution (European Commission) that undertook to harmonise areas of company law (without touching the core). While the original legislative strategy satisfied the objectives of the

Member States, the European Commission expanded their own lawmaking agenda by developing truly 'European' company forms. To the extent this (vertical) approach limited the lawmaking discretion of Member States, their support for top-down lawmaking was gradually eroded.

54 High Level Group of Company Law Experts (2002), 'A Modern Regulatory Framework for Company Law in Europe: A Consultative Document'. See also H.J. De Kluiver, 'Disparities and Similarities in European and American Company Law: What about Living Apart Together?', in J. Wouters and H. Schneider (eds), *Current Issues of Cross-Border Establishment of Companies in The European Union* (Maklu, 1995), at 300.

55 See Case 120/78 *Rewe Zentral AG v Bundesmonopolverwaltung für Branntwein* [*'Cassis de Dijon'*] [1979] ECR 1979; European Commission (1985).

56 See G. Majone, 'Mutual Recognition In Federal Type Systems', (1993) EUI Working Paper SPS No. 1, at 1–3: '[t]he immediate reason for introducing this new strategy was to reduce the burden on the Commission in harmonizing national rules'.

57 See Inman and Rubinfeld, op. cit. note 48 supra, at 549: '[b]orn in part from the frustration over the slow pace of integration of the advantages such reforms might have in combating Europe's declining economic fortunes (known as 'Eurosclerosis'), the ten members of the Community put aside the Luxembourg Compromise and decentralized federalism and adopted in 1986 the Single European Act (SEA) and a new institutional structure closely approximating that of centralized federalism'. Cf. M.E. Streit and W. Mussler, 'Evolution of the economic constitution of the European Union', in P. Newman (ed.), The New *Palgrave Dictionary of Economics and the Law*, vol. 2 (Macmillan Reference Limited, 1998), at 104–105.

58 In 1986, Spain, Portugal and Greece entered the EU.

59 See Inman and Rubinfeld *op. cit.* note 48 *supra*, at 549; M.A. Pollack, *The Engines of European Integration, Delegation, Agency, and Agenda Setting in the EU* (Oxford University Press, 2003).

60 Eleventh Council Directive [1989] OJ L395/36; Twelfth Council Directive [1989] OJ L395/40.

61 See A. Heritier, C. Knill and S. Mingers, *Ringing the Changes in Europe: Regulatory Competition and Redefinition of the State: Britain, France, Germany, Berlin* (de Gruyter, 1996), at 149. Cf. D. Caruso, 'The Missing View of the Cathedral: The Private Law Paradigm of European Legal Integration', (1997) 3 *European Law Journal* 3, arguing that entrenched in legal formalism, obstinate in the defence of the doctrinal coherence of their codes and unwilling to discuss the political merits of their consolidated policies, European legal actors manage to slow down, and even at times to halt, the process of private law integration; Halbhuber, H., *op. cit.* note 42 *supra*, at 1409–1411, arguing that domestic doctrinal structures appear to play an important role in shaping the German understanding of European company law materials.

62 See F. Scharpf, *Governing in Europe, Effective and Democratic?* (Oxford University Press, 1999).

63 See Carney, *op. cit.* note 42 *supra*, at 317 and 329.

64 Besides constraining the Commission's role through the subsidiarity principle, the Maastricht Treaty also introduced the co-decision procedure. As a consequence, the European Union's decision-making structure closely resembles the constitutional form of democratic federalism in which central government policies are agreed to by a simple majority of elected representatives from lower-tier governments. See R. P. Inman, and D.L. Rubinfeld, 'Rethinking Federalism', (1997), 11 *Journal of Economic Perspectives*, pp. 43–63; Inman and Rubinfeld, *op. cit.* note 48 *supra*, at 550.

65 Areas within the exclusive competence of the Union are subject to the proportionality test. Art 5(3) TEU provides that 'any action by the Community shall not go beyond what is necessary to achieve objectives of the Treaty'.

66 First of all, it has to be determined whether there is a power under the Treaty to take action. The subsidiarity principle then determines whether and how the Community may act. It must be shown that the objectives of the proposed action cannot be sufficiently achieved by the Member States. The finding must then justify the further conclusion that in view of the measure the objective can be better achieved at Community level. Eventually, the proportionality test as defined in Art 5(3) has to be satisfied. See Micklitz and Weatherill *op. cit.* note 7 *supra*, at 16. See also G. A. Bermann, 'Taking Subsidiarity Seriously: Federalism in the European Community and the United States', (1994) 94 *Columbia Law Review* 331, at 334: '[t]he drafters' apparent purpose was to reassure Member State populations, and subcommunities within those populations, the Community's seemingly inexorable march toward greater legal and political integration would not needlessly trample their legitimate claims to democratic self-governance and cultural diversity'.

67 See COM (2001) 428 final, 'White Paper on European Governance' and A. Cygan, 'The White Paper on European Governance—Have Glasnost and Perestroika Finally Arrived to the European Union?', (2002) 65 *Modern Law Review* 229, at 240; '[t]he main criticism against the contents of the White Paper is that it promotes the institutional self-interest of the Commission, at the expense of substantive concerns of many EU citizens'.

68 See S. Deakin, 'Regulatory Competition Versus Harmonization in European Company Law', in D.C. Esty and D. Geradin (eds), Regulatory Competition and Economic Integration (Clarendon Press, 2001), at 192–195.

69 Cf. C.M. Forstinger, *Takeover Law in EU & USA, A Comparative Analysis* (Kluwer Law International, 2002), at 34; J.A. McCahery and L. Renneboog, 'The Economics of the Proposed Takeover Directive', (2003) Centre for European Policy Studies Research Report in Finance and Banking No. 32., at 46–51.

70 Powerful insiders that derive private benefits from blockholding arrangements and non-stakeholder interests have few incentives to optimise national corporate governance régimes for the benefit of share-holders. See, e.g., M. Roe, 'Rents and Their Corporate

FOUR

Law Consequences', (2001) 53 *Stanford Law Review* 1463, noting that as nations with norms and corporate rules that harm shareholders become more competitive through customs unions and single-currency areas, pressure on these norms, these corporate law and labour law rules, and old politics rises (as it has been doing).

71 Council Regulation 2157/2001/EC OJ L 294/1 (2001).

72 See B. Keller, 'The European Company Statute: Employee Involvement and Beyond', (2002) Paper Presented at the IIRA/CIRA 4th Regional Congress of the Americas, University of Toronto, 25–29 June.

73 Generally the European Company may be formed by consequence of: (1) a merger of two or more existing companies originating from at least two Member States; (2) the formation of a holding company promoted by public or private limited companies; (3) the formation of jointly held subsidiary; and (4) the conversion of an existing public limited company. See Art 2 and Title II of the Regulation.

74 Article 38(b) of the Regulation.

75 Provisions for participation of employees in the European Company, See Council Directive 2001/86/EC OJ L 294/22 (2001).

76 Section II of the Directive.

77 See B. Springael, 'Taxation Issues and the Single European Company: a Preliminary Look at Societas Europaea', (2002) 14 *EuroWatch* 1 (arguing that the European Company is not a uniform company type, as originally intended, but instead a 'national European Company'); C. Hampton, 'European Company Law Reforms Make Uneven Progress', (2002) 14 *EuroWatch* 1, at 1, arguing that without an EU-wide régime for tax it offers little that cannot be achieved already.

78 The Regulation addresses the Formation (Title II), the Structure of the SE (Title III), Annual Account and Consolidated Accounts (Title IV) and Winding Up, Liquidation, Insolvency and Cessation of Payments (Title V).

79 Title II, section 2 of the Regulation. See also Enriques, *op. cit.* note 3 *supra*; H.J. De Kluiver, S.H.M.A. Dumoulin, P.A.M. Witteveen and J.W. Bellingwout, *De Europese Vennootschap (SE), Preadvies van de Vereeniging 'Handelsrecht'* (Kluwer, 2004) at 62–63.

80 F. Bolkestein, 'The New European Company: Opportunity in Diversity' in J. Rickford (ed.), *The European Company, Developing a Community Law of Corporations* (Intersentia, 2003) at 43–44. It is worth pointing out that, unlike earlier drafts, the Statute lacks any tax provisions at the EU level. Indeed, the tax position of the SE is identical to any other national public limited company. See B.J.M. Terra and P.J. Wattel, *European Tax Law* (Kluwer, 2001) at 429–430.

81 See C. Thommes, 'EC Law Aspects of the Transfer of Seat of an SE', (2004) 44 *European Taxation* 22, at 23–25 (noting that transfer abroad of the real seat of an SE will trigger an obligation to pay exit taxes to the Member State that it wishes to depart). See also, International Bureau of Fiscal Documentation, Survey on the Societas Europaea (2003).

82 See P. Davies, 'Employee Involvement in the European Company', in Rickford *op. cit.* note 80 *supra* at 67 and

81–82; K.J. Hopt, 'Board Structures—The Significance of the Rules on the Board of the European Company', in Rickford *op. cit.* note 80 *supra*, at 53–54.

83 It could be argued that French company law could obtain cost-saving benefits as a result of the introduction of the European Company Statute since firms can easily opt into the flexible corporate business form, namely the Société par Actions Simplifiée (SAS) regulation. S.M. Bartman, 'Fransen winnen slag om SE', Financieele Dagblad, 21 October 2004.

84 Cf. J. Garrido, 'Company Law and Capital Markets', in Rickford, *op. cit.* note 80 *supra*.

85 European Commission, 'Communication from the Commission to the Council and the European Parliament on Preventing and Combining and Combating Corporate and Financial Malpractice', Brussels, 27.09.2004, COM(2004) 611 final.

86 See G. Hertig and J.A. McCahery, 'An Agenda for Reform: Company and Takeover Law in Europe', in G. Ferrarini, K.J. Hopt, J. Winter and E. Wymeersch (eds), *Company and Takeover Law in Europe* (Oxford University Press, 2004).

87 See F. Kübler, 'A Shifting Paradigm of European Company Law?', (2004) Working Paper.

88 It follows, perhaps, that the Court of Justice's recent judgments in Centros, Überseering and Inspire Art—and their implications for the real seat theory—could, along with the pressure from the introduction of the European Company, induce the European Union to embark on a new, market-based approach to the process of business organisation lawmaking. See J.A. McCahery and E.P.M. Vermeulen, 'The Evolution of Closely Held Business Forms in Europe', (2001) 26 *Journal of Corporation Law* 857; J.A. McCahery and E.P.M. Vermeulen, 'The Changing Landscape of European Company Law', (2004) TILEC Discussion Paper no. 023. Now that the EU has opened its door to new Member States, national lawmakers must be on their guard against highly incentivised Central and Eastern European legislatures that may be considering modern and attractive company law legislation.

89 See High Level Group of Company Law Experts, 'European Corporate Governance in Company Law Codes', Report Prepared for the European Corporate Governance Conference, The Hague, 18 October 2004, at 67.

90 See B. Groom and I. Bickerton, 'Architect of Corporate Reform Warns Against Convergence', *Financial Times* 26 December 2004.

91 The introduction of the European Company has stimulated discussion about the transformation of board-level labour representation régimes within the EU (M. Karnitschnig 'German Law on Board Seats Targeted', *Wall Street Journal Europe* 26 October 2004.) For instance, the possibility of circumventing the rigid labour representation laws through a merger with an English public company has given company law reformers more political leverage in their efforts to alter home country legislation; 'Duitse werkgevers willen medezeggenschap hervormen', *Financieele Dagblad*, 11 November 2004.

92 The recent meeting of the ECOFIN Council on 7 December 2004 expressed support for the European Commission's efforts to facilitate cross-border reorganisations by providing for tax deferral in the case of cross-border mergers.

F
O
U
R

13 "UK Corporate Governance: To What End a New Regulatory State?"

from West European Politics (2006)

Alistair Howard

SUMMARY

This chapter questions the importance of recent changes in the regulation of UK corporate governance. Michael Moran has observed that a new regulatory state is emerging. In the case presented here new authority was created but little changed substantively. Under Labour and Conservative ministers, governance policy was reactive and cautious. For all the new institutional capacity, governance problems and policies were conceived within existing structures of power and advantage. Any ambitions to social control that threatened the political–economic status quo were ruled out. While this may be no surprise, it suggests regulatory reorganisation need not herald dramatic change, even when politicised.

Corporate governance is a normally settled policy domain involving corporate boards, shareholders, and financial reporting. Beginning in the early 1990s extraordinary politicisation and institutional development challenged Britain's characteristically laissez-faire governance style (Howard 2005). This resulted from scandalous corporate failures at the outset of the period and again a decade later with closely watched frauds at Enron and WorldCom. In the interim, rapidly escalating boardroom pay further eroded business legitimacy even as equities peaked and burst. And finally, the 1997 Labour Government briefly debated a Third Way 'stakeholding' alternative to the UK's shareholder-centric governance system. These reforms – supported by unions but quickly rejected – would have given workers and environmentalists a significant role in company law. Overall, the period saw a significant expansion of policy authority, first in the private sector and later under more direct state influence.

These events echo Michael Moran's recent argument that a new, modernist regulatory state is emerging in Britain (Moran 2001, 2003). For Moran, explicit, formal, and juridical authority is displacing informal or private coordination in a range of policy domains. Although Moran's argument is historical rather than predictive, he nonetheless expects – and business fears – that the new regulatory state will be ambitious. As coordination or regulation become politicised, policies may change too. Agenda expansion can lead to new policy goals and even efforts at social transformation.

In the case of corporate governance, however, not much has changed beyond the nature and location of regulatory authority. While the governance agenda widened after 1998, there was no serious effort to reshape policy fundamentals. This may not be surprising, and ministers would argue that more dramatic change was unnecessary. But even where intervention might have been expected to improve the system on its own terms (in effect, for shareholders), state intervention was restrained. On executive pay, threatened action was withheld. And on stakeholding reform, only mild and management-led reporting requirements were imposed. Instead, there was a pattern of ministerial cajoling, protracted consultation, ministerial pleading, and, finally, feeble disclosure requirements. In no case were the benefits and burdens of regulation significantly redistributed.

Evidence from one policy domain cannot, of course, overturn an argument as broad and compelling as Moran's – and that is not the present intention. On the contrary, the evidence on institutional development set out below is very much consistent with Moran's argument. But this chapter goes further, comparing policy evolution with what might be expected under the circumstances, and briefly considering why greater change was not forthcoming despite the regulatory reorganisation. Before reviewing the evidence, the first section below locates Moran's thesis in the literature on the UK state and derives broad expectations. Subsequently, relevant institutional and policy changes are outlined for each of three key governance mechanisms (board, shareholder, transparency) over both Conservative and Labour Governments.

COMPETING PERSPECTIVES ON BRITISH REGULATION

The UK state is something of a paradox for policy scholars and political economists. It is historically liberal in its approach to business – especially in industrial relations and corporate governance. It avoided statutory prescription and litigation. It had neither US-style Progressive-era public regulators nor a Continental tradition of corporatist coordination. Despite bouts of nationalising Labourism, no social- (or Christian-) democratic critique of contract and capital took hold. Companies were private affairs and industrial relations were a matter for employers and independent unions. Thatcherite Conservatives, of course, clarified this privatism while attacking trade unions' strength. In doing so they demonstrated the other, more muscular side of the British state. Central government has great formal and political potential for decisive action; there are constitutionally few legislative or judicial veto points. Plurality elections produce large majorities and governing party leaderships are relatively unconstrained politically. And ministers guard their role closely, even when deferring regulation to private groups or incorporating European Union initiatives.

Despite this mixed picture, the conventional view is that Britain's core state has retreated before the forces of globalisation and the advocates of smaller, flatter government (Rhodes 1996). In this account, the organisational capacities of Westminster were dispersed among a diverse array of governmental, non-governmental, and quasi-governmental bodies, and

its jurisdiction was shared upward with the European Union and downward to the regions and local authorities (Richards and Smith 2001: 148). Even if new regulators were established to ensure market effciency in privatised utilities sectors, the overall tendency was centrifugal rather than centralising. At the same time the state was marginalised ideologically by neo-liberalism, the 'new public management', and the Third Way. Thus, steering replaces control, and networks or markets replace closed, hierarchical regulation.

Moran offers a contrasting narrative of regulatory centralisation. Since the 1980s, Britain's uniquely privatised systems of self-regulation in labour, services, and goods have been replaced or colonised by direct state organised and controlled regulation (Moran 2003: 3). The creation of the Financial Services Authority in 2000 is emblematic. An expansive and newly juridified regime of agency-based regulation displaced narrow, informal, and privatised self-regulation. Close, legislated surveillance of business has become the norm. At the same time, Moran stresses the ad hoc and provisional character of the movement. Rather than comprehensive review and abolition of existing forms, there is absorption, cooption, or marginalisation of older bodies. Existing self-regulatory arrangements (in the professions, for example) may have to coexist and compete with new state agencies. In short, there are institutional 'irrationalities, perversities, and contradictions' (Moran 2003: 154).

Moran's discussion of the consequences of the new regulation is highly generalised. It is clear, however, that he expects more than the reorganisation of authority. The modernist regulatory state entails 'command-like ambitions' (Moran 2003: 162). We can expect an attempt, 'above all, to equip the state with the capacity to have a synoptic, standardized view of regulated domains, and to use that synoptic view to pursue a wide range of projects of social control' (Moran 2003: 168, emphasis added). Business representatives, the Conservative Party, and Liberal Democrat spokes-people echo Moran's analysis, bemoaning the hyper-innovative tendencies of the new regulatory state. Britain is struggling, they charge, under a dense web of red tape.

Corporate governance: new regulators but still the end of history

The organisational developments outlined in the next two sections of this paper fit the new regulatory state narrative.[1] What is not apparent, however, is any substantial policy change. Even as new authority was created – first by private actors and later by ministers – the distribution of regulatory requirements, burdens and benefits did not dramatically change. Arguably this should be no surprise. First, the initial reforms of the mid-1990s were widely touted as a success. The Anglo-capitalist model of shareholder-friendly governance was near-hegemonic in the days prior to Enron and WorldCom, when one droll article announced the 'end of history for corporate law' (Hansmann and Kraakman 2000). Second, Labour had of course followed the Conservatives to the right in opposition (Heffernan 2000) and had no desire to alienate business. For these and other reasons the presumption was against change in the corporate governance domain.

However, this conclusion suggests two preliminary theoretical questions. First, what is the relative importance of political-institutional change for policy continuity? And, second, with regard to corporate governance, why might distributive conflicts between investors, managers and employees play out in public policy at this time and in this way?

Debates about the organisation of the state are important if change affects policies or outcomes about which people care. Broader socio-economic antagonisms can become suddenly relevant when market-based or inconspicuously technocratic coordination falls under direct ministerial or parliamentary influence. Interest groups (and politicians claiming the mantle of public interest) can exploit new jurisdictional opportunities, in due course widening problem and decision agendas. Furthermore, the institutional locus of final decisions may also condition policy change, as when it increases the number of veto points or players. Thus, political institutions may be important predictors of policy adventurism. Two non-institutional factors will also be important however: the merits and qualities of policy arguments and the broader structure of political-economic power. Emphasising organisational changes in the state should not distract from the deeper structural factors (or contingent events) that drive policy outcomes. Careful empirical research will be needed to establish the role of each.

With regard to change in the corporate governance case, major policy shifts might have occurred for three reasons: because of unresolved concerns about managerial accountability (especially after 2001), because of popular anger over managerial pay,

and because of support for a 'stakeholding' departure in Labour circles and among their trade union friends. Britain's reputation as a safe jurisdiction for shareholders should not obscure possible enhancements. Above all there was reason and opportunity to require greater shareholder involvement in governing companies (on pay, for example) and to reduce conflicts of interest in audit (by preventing auditors from selling other services to companies). Arguably these dramatic reforms would have benefited the economy as a whole as well as shareholder value.

Yet the quite separate and purportedly futile argument about stakeholding reform should also be taken seriously. Indeed, some legal scholars see Labour's new disclosure requirements as a significant departure from the shareholder model (Williams and Conley 2005). Others find evidence of a system in flux, with aspects of insolvency law, employee representation and even institutional investment offering an opening to stakeholder interests (Armour et al. 2003). The analysis below is less sanguine, highlighting instead Labour's recoil from anything too distasteful to investors and managers. But nonetheless the stakeholding debate was an attempt by employee groups and policy entrepreneurs to confront both managerial and investor power. Its appearance forces governance scholars to go beyond their accustomed emphasis on efficiency to consider politically conceived notions of power, equity and justice. Viewed from this perspective, the work of the Trades Union Congress on stakeholding reform is a creative – if improbable – effort to reanimate governance history.

NEW AUTHORITY IN CORPORATE GOVERNANCE: 1990–97

Corporate governance refers to the ways companies are directed and controlled. In the liberal, Anglo-capitalist tradition, corporations exist for their shareholders' benefit. Governance, it follows, is about ensuring that managers are accountable to share-owners. But accountability is difficult because of conflicts of interest, collective action problems, and information asymmetries. When things go wrong, reformers emphasise some combination of the following: how boards work, what shareholders themselves might do, and the transparency arrangements including audit that supply information to the markets.

While states do not directly govern companies, they do define corporate forms and set minimal accountability requirements. They generally revisit these only under duress – elections are not fought on questions of company law and accounting practice. Since 1990, however, Britain has endured two periods of governance crisis and protracted concerns about unjustified managerial pay increases. The first began with the failure of Polly Peck, criminal fraud at Maxwell Group and the Bank of Credit and Commerce International, large losses at Allied Lyons and Queens Moat Houses and, in 1995, the Bank of Barings trading crisis. These failures devastated shareholders, creditors, and workers. They were joined by the media to more general concerns about Britain's industrial underperformance. The bulk of the institutional and policy reforms described in this chapter came as a result of this first round of collapse. The following sections summarise reforms in each of the major governance mechanisms.

Early board reform

Boards personify their companies and are obvious targets for blame when the unexpected happens. Moreover, for decades critics had decried systemic problems of UK board membership and structure, arguing that companies were failing shareholders and society (Mills 1981: 74). Too often, directorships were sinecures and directors were complacent and conservative. Board members who were also executives or former executives lacked the independence necessary to monitor and supervise managers. Often the company's chief executive might chair – and dominate – the board. But neither public nor private authority had much to say about these problems. The Department of Trade and Industry (DTI) is responsible for UK company law and prosecutions. But the DTI's responsibilities range across industrial policy and regulation and its company law division is tiny. Through Conservative and Labour administrations the ideological presumption on these matters was laissez faire (Gamble and Kelly 2000: 48). Nor was there any obvious private way to coordinate change: there was no professional self-regulation of the sort found in the legal and medical professions. As a result, critics argued that directors' duties to shareholders should be clearer in law and more easily enforceable in court.[2]

A stronger reform agenda would address conflicts of interest by limiting directors' terms, uniformly increasing the number of non-executive and independent directors, and by ensuring independent board committees handle sensitive tasks such as audit, remuneration, and nominations. It would modify pay structures to better align directors' and shareholders' interests.

As the crises broke, Conservative ministers rejected a legislative response out of hand, opting instead to prosecute malfeasance under existing law. In Parliament they asserted that shareholders should do more with their governance powers. When it became clear that a systemic approach was needed, ministers advocated a private, code-based approach to reform to balance the twin goals of investor protection and managerial flexibility. From 1991, ministers joined the Bank of England, the existing private accountancy bodies, and trade associations in promoting three reform committees, each named for their chairmen. The Cadbury, Greenbury, and Hampel groups were dominated by leading managers and accountants who operated under the assumption that legislation was likely if business did not put its own house in order. In 1998 their results were compiled as the 'Combined Code' and they apply to all listed companies. Albeit private in nature, the committees and the Code dramatically increased non-market coordination of UK board governance.

Still, they were remarkable less for their substance than for their regulatory style. They broadly succeeded in promoting greater independence from management. Cadbury, for example, recommended splitting the posts of Chairman and Chief Executive and new independent board committees to set directors' pay, nominate directors, and oversee audit (Committee on the Financial Aspects of Corporate Governance (UK) 1992). These were commonly adopted. But the Cadbury Code is most admired for its principles-based regulatory style. It extolled the virtues of flexibility, avoiding 'one-size-fits-all' rules and a 'box-ticking' approach to compliance. Specifically, it introduced the notion of 'comply or explain', by which companies acknowledge compliance or explain why they are departing from the norm. This flexibility was the main virtue of the Code for managers. Investors could judge for themselves whether departures from the Code's recommendations were warranted in particular circumstances, and adjust their shareholding accordingly. Its provisions spread quickly through the corporate population. The Code is widely admired by liberal governance experts as an alternative to the costly and prescriptive legislation seen in the US after Enron and WorldCom.

Not all was well, however. While companies responded to the Cadbury Code by reorganising their boards, executive pay rose unabated. The issue peaked first in 1995, embarrassing an already unpopular Tory government. Prime Minister John Major met the heads of both the Institute of Directors and the Confederation of British Industry (CBI) to press for change (Gribben 1995). In the Commons, he and Michael Heseltine threatened legislation. Simultaneously, though, the Government expressed confidence in private action, and the Greenbury Committee was convened by the CBI and others (Written Answers: Treasury Questions 1995).

The political pressure to produce results was strong, especially given the imminence of a Labour Government. Still, the Committee was dominated by those it was supposed to regulate, including the head of the leading association of board members (the Institute of Directors, IoD). In the end the Greenbury Code required disclosure but little else. Companies' board remuneration committees would report to investors but the report would not have to be approved by shareholder vote. The reporting requirement was taken into Stock Exchange rules and a Statutory Instrument (regulation) made them law. But the Government did not go beyond Greenbury, and in fact the rules were less stringent for unlisted companies. In something of a blow to the transparency approach, the Greenbury disclosure rules probably contributed to rising pay as companies and directors tried to keep up with their peers.

By then, the private, Code-based approach to board reform was itself becoming controversial. As anticipated by Cadbury, a consolidating follow-up committee met from 1996. Its chairman, Ronnie Hampel, believed little additional reform was necessary, and even opined that the governance–performance link was not actually proven (Martinson 1998). His Report implicitly criticised the corporate governance movement for threatening board and pay 'flexibility' (Committee on Corporate Governance 1997: 10). The rapid take-up of Cadbury's best practice, he implied, led to a regrettable 'box-ticking' approach to the codes. Directors might spend more time ensuring compliance than implementing the spirit and intent of codes. But despite their complaints, Hampel's Combined Code was only mildly burdensome to managers; it did not mandate an exact proportion of non-executive directors, require a permanent governance board committee or ensure shareholder approval of board pay. The one really significant proposal was that a senior non-executive director be identified for each board. This, managers said, would sow confusion about who was really running the company.

Shareholders as proprietors

As ministers pointed out, UK law assumes shareholders will govern companies, at least by voting at annual meetings and replacing unsatisfactory directors (Dine 2001: 292). But it does not require any governance role, and monitoring managers of individual companies is rarely rational for shareholders who hold less than a majority of one company's stock. This explains, in part, why investors diversify their holdings into many companies and sell shares when managers under-perform. These diversified shareholders are protected (and more so in Britain than in the United States) by a tight regime of takeover rules to prevent managers blocking hostile bids when the market moves against them. Shareholders do not need, it follows, to be company proprietors, but can instead rely on the more or less effectively functioning equities markets to signal corporate governance concerns.

Still, shareholders are sometimes visible governance players, and they are of two kinds. The first are private individuals who are more of an irritant than a real force. Beyond selling shares in under-performing companies, their role is limited to voice and vote at the annual meetings. Legal action is possible if aggrieved, but the obstacles are very high and shareholder suits are much rarer than in the US. Interventions at meetings are hindered by cost and logistics. Both institutional investors (who do not attend) and directors (who must) view the meetings as an expensive waste of time and money (Ezzamel and Watson 1997: 67; OECD 1997: 134). Making a difference at the AGM is challenging because institutions and directors control the bulk of shares. Shareholders attempted to rein in executive pay at British Gas, for example, but the cost of circulating a resolution for the annual meeting was prohibitive. The Commons Employment Committee joined a small shareholder lobbying association in calling for reform, and ministers launched two consultations on what might be changed. Separately, the Law Commission reviewed legal remedies available to shareholders (Law Commission 1997). Ultimately, however, work flagged on both fronts.

The second class of shareholder comprises institutional investors. By 1990 most people with an interest in equities were invested through financial intermediaries such as pension funds, investment companies, or insurers. These institutions are the greatest actual and potential force in corporate governance. Critics argue they should take longer-term positions in companies, monitor managers more aggressively, or at the very least vote their shares. But the main structural problem is that institutions do not have strong incentives to intervene, and may have good reason not to (Plender 1997a; Goergen and Renneboog 1998). The London Stock Exchange argued that there was, in fact, enough shareholder governance – but that it was informal and hidden. Still, despite evidence of occasional interventions, commentators insisted that they should do more (and do more publicly). State action on this front was widely opposed, and would have been very difficult given the great number of UK shares owned by overseas investors. But some would have gone so far as to make institutional investor voting compulsory. Indeed, under US law pension funds covered by Federal guarantees are expected to vote their shares.

The Cadbury, Greenbury, and Hampel committees each charged institutional investors with neglect. Still, they were in no position to compel action: it was beyond their remit, was strongly resisted by shareholders themselves, and was not perhaps in their interests as management-dominated bodies. Nor was there any coordinating body of investors capable of imposing new rules on its members. The leading associations did fund extensive research and launched promotional campaigns among their members. Institutional Shareholders Committee members, for example, were asked to contact management regularly, encourage non-executive directors and board committees, and discourage concentrations of power at the head of the board.[3] While these moves appear to have encouraged normative change, they were not authoritative.

More important than legal reform and trade association initiatives was the activism of public pension funds. These fund managers invest public sector workers' retirement savings. They do not face the same conflicts of interest as for-profit financial institutions who are also marketing other services to companies. Nor are they run by company directors who dislike investor activism, as are company pension funds. Most prominent was the California Public Employees Retirement System (CALPERS), a leading voice in US governance. Systematically and with panache, CALPERS announced their governance criteria, compiled 'watch' lists of companies, and adjusted their buying, selling, and voting intentions accordingly. Managers did not welcome the attention, even joining unions and the Left in condemning the increased emphasis on short-term returns and market capitalisation. Governance experts applauded these new trans-Atlantic shareholder proprietors, although evidence on their impact is mixed.

Improving corporate transparency

Without reliable information boards cannot direct managers and shareholders cannot govern companies. Details about what must be disclosed to markets are mandated by the state, but the standards for reporting are set by authorised private bodies. The self-regulatory structure of the accounting industry may have contributed to transparency problems. Occasional reorganisations of this regime were prompted by ministers but were delegated to coalitions of professional groups rather than some state regulator.[4] Moreover, a 1990 judicial ruling that auditors have no duty of care (or liability) to shareholders or potential shareholders compounded these problems.[5] Even the Bank of England admitted systemic problems of transparency during the early 1990s (Charkham 1993). Indeed, creative accounting, careless audit, and obscured misappropriations of funds were features of the corporate scandals (Keasey and Wright 1997; Smerdon 1998).

Still, the Conservative Government was reluctant to take direct regulatory control. The 1989 Companies Act implemented an EU directive on audit and extended the Secretary of State's power to regulate the accountancy profession. That power was not used. Citing flexibility concerns, ministers preferred not to put the EU-mandated audit standards on a statutory footing.[6] They were delegated instead to the newly created Financial Reporting Council and Auditing Practices Board. It is true, however, that courts were empowered for the first time to order financial restatements where a 'true and fair' view of accounts was not given by companies.

Another long understood transparency problem is auditor conflict of interest (Coggan 1989). This results from overly close relationships between auditors and the executives with whom they work. Even more problematic is the provision of multiple services by the auditor to a single client. Can a firm making more money from, for example, tax preparation also conduct an objective audit which may be worth considerably less? The obvious incentive is not to antagonise the client. In 1991 EU-mandated regulations were introduced to UK law to reduce conflicts by requiring companies to disclose non-audit fees paid to their auditing firm.[7] This was a longstanding desire of the institutional investors, but was opposed by accountancy firms. Always resistant to European injunctions, the Government subsequently reduced the non-audit work falling within the regulations' scope.[8]

Summary: reticent ministers and new private authority

Between the technical changes of the Companies Act of 1989 and Labour's 1997 election, the Conservatives introduced no significant governance legislation. Neither investors nor managers could complain about burdensome state regulation during this period.[9] This is not, perhaps, surprising. There was neither precedent nor institutional framework for intervention, except in advancing transparency minima. Neoliberal Conservative ministers were committed to self-regulation. Nor, aside from the unions, were interest groups demanding action. On the contrary, all the relevant trade associations and professional bodies opposed new legal rules. And finally, the encroachment of aggressive investor-activists from the United States hinted that market solutions were emerging broadly as ministers predicted.

The governance committees and their codes were, however, a remarkable advance in private institutionalised authority over governance. This made explicit expectations that had long held in business, and sought to codify emerging best practice. The result was coordinated change in board and transparency structures that favoured investors while forcing recalcitrant managers to reshape their boards. Indeed, one senior participant went so far as to say that the Code and its precursors 'represent a new area of company law, opening up new techniques of concretization of legal norms and for their implementation' (Rickford 2000: 30).

Although the Codes are widely admired for their consensual and non-prescriptive nature, they were not representative of interest groups (like employees or environmentalists) outside the conventional governance community. They were thus able to limit the agenda to managerial and investor concerns and

better obtain essential reforms. They did offer, however, an easy target for future intervention and the politicisation that state oversight brings. This is all the more true on executive pay where they must be seen as having failed.

EXTENDING STATE REGULATION: 1998–2004

Beyond executive pay, corporate governance was not generating significant headlines during the late 1990s, and was not central to New Labour's election manifesto. But even New Labour endorsed the familiar twin critique of British capitalism: that companies were overly concerned with short-term returns and so were insufficiently competitive in high-value added global trade (on the one hand) and were insensitive to its employee stakeholders (on the other).

Prior to the scandals of 2001–02, governance policy took two institutional directions: an independent review of company (corporations) law and a separate, ministerially controlled track on restraining executive pay. The first consumed vast amounts of time and energy in consultation and its proposals for legal rationalisation were finally legislated in late 2005. It was notable, however, for giving a prominent forum to critics of the shareholder orientation of British companies. On executive pay, the Government cajoled, threatened, and finally supplemented private regulation with statutory regulation – although it did not move away from the disclosure approach.

The Company Law Review and stakeholding reform

The Company Law Review (1998–2001) was a blue ribbon panel convened by the Department of Trade and Industry to propose rationalising reform of the statutes underpinning governance. Ministers justifiably saw the archaic jumble of law governing companies as a costly burden, and lawyers had wanted reform for decades. But there was more at issue than legal complexity. The Review's 'root and branch' mandate meant it crossed paths with the substantive problems of governance, as well as the proper mix of private, market, and public authority. On the latter question there was little controversy: the presumption against state intervention held. But there were interesting developments on the first. At its inception Secretary Margaret Beckett asked the Review to evaluate the merits of stakeholding reform.

This threatened managers and shareholders alike. The result was an extended discussion, carried on in the Review's Steering Group and Consultative Committee meetings, in consultation documents, and in the copious responses of interested parties. The innocuous outcome of this debate demonstrates just how reluctant the Government has been to use its power to reorder corporate governance.

The stakeholding critique was best articulated prior to the 1997 election in Will Hutton's startlingly successful book *The State We're In*, and its policy implications were carefully detailed by the Trade Union Congress (TUC) and academics (Hutton 1995; TUC 1996; Kelly *et al.* 1997). At its core was the sense that the legal and theoretical underpinnings of companies were insufficiently embedded in society. First, managers are not obliged to balance shareholders' interests with those of employees, suppliers and contractors, customers, communities, and even the environment. The TUC urged the Company Law Review (CLR) – and ministers – to embrace a more pluralistic governance structure, modelled in part on German codetermination arrangements. Indeed, European Union directives were pressing works councils on Europe-wide companies and new information and consultation rights for all EU companies. For managerial representatives all this echoed Britain's 'industrial democracy' movement of the 1970s. Others took the more sympathetic position that stakeholder companies actually *promote* shareholder gain over the long term (Royal Society for the Arts 1995; Kay 1997).

Second, stakeholding indicted financial markets for inducing short-term managerial investment horizons (Kay 1996; Plender 1997b; Wheeler and Sillanpaa 1997). Appropriate shareholder governance, in this view, is not about improving short-term capital and dividend growth but about ensuring that companies are competitive over the long term. This requires investment in research and development, human capital creation, and productivity raising technology. Fears that institutional shareholders held back the patient capital needed for these outlays were a long-standing complaint (Charkham 1994: 255). They were even given voice by Michael Heseltine at Trade and Industry (Department of Trade and Industry 1995). The 1997 Labour manifesto rehearsed the new Government's concerns and Gordon Brown criticised

investors for holding back 'UK Plc'. The Company Law Review took up this issue but was rapidly preempted by more ministerial action. In 1999 the Government required pension schemes to state with their investment principles 'their policy (if any) in relation to the exercise of the rights (including voting rights) attaching to investments'.[10] This did not *require* exercising those rights, and was essentially a prescription for boilerplate.

In the end, the only meaningful stakeholder-friendly outcome of the Company Law Review and subsequent consultations was the Operating and Financial Review (OFR). This increases disclosure in corporate Annual Reports on employee, environmental, and social issues. Although it caused some discomfort to managers, it was entirely consistent with the liberal and voluntarist history of British corporate governance. The content of the OFR was to be left to managerial discretion. Equally mild was the statutory clarification of directors' duties so that they were not limited to short-run investor interest. This was already the legal reality if not the statutory language. Neither introduced new managerial liabilities or provided any means for judicial enforcement. The sense in the trade union movement is of a missed opportunity (Williamson 2003). This was only compounded in November 2005 when, with little consultation of the wider governance policy community, Chancellor Gordon Brown told CBI he would withdraw the mandatory OFR so as to help cut 'red tape'.

The chronic problem of executive pay

Executive pay rose unabated during the late 1990s and early 2000s – even as equities peaked and then crashed. This indicates, perhaps, the limited efficacy of disclosure as a regulatory strategy and the ability of private governance authorities to impose discipline. Greenbury's disclosure requirements helped raise average pay by revealing peer earnings, and companies were not presenting pay reports to shareholders for approval. Investors increasingly joined trade unions in decrying managerial rapacity. The Government, meanwhile, sent mixed signals. Peter Mandelson issued a 'final warning' in 1998 (Wighton 1998). Christopher Haskins of the Better Regulation Task Force appealed for more shareholder activism 'in desperation' (Haskins 1998). Trade Secretary Byers (1999) even threatened to compel institutional voting. Reportedly, Chancellor Gordon Brown was ready to go even further than Byers (Shrimsley and Targett 2001). Ministerial faith in managerial self-discipline, market forces, and private authority was confounded.

Still, the Government acted without celerity, apparently because of reticence at Number Ten. The Company Law Review's remit on pay had been preempted by a ministerial consultation in 1999, but three years and another consultation passed before the final, mild regulations were laid before Parliament (Department of Trade and Industry 1999). During this time ministers announced the same package of reforms several times before sending it to Parliament in June 2002. The final proposals were 'a compromise approved by Downing Street' (Shrimsley and Targett 2001).

The main problem, according to the Government, was still the lack of disclosure – not of individual directors' pay, but of the board's overall pay policy. The new rule required better explanation and equity performance comparisons. Shareholders would have an 'advisory' vote on the report, but not on the policy itself. The Law Society was quick to point out the meaningless ambiguity of an 'advisory' shareholder vote. Otherwise, reaction was mixed. The Association of British Insurers wanted no less than a vote on the policy itself. The other major shareholder representative, NAPF, was more satisfied. The Trades Union Congress saw the Government's new thinking as a modest success, particularly as it required comparing top and bottom pay rates within companies. Managers, who had opposed the regulation, were mildly aggrieved. The IoD was most hostile, saying that abuse was rare. Still, it might have been worse. The CBI welcomed the final regulation, hoping that it would close the issue.

It did not. In early 2003, with headlines focusing now on the fees paid to retired and fired executives, the Government announced yet another consultation.[11] This addressed more explicitly the mix of statute and private guidance and – since giving markets more information appeared to be an exhausted strategy – threatened direct controls. The most radical option was to amend the Companies Act to permit only 'fair and reasonable' compensation on loss of office. The CBI's Director-General told the press that, 'it won't just be David Beckham who leaves the country' if limits were imposed. He need not have worried: even in the Consultation document, ministers expressed their aversion to direct controls. They had already allowed a private member's Bill limiting 'rewards for failure' to fail.

In March 2004 the Government again refused to legislate, issued yet another threat, and demanded once more that shareholders do their proprietary duty to restrain managers. Indeed, 2003 was a remarkable year for activism. Several prominent company chiefs lost their jobs. Shareholders rejected GlaxoSmithKline's remuneration report because of a possible severance payment of £22m to its chief executive. Finally, in January 2005 the Government announced that it was satisfied that legislation was not needed.

Board direction after Enron/WorldCom

In late 2001 and 2002 the collapses of Enron, its accountant, Arthur Andersen, and the US telecommunications firm WorldCom swept through the UK governance community. Both symbolic and economic factors explain the trans-Atlantic significance of these collapses. First, Enron embodied the integration of free-market US and UK capitalism.[12] It had bought into UK privatisations and was a significant employer. Enron's auditor, Arthur Andersen, handled over 10 percent of the UK's £3.1bn oligopolistic accounting market and cast doubt on the profession generally. There was also significant financial spillover related to the broader loss of confidence in equities. The FTSE 100 share index fell almost in tandem with the Dow, losing 20 percent of its value between September 2000 and March 2001. It was down 40 percent from its January peak by that summer. On the June day after WorldCom revealed its crimes every share on the FTSE 100 fell. Britons were also heavily invested in US equities (in 2000, more than any other foreign nation), meaning that governance on Wall Street affects UK retirement savings. Foreign equities worth £429.3bn in 2000 dropped in value to £333.6bn two years later. Home grown collapses at Marconi and Cable and Wireless only added to the sense that the Anglo-capitalist model was in crisis.

These developments were met by calls for reform by the Parliamentary committees and the press (House of Commons Select Committee on Treasury 2002). Although clearly preferring a non-statutory approach, ministers responded by exerting direct influence over enhancements to the Combined Code. The Secretary of Trade and Industry created two study groups to recommend board reforms from which she would choose. The most controversial investigated how non-executive directors' (NEDs) influence might be strengthened. This caused significant consternation. Dismissing ministerial influence as 'dangerous nonsense', the outgoing head of the Institute of Directors went so far as to call for the abolition of non-executive directorships. He suggested the only result of a decade of 'well-meaning, but ... misguided effort' was 'that we are more concerned about corporate governance than ever' (Roberts 2002). In this atmosphere, the Government had problems finding someone to chair its NED review. Ministers chose Derek Higgs, who was praised by one banker as 'not a theoretician who will go away and work out how things should be'. Instead he would test reform 'against the benchmark of practicality' (Adams 2002).

Higgs' proposals were, in the end, rather radical. He wanted non-executives to meet without the rest of the board and a lead independent director to hear shareholder concerns privately. This would have moved UK boards towards a two-tier structure, splitting supervisory and managerial functions. In addition, he proposed that fully half of board members be independent and urged that directors chair no more than one company.[13] Investors were essentially supportive of this programme, but managers were aghast. It would, they said, threaten board comity and shrink the pool of qualified candidates while eroding the lucrative practice of collecting directorships. The fact that none of it was compulsory was little consolation. Although Higgs continued Cadbury's norm-based approach of 'comply or explain', managers complained that even this was too burdensome, because the new norms spread so quickly.

Given these reactions, ministers back-pedalled. In concluding the reform process in January 2003, Secretary of State Hewitt avoided mentioning the controversial proposal that lead non-executives should meet shareholders separately from the board Chairman. She was asked about this in the Commons by her Conservative shadow but did not respond directly. Instead, she assured the House that the Higgs reforms were not 'one size fits all' regulation. The Financial Reporting Council (FRC), with formal responsibility for revising the Code, followed this political lead when it published the new Combined Code in late 2003 (Financial Reporting Council 2003). The Chairman would retain his/her responsibilities as the leader of non-executives and the main source of information about shareholder's views. He (or she) would be able to chair the nomination committee and so preserve their influence on board composition. Finally, smaller listed companies could escape with 'at least two'

independents rather than the 50 percent proposed by Higgs. And the FRC opened new avenues of flexibility through Byzantine distinctions between 'principles', 'provisions', and 'supporting principles'. Managers and investors welcomed the changes, which must be seen as a significant climb-down.

Cajoling investors

The Company Law Review had considered the role of shareholders, first in the context of stakeholding critique (which is, essentially, that they have too much power) and then in the context of investor protection (where they do not exercise enough power, or least are too short term in their orientations to properly husband successful business). On the latter front, the CLR summarised the underlying situation facing investors: a lack of governance expertise, free rider problems, insider trading rules, and conflicts of interest. While the debate (and the Government's response) occurred before Enron/ WorldCom, it nonetheless helps stake out Labour's position.

Investor conflicts of interest were the most intractable problem, since resolving them might foreclose lucrative business opportunities to the large financial services firms. The matter was considered nonetheless, largely at the urging of John Plender, a journalist and former chairman of a consultancy with close ties to the public sector pension funds. The CLR steering group concurred with Plender that conflicts were indeed a public interest issue, and typically proposed disclosure as a solution. Companies might be required to publicise their relationship with financial services firms which were, at the same time, shareholders. Conversely, large institutional shareholders might have to disclose or explain their holdings and governance votes to the public. The usual lines were drawn in response. The CBI and IoD denied there were any conflicts of interest or even any collective action problems facing investors. Institutional investors acknowledged the problems but opposed legislative action – again with the exception of the public pension funds. As might be expected, accountants supported new disclosure. Responding to the Review's proposals, the Government mused that conflicts of interest were 'difficult and controversial' and deferred action (Department of Trade and Industry 2002: 24).

Meanwhile, there were simultaneous calls for reform from other areas of the regulatory establishment. The Treasury held a broader inquiry into the

UK's shambolic pension savings and investment system. The resulting 2001 Myners report recommended that fund managers be legally bound to intervene where it would benefit retirement plan beneficiaries. This mimicked a famous US Department of Labor instruction to trustees covered by the Employee Retirement Income Security Act. Shortly thereafter, the Department for Work and Pensions joined the Treasury in consulting on just such a duty (Department for Work and Pensions 2003). But forcing voting would be a dramatic increase in state control over the City, and Labour was reluctant to go that far. And again, private actors sought to stave off intervention. The Institutional Shareholders' Committee issued yet another code for investors, again stressing procedure (investors must have a *policy* on investment). In 2002, ministers announced that they would put legislation on hold for two years to await results of the private approach.[14]

Since then the emphasis has shifted from compelling institutional action to the relationship between the institutions and their beneficiaries. In its recent White Paper, the Government wants to promote better information flows from companies to shareholder beneficiaries, and to better enable them to exercise their governance rights when they so wish (Department of Trade and Industry 2005). Registered shareholders are to be given proxy rights (enabling them to instruct others to vote on their behalf at annual meetings). After a good deal of promotion by the investor trade associations more companies are arranging electronic voting of shares, which obviously makes individual shareholder input easier. Mixed with its mild reforms, the Government is reserving to itself powers to compel further action if markets do not continue to improve. These latest moves are likely to reduce the costs of shareholder governance, in part by reducing information asymmetries, but they do not directly address systemic conflicts of interest and collective action problems.

Transparency revisited

Even before Enron there was movement on accountancy and audit. This took two tracks: regulation of the profession itself, and rules about the auditor–client relationship. In 1998 Labour's DTI launched a review of the eight-year-old accounting regulatory regime. The party's Business Manifesto had called for more independent regulation, and some academics urged

the creation of a single, 'SEC-type', state regulator. This would have resolved jurisdictional confusion and increased political control. Ministers apparently pursued the former while avoiding the latter. The new structure, created in 2000, did not depart significantly from the design offered by the industry's Consultative Committee of Accountancy Bodies.[15]

As in the early 1990s, however, the new arrangements were immediately challenged by corporate fraud and collapse. Again, there were calls in the Commons to bring regulation under central control and to break the hold of the largest five (suddenly now four) firms on blue chip auditing. A second review was announced and its recommendations are now being implemented. These shift authority between two semi-public bodies: from the Accountancy Foundation to the Financial Reporting Council. While this is clearly another case of regulatory centralisation, little of substance has changed. Most significantly, ministers did not insist that the Competition Commission investigate the profession's oligopolistic market structure.

The separate problem of auditor independence was acknowledged early in the Company Law Reviews deliberations (Company Law Review Steering Group 1999: 6.23). Still, without a crisis there was little pressure for action. Investor and management groups did not express great interest, and the accounting industry uniformly opposed any change. In the end, the Review's Steering Group deferred action, and the Government's 2001 White Paper on company law ignored the issue. After Enron/WorldCom the Commons Treasury Committee urged that audit contracts be regularly re-tendered, and that firms or at least audit partners be rotated periodically. Equally, the Committees wanted to improve industry standards on 'revenue recognition' and 'aggressive earnings management' – the sometimes unsubtle ways numbers can be interpreted in compiling financial accounts (House of Commons Select Committee on Treasury 2002).

Initially it appeared that ministers might take decisive action. In July 2002 a censorious press release threatened mandatory rotation, re-tendering and possibly also some statutory enforcement of the Combined Code's injunction that boards have audit committees. But by winter 2002–03 the familiar cycle of threat, review and retreat was complete. Auditor conflicts of interest would be ameliorated flexibly through a 'principles-based framework'. No rotation would be mandated, the Code's provisions would not be enforced, and audit firm transparency would be voluntary. There was no ministerial review of accounting standards and again the industry was not to be investigated.

In the Government's 2005 company law bill, ministers met a longstanding demand from the profession that auditor liabilities be limited in negligence suits brought for opinions that prove inaccurate. The Bill is to include a new criminal offence of knowingly or recklessly giving a misleading, false, or deceptive opinion. Again, the wording of the Bill was closely influenced by the accountancy profession. Investors are disappointed as criminal prosecutions tend to raise the bar significantly.

Evaluating corporate governance under Labour

Overall the period marks a strengthening of state authority over the board, shareholder, and transparency mechanisms. The major vehicle for reform – the Combined Code – is kept under review by the state-sponsored independent Financial Reporting Council. Influencing changes is clearly a ministerial prerogative, and it is widely regarded as a public policy vehicle onto which further rules might be loaded.[16] This was a significant change from the era of Cadbury, Greenbury, and Hampel, which was itself a departure from the UK's laissez faire governance tradition. Shareholder rights are being improved through minor changes and the takeover mechanism remains a strong disciplining force. And, finally, accountants endured new bouts of regulatory reorganisation but as before had much to say about implementation. Overall the picture is of a centralising and interfering – but not particularly aggressive – regulatory style.

Yet how were regulatory benefits and burdens distributed among the relevant interests? Only managers could have any self-interested reason to grumble: board structures and pay are obviously subject to wider scrutiny and control. But under the 'comply or explain' principle, companies are free not to adopt the reforms, as long as they justify their rejection. Conceivably non-conformity could become more widespread. Managers may have more grounds for complaint on new pay disclosures and greater investor activism on employment contract issues. But their pay has not suffered and activism remains the exception rather than the rule.

Investors fared even better. Board and accountancy reforms were, after all, designed to protect them.

More important, though, is what did not happen. Despite their own lax custodial exertions, institutional fund managers have not been compelled to do more to protect beneficiary interests. They must state their policy on voting shares, but need not actually have such a policy. High profile cases of shareholder activism during the early 2000s perhaps took the sting out of charges that institutions were not doing enough. Institutions were able to show that any regulatory mandate would drive up capital costs in a global financial market. Thus, they enjoy the benefits of governance without its burdens.

The Government would argue that its measured, cautious approach to investor protection was more appropriate than the hasty extension of law seen in the US during 2002. Unburdened by the push and pull of an aggressive Congress and ambitious state attorneys-general, British ministers viewed the Washington experience with horror. The DTI's annual report said it opposed 'anything which could lead to Sarbanes-Oxley type prescriptive legislation' (Department of Trade and Industry 2003: 13). DTI Secretary Hewitt thought it 'an example of legislating in haste, repenting at leisure' (Hewitt 2002) Thus, despite their willingness to use more muscular state influence on the private sector, they stood by their view that governance should be based on principles rather than rules and statute.

Finally, on the question of stakeholding, employees, ecologists, and other activists gained little from the new regulation. By virtue of the politicisation of authority they have greater access to debates. Through access to ministers and tactical effectiveness they achieved agenda expansion, but policy decisions largely went against them. This is equally true for Britain's implementation of European Union rules about employee consultation. Opponents convincingly argued that any infraction on managerial autonomy or short-term investor interests would result in lost competitiveness or capital flight. Labour ministers largely agreed with this conceptualisation of competitiveness and were unwilling to consider complementary reforms (for example, on capital mobility) to combat such risks. This is not surprising, given the structural importance of financial services to the British economy and the essential place of institutional investors in underwriting British retirement pensions. Any perceived threat to returns must be avoided. As a result, new disclosure requirements, now being implemented, are objectionable neither to investors (who like new sources of information on principle) nor to managers (who have wide discretion on what to disclose). The Government reconceptualised further stakeholder concerns as a matter for its promotional campaign for corporate social responsibility. And, finally, European Union directives on employee consultation have been implemented in very mild fashion.

CONCLUSION

The history recounted here suggests that even an extended regulatory state can be substantively contained. Under both Labour and Conservative ministers, corporate governance policy was both reactive and cautious. First, the state was not as aggressive as we might expect, even on conventional concerns. Investor protection did not elicit the kinds of legislation seen in the United States after Enron/WorldCom, despite fears that the same conflicts of interest in audit afflicted British companies. On executive pay there was ample scope for action but managers were hardly burdened. Nor were fund managers required to step up their governance role, even when it would serve their beneficiaries' interests. Second, when the state might have reformed governance in favour of employees or ecological concerns – that is, when transformational reform was on the agenda – it did not do so. Stakeholding reform was rejected in favour of paeans to 'enlightened shareholder value' and only the mildest disclosure requirements. For all the new institutional capacity, governance problems and policies were conceived within existing structures of power and advantage. Any ambitions to social control that threatened the political-economic status quo were quickly ruled out. While research in other policy domains is required to comprehensively evaluate Britain's new regulatory state, the case described here is not one of dramatic policy effects.

ACKNOWLEDGEMENTS

I am grateful for comments on an earlier draft from Terrence Casey, Deirdre Martinez, two anonymous reviewers, and participants in the Penn Temple European Studies Colloquium.

NOTES

1. Indeed, two of Moran's case studies (financial services and accountancy regulation) are directly linked to corporate governance.
2. Although there are detailed prescriptions and proscriptions to prevent directors' self-dealing, the law is almost silent on how boards should do their job. They must exercise the care of a reasonable person but are liable only for gross negligence. Imprudence and errors of judgement are not covered by liability.
3. Texts are archived online at: http://www.ivis.co.UK/pages/guidelines.html#sectioneight (accessed 27 July 2005). Separately, the Association of British Insurers (ABI) and National Association of Pension Funds (NAPF) issued similar guidance.
4. The Consultative Committee of Accounting Bodies brought together the various Institutes.
5. *Caparo Industries plc v Dickman* [1990] 2 A.C. 605.
6. John Redwood, Commons Hansard, 25 October 1989.
7. Companies Act 1985 (Disclosure of Remuneration for Non-Audit Work) Regulations 1991.
8. Disclosure of Interests in Shares (Amendment) Regulations 1993, 27 May 1993.
9. The Criminal Justice Act of 1993 somewhat tightened insider-trading rules.
10. The Occupational Pension Schemes (Investment, and Assignment, Forfeiture, Bankruptcy etc.) Amendment Regulations 1999. The regulations required an additional statement on whether the scheme took into account social, environmental, or ethical matters in selecting investments.
11. Commons Hansard, 29 January 2003, Col. 890. The proposals for comment came in June.
12. Enron's UK utility interests included a major Teeside power station and Wessex Water, a privatised company serving 2.5 million customers. Enron Europe's trading operations were centred in London, and 1,400 jobs were lost there. The company's banks and advisors were as prominent in the City as they were on Wall Street. A former Tory energy minister, Lord Wakeham, sat on the board's audit and nominations committees. And finally, Barclays, the Royal Bank of Scotland, and Abbey National had significant financial exposure to the company.
13. Higgs had not entirely ignored managerial demands. For example, he opted for the CBI's preferred disclosure by NEDs of their multiple commitments and the extent of their availability rather than (as proposed by TUC, the Institute of Directors, and Tomorrow's Company) a mandatory limit on directorships. Nonetheless, the proposals were received very badly.
14. Shareholders do have new rights to vote in AGMs. Under the Political Parties, Elections and Referendums Act 2000 political donations must now be approved by shareholder vote. Finally, some provisions to encourage electronic voting of share proxies have been introduced.
15. This established the Accountancy Foundation, together with its subsidiaries on Auditing Practices, Ethics

Standards, Investigations and Discipline, and the Review Board. The DTI was to be represented as an observer on each. Notably, the Foundation was peopled with client representatives rather than practising accountants. Its membership was nominated by: the National Association of Pension Funds, the Bank of England, Public Sector Audit Commission, the National Consumer Council, the Trade Union Congress, the Confederation of British Industry, and the Central Bank of Ireland.

16. John Parkinson, Interview with author, Bristol, 5 June 2000.

REFERENCES

Adams, Christopher (2002). 'Heavyweight Riding to Rescue of Boardroom Review', *Financial Times*, 16 April, 22.

Armour, John, Simon Deakin and Suzanne J. Konzelmann (2003). 'Shareholder Primacy and the Trajectory of UK Corporate Governance', *British Journal of Industrial Relations*, 41:3, 531–55.

Byers, Stephen (1999). Directors' Remuneration and Institutional Investor Voting: Speech to an ABI and NAPF Seminar. London: Department of Trade and Industry.

Charkham, Jonathan P. (1993). 'The Bank and Corporate Governance: Past, Present and Future', *Bank of England Quarterly Journal*, August, 388–92.

Charkham, Jonathan P. (1994). *Keeping Good Company: A Study of Corporate Governance in Five Countries*. Oxford: Clarendon Press.

Coggan, Philip (1989). 'Anxieties Over the Effectiveness of Analysis', *Financial Times*, 20 June, 29.

Committee on Corporate Governance (1995). *Directors' Remuneration: Report of a Study Group Chaired by Sir Richard Greenbury*. London: Gee.

Committee on Corporate Governance (1997). *Committee on Corporate Governance: Final Report (Hampel Report)*. London: Gee Publishing.

Committee on the Financial Aspects of Corporate Governance (UK) (1992). *Report of the Committee on the Financial Aspects of Corporate Governance (Cadbury Report)*. London: Gee/Professional Publishing Ltd.

Company Law Review Steering Group (1999). *Modern Company Law for a Competitive Economy: The Strategic Framework*. London: Department of Trade and Industry.

Department for Work and Pensions (2003). *Encouraging Shareholder Activism: A Consultation Document*. London: Department of Work and Pensions.

Department of Trade and Industry (1995). *Developing a Winning Partnership*. London: DTI.

Department of Trade and Industry (1999). *Directors' Remuneration: A Consultative Document*. London: DTI.

Department of Trade and Industry (2002). *Modernising Company Law*. London: HMSO.

Department of Trade and Industry (2003). *Companies in 2002–2003*. London: The Stationery Office.

Department of Trade and Industry (2005). *Company Law Reform (Cm 6456)*. London: The Stationery Office.

Dine, Janet (2001). *Company Law*, 4th ed.. London: Palgrave.

Ezzamel, Mahmoud, and Robert Watson (1997). 'Executive Remuneration and Corporate Performance', in K. Keasey and M. Wright (eds.), *Corporate Governance: Responsibilities, Risks and Remuneration*. New York: John Wiley & Sons.

Financial Reporting Council (2003). *FRC issues revised Combined Code*. London: FRC.

Gamble, Andrew, and Gavin Kelly (2000). 'The Politics of the Company', in J. Parkinson, A. Gamble and G. Kelly (eds.), *The Political Economy of the Company*. Portland, OR: Hart Publishing.

Goergen, Marc, and Luc Renneboog (1998). *Strong Managers and Passive Institutional Investors in the UK*, European Corporate Governance Network Working paper.

Gribben, Roland (1995). 'CBI Committee To Focus On Pay', *The Daily Telegraph*, 16 January, 23.

Hansmann, Henry, and Reinier Kraakman (2000). 'The End of History for Corporate Law'. Discussion paper no. 280. Cambridge, MA: Harvard Law School.

Haskins, Christopher (1998). 'Setting the Agenda on Boardroom Excess', *Guardian*, 31 October, 27.

Heffernan, Richard (2000). *New Labour and Thatcherism*. New York: St. Martin's Press.

Hewitt, Patricia (2002). *100 Group Speech: Institute of Directors*. London: Department of Trade and Industry.

House of Commons Select Committee on Treasury (2002). *The Financial Regulation of Public Limited Companies*. Sixth Report of the 2001–2002 Session. Select Committee on Treasury. London: The Committee.

Howard, Alistair (2005). 'The Governance of Flexibility: Contemporary Politics and the British Company', Unpublished doctoral thesis, Political Science Department, George Washington University, Washington, DC.

Hutton, Will (1995). *The State We're In*. London: Jonathan Cape.

Kay, John (1996). 'The Root of the Matter: The Stakeholding Corporation Has More Than One Responsibility and Measure of Success', *Financial Times (London Edition)*, 16 February, 17.

Kay, John (1997). 'The Stakeholder Corporation', in G. Kelly, D. Kelly and A. Gamble (eds.), *Stakeholder Capitalism*. London: Macmillan/Political Economy Research Centre.

Keasey, Kevin, and Mike Wright, eds. (1997). *Corporate Governance: Responsibilities, Risks and Remuneration*. New York: John Wiley & Sons.

Kelly, Gavin, Dominic Kelly and Andrew Gamble, eds. (1997). *Stakeholder Capitalism*. London: Macmillan Press.

Law Commission (1997). *Shareholder Remedies*. London: The Stationery Office.

Martinson, Jane (1998). 'Plea to Give Self-regulation "Time to Work" Final Hampel Report on Corporate Governance Published Yesterday Accepts Need for Tougher Action', *Financial Times*, 29 January, 11.

Mills, Geoffrey (1981). On the Board. London: Gower/Institute of Directors.

F
O
U
R

Moran, Michael (2001). 'The Rise of the Regulatory State in Britain', *Parliamentary Affairs*, 54:1, 19–34.

Moran, Michael (2003). The British Regulatory State. New York: Oxford University Press.

OECD (1997). *OECD Economic Surveys: United Kingdom, 1997–98*. Paris: Organization for Economic Cooperation and Development.

Plender, John (1997a). 'Hampel's Rotten Boroughs', *Financial Times*, 6 August, 18.

Plender, John (1997b). *A Stake in the Future: The Stakeholding Solution*. London: Nicholas Brealey.

Rhodes, R.A.W. (1996). 'The New Governance: Governing without Government', *Political Studies*, 44, 652–67.

Richards, David, and Martin J. Smith (2001). 'New Labour, The Constitution and Reforming the State', in S. Ludlam and M.J. Smith (eds.), *New Labour in Government*. New York: St. Martin's Press.

Rickford, Jonathan (2000). 'Do Good Governance Recommendations Change the Rules for the Board of Directors?' Paper read at Conference on Company Law and Capital Market Law, 30–31 March, at Siena.

Roberts, Dan (2002). 'Institute of Directors Head Calls for Non-executive Posts to be Abolished', *Financial Times*, 25 April, 1.

Royal Society for the Arts (1995). *Tomorrow's Company Inquiry Report*. London: Royal Society for the Arts.

Shrimsley, Robert, and Simon Targett (2001). 'Spotlight on Boardroom Pay Deals', *Financial Times (London Edition 1)*, 8 March, 1, 33.

Smerdon, Richard (1998). *A Practical Guide to Corporate Governance*. London: Sweet & Maxwell.

TUC (1996). *Your Stake At Work*. London: Trades Union Congress.

Wheeler, David, and Maria Sillanpaa (1997). *The Stakeholder Corporation: The Body Shop*, Blueprint for Maximizing Stakeholder Value. London: Pitman Publishing.

Wighton, David (1998). 'Mandelson Gives Final Warning on Executive Salaries', *Financial Times*, 3 December, 10.

Williams, Cynthia A., and John M. Conley (2005). 'An Emerging Third Way? The Erosion of the Anglo-American Shareholder Construct', *Cornell International Law Journal*, 39:2, 493.

Williamson, Janet (2003). 'A Trade Union Congress Perspective on the Company Law Review and Corporate Governance Reform since 1997', *British Journal of Industrial Relations*, 41:3, 511–30.

Written Answers: Treasury Questions (1995). *In Parliamentary Debates: Commons Hansard*, 2 February, Col. 791–2. London.

14 "Varieties of Institutional Investors and National Models of Capitalism: The Transformation of Corporate Governance in France and Germany"

from Politics and Society (2006)

Michel Goyer

SUMMARY

This chapter examines the rise of foreign ownership in France and Germany. I argue that the firm-level institutional arrangements of workplace organization constitute the most significant variable to account for the greater attractiveness of French firms over their German counterparts to short-term, impatient capital— namely, hedge and mutual funds. I demonstrate how key notions of the Varieties of Capitalism perspective—institutional interaction, institutional latency, and the distinction between institutional framework and the mode of coordination that follows from these institutions—provide important theoretical insights to account for the different structures of foreign ownership in France and Germany.

INTRODUCTION

The chapter examines the transformation of the system of corporate governance in France and Germany from the mid-1990s to 2005, a period of tremendous change in European finance. The topic of corporate governance—the system by which firms are controlled and operated, the rules and practices that govern the relationship between managers and shareholders, and the overall process by which investment capital is allocated—has become an important issue for policymakers and scholars in recent years in the wake of financial scandals in Europe and in the United States.[1] The increasing importance of corporate governance in Europe, however, goes beyond the advent of recent acts of corporate malfeasance. It reflects the importance of critical trends with serious political implications for advanced European capitalist economies.[2] Tremendous changes have pushed these systems toward the adoption of greater shareholder value in the strategy of companies in recent years.[3] Will the globalization of finance and investment lead to convergence across European systems of corporate governance along the lines of the American model?

The research question of this chapter on France and Germany is two-pronged: to account for the different patterns of transformation of the two systems of corporate governance, and to assess its implications for their respective national models of capitalism. I focus on the rise of foreign ownership as a key indicator of shifts in corporate governance. Two critical methodological considerations serve as motivation for the research question of this article. First, how does one assess the advent of institutional change in corporate governance? As Campbell (2004) reminds us, we often mistake evolutionary shifts for more revolutionary developments and vice versa.[4] The absence of an analytical framework to distinguish between patterns of institutional change leaves us powerless to distinguish between them and to understand their consequences. Changes in corporate governance might be a more recent development in continental Europe, but advanced capitalist economies underwent substantial institutional change in many areas in the last 25 years without resulting in either internally revolutionary transformation or in cross-national convergence.[5] Second, the current interest in accounting for institutional change is understandable given the predominant consensus that institutions do matter for economic, political, and social outcomes.[6] The design of institutional frameworks is seen by scholars and policymakers as the key variable for important public policy issues.

The argument presented in this chapter is the following. First, an assessment of the consequences associated with the rise of foreign ownership and the growth of securities markets in France and Germany requires a sophisticated differentiation between investors. The rise of foreign ownership in the form of institutional investors pushing for a greater shareholder value orientation cannot by itself constitute a radical transformation of European corporate governance. I distinguish primarily between pension and mutual/hedge funds. Pension funds constitute long-term investors that acquire an equity stake in corporations primarily for diversification purposes; mutual/hedge funds seek to maximize assets under their management as they possess a shorter-term horizon and operate under competitive pressures to beat market benchmarks. The importance of this distinction between different types of investors is primarily driven by its implication for the mode of coordination of firms. As Hall and Soskice (2001) have argued, access to patient capital constitutes a key feature of coordinated market economies, as opposed to liberal market economies that rely on short-term, risk capital. The investment strategies and time horizons of mutual/hedge and pension funds have different consequences for the sustainability of national models of European capitalism.

Second, I argue that the firm-level institutional arrangements of workplace organization constitute the most significant variable to account for the diverging ability of French and German firms to attract funds from Anglo-Saxon institutional investors. Mutual and hedge funds possess short-term investment strategies and time horizons. They also exhibit firm-specific preferences since the performance of their portfolio is shaped by the behavior of a smaller number of companies than is the case for pension funds. The degree of fit between their preferences and the firm-level institutional arrangements of advanced capitalist economies reflects the ability of the CEO and top managers to reorganize the workplace in a unilateral fashion. It fits well with the corporate decision-making process in France, which is management-led and excludes the workforce. French firm-level institutions are characterized by the concentration of power in the CEO that, in turn, allows for a rapid reorganization of the workplace under the guidance of a small number of corporate officials.[7] The strategies of mutual and hedge funds, in contrast, do not fit well with the firm-level institutions found in Germany. Firm-level institutions impose several constraints on the ability of management to develop and implement strategies in a unilateral fashion. Several legal obstacles stand in the way of a rapid and unilateral reorganization of the shop floor. Adjustments to external pressures in Germany are the result of negotiation between management and employees.[8] As a result, hedge and mutual funds—two categories of short-term, impatient capital—displayed an overwhelming preference for France over Germany as an investment site.

I draw on notions from the Varieties of Capitalism (VoC) theoretical perspective to understand both institutional transformation and the maintenance of differences between contemporary capitalist economies. The VoC perspective emphasizes the critical importance of patterns of institutional complementarities across the various sub-spheres (finance and corporate governance, industrial relations, innovation system, and inter-firm relations) of the economy that lead to diverging forms of behavior on the part of economic actors. The key insight is that the impact of an institution cannot be studied in isolation as it is mediated by its interaction with other features of the national institutional framework, therefore implying that different types of institutional fit are possible.[9] In other words, national institutional frameworks engender interaction effects that shape in different ways the behavior of economic actors according to the particular combination of institutions found in the national setting. The outcome is that developed economies are distinguished by their specific configuration of interdependent institutions.[10] Moreover, these national institutional configurations of interlocking and interdependent institutions reinforce each other, thereby proving resistant to change.

Finally, the VoC perspective contends that superior economic performance and the development of competitive advantage result from the extent to which patterns of institutional complementarity support the development of firm competencies.[11] In other words, each institutional feature fits with the others and makes them more effective than they would be on their own. The notion of competitive advantage is institutionally based as firm performance lies in the achievement of a proper fit between their organizational features and the requirements associated with specific market niches. The presence of institutional complementarity constitutes a source of economic efficiency as it contributes to solving coordination problems since the actions a firm takes in one sphere of the economy are contingent on the actions of others in different spheres.[12] As a result, different patterns of institutional fit across nations should be good at excelling at different types of activities, thereby leading to different types of specialization.[13]

However, the VoC theoretical perspective has come under attack in recent years. The broad line of criticism is that the tools developed by comparative political economists in the last twenty years have provided us with a better understanding of institutional resiliency, but have not been as helpful in accounting for institutional transformation.[14] The theoretical insights of the concept might be quite useful in accounting for stability, but they are far too static to account for institutional discontinuity. This theoretical challenge to the VoC perspective is comprised of several elements. First, processes of incremental and continual institutional change can lead to significant discontinuity without requiring dramatic disruptions.[15] Rather than radical change breaking current patterns of institutional complementarity and re-shaping the preferences of actors, the process of institutional transformation often results from ongoing and accumulating dynamics that involve small adjustments. Thus, institutional transformation frequently is an evolutionary process that unfolds in an incremental manner and without major disruptions over long periods of time and resulting in profound change.[16] Second, and related to the previous line of criticism, the transformation of the dynamics found in capitalist societies can take place without formal institutional change. A process of functional conversion, whereby institutions are redirected to new purposes, can occur in the presence of formal institutional stability.[17] In other words, the practice associated with an institution can change without a similar transformation in its formal structure. Major changes in institutional practices are coupled with the stability in institutional structures. Third, the environment faced by firms is increasingly characterized by the presence of institutional hybridization with the consequence that advanced capitalist economies might no longer fit neatly into a single model. This process of hybridization can result from firms borrowing from the features of different models as the process of institutional adoption tends to be piecemeal rather than full scale.[18] These three lines of criticism constitute a serious challenge. If the VoC perspective's ability to explain institutional change is less successful than its account of divergence, its theoretical contribution would be seriously weakened.

What does my analysis of the investment patterns of institutional investors in France and Germany entail for the VoC theoretical perspective? The argument presented in this chapter testifies to the importance of national institutional frameworks for the study of institutional change. First, the transformation of corporate governance in France and Germany was deeply influenced by the character of existing institutional arrangements. Domestic institutions interact to complement each other and consequently cannot be studied in isolation regardless of whether one is analyzing the presence of stability or the occurrence of change in the broader institutional framework. The effects of a single institutional variable vary according to the presence of other institutions in the economy.[19] This is particularly true since institutional change is almost invariably piecemeal rather than full scale, thereby highlighting the importance of the interaction between the new institutions and those already in place. I recognize that processes of institutional conversion and hybridization can, and do, occur. Nonetheless, their occurrence still requires an argument to assess whether institutional conversion or hybridization constitutes a revolutionary or evolutionary transformation. The notion of interaction among the various elements of an institutional framework represents a highly helpful indicator to assess the consequences associated with the process of institutional transformation. Second, institutions are characterized by an element of latency, their effects and importance changing over time. In the case of France, for example, the firm-level institutional arrangements that are proving highly attractive for short-term, impatient capital cannot be held solely responsible for the inability of companies to access long-term finance since they have been largely stable over the last three decades. The present inability of firms to secure long-term, patient capital is a recent phenomenon, but the institutionally based concentration of power in the CEO is not something new. Prior to the mid1990s, the CEO's power was associated with the provision of long-term, patient capital in the form of bank loans since policymakers impeded the development of direct (bonds and stocks) finance, fixed interest rates at low levels, and implemented preferential credit policies.[20] The concentration of power in French firms, as embodied in the institutional arrangements of workplace organization, came to be conducive to short-term capital in the second half of the 1990s because of the deregulation of the banking system and the decision of long-term domestic shareholders to sell their holdings—as well as by the advent of the international strategy of institutional investors. International shifts came to have a substantial impact after internal changes in corporate governance.

Finally, and perhaps more importantly, I highlight in this chapter the need to distinguish between institutions and the mode of coordination that follows from these institutions.[21] I argue that the divergent patterns of investment of institutional investors were deeply influenced by differences in the power structure of French and German firms. But power concentration (diffusion) has been a stable feature of French (German) firms at the same time as tremendous changes in several institutional spheres took place. It is important to note that while institutions have undergone tremendous change in the two countries, the effects of this change on the mode of coordination of large blue-chip firms have been marginal.[22] In particular, the process by which large French and German firms develop and sustain their innovative capabilities has remained largely unchanged despite important changes in corporate governance. The coordination of activities in French firms is characterized by the vesting of unilateral authority in top managers and senior technical staff. The bulk of the workforce does not contribute to the development of the organizational capabilities of the firm.[23] In the coordination of activities of German companies, by contrast, authority is shared with the bulk of the workforce to a high degree. The development of innovative capabilities takes place on the basis of the long-term contribution of skilled employees through institutionalized career paths.[24] This stark divergence in the development of innovative capabilities remains stable despite impressive changes in corporate governance. Thus, the

presence of institutional hybridization and the occurrence of functional conversion are not sufficient to conclude that countries and firms are experiencing revolutionary developments that will undermine their nationally specific capacities for strategic coordination.

The roadmap for this chapter is the following. First, I provide an overview of the changes in the external environment in which French and German companies are embedded. Second, I empirically analyze the transformation of these two systems of corporate governance by highlighting the differences in the nature of foreign capital attracted by domestic companies in the two countries. Third, I highlight the critical importance of the institutions of workplace organization to account for the direction of change of corporate governance. Fourth, I conclude by presenting the theoretical implications for the analysis of institutional change that emerges from the study of French and German corporate governance.

I STRUCTURAL CHANGES IN EUROPEAN FINANCE

The French and German systems of corporate governance have experienced an important transformation resulting from a series of cumulatively far-reaching changes. These developments have decreased the importance of bank loans as a source of finance and have heightened the importance of stock markets. The two systems of corporate governance were previously characterized by three features. First, corporations had a high debt-equity ratio, i.e., bank loans were more important than stock issues as a source of external finance.[25] Second, the ownership structure of blue-chip firms was highly concentrated in the hands of friendly cross-shareholdings among companies, a large owner in the form of a family firm, banks' direct share and proxy voting in Germany, and extensive public sector in the French case.[26] Third, the market for corporate control was fairly restricted.[27] In particular, hostile takeovers were a rarity.

The bank-based system of corporate governance of the two countries crumbled under the impact of several factors. First, their financial system underwent a massive process of deregulation: the use of credit ceilings as a means to control inflation has been replaced by the discipline of central bank independence and of high real interest rates, capital controls have been removed under pressures from the EMS and the suspension of the dollar's convertibility into gold, and the bond market has been deregulated.[28] Second, the transformation of corporate governance is the result of developments that have raised the importance of equity capital. Two key factors account for the rise in importance of the stock market capitalization of firms. In the first place, the removal of capital controls by European policymakers enabled institutional investors to pursue a strategy of international diversification of their assets. The growth of foreign equity held by American institutional investors increased from $128.7 billion in 1988 to $178.7 billion in 2000.[29] The resulting impact of these developments on the strategy of large companies should not be underestimated. Institutional investors have expressed clear preferences for the adoption of shareholder value practices that maximize return on equity. Moreover, the rise of foreign ownership in the French case came at the expense of domestic cross-shareholdings among large domestic firms.[30]

Another development that has increased the importance of securities markets is the changing conditions associated with the successful completion of a takeover bid in the United States in the last decade. The importance of equity swap, whereby companies issue additional stocks to pay for the shares of the target firm, has increased dramatically. In 1988, nearly 60 percent of the total value of deals over $100 million in the United States was paid for entirely in cash. The similar figure for deals paid in stock was less than 2 percent. By contrast, about half of the value of large deals in 1998 was paid entirely in stock—and 17 percent was solely financed in cash.[31] What is the significance of the changing characteristics of takeover activity in the United States for European corporate governance? The importance of takeover activity in the United States for European corporate governance is intimately related to the process by which firms build their innovative capabilities. Large French and German firms are engaged in a process of institutional arbitrage.[32] They have sought to pursue radical types of innovation, thereby gaining access to new innovative capabilities, through the acquisition of companies in the United States via takeovers. Firms with higher stock market capitalization possess a substantial advantage in the global merger marketplace in using equity swap.[33]

II THE TRANSFORMATION OF FRENCH AND GERMAN CORPORATE GOVERNANCE: AN EMPIRICAL EVALUATION

The previous section has highlighted changes in the external financial environment of French and German firms. Anglo-American institutional investors are operating in the new European financial environment that is characterized by the importance of stock market capitalization for blue-chip companies. The greater mobility of capital and the strategy of international diversification of Anglo-American institutional investors, however, mask substantial divergence in regard to the composition of foreign ownership in France and Germany. First, the growth of securities markets in France has been far more impressive than that of Germany. The traditional measure of the importance of securities markets in an economy is the aggregate market capitalization of domestic companies divided by the gross domestic product. These figures on stock market capitalization are presented in Table 14.1. Equity finance was marginal in continental European countries associated with an insider model of corporate governance until the mid-1990s. The rates of growth of the stock market capitalization among advanced industrialized countries in the second half of the 1990s did not exhibit a common trajectory. France experienced a bigger explosion of its securities markets than Germany and Japan during the bull market of 1995–2001. Moreover, the relative decline of stock markets between 2000–2001 and 2003, and the reversal of this trend since 2003, also put France in a very favorable position. However, it is important to note that the growth of stock markets does not constitute the research question of this article. The focus is on the composition of foreign ownership of French and German companies under a new financial environment of heightened importance for the level of their stock market capitalization. Second, foreign ownership in France has grown significantly during the 1990s while the German picture is best characterized by a more modest progression. The foreign penetration of the French market increased from 17.4 to 36.1 percent from 1990 to 2000. The growth of foreign ownership in Germany, by contrast, remained largely stable from 22.7 to 23.6 percent for the same period.[34]

Third, an analysis of financial markets in Europe requires a nuanced understanding of the preferences and strategies of investors. Theoretical inferences cannot be drawn simply from the growing importance of capital mobility across borders since Anglo-American institutional investors do not constitute a monolithic bloc. I distinguish primarily between pension versus hedge and mutual funds. These three categories of investors possess preferences and time horizons that can clash or fit with the institutions of European companies. Pension funds constitute long-term investors that acquire an equity stake in corporations primarily for diversification purposes. The incentives of managers of pension funds lie in the generation of a certain minimum amount of revenues required to cover regular payments to retirees. Mutual funds, in contrast, possess a shorter-term horizon as they face greater liquidity concerns, since funds under their management are redeemable on demand by investors. Mutual fund managers seek to maximize assets under their management by picking firms undervalued in financial markets. Hedge funds are largely unregulated limited partnerships characterized by arbitrage strategies, high turnover and aggressive trading, and heightened managerial incentives to outperform financial benchmarks. Hedge funds collect funds from wealthy and more sophisticated investors willing to assume higher levels of risk for potentially superior returns.

The growth of foreign ownership in France and Germany has been characterized by substantial divergence in regard to its composition. Large firms in the two countries have been a favorite destination for the international diversification strategy of pension funds.[35] This reflects the fact that corporate law in the two countries provides an adequately acceptable level of financial transparency, a sufficient level of protection for minority shareholders, and that the quality of law enforcement is excellent.[36] Mutual and hedge funds, on the other hand, have primarily chosen France over Germany as a site for investment in continental Europe. I argue in the next section that the fit between the investment strategies of these two categories of investors and the institutional arrangements of advanced industrialized countries depends on the ability of the CEO and top managers to reorganize the workplace in a unilateral fashion. They fit well with the decision-making and adjustment processes in France, which is management-led with the exclusion of the workforce from the decision-making process. Workers possess fewer opportunities to block managerial initiatives.[37] French firm-level institutions are characterized by the concentration of power in the CEO that, in turn, allows for a rapid reorganization of the workplace under the guidance of a small number of corporate officials. The strategies of mutual and hedge funds, in contrast, do not fit well with the firm-level institutions found in Germany. Those institutions impose several constraints on the ability of management to develop and implement strategies in a unilateral fashion. The process of adjustment in Germany is the result of negotiation between management and employee representatives.[38] The rest of this section is divided in two parts. First, I provide an overview of the differences between these three groups of investors. Second, I present data on the presence of mutual and hedge funds in the two countries.

A. Hedge, mutual, and pension funds

Four features set apart these groups of institutional investors with systematic consequences for comparative corporate governance: mode of collecting funds and issuing payments, time horizon and liquidity constraints, managerial incentives, and process of picking portfolio companies. First, a key difference between these types of institutional investors lies in their mode

	1980	1985	1990	1995	1999	2001	2002	2003	2004
France	8	15	26	35	105	103	68	93	110
Germany	9	29	22	28	68	61	35	54	62
Japan	36	71	99	81	102	73	52	74	N/A
United Kingdom	37	77	87	98	198	166	114	148	178
United States	48	57	56	78	181	152	106	134	150

Source: World Bank, *World Development Indicators* (New York: World Bank, various years); and Christoph Van Der Elst, "The Equity Markets, Ownership Structures and Control: Towards an International Harmonization?" in *Capital Markets and Company Law*, ed. Klaus Hopt and Eddy Wymeersch (New York: Oxford University Press, 2003), 11.

Table 14.1 **Evolution of market capitalization as percentage of GDP, 1980–2004**

of collecting funds and issuing payments "held in trust" for the beneficiaries. Defined benefits (DB) schemes guarantee the level of benefits the fund will pay and the method of determining those benefits, but not the amount of the contributions. DB schemes guarantee a fixed payment in the future. Defined contribution (DC) schemes, on the other hand, specify the level of contributions but not the amount of the benefits to be paid. The amount available to the beneficiaries results from both the portfolio performance and the amount initially invested. The existence of an almost perfect correlation characterizes the relationship between the method of collecting funds and the type of institutional investors. Pension funds are relying, to a substantial extent, on a DB scheme to collect and distribute assets.[39] The assets of mutual funds, by contrast, are managed almost exclusively on a DC scheme.[40] This is not surprising since mutual funds are investment companies that pool funds from individuals and corporations with the provision that the money invested is redeemable on demand.[41] The funds paid to investors are dependent on the market performance of the mutual fund. Moreover, it is also important to note that pension funds do manage directly only a small percentage of the assets collected by them. The pension fund industry is increasingly dominated by reliance on mutual fund managers for asset management since 401(k) plans allow firms to more easily outsource direct contribution pension plans to external DC fund managers.

Second, the time horizon of institutional investors diverges considerably in regard to their patterns of trading. The annual average turnover rate of American public pension funds in 1997 was 19.3 percent.[42] The similar figure for mutual fund managers and external money managers was 42.5 percent.[43] The time horizons of the largest mutual funds, in particular, are considerably short.[44] The average amount of time a share is held for Fidelity and Templeton (mutual funds) were respectively 2.63 and 2.22 years in 1999.[45] By contrast, most public pension funds have longer-term horizons as witnessed by their turnover rates: Florida state (12.5 years) and California State Teachers (7.6 years).[46]

Hedge funds also display reliance on short-term trading, albeit in a different way from mutual funds.[47] The investment strategies of hedge funds entail high turnover and aggressive trading on short-lived information, but not because of liquidity concerns. Investors face an initial lock-up period of one year and subsequent restrictions to quarterly intervals. Instead,

the short-time horizon of hedge funds results from their investment strategies. Hedge funds practice statistical arbitrage that involves balancing positions in assets (equity, government bonds, and national currencies) that are believed to be undervalued against others that are expected to fall in value. Hedge funds are putting bets that an asset will go above a designated target or will fall below it. They tend to quickly sell their positions in assets once these targets have been reached, thereby accounting for their propensity to rely on a short-term trading strategy.

Third, the incentives of fund managers are strikingly different. Increases in the level of the financial compensation of fund managers can come from maximizing the value of assets under management or from attracting new flows of funds. In other words, managerial remuneration is based on the volume of assets under management and on the performance of the portfolio. Public pension fund managers, however, face constraints that deter them from maximizing the value of their portfolio. The first constraint consists of state regulations that impose caps on the salary of managers.[48] In other words, the link between compensation and size of assets under management does not hold above a certain level— thereby resulting in overall lower salaries for public pension fund managers. Moreover, the number of beneficiaries in public fund schemes is limited by the size of the contributing workforce—a factor over which public pension fund managers have no control. The second constraint on public pension fund managers lies in the absence of any financial incentives tied to fund performance. The primary objective of DB public pension funds is to generate a certain minimum amount of revenues through the management of the assets under their control. Contributions are determined actuarially on the basis of the level of the benefits expected to become payable to the retirees. Fund managers earn a civil service salary and would not receive proportional extra rewards for achieving returns beyond the mandated averages.[49] Finally, public pension fund managers are elected state officials or political appointees facing different types of pressure from their mutual and hedge fund counterparts.[50]

The incentives faced by mutual/hedge fund managers stand at the opposite end of the spectrum. The compensation for mutual fund managers is based on a percentage of assets under management without any caps.[51] Moreover, the behavior of investors in mutual funds exhibits a marked tendency to flock to "winners." Funds displaying high returns during an assessment period will experience an inward surge of new investment inflows in subsequent periods. In particular, capital inflows are highly correlated with a fund outperforming a market benchmark. Managers desirous of increasing the value of the fund—and to augment their compensation—face highly powerful incentives to increase the size of assets under management by increasing the flows of new investment. This strategy invariably entails the revision of the composition of the portfolio.[52] As well as being relative to the performance of other funds, the compensation of mutual fund managers is driven by internal performance and rankings. Numerous mutual funds are using a ranking system to evaluate their managers. At Fidelity, for example, each manager's returns are compared to benchmarks reflecting the risk specificity of the particular fund they manage.[53] Finally, hedge fund managers possess serious financial incentives to "beat" average market returns. As their mutual funds counterparts, managers of hedge funds are also compensated on the basis of the volume of assets under management and are given mandates to beat recognized financial benchmarks. However, the financial incentives of hedge fund managers differ in one fundamental way from those prevalent at mutual funds. Their compensation comprises both substantial incentive fees as well as the amount of assets under management, the former being paid only in the event of a positive return. The typical remuneration of hedge fund managers is characterized by 1 to 2 percent of assets under management and 5 to 25 percent of profits realized.[54]

Fourth, the criteria and processes by which funds select companies for investment also differ, thereby resulting in a different composition of the stock portfolio. The composition of the stock portfolio for the great majority of pension funds is increasingly based on an index strategy. The growing recourse to indexing reflects their assessment that active management of the equity portfolio produces results inferior to market indexing. Pension funds often lack the firm-specific knowledge needed to take actions aimed at transforming the strategy of portfolio companies. Mutual funds, by contrast, do not acquire an equity stake in a corporation because it is part of an index. Managers are in stiff competition with other funds for the assets of investors that, in turn, can be redeemed at any moment. The structural characteristics of the mutual fund industry compel managers to achieve high returns, not simply matching an index. Mutual

funds behave like stock pickers and are in many ways the mirror image of DB pension funds.[55] Finally, the compensation of hedge funds managers derives from the amount of assets under management and, to a substantial extent, from incentive fees. These incentive fees are paid only in the event of the returns on the portfolio exceeding financial benchmarks. The raison d'être of hedge funds is to pursue flexible and aggressive strategies that entail above-normal risks and potentially high returns.

The importance of specific firms for the overall financial performance of the fund also illustrates the differences in the composition of the portfolio of mutual and pension funds. The use of an index as an investment strategy by pension funds entails that their aim is to reproduce as closely as possible the economic profile of a sector/country. The investment strategy of mutual funds, in contrast, aims at picking undervalued firms that are likely to outperform the market in the short term. These different investment strategies, in turn, entail diverging degrees of dependence on the performance of specific portfolio companies. The top portfolio companies for mutual funds account for a greater percentage of their overall investment than the top portfolio companies for pension funds.[56] The financial returns of mutual funds are more dependent on the performance of a selected number of portfolio companies than they are for pension funds.[57]

B. Presence of mutual and hedge funds in France and Germany

I computed data on the presence of mutual and hedge funds in France and Germany with the use of two indicators. The first indicator is related to the disclosure requirements of listed companies. EU regulation requires shareholders owning 5 percent or more of the outstanding equity capital of a corporation to notify the national securities regulations authorities. I recorded data on equity stake above the 5 percent threshold from September 1997 to May 2005 for both France and Germany.[58] I recorded every instance of acquisitions of equity capital over the 5 percent threshold by hedge and mutual funds under the following conditions. First, I discarded acquisitions above the 5 percent threshold by subsidiaries of non-financial firms from the database. Second, my sample is composed of domestically based firms in France and Germany. Third, I also discarded movements of capital above and below the 5 percent threshold within a thirty-day period. Some funds have adopted a policy of automatic sale of stocks if their equity stake goes above the mandatory disclosure requirement. Moreover, movements above and below the 5 percent threshold might reflect a share buyback program by a portfolio corporation rather than an intended strategy by an institutional investor. Fourth, I selected equity capital in a firm rather than voting rights as the indicator of movement of capital above the 5 percent threshold. Finally, I cross-checked the data collected by relying on two national business directories: DAFSA Annuaire des Sociétés for France and Rudiger Liedtke's Wem Gehört die Republik for Germany.[59] These two annual publications provide a full list of shareholders of listed companies and serve as useful reliability check mechanisms.

Data on the presence of short-term institutional investors in France and Germany reveal striking patterns of divergence. The attractiveness of France over Germany is evident as mutual and hedge funds have invested massively in the former, as measured by the overall number of stakes over the 5 percent threshold.[60] For the top twenty French firms by market capitalization, ten of them recorded twenty-five instances of investment over the 5 percent threshold by short-term Anglo-Saxon institutional investors. Because a firm can receive more than one investment from a single institutional investor, the number of investments is always higher than the number of companies receiving investment. For the top twenty German firms by market capitalization, only five of them recorded twelve instances of investment over the 5 percent threshold by Anglo-Saxon institutional investors. For the top forty firms in the two markets, twenty-six French firms recorded sixty-six instances of investment over the 5 percent threshold; the corresponding figures for Germany were twelve firms and twenty-four acquisitions. For the top eighty companies, fifty-two French firms recorded 139 instances of investment over the 5 percent threshold; the corresponding figures for Germany were twenty-eight and forty-eight. For blue-chip companies, therefore, twice as many French firms recorded an investment from short-term Anglo-Saxon institutional investors than their German counterparts: and their total overall number of acquisitions was a little less than three times those recorded for German companies.[61]

The second source of data concerning the presence of short-term institutional investors is taken from the analysis performed by Morningstar, Inc., the Chicago-based rating agency. Morningstar, Inc., is the leading provider of independent research on American mutual funds and is highly influential with investors. Data on the importance of mutual funds is collected from *Morningstar Funds 500*, an annual publication that evaluates the performance of the biggest 500 funds in the United States. Most of the funds covered in this publication have assets invested in domestic stocks and bonds.[62] About seventy-five funds per year are involved in international equity. For each of these internationally oriented funds, *Morningstar Funds 500* lists the five top countries of exposure.

I compiled data on the importance of the French and German markets by computing the number of times they appear among the top three foreign investment destinations of individual mutual funds. I also collected for comparability purposes data for the United Kingdom, a liberal market economy with a system of corporate governance most similar to that of the United States. The results are presented in Table 14.2. The attractiveness of the French market over that of Germany for mutual funds is further confirmed. Investment in France is almost twice as important as investment in Germany in regard to country of exposure of internationally oriented American mutual funds.

The conclusion that German workplace institutions deter short-term investors receives further confirmation from a comparison of the price/earnings (p/e) ratio of companies. German firms possess an overall lower p/e ratio than their French counterparts (see Table 14.3). The p/e ratio is an indicator of how cheap or expensive the shares of a company are. It is calculated by dividing the price per share by its earnings per share. The p/e ratio is a valuation of the firm's share price compared to its per-share earnings. It shows how much shareholders are willing to pay per dollar of earnings. The higher p/e ratio of French firms indicates that value investors must pay relatively more for a given amount of earnings as compared to in the German market. In other words, the attractiveness of French firms for short-term, impatient capital cannot be attributed to low share price compared to per-share earnings. But the higher p/e ratios of French firms also reflect the expectations of higher streams of earnings in the future. Growth investors have expressed higher confidence in the future earnings stream of French companies.[63] Further confirmation of the divergent attractiveness of the two countries is also provided by anecdotal evidence from practitioners. The concerns of institutional investors of the French market have tended to revolve around the questions of unequal voting rights and the lack of financial transparency—two issues that are dear to pension funds who rely on publicly available mechanisms to monitor portfolio firms.[64] German firms have largely met the preferences of foreign institutional investors on these two issues. By contrast, hedge and mutual funds have expressed concerns about corporate and workplace governance in Germany.[65] Their fear is that employees can act as insiders with management—a situation less likely to occur in France, as the discussion in the next section will illustrate. That fear, moreover, has to be contrasted against evidence that one category of shareholders, namely, long-term pension funds, has been able to act as a coalition partner with German employees against instances of managerial opportunism.[66]

III FIRM-LEVEL INSTITUTIONS IN FRANCE AND GERMANY

The lack of convergence in the composition of foreign ownership of French and German firms, as documented in the previous section, reflects in great part the ability of companies to attract capital from the world's biggest investors, namely, mutual and hedge funds. The argument presented in this section is that the firm-level institutions of companies provide different degrees of fit with the preferences and strategies of these investors. I argue that the degree of fit between the investment strategies of mutual/hedge funds and the firm-level institutions of advanced industrialized nations reflects the ability of the CEO and top managers to reorganize the workplace in a unilateral fashion. The divergence in the institutional arrangements of firm-level organization between France and Germany impacts on the ability of

Year	Germany	France	United Kingdom
1997	9	24	39
1998	22	39	56
1999	7	26	48
2000	10	29	52
2001	11	22	50
2002	6	31	46
2003	8	20	53
2004	8	25	53
2005	3	20	51

Source: Adapted from Michel Goyer, "Institutional Investors in French and German Corporate Governance," working paper (Cambridge, Mass.: Center for European Studies at Harvard University, 2006), Table 7.

Table 14.2 **Number of times countries appear among the top three foreign investment destinations of individual mutual funds**

Year	DAX 30 (Germany)	CAC 40 (France)	DAX 100 (Germany)	SBF 120 (France)
1998	21.7	21.7	N/A	21.4
1999	19.4	22.4	14.1	21.3
2000	24.9	28.2	16.9	27.1
2001	17.7	16.6	20.8	16.5
2002	18.8	19.3	12.4	19.0
2003	10.6	13.5	11.2	13.3
2004	12.1	15.6	19.1	16.0
2005	11.0	13.9	15.2	14.5

Source: Adapted from Michel Goyer, "Institutional Investors in French and German Corporate Governance," working paper (Cambridge, Mass.: Center for European Studies at Harvard University, 2006), Table 8.

Table 14.3 **Price-earnings ratio, French and German stocks**

management to implement reorganization schemes in a unilateral manner, thereby providing specific incentives for the managers of mutual and hedge funds. The short-time horizon of these investors does fit well with the decision-making and adjustment processes of large French firms—which are management-led and provide the workforce with fewer opportunities to block managerial initiatives.[67] The primary goal of mutual and hedge funds is to convince the CEO of the value of specific strategic changes. This is because the implementation of restructuring policies requires, almost solely, the CEO's approval given that employees have no means of intervention for employees. The diffusion of power inside German firms, by contrast, means that the consent of works councils as well as that of top management are necessary for the introduction of new strategies.[68] The legal rights of works councils and the regulations regarding training provide employees with means to derail unwanted measures.[69]

The rest of this section is organized in the following manner. First, I identify the institutional arrangements of firm-level organization that stand prominently in illustrating the concentration of power at the top of French companies and the constraints on managerial autonomy in Germany. I discuss two key areas of firm-level organization—skill certification and formation, and segmentation of activities and the autonomy of employees in problem-solving tasks. Second, I analyze how these institutional arrangements shape the adjustment process of companies which, in turn, provides for different degrees of fit with the preferences and strategies of funds.

A. Training and the building of firm competencies

The first key firm-level institutions are those related to the process of skill formation and certification of the workforce, i.e., training. The matching of jobs and worker competencies in the two countries shapes, in different ways, the ability of management to implement restructuring measures in a unilateral manner. The German economy is organized around the presence of a majority of employees with certifiable skills as a strategy for firms to develop their capabilities. By contrast, French companies build their competencies around mid-level management and technical specialists rather than investing in the improvement of the skills of the bulk of the workforce.

The divergent method of coupling tasks and competencies is first reflected in the role of vocational training in the two countries. Vocational training is prominent in Germany and relatively neglected in France. The German system of occupational training is both prominent and autonomous. A substantially higher proportion of workers in Germany have received some vocational training. In 1995, the average number of trainees for large German firms (over 500 employees) was six per 100 workers with a retention rate of 85 percent.[70] The corresponding figure for large French companies was 2.2 per 100 workers in 1996 with a retention rate of 35 percent.[71] Second, the different patterns by which competencies and jobs are matched in the two countries are also visible throughout the entire career of employees—and are not simply limited to vocational training. The qualification of German employees determines the definition of jobs. The access to a majority of jobs in large firms is based upon the holding of a recognized diploma or qualification. Training is invariably a prerequisite for employment and promotion.[72] The influence of firm-level works councils is paramount, as they have consistently insisted that different types of occupations should be associated with different levels of skills. Managers cannot move employees within the firm without prior appropriate training. The promotion process in German firms reflects the acquisition of the required technical expertise and completion of the relevant training. This process ensures that the authority of projects managers rests on technical competence and is not based on their access to higher levels of managerial authority. By contrast, French employers use their own criteria to define jobs to which employees adapt either in training programs (blue collar) or through the obtainment of university diplomas (white collar), the promotion system of French firms being a reflection of a change of status unilaterally decided by top management rather than being the acquisition of technical expertise. The relationship between training and promotion is reversed in France. Management selects workers to be promoted, and then provides them with the appropriate training.[73] Firms provide in-house training for employees who usually have a substantial experience.

The German training system, moreover, is well established and autonomous from managerial interference—in addition to being prominent. The presence of a majority of workers with certifiable skills in the German economy is legally based and protected from outside intervention.[74] First, a high number of jobs require certifiable skills that are acquired in vocational training programs. Second, industrial or regional chambers must certify the training programs of firms, and any change in the content of training certification—the modification of an existing certification or the introduction of a new one—requires the approval of a body of experts in which national industrial unions occupy half of the seats. In turn, works councils have been instrumental in setting training standards as well as overseeing the implementation of training programs in the firm. The veto power of employees on the board of the industrial and regional training commissions prevents significant modifications of the system and ensures a stable demand for certified employees. Third, firm-level works councils possess a full veto power over hiring, thereby constraining managerial ability to rely on outside experts.[75] New jobs must be offered first to the current members of the workforce. In other words, the position of organized labor and the works councils in the training system has enabled them to impose significant constraints on hiring new employees when a company scaled back its activities to a few core competencies: since new training programs have to be approved by an expert body in which organized labor holds half of the seats, they have de facto veto power over these programs. The institutions of training constrain management on several fronts: skills are a prerequisite for jobs, management must provide the relevant training to employees, the content of these programs must be certified by an outside body where labor possesses a veto, and the hiring of new employees with the requisite skills is subject to the approval of works councils.

By contrast, the development of the core competencies of French firms is not based on the skills of the bulk of the workforce. The educational system remains the primary mechanism by which employees are assigned to skilled positions.[76] The French case is characterized by the absence of legal requirement to assign specific jobs to workers with certifiable skills. First, attempts by state officials to impose the recognition of training (vocational or on the job) as a prerequisite for holding jobs have been defeated by French employers.[77] As discussed above, managers use their own criteria to define jobs to which employees adapt either through participation in training programs (blue collar) or through the obtainment of university diplomas (white collar). The content of training and the place of employees in the production

process represent areas of pure managerial prerogative.[78] Second, boards of experts (business associations and employee committees) on training play a simple consultative role.[79] In the case of vocational training, moreover, it is the Ministry of Education that is responsible for the elaboration of the standards. Third, firm-level works councils possess limited information rights on the hiring of new staff—not a full veto power that could prevent employers from replacing current workers with new employees.[80] Relying on outside experts has, in fact, proven to be a privileged strategy of adjustment for French companies.[81]

B. Work Organization and the Segmentation of Activities

The second major difference between the organization of the workplace in France and Germany concerns the extent to which activities are segmented, i.e., the degree of managerial control over the organization of the production process, especially in regard to how employers rely on the bulk of the workforce in organizing and carrying out tasks.[82] The French case is characterized by the segmentation of production activities and responsibilities between blue-collar employees and managers, a rather rigid system of rules, and an emphasis on narrow and specialized skills.[83] Firms rely on the presence of rules that regulate the nature of the tasks to be accomplished—rather than the functions to be performed—to organize the production process.[84] The implementation of the firm strategy is accomplished through numerous sets of rules designed to specify the terms of exchange among parties. The organization of work is divided into fragmentary tasks. Highly qualified engineers elaborate the conception of products, and employees carry out the tasks following instructions.[85] The separation between planning and execution limits the ability of blue-collar employees to participate in the conduct of the business strategy of the firm since they possess a limited view of its operations. This limitation, in turn, contributes to the concentration of power at the top of the managerial hierarchy.

The initial rationale for this specific organization of the workplace in France is best explained by Crozier's notion of the avoidance of face-to-face relationships and Hofstede's classification of France as a country in which individualism ranks high as a value.[86] The

French propensity for uncertainty avoidance, combined with the antagonistic nature of industrial relations, led firms to adopt mechanisms designed both to prevent the involvement of employees in the conduct of the strategy of the firm as well as to protect them from unpredictable and unwarranted intrusion. However, the advent of firm-level flexibility and the increasing importance of microprocessor technology did raise the costs associated with the maintenance of this separation between elaboration and implementation of tasks. The need for companies to adapt quickly to a changing environment requires a change of attitude of workers. Employees must enter into a dialogue with management and different functional departments in order to achieve flexibility, quality, and speed. Consequently, greater participation by employees in the modification of their environment has taken place inside large French companies in the last fifteen years.[87] Employees are given a greater choice of tasks by management. They have become more involved in problem solving and contribute in monitoring and evaluating performance, as more is expected of them from management.[88] Nonetheless, the separation between planning and execution is still predominant and the organization of work has not lost its key Fordist component.[89] Shop floor restructuring in the last fifteen years might have provided for greater employee involvement, but does not allow for their influence over what tasks they perform and the conditions under which work takes place. Hierarchical relationships are still predominant inside French firms.[90]

The organization of work in Germany, on the other hand, is more straightforward and characterized by the application of rules to broad functions, rather than by trying to predict contingencies on the shop floor through heavy reliance on explicit instructions. The predominance of employees with certifiable skills and the subsequent reliance of management on the bulk of the workforce as a strategy to develop the capabilities of the firm constitute critical factors that have bridged the gap between conception and implementation in Germany.[91] The role of training is particularly important in this process as employees are grouped according to the types of qualifications they possess, and tasks are organized according to their skill requirements.[92] The outcome is one where the institutional arrangements of the workplace are characterized by blurred organizational boundaries and reduced segmentation, the delegation of control over the nature of work processes resulting in the involvement of employees in many tasks.[93]

The differences exhibited by French and German companies in regard to the separation of task execution and implementation, in turn, impact on the extent to which workers exercise discretion over how tasks are performed and their ability to contribute to problem solving. The institutional arrangements of workplace organization in Germany provide for substantial autonomy in the definition of tasks and autonomy in their implementation.[94] High levels of authority sharing, the development of firm competencies via the institutions of training, and the involvement of workers beyond the managerial hierarchy in the elaboration of the strategy of the firm link the fate of employees to that of management.[95] Skilled employees possess strong incentives to develop problem-solving capabilities, given the firm-specific stakes of their career development. Moreover, the capabilities of German employees are shaped in a profound manner by the content of their skills. The involvement of employer associations in the certification process ensures that skills would be relevant to their strategic needs. The involvement of national union representatives in the certification process, on the other hand, ensures that skills will be of general character and fit with broad job descriptions.[96] The content of the skill certification of employees is not tightly connected to specific jobs. Finally, the use of job rotations enhances the degree of polyvalence of German employees, thereby increasing their capabilities to engage in problem-solving tasks.[97] Job rotation allows companies to rely on employees with broad skills to tackle shifts in work demands.[98] The degree of polyvalence of workers is high since the organization of the workplace favors the acquisition of broad-based skills.[99]

The institutional arrangements of workplace organization in France, by contrast, do not contribute to the development of the firm-specific problem-solving capabilities of employees. First, job rotations in French enterprises are less frequent than in Germany.[100] The working life of employees tends to be associated with specific tasks, therefore leading to segmentation of work roles and functional specialization. Second, job demarcations are stricter. The segmentation of the activities of the firm between elaboration and execution and the narrow skills of French employees entail that they possess a limited view of the totality of the operations of the firm and rely on top management for coordination. Their ability to develop firm-specific problem-solving capabilities are seriously limited since they have a limited view of the operations of the firm.[101] The process of problem solving is management-led with the involvement of a few highly qualified technical specialists.

C. Firm-level institutional arrangements and paths of adjustment

The firm-level institutional arrangements of German firms place serious constraints on the ability of managers to conduct the business strategy of the firm in a unilateral manner. Nonetheless, companies have exhibited flexibility in adjusting internally to shifts in demand on markets—although not in a manner that fits well with the preferences of mutual and hedge funds. Firms have traditionally responded to the volatility of markets by redeploying the capabilities of employees to new uses—instead of relying on firings and other types of market-based adjustments. This adjustment process is possible because the skills of employees are broad enough to accomplish a wide range of tasks in a context where labor laws make it difficult to proceed to dismissals. Broad skills and blurred organizational boundaries provide employees with the skills for problem-solving activities.[102] Training curricula and regulations are broadly defined to avoid overspecialization in narrow skill assignments, and the blurring of boundaries and responsibilities allows employees to switch between different functions. The skills of employees shape their ability to solve problems that, in turn, present management with opportunities to reorganize the production process. The possession of broad skills by employees provides German companies with the capacity for retooling in response to new market demands.[103] This strategy, however, does not fit well with the preferences and tactics of mutual/hedge funds. The redeployment of the skills of employees to new economic circumstances is unlikely to be accomplished as rapidly as external mechanisms of adjustment that rely on dismissals and other types of market-based adjustment. This is particularly true in times of rapid technological change that require a radical transformation in skill content. The German system is plagued by serious rigidities. The introduction of a new product invariably gives rise to jurisdictional disputes between various employees.[104] The respective role to be performed by each of the skill categories in the introduction of new products must be bargained out.[105]

The centralized and functionally differentiated work organization of large French firms, on the other hand, militates against experimentation with skill redeployment. It instead entails a separation between categories of workers: a small number of highly qualified employees sealed off from the implementation process, and the bulk of the workforce composed of low-skilled workers with narrowly specialized tasks that cannot be redeployed with unpredictable shifts in demand. The importance of the failure of state officials to impose the recognition of training as a prerequisite for holding specific jobs becomes apparent in this context. Differences in training between France and Germany are not simply a quantitative issue—i.e., more workers possessing certified skills in the latter. Despite state regulation that imposes a legal obligation on French firms to spend a percentage of their wage bill on training, flows of funds have been concentrated on managerial staff with already high levels of skill.[106] The sharp segmentation of production activities and responsibilities between blue-collar employees and managers, a rigid system of rules, and the emphasis on narrow and specialized skills limit the ability of workers to participate in the conduct of the business strategy, thereby lessening the dependence of management on the skills of the bulk of the workforce.

CONCLUSIONS AND IMPLICATIONS

The argument presented in this chapter has several implications for the study of comparative corporate governance and national models of capitalism under conditions of financial globalization and increasing capital mobility across borders. The chapter took a two-pronged approach to these issues by asking the following: what accounts for the diverging ability of French and German firms to attract capital from Anglo-Saxon investors, and what are the consequences associated with the growth of foreign ownership? The issue of accounting for institutional change and its effects has become critical for comparative political economists, given that the field has long focused on using institutions to account for divergence across countries. The argument of this chapter has highlighted the continuing usefulness of taking seriously institutional frameworks as an independent variable for middle-range theoretical projects. Key institutions (workplace organization) constitute the single most important variable to account for change in the specific case of the foreign ownership structure of French and German firms.

First, institutional arrangements interact to complement each other and consequently cannot be studied in isolation, whether analyzing the presence of stability or the occurrence of change in the broader institutional framework of countries.[107] The introduction of a profound institutional change in the ownership structure of French and German companies does not annul the theoretical importance of institutions. Substantial institutional differences remain in other areas, and these persisting cross-national differences form a distinctive constellation that produces different outcomes across nations. The impact associated with institutional change on the overall operation of the political economy is dependent on the interaction of the new institutions with those already in place, as institutional change is almost invariably piecemeal rather than full-scale. This is a significant and worthy aspect of analysis, since the occurrence of institutional change is not sufficient in order to assess whether change is evolutionary or radical.[108] Different processes of change (abrupt and incremental) can both result in an evolutionary or radical transformation of the system.

Second, the institutions of workplace organization in the two countries have become more salient in the new context of financial globalization after having been characterized by an element of latency prior to financial deregulation.[109] The long-term cross-national differences in work organization contributed to the differences in the patterns of economic specialization of the two countries, but they had nothing to do with the ownership structure of large domestic companies given the lack of international diversification of Anglo-Saxon investors prior to the early to mid-1990s. This last point about latency illustrates quite well the importance of the interactive effects associated with an institutional matrix. Prior to the mid-1990s, France and Germany were two bank-based financial systems with long-term patient capital despite differences in the institutions of workplace organization. The provision of patient capital in France was previously made possible through a combination of state regulation of the banking sector that facilitated access to long-term capital through bank loans, and cross-shareholdings among large companies.[110] The deregulation of the banking sector and the decline of cross-shareholdings in France entail that the provision of long-term capital in the form of debt finance is no longer available; it has instead been replaced by the presence of short-term, impatient capital. A key insight is that while the institutions of workplace organization have not

fundamentally changed, the external environment in which they are embedded has. The concentration of power in top management was previously interacting with state policies and patterns of cross-shareholdings that enabled firms to have access to long-term capital. This outcome contrasts with the German situation. The provision of long-term capital in Germany resulted from concentrated ownership and the ability of shareholders to monitor companies via non-market mechanisms. The provision of long-term capital has not been affected by recent developments. The ownership concentration of large companies has remained intact despite the increasing importance of Anglo-American pension funds that are, moreover, themselves long-term owners.[111]

Third, the theoretical importance of the degree of power concentration associated with the institutions of workplace organization as an explanation of the ability of companies to attract foreign capital is contingent upon its resilience and its ability to sustain cross-national comparisons. The research design of this article and the ability to draw causal inferences would be uncertain if both the power concentration inside companies and the ownership structure of large firms had changed in recent years, given the problem of over-determination. The degree of power concentration of large French and German companies, and the process by which they develop their innovative capabilities, have been relatively stable and exhibited striking differences between the two countries for the last thirty years despite changes in ownership structure. A key insight of this chapter is that one must distinguish between the character of coordination of firms and the institutional framework that supports it.[112] Change in the former does not entail a modification in the latter. The sustainability of national models of corporate governance and capitalism cannot rest on the total absence of institutional change. The presence of institutional change does not imply inertia.[113] Instead, the central issue is whether the transformation of the ownership structure of large firms sustains their mode of coordination and the complementarities of the model.

The distribution of power of French and German companies has remained stable over a period of time in which their ownership structure underwent a significant transformation. The mode of coordination of the activities of large companies in the two countries is best understood by analyzing the process by which they develop and sustain their innovative competences. The development of innovative capabilities by firms requires the involvement of employees in complex problem-solving activities as well as the ability to develop a viable strategy that will enable them to compete in different sectors and technology. However, the nature of the integration of employees in the development of organizational capabilities varies quite sharply between France and Germany. The coordination of activities in large French companies is characterized by the vesting of unilateral authority in top managers and senior staff. The acquisition of new competences often takes place through the hiring of specialists on external labor markets. The bulk of the workforce does not contribute to the development of the organizational learning capabilities of the firm. The hierarchical patterns of differentiation and the concentration of power inside French companies not only reflect organizational politics, but also constitute the key mode of coordination by which they develop their competitive competences. The coordination of activities of large German firms, in contrast, involves high levels of authority sharing with the bulk of the workforce. The development of innovative capabilities takes place on the basis of the long-term contribution of skilled employees through institutionalized career paths. Continuing job rotations across functions as well as lateral coordination enable the bulk of employees to contribute to the improvement of the organizational problem-solving capabilities of firms. The rise of foreign ownership in France and Germany does not constitute a challenge to the mode of coordination of large domestic firms; it does contribute to reinforce the process of development of their innovative capabilities. I argue in this chapter that the relative attractiveness of French and German firms for Anglo-American institutional investors is shaped by the different institutional arrangements of workplace organization and the power relationships embodied in them. The concentration of power in the CEO of French companies is valued by mutual and hedge funds, since it makes it easier to reorganize the strategy of the firm quickly—a key aspect of the preferences of this type of investors given their short-time horizons. By contrast, the relative absence of mutual and hedge funds, coupled with the growing strength of pension funds with their demands for financial transparency and long-term horizon, constitutes a stabilizing factor for the institutional arrangements of workplace organization of German companies. The globalization of financial markets and the greater mobility of capital across borders have not undermined the institutions of work

organization in France and Germany, a key feature of these two distinctive models of capitalism.

NOTES

1   A good overview of the causes and dynamics of recent corporate scandals in Europe and the United States is provided in John Coffee, "A Theory of Corporate Scandals: Why the USA and Europe Differ," *Oxford Review of Economic Policy* 21, no. 2 (Summer 2005): 198–211.

2   Excellent analyses of the political dimensions of the transformation of national systems of corporate governance are Peter Gourevitch and James Shinn, *Political Power and Corporate Control: The New Global Politics of Corporate Governance* (Princeton, N.J.: Princeton University Press, 2005); and Mark Roe, "Political Preconditions to Separating Ownership from Corporate Control," *Stanford Law Review* 53, no. 3 (December 2000): 539–606.

3   For comprehensive overviews of the rise of shareholder value practices in France and Germany, see Richard Deeg, "The Comeback of Modell Deutschland?" *German Politics* 14, no. 3 (September 2005): 332–53; Michel Goyer, "Corporate Governance, Employees, and Core Competencies in France and Germany," in *Global Markets, Domestic Institutions: Corporate Law and Governance in a New Era of Cross-Border Deals*, ed. Curtis Milhaupt (New York: Columbia University Press, 2003); and Martin Hoepner, "Corporate Governance in Transition: Ten Empirical Findings on Shareholder Value and Industrial Relations in Germany," Discussion Paper no. 01/5 (Cologne: Max Planck Institute, 2001). For a theoretical overview of the issue of convergence in corporate governance, see Ruth Aguilera and Gregory Jackson, "The Cross-National Diversity of Corporate Governance: Dimensions and Determinants," *Academy of Management Review* 28, no. 3 (July 2003): 432–46.

4   John Campbell, *Institutional Change and Globalization* (Princeton, N.J.: Princeton University Press, 2004).

5   The case for divergence is best asserted in Suzanne Berger, "Introduction," in *National Diversity and Global Capitalism*, ed. Suzanne Berger and Ronald Dore (Ithaca, N.Y.: Cornell University Press, 1996); and Peter Hall and David Soskice, "An Introduction to Varieties of Capitalism," in *Varieties of Capitalism: The Institutional Foundations of Comparative Advantage*, ed. Peter Hall and David Soskice (New York: Oxford University Press, 2001).

6   See Campbell, *Institutional Change and Globalization*, 1–9; and Douglass North, *Understanding the Process of Economic Change* (Princeton, N.J.: Princeton University Press, 2005).

7   Excellent analyses of patterns of adjustment in French firms are Bob Hancké, *Large Firms and Industrial Adjustment: Industrial Renewal and Economic Restructuring in France* (New York: Oxford University Press, 2002); and Vivien Schmidt, *From State to the*

Market? The Transformation of French Business under Mitterrand (New York: Cambridge University Press, 1996).

8   The key readings on the negotiated process of firm-level adjustment in Germany are Wolfgang Streeck, *Social Institutions and Economic Performance* (London: Sage, 1992); and Kathleen Thelen, *Unions of Parts: Labor Politics in Postwar Germany* (Ithaca, N.Y.: Cornell University Press, 1991).

9   The classic statement on the Varieties of Capitalism theoretical perspective is Hall and Soskice, "An Introduction to Varieties of Capitalism," 1–71.

10 Hall and Soskice argue that two dominant clusters of interdependent institutions exist: liberal market economies and coordinated market economies. These two clusters constitute different ways to solve coordination problems faced by firms—market instruments being predominant in the former, while a greater range of institutions such as peak associations, network monitoring based on the exchange of private information, and relational contracting constitute the hallmarks of adjustment processes for the latter.

11 See Peter Hall and Daniel Gingerich, "Varieties of Capitalism and Institutional Complementarities in the Macroeconomy: An Empirical Analysis," Discussion Paper no. 04/5 (Cologne: Max Planck Institute, 2004); and David Soskice, "Divergent Production Regimes: Coordinated and Uncoordinated Market Economies in the 1980s and 1990s," in *Continuity and Change in Contemporary Capitalism*, ed. Herbert Kitschelt, Peter Lange, Gary Marks, and John Stephens (New York: Cambridge University Press, 1999).

12 An excellent analysis of the problem of economic coordination in regard to the question of training is Pepper Culpepper, *Creating Cooperation: How States Develop Human Capital in Europe* (Ithaca, N.Y.: Cornell University Press, 2003).

13 Hall and Soskice, "An Introduction to Varieties of Capitalism," 36–44.

14 The broadest theoretical critiques of the Varieties of Capitalism perspective are Colin Crouch, *Capitalist Diversity and Change* (New York: Oxford University Press, 2005); Chris Howell, "Varieties of Capitalism: And Then There Was One?" *Comparative Politics* 36, no. 1 (October 2003): 103-24; and Glenn Morgan, "Institutional Complementarities, Path Dependency, and the Dynamics of Firm," in *Changing Capitalisms? Internationalization, Institutional Change, and Systems of Economic Organization*, ed. Glenn Morgan, Richard Whitley, and Eli Moen (New York: Oxford University Press, 2005).

15 The thesis of significant transformation via incremental processes of change is best provided in Wolfgang Streeck and Kathleen Thelen, "Introduction: Institutional Change in Advanced Political Economies," in *Beyond Continuity: Institutional Change in Advanced Political Economies*, ed. Wolfgang Streeck and Kathleen Thelen (New York: Oxford University Press, 2005).

16 This theoretical perspective of institutional change constitutes an explicit criticism of punctuated equilibrium models whereby prolonged periods of institutional stability are interrupted suddenly by critical exogenous shocks that result in a conflictual period of transition until a new pattern of institutional complementarity is established, thereby resulting in a new stable equilibrium.

17 See Ronald Gilson, "Globalizing Corporate Governance: Convergence of Form or Function," *American Journal of Comparative Law* 49, no. 2 (Spring 2003): 329–57; and Kathleen Thelen, "How Institutions Evolve: Insights from Comparative Historical Analysis," in *Comparative Historical Analysis in the Social Sciences*, ed. James Mahoney and Dietrich Rueschemeyer (New York: Cambridge University Press, 2003).

18 See Marino Regini, "Between Deregulation and Social Pacts: The Responses of European Economies to Globalization," *Politics and Society* 28, no. 1 (March 2000): 5–33.

19 This argument is best developed in Peter Hall, "Central Bank Independence and Coordinated Wage Bargaining: Their Interaction in Germany," *German Politics and Society*, no. 31 (Spring 1994): 1–23; and Peter Hall and Robert Franzese, "Mixed Signals: Central Bank Independence, Coordinated Wage Bargaining, and European Monetary Union," *International Organization* 52, no. 3 (Summer 1998): 505–35.

20 See Michael Loriaux, *France after Hegemony: International Change and Financial Reform* (Ithaca, N.Y.: Cornell University Press, 1991); and John Zysman, *Governments, Markets, and Growth* (Ithaca, N.Y.: Cornell University Press, 1983), 99–169, for historical analyses of the French financial system.

21 The original thesis is Peter Hall and Kathleen Thelen, "Institutional Change and the Varieties of Capitalism" (paper presented to the APSA annual meeting, Washington, D.C., September 1–4, 2005).

22 A good example of this dichotomy between coordination and institutional change is the transfer of Japanese methods of production (just-in-time, teamwork) to France and Germany in the last twenty years. In France, the introduction of such methods served as an additional means of control for management at the same time as constituting a source of productivity. In Germany, the same event strengthened the position of the Meister and the central role of training in the production process. See Peter Doeringer, Edward Lorenz, and David Terkla, "The Adoption and Diffusion of High-Performance Management: Lessons from Japanese Multinationals in the West," *Cambridge Journal of Economics* 27, no. 2 (March 2003): 265–86; and Mari Sako, "Training, Productivity and Quality Control in Japanese Multinational Companies," in *The Japanese Firm*, ed. Masahiko Aoki and Ronald Dore (New York: Oxford University Press, 1996).

23 See Robert Boyer, "Wage Austerity and/or an Education Push: The French Dilemma," Labour 9, special issue (1995): 19-65; and Pepper Culpepper, "Individual Choice, Collective Action, and the Problem of Training Reform: Insights from France and Eastern

Germany," in *The German Skills Machine: Comparative Perspectives on Systems of Education and Training*, ed. Pepper Culpepper and David Finegold (New York: Berghahn, 1998).

24   See Arndt Sorge, *The Global and the Local: Understanding the Dialectics of Business Systems* (New York: Oxford University Press, 2005), ch. 5; and Richard Whitley, "The Institutional Structuring of Organizational Capabilities: The Role of Authority Sharing and Organizational Careers," *Organization Studies* 24, no. 5 (June 2003): 667–95.

25   Zysman, *Governments, Markets, and Growth*, 69–75.

26   See Jeremy Edwards and Klaus Fisher, *Banks, Finance and Investment in Germany* (New York: Cambridge University Press, 1994); and François Morin, *La Structure Financière du Capitalisme Français* (Paris: Calmann-Levy, 1974).

27   Julian Franks and Colin Mayer, "Corporate Ownership and Control in the UK, Germany, and France," *Journal of Applied Corporate Finance* 9, no. 4 (Winter 1997): 30–45.

28   See Loriaux, *France after Hegemony*; and Jonathan Story, "Finanzplatz Deutschland: National or European Response to Internationalization?" *German Politics* 5, no. 3 (December 1996): 371–94.

29   Conference Board, "Equity Ownership and Investment Strategies of US and International Institutional Investors," *Institutional Investment Report* 4, nos. 2-3 (May 2002): 1–45.

30   François Morin and Eric Rigamonti, "Evolution et Structure de l'Actionnariat en France," *Revue Française de Gestion* 28, no. 141 (November–December 2002): 155–81.

31   Alfred Rappaport and Mark Sirower, "Stock or Cash? The Trade-Offs for Buyers and Sellers in Mergers and Acquisitions," *Harvard Business Review* 77, no. 6 (November–December 1999): 147–58.

32   Hall and Soskice, "An Introduction to Varieties of Capitalism," 57. Data on the distribution of activities of French and German firms between the home base and American subsidiaries are presented in Manuel Separio and Donald Dalton, "Globalization of Industrial R&D: An Examination of Foreign Direct Investments in R&D in the United States," *Research Policy* 28, nos. 2–3 (March 1999): 303–16.

33   John Coffee, "The Future as History: The Prospects for Global Convergence in Corporate Governance," *Northwestern University Law Review* 93, no. 3 (1999): 641–708.

34   Gourevitch and Shinn, *Political Power and Corporate Control*, 105. It must be noted, however, that foreign ownership for large companies is substantially higher than for the rest of the German corporate sector. See Michel Goyer, "Institutional Investors in French and German Corporate Governance," working paper (Cambridge, Mass.: Center for European Studies at Harvard University, 2006), Table 2.

35   See Goyer, "Institutional Investors in French and German Corporate Governance," Table 4.

36   See, for example, Mark Roe, "Corporate Law's Limits," *Journal of Legal Studies* 31, no. 2 (June 2002): 233–71.

37   See Hancké, *Large Firms and Industrial Adjustment*, 57–87; and Schmidt, *From State to the Market?* 393–416.

38   See Kathleen Thelen, *Unions of Parts*, 25–104.

39   *Pensions & Investments*, January 26, 2004, 16.

40   Robert Pozen, *Mutual Fund Business* (Cambridge, Mass.: MIT Press, 1998), 397–423.

41   Hedge funds, on the other hand, are traditionally set up as limited partnerships that are limited to a restricted number of wealthy individuals (500) with personal assets of at least $5 million who are willing to adopt highly risky short-term strategies and borrow on financial markets in exchange for high return potential. Hedge funds are managed on a DC scheme with investors uncertain to recover their investment since fund managers are typically given mandates to make an absolute return target regardless of the market environment. But in contrast to mutual funds schemes, hedge funds impose initial lock-up periods of at least one year as funds are not redeemable on demand. This difference aside, hedge and mutual funds constitute two forms of short-term, impatient capital. For an overview, see Stephen Brown and William Goetzmann, "Hedge Funds with Style," NBER working paper no. 8173 (Cambridge, Mass.: NBER, 2001).

42   Conference Board, "Turnover, Investment Strategies, and Ownership Patterns," *Institutional Investment Report* 2, no. 2 (August 1998): 1–51.

43   Ibid.

44   See Daniel Bandru, Stéphanie Lavigne, and François Morin, "Les Investisseurs Institutionnels Internationaux: Une Analyse du Comportement des Investisseurs Américains," *Revue Économie Financière*, no. 61 (2001): 121–37.

45   Ibid., 125.

46   Ibid., 126.

47   For an overview of the investment strategies of hedge funds, see Carl Ackermann, Richard McEnally, and David Ravenscraft, "The Performance of Hedge Funds: Risk, Return, and Incentives," *Journal of Finance* 54, no. 3 (June 1999): 833–74.

48   See Tracy Woidtke, "Agents Watching Agents? Evidence from Pension Fund Ownership and Value," *Journal of Financial Economics* 63, no. 1 (January 2002): 99-131.

49   Robert Monks and Nell Minow, *Corporate Governance* (Cambridge, Mass.: Blackwell, 1995), 125.

50   An excellent review of the motivations of pension fund officials is provided in Roberta Romano, "Public Pension Fund Activism in Corporate Governance Reconsidered," *Columbia Law Review* 93, no. 4 (May 1993): 795-853.

51   See Edwin Elton, Martin Gruber, and Christopher Blake, "Incentives Fees and Mutual Funds," *Journal of Finance* 58, no. 2 (April 2003): 779–804.

52   Mutual fund managers whose fund's performance lags behind rivals at the mid-point of an assessment period are likely to shift the composition of their portfolio by investing in a greater number of riskier companies, thereby increasing the volatility of the fund but also the probability of increasing its performance. See Judith

Chevalier and Glenn Ellison, "Risk Taking by Mutual Funds as a Response to Incentives," *Journal of Political Economy* 105, no. 6 (December 1997): 1167–200.

53 Ian McDonald, "Fidelity Managers Gets Ranked," *Wall Street Journal Europe*, January 21, 2003.

54 Brown and Goetzmann, "Hedge Funds with Style," 2.

55 Monks and Minow, *Corporate Governance*, 163; and Robert Pozen, "Institutional Investors: The Reluctant Activists," *Harvard Business Review* 72, no. 1 (January–February 1994): 140–49.

56 See Goyer, "Institutional Investors in French and German Corporate Governance," Table 5.

57 Hedge funds do not have to reveal the composition of their portfolio, and materials distributed to investors are often available on a restricted basis and published at irregular intervals. Their low-profile and secretive nature is designed to minimize regulatory and tax oversights. As a result, it is often impossible to acquire credible data on the holdings of hedge funds. On the other hand, however, financial regulation in the European Union obliges shareholders to disclose equity stake above the 5 percent threshold. Thus, it becomes possible to track the investment targets of hedge funds when their equity stake exceeds this threshold. Data on the presence of hedge funds in France and Germany are provided in the next section.

58 I collected data from the two official governmental databases of the financial regulation authority of the two countries: http://www.amf-france.org and http://www.bawe.de.

59 Dafsaliens, *Annuaire DAFSA* (Paris: Editions Dafsa, annually); and Rudiger Liedtke, *Wem Gehort die Republik?* (Frankfurt: Eichborn, annually).

60 A detailed and complete listing of acquisitions over the 5 percent threshold in France and Germany is provided in Goyer, "Institutional Investors in French and German Corporate Governance."

61 A similar divergence characterizes the investment of Anglo-Saxon institutional investors in the two countries outside the blue-chip company category. From September 1997 to May 2005, ninety-three German firms received a total of 130 instances of an investment over the 5 percent threshold by an Anglo-Saxon institutional investor. If we deduct the top eighty companies from this sample, this leaves us with sixty-five German firms recording eighty-two investments over the 5 percent threshold. For the same period, 211 French companies recorded 416 instances of an investment over the 5 percent threshold. The same figures, if we deduct the top eighty French companies from the sample, are 159 and 277.

62 Morningstar, *Morningstar Funds 500* (Hoboken, N.J.: John Wiley, annually).

63 For a complete discussion of the link between price/earning ratio and managerial autonomy, see Goyer, "Institutional Investors in French and German Corporate Governance."

64 Nicolas Daniels, "Les Points Noirs du Gouvernement d'Entreprise a la Française," *Figaro Economie*, May 10, 2001; and Davis Global Advisors, *Leading Corporate Governance Indicators* (Newton, Mass.: Davis Global Advisors, annual publication). See also Goyer, "Corporate Governance, Employees, and Core Competencies in France and Germany," 191–98.

65 See Detley Karg, "For Sale: Germany, Inc.," *Deutsche Welle*, May 15, 2005; and Richard Milne, "Tweedy May Review Its German links over VW Row," *Financial Times*, December 2, 2005.

66 See Gourevitch and Shinn, *Political Power and Corporate Control*, 205–28; and Hoepner, "Corporate Governance in Transition," 27–28.

67 Hancké, *Large Firms and Industrial Adjustment*, 57-87; and Schmidt, From State to the Market? 393-416.

68 See Michel Goyer, "The Transformation of Corporate Governance in France and Germany: The Role of Workplace Institutions," working paper no. 02/10 (Cologne: Max Planck Institute, 2002); and Peter Hall, "The Politics of Adjustment in Germany," in *Ökonomische Leistungsfähigkeit und Institutionelle Innovation*, ed. F. Naschold, D. Soskice, B. Hancké, and Ü. Jurgens (Berlin: Edition Sigma, 1997).

69 See Streeck, *Social Institutions and Economic Performance*, 49–55.

70 Culpepper, "Individual Choice, Collective Action, and the Problem of Training Reform," 286.

71 Ibid., 301.

72 See Marc Maurice, François Sellier, and Jean-Jacques Silvestre, *The Social Foundations of Industrial Power: A Comparison of France and Germany* (Cambridge, Mass.: MIT Press, 1986), 65–73.

73 Ibid., 77.

74 See Culpepper, "Individual Choice, Collective Action, and the Problem of Training Reform," 276–77; and Walter Muller-Jentsch, "Germany: From Collective Voice to Co-management," in *Works Councils: Consultation, Representation and Cooperation in Industrial Relations*, ed. Joel Rogers and Wolfgang Streeck (Chicago: University of Chicago Press, 1995).

75 Michel Goyer, "The Transformation of Corporate Governance in France and Germany," 26; and Wolfgang Streeck, "Successful Adjustment to Turbulent Markets: The Automobile Industry," in *Industry and Politics in West Germany: Toward the Third Republic*, ed. Peter Katzenstein (Ithaca, N.Y.: Cornell University Press, 1989), 129.

76 David Marsden, *A Theory of Employment Systems* (New York: Oxford University Press, 1999), 121–38.

77 Ibid., 98.

78 A good analysis of the reorganization of the practices of work floor organization in France is Danièle Linhart, *La Modernisation des Entreprises* (Paris: La Découverte, 1994).

79 Culpepper, "Individual Choice, Collective Action, and the Problem of Training Reform," 278.

80 Goyer, "The Transformation of Corporate Governance in France and Germany," 25.

81 See Hancké, *Large Firms and Industrial Adjustment*, 57–82.

82 Richard Whitley, *Divergent Capitalisms: The Social Structuring and Change of Business Systems* (New York: Oxford University Press, 1999), 38–44.

F
O
U
R

83 See Linhart, *La Modernisation des Entreprises*, 57–64; and Arndt Sorge, "Strategic Fit and the Societal Effect: Interpreting Cross-National Comparisons of Technology, Organization and Human Resources," *Organization Studies* 12, no. 2 (1991): 161–90.

84 See David Marsden, *A Theory of Employment Systems*, 103–4; and Maurice, Sellier, and Silvestre, *The Social Foundations of Industrial Power*, 60–65.

85 See Maurice, Sellier, and Silvestre, *The Social Foundations of Industrial Power*, 59–120.

86 Michel Crozier, *Le Phénomène Bureaucratique* (Paris: Le Seuil, 1963); and Geert Hofstede, *Culture's Consequences: International Differences in Work Related Values* (London: Sage, 1980).

87 See Linhart, *La Modernisation des Entreprises*, 23–47.

88 See Danièle Linhart, "The Shortcomings of an Organizational Revolution That Is out of Step," *Economic and Industrial Democracy* 14, no. 1 (February 1993): 49–64.

89 See Linhart, *La Modernisation des Entreprises*, 48–64; and Sorge, *The Global and the Local*, 180–82.

90 The dual nature of this development—change in practices of workplace organization combined with stability in power relationships—testifies to the importance of the distinction between institutional framework and the mode of coordination that follows from these institutions. See Hall and Thelen, "Institutional Change and the Varieties of Capitalism," for an analysis of this crucial distinction.

91 See Whitley, "The Institutional Structuring of Organizational Capabilities," 669–79.

92 Marsden, *A Theory of Employment Systems*, 38.

93 Carl Kester, "Industrial Groups as Systems of Corporate Governance," *Oxford Review of Economic Policy* 8, no. 3 (Autumn 1992): 24–44.

94 Maurice, Sellier, and Silvestre, *The Social Foundations of Industrial Power*, 90–100.

95 Whitley, "The Institutional Structuring of Organizational Capabilities," 669–79.

96 See Streeck, "Successful Adjustment to Turbulent Markets," 131–32.

97 Maurice, Sellier, and Silvestre, *The Social Foundations of Industrial Power*, 79–84.

98 Marsden, *A Theory of Employment Systems*, 133.

99 See Maurice, Sellier, and Silvestre, *The Social Foundations of Industrial Power*, 69–73; and Streeck, *Social Institutions and Economic Performance*, 36–40.

100 Maurice, Sellier, and Silvestre, *The Social Foundations of Industrial Power*, 79–84.

101 See Sorge, "Strategic Fit and the Societal Effect," 168–76.

102 See Whitley, "The Institutional Structuring of Organizational Capabilities," 669–79.

103 See Streeck, *Social Institutions and Economic Performance*, 36–40.

104 For a discussion of the problems engendered by the constant modification to the codes of training practices, see Gary Herrigel and Charles Sabel, "Craft Production in Crisis: Industrial Restructuring in Germany during the 1990s," in Culpepper and Finegold, *The German Skills Machine*.

105 For example, thirty-one new occupations were defined and ninety-seven were updated and modernized between 1996 and 1999. See Jill Rubery and Damian Grimshaw, *The Organization of Employment: An International Perspective* (London: Palgrave Macmillan, 2003), 130.

106 Culpepper, *Creating Cooperation*, 57.

107 For a full discussion of the macro effects of interaction between institutions in different spheres of the economy, see Hall and Franzese, "Mixed Signals"; and Hall and Soskice, "An Introduction to Varieties of Capitalism," 17–33.

108 See Campbell, *Institutional Change and Globalization*, for a subtle analysis of the problem of measuring and assessing institutional change.

109 For a discussion of the concept of latent institutions, see Kathleen Thelen and Sven Steinmo, "Institutionalism in Comparative Politics," in *Structuring Politics: Historical Institutionalism in Comparative Analysis*, ed. Sven Steinmo, Kathleen Thelen, and Frank Longstreth (New York: Cambridge University Press, 1992), 16–18.

110 See Zysman, *Governments, Markets, and Growth*, 99–169.

111 See Culpepper, "Institutional Change in Contemporary Capitalism," *World Politics* 57, no. 2 (January 2005): 173–99, for an analysis of the stability of ownership concentration in Germany.

112 See Hall and Thelen, "Institutional Change and the Varieties of Capitalism," 30–37.

113 The original thesis of this argument is Kathleen Thelen, *How Institutions Evolve: The Political Economy of Skills in Germany, Britain, the United States, and Japan* (New York: Cambridge University Press, 2004).

15 "Corporate Governance Reforms in Continental Europe"

from *Journal of Economic Perspectives* (2007)

Luca Enriques and Paolo Volpin

The fundamental problem of corporate governance in the United States is to alleviate the conflict of interest between dispersed small shareowners and powerful controlling managers. Classic works like Berle and Means (1932) and Jensen and Meckling (1976) discussed this separation of ownership and control and its consequences. Although some companies in the United States are controlled by large blockholders—for instance, Microsoft, Ford, and Wal-Mart—such firms are relatively few and have thus drawn less attention in the corporate governance debate (Anderson and Reeb, 2003).

In contrast, the fundamental problem of corporate governance in continental Europe and in most of the world is different. There, few listed companies are widely held. Instead, the typical firm in stock exchanges around the world has a dominant shareholder, usually an individual or a family, who controls the majority of votes. Often, the controlling shareholder exercises control without owning a large fraction of the cash flow rights by using pyramidal ownership, shareholder agreements, and dual classes of shares (La Porta, Lopez-de-Silanes, and Shleifer, 1999).

These differences in ownership structure have two obvious consequences for corporate governance, as surveyed in Morck, Wolfenzon, and Yeung (2005). On the one hand, dominant shareholders have both the incentive and the power to discipline management. On the other hand, concentrated ownership can create conditions for a new agency problem, because the interests of controlling and minority shareholders are not aligned.

In this chapter, we begin by describing the differences in the ownership structure of companies in the three main economies of continental Europe—Germany, France, and Italy—with comparisons to the United States and the United Kingdom. We next summarize the corporate governance issues that arise in firms with a dominant shareholder. We take a look at the major European corporate scandal, Parmalat, as an extreme example of investor expropriation in a family-controlled corporation. We outline in general the legal tools that can be used to tackle abuses by controlling shareholders. Finally, we describe the corporate governance reforms enacted by France, Germany, and Italy between 1991 and 2005 and assess the way in which investor protection in the three countries has changed.

CONCENTRATED OWNERSHIP ACROSS COUNTRIES

A common measure of ownership concentration is whether one shareholder owns at least 20 percent of a company's voting rights; such a shareholder is called a "controlling shareholder." The first column of Table 15.1 shows what percentage of the 20 largest listed companies in France, Germany, Italy, the United Kingdom, and the United States are widely held, or do not have a controlling shareholder. Dispersed ownership is common in the United States and United Kingdom and very rare in Italy, with Germany and France falling in the middle. The second column shows that, with the exception of Britain, family control is quite common even among the largest corporations. Pyramidal ownership is a common way of holding control in continental

Europe. A pyramid is defined as an ownership structure in which the controlling shareholder exercises control of one company through ownership of at least one other listed company. Column 3 shows that pyramidal ownership is absent in Britain and America, but is found even among the top 20 corporations in France, Germany, and Italy.

Why do no pyramids exist in the United States or the United Kingdom? The answer probably lies in historical differences in regulation: Morck and Yeung (2005) suggested that the taxation of intercompany dividends introduced in 1935 could explain the disappearance of pyramids in the United States. According to Franks, Mayer, and Rossi (2005), the introduction of the mandatory takeover bid in 1968 may explain the disappearance of pyramids in the United Kingdom.

The difference between the United States and the United Kingdom on the one hand and continental Europe on the other is not restricted to the largest corporations. Going by the median fraction of votes owned by the largest shareholder in all listed companies, shown in column 4 of Table 1, ownership is highly concentrated in Germany and Italy, and diffused in Britain and America, with France in an intermediate position. Remarkably, in half of German and Italian listed companies, one blockholder owns at least 57 percent or 55 percent, respectively, of the votes. A final measure of ownership concentration is the share of a country's total stock market capitalization held by the ten richest families. By this measure,

displayed in column 5, company ownership in continental Europe is concentrated in the hands of a small number of wealthy individuals.

To understand how pyramids, shareholder agreements, and dual classes of shares work, consider three prominent examples. Louis Vuitton Moët Hennessy (LVMH) is the world leader in luxury goods and one of the largest companies listed on the Paris Bourse, with a market capitalization of about $45 billion. The firm has an ultimate owner, Bernard Arnault, who is also the chief executive officer and chairman of the board. The firm is controlled via a pyramidal group that includes several nonlisted and one listed company (Christian Dior). Figure 15.1 plots this control chain. The number above each company to the right of the arrow shows the fraction of the shareholder votes owned by the entity listed above it. The numbers on the left of the figure show for each company the fraction of its cash flow rights that are owned either directly or indirectly by the controlling shareholder. For example, Arnault owns 98.7 percent of the cash rights in Semyrhamis, and this company owns 70 percent of Christian Dior SA, so Arnault owns 69.1 percent of the cash flows in Dior (that is, 98.7 percent multiplied by 70 percent). As a consequence of this control structure, he controls 47 (42 plus 5) percent of the voting rights in LVMH with a direct and indirect ownership of 34 percent of the cash flow rights.

The separation of ownership from control is more dramatic in Telecom Italia, one of the world's largest telecom companies with a market capitalization of

	Widely held	Family control	Pyramid control	Median largest voting block	Family wealth
France	60%	20%	15%	20%	29%
Germany	50%	10%	20%	57%	21%
Italy	20%	15%	20%	55%	20%
United Kingdom	100%	0%	0%	10%	6%
United States	80%	20%	0%	5% (NYSE) 9% (Nasdaq)	N.A.

Sources: For "Widely held" and "Family control," La Porta, Lopez-de-Silanes, and Shleifer (1999, Table 2); for "Pyramid control," La Porta, Lopez-de-Silanes, and Shleifer (1999, Table 4); for "Median largest voting block," Barca and Becht (2001); for "Family wealth," Faccio and Lang (2002, Table 10). *Notes:* "Widely held" is the fraction of firms with no controlling shareholder among the 20 largest companies by stock market capitalization at the end of 1995. A company has a controlling shareholder if the sum of a shareholder's direct and indirect voting rights exceeds 20 percent. "Family control" is the fraction of the 20 largest companies where the controlling shareholder is an individual. "Pyramid control" is the fraction of the 20 largest companies, where the controlling shareholder exercises control through at least one publicly traded company. "Median largest voting block" is the median size of the largest ultimate voting block for listed industrial companies. "Family wealth" is the percentage of total stock market capitalization controlled by the ten richest families.

Table 15.1 **Ownership concentration**

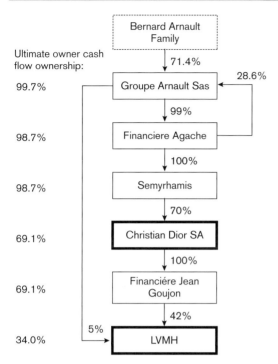

Figure 15.1 Ownership structure of LVMH in 2005

Source: Amadeus and Factiva databases.

Note: The ultimate owner is indicated in a box at the top. Single-bordered boxes represent nonlisted companies. Bold-bordered boxes represent listed companies. The arrows indicate the direction of control. The numbers next to the arrows indicate the fraction of votes owned. The numbers on the left represent the fraction of cash-flow rights owned directly and indirectly by the controlling shareholder in each of the companies in the pyramid.

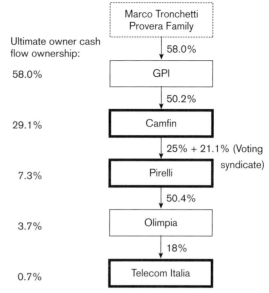

Figure 15.2 Ownership structure of Telecom Italia in 2005

Source: Consob webpage.

Note: The ultimate owner is indicated in a box at the top. Single-bordered boxes represent nonlisted companies. Bold-bordered boxes represent listed companies. The arrows indicate the direction of control. The numbers next to the arrows indicate the fraction of votes owned. The numbers on the left represent the fraction of cash-flow rights owned directly and indirectly by the controlling shareholder in each of the companies in the pyramid.

about $40 billion. The pyramidal group includes three listed companies and two non-listed companies, shown in Figure 15.2. Marco Tronchetti Provera controls 18 percent of the votes in Telecom Italia (and is by far its largest shareholder), although he holds only 0.7 percent of the cash flow rights. Notice that the control over one of the companies in the pyramid (Pirelli) is strengthened via an agreement with other large shareholders on how to vote shares, known as a *voting syndicate*. Because of this agreement, Tronchetti Provera controls 46.1 percent of the votes in Pirelli: 25 percent directly owned by his holding company Camfin and 21.1 percent provided by other friendly blockholders.

As a third example (Figure 15.3), consider the ownership structure of Volkswagen AG, which has a market capitalization of about $25 billion. The largest shareholder in this company is another listed company, Porsche AG. Because Volkswagen AG also has nonvoting preferred shares, Porsche AG owns 25.1 percent of the common shares but only 18.9 percent of the equity. A 1960 law (the "Volkswagen Law") caps the voting power of any shareholder at 20 percent. Hence, Porsche AG does not technically control Volkswagen AG, but as its largest shareholder, it holds a blocking minority. Porsche AG, in turn, is controlled by the family of the company's founder, Ferdinand Porsche. The Porsche family owns 100 percent of the common (voting) shares but only 50 percent of Porsche's equity, half of which consists of preferred (nonvoting) shares. Because of the combined effect of the dual classes of shares and the pyramidal structure, the Porsche family controls 25.1 percent of the votes in Volkswagen AG but owns only 9.44 percent of its cash flow rights.

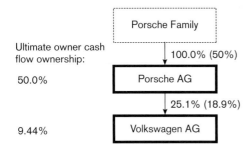

Figure 15.3 Ownership Structure of Volkswagen AG in June 2006

Source: Porsche AG and Volkswagen AG websites.

Note: The ultimate owner is indicated in a dash-line bordered box at the top. Bold-bordered boxes represent listed companies. The arrows indicate the direction of control. The numbers next to the arrows indicate the fraction of votes owned. The numbers on the left represent the fraction of cash-flow rights owned directly and indirectly by the controlling shareholder in each of the companies in the pyramid. In parentheses, we report the fraction of equity owned by the direct controlling shareholder. The latter differs from the fraction of votes owned in this case because companies have both common (voting) shares and preferred (nonvoting) shares.

CORPORATE GOVERNANCE IN FAMILY-CONTROLLED COMPANIES

On average, family-controlled firms are better managed than widely held ones. In a sample of large US companies, Anderson and Reeb (2003) find a significantly higher Tobin's q for family-controlled firms (a third of their sample) than for widely held companies. Barontini and Caprio (2005) find a similar result for European companies. Tobin's q is the ratio of the market value of a firm to the replacement value of its assets, typically measured as the book value of the firm's assets. A higher (industry-adjusted) Tobin's q suggests that the assets are used efficiently—that is, they are worth more within the firm than in alternative uses.

Of course, these findings do not imply that family-controlled firms are always better governed than widely held ones. Family control does help to protect shareholders' interest against managerial abuses, since the controlling owner and the manager are often the same person. Moreover, the controlling family is likely to commit more human capital to the firm and to care more about its long-run value (Bertrand and Schoar, 2006). However, families, like managers in a widely held company, can abuse their power and use corporate resources to their own advantage. When this happens in a family-controlled firm, things are even worse than in a widely held company, because controlling families cannot be ousted through a hostile takeover or replaced by the board of directors or by the shareholders' meeting.

Self-dealing or *tunnelling* is the transfer of value from firms where the controlling shareholder owns a small fraction of the cash-flow rights (lower down in the pyramid) to firms where the controlling shareholder owns a large fraction of cash-flow rights (higher up in the pyramid) (Johnson, La Porta, Lopez-de-Silanes, and Shleifer, 2000). Value can be transferred in many ways: related-party transactions (transactions with the dominant shareholder, a director, or parties associated with them) at other than arm's-length terms; the biased allocation of intangible assets and liabilities; excessive director compensation; and others.

A hypothetical example may help to clarify how tunnelling works. In the pyramidal group described in Figure 15.2, imagine what would happen if Marco Tronchetti Provera forced Telecom Italia to buy inputs from Camfin at above-market prices. This related-party transaction neither creates nor destroys value, because the loss for Telecom Italia is equal to the gain for Camfin. But Tronchetti Provera would be better off, because he pockets 29.1 percent of Camfin's gain and suffers only 0.7 percent of Telecom Italia's loss.

The power of a controlling shareholder to use corporate resources for private advantage is likely to create a wedge between the value of a company for the controlling shareholder and for the other (minority) shareholders. This difference in value is known as the private benefits of control. One empirical measure of such benefits is the "block premium," which is the difference between the price per share paid in a block transaction and the market price after the transaction. The first column of Table 15.2 shows that block premiums are somewhat larger in Germany and much larger in Italy than in the United States, the United Kingdom, or France. Another measure is the "voting premium," which is the difference between the market prices of voting and nonvoting shares. The second column of Table 15.2 shows that the voting premium is much higher in France and Italy, moderate in Germany and the United Kingdom, and low in the United States. These results suggest that the value of control is larger in continental Europe than in the United States and the United Kingdom.

	Block premium	Voting premium
France	2%	28%
Germany	10%	10%
Italy	37%	29%
United Kingdom	2%	10%
United States	2%	2%

Table 15.2 **Private benefits of control**

Notes: "Block premium" is the country average of the difference between the price per share paid in a transaction for a control block of shares and the trading price two days after the announcement of a control transaction. See Dyck and Zingales (2004, Table 2) for details. "Voting premium" is the country average of the estimated value of a vote as a percent of firm value. See Nenova (2003, Table 5) for details.

THE PARMALAT COLLAPSE

Parmalat is the most glaring example to date of corporate governance abuses in insider-dominated countries. Our account here draws on Ferrarini and Giudici (2005). The story begins when Calisto Tanzi inherited a small family business in the 1960s and the firm started a pattern of ever-accelerating growth. When it listed on the Milan stock exchange in 1989, Parmalat Finanziaria was the holding company of a group comprising 58 companies (33 based outside Italy) with aggregate sales of $720 million. The Tanzi family was the controlling shareholder via a nonlisted company. The acquisition drive became even more intense in the 1990s, with aggregate sales reaching $3.6 billion in 1996 and almost $10 billion in 2002.

Most of the group's expansion was in milk and dairy products, especially in South America. But the Tanzis also diversified outside the food industry, mainly into soccer, the pet project of Calisto Tanzi's son Stefano, and tourism, the pet project of Tanzi's daughter Francesca. Most of the acquisitions were financed with debt. The peculiar characteristic of Parmalat's balance sheet was the simultaneous presence of high levels of debt and cash. In 2002, the annual report indicated $4.3 billion in cash and equivalent against $9.3 billion of debt. The reality was that most of the cash reported in the balance sheet no longer existed: it had already been consumed.

Tanzi's empire collapsed in December 2003. After several unsuccessful attempts to refinance its debt, on December 8 Parmalat informed the market that it could not repay bonds that were maturing. Following the bonds' downgrade to junk level, the share price collapsed. Meanwhile, Consob (the Italian securities and exchange commission) required confirmation of the existence of a bank account with Bank of America where all $4.3 billion of Parmalat's cash was supposedly deposited (via a Cayman Islands company called Bonlat). Bank of America soon replied that there was no such account, Parmalat Finanziaria was declared insolvent, and Calisto Tanzi was jailed.

According to an estimation of the sources and uses of funds reported in Table 15.3, from 1990 to December 2003, the Parmalat group used a total of $18.2 billion of financial resources, including $16.9 billion raised from debt. Over that period of time, the family siphoned off (in "unknown" uses) about $3 billion. This amount is a lower bound of the expropriation, because overpayment for the acquisition of assets would be classified as acquisitions or other capital expenditures. Most of these resources were transferred to the other businesses directly owned by the Tanzis. The techniques used to conceal the fraud were rudimentary. Parmalat hid losses, overstated assets, recorded nonexistent assets, understated debt, forged bank documents, and diverted cash to the Tanzi family.

As in any large financial scandal, the designated watchdogs like auditors, investment banks, and regulators are partly to blame for not detecting the patterns of negligence, fraud, and corruption. However,

Sources		Uses	
Internal funds	1.3	Interests & fees	6.8
Debt	16.9	Acquisitions	4.8
		Other capital expenditures	3.6
		Unknown (diverted)	3.0
Total sources	18.2	Total uses	18.2

Table 15.3 **Parmalat group: uses and sources of funds (aggregate estimates for the 1990–2003 period in billions of US dollars)**

Source: Ferrarini and Giudici (2005).

Parmalat is mainly an example of outright expropriation of both shareholders and creditors by a family that treated company resources as their own. Although it represents an extreme case (given the scale of the expropriation), the evidence on private benefits of control reported in Table 15.2 indicates that minor forms of expropriation are systemic in continental Europe.

Financial scandals in companies with concentrated ownership, like Parmalat, usually differ from those with diffused ownership, like Enron and Worldcom. In Enron and Worldcom (as well as in Vivendi and Royal Ahold, two European widely held companies) corporate managers engaged in earnings manipulation and accounting irregularities to inflate the stock price and gain from their equity and options holdings. In Parmalat (as well as in Adelphia, a US company with concentrated ownership), the controlling shareholders expropriated corporate resources via self-dealing. These differences should lead to different regulatory responses in different countries (Coffee, 2005).

FOUR LEGAL TOOLS

Dominant shareholders (and insiders more generally) have opportunities to expropriate investors. Can this problem be solved without regulation, namely via private contracting and social norms? From the available evidence, the answer is no. For instance, we know that countries with weaker investor protection have less-developed financial markets (La Porta, Lopez-de-Silanes, Shleifer, and Vishny, 1997; La Porta, Lopez-de-Silanes, and Shleifer, 2006) and that weaker insider trading legislation and enforcement is associated with higher cost of capital (Bhattacharya and Daouk, 2002). Because finance matters for growth (Rajan and Zingales, 1998), financial regulation matters. In this section, we briefly describe four legal tools that are commonly used to protect investors. In the following section, we discuss the evolution of these tools in the three major economies of continental Europe—France, Germany, and Italy—and compare it with the United States.

Strengthening internal governance mechanisms

The board of directors is the primary institution of corporate governance. Its main task is to hire and

monitor top management on behalf of shareholders, and it is best placed to screen related-party transactions. Whether firms are widely held or family-controlled, the danger is that boards, rather than represent the interests of faceless shareholders, will bond with management, whom they interact with regularly, or with the family, who has the ultimate power to select and remove them.

Regulations mandating greater independence for directors and defining the board's functions, powers, and internal workings—including matters like auditing, setting executive compensation, screening related-party transactions, and disclosure of information flows—may give the board of directors some power to challenge the dominant shareholder. So far, though, little evidence exists that these reforms have curbed controlling shareholders' abuses (Denis and McConnell, 2003).[1]

Empowering shareholders

The law traditionally protects shareholders by enhancing their rights to sell, sue, and vote. First, in widely held companies, the shareholders' right to sell their shares allows for a market for corporate control to emerge as a mechanism to limit insider abuses (Manne, 1965). However, where ownership is highly concentrated, as in continental Europe, this market only disciplines the insiders of the relatively few companies that are widely held (Rossi and Volpin, 2004).

Second, regulators may empower shareholders by granting them the right to sue the company and its directors. The effect of such suits will depend on how easy or costly it is to bring them and how efficient the court system is.

Third, regulation can empower shareholders by giving them a say over key corporate governance issues. For this purpose, regulators can extend the subject matters to be decided by the shareholder meeting, mandate super-majority requirements, lower the cost of voting, limit deviations from one-share-one-vote, and mandate minority shareholders' representation on the board. The evidence in Djankov, La Porta, Lopez-de-Silanes, and Shleifer (2006) indicates that shareholders' right to vote on self-dealing transactions is particularly important.

Control transactions may also provide the occasion for self-dealing (Kirchmaier and Grant, 2005). Controlling shareholders may reject value-maximizing takeovers (if they are not fully compensated for the foregone private benefits of control), and accept value-destroying ones that let them appropriate the control premium. The law can protect minority shareholders by allowing them to share the control premium with majority shareholders (so as to align the incentives of controlling and minority shareholders). Bebchuk (1994) discusses extensively the trade-off between investor protection via equal treatment clauses, and efficiency of the market for corporate control.

Enhancing disclosure requirements

Whether shareholders effectively exercise their rights to sell, vote, and sue depends on their access to information. An extensive regime of disclosure may help alleviate agency problems in listed corporations: as Louis Brandeis (1914, p. 62) once famously wrote, sunshine is "the best of disinfectants." For example, mandatory disclosure of related-party transactions and of directors' compensation can be an effective tool to limit self-dealing by those in control. Disclosure of price-sensitive information helps prevent insider trading. Well-designed accounting standards and independent and skilful audits can detect Parmalat-style frauds early on.

Tougher public enforcement

Another type of regulatory intervention is enforcement of corporate and securities laws through supervisory agencies and criminal sanctions. Little evidence exists that public enforcement matters (Djankov, Las Porta, Lopez-de-Silanes, and Shleifer, 2006). Yet public enforcement may be the most effective tool to prevent specific forms of expropriation, like insider trading, which are otherwise hard to detect. It may also be needed to impose sufficiently severe sanctions, like prison terms, in extreme cases.

CORPORATE GOVERNANCE REFORMS IN FRANCE, GERMANY, AND ITALY

In the last 15 years, reforms have been enacted in France, Germany, and Italy to improve internal governance mechanisms, empower shareholders, enhance disclosure, and strengthen public enforcement. To understand the impact of these reforms, it is helpful to start by offering some comparisons with the United States.

In the United States, the directors make all the decisions (or have an exclusive power to initiate them if a shareholder vote is mandated). In Europe, shareholders have a final say on a larger number of issues, such as share buy-backs, dividend payments, and new issues. European shareholders also have much greater power to set the shareholder meeting agenda (Cools, 2005). This allocation of power backs up the prevailing ownership structures: in both cases, the law grants the controllers (management in the United States, dominant shareholders in Europe) the right to exercise and retain control.

The US central government has long played a much more important role in regulating corporate governance than the European Community on the other side of the Atlantic: US securities regulation has developed since the 1930s and deals with many crucial corporate governance issues, such as shareholder meetings and voting, insider trading, takeovers, securities fraud, and now, with the Sarbanes–Oxley Act, even board composition and functioning (Roe, 2003). By contrast, the European Community, despite its power to enact binding regulations and directives in corporate law matters, has traditionally had a much lower impact on European companies' corporate governance (Enriques, 2006).

Furthermore, US securities regulation provides for a system of mandatory disclosure that is traditionally far more comprehensive than Europe's. Its effectiveness is ensured by an aggressive set of enforcement institutions, such as the securities plaintiff bar (lawyers who bring class action suits on behalf of large numbers of investors), the Securities and Exchange Commission (SEC), and the US Department of Justice. In Europe, enforcement is in the hands of member states, which have traditionally been far from aggressive in tackling violations of corporate and securities laws via public enforcement. With no plaintiff bar and long-standing legal hurdles to shareholder litigation, private enforcement of directors' duties is almost unheard of. This pattern is in sharp contrast with the United States, where corporate directors face a high risk of being sued if they engage in self-dealing. When such a lawsuit occurs, the courts, especially in Delaware, are very strict in judging a director's loyalty to the corporation.

While the various continental European corporate governance systems can look rather similar, especially when compared with the US system, each also has its own distinctive traits.

German law mandates a two-tier board structure, made up of a "supervisory board" and a "managerial board." In companies with more than 2,000 employees, the supervisory board must be composed of equal numbers of shareholder-elected and employee-chosen members (so-called "co-determination"). Banks have traditionally played a central role in the supervisory boards of listed companies, as a result of their shareholdings and of their acting as their clients' proxies in shareholder meetings (Fohlin, 2005). Unsurprisingly, supervisory boards, packed with employees and bank representatives, have been quite ineffective in monitoring management (and dominant shareholders) on behalf of outside investors (Theisen, 1998).

In France, managerial power has historically been concentrated in the hands of the chief executive officer, who, by law, also acted as chairman of the board. At least on paper, corporate law has traditionally been friendlier to minority shareholders in France than in Germany or Italy. As one example, individual shareholders of French companies have long been able to sue directors derivatively and a special regime has always applied to related-party transactions involving board members: these transactions need to be approved by the board and ratified by the shareholder meeting, unless they are deemed to be routine "current transactions entered into at normal conditions." In general, however, judges and practitioners have traditionally provided a mild interpretation of this regime; for example, by classifying most transactions with companies of a same group as routine (Enriques, 2004).

In Italy, a separate board of auditors—an internal body composed exclusively of formally independent members—has traditionally performed the internal audit functions. Neither the board of directors nor the board of auditors have ever been able to exercise effective control over managers (and hence over the dominant shareholders who appoint them), as the Parmalat scandal vividly illustrated. More generally, Italian corporate law has historically provided poor protection for investors, while enforcement institutions, like courts or the Italian securities and exchange commission (Consob), have been unable to make up for the deficiencies of the law (Aganin and Volpin, 2005).

Three main factors have driven the reforms in continental European corporate governance over the last two decades. First, reforms aimed to make national capital markets more attractive at a time when international competition for equity capital was increasing due to deregulation, globalization, and large-scale privatizations (Kamar, 2006). Second, changes were spurred as part of the European Community's efforts to institute a common regulatory framework for European financial markets, especially on disclosure issues (Ferran, 2004). Finally, many of the corporate law reforms recently enacted in Europe have come as a response to corporate scandals, including both the well-publicized cases like Enron and Parmalat, and many other scandals, like the recent financial frauds in France and Germany discussed in Enriques (2003). For example, a 1998 German corporate governance reform was enacted after Metallgesellschaft and other corporate scandals exposed German corporations' defective internal control mechanisms (Cioffi, 2002).

The discussion that follows highlights the efforts of lawmakers to enact corporate governance reforms that may help protect minority shareholders of listed corporations.[2] Tables 15.4 to 15.7 summarize the relevant reforms. For general overviews of European corporate law reforms, see Nowak (2004) and Noack and Zetzsche (2005) (Germany); Conac (forthcoming) (France); and Bianchi and Enriques (2005) and Ferrarini, Giudici, and Stella Richter (2005) (Italy). Enriques and Gatti (2006) provide an overview of recent reforms at the European Community level.

Strengthening internal governance mechanisms

In the wake of US scandals, reforms enacted by the US Congress and the main stock exchanges (NYSE and Nasdaq) have required that a majority of directors be independent, that audit committees be entirely composed of independent directors and that companies have adequate internal control mechanisms. Further, independence requirements have been tightened and audit committees' powers and responsibilities have been extended. Finally, attempts to curb self-dealing have been imposed by requiring that companies have a compensation committee entirely composed of independent directors and by banning corporate loans to directors. None of the European countries considered here have gone as far as the United States in their attempts to strengthen internal governance mechanisms. Table 15.4 shows the internal governance reforms in continental Europe that involve improving *board effectiveness* or tightening rules on *related-party transactions.*

In Germany, the 1998 reform sought to improve internal corporate governance by redefining the functions of both the management board and the supervisory board. The management board now must ensure that adequate risk management and internal audit systems are in place and must report to the supervisory board over risk management issues, budget, and business plans. Supervisory boards must meet at least four times a year and have an increased role in the choice of, and relationship with, the auditor.

French law has done little to empower the board of directors, other than to *allow* companies to separate the roles of chairman of the board and chief executive officer. Some attempts were made to give more information to directors from outside the firm. In 2001, a new law stated that "each director should receive all information needed to fulfill his duties" and that "each director can obtain any and all documents that he sees fit to request" (Menjucq, 2005, p. 702). But two years later, French lawmakers scrapped the latter provision, preventing individual board members from accessing the company's documents directly.

In Italy, reforms strengthened internal governance mechanisms by requiring that executive directors regularly inform the board of directors and the board of auditors of business developments and related-party transactions, and most importantly, that at least one director and one board-of-auditors member be elected by minority shareholders. The reforms also entrusted the board of auditors with greater powers and somewhat tightened their members' independence requirements.

France and Italy have strengthened their rules on self-dealing transactions by dominant shareholders. France made its special regime on directors' related-party transactions also applicable to transactions involving the parent company or any shareholder holding more than 10 percent of the voting rights and to executive compensation packages granting a lump-sum bonus at the time of appointment or dismissal.

In its 2003 corporate law reform, Italy revised its previously lax regime on self-dealing transactions to "strengthen its prophylactic character" (Ferrarini, Giudici, and Stella Richter, 2005, p. 680). Directors now have to disclose to the whole board and to the board of auditors any direct or indirect interest they might have in a transaction. Prior board-of-directors approval is required for transactions in which the chief executive officer has an interest. While interested directors need not abstain from voting, the

France	Germany	Italy
Board effectiveness		
Separation of Chairman and CEO allowed (2001).	Greater role for supervisory board (1998).	New rules on board's information (1998 and 2003).
New rules on board's information (2001 and 2003).	Specific duties on risk management and internal controls (1998)	Minorities represented in board of directors (2005) and in board of auditors (1998).
		Greater role and powers for board of auditors. Stricter independence requirements for its members (1998 and 2005).
Internal governance and self-dealing		
Board approval of nonroutine transactions with significant shareholders and of some forms of executive compensation; board disclosure of nontrivial routine self-dealing transactions mandated (2001, 2003, and 2005).		Increased board disclosure and procedural requirements on related-party transactions (2003).

Table 15.4 **Internal governance reforms in France, Germany, and Italy**

board resolution must "adequately explain the reasons for the transaction and the benefits deriving to the company" (p. 681). This mandatory justification of the transaction's fairness has to be more detailed and analytical when the corporation decides for it under the influence of its parent company.

By contrast, no new internal governance rules for related-party transactions have been enacted in Germany over the past 15 years.

Empowering shareholders

In the United States, shareholders have become louder and more powerful. The two main stock exchanges amended their listing rules in 2003 to require shareholder approval of stock-based compensation plans, and also prohibited brokers from voting their clients' shares to approve such plans, unless the clients instruct them on how to vote. Restrictions on brokers' discretionary voting (they usually back management's proposals) are now being discussed with reference to board elections, an issue where recent developments at the state and federal level have strengthened shareholders' power (Klingsberg, 2006; for the policy debate see Bebchuk, 2005, and Bainbridge, 2006).

Lawmakers in continental Europe have taken various steps to increase minority shareholders' powers vis-à-vis managers and dominant shareholders, as summarized in Table 15.5. They have *strengthened shareholders' voice* in corporate governance. Shareholders now have the power to authorize or ratify some transactions and resolutions in a potential conflict of interest. As noted, in France the general meeting has to ratify any nonroutine transactions with a major shareholder and some forms of executive compensation. In Italy, a specific provision now requires the meeting's approval of any form of stock-based compensation.

In each of the three countries, shareholders now face lower costs for voting. Companies can allow remote voting via Internet and telecommunications technology. France and Germany have also introduced rules to reduce technical barriers to voting by shareholders residing abroad and to facilitate the circulation of documents, including shareholder proposals, prior to the meeting.

Italian companies' shareholders formerly had to deposit their shares with a bank five days prior to the meeting, which prevented them from selling their shares during those five days and hence severely discouraged voting, especially by institutional investors. In 2003 this provision was repealed; the default rule is now no deposit obligation, although company bylaws may require an up to two-day deposit obligation. No such requirement exists in Germany, where a new law has clarified this point. In France, corporate bylaws can require the deposit of shares for up to five days prior to the meeting, but a 2002 decree provides that shareholders remain free to sell their shares up until the day before the meeting.

To limit the power of controlling shareholders, special majorities for "nonroutine" shareholder resolutions have traditionally been in place in France and Germany. In Italy, since 1998, a two-thirds majority of the shares represented at the meeting has been required for various kinds of resolutions, including new issues, mergers, and amendments to the bylaws. The purpose is to allocate some power to large minority shareholders, in hopes that they monitor the controlling shareholder.

France and Italy also lowered the ownership thresholds for some minority shareholder rights, such as the right to call a meeting (from 10 to 5 percent and from 20 to 10 percent, respectively) or to ask a court to appoint an expert for the review of transactions (from 10 to 5 percent in both countries).[3]

Of these three countries, Germany has done the most to *limit deviations from the one-share-one-vote principle*, but Italy has also taken steps in this direction. Germany banned multiple-voting shares in 1998, and also prohibited banks from acting as a clients' proxy if they own more than 5 percent of the shares. More generally, the rules on bank voting of clients' shares were revised to discourage the clients' tendency to let banks decide freely on how to vote and hence, as a rule, support management. In 2002, Germany revised its tax code to exempt from taxation capital gains from sales of shareholdings held by corporations. The aim was to encourage firms and financial institutions to disentangle their cross-shareholdings. Italy did the same in 2003. In both countries, the exemption also applies to newly acquired holdings, so that it is not obvious that it should lead to a lower number of corporate shareholdings. In fact, while in Germany firms did disentangle their cross-shareholdings, a process that was already under way when the tax-break was enacted (Fohlin, 2005), in Italy the tax-break was followed by an increase in the number of corporate block-holdings (Bianchi and Bianco, 2006).

Italy also reformed its corporate law to counter

France	Germany	Italy
Greater voice for shareholders		
Annual ratification by shareholder meeting of nonroutine transactions with significant shareholders and of some forms of executive compensation (2001, 2003, and 2005). Exercise of voting rights made easier (2001). Lower thresholds for minority shareholder rights (2002).	Exercise of voting rights made easier (2001). Communication among shareholders facilitated (2005).	Shareholder approval of stock-based compensation (2005). Exercise of voting rights made easier (2003). Qualified majority for major resolutions (1998). Lower thresholds for minority shareholder rights (1998 and 2005).
One-share-one-vote rules		
	Multiple voting shares banned and banks' influence over shareholder meetings curbed (1998). Sale of corporate shareholdings tax-exempt (2002).	Voting caps banned (2003). Limits on validity of shareholder agreements (1998). Sale of corporate shareholdings tax-exempt (2003).
Private enforcement		
(Individual shareholders were already allowed to bring derivative suits.)	Derivative suits made easier (2005). Civil actions for securities fraud made easier (2003).	Derivative suits for minorities representing at least 2.5 percent of shares allowed (1998 and 2005). Contingency fees allowed (2006). Direct shareholder suit against parent company for damages stemming from abuse of corporate control introduced (2003).
Control transactions		
Mandatory bid rule (1992).	Mandatory bid rule (2002).	Mandatory bid rule (1998).

Table 15.5 **Shareholder empowerment reforms in France, Germany, and Italy**

various forms of deviation from one-share-one-vote. In 1998 the so-called "Draghi Law" tackled shareholder agreements—that is, pacts among blockholders to set a common voting policy and/or restrict their freedom to sell shares. These agreements, which are very common in Italy's large listed companies, stabilize control in the hands of the blockholders, who are often linked by a web of cross-holdings (Ferrarini, 2001). The 1998 law introduced a three-year time limit for these agreements, so that parties are free to back off from them every three years. The law also provides that in the event of a takeover bid the parties

are free to tender their shares, no matter what restrictions the agreements would impose on their sale.

Another mechanism by which shareholders can have more say is *private enforcement by shareholder lawsuits.* Germany and Italy have enacted reforms favoring derivative suits, which are shareholder actions for damages against directors on behalf of the corporation.

In Italy, derivative suits were first permitted in 1998, but standing to sue was restricted to shareholders holding at least 5 percent of the shares. No derivative action has yet been brought, probably because of this high threshold and other hurdles. For example, in Italy the losing party in a suit has to pay the winner's lawyer fees. Also, shareholder plaintiffs can find it almost impossible to obtain the evidence they need to substantiate their claims, in the absence of US-style rules providing for pre-trial discovery (Enriques, 2004). However, Italy has made some changes. Contingency fees (lawyers' fees that are owed only if the client wins or settles) were made legal in 2006, and the threshold for a shareholder suit was reduced to 2.5 percent in 2005.[4] Further, any shareholder may sue the parent company for damages, if it has abused its control powers.

Of the three countries, Germany has enacted the most extensive revisions to encourage US-style shareholder litigation. For example, rules introduced in 2005 make it possible for shareholders representing at least 1 percent of shares or shares worth at least €100,000 to bring a derivative suit against directors. Settlement agreements have to be disclosed to the public, and a special regime on lawyers' fees more favorable to plaintiff shareholders has been introduced.

Germany also enacted rules to facilitate shareholder suits for damages stemming from violations of issuers' duty to disclose material information. Such suits were first allowed in 2003. Two years later, procedural rules were introduced to facilitate securities class action lawsuits. No such procedural rules exist in Italy or in France.

European lawmakers have also been active in the field of *control transactions*. All three countries have introduced a "mandatory bid rule": that is, the acquirer of a control block must offer to acquire all the remaining shares at a price usually above market.

Enhancing disclosure requirements

The regulatory framework for disclosure has improved on both sides of the Atlantic. After its own corporate scandals, the United States imposed additional disclosure obligations and enhanced the role of auditors (as Coates discusses in this issue). In continental Europe in the last 15 years, major disclosure reforms have been enacted, that mainly cover four spheres: 1) corporate governance; 2) self-dealing and insider trading; 3) compensation; and 4) financial reporting. Table 15.6 summarizes these changes.

In France, companies are required to disclose *corporate governance arrangements* in a detailed report, which must also state whether they comply with the relevant corporate governance code. In Italy companies must declare whether they comply with the stock exchange corporate governance code, in Germany with the official code.

Disclosure of self-dealing has also improved. Following a 2002 European Community Regulation, starting in 2006 the annual accounts of listed companies must be drawn according to the International Financial Reporting Standards (IFRS), whose Standard 24 requires detailed and specific disclosure of related-party transactions. Annual disclosure of related-party transactions was already the rule in France, although in practice shareholder meetings had traditionally been given little specific information about them (Enriques, 2004). Italy, at least on paper, went further. In 2002, Consob (the Italian securities and exchange commission) issued new rules requiring prompt, ongoing disclosure of *material* related-party transactions. However, companies rarely disclose such transactions (Consob, 2005), taking advantage of the vagueness of the criteria used to identify materiality.

A 2003 European Community directive on "market abuse"—the short name for insider trading and securities fraud—contains disclosure provisions aimed to prevent it (Ferrarini, 2004). The directive extends the definition of inside price-sensitive information requiring immediate disclosure. It also requires disclosure of trading activity on a company's shares by its directors and persons closely connected with them. Between 2003 and 2005, all three countries have changed their laws to incorporate these provisions. Only Italy followed the US example and extended the disclosure requirement to trading activity by controlling shareholders.

Until recently, *compensation* received by European companies' directors was a well-guarded secret. Reforms have now mandated complete disclosure of the compensation of individual board members, including stock options: Italy has required annual disclosure since 1999, France since 2001, and Germany since 2006.

However, German companies, upon a vote of shareholders representing at least 75 percent of the shares, may opt out of the new disclosure requirement until 2011.

Companies from continental European countries used to accumulate hidden reserves due to conservative accounting policies. Under the new IFRS rules on *financial reporting,* the principle of "fair value accounting" forces companies to disclose such reserves. As a

France	Germany	Italy
Corporate governance		
Corporate governance report mandated; corporate governance code mandated on a comply-or-explain basis (2003).	Corporate governance code mandated on a comply-or-explain basis (2002).	Corporate governance code mandated on comply-or-explain basis (2005).
Self-dealing and compensation		
IAS/IFRS 24 (2002, effective 2006).	*IAS/IFRS 24* (2002, effective 2006).	*IAS/IFRS 24* (2002, effective 2006).
Annual disclosure of nonroutine transactions with significant shareholders and of some forms of executive compensation (2001, 2003, and 2005).	*Price-sensitive information to be immediately disclosed* (1994 and 2004).	Immediate disclosure of material related-party transactions (2002).
Price-sensitive information to be immediately disclosed (pre-existing; revised in 2005).	*Disclosure of directors' and officers' trading* (2004).	*Price sensitive information to be immediately disclosed* (1991 and 2005).
Disclosure of directors' and officers' trading (2005).	Annual disclosure of individual directors' compensation (2006).	*Disclosure of directors' and officers' trading* (2005).
Annual disclosure of individual directors' compensation (2001).		Disclosure of major shareholders' trading (2005).
		Annual disclosure of individual directors' compensation (1999).
Financial reporting and audit		
IFRS reporting mandated (2002, effective 2006).	*IFRS reporting mandated* (2002, effective 2006).	*IFRS reporting mandated* (2002, effective 2006).
CEO abstains from proposal of auditors (2003).	Increased cooperation between supervisory board and auditor (1998).	Increased cooperation between supervisory board and auditor (1998).
Audit partner rotation (6 yrs) (2003).	Audit partner rotation (7 yrs) (1998).	General manager's and CFO's statement on truth of financial reports and adequacy of accounting procedures (2005).
Prohibition on nonaudit services to audit clients (2003).	Prohibition on nonaudit services to audit clients (2004).	Audit partner rotation (6 yrs) and audit firm rotation (12 yrs) (2005).
		Prohibition on nonaudit services to audit clients (2005).

Table 15.6 **Disclosure reforms in France, Germany, and Italy *(European Community reforms in italics)***

consequence, investors should be better able to understand whether companies retain excessive cash in the effort to maximize the size of the firm and the private benefits that size can bring.

Finally, continental European jurisdictions have also taken steps to strengthen auditors' independence and effectiveness, similar to the US rules imposed under the Sarbanes–Oxley legislation.

Tougher public enforcement

By international standards, the United States has very strict public enforcement of corporate governance rules, which the post-scandal reforms have made even tougher. As Coates explains in this issue, the US Congress has raised SEC resources, increased criminal sanctions for fraud, and set up a body to supervise auditors, the Public Company Accounting Oversight Board, or PCAOB. Table 15.7 summarizes the changes in France, Germany, and Italy in the area of tougher public enforcement.

France, Germany, and Italy have all reshaped and strengthened their public enforcement structures in the past 15 years. Germany has done the most in the area of *supervisory authority's powers* for the remarkable reason that prior to 1994 it had no authority for supervising securities markets. Germany has thus had to build this authority from scratch. Italy has granted Consob greater powers. France, which already had a powerful public enforcement agency in place, merged (like Germany) all its financial supervision into one authority, the AMF (Autorité des Marchés Financiers); Germany's new financial supervision authority is the Federal Financial Supervisory Authority (BaFin).

France, Germany, and Italy all now provide for criminal *sanctions in cases of market abuse*. France has done so since 1970; since 1996, fines for insider trading violations can also be imposed on corporations. Italy prohibited insider trading and market manipulation, respectively, in 1991 and 1998; Germany in 1994 and 2002. With the adoption of the Market Abuse Directive in 2003, all three countries had to tighten their regime with various measures to facilitate the punishment of insider trading and market manipulation. For example, Italy increased the

maximum prison term and the fines for the two crimes; coupled the criminal sanction with an administrative one that Consob can impose directly (as a remedy to the frequent inertia of public prosecutors); and strengthened Consob's investigative powers.

All three countries have strengthened their public enforcement apparatus on *financial reporting and auditing*. Germany and Italy have introduced rules providing for the supervisory agency's review of companies' financial reports. All three countries have introduced or strengthened the public oversight on auditors. France in 2003 and Germany in 2004 instituted an equivalent of the US Public Company Accounting Oversight Board (PCAOB). Italy's Consob supervisory powers over audit firms were greatly extended in 2005 (after they had been reduced by the 1998 reform).

CONCLUSION

Corporate governance in continental Europe traditionally differs from that in the United States in two important ways: first, most European companies have controlling shareholders, while most American corporations are widely held; second, the regulations on self-dealing have traditionally been stricter in the United States.

France	Germany	Italy
Powers of supervisory authority		
Merger of securities and banking authorities (2003).	Securities regulator set up (1994) and granted extensive investigative and sanctioning power (various years). Merger of securities and banking authorities (2002).	Increased regulator's investigative and sanctioning power (1998 and 2005).
Sanctions against market abuse		
Market abuse regime tightened (2005).	Criminal sanctions for *insider trading* (1994) and market manipulation (2002). *Market abuse regime tightened (2002 and 2004).*	Criminal sanctions for *insider trading* (1991) and market manipulation (1998). *Market abuse regime tightened (2005).*
Enforcing rules concerning financial reporting and auditing		
French "PCAOB" (2003).	Securities' agency review of financial reports (2004). German "PCAOB" (2004).	Securities' agency review of financial reports (2005). Securities agency's powers on audit firms strengthened (2005).

Table 15.7 **Public enforcement reforms in France, Germany, and Italy** *(European Community reforms in italics)*

In the last 15 years, France, Germany, and Italy have enacted significant corporate law reforms to strengthen the mechanisms of internal governance, empower shareholders, enhance disclosure requirements, and toughen public enforcement. Special emphasis was placed on empowering minority shareholders and on disclosure, which are the most effective tools for countering abuses by dominant shareholders.

However, before concluding the reforms have benefited investors, a few words of caution are in order. First, far too little has been done to resolve the problem of related-party transactions, which is the most common form of self-dealing for dominant shareholders in Europe. Germany has done nothing to improve its law on this matter. France and Italy have introduced stricter rules on such transactions but have not done enough to strengthen private enforcement, which is an absolute necessity for giving these rules "teeth," making them effective in the real world.

Second, a good part of the European reforms have been patterned after US corporate and securities law. America does have a well-developed legal framework for corporate governance, which has been further improved by the post-scandal reforms. However, the fundamental differences in ownership structure between Europe and the United States mean that emulating laws whose focus is on curbing managerial opportunism may not be an appropriate way to prevent self-dealing by controlling shareholders. Indeed, a cynical observer might argue that when European policymakers adopt US-style solutions designed to tackle managerial agency problems, they can appear to be doing something to reform European corporate governance while actually leaving the rents of Europe's dominant shareholders perfectly intact.

In view of its recent evolution, corporate governance law in Europe is often described as being in a "state of permanent reform" (Noack and Zetzsche, 2005). The reform effort needs to continue if continental Europe is to address in an effective manner the basic problems of corporate governance that are posed by the power of dominant shareholders.

Acknowledgement:

We wish to thank Gabriele Apfelbacher, Andrea Carinci, Holger Fleischer, Philipp Heer, Virginie Henry, Federico Mucciarelli, Giuseppe Scassellati Sforzolini, and especially Andrei Shleifer for helpful discussions and suggestions. We received helpful comments on earlier drafts from Pierre-Henri Conac, Lorenzo Forni, James Hines, Martin Gelter, Peter Mülbert, Thomas Paul, Timothy Taylor, Michael Waldman, Dirk Zetzsche, Daniel Zimmer, and seminar participants at the London School of Economics. Marco De Nadai and Andrea Zorzi provided valuable research assistance. Usual disclaimers apply.

NOTES

1 A similar skeptical view applies to compensation schemes for executives, which are unlikely to alleviate the abuses of controlling shareholders, if—as it seems—compensation schemes are not immune from managerial abuses in widely held corporations (Bebchuk and Fried, 2004).

2 Case law, including the core area of fiduciary duties, is outside the scope of this paper. Fleischer (2005) discusses the "transplant" of Anglo-American fiduciary duty doctrines in continental Europe.

3 French law provides that shareholders may petition the court for the appointment of such an expert in order to gather information about suspicious transactions. Italian law grants minority shareholders a similar right, but where serious irregularities in the company's management are found, the court may take further measures, such as convening the general meeting or even removing the directors.

4 The ban on contingency fees and the procedural hurdles also exists in France and may explain why derivative suits have always been extremely rare there, despite the absence of any ownership threshold (Enriques, 2004).

REFERENCES

Aganin, Alexander, and Paolo Volpin. 2005. "The History of Corporate Ownership in Italy." In *A History of Corporate Governance around the World*, ed. Randall K. Morck, 325–361. Chicago and London: The University of Chicago Press.

Anderson, Ronald C. and David M. Reeb. 2003. ("Founding Family Ownership and Firm Performance." *Journal of Finance.* 58(3): 1301–28.

Bainbridge, Stephen M. 2006. "Director Primacy and Shareholder Disempowerment." *Harvard Law Review.* 119(6): 1735–58.

Barca, Fabrizio, and Marco Becht, eds. 2001. *The Control of Corporate Europe.* Oxford: Oxford University Press.

Barontini, Roberto, and Lorenzo Caprio. 2005. "The Effect of Family Control on Firm Value and Performance. Evidence from Continental Europe." ECGI Finance Working Paper 88/2005.

Bebchuk, Lucian A. 1994. "Efficient and Inefficient Sales of Corporate Control." *Quarterly Journal of Economics,* November, 109(4): 957–93.

Bebchuk, Lucian A. 2005. "The Case for Increasing Shareholder Power." *Harvard Law Review*, 118(3): 833–917.

Bebchuk, Lucian A., and Jesse M. Fried. 2004. *Pay Without Performance.* Cambridge and London: Harvard University Press.

Berle, Adolf, and Gardiner Means. 1932. *The Modern Corporation and Private Property.* New York: Macmillan.

Bertrand, Marianne, and Antoinette Schoar. 2006. "The Role of Family in Family Firms." *Journal of Economic Perspectives*, 20(2): 73–96.

Bhattacharya, Utpal, and Hazem Daouk. 2002. "The World Price of Insider Trading." *Journal of Finance*, 57(1): 75–108.

Bianchi, Marcello, and Magda Bianco. 2006. "Italian Corporate Governance in the Last 15 Years: From Pyramids to Coalitions?" Unpublished paper.

Bianchi, Marcello, and Luca Enriques. 2005. "Corporate Governance in Italy after the 1998 Reform: What Role for Institutional Investors?" *Corporate Ownership & Control*, 2(4): 11–31.

Brandeis, Louis D. 1914. *Others People's Money and How the Bankers Use It.* New York: Stokes.

Cioffi, John W. 2002. "Reforming 'Germany Inc.': The Politics of Company and Takeover Law Reform in Germany and the European Union." *Law & Policy*, 24(4): 355–402.

Coffee Jr., John C. 2005. "A Theory of Corporate Scandals: Why the US and Europe Differ." *Oxford Review of Economic Policy*, 21(2): 198–211.

Conac, Pierre-Henri. Forthcoming. "French Corporate Governance Law—Current Issues." In *Modern Company Law for a European Economy. Ways and Means,* ed. Ulf Bernitz. Stockholm: Norstedt Juridik.

Consob. 2005. *Annual Report 2004.* Rome, March, 31.

Cools, Sofie. 2005. "The Real Difference in Corporate Law between the United States and Continental Europe: Distribution of Powers." *Delaware Journal of Corporate Law*, 30(3): 697–766.

Denis, Diane, and John J. Mc Connell. 2003. "International Corporate Governance." *Journal of Financial and Quantitative Analysis*, 38(1): 1–36.

Djankov, Simeon, Rafael La Porta, Florencio Lopez-de-Silanes, and Andrei Shleifer. 2006. "The Law and Economics of Self-Dealing." NBER Working Paper 11883.

Dyck, Alexander, and Luigi Zingales. 2004. "Private Benefits of Control: An International Comparison." *Journal of Finance*, 59(2): 537–600.

Enriques, Luca. 2003. "Bad Apples, Bad Oranges: A Comment from Old Europe on Post-Enron Corporate Governance Reforms." *Wake Forest Law Review*, 38(3): 911–34.

Enriques, Luca. 2004. "Book Review: The Comparative Anatomy of Corporate Law." *American Journal of Comparative Law*, 52(4): 1011–36.

Enriques, Luca. 2006. "EC Company Law Directives and Regulations: How Trivial Are They?" *University of Pennsylvania Journal of International Economic Law*, 27(1): 1–78.

Enriques, Luca, and Matteo Gatti. 2006. "EC Reforms of Corporate Governance and Capital Markets Law: Do They Tackle Insiders' Opportunism?" http://papers.ssrn.com/sol3/papers.cfm?abstract_id=886345.

Faccio, Mara, and Larry Lang. 2002. "The Ultimate Owner of Western European Corporations." *Journal of Financial Economics*, 65(3): 365–95.

Ferran, Eilis. 2004. *Building an EU Securities Market.* Cambridge: Cambridge University Press.

Ferrarini, Guido A. 2001. "'Share Ownership, Takeover Law and the Contestability of Corporate Control. A Comparative Outlook of Current Trends." http://papers.ssrn.com/sol3/papers.cfm?abstract_id=265429.

Ferrarini, Guido A. 2004. "The European Market Abuse Directive." *Common Market Law Review*, 41(3): 711–41.

Ferrarini, Guido A., and Paolo Giudici. 2005. "Financial Scandals and the Role of Private Enforcement: The Parmalat Case." ECGI Law Working Paper 40/2005.

Ferrarini, Guido A., Paolo Giudici, and Mario Stella Richter. 2005. "Company Law Reform in Italy: Real Progress?" *Rabels Zeitschrift für ausländisches und internationales Privatrecht.* 69(4): 658–97.

Fleischer, Holger. 2005. "Legal Transplants in European Company Law—The Case of Fiduciary Duties." *European Corporate and Financial Law Review*, 2(3): 378–97.

Fohlin, Caroline. 2005. "The History of Corporate Ownership and Control in Germany." In *A History of Corporate Governance around the World,* ed. Randall K. Morck, 223–277. Chicago and London: The University of Chicago Press.

Franks, Julian, Colin Mayer, and Stefano Rossi. 2005. "Spending Less Time with the Family: The Decline of Family Ownership in the United Kingdom." In *A History of Corporate Governance Around the World,* ed. Randall K. Morck, 581–607. Chicago: The University of Chicago Press.

Jensen, Michael, and William Meckling. 1976. "Theory of the Firm: Managerial Behavior, Agency Costs, and Ownership Structure." *Journal of Financial Economics*, 3(1): 305–60.

Johnson, Simon, Rafael La Porta, Florencio Lopez-de-Silanes, and Andrei Shleifer. 2000. "Tunneling." *American Economic Review Papers and Proceedings*, 90(2): 22–27.

Kamar, Ehud. 2006. "Beyond Competition for Incorporations." *Georgetown Law Journal.* 94(6): 1725–70.

Kirchmaier, Tom, and Jeremy Grant. 2005. "Financial Tunnelling and the Revenge of the Insider System." FMG Discussion Papers dp536, Financial Markets Group. http://ideas.repec.org/p/fmg/fmgdps/dp536.html.

Klingsberg, Ethan. 2006. "New Court Decisions, Regulatory Positions and Legislation Provide New Tools for Stockholder Activists: Increases in Stockholder-Adopted By-laws and Proxy Contests on the Horizon." *Cleary Gottlieb M&A and Corporate Governance Report. September 2006.* http://www.cgsh.com/files/tbl_s47Details%5CFileUpload65%5C646%5CCGSH_72-2006.pdf.

La Porta, Rafael, Florencio Lopez-de-Silanes, and Andrei Shleifer. 1999. "Corporate Ownership Around the World." *Journal of Finance,* 54(2): 471–517.

La Porta, Rafael, Florencio Lopez-de-Silanes, and Andrei Shleifer. 2006. "What Works in Securities Laws?" *Journal of Finance*, 61(1): 1–32.

La Porta, Rafael, Florencio Lopez-de-Silanes, Andrei Shleifer, and Robert W. Vishny. 1997. "Legal Determinants of external Finance." *Journal of Finance*, 52(3): 1131–50.

Manne, Henry. 1965. "Mergers and the Market for Corporate Control." *Journal of Political Economy,* 73(2): 110–20.

Menjucq, Michel. 2005. "The Company Law Reform in France." *Rabels Zeitschrift für ausländisches und internationales Privatrecht,* 69(4): 698–711.

Morck, Randall, Daniel Wolfenzon, and Bernard Yeung. 2005. "Corporate Governance, Economic Entrenchment and Growth." *Journal of Economic Literature,* 43:3, pp. 655–720.

Morck, Randall, and Bernard Yeung. 2005. "Dividend Taxation and Corporate Governance." *Journal of Economic Perspectives,* 19(3): 163–80.

Nenova, Tatiana. 2003. "The Value of Corporate Voting Rights and Control: A Cross-country Analysis." *Journal of Financial Economics,* 68(3): 325–51.

Noack, Ulrich, and Dirk A. Zetzsche. 2005. "Corporate Reform in Germany: The Second Decade." *European Business Law Review,* 16:5, pp. 1033–64.

Nowak, Erik. 2004. "Investor Protection and Capital Market Regulation in Germany." In *The German Financial System,* ed. Jan P. Krahnen and Reinhard H. Schmidt, 425–49. Oxford: Oxford University Press.

Rajan, Raghuram, and Luigi Zingales. 1998. "Financial Dependence and Growth." *American Economic Review,* 88(2): 559–86.

Roe, Mark J. 2003. "Delaware's Competition." *Harvard Law Review,* 117(2): 588 –646.

Rossi, Stefano, and Paolo Volpin. 2004. "Cross-Country Determinants of Mergers and Acquisitions." *Journal of Financial Economics,* 74(2): 277–304.

Theisen, Manuel R. 1998. "Empirical Evidence and Economic Comments on Board Structure in Germany." In *Comparative Corporate Governance: The State of the Art and Emerging Research,* ed. Klaus J. Hopt, Hideki Kanda, Mark J. Roe, Eddy Wymeersch, and Stefan Prigge, 259–65. Oxford: Oxford University Press.

F
O
U
R

PART FIVE

The Impact of Shareholder Value

INTRODUCTION TO PART FIVE

The sharpest point of the advance of Anglo-Saxon modes of corporate governance is the principle of shareholder value as the central objective of corporations. Technically shareholder value is the capacity of the firm to generate value by achieving a cash return greater than the cost of capital itself. However, what is contentious is first the methods employed to generate this shareholder value, often short-term reduction of costs, sometimes directed at investments essential for the future, such as research and development, or employment and training. Second is the impact of an excessive focus on one financial indicator, potentially leading to a relative neglect on product quality or customer satisfaction for example. Finally there is the objection to the assumption that all value created is essentially for the shareholders, again potentially limiting the capacity to invest in the development and growth of the company. Ultimately the direction of the development of corporate governance in Europe will be determined by the extent to which shareholder value orientations and their accompanying managerial practices take hold.

The problematic nature of the concept of shareholder value is debated by Michel Aglietta and Antoine Rebérioux. While historically there may have been some credibility to the claims of entrepreneurs who completed all of the functions of management, production and marketing to the profit of the company, in the large managerial firm there is a collaborative corporate basis to the production of profit, and it is not convincing that the profit is the exclusive preserve of shareholders (Blair and Stout 1999). Similarly with risk, if in the past shareholders were identified as the risk takers with a right as residual claimants to the profits of the company, there is an increasing realization of the risks that have been effectively transferred to employees through flexibility, short-term contracts and other employment practices. In the US there has been a progressive rise in dividend payments to shareholders apparently excluding any possibility that there could be a reduction in the cash flow paid to shareholders. This one-sidedness neglects the plurality of the process of value creation, the critical importance of human capital, and the essential role played by numerous stakeholders. The interests of this wider group must be reflected in the fiduciary duties of company directors, and not just the interests of shareholders, as a practical necessity, if not as an ethical imperative. This returns to a holistic conception of the firm, as Berle and Means (1933) outlined, that focuses on its autonomous and collective nature, which cannot be reduced to a contractual set of inter-individual relationships.

Jürgens *et al.* survey the changes in corporate governance towards a shareholder value orientation in a group of flagship European car companies. Identified as an industry that destroys value, the share price of these companies has fallen to the point where their low market capitalization makes them vulnerable to hostile takeovers. As a result they have come under insistent pressures to change their corporate governance systems and performance measures. Fiat, PSA Peugeot–Citroën, Renault and the Volkswagen Group have in the past made limited use of the stock market, and had limited exposure to it. Fiat and Peugeot–Citroën have relied on majority family ownership, and Renault and Volkswagen have both had state majority ownership. None of the companies made use of the stock market in terms of their operational need for capital, or in their investment in innovation, or in their international expansion and acquisition strategies, employing internally generated finance and bank finance. During the period studied, from 1991 to 2000, each of the companies put greater emphasis on developing products and volumes. However, each also adopted a greater emphasis on advancing shareholder value. Fiat and Renault adopted a more determined policy of focusing on financial targets for shareholder value. Peugeot–Citroën and Volkswagen adopted a less intensive shareholder value orientation and capital market orientation. However all of the companies made considerable efforts to prevent any shift in their ownership structure, protecting their executives effectively from the capital market. Interestingly, Jürgens *et al.* record that the economic performance of the four companies was in reverse order to their commitment to shareholder value indicating that product development and production values might contribute more to performance than shareholder value management.

Since Jürgens *et al.* completed their survey, further dramatic changes have occurred in the international car industry. The industry has further internationalized both production and sales, with the expansion of new markets in China and other developing countries. Intensification of competition, falling profitability and falling share prices of most large international car companies (with the notable exception of Toyota), have left companies more vulnerable to takeover. However the eventual failure of the Daimler–Chrysler merger after years of investment and effort on the part of Daimler, indicates that integrating different corporate strategies and cultures is not an easy task. (Similarly the GM–Fiat alliance failed, though the Renault–Nissan alliance continues to be effective.) Problems of overcapacity and weak performance have caused recurrent restructuring in the industry with major redundancies and plant closures in most European and American car companies. In the US, the largest number of plant closures and redundancies in the history of American manufacturing industry were announced by GM, Ford and Chysler in a desperate bid to contain costs and restore profitability, in a context of falling sales and huge legacy costs in pensions and health care that were neglected in the past. In Europe Fiat has made the largest cuts, closing 12 plants and cutting the workforce by over 12,000 worldwide; however, even Volkswagen, which increased employment in 2002/03 subsequently reduced staff in 2005. Volkswagen consolidated its position as leader in the European market, followed by PSA and Renault–Nissan, as the market share of Fiat has fallen badly.

However Volkswagen remained an attractive takeover target, and in October 2005 Porsche acquired an 18.53 percent stake in Volkswagen as the European Union moved against Volkswagen's protective company instrument that prevented any owner from exercising more than 20 percent of the firm's voting rights regardless of their stockholding, which originated in a special VW law in 1960 when Volkswagen was privatized. The European Court of Justice declared this instrument illegal in October 2007. There were concerns in Germany that a hedge fund or other international investment institution might secure control of Volkswagen simply to realize its inherent value by breaking it up. In March 2007 Porsche took its holding to 30.9 percent, triggering the European takeover provisions, and in March 2008 the Supervisory Board of the Volkswagen Group, AG, approved Porsche taking majority control of the company with a 51 percent stake. Porsche AG is majority-owned by the Porsche and Piëch families, and Ferdinand Piëch was chairman and CEO of the Volkswagen Group from 1993 to 2002, and remains chairman of the Supervisory Board of Volkswagen. Though a much smaller company than Volkswagen, Porsche was able to effect this takeover because it remained financially stronger, and it is likely it will introduce greater financial controls in the operations of Volkswagen. This will probably include a greater orientation towards shareholder value, and higher executive rewards.

In another study focused on companies in Germany, Jürgens, Naumann and Rupp (2000) suggest the most visible manifestations of change in the direction of a shareholder value economy in Germany are the internal changes by management introducing shareholder value-oriented management control and incentive systems. However, they claim that these changes have primarily affected a handful of large companies such as Daimler–Chrysler and Siemens, though these flagship companies have linkages that flow through to the rest of the economy. Other recent changes include the role of the banks, the loosening of traditional cross-holdings and inter-locking directorate structures, and the growing influence of institutional investors with value orientations. However they contrast German society, where private pension schemes are just developing, with Anglo-Saxon countries where the interests and behavior of private households drives shareholder value orientation more aggressively.

Beyer and Hassel (2005:171) examine the interdependence between economic institutions captured in the idea of *institutional complementarities* and the impact upon this of internationalization, with reference to the changing distribution of net value added in large German firms. The German corporate governance regime is not only bank-based, but also has weak rights for minority shareholders, a lower rate of return for shareholders and a weakly developed market for corporate control. Moreover, it coincides with a system of co-determination and centralized wage bargaining which gives labour a prominent role in the firm's decisions on restructuring and pursuing product market strategies. All of this appears to fit together; for example, the lower return to shareholders is possible with a weak market for corporate control since managers cannot be pressured by the threat of hostile takeovers, and lower returns for shareholders implies higher rates of retained earnings which enables a more consensus-oriented approach to restructuring in line with a higher skill level and employee involvement in the firm. In their survey of large German firms, Beyer and Hassel find a small but significant change in the distribution of net value added towards shareholders in the payment of dividends, resulting from the increasing orientation of firms towards international financial markets and the increasing importance of the market for corporate control, though this does not as yet appear to have affected the relationship between management and employees, though this might happen in time. The direction of changes of the German system will be negotiated for some time to come. Undoubtedly, however, there will be changes from the closed financial networks of the past towards a more internationalized system, with consequent developments towards international accounting standards, auditing, and board supervision.

BIBLIOGRAPHY

Aglietta, M. and Rebérioux, A. (2005) *Corporate Governance Adrift: A Critique of Shareholder Value*, Cheltenham: Edward Elgar.

Berle, A.A. and Means, G.C. (1933) *The Modern Corporation and Private Property*, Amsterdam: Commerce Clearing House.

Beyer, J. and Hassel, A. (2002) The Market for Corporate Control and Financial Internationalisation of German Firms, *Economy and Society*, 31.

Beyer, J. and Hassel, A. (2005) The Effects of Convergence: Internationalisation and the Changing Distribution of Net Value Added in Large German Firms, in Clarke, T. (ed.) *Corporate Governance: Critical Perspectives on Business and Management, vol. III: European Corporate Governance*, London: Routledge.

Blair, M.M. (2003) Director's Duties in a Post-Enron World, *Wake Forest Law Review*, 38: 885–910.

Blair, M.M. (2004) The Neglected Benefits of the Corporate Form: Entity Status and the Separation of Asset Ownership from Control, in A. Grandori (ed.), *Corporate Governance and Firm Organisation: Microfoundations and Structural Forms*, pp. 45–66, Oxford: Oxford University Press.

Blair, M.M. and Stout, L.A. (1999) A Team Production Theory of Corporate Law, V*irginia Law Review*, 85(2): 247–328.

Bratton, W. (2002) Enron and the Dark Side of Shareholder Value, *Tulane Law Review*, 76: 1275–1361.

Deakin, S. (2005) The Coming Transformation of Shareholder Value, *Corporate Governance: An International Review*, 13(1): 11–18.

Froud, J., Haslam, C., Johal, S. and Williams, K. (2000) Shareholder Value and Financialisation, *Economy and Society*, 29(1): 80–110.

Jürgens, U., Naumann, K. and Rupp, J. (2000) Shareholder Value in an Adverse Environment: The German Case, *Economy and Society*, 29(1): pp. 54–79.

16 "The Arrival of Shareholder Value in the European Auto Industry: A Case Study Comparison of Four Car Makers"

from Competition and Change (2002)

Ulrich Jürgens, Yannick Lung, Giuseppe Volpato and Vincent Frigant

SUMMARY

The chapter deals with changes in the corporate governance systems of major European flagship companies in the car industry – Fiat, PSA, Renault and Volkswagen. While all four companies are protected from immediate capital market pressures either by family or state ownership, they have clearly opened up to shareholder value principles in recent years. The central questions of the paper are: to what extent traditional characteristics of corporate governance have converged under the pressure of capital markets; the different approaches companies take to governance and how this affects their performance. To answer these questions, the paper discusses the recent developments of a shareholder value policy and the corresponding changes of targets and controls, as well as of incentive systems, in these companies. The paper also assesses what these companies use the capital markets for: do companies need the stock market to finance their operations? Or does the importance of the stock market rather lie in its function as a market for corporate control? What comes out clearly from the analysis is that none of the companies used the stock market for their operational activities, including major investments. The most important influence of the stock markets lies in the potential for hostile takeover. Even though all four companies investigated are to some degree protected by family or state ownership, they feel the need to raise a defence against this potential danger. As to performance indicators, the analysis shows that a shareholder value policy does not necessarily lead to better economic performance. On the contrary, the analysis shows that the more engaged companies are towards shareholder value policy, the less well they performed in terms of profit margins and returns on capital.

INTRODUCTION

The car industry has come under pressure from the capital markets. It has been singled out as one of the major value destroyers in terms of shareholder value in recent years. The low market capitalisation of some of the companies has put them under threat of a hostile takeover, while institutional investors have voiced their discontent about corporate governance structures in the car industry. In sum, there is a strong pressure on companies to change their traditional corporate governance systems.

However, in terms of ownership most of the European carmakers have only a limited exposure to the stock markets. At all events, this is true for the companies considered in this paper: Fiat, PSA Peugeot-Citroën, Renault and Volkswagen Group. While the first two can still rely on family ownership, the latter two have the state as dominant owner. Nevertheless, recently all four companies have put shareholder interests higher on their priority lists and shown signs of a change in their corporate governance systems. The central question in the following will be: how far will pressure from the capital markets remove differences in the traditional characteristics of corporate governance? Do companies with different corporate governance systems take different approaches when under the pressure of capital markets? This leads to the general issue of what the companies use the capital markets for. Do companies need the stock markets at all to finance their operations? Or, does the importance of the stock market lie in its functions as a market for corporate control?

The chapter is based on case studies of Fiat, PSA, Renault and Volkswagen, which the authors have carried out in the context of a wider research project.[1] The second section gives a brief account of the corporate governance characteristics of each of the four companies. An analysis of the differences in the strategic challenges and responses of these companies and their influence on long-term investment patterns follow this. The next section discusses the recent changes towards a shareholder value policy and corresponding changes in targets, controlling systems and incentive systems. The final section analyses the importance of the stock markets as a means of financing the operations of companies *vis-à-vis* its role in relation to acquisitions and potential hostile takeovers. The chapter ends with a summary and conclusions.

CORPORATE GOVERNANCE CHARACTERISTICS

One key issue in corporate governance relates to the role of the ownership structure. Table 16.1 shows that Fiat and PSA are still to a large extent family-dominated companies, whereas Renault and VW are state-dominated companies. The following account describes this background first for the two family firms, Fiat and PSA, then for the two firms where the state is still the dominant owner, Renault and

Volkswagen. In order to understand their distinctive systems of corporate governance, it is necessary to briefly describe the different trajectories of the four companies.

The two family companies: Fiat and PSA

Fiat

Since Senator Giovanni Agnelli became undisputed leader among the founding partners of 1902, the Fiat Group has been an embodiment of a form of family-driven capitalism. It shared this characteristic with most Italian firms although Fiat was, of course, exceptional in being, until a few years ago, the largest private Italian company. This strong and permeating presence of the family, capable of aggregating "friendly" investors around it, not only gave to the family the assurance of the share of capital necessary to lead the company without uncertainties over financial control but also developed alongside other reinforcing elements. Much of this still applies (Volpato, 1998; 2001) despite the recent signs of a transformation, not yet completed, towards a clearer separation of property and control.

In any event, Fiat in the Italian landscape cannot be compared to any other firm, however large and important. In order to understand the significance of Fiat, particularly within the Piedmont milieu, one must interpret the company as a sort of kingdom in which the Agnelli family has all the traits of a dynasty and its managers must be regarded as a priest-like caste which tends to come together with the family dynastic interests. Moreover, until recently, to be employed at middle management level at Fiat meant holding a sort of nobility and with it a sense of identification and loyalty to the family and to the charismatic lead of Avvocato Agnelli. Even blue-collar workers, who in some instances could manifest conflictual expressions with the company and the management hierarchy, shared a sense of being part of a blue-collar aristocracy. Fiat, in these respects, was not a company but "The Company", a true symbol of Italy's efficiency and of its capacity to compete in international markets.

Clearly such a priest-like view of the duties of the Fiat manager has gradually softened, but there is no doubt that for a significant proportion of the employees, and particularly for those coming from Piedmont and Turin, such a sense of belonging is in part still present. Therefore it would be completely misleading,

Car maker	Family/State control	Self-control[1]	Traditional allies		Institutional investors[2]			Floating capital[3]
			Industrial	Financial	National	Other European	USA	
Fiat Group	30.6% Agnelli family (4)	—	[4]	12.2%	11%	15%		31.2%
PSA	24.6% Peugot family	6.6%	5.35% Michelin, Lafargue	6.5% (Société Générale, CDC)	8.0%	5.3%	3.7%	40.0%
Renault	44.2% French State	4.9%	1.5% Lagardère		11.3%	4.6%	4.9%	28.6%
VW	20% State of Niedersachsen	10.2%			12.1%	3.5%	3.0%	51.4%

Source: Shareworld-LEREPS in Dupoy and Lung (2002): company annual report and accounts.

Notes:

[1] Stakes owned by the company and its employees.

[2] Except financial allies.

[3] Shareholders non-identified.

[4] GM owns no share of Fiat SpA (holding of the Group), but 20 percent of Fiat Partecipazioni B.V., the company that controls 100 percent of Fiat Auto SpA.

Table 16.1 Ownership structure and control of four European car makers (as at 31st December 2000)

in order to understand the model of corporate governance at Fiat, to adopt a view which is exclusively based upon the share of capital held by the Agnelli family and by the number of family members directly involved in managerial responsibilities.

PSA

The key role of the founding family must be stressed as well as its ties to a few major industrial actors (Loubet, 1998; Frigant and Lung, 2001). Originally a family-run business, the Peugeots have maintained their influence despite the many changes that have affected the business, as Table 16.1 shows. Operating through a variety of different companies, the family has maintained on average around one quarter of PSA's capital. In fact, the company's shareholders are structured around two main blocks. On the one hand, there is a block of stable shareholders (surrounding the extended family with industrial investors like Michelin and Lafarge Cement) that seek a stable long-term investment with an approach that emphasises industrial development and economic profitability. On the other hand, there are the institutional investors, who are mainly guided by the logic of financial profitability. The entry of foreign investors at PSA is old news stemming from the sale of Chrysler's stake in the company. In fact, a share swaps programme accompanied PSA's takeover of Chrysler Europe. The American carmaker's quasi-bankrupt condition at the time induced it to sell its PSA shares on the market, opening the door to US investors.

For the modernisation of the company, Jacques Calvet, who became CEO in 1982, was of particular importance. With a background in finance (he had previously been President of the Banque Nationale de Paris), Calvet focused on curtailing the company's debts and reducing its break-even point. In manufacturing, he insisted on rationalisation via integration of the two companies and brands, Peugeot and Citroën. Over a period of 15 years and with the support of the Peugeot family, he managed the company, insisting on financial autonomy and on a type of industrial rationalisation that was facilitated by a prudential and systematic policy. The 1997 arrival of Jean-Martin Folz as the new CEO changed for good the firm's attitude towards corporate governance, making efforts to ensure more transparency and to seek more direct relationships with the financial community.

The two state companies: Renault and VW

Renault

Renault is certainly the French car firm that has experienced the greatest change over the past twenty years (Freyssenet, 1998). Previously a fully state-owned enterprise, and once the symbol of a French model of "mixed capitalism", Renault has been discreetly turned into a champion of corporate governance by Louis Schweitzer who personifies a typically French managerial career path. Having been Chief of Staff for Laurent Fabius when the latter was Prime Minister, Schweitzer had taken an "Enarque" professional trajectory as far as he could before starting a career in industry.

Renault's status as a state enterprise kept the firm going during the seven consecutive years that it made losses (1980–86), especially during an extreme crisis period (1984–86) when its cumulated financial losses reached nearly 30 billion Francs. This crisis led to a significant turnaround. It signalled the end of previous compromises between stakeholders as well as changes in company rules and routines. The implicit partnership between Renault and its labour unions was halted and then, after a number of serious confrontations during the 1980s, the partnership vanished completely. The state progressively withdrew from direct intervention in the firm's decision-making processes, and managers now have a great deal of autonomy in terms of policymaking. In fact, Renault's managers were ultimately the ones to have introduced its new business orientation.

Renault's privatisation, starting back in 1994 and 1995, has served to confirm these changes. The French State remains the main shareholder with a 44 percent holding, but it has been maintaining a largely passive attitude, without any direct intervention in strategic decision-making. Today the global alliance with Nissan offers an opportunity to reduce the share of the company held by the state. In October 2001, the French and Japanese auto-makers announced that Renault would increase its stake from 36.8 percent (acquired in 1999) to 44.4 percent, while Nissan would acquire 15 percent of the French automaker. This last operation implied a decline of the state share (to 37.6 percent) with a further reduction of 25 percent planned for the future.

Volkswagen

VW's governance structure has often been discussed as an example of German neocorporatism (Jürgens,

1998). The Volkswagen works were run as a state company after the British allied force withdrew in 1949. In 1960 Volkswagen Works Limited became a stock corporation (AG) and was partially privatised. State institutions owned 40 percent of the shares, with the state of Lower Saxony and the German Federal Government each holding 20 percent. The remaining shares were widely spread among banks, insurance companies and private shareholders, many of whom were Volkswagen employees. Governmental influence on VW remained strong, even after 1988 when the federal government sold its Volkswagen shares, since the Lower Saxony government with around 20 percent remained the single most important shareholder.

The distinctiveness of VW's governance structure is based on a special law, the "VW Act" of 1960 when Volkswagen was privatised, and on a corresponding company statute. On this basis, the state of Lower Saxony has a guaranteed status as the dominant shareowner:

- Any increase in shareholder ownership beyond 20 percent of total shares does not lead to further voting rights; this holds true also for indirectly controlled shares or attempts at share pooling; in this way Lower Saxony with its 20 percent share ownership could not be outvoted by another block owner. In addition, the state owners were guaranteed the right to fill two positions on the supervisory board.
- Decisions on new plants or plant relocation require a two-thirds majority on the supervisory board. In this way government and labour representatives could hardly be overruled in decisions concerning changes of location and employment security.
- The VW Act requires banks to receive authorisation for proxy voting from each shareholder in advance of each general shareholder assembly. In view of the effort this would require banks have never attained the same degree of proxy voting power at VW as they had in other German companies.

Various political initiatives have been taken in the past which attempted to abolish the VW Act. More recently in 2000/01, and allegedly by request of a German Bank and, latterly, a group of British investors, the EU has been scrutinising the legal situation and has already declared it to be an impediment to free capital flow within the EU. It is clear that the protection the VW Act has provided for Volkswagen up to now can no longer be taken for granted.

Concerning labour union influence, the chairman of IG Metall traditionally has been a member of Volkswagen's supervisory board. The chairmen of the Works Councils of most of VW's German plants were also members of the board. Thus labour's standpoint has always been strongly represented on the board and greatly influenced the selection of the chief officers who ran the company. Labour relations at Volkswagen are characterised by a high degree of "jointness" between management and works councils in company policy beyond what is stipulated by Germany's co-determination laws (Haipeter, 2000; Jürgens, 1998). This jointness was reflected by a partnership between the heads of the executive board and the corporate works council. Such close co-operation is characteristic throughout Volkswagen's postwar history and re-established itself in almost all cases after new leaders came in.

Summarising, each of the four companies has a distinctive corporate governance system that cannot be fully explained by differences of ownership. Thus the role of the families in the cases of Fiat and PSA remains predominant for strategic decisions, even if the Agnelli and Peugeot families have each, although to differing degrees, to negotiate with outsider CEOs and to take into account the place of institutional investors. In contrast, the role of the state in the case of Renault and Volkswagen is reduced to a supervisory board with no actual involvement in running the companies. But the state remains a dominant stakeholder in both cases. The role of labour is now quite different in these two companies: at Volkswagen, labour remains an important stakeholder with an institutionalised presence in Volkswagen's corporate governance system; at Renault, labour has lost its direct influence.

DIFFERENCES IN STRATEGIC CHALLENGES AND RESPONSES

In the debate about the recent changes of corporate governance, the negative consequences of short-termism and the threat of undermining the innovation potential and human resource base of the companies were brought forward by critics of the shift towards a finance orientation and shareholder value. There could be several reasons behind such criticisms. Firstly, greater stress on financial indicators could lead to changes in investment levels – in the short term, financial targets can be met just by reducing investment. Secondly, they could suggest a need for outsourcing and downsizing – alleviating the balance sheet in this way could also be a short-term measure to meet financial targets. Thirdly, investment could be redirected to other businesses where higher returns are expected.

Capital market pressures, however, cannot simply explain decisions on investment, disinvestment and outsourcing. They also reflect differences in the strategic challenges and in the responses of companies to product market pressures. Broadening the product range, shortening time-to-market and establishing new facilities in emerging markets were strategic challenges all carmakers were facing in the 1990s. At the same time, market conditions and product market success varied between companies thereby setting different constraints and opportunities. The following analysis of the differences between the four companies focuses on the development of investment in tangible assets and in R&D in the 1990s (Table 16.2).

Development at Fiat was marked by extremely high investment in the early 1990s, related to globalisation and new product development, and by a continuous reduction of investment levels in the following years due to rising difficulties in the product markets.

In the early 1990s, the competitiveness of Fiat was deteriorating both in the European market and domestically. The negative effects of this on the Group's financial situation led to a reduction of R&D expenditure from its level in the early nineties (when between 1991 and 1993 it represented over 4.5 percent of sales

in the auto sector and over 4 percent in the whole of the group) (Table 16.2). The decline in competitiveness, worsened further in 1993 with a sales downturn in the domestic market that forced a reduction in R&D investment. For the rest of the decade R&D investment fell below the threshold level of 3 percent of sales, with the auto sector being comparatively lower than the rest of the group.

The downward economic trend in the auto sector of Fiat dominated the 1990s with negative operational results in 1992 and 1993, modest results between 1994 and 1997, negative results again in 1998 and 1999, and a modest comeback in the year 2000. Such a trend cannot but raise worries since, as is obvious, the adverse economic trend in the sector makes it harder to find resources to be invested in the development of new models. Equally obvious, a revival of competitiveness can take place only through a policy of profound renovation of the product range.

The simple data on R&D spending gives an excessively pessimistic impression, which is eased in the light of the policy of re-defining the overall activities of the Group. This has been aimed at privileging the so-called core business and at reducing the degree of vertical integration in the automobile sector. In fact with these two policies, the Fiat Group has reduced its industrial activities in the areas of investment goods (railway sector), intermediate products (fibres) and automotive components. As a consequence, the increase of R&D investment recorded between 1997 and 2000 has been greater than the headline figures seem to indicate: there has been a greater concentration of R&D effort, with the focus mainly on total

	1991	1992	1993	1994	1995	1996	1997	1998	1999	2000
Capital investments in tangible fixed assets as a % of sales										
Fiat Group	7.4	10.0	12.4	6.9	7.5	6.8	5.1	5.3	5.9	6.3
PSA	9.7	8.9	7.7	6.3	6.7	5.9	5.5	4.9	5.3	6.6
Renault	5.7	6.3	6.6	8.3	8.3	8.8	7.5	5.9	6.5	7.5
VW AG	10.9	9.4	5.3	5.0	5.0	7.2	7.2	7.3	8.0	6.6
R&D as a % of sales										
Fiat Group	4.4	4.4	4.2	2.9	2.8	2.8	2.5	2.7	2.9	3.0
PSA	4.2	3.4	3.8	3.5	3.6	3.5	4.6	3.9	3.9	3.7
Renault	3.6	3.5	4.1	4.3	4.3	5.0	4.4	4.2	4.8	5.1
VW AG	3.2	3.2	3.7	3.6	4.5	4.4	4.2	4.2	5.6	6.0

Source: Company annual report and accounts, various years.

Table 16.2 **Investments in tangible assets and R&D, 1991–2000.**

vehicle design and on reducing the involvement in components. In this respect it can reasonably be argued that over the coming years the total investment is likely to return to high levels, both due to innovation initiatives stemming from co-operation agreements with General Motors, and due to Fiat's recently announced renovation programme of the whole auto-mobile product range. This programme includes the launch of 19 new models in the 2001–2005 period with a total investment of 14 billion euros.

PSA reduced its rate of investment during the 1990s, but this was not related to any change in the company's corporate governance. Capital expendi-ture represented about 8 percent of sales in the first half of the 1990s, and less than 6 percent in the second half. Comparing this evolution with its competitors'– PSA has the lowest proportion of capital expenditure among the four carmakers studied – two factors could explain the divergence. Firstly, the cycle of invest-ment is specific to each firm. Secondly, PSA has been less ambitious in its internationalisation strategy pre-ferring to advance slowly in emerging markets like China and Mercosur, whereas its competitors have been engaged either in many acquisitions of different brands (Seat, Skoda, Bentley and Bugatti by VW; Dacia and Samsung by Renault) or in global alliances (GM-Fiat, Renault-Nissan) in order to accelerate the transition towards global player status.

If we consider the degree of involvement in the component sector, PSA in contrast to its competitors has been reinforcing its activities. Its component divi-sion (ECIA) merged with Bertrand Faure in 1997–98 to form a new company Faurecia, 52.6 percent con-trolled by PSA. The acquisition of Sommer-Allibert by Faurecia in 2001– where PSA will hold about 70 percent of the new company's capital at the end of the process – gives the company a leading position in the European supplier industry in some key module markets: vehicle interiors (seats, cockpit), exhaust systems and front end modules. For PSA, the design and manufacturing of the key mechanical elements of the car remain evidently part of its core business.

Whilst its R&D did not grow significantly at the end of the decade, as Table 16.2 shows, PSA compen-sated for this in various ways. It restructured its R&D organisation and developed several alliances with competitors for specific products (V6 engine and automatic transmission with Renault, minivan and commercial vehicles with Fiat, diesel engines with Ford) as well as with suppliers in vertical co-opera-tions, in order to secure access to specific capabilities,

including new services (such as communicating cars with IBM and B2C with Vivendi). PSA has also devel-oped its services associated with the sales of new cars, such as finance and insurance, but does not focus on these activities to replace the ones in tradi-tional manufacturing.

In considering the approach of the other French competitor Renault, we found some clear differences. After peaking in 1994–96 when capital expenditure represented more than 8 percent of the company's revenue, the rate of investment decreased to about 6–7 percent at the end of the 1990s. Renault decided to accelerate its internationalisation through the deal with Nissan, concluded in 1999, as well as through investment in Brazil and Russia, and the acquisition of Samsung Motors in South Korea and Dacia in Romania to constitute a multi-brand portfolio to rein-force its presence in emerging markets. The alliance between Renault and Nissan put this group in fifth place amongst global vehicle producers, with evident geographical complementarities, which allow it to have a worldwide presence. To integrate the Euro-pean activities of the Japanese with its own activities, Renault pursued a coherent plan of rationalisation of purchasing, distribution and common platform in Europe, with the closure of three assembly plants: Bil-lancourt in France (1992), Setubal in Portugal (1996) and Vilvorde, Belgium (1997), and the sale of the Chausson plant in France (previously a commercial vehicle assembly joint venture with PSA). Renault adopted a profit strategy based on innovation, launch-ing new types of vehicles (such as the minivan and compact minivan) on the market, as well as develop-ing products for the upper segments and forging alli-ances for some sectors (such as with GM for commercial vehicles).

With such an ambitious horizontal growth strategy, Renault accelerated its outsourcing policy. Several activities that were not considered as core competen-cies have been separated: sales of mechanical plants, prototyping, foundry and robotics. The new innova-tion policy corresponds with one of the golden rules associated with corporate governance, that non-specific capabilities should be outsourced, and that focus should be placed on the core business. This strategy has been pursued through:

■ the outsourcing of technological research to first tier suppliers who are supposed to develop their own R&D capabilities, and to offer technological innovations;

■ focus on Renault's core competencies, defined as the *ability to integrate* different (supplier developed) technologies so as to design an innovative product that is valuable and firm-specific.

Nevertheless, this has not led to a reduction of expenditure on R&D. On the contrary R&D represented 3.9 percent of Renault sales in 1991–95 and jumped to 4.7 percent in 1996–2000 and 5.1 percent in 2001. The building of the Renault Technocentre engineering plant near Paris, which brings together the human resources of the company and its suppliers dedicated to the design activities, can be seen as the manifestation of this new innovation policy.

For Volkswagen, the development of capital investment shows no effect of a change of policy during the years 1995–2000. Capital investment in tangible fixed assets as a percentage of sales for the automobile business during the six years 1995–2000 was around 8 percent explained mainly by high expenditures for new product development. Despite the savings attributed to Volkswagen's common platform approach the company claims to have invested more in its new product programmes than the average of its competitors during this period (Adelt, 2000).

In considering the process of investment planning the role of the Works Council has to be stressed, which brings us back to the distinct corporate governance situation at Volkswagen. The Works Council is closely involved throughout the planning process and with the increased emphasis on financial targets the council representatives in many cases take over the role of guardians of innovation. Return on investment figures for projects are intensively scrutinised by the Works Councils. In cases when negative long-term employment effects are expected – as in decisions on technology development projects or further training outlays for instance – Works Council representatives may try to overrule "narrow" financial considerations.

Volkswagen clearly has not followed a policy of "downsize and distribute": it clearly has not tried to downsize in terms of workforce reduction and plant closures. (This policy has been explained by Volkswagen's labour directors in various publications, cf. Briam, 1986; Hartz, 1994; 1996.) When the pressure was there, during the crisis years of the early 1990s, it pursued a policy of reducing weekly working hours. Thus, by 1993 when it had become evident that 30,000 employees out of VW AG's 108,000 would have to be made redundant, an agreement was struck

with IG Metall to reduce working time by 20 percent (to a regular working week of 28.2 hours) thereby securing 20,000 jobs. With some modification, the agreement is still in place.

There has been no major case of outsourcing at VW. Despite considerable activities in this sector, Volkswagen has not (yet) established a separate business unit for automotive supplies. Besides engines and transmissions, VW still produces drive train components such as axles, steering gear and brakes, while it also retains production of instrument panels and seating components. Instead of outsourcing its component production Volkswagen has pursued a policy of upgrading the capabilities of its component production units (specifically in the area of braking systems and drive train parts), to increase their R&D potential and develop them into systems suppliers. They have to compete with external suppliers in the bidding process for new production programmes and thereby demonstrate their cost competitiveness. In view of the increasing relevance of electronics and software, the company has also developed an "electronics strategy" to initiate in-sourcing in core areas.

Finally, has the company pursued a policy of value migration out of the automotive business? After the sale of Triumph-Adler (bought in 1978 and sold in 1985) which was VW's only attempt to diversify out of the automotive business, any trend towards value migration could only be realised through the financial services division. The aim clearly is to profit from the continuous extension of the automotive value chains. Volkswagen's chief executive, Ferdinand Piëch, made it clear that he expected financial services to contribute one third to Volkswagen's overall profits. Volkswagen is clearly interested in benefiting from the higher rates of return of financial services. In one of his first statements as nominated successor to Piëch, Pischetsrieder declared that without contributions from financing new car sales, fleet management and used-car retailing the return on sales margins would be no more than 3–4 percent. In view of Volkswagen's target of 6–7 percent he stated: "Six to seven percent is a possible target including Financial Services, which is a precondition for a successful car business" (*Financial Times* 12.9.2001). Thus, it can be expected that Volkswagen will expand its financial services business. There is, however, no official policy to migrate out of the automotive business which, as of 2000, contributed 80 percent of its revenues.

In summary, we do not observe a marked reduction of investment levels nor a substantial disinvestment process for the four carmakers during the period studied, but we do observe a greater emphasis towards more products and higher volumes. Some differences can be observed but they are mainly explained by specific product development cycles, rather than by any short-termism: growth is also a necessary component of the shareholder value policy. Differences were also found with regard to the outsourcing of automotive components where PSA and VW exhibited a more "productionist approach", while Fiat and Renault seemed to be more eager to disinvest in these areas and possibly move into new areas of business. Interestingly, these differences do not correspond with the family/state divide in their corporate governance characteristics.

SHAREHOLDER VALUE POLICY

Shareholder value principles were adopted by all four companies but with different degrees of emphasis. The two family-based companies adopted these principles at an earlier stage and with more emphasis, with Fiat giving the policy a higher profile.

At Fiat, the most significant change in terms of corporate governance occurred at the end of 1996 with the adoption of a policy of Value-Based Management, oriented towards the creation of value defined as the "capability of the firm to generate a cash return with return on invested capital higher than the cost of capital itself". The principles of this policy were outlined in the corresponding company document:

> Value creation is the obligation we have towards our shareholders. Each of us holds the responsibility of contributing to the development of the Group and hence to hand over to those who will follow, shareholders and employees, a Company with higher value. All decisions and actions must respond to the objective of increasing the economic value of the Group as a whole. Value creation is meant and measured as the share of operating income exceeding the cost of capital employed to obtain it. *I Valori del Gruppo Fiat*, 1998.

The new policy was implemented in phases beginning with the definition of the "Fiat formula" of value creation, followed by its communication and training activities at various levels and finally by various efforts to transform the management culture within the Fiat Group. This started in 1997 and ended in 1998, involving in excess of 450 people in the top management tier, 3500 managers and more than 23,000 staff of all controlled companies.

The reasons for this change in corporate strategy are related to Fiat's policy of globalisation. The amount of capital necessary to carry out the globalisation project for Fiat was a relevant consideration because mere self-financing was insufficient and a massive use of international capital markets was needed. There was also the need for Fiat to be able to stand up in front of the international financial community as a company led by the same economic guidelines as that community. In other words, the company has defined itself as "international" not only in terms of its world-wide activities, but also by having a managing culture which warranted the same forms of behaviour towards the main stakeholders and, especially, towards shareholders. The fact that "value creation" has become such an important parameter in evaluating the strategic moves of a firm by the international financial community, represented by banks, institutional investors and rating companies, means that this is a test that cannot be avoided.

The strategic industrial alliance that Fiat and General Motors (GM) put in operation in the year 2000 (Camuffo and Volpato, 2001) will undoubtedly contribute to the strategy of value creation. From 1st July 2000, Fiat Auto SpA (now Fiat Auto Partecipazioni SpA) has de-merged its operational activities which have been transferred to a new head company Fiat Auto Holdings B.V. At the same time, General Motors Corporation has acquired a stake in Fiat Auto Holdings B.V. of 20 percent, while Fiat has acquired a stake of about 6 percent in General Motors. It is likely that the Fiat-GM alliance will generate interesting results in other fields. For example, Fiat's communications with private and institutional investors has already been improved through a rich programme of initiatives aimed at improving "investor relations". It appears likely that the Fiat-GM co-operation will increasingly introduce routine US habits and practices into the Italian Group management: a symbol of this may be the hiring of Jack Welch, General Electric's former CEO, in December 2001 as a consultant to help Fiat restructure its operations.

Until recently, PSA based its strategic policies on exclusively industrial criteria: the importance of customer satisfaction; searching for internal savings; recognising the role of product innovation as a factor of competitiveness; and the need for a carmaker which was still far too focused on Europe (and even on France) to become more internationalised. In the late 1990s, however, PSA began to view shareholder interests as an integral part of their strategic objectives. In January 1998, the new CEO, Jean-Martin Folz, announced three priorities for the company that he would actually start to run a year later: growth, innovation and profitability. The implementation of financial profitability presupposes changes in the way strategic and operational decisions are made.

Two complementary criteria were chosen. The first was the pre-tax Return on Capital Employed (ROCE). This rate is the principal criteria for the company, which each year sets itself a target where the ROCE represents an estimate of the cost of capital that the company has used. The group is committed to achieving a return of at least 8.5 percent (after tax) on capital employed. Effectively, the rate has risen significantly over the past few years, to 13.5 percent after tax in 2001, as the original targets have been exceeded. This first indicator involves the entire company, whereas the second (the operating margin) focuses on its core car business. Here, PSA has set a minimum threshold based on the ratio between its gross operating margins and the turnover of its automobile activities. Revised annually, the automotive division target operating margin was 3.0 percent in 1999, 4.5 percent in 2000, 4.8 percent in 2001 and 6 percent in 2002.

In contrast to the two family-owned companies, the two state-owned companies seemed to embrace shareholder value principles in a more ambiguous and reluctant way. However, clear differences in approach can be observed here also.

For nearly a dozen years, all of Renault's economic projects have been evaluated according to three criteria:

- positive net present value for the investment, using a discount rate of 14 percent;
- gross operating margin of 4 percent; and
- return on equity of 11 percent.

These criteria have been introduced since the quasi-bankruptcy of the company in 1984–86, and they have become increasingly stringent in recent years. Firstly, the European Commission's competition policy accepted final financial help (recapitalisation) from the French government to Renault in the light of its partial privatisation in 1994–95. Secondly, the tight relationship that Renault managers want to develop with the financial market implies the respect of strict financial criteria. Announced at the beginning of 1997, the closure of the Vilvevorde assembly plant in Belgium was a sign of this new attitude, which sent a clear message both internally and externally to the financial community. Carlos Ghosn's arrival accentuated this shift towards the use of profitability as a "guide for action". The firm began to view shareholder interests as an integral part of its strategic objectives. In 1998, he officially proclaimed that one of its strategic goals was to "generate profits to meet *shareholders' expectations* [our emphasis] and finance our development". Nowadays, even strategic decisions such as the Nissan takeover must satisfy these three criteria.

However, if shareholder value is now a clear goal for Renault, the main objective is still to promote profitable growth based on industrial development. The three priorities are:

- "developing a brand identity focused on innovation in products and services for complete customer satisfaction";
- "becoming the most competitive manufacturer in our markets in terms of quality, costs and delivery times";
- "expanding our international scope to play a central role in automotive development throughout the world".

At Volkswagen, shareholder value has only recently been accepted as a goal to be achieved by the company, and even then, it has been balanced with other goals. In this way, VW has made clear that it was following a general stakeholder approach. Nonetheless accepting shareholder value principles has been a process driven by the top management in the company. In view of the dismal record of profitability of the company, after taking the position of the head of the Executive Board in 1993, Piëch stressed the need for profitability. Responding to critiques by investors, he declared his commitment to realise a return on sales target of 8 percent "in the mid-term". This target was later reduced to 6.5 percent and was complemented by a target for a return on capital. Since 1998, Piëch seems to have taken these targets more and more seriously, requiring their achievement by the last year before his retirement in April 2002. With his well-known autocratic management style there was no doubt that he made the adopting of and adapting to these goals a "must" for the company. In the final years of his tenure, Piëch pursued the achievement of the financial and profitability goals with the same vigour as he had pursued the productionist targets for improving product quality during the first half of his reign.

The year 2000 marked a decisive shift in the new direction. The "planning round" of this year – a yearly process of determining investment in products and processes for the following five years – gave firm and specific goals for the new financial performance orientation of the company. The financial targets set in this round were:

- Return on capital (ROCE) should be within a corridor between 9 percent and 11 percent;
- Break-even at maximum 60 percent of full capacity production;
- Return on sales should reach 4.7 percent in the following year and increase to 6.5 percent by 2005;
- Investment should be covered by internal cash flow and should not exceed 6 billion DM.

As of the beginning of 2000, Volkswagen also introduced a new results-oriented system for exercising control. In effect this has meant abandoning its traditional budget system for a new method based on capital costs and return on capital as target indicators, with the aim of measuring in detail the success of the individual brands and regions of the group, and also of the different products and projects.

Also, in 2000 a number of measures were taken by Volkswagen to step up "efforts to enhance communication with its investors", as VW's 2000 Annual Report stated. Thus, among other steps, over 100 one-to-one meetings were held to explain corporate strategy and to answer questions from financial analysts and investors. The investor relations function was restructured and an office was established in London to promote contacts with international financial analysts.

Within the company, the policy of a cautious opening up to the expectations of the capital market was carried out jointly by management and the Works Council. The clear driving force has been the fear of a hostile takeover, an issue on which management and Works Councils were united. With a market value of 15 billion Euro, Volkswagen seemed an easy prey for any group of investors, had it not been for the blocking stake of the Lower Saxony State government. The Mannesmann case was seen as the writing on the wall and, although Volkswagen was at the forefront of those who lobbied against the takeover directive proposed by the EU, it was obvious that it could not rely on state government protection forever.

At the same time, the concept of "workholder value" developed by Volkswagen's labour director in 1999 showed the uneasiness felt by company management and the search for a compromise. According to this concept, personnel policy should combine two sets of goals in the future. One is workholder value with social responsibility, knowledge management, employability and flexibility as central elements; the other is shareholder value aiming to increase company value, and to improve results such as value added per employee. Although the workholder value concept was not given a high profile in its public relations activities, internally at VW it certainly reflected a widespread consensus. In any case, shareholder value at Volkswagen has not become the dominant goal; it is part of a policy of balancing the interests of stakeholders in order to secure the long-term viability of the company.

The introduction of finance-oriented targets and shareholder-value principles in all four companies went along with stock option programmes. In addition to introducing stock options all companies have changed their systems of management compensation (some also their remuneration systems for ordinary employees) in order to create incentives to increase performance and meet their financial targets. Those measures will not be elaborated here.

To summarise, all four companies have moved towards a shareholder value orientation, but clearly with different degrees of emphasis. It seems that Fiat and Renault have adopted a far more stringent policy of setting financial targets. This is related to the strong position of finance-oriented CEOs in both companies. Fiat, as was shown, has reorganised its targets system explicitly towards the goal of "value creation"; PSA, while making similar moves, remains reluctant to introduce as intensively as Fiat the new rules of shareholder value management. Paradoxically, Renault managers appear to have retained more autonomy from their main shareholder (the State) than PSA (Peugeot family) in such changes. In the case of Volkswagen, the year 2000 marks the beginning of a capital market-oriented target system. A number of measures were taken to enhance communication with investors. At the same time, the company refrains from putting shareholder value at the top of its priority list. Instead, it seeks a balance between shareholder and workholder values.

THE ROLE OF STOCK MARKETS IN COMPANY FINANCING

We have seen that all four companies make great efforts to meet shareholder value expectations, to become more investor friendly, to adopt financial targets and to increase returns. In this section, we will explore to what extent companies actually use the capital markets for financing their operations or for acquisition purposes. To what extent do the companies need the stock market for financing operations and investment, for coping with crisis situations, and for expanding operations as part of a globalisation or diversification policy? Or is the stock market's role primarily related to acquisition policy or to a fear of loss of control?

At Fiat, as a general rule, the Agnelli family tried to avoid operations that required stock augmentation because the family lacked the financial resources to underwrite a proportional share of the new stock capital and they are, of course, against a dilution of their control of the company. This rule could be easily followed in periods when the car business was going well and generating a huge cash flow (like 1983–1987). Under such favourable conditions, Fiat pursued an "aggressive" investment policy, financed, in order of priority, by:

- internal cash flow
- financial borrowing from banks
- increasing the capital stock through subscriptions from IFI and IFIL (the two financial companies controlled by the Agnelli family). At that time, the two companies had no particular problem in participating in the capital stock increase thanks to dividends paid by Fiat SpA to IFI and IFIL, and in any case, the two companies could temporarily borrow money from banks.

A different approach had to be taken in times when the car business was less successful and the company needed external financing in order to invest in new car models or consolidate its competitive position. This situation occurred in 1969–1978 and in 1989–1993. In these circumstances, new investments are "defensive" and financed in order of priority by:

- divestments of non-core activities.
- financial (long-term) borrowing from banks. (Between 1997 and 2000 Fiat moved from being a net depositor to having net debts of some 8 billion Euro.)
- by increasing the capital stock with the help of "friends" who underwrite shares and who join the Board of Directors. This role of a "friendly institution" in the past has been played by the merchant bank Mediobanca, the insurance company Assicurazioni Generali, by the French company Alcatel Alsthom and by IFI and IFIL, the two family-controlled investment funds. In view of the globalisation strategy of Fiat in the late 1990s as we have seen above, financing through capital markets became more of a concern.

From the background of its strained financial situation, it can be explained that Fiat used share buybacks to a very small extent, and only for its stock option programme (about 0.5 percent per annum). Family control could be secured through the structure of cross shareholdings and financing through "friends", and, more recently, through the alliance with General Motors.

Like Fiat, in its policy towards the use of capital markets for financing, PSA's first priority was to maintain family control. The period from 1999 combined contradictory phenomena. On the one hand, the capital continued to rise through the continued operation of the automatic mechanisms that had been in effect during the preceding period: options exercises and bond conversions. On the other hand, this period corresponded to a new stage in PSA's relationship with the capital markets. The company did not at this stage use the stock market as a source of funding, and even indulged in negative financing operations: 9.3 percent of the capital was cancelled in 1999. Thus this year marked a new period, especially since PSA repurchased some of its shares in the market, both to cover its internal options programmes and also because it was planning to launch further share cancellation programmes.

For the three years from 1998 to 2000, the carmaker did not make any use of share swaps in the funding of its acquisitions. This may appear logical at the PSA parent company level, given the absence of any deals equivalent to those that Renault was making, but its transport (Gefco) and automobile equipment (Faurecia) subsidiaries did pursue their external growth by means of cash purchases. PSA used part of its cash flow to fund its investment operations, and at the same time increased its level of debt. This rise in indebtedness constituted a clear break with the company's previous policies. Under Jacques Calvet, PSA had taken great pains to reduce its debt. Jean-Martin Folz's arrival coincided with its adoption of a more flexible attitude. Henceforth the objective became a sustainable increase in debt levels.

Jean-Martin Folz's strategy of relying on debt whenever the opportunity is presented by bond market conditions is clearly visible in the changes in PSA's long-term borrowings, both in absolute terms and as a percentage of shareholder equity. Nevertheless, it is clear that this increased indebtedness has been subject to tight control. Pursuing Folz's predecessor's approach, PSA has been working hard to preserve a healthy financial situation. For three years, it succeeded in generating cash surpluses. Despite the rise in investment outlays and the share repurchase programmes, the car company succeeded in lowering its long-term debts in 2000.

PSA's strategy is to rely on borrowings as long as costs are low. It wants to be able to preserve its ability to raise funds rapidly as the need arises and avoid causing the financial markets any undue concerns. PSA tries to present a company image geared towards an industrial logic whose financial situation is healthy. Part of this message seems to stem from a desire to dissociate itself from its French rival, which since its denationalisation, has been presenting the image of an overly indebted company. Also, in contrast to Fiat, PSA used the instrument of share buy-backs intensively as a means to forestall a hostile takeover. PSA has launched several purchasing programmes over the past two years, accompanied by stock cancellation. The stock repurchases announced in 1999, 2000 and 2001 represent a change in company policy. Repurchases were accompanied by a partial share-cancellation programme: PSA cancelled 4.65 million shares in November 1999, and is authorised to cancel further shares in future months. In parallel, and a few months after this operation, the company called in 2.38 million convertible bonds, again so as to counter any previous dilution of its capital.

The cancellation of convertible bonds may be part of this effort to improve the securities' yield, but it can also be seen as a means of increasing control over the firm's capital. The company's relatively small size means that it is more vulnerable to takeover by competitors. PSA is sensitive to the risk of take-over, as witnessed by the authorisations that it submits to voting during shareholder meetings. With this in mind, the share repurchase programme

when followed by a cancellation of securities has two purposes: creating shareholder loyalty by enhancing the securities' yield; and increasing the relative percentage of capital that is held by family shareholders.

Financing through issuing new stock for Renault was a necessity in its struggle for survival during the 1980s and up until 1992. The firm's quasi-bankrupt condition forced the state as its shareholder to recapitalise it on several occasions[2] – but the European Community did not approve of this aid, seeing it as contradicting the EU's tenets of fair trade. In 1990 for example, the EU Commission only accepted a new recapitalisation plan under the condition that the firm reimburse a 3.5 billion FF subsidy that it had received in 1988 and that it change its legal status. This happened that very same year, leading to AB Volvo's entrance into Renault's capital.

With partial privatisation in 1994, a new phase began, with capital issuance operations becoming more and more marginal. Since 1997, the carmaker has refused to issue any new capital, and the stock in circulation has remained stable. For five years now, Renault has not used the stock market as a source of primary funding, despite the rapid growth it has experienced (above all internationally).

Given Renault's strong external growth over the past few years, we could legitimately assume that it uses the stock market as a lever to finance its deals. The parent company's biggest acquisitions have involved the takeover and/or purchase of a stake in major competitor automakers (Samsung, Dacia and Nissan Motor including Nissan Diesel). Yet in all three cases, Renault did not use equity swap as a lever. It is true that its agreement with Nissan foresees the acquisition by this latter firm of a stake in the French company, but it has not yet taken advantage of this possibility. One reason that Renault gives for this is its desire to maintain control over its capital. C. Dor, the CFO, stated that "to realise the Nissan operation, our constant concern was to avoid dilution for our shareholders" (*Options Finances*, no. 60, 1999 p.16).[3]

Despite its efforts to reduce its overall debt levels, Renault's growth strategy has forced it to increase borrowings and to draw on its bank reserves. The consequence is that Renault has had a negative net cash position for the past few years. Moreover, this indebtedness increased by 77.5 percent between 1999 and 2000, following the acquisition of Volvo and Benetton Formula, with the increase in fixed tangible assets and with the rise in the need for working capital needs stemming from the major economic slowdown that began to affect the company at the end of 2000.

As for share buy-backs, Renault, just like PSA, has had its general shareholders' meeting adopt resolutions authorising the firm to repurchase its own shares up to 10 percent of its total capital. The 1999 and 2000 repurchase programmes were entirely allocated to cover staff share ownership schemes. For the first time, the 2001 general shareholder meeting allowed Renault to cancel capital. This is a new stage, even if Renault has not yet used this authorisation. Indeed, share cancellation is a delicate proposition. On the one hand, cancelling shares that were acquired in the marketplace would automatically lead to an increase in the percentage of the state's holding. Despite the discreet role that the state plays, analysts could interpret this change negatively. On the other hand, the company has had a relatively poor cash position because of its recent deals, and would have to borrow funds to finance the cancellation. At the current time, Renault has little room for manoeuvre in this regard.

At Volkswagen, the stock market has only very recently been regarded as important for company policy. On the rare occasions in the past when the company increased its equity base, all measures were taken to maintain the existing ownership structure. Capital intake from the stock market was in most cases linked to major acquisitions. This was the case in 1965 when Volkswagen bought Audi Union from Daimler Benz, again in 1977 in the context of the purchase of Triumph-Adler, and in 1986 for the acquisition of Seat. At this point, Volkswagen decided to introduce preference shares, which have no voting rights. In this way, VW could mobilise new capital without affecting the existing ownership structure. New preference shares were issued several times in the 1990s. In 2000, preference shares made up one fourth of total shares. 1990 also saw an increase in common shares necessarily arising from the full acquisition of Seat and 30 percent of Skoda, which was raised stepwise to 70 percent in 1994 and 1995 and to 100 percent in 2000. In the second half of the 1990s, under the reign of Piëch, new common or preference shares were issued almost every second year. Although these were in small amounts, there was a total increase of 22 percent in the equity base between 1995 and 2000.

As to financing investment and regular operations, the stated policy of the company is that this should be done out of cash flow. Given the development of cash flow as a percentage of capital investments in tangible fixed assets during the 1990s this did not pose a problem for the Volkswagen Group.

While the automobile business could largely be financed out of cash flow, the expansion of the finance service business required a more frequent interchange with the capital markets and led to a diversification of the means of re-financing. An analysis of the changes in Volkswagen's liability structure shows an increased importance of bonds (increased by 69 percent from 1995 to 2000), and of credits from banks (increased by 31 percent). Most importantly, however, re-financing occurred through the use of commercial paper and a multi-currency Euro medium-term note (EMTN) programme as well as through internal company loans.

The special attention the company has paid to stock market development in recent times is clearly linked to its acquisition policy and its concern about a hostile takeover. Rumours of Ford's interest in acquiring Volkswagen, the European Commission scrutinising the VW Act and the low market capitalisation of Volkswagen all contributed to a rising fear of a hostile takeover which almost became a phobia in 2000/2001. With the authorisation of the 2000 general shareholder meeting, Volkswagen has already bought back 10 percent of its shares and the 2001 general assembly again authorised another share buy-back. While Volkswagen is not allowed to hold more than 10 percent of its own shares, it could exchange these shares with "friendly" companies (Deutsche Post and Thyssen-Krupp were mentioned as such possible partners), then buy another 10 percent to be used in the same manner. In 2001, various possibilities to build a protective wall around Volkswagen were played through with the help of consultants. The 20 percent share block of Lower Saxony, together with the cross shareholdings held with other companies, would effectively block off any hostile takeover attempt.

In summary, none of the four companies used the stock markets for regular operations and investment. Only at Renault, under special conditions of near bankruptcy and EU directives to reduce state ownership as a precondition for allowing a 'rescue' subsidy, was there a substantial shift in the ownership structure. Fiat as well as PSA and Volkswagen made great efforts not to allow any shift of ownership structure that could endanger the existing top management group. The share swap between Fiat and GM to a certain degree fits into this policy framework as long as GM does not exercise its option to acquire a majority ownership of Fiat. The stock market policies of PSA and Volkswagen have been dominated by the perceived need to avoid a takeover and have been mainly implemented by buying back their own shares.

SUMMARY AND CONCLUSIONS

The case studies of the four car companies lead to the conclusion that the introduction of new rules and routines associated with shareholder value policy has taken diverse forms within the European automobile industry. There is a big gap between the rapid introduction of shareholder value criteria at Fiat and VW's attempt to develop a more symmetrical consideration between labour and capital. The type of capital control does not explain such differences, whether family or state.

At Fiat and PSA, the Agnelli and Peugeot families are deeply involved in the strategic decisions concerning their companies, but the family control has recently been evolving differently: the French company appears to have been more cautious in the introduction of shareholder policy. The reinforcement of control by the Peugeot family has clearly indicated this new direction. In contrast, the Agnelli family seems now to accept a need to share the control of Fiat Auto with other partners. The global alliance with GM, and the arrival of managers from General Electric have accelerated the transition toward a more Anglo-American style of shareholder policy. This policy is definitely an element in all Fiat official documents, while shareholder value figures less prominently at PSA. There are other differences. The Italian company adopts a clear policy of stock options, while it remains limited for the French one. The stock market has been used to reinforce the control of Peugeot family on PSA: although this policy was also followed by the Agnelli family until the mid-1990s, the ambitious globalisation strategy then took the leading role in determining policy. PSA has clearly reinforced its activities in the component sector while Fiat is engaged in an exit strategy for this sector with the spin-off and sales of several departments of Magneti-Marelli, its component division. Building up the contribution to company revenues from services associated with the automobile product – as the US car makers Ford and GM are doing (Froud et al., 2002) seems a possible trajectory for Fiat, but not for PSA.

We also found divergences in the transition of the state-controlled car companies towards a new corporate governance. In both cases, the state has been reduced to a role of supervision without direct involvement in running the company. But this reduced control of the dominant shareholder has had different consequences. At VW, the co-management policy remains strong and Works Council/union members are represented on the supervisory board and thereby involved in strategic decision making. At Renault, the implicit compromise between unions (mainly the CGT) and management, which had governed the company from the Second World War until the mid-1980s, has been broken. The managers of the French company have definitely been moving towards a shareholder value policy, and although this was not so evident as in the Fiat case, it gave clear messages to the financial market and community, and could lead to a possible future total privatisation of the company.

In both Renault and Volkswagen, financial criteria play a growing role in investment decisions, but this is not an indication of a full shareholder value policy. It is related to the declining role of the main shareholder, the state, as an active source of new funds and follows from the European Commission's competition policy which implies that firms have to be autonomous in financing their investment and growth policy. For institutional reasons, and due to available cash generated by profits or sales of previous stakes (e.g. Volvo Car by Renault), the financial market played no role in financing investment, acquisitions or alliances. Finally, the German maker seems more committed to the development of new technologies, especially for electronics, while Renault is evolving towards a role of co-ordination of product development (associating suppliers which would have the role of technological innovators) and a closer relationship with the final market.

A result, which comes out most clearly from our research, is that none of the companies needed the stock market for its operational activities, including major investment in new facilities and new product programmes. The same is true to a large extent even for the financing of acquisitions although the issue of getting access to "acquisition currency" has played an increased role in the debate and some companies have declared a future intention to play a more active role in this area. Neither has the use of stock options as an incentive in motivating and retaining personnel, primarily management, played an important role. The most important influence of the stock market lies in its potential for allowing a hostile takeover. Interestingly, even though the four companies investigated were protected to some degree by family or state ownership, they all felt the need to brace themselves against this potential danger. In response, the companies have followed a dual strategy of trying to enhance their stock market valuation on the one hand and of erecting protective barriers against hostile takeovers on the other.

With all four companies introducing some kind of a shareholder value management policy, how does this influence the economic performance of the car companies? If we rank the degree of movement towards a shareholder value management policy for the four car companies studied, the rank order is VW (least), to PSA, then Renault and, finally, Fiat (most). Clearly, Family or State control does not affect the rank order. Any explanation of the trajectories of these firms clearly needs to consider additional factors and hypotheses; Boyer and Freyssenet (2000), for example, provide strong confirmation of the limited explanatory role of ownership structures.

The level of employment and the development of gross profit margins could reasonably be taken as the two best economic performance indicators to represent, on the one hand, the interests of employees, and, on the other, the interests of shareholders. On this basis it is interesting that these companies rank almost in reverse order to their ranking in terms of the degree of adoption of shareholder value policies. The companies (Fiat and Renault) which have moved most in terms of the use of financial indicators have the worst performance in terms of the indicators of both capital and labour. The better performers in these respects have been those which have been more reluctant to introduce shareholder value policies (PSA and VW).[4] In view of our findings we may even reverse the causality and claim that the companies which achieve better economic performance have been less under pressure from shareholders, especially institutional investors (Dupuy and Lung, 2002). In the short term, it seems to be clear that economic performance in the auto industry is explained by other factors, especially by the success of product policies. But the changing of corporate governance may have an effect on the medium to long term, as it implies a progressive change in the routines of the companies at all levels.

NOTES

1   This project entitled "Corporate Governance, Innovation and Economic Performance" is co-ordinated by Mary O' Sullivan and William Lazonick based at INSEAD and financed by the European TSER Programme.
2   Between 1980 and 1986, the various re-capitalisation plans caused the State as principal shareholder to inject more than 22 billion FF into Renault.
3   Although Renault's largest deals have not involved any share swaps, it has utilised this method for secondary operations involving its subsidiaries. For example, in RVI's sale to Volvo, finalised in July 2000, Renault sold 100 percent of its RVI-Mack shares for 15 percent of the capital of Volvo AB (with 5 percent more being acquired on the market). Similarly, starting on 1 January 1999 Renault acquired 33.5 percent of Teksid's capital in exchange for the firm's own foundry subsidiaries.
4   Another source confirms this result: in July 2001, the Total Shareholder Return Index calculated by PricewaterhouseCoopers and published by Automotive News Europe indicated that PSA Peugeot-Citroën outperformed during the last twelve months – as well as the last 3 years – in the European car industry, while Fiat is the worst destroyer of shareholder value. VW follows PSA, performing better than Renault for 2000/2001.

	1995	1996	1997	1998	1999	2000
Index of employment growth (1995 = 100)						
Fiat Group	100.0	100.2	102.1	92.9	93.2	94.3
PSA	100.0	99.4	100.2	111.9	118.5	122.9
Renault	100.0	100.7	101.0	98.8	114.0	118.7
VW AG	100.0	107.5	113.3	122.9	126.3	133.8
Gross profit margin % (Profit before tax/Revenue)						
Fiat Group	4.5%	4.9%	4.7%	3.2%	2.1%	1.8%
PSA	1.3%	0.4%	−0.2%	2.4%	3.1%	5.0%
Renault	1.1%	3.1%	2.0%	4.6%	3.1%	4.3%
VW AG	1.3%	2.0%	3.4%	4.7%	5.0%	4.8%

Source: Company annual report and accounts, various years.

Table 16.3 **Two criteria for economic performance in the 1990's: Employment and gross profit margin**

REFERENCES

Adelt, B. (2000) Presentation to the Association of European Automotive Analysts' Meeting, 6.12.2000 (http://www.Volkswagen-ir.de/deutsch/08/htm1/adelt.html of 25.9.2001).

Boyer, R. and Freyssenet, M. (2000) *Les Modèles Productifs*. Editions La Découverte, Paris; *Productive Models*, English translation. Palgrave, London (forthcoming).

Briam, K.-H. (1986) *Arbeiten Ohne Angst: Arbeitsmanagement in Technischen Wandel* [Working without Fear: Labour Management in Times of Technological Change]. ECON-Verlag, Düsseldorf, Wien.

Camuffo, A. and Volpato, G. (2001) The Fiat-GM strategic alliance. In: *Reconfiguring the Auto Industry: Merger and Acquisition, Alliances and Exit, Proceedings of the Ninth GERPISA International Colloquium 2001*, Palais du Luxembourg, Paris, 7–9 June.

Dupuy, C. and Lung, Y. (2002) Institutional investors and the car industry. Geographic focalisation and industrial strategies. *Competition and Change*, 6(3)

Freyssenet, M. (1998) Renault: From diversified mass production to innovative flexible production. In: Freyssenet, M., Mair, A., Shimizu, K. and Volpato, G. (eds), *One Best Way? Trajectories and Industrial Models of the World's Automobile Producers*. Oxford University Press, Oxford.

Frigant, V. and Lung, Y. (2001) Are the French car companies PSA and Renault the European automobile industry's champions of shareholder value? *Corporate Governance, Innovation and Economic Performance in the EU*, Report to the CGEP Project. INSEAD, Fontainebleau.

Froud, J., Haslam, C., Johal, S. and Williams, K. (2002) Cars after financialisation: A case study in financial under-performance, constraints and consequences. *Competition and Change*, 6(3): (page numbers to be added).

Haipeter, T. (2000) *Mitbestimmung bei VW: Neue Chancen für die Betriebliche Interessenvertretung?* [Co-determination at VW: New Possibilities for Company-Level Interest Representation?]. Verlag Westfälisches Dampfboot, Schriftenreihe der Hans-Böckler-Stiftung, Münster.

Hartz, P. (1994) *Jeder Arbeitsplatz hat ein Gesicht: Die Volkswagen-Lösung* [Each Workplace has a Human Face: The Volkswagen Solution]. Campus Verlag, Frankfurt on Main, New York.

Hartz, P. (1996) *Das Atmende Unternehmen: Jeder Arbeitsplatz hat einen Kunden* [The Breathing Company: Each Workplace has a Customer]. Campus Verlag, Frankfurt on Main, New York.

Jürgens, U. (1998) The development of Volkswagen's industrial model, 1967–1995. In: Freyssenet, M., Mair, A., Shimizu, K. and Volpato, G. (eds), *One Best Way? Trajectories and Industrial Models of the World's Automobile Producers*. Oxford University Press, Oxford, pp. 273–310.

Loubet, J.L. (1998) Peugeot meets Ford, Sloan and Toyota. In: Freyssenet, M., Mair, A., Shimizu, K. and Volpato, G. (eds), *One Best Way? Trajectories and Industrial Models of World's Automobile Producers*. Oxford University Press, Oxford, pp. 338–363.

Volpato, G. (1998). Fiat auto and magneti marelli: Toward globalization. *Internationalization of Firms: Strategies and Trajectories*, Actes du GERPISA, 22, Paris.

Volpato, G. (2001). Corporate governance at Fiat SpA. *Corporate Governance, Innovation and Economic Performance in the EU*, Report to the CEGP Research Project. INSEAD, Fontainebleau.

17 "The Theory of the Firm and Shareholder Value"

from Corporate Governance Adrift: A Critique of Shareholder Value (2005)

Michel Aglietta and Antoine Rebérioux

The key question remains to be answered: in the agency model, what are the theoretical foundations for the preference given to shareholders? In other words, why are corporate executives designated as the agents of the shareholders? Or, put in another way, why should the board of directors – the central organ of the firm – be reserved exclusively for shareholder representatives? What economic arguments are put forward? The problematic nature of these arguments has led to the creation of a new path of research, focusing on the question of the incompleteness of contracts.

THE PROFIT ARGUMENT

This argument is founded on the idea that in a market economy a firm's objective is to maximize its profits. If we add that these profits are the remuneration of capital providers, shareholder value would be justified. It would be, in some way, inscribed within capitalism itself. This analysis may be correct in the case of an entrepreneurial firm, but it is, on the contrary, much more problematic in the case of a managerial firm.[1] Let us explore this point in more detail.

Entrepreneurial firms are unique in that one and the same person (the central agent) fulfils the following four functions: entrepreneur (knowing the trade, the markets, managing uncertainty, etc.), manager (organizing the firm), capitalist (owning the means of production) and worker. The share of total revenues which comes back to him or her, once the (other)

factors of production have been remunerated, can be considered as the profit. This profit is composed of various elements, deriving from the different functions: wages for managerial and non-managerial work, interest for capital contribution, and a 'pure' profit for the entrepreneurial activity – a mix of risk-taking and a capacity to lead the business in the midst of uncertainty. In the case of a managerial firm (or listed company), these functions are separated and performed by collective units rather than individuals. The functions of entrepreneur and manager are grouped together within the executive team, which is salaried. The company itself, as a legal entity, is the owner of the means of production. The shareholders receive residual earnings in the form of dividends by virtue of their contract; this function has no equivalent in the entrepreneurial firm. What then is profit? For the entrepreneurial firm, we have identified it in terms of its destination (the share that comes back to the central agent) and not by its origin (which is diverse, as we have seen). For the managerial firm, this attribution is no longer possible. The very concept of profit becomes muddled: it no longer designates the remuneration of a specific agent. Different stakeholders in the firm may be remunerated on the basis of the book profits. Thus shareholders receive part of it if dividends are paid; so may employees, if their remuneration includes an incentive scheme. Finally, it may be reinvested. In no case, either legally, contractually or statutorily, does profit belong exclusively to the shareholders. Bernstein (1953) highlighted the distance between the concept of profit in the cases of managerial and entrepreneurial firms in the following passage:

> [in the case of a large corporation] the profit has an 'impersonality' about it, whereas in the case of small business, the relationship between the entrepreneur and his company's earning is very intimate indeed. [...] In brief, while conceptually small business profit seems to accrue to people, big business profit belongs to 'the corporation'. (1969, p. 243)

This makes it easier to understand the mistake made in basing shareholder value on the concept of profit maximization: the fact that the objective of the firm is to maximize its profit does not imply that the firm must be managed in the exclusive interest of its shareholders; profit is not reserved for their exclusive remuneration. In other words, in the case of a managerial firm, the principle of profit maximization does not, in itself, convey any criterion for the distribution of profit between the different constituents (shareholders, employees or the firm itself).

THE RISK ARGUMENT

From an economic point of view, the second argument is the most widely used to justify shareholder value: it is because the shareholders are the risk-bearers in the firm that they should take precedence in the distribution of power and profit. The idea that the shareholders are the party which incurs the risk is very widespread: it derives from the fact that the remuneration of equity holders is not specified beforehand in the contract which binds them to the company, unlike the remunerations of wage earners and creditors. An allocation of power in favour of shareholders is the only one that respects the basic principle of externality management, according to which the capacity to impact the income from an asset should be conferred on the person receiving those revenues. All institutional mechanisms which contribute to returning control to the risk-bearers thus make it possible to draw closer to the optimum. They participate in the internalization of externalities. On this subject, Easterbrook and Fischel (1993), promoters of contract theory in the economic analysis of law, wrote:

> voting rights are universally held by shareholders, to the exclusion of creditors, managers and other

employees. [...] The reason is that shareholders are the residual claimants to the firm's income. [...] As the residual claimants, shareholders have the appropriate incentives [...] to make discretionary decisions. (pp. 67–8)

Nevertheless, this link between risk-taking and the right to control is a fragile foundation on which to base shareholder value. In fact, the intensity of the risk taken by shareholders can be challenged as soon as we move away from the question of the residual nature of their remuneration as defined in their contract. First, their liability is limited: the losses they sustain in the event of bankruptcy of the firm are limited to the value of their capital contributions. Second, the tradable nature of their assets and the growing liquidity of stock markets provides them with a capacity for exit and diversification without equal, in any case much higher than that of the employees. Current developments tend further to reduce the risk incurred by shareholders, reinforcing our scepticism about the validity of risk as a justification. One example of this trend is the spread of the principle of the creation of value for the shareholder.... Thus Economic Value Added (EVA) affirms the idea that there exists a minimum remuneration for the shareholder, namely the cost of capital as evaluated by the market. Only financial profitability over and above this cost is considered to create value. The pursuit of a strategy oriented towards the creation of value for the shareholder thus necessitates the (internal) setting of a profitability threshold which must be exceeded. Obviously, the application of this principle remarkably modifies that status of the shareholder (Lordon, 2000): from a residual creditor, the shareholder is transformed (thanks to EVA) into a secured creditor, similar to lenders. Shareholders acquire guarantees of return on their investment, which may not be legally binding (contractual), but which are nevertheless very real. To observe this change, we need to go beyond the contractual clauses and examine the *actual* unfolding of the relationships. The reduction in the risk incurred by shareholders is necessarily accompanied by an increase in the risk incurred by the other stakeholders, and notably by the employees. The development of the individualization of remunerations, for managers, white-collar workers and blue-collar workers, forms part of this movement of the transfer of risk (Coutrot, 1998; H. Petit, 2003). Increased work flexibility throughout all Western countries has also been part of this movement: the growing use of specific forms of employment (short-term and temporary contracts), along with the generalization of subsidiary and outsourcing strategies, make it possible to adjust the wage bill to suit industrial requirements. In short, the rise to power of the doctrine of shareholder value is turning the traditional roles upside-down: employees are incurring an ever greater share of the risk as the shareholders succeed in taking advantage of a favourable balance of power to guarantee partially their income.

The statistics for the evolution of dividends as a proportion of profit in the United States give an idea of the scale of this movement (see Figure 17.1). During the 1980s, while profits remained globally stable, the size of dividends rose as pressure from the capital markets increased: dividends as a proportion of profit doubled, from 24.7 percent in 1980 to 50.1 percent in 1990. From 1992 to 1997, dividends continued to rise, but with profits climbing as well: the share of dividends settled at around 50 percent. In 1998, a new trend began to form, one that would appear fully in 2001, 2002 and 2003: profits fell, yet dividends continued on their upward movement started at the beginning of the 1980s. Consequently, dividends as a proportion of profits exploded, reaching 87.3 percent in the second quarter of 2003. Thus, for more than 20 years, we have been observing a regular rise in dividends, completely detached from

movements in profits. This ratcheting up, which appears to exclude any possibility of a reduction in the cash flow paid to shareholders, clearly highlights the developments described above; for the last two decades shareholders have succeeded in partially guaranteeing their income against trading fluctuations, thus significantly reducing the risk they incur. Consequently, the argument that the firm should be managed in the exclusive interest of its shareholders because they are the ones incurring the risk loses a lot of its validity.

THE INCOMPLETE CONTRACT APPROACH

The above discussion underlines that the relative position of a given stakeholder should not be evaluated exclusively through the contract between that party and the company; the actual development of their relationship must also be taken into account. If shareholders are sometimes judged to be the only residual creditors of the firm, that is because analysis has focused exclusively on the equity contract. As we have seen, conclusions are substantially modified when we take into account the *ex post* dimension of contracts, in other words their actual unfolding. This observation has led to a renewal of the normative

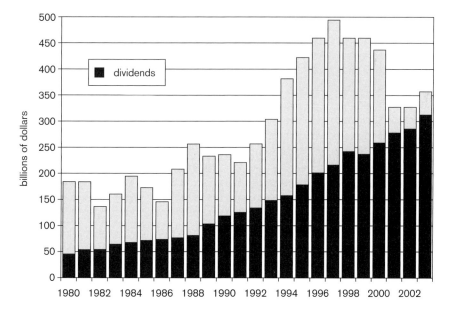

Source: Flow of funds (Federal Reserve), Tables F.102.

Figure 17.1 **Evolution of dividends as a proportion of total profits (before tax) for non-financial companies (excluding farming) in the USA**

approach to corporate governance, focusing analysis on the question of contractual incompleteness. The hypothesis of incompleteness represents the translation of the above idea into the syntax of contract theory: affirming that we need to analyse the actual realization of the relationship means recognizing that contracts signed *ex ante* do not cover this relationship exhaustively. In other words, we consider that these contracts are incomplete; certain decisive elements of the relationship cannot be contracted at the start, giving it an indeterminate character from the outset. In terms of governance, the importance of the hypothesis of contractual incompleteness is particularly evident, as Hart (1995) points out: 'Governance structure matters when some actions have to be decided in the future that have not been specified in an initial contract' (p. 679).

The securing of investments in financial and human capital

The hypothesis of contractual incompleteness lies at the heart of the contemporary theory of the firm. It is one of the foundations of transaction cost theory, pioneered by Williamson (1975, 1985), and of modern property rights theory, developed by Grossman and Hart (1986). These two approaches both explore the way in which parties to a transaction secure their reciprocal investments when contracts are incomplete. In this context, protection of specific, non-redeployable investments cannot be achieved beforehand by the establishment of a contract providing for every possible contingency. Consequently, the parties to the contract are led to establish institutional devices, enabling them to appropriate a share of the organizational quasi-rent as a return on their investment. When applied to corporate governance, this schema considers rights on the board of directors as a tool for securing investments. Thus Zingales (1998) writes of the 'incomplete contracts approach to corporate governance'.

This path was first explored by Williamson in Chapter 12, entitled 'Corporate Governance', of his seminal 1985 book *The Economic Institutions of Capitalism*. His argument is taken up and furthered in two articles, one by Williamson and Bercovitz (1996), the other by Romano (1996). These works recognize that shareholders are not the only risk-takers within the firm. This assertion, however, is not based on the observation, made above, of a transfer of risk from shareholders to employees, but on the development of a risk that is *internal* to the workforce. This new risk derives from a trend, noted by many observers, of an increase in the specificity of human capital (see also Blair, 1995). This increase does indeed constitute a risk-taking factor: workers' payoff depends on the future distribution of the quasi-rent generated by the investment in human capital, which is fundamentally uncertain. This risk is all the stronger as the specificity of capital, in other words its non-redeployable nature, places employees in a disadvantageous position at the time of (re-)negotiation of the allocation of the quasi-rent. Reflection is thus focused on the measures capable of efficiently protecting those parties which incur the greatest risk (shareholders and employees), whereas contracts are incomplete. These authors reach the following conclusion: shareholders should be protected through rights of control over the board of directors. As for employees' investments, they should be secured by means of various devices: a pre-defined system of promotion, severance packages and procedures for settling internal disputes. Employee participation on the board of directors, however, is not envisaged. One may be surprised by this asymmetry between the treatment of shareholders and that of employees: in one case, the recognition of a weakness gives the right to control; in the other, it gives the right to protection against the arbitrary nature of decisions. The conclusion of Romano is clear: 'Transaction cost economics offers no analytical support for expanding board representation to non-shareholder groups, and indeed, cautions against such proposals' (1996, p. 293). The German model, in which employee representatives sit on the supervisory board,[2] is deemed to be inefficient.

Towards a questioning of shareholder value

The work of Zingales (1998, 2000) and of Blair and Stout (1999) has developed the incomplete contract approach to corporate governance pioneered by Williamson. This work offers, following Blair (1995), a new conception of the process of value creation within the firm. Thus it is observed that the quasi-rent created by the firm derives from the pooling of complementary factors of production, in the form of tangible, intangible, human and financial capital. Compared with the work of Williamson, more emphasis is placed on the incomplete nature of contracts and on the synergies that come into play between the investments of the different stakeholders. The firm is conceptualized as a 'nexus of specific investments'. The allocation of rights of control over the entity thus created plays a decisive role, in that this allocation will determine how the value created is divided up. Consequently, each stakeholder will be more or less motivated to commit to the firm, and this will influence the very level of the organizational quasi-rent.

Taking into account the complexity of the relationships formed between the different stakeholders and the plurality of centres of value creation, Zingales (1998) and Blair and Stout (1999) propose a solution that moves away from the doctrine of shareholder value: the stakeholders should delegate their powers to an independent third party – the board of directors – whose objective is to best serve the interest of the constituted entity. In this context, the directors are no longer simply the agents of the shareholders; their fiduciary duties must be exercised towards the whole firm, in accordance with what is today the most widely accepted analysis of the contents of these duties in US corporate law. Thus the productive assets of the firm must be managed in the interest of the firm itself. This point is new compared with the work of Williamson, for whom the role of the board of directors was to serve the interests of the shareholders. In short, the primacy of shareholders is partially challenged.

For Zingales (1998) and for Blair and Stout (1999), however, ultimate control of the board of directors should remain in the hands of shareholders, because of their contractually weak position. Here, we find a mode of reasoning analogous to that of Williamson who, after recognizing the importance of employees in terms of the creation of value (through their specific investments), excludes them from board-level participation. This conclusion, it must be noted, upholds the optimality of the US model of governance, in which the managers, while having their fiduciary duties extended, are exclusively controlled by their shareholders through the board of directors.

Zingales (2000) goes one step further in an article of a very prospective nature entitled 'In Search of New Foundations'. This title reveals his ambition: in terms of corporate governance, he seeks to grasp the implications of transformations in forms of coordination, which have become more flexible, and in methods of value creation, which are more closely focused on workers' skills. His conclusion moves even further away from the doctrine of shareholder value: 'In the current environment, where human capital is crucial and *contracts are highly incomplete*, the primary goal of a corporate governance system should be to protect the integrity of the firm, and new precepts need to be worked out' (p. 1645, our italics). Despite this call for further reflection, Zingales offers no 'solutions'; his article is essentially devoted to describing the limits of existing theories.

The issue of contractual incompleteness

Examination of the contributions of Zingales (1998, 2000) and of Blair and Stout (1999) brings out a remarkable principle: the stronger the emphasis on contractual incompleteness, the more managers' responsibility is extended. Zingales (2000) thus calls for reflection on new principles of governance in light of the current situation in which contracts are 'highly incomplete'. The corollary of this increased incompleteness is an affirmation of the collective nature of the firm: from a form strictly centred on shareholders (Williamson, 1985), principles of governance were first extended to collective management of productive assets (Zingales, 1998; Blair and Stout 1999), before finally embracing protection of the integrity of the firm (Zingales, 2000).

It should be noted, however, that this principle, by which the widening of the field of incompleteness is accompanied by an extension of the responsibility of managerial power, raises its own problems. The widening of the field of incompleteness progressively reduces the validity of the contractual analysis on which the work of Zingales and of Blair and Stout is founded. To say that contracts are incomplete is to acknowledge that the 'off-contract' plays a role in coordination. As this incompleteness increases, the scope of contractual analysis therefore tends, by definition, to shrink (Favereau, 1997). The less we understand the nature of the interactions at work within the firm, the more *ad hoc* becomes the description of any particular model as efficient. Consequently, we may consider that Zingales (1998) and Blair and Stout (1999) give voting rights to shareholders less for analytical reasons specific to their model and more for shaping this model to fit the US reality. In doing so, they give 'scientific' credit to this model of governance.[3] Indeed, this difficulty is recognized implicitly by Zingales (1998), for whom 'at the current state of knowledge the [incomplete contracts approach to corporate governance] lacks theoretical foundations'

(p. 502). The author adds by way of conclusion: 'Without a better understanding of why contracts are incomplete, all the results are merely provisional' (p. 502).

We can draw two conclusions from this presentation of the incomplete contract approach to corporate governance, one negative and the other positive:

1. As it stands, this approach appears to display a certain conservatism. These works conclude that the model under consideration (the US model) is efficient, to the exclusion of every other model. This conclusion is all the more fragile because it relies on strictly microeconomic and contractual reasoning, placing the emphasis precisely on the massively incomplete nature of contracts. The risk of 'ad hocness' are heightened as a result.

2. On the other hand, this approach highlights the specifically collective dimension of the firm as a locus of coordination and actualization of specific and complementary skills. This coordination cannot be reduced to a set of contracts, except in the case where these contracts are assumed to be largely incomplete. This ultimately amounts to concluding that intra-firm coordination is partially outside the realm of contractual order. In terms of governance the conclusions of this recognition of the collective nature of the firm are also interesting, in that they represent a move away from the doctrine of shareholder value.

FOR A PARTNERSHIP THEORY OF THE FIRM

The 'discovery' of the collective nature of the company (beyond the sphere of contracts) by the contractual theory of the firm is all the more remarkable in that it rejoins a whole tradition of thought which has been largely ignored for nearly 40 years. This tradition, having more of a legal origin, fell into oblivion through a curious turn of history that saw its message attacked by both neoclassical and Marxist theorists.

In the United States, Berle and Means (1932) can be connected to this tradition, which proposes of a holistic conception of the firm. By 'holistic', we mean a conception of the firm that focuses on its autonomous and collective nature. The firm exists in and of itself; it cannot be reduced to a set of inter-individual relation ships. We have already described the way in which Berle and Means's analysis of the changes in private

property, subsequent to the growth in capital market liquidity, led them to argue for an 'empowerment' of the firm in relation to its shareholders. We have also pointed out that this thesis, contrary to that of the 'separation of ownership and control', was carefully buried by the firm theorists from the 1960s onwards.

The point of view upheld by Berle and Means has also been espoused by certain legal theorists in Europe. In France, the 'institutional theory of the firm' (*théorie institutionnelle de l'enterprise*), developed just after the Second World War, provides a particularly rich interpretation of the nature of the firm and the conclusions to be drawn in terms of corporate governance.

To understand the foundations of this 'institutional' theory, the first thing to bear in mind is that *the firm does not exist in law*. Only the corporation, grouping together the shareholders, has a legal existence. This is because the only methods of coordination recognized by the law are contracts and associations (Ripert, 1951): the firm remains hidden behind a network of contracts (corporate and labour).[4]

In response to what they saw as a lack, different legal specialists have sought to unveil the collective nature of the firm: first, by observing the existence of a sociological and economic reality of the firm; and second, by detecting, within current legislation, the premises of a recognition of the substance of the firm, and calling for further progress in that direction. This unveiling of the firm as an autonomous collective – which deserves to be treated as a person in the eyes of the law – has been based, in France, on German legal scholarship and on the 'theory of the institution' developed in public law:

- German legal culture established a 'labour relations doctrine', conceiving of employment relations as a relationship founded on the personal commitment of the employee, and not as a purely contractual relationship. This approach was extended into a community vision of the firm in the work of Gierke (1874).

- The 'legal theory of the institution', developed in France by Hauriou (1910), analysed an institution as an activity or idea which becomes autonomous in relation to its creator. Its management is thus driven by the search to satisfy the general interest of the institution, which reaches beyond the specific (and sometimes divergent) interests of the different parties involved. This analysis is very close to that of Berle and Means, for whom the concentration of power in the hands of managers was only acceptable when that power was 'contained', in other words given objectives distinct from the interests of those wielding the power.

The 'institutional theory of the firm' was born out of a synthesis of these two approaches through the work of Durand (1947) and Ripert (1951). Durand saw the firm as a 'grouping organized in relation to a common purpose' (vol. 1, Section 339, our translation), while Ripert proposed to 'bring to light the collective action, the solidarity between all the members of the same firm, the natural society created by the community of work' (p. 275, our translation). The key idea in this theory is that intra-firm activity is based on the cooperation between the different stakeholders (employees and capitalists), and that this cooperation aims at a common objective. Consequently, the firm displays the characteristics of an institution: it is autonomous in relation to its members, and the objective defined by its management must be to satisfy the general interest, which both synthesizes and transcends the motivations of its different constituents. The closeness of this thesis to the principles upheld by Berle and Means in Book IV of *The Modern Corporation* can be clearly observed on reading the following passage from *Aspects juridiques du capitalisme moderne* ('Juridicial Aspects of Modern Capitalism') by Ripert (1951):

> In the grouping of forces constituted by the firm, the end pursued becomes of capital importance. This end is the common good of all the people who cooperate in the firm. It is no longer solely the limitless remuneration of capital through the profits made, it is also the guarantee of the livelihood of the people who work in the firm and the families of these people. Capital and labour must each find satisfaction in the firm, but of a different nature, and if the firm cannot provide this, it does not deserve to survive. (p. 279, our translation)

Thus, for Ripert (1951), 'it is essential to render management independent of capital. We should not consider managers and directors to be the agents of the shareholders' (p. 285, our translation). Note that the foundations of the legal concept of the 'interest of the firm', which plays a key role in the French legal framework of collective layoffs, are found in institutional theory.

The progressive obliteration of this 'holistic' vision can be attributed to its awkward positioning, out of plumb with the two dominant post-Second World War conceptions of the firm – the neoclassical approach (in economics) on the one hand, and the Marxist approach (in labour law) on the other (see Box 17.1). The neoclassical approach has appeared in numerous variations (normative and positive agency theory, property rights theory, etc.), but these variants are unanimous in reducing the firm to a nexus of contracts agreed between autonomous agents. This vision is clearly antithetic to the holistic approach, which confers primacy to the entity over the stakeholders. Paradoxically, the Marxist approach also claims to adopt a 'contractual' approach (see Lyon-Caen, 1955). In this context, the term 'contractual' is used in opposition to the institutionalist (holistic) approach, of which the community connotations run counter to an analysis in terms of class struggle. If we add that the paternalistic character of institutional theory evoked, for certain authors, too much of the principles of Vichist ideology, it is easy to understand why holistic theory was struck by an 'anti-community taboo' after the Liberation (Segrestin, 1992). This taboo can also be observed in Germany and Italy.

Economic analysis of the firm, in its most modern developments, is tending to return to the central message of these theories. We have already described the way in which emphasis on the incomplete nature of contracts has driven the contractual approach to consider the firm as an entity in itself, whose management must be oriented towards the satisfaction of a transcendent interest. This is all the more for cognitive approaches to the firm. Unlike contractual theory, for which the firm is above all an incentive structure, cognitive approaches explore the way in which the firm constructs, maintains and develops tacit and collective productive knowledge. The competitiveness of the firm depends on the quality of the 'cognitive' process. The economics of conventions focuses particularly on the conditions for realizing these processes of collective learning (Favereau, 1994; Eymard-Duvernay, 2001): the concept of cooperation, around an objective shared by both the employees and the shareholders, is given a central role. This underscores the 'partnership' dimension of the firm. A partnership is defined generically as an association which has the aim of performing a common action. Today, this concept, rather than the term 'holistic', lies at the heart of different analyses seeking to define the essence of the firm. These analyses, be they British (Wheeler, 1997) or French (Charreaux and Desbrières, 1998), share the idea that the firm is collective

---

Box 17.1   The Marxist theory of the firm

The 'traditional' Marxist approach emphasizes a contradiction in labour relations. These are both a market relationship, which can be interpreted in contract terms, and a subordinative relationship of the employees to the managers in the performance of the contract, in other words in their work. The contract is therefore highly incomplete, and this fact is also recognized by neoclassical efficiency wage theories.

We need to go further by rethinking labour relations in a monetary economy. In this case, they are clearly not a market relationship. They are in fact a social division which deprives employees of the possibility of becoming autonomous producers. Not being owners, employees cannot be the subject of contracts. This means that labour relations are not only an incomplete contract, in the sense of an agreement between two subjects who are formally equal because they are both traders, but also a *sui generis* institution resulting from the private appropriation of the means of production. This institution is a mediation which establishes, enforces and legitimizes a system of rules concerning wages,

working conditions, labour mobility, and so on. Thus conceived of, labour relations correlatively build the capitalist firm into an autonomous entity capable of subordinating employees through the power of labour coordination.

This structure is reflected in the access to money enjoyed by firms and employees. Firms have the monetary initiative to be able to produce. It is their access to monetary creation, either directly through the banks or indirectly through share issues, which enables them to draw resources from society, foremost among which are the human capacities of employees to produce in order to sell. It follows that the monetary initiative of firms is built on the anticipation of the accumulation of capital gathered in the collective entity and considered as a whole. This confers strategic power on the managers of the firm, because the definition of a global objective is indispensable for access to credit…. Access of the employees to money, on the contrary, depends on the firm. This validates the mediation (role) of labour relations in the formation of the monetary wealth of the economy.

---

in nature, in the style of Berle and Means or Ripert. As things stand, this term appears to us to be both the most illuminating and the most unifying, if an alternative has to be found for the contractual qualifier of the firm.

Clearly, the firm is not a pure partnership, and much work remains to be done in this direction. One cannot deny the existence of power struggles, asymmetries, and so on, just as one cannot deny all partnerial foundation to the firm. The firm has a partnerial dimension because it develops on the basis of cooperation oriented towards a common goal.

While the current movement towards employment insecurity has led certain authors to refuse to accept the partnerial dimension of the firm, it is also possible, conversely, to treat this movement as an opportunity to reaffirm the partnerial essence of the firm – from a reformist point of view (Kay and Silberson, 1995). We believe that the following remarks by Catala, in the introduction to the fourth volume of the general survey of labour law directed by Camerlynck in 1980, are more relevant than ever:

The view we adopt concerning the nature of the firm is therefore lacking neither in practical implications nor in political repercussions. As things stand, it may be illusory or premature to detect an institution therein. However, to deny that the interests of those who contribute their energy, skills or capital converge, at least partially, within the firm, is not only to deny a reality, it is also to condemn *a priori* any institutional participation, any social organization of the firm, any effort to construct within the firm, by means of bodies and mechanisms that may be imperfect but are perfectible, a balance that respects the vested interests. (p. IX, our translation)

CONCLUSION

The conclusion of this chapter, which set out to assess the normative dimension of the 'end of history' thesis, is clear: shareholder value, or the agency perspective of corporate governance, is less a theoretically founded model than a position of principle. Contrary to the affirmations of its champions, it cannot lay claim to any scientific legitimacy: no economic reasoning can justify the assertion that the firm should be managed exclusively in the interest of its shareholders. Attempts at justification come up against the distributed nature of risk within the firm. Moreover, instead of the 'widespread normative consensus' (see above, Hansmann and Kraakman, 2001) on the intrinsic qualities of shareholder value, the most recent works (Zingales, 1998, 2000; Blair and Stout, 1999) propose a more contrasting, if not contradictory, conclusion – although one may observe the fragility of these results. Study of the creation of value within the firm thus brings out the collective nature of this process, which combines a group of specific productive resources under the authority of managers and directors. The implications in terms of the organization of power within the firm are noteworthy: management of the firm must be oriented to satisfying the interests of the entity itself, and not the interests of one of its constituents. In other words, the holistic, or partnerial, conception of the firm and its governance are reaffirmed by an economic analysis of the processes of value creation in the firm. The shift towards approaches which focus more on the cognitive dimension and less on the incentive dimension of the firm strengthens this conclusion.[5]

Economic analysis has yet to produce any argument capable of challenging the analysis of Berle and Means (1932), despite the efforts made in this direction ever since the success, during the 1970s, of agency theory. It could even be argued that current economic theory is moving towards the normative conclusions of *The Modern Corporation and Private Property*. In this work, Berle and Means provided a dual interpretation, both positive and normative. On the positive level, they diagnosed a fundamental transformation in the concept of property due to the growth in capital market liquidity. Although this diagnosis was very widely accepted, the remedy proposed was, on the contrary, firmly challenged and/or progressively forgotten by the dominant economic approach (contract theory). While the mainstream reaffirmed a shareholder sovereignty, thus founding the set of themes of corporate governance on a logic of dispossession and control, Berle and Means called for a redefinition of the nature of power in the firm, this power to be exercised in the name of the firm as a collective. The intuition of these two authors, which

has been taken up in France by Ripert, is therefore that shareholder value is not inscribed within capitalism. For them, the choice of liquidity made by the shareholders should logically be paid for by relinquishment of control over the wealth-creating entity, which becomes autonomous. This intuition has stronger foundations today than it had in 1930, due to the rise to power of institutional investors in the stock markets. By definition, these investors are only interested in the (relative or absolute) return on their portfolios. Investment in a firm is nether guided by a desire to get more involved with the entity, not concerned with understanding its business or strategies. Financial profitability in relation to the risk taken is the unique criterion of choice. Consequently, the idea that the firm is an autonomous entity is today even more obvious than during Berle and Means's time.

Finally, the tradability of shares and the liquidity of stock markets call for a form of governance that emancipates the firm from the grip of its shareholders. The partnerial dimension of the firm must be reaffirmed: this dimension comes from bringing together the strategic, cognitive and financial skills necessary for the development and competitiveness of the entity thus constituted. Central power is conferred on the managers and directors, entrusted with the task of setting this productive force into motion in the temporal dimension. However, this power must be given objectives, in other words it must be exercised in the interest of the entity, which both synthesizes and transcends the interests of the main stakeholders (shareholders and employees). Making managerial power binding thus calls for a form of governance quite different from that championed by the doctrine of shareholder value, where managers must act in the strict interest of the shareholders, under the watchful eye of a board of directors composed exclusively of shareholder representatives.

In addition to a new normative vision of the governance of listed companies, the analysis conducted in this chapter argues in favour of a second shift: the reintegration of the wage–labour nexus into positive discussions on governance. There is nothing to justify the fact that debates on governance are focused exclusively on institutions relating to capital markets. This type of analysis, particularly used to examine the convergence of national models, confirms the partition between *corporate governance* on the one hand, lying within the scope of stock market law and corporate law, and *labour governance* on the other, lying within the scope of labour or industrial law. [We] propose an analytical framework which takes into account simultaneously the influence of the financial sphere and labour relations in the exercise of power in large companies.

NOTES

1 The term 'entrepreneurial firm' is commonly used to designate individual companies, or unlisted companies. The term 'managerial firm', on the other hand, designates all firms established on the basis of a public limited company.
2 Here, the difference between the board of directors and the supervisory board is of little importance. In both cases, we are dealing with the central strategic organ of the firm.
3 In the process, the French model, which is identical to the US model from this point of view, is seen as efficient. The German model, on the other hand, is once more perceived as being sub-optimal.
4 'Association' is a legal technique which is, by nature, foreign to intra-firm coordination, as it designates a gathering or a group brought together with the view of satisfying non-financial interests.
5 For developments on this point, see O'Sullivan (2000) and Rebérioux (2003b).

REFERENCES

Berle, A.A. and Means, G.C. (1932) *The Modern Corporation and Private Property*, New York: Harcourt, Brace and World.
Bernstein, P. (1953) Profit Theory – Where Do We Go From Here?, *Quarterly Journal of Economics*, 67, 401–22, reprinted in S. Blumner (ed.) (1969) *Readings in Microeconomics*, Scranton: International Textbook Company, pp. 239–52.
Blair, M.M. (1995) *Ownership and Control: Rethinking Corporate Governance for the 21st Century*, Washington DC: Brookings Institute.
Blair, M.M. and Stout, L.A. (1999) A Team Production Theory of Corporate Law, *Virginia Law Review* 85(2): 247–328.
Charreaux, G. and Desbrières, P. (1998) Gouvernance des Enterprises: Valeur Partenariale Contre Valeur Actionnariale, *Finance, Controle, Stategie*, 1, 57–88.
Coutrot, T. (1998) *L'Enterprise Neo-Libérale: Une Nouvelle Utopie Capitalist?* Paris : La Decouverte.
Durand, P. (1947) *Traité de Droit du Travail*, Paris: Dalloz.
Easterbrook, F. and Fischel, D. (1993) *The Economic Structure of Corporate Law*, Cambridge, MA and London: Harvard University Press.
Eymard-Duvernay, F. (2001) L'Economie des Conventione A-t-Elle une Théorie Politique, in P. Batifoulier (ed.) *Théorie des Conventions*, Paris: Economica, coll. Forum, pp. 279.

Favereau, O. (1994) Règles, Organisation et Apprentissage Collectif: Un Paradigme non Standard pour Trois Théories Heterodoxes, in A. Orlean (ed.), *Analyse économique des conventions*, Paris: PUF, pp. 113–37.
Favereau, O. (1997) L'Incompletude n'est pas le Problem, c'est la Solution, in B. Reynaud (ed.) *Les Limites de la Rationalité. Tome 2: Les Figures du Collectif*, Paris: La Decouverte.
Gierke, O. (1874) *Die Grunbegriffe des Staatsrechts und die Neuesten Staatrsrechtstheorien*, Second Edition, Tübingen: Mohr, 1915.
Grossman, S. and Hart, O. (1986) The Costs and Benefits of Ownership: A Theory of Vertical and Lateral Integration, *Journal of Political Economy*, 94, 691–719.
Hansmann, H. and Kraakman, R. (2001) The End of History for Corporate Law, *Georgetown Law Journal*, 89: 439.
Hart, O. (1995) Corporate Governance: Some Theory and Implications, *The Economic Journal*, 105, 678–89.
Hauriou, M. (1910) La Théorie de L'Institution et de la Fondation, Cahiers de la Nouvelle Journée, 4.
Kay, J. and Silverton, A. (1995) Corporate Governance, *National Institute Economic Review*, August: 84–97.
Lordon, F. (2002) *La Politique du Capital*, Paris: Odile Jacob
Lyon-Caen, G. (1955) *Manuel de Droit du Travail et de la Securité Sociale*, Paris: Dalloz.
O'Sullivan, M. (2000) *Contests for Corporate Control: Corporate Governance and Economic Performance in the United States and Germany*, Oxford: Oxford University Press.
Petit, H. (2003) Les Determinants de la Mise en Oeuvre d'un Mode de Gestion de L'Emploi, *Economie et Statistique*, 361, 53–70.
Rebérioux, A. (2003) Les Marchés Financiers et la Participation des Salaries aux Decisions, *Travail et Emploi*, 93, January, 23–41.
Rebérioux, A. (2003b) Governance d'enterprise et théorie de la firme: quelle(s) alternative(s) a la valeur actionnariale? *Revue d'economie industrielle*, 103, 4, 85–110.
Ripert, G. (1951) *Aspects Juridiques Du Capitalisme Moderne*, Paris: LGDJ.
Romano, R. (1996) Corporate Law and Corporate Governance, *Industrial and Corporate Change*, 5, 277–339.
Segrestin, D. (1992) *Sociologie de l'Entreprise*, Paris: Armand Colin.
Wheeler, S. (1997) Works Councils: Towards Stakeholding? *Journal of Law and Society*, 24, 44–64.
Williamson, O. (1975) *Markets and Hierarchies: Analysis and Antitrust Implications*, New York: Free Press.
Williamson, O. (1985) *The Economic Institutions of Capitalism*, New York: Free Press.
Williamson, O. and Bercovitz, J. (1996) The Modern Corporation as an Efficiency Instrument: The Comparative Contracting Perspective, in C. Kaysen (ed.) *The American Corporation Today*, New York and Oxford: Oxford University Press, pp. 327–55.
Zingales, L. (1998) Corporate Governance, in P. Newman (ed.) *The New Palgrave Dictionary of Economics and the Law*, London: Stockton Press, pp. 497–502.
Zingales, L. (2000) In Search of New Foundations, *Journal of Finance*, 55, 1623–53.

18 "Negotiated Shareholder Value: the German Variant of an Anglo-American Practice"

from Competition and Change (2004)

Sigurt Vitols

SUMMARY

In comparative political economy it has become commonplace to distinguish between two types of corporate governance systems. In shareholder systems, influence over company management is concentrated with institutional investors holding small percentages of companies' shares. In stakeholder systems, influence is shared between large shareholders, employees, the community and suppliers and customers. This chapter contributes to the literature addressing recent changes in the German variant of the stakeholder system by proposing a few new concepts. On the level of institutions, it is argued that the stakeholder system is not being replaced by a shareholder system in Germany. Rather, an augmented stakeholder system is emerging through the inclusion of institutional investors in the old stakeholder coalition of interests. On the level of practice, it is argued that negotiated shareholder value is being adopted in Germany. This German variant of shareholder value is distinct from Anglo-American practice because major changes implementing shareholder value must be negotiated within the augmented stakeholder coalition. As a result, performance incentives for employees tend to be less strong than is the case in the USA and UK.

INTRODUCTION

In comparative political economy it has become commonplace to distinguish between two types of corporate governance systems (Kelly *et al.* 1997; Hopt *et al.* 1998; Jackson 2001a; McCahery *et al.* 2002). In shareholder systems, shareholders are the dominant interest group exercising influence on management, and the major goal pursued by companies is the maximization of shareholder value, that is, of the financial value of the firm. The USA and UK are the best known examples of shareholder systems. In stakeholder systems, in contrast, power is shared between shareholders and other groups with an interest in the firm, particularly employees. Reflecting the diverse interests of these different groups, increasing the value of the firm may be only one of a number of key goals pursued by firms in these types of systems. Germany and Japan are exemplars of stakeholder systems.

A major point of controversy is the extent to which stakeholder systems like Germany are currently facing pressures to change. At issue is the extent of influence of institutional investors, such as pension funds and mutual funds, that hold small amounts of stock in each of a large number of companies. These types of investors, who are particularly strong advocates of shareholder value, have accounted for a steadily increasing proportion of share ownership in the recent past. Given the stark choices offered by the shareholder versus stakeholder dichotomy, one position in the debate is that these institutional investors are powerful enough to force stakeholder systems to convergence on the shareholder model (Itami 1999; Eckert 2000). A second position is that these investors do not exercise enough influence to change the fundamental features of stakeholder systems, *i.e.* that heterogeneity in corporate governance systems will continue to exist (Hall and Soskice 2001; Jürgens *et al.* 2000; Van Den Berghe *et al.* 2002).

Recently, however, a number of researchers have been arguing that the stakeholder–shareholder dichotomy is inadequate to describe the changes occurring in stakeholder systems. In Germany, for example, although the financial system and its role in corporate governance has evolved in an Anglo-American direction, labour has maintained its strong influence within the company through works councils and board representation (Cioffi 2000; Goyer 2002). Attempts to theorize this process include the concept of 'hybrid' systems (Vitols 1999), multi-dimensional schemes for classifying corporate governance systems (Jackson and Aguilera 2003) and greater attention to the process of change (Höpner 2003).

This chapter seeks to contribute to this new body of research by developing a few ideas for conceptualizing recent changes in Germany. On the whole these recent developments are characterized as incremental changes in the German variant of the stakeholder model. These changes have occurred both at the level of institutions and of practice. At the institutional level, the post-war coalition of stakeholders influencing the firm (large shareholders, employees, the community, suppliers and customers) has not been replaced by or driven out by institutional investors. Instead, this post-war coalition has been augmented through the integration of institutional investors into the coalition. One can, therefore, speak of the emergence of an augmented stakeholder coalition in Germany. At the level of practice, the typical goals that German companies have focused on after World War II (sales growth, employment stability and product quality) have also have been enhanced, rather than replaced, by shareholder value. In contrast with the variant of shareholder value practised in the USA and UK, the German variant can be characterized as negotiated shareholder value, which has two key distinguishing features. First, the implementation of measures designed to achieve shareholder value in the interests of institutional investors cannot simply be imposed by management. Rather, they must first be negotiated with other members of the stakeholder coalition, particularly large shareholders and employee representatives. Secondly, reflecting the balance of power in this augmented stakeholder coalition, measures designed to achieve shareholder value are typically modified during the process of negotiation to take into account the interests of other

stakeholder groups. Many shareholder value measures, such as remuneration incentives designed to align the interests of shareholders, managers and employees, thus take significantly different forms in Germany than in the USA and UK, particularly where the interests of labour are concerned.

The second section of this chapter summarizes the debate on the extent to which the German stakeholder model is changing. The third and fourth sections provide evidence supporting the 'incremental change' interpretation of current developments. On the level of institutions, the third section analyses changes leading to the emergence of the augmented stakeholder coalition. On the level of practice, the fourth section focuses on specific examples of negotiated shareholder value, as well as on general indicators indicating differences relative to the Anglo-American variant of shareholder value. The final section summarizes and concludes.

The debate on the nature of change in the German stakeholder model

In analysing systems of corporate governance it is useful to distinguish between two levels. At the institutional level, national institutions influence the relative power of different groups with an interest in the firm. This includes both institutions structuring the internal organization and cohesion of interest groups, such as laws regarding trade union organization, and institutions regulating the interaction of these interest groups, such as company law. At the level of practice, companies embedded in different national institutional settings are distinguished by different mixes of strategic goals pursued, differing distributions of value added, and different organizational and operational characteristics. Drawing on Hirschman's (1970) concept of 'Exit, Voice, Loyalty', interest groups thus differ in the extent to which they can exercise 'voice' within the firm's strategic decision-making processes and in the possibilities they have to 'exit' their relationship with the firm.

In stakeholder systems, power is dispersed across a number of groups with an interest in the firm (Hutton 1995; Kelly *et al.* 1997; Vitols *et al.* 1997). These stakeholders typically include not only owners but also lenders, employees, customers and suppliers, and the community in which the firm is located (see Figure 18.1). Stakeholder systems are 'insider' systems, in which interested groups are closely tied to the firm

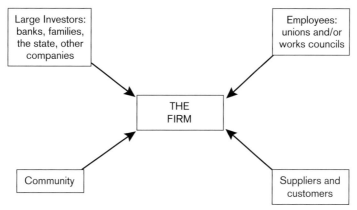

Figure 18.1 **The stakeholder model**

and exercise influence through institutional mechanisms for expressing (in Hirschman's terms) 'voice' within the firm.

In shareholder systems, power is concentrated in the hands of shareholders, while other groups have little or no influence (see Figure 18.2). Shareholder systems are 'outsider' systems, in which market mechanisms play a much stronger role in governance, and owners exert influence on management through the threat of 'exit' (selling shares). Owners in insider systems frequently hold large blocks of shares, often majority or controlling interests.[1] Owners in outsider systems, in contrast, tend to hold much smaller percentages of shares, leading to a highly dispersed system of ownership.

This heterogeneity in the distribution of influence is reflected in differences in company practice between corporate governance systems. The dominant goal of companies in shareholder systems is understood to be the maximization of the financial value of the firm (shareholder value), since this is the primary interest of shareholders. Correspondingly, firms in stakeholder systems are understood to be concerned with a broader mix of strategic goals, such as sales growth and employment security, than shareholder firms. Although profitability is a consideration in stakeholder systems, it will not be maximized if it conflicts with the interests of key stakeholders. Employees, for example, may have a greater interest in sales growth than in profitability, since sales growth implies an expanding firm and, thus, greater employment stability.

In practice Germany has become one of the most prominent national examples of an insider or stakeholder system of corporate governance. A recent large cross-national study showed that Germany had

the highest levels of shareholding concentration among the countries examined (see Table 18.1). According to the study, the median size of the largest shareholder for German companies listed on the stock exchange was 57 percent. In the USA, in contrast, the median size of the largest shareholder for companies listed on the New York Stock Exchange (the largest stock exchange in the USA) was 5.4 percent.

The role of large private banks has received special attention in the system of ownership in Germany. In contrast with banks in other countries, such as the USA, German banks are allowed to hold large blocks of shares in industrial companies on their own account. Furthermore, to a much greater extent than in the USA or UK, individuals purchase their shares through banks and leave these shares on deposit with the banks. Banks have been able to exercise votes on the shares of these small, largely passive individual investors through a system of proxy voting. Banks have, thus, been able to control upwards of 90 percent of the votes exercised at many shareholder meetings (Pfeiffer 1986; 1993).

A powerful institutional mechanism supporting the influence of the banks is the dual board system, which is mandatory for joint stock companies in Germany. The supervisory board is responsible for making key financial and strategic decisions and for appointing top management in the firm. Day-to-day managers may only be members of the executive board. Banks insisted on this governance form in the reform of German company law in the wake of a wave of bankruptcies in the late 1800s (Jackson 2001b). Banks nominate representatives to the supervisory boards of most large companies, including the chairs of these supervisory boards where their voting power is particularly large.

Figure 18.2 The shareholder model

Country	Largest voting block: median (%)
Germany	57.0
Belgium	56.0
Italy	54.5
Austria	52.0
Netherlands	43.5
Sweden	34.9
Spain	34.5
France (CAC 40)	20.0
UK	9.9
US, NYSE	5.4
US, NASDAQ	8.6

Source: Adapted from Barca and Becht (2001: 19, Table 1.1).

Table 18.1 Median size of largest shareholding block, mid-1990s

Although receiving less attention than banks, other types of large shareholders have also played a key role in corporate governance, including founders and families (e.g. BMW, Krupp, Thyssen, Siemens, SAP), the state (e.g. VW, Preussag, RWE, VEBA) and other companies (e.g. Degussa, Fresenius Medical Care). These large owners are also represented on company supervisory boards, typically as chairpersons where they are the largest owners.

Employees are a second key stakeholder group in the German model. Employees enjoy particularly strong rights of representation within the firm through the institution of the works council. Employees have the right to elect delegates to works councils at the plant level. This works council enjoys a wide variety of information, consultation and co-determination rights *vis-à-vis* management. In multi-plant companies, plant works councils appoint delegates to a company works council. Furthermore, in large companies up to half of supervisory board members are employee representatives. These include both representatives elected by the workforce (typically top works councilors) and appointed by external trade unions.

The community in which the firm is located and suppliers and customers have also frequently been mentioned as two other important stakeholder groups in Germany (Hutton 1995). However, formal community influence is limited to companies where local or regional governments have ownership stakes and board representation (Bamberg *et al.* 1987). This is the case mainly in companies involved in transportation, utilities or other local service provision. Community is, therefore, an important stakeholder group mainly through the ownership mechanism in a minority of companies. The importance of customers and suppliers as stakeholders in Germany has also probably been overstated. Customers and suppliers probably played their most prominent role in governance during the 1920s through a corporatist system of cartel regulation. Although one frequently finds prominent customers or suppliers represented on company boards, this appears to be due more to the usefulness of having powerful and well-connected industrialists on supervisory boards than to any intent to formally represent the interests of customers and suppliers (Vitols *et al.* 1997).

The shareholder (or outsider) model, which is predominant in the USA and UK, is institutionally a much simpler construct. Ownership is dominated by institutional investors, such as mutual funds, pension funds and insurance companies, who are generally reluctant to hold ownership stakes of more than one or two percent, and who, in principle, do not wish to be represented on company boards. Other stakeholders such as employees generally do not enjoy voice in the company through formal representation. These countries have a single board system, and this board has in the past often been dominated by a single strong manager who assumed the role of both chairperson and CEO.[2]

In the mid-1990s, a number of developments triggered a debate on the extent to which the German stakeholder system is changing. The first development was the increasing activism of foreign funds in Germany, such as Calpers (the California public employee pension fund), who stated that they would try to use their influence to make German companies pay more attention to small shareholders. A second development was the announcement by the two largest banks, Deutsche Bank and Dresdner Bank, and by the largest insurance company, Allianz, that they wished to reduce their presence on company boards and manage their share portfolios more according to 'shareholder value' principles. Changes in tax law in 2000, in fact, were designed to make it less costly for the banks to reduce their shareholdings (Höpner 2000). A third development was Vodafone's takeover of Mannesmann, the first major hostile take-over in Germany (Höpner & Jackson 2003). A fourth development was that a number of large companies announced that they were adopting 'shareholder value' as a key strategic goal; some of these compa-nies made an explicit link between this step and the previous developments, such as the chemical/phar-maceutical company Hoechst (Eckert 2000).

The dichotomous nature of shareholder–stake-holder typology initially forced people to decide between the alternatives of 'convergence' and 'diver-gence' (convergence to the shareholder model versus continuing distinctiveness) in this debate. Conver-gence advocates argue that the changes currently taking place in Germany – as well as in other stake-holder countries – represent the transformation of a stakeholder into a shareholder system. Large 'inside' investors are gradually being replaced by internation-ally-active investors, who increasingly have the capacity to cut off funding to companies that do not fulfill their demands for shareholder value (Dore 2000; Inagami 2001). Wojcik (2001) finds some statistical evidence consistent with the convergence thesis. In particular, the median size of the largest shareholder has decreased by roughly five percentage points (from 65 percent to 60 percent) between 1997 and 2001. In a provocative article entitled 'Deutschland AG – a.D', Beyer (2003) found that the number of bank representatives on company boards has declined substantially since the mid-1990s. Höpner (2003) found a positive correlation between the degree of internationalization of share ownership and the adop-tion of shareholder value strategies by company management.

On the other side of the debate, others have empha-sized continuity in the German system of corporate governance and argued that current changes are only minor (Vitols *et al.* 1997; Jürgens *et al.* 2000). Vitols (2002), Jürgens (2002) and Kädtler and Sperling (2001) have argued that the degree of influence share-holders have over management in industries such as chemicals and autos has been overestimated by con-vergence advocates. The Varieties of Capitalism paradigm (Hall and Soskice 2001) provides a theoretical explanation of why shifts in ownership might result in only incremental changes in the overall co-ordinated market economy (CME) system. The existence of complementarities between different elements of a CME limits the overall impact that changes in one subsystem might have on the per-formance of a system as a whole. Hall and Soskice, however, leave open the possibility that changes in finance might eventually lead to a crossing of the 'tipping point' and, thus, a hop to a new equilibrium (i.e. the introduction of a liberal market economy or LME system) in Germany.

Out of frustration with the strict corset of the 'insider–outsider' dichotomy, a number of research-ers have been trying to develop a more nuanced approach to classifying corporate governance systems and understanding processes of change within them. One key fact is that, although the partial 'Americanization' of the German financial system and ownership is unmistakable, the labour relations system has remained quite stable and that works councils are still powerful (Cioffi 2000). Goyer (2002) has argued that labour in Germany exerts a veto right and, thus, has blocked the introduction of the most important parts of shareholder value in Germany. One approach has been to conceptualize change as a process of 'hybridization', whereby elements of both the insider and outsider models are combined (Vitols 1999). Another approach has been to introduce mul-tiple dimensions for classifying corporate governance systems; for example, Jackson and Aguilera (2003) claim that there are three key dimensions of corpo-rate governance – capital, labour and management – and that each dimension can be conceptualized as a continuum. A further approach is to focus on change in Germany as a long-term process with multiple determinants and an uncertain ultimate outcome (Höpner 2003).

THE EMERGENCE OF AN AUGMENTED STAKEHOLDER COALITION IN GERMANY

In an effort to contribute to this more nuanced approach, this paper proposes two new ideas for helping conceptualize the process of change in the German stakeholder system. Drawing on the distinc-tion made earlier between the institutional level and the level of practice, the first idea is that institutional changes have encouraged the emergence of a mixed system of ownership in which both large shareholders and institutional investors play a significant role. The result has been an augmented stakeholder coalition, which involves the integration of pro-shareholder value institutional investors into the postwar coalition of stakeholders, of which the most important members were large shareholders and employees (see Figure 18.3).

Towards a 'mixed' system of ownership by large and small shareholders

A key argument of the convergence thesis is that, within the German system of ownership, large shareholders are being replaced by institutional investors who, as a rule, hold less than five percent of shares of individual companies. A statistically significant decline in the median size of the largest shareholder in the late 1990s is an important piece of evidence drawn upon by supporters of the convergence thesis. However, three critical points regarding the convergence thesis can be made here.

First, even with the decline in the late 1990s, large shareholdings in Germany are still many orders of magnitude apart from the USA. The median size of the largest shareholding in German listed companies in 2000 was still around 60 percent, as opposed to around five percent for companies listed on the New York Stock Exchange. Even with a continued decline of five percentage points every half decade in Germany, it would take another 55 years to decline to the US level.

In this respect a comparison of the Dow Jones Industrial Index and the DAX (the Deutsches Aktienindex), the 30 largest companies in both countries, is instructive. In the USA the median largest shareholding in the Dow Jones 30 Industrial (the 30 largest companies in the USA listed on the stock exchange) is below five percent (see Table 18.2). Sixteen of the 30 companies had no identifiable shareholder with a stake of at least five percent. An institutional investor was the largest shareholder in 11 of the 14 cases where a company had a blockholder. Typically this institutional investor was a fund group. Since fund groups can be composed of dozens of individual equity funds which do not co-ordinate with each other, no individual fund is likely to have voting power approaching five percent in these cases.

When examining the individual companies in the DAX, the index of the 30 largest German listed companies, one sees the continuing influence of large shareholders. Only four of the DAX companies at the end of 2002 had no large shareholder: Addidas-Salomon, Deutsche Bank, E.on and Siemens (see Table 18.3). Of these companies with large shareholders, banks were the largest shareholders at only two of the firms, versus insurance companies at ten, founders and families at six, federal or local government at four, and other companies at two. Foreign institutional investors also were the largest investor at two of the DAX 30 companies.

Second, it is not clear that the trend can continue at this pace, or even at all. The increasing importance of institutional investors is predicated on their ability to capture a greater share of the flow of funds by the ultimate investors, namely households. The late 1990s were characterized precisely by this development. German households increased their investments in stocks and stock funds, reaching a high of a combined total of €84 billion in 2000, the peak year of the bubble (see Table 4). The increase in indirect investment in stocks (through equity mutual funds) was particularly

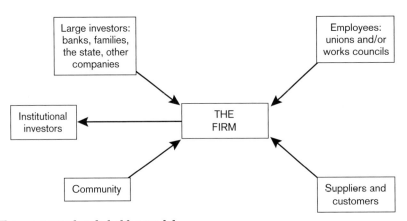

Figure 18.3 **The augmented stakeholder model**

Company	Largest shareholding		Type
	% of shares	Shareholder	
3M	6.2	Fidelity Mutual Fund Group	Institutional investor
Alcoa	6	Wellington Management	Institutional investor
Altria Group	7.2	Capital Research and Management	Institutional investor
American Express	11.7	Berkshire Hathaway	Institutional investor
AT&T	10.6	Dodge & Cox	Institutional investor
Boeing	5.2	Capital Research and Management	Institutional investor
Caterpillar	5.6	Capital Research and Management	Institutional investor
Citigroup	<5		
Coca-Cola	<5		
DuPont	<5		
Eastman Kodak	11.6	Legg Mason Funds	Institutional investor
Exxon Mobil	<5		
General Electric	<5		
General Motors	11.1	Capital Research and Management	Institutional investor
Hewlett-Packard	5.4	The Packard Foundation	Founder/family
Home Depot	<5		
Honeywell	<5		
Intel	<5		
IBM	<5		
International Paper	11.0	Capital Research and Management	Institutional investor
J.P. Morgan Chase	<5		
Johnson & Johnson	<5		
McDonald's Corp.	5.2	Fidelity Mutual Fund Group	Institutional investor
Merck & Co.	<5		
Microsoft	10.1	William H. Gates	Founder/family
Procter & Gamble	<5		
SBC Communications	<5		
United Technologies	<5		
Wal-Mart	39.7	John T. Walton	Founder/family
Walt Disney	<5		
Median	<5		

Source: Company proxy filings with the Security Exchange Commission.

Table 18.2 **Largest shareholders in the 30 Dow Jones companies (2003)**

pronounced, from negligible levels in the early 1990s to a high of €66 billion in 2000. Direct ownership of shares by households also increased significantly, to €18 billion in that same year. However, with the bursting of the bubble, the German household sector has rapidly exited the stock market, withdrawing €20 billion of equity in 2001 and €57 billion in 2002. This exiting has occurred mainly through the liquidation of direct equity holdings, rather than through the sale of equity funds.

Although some of this volatility may be driven by short-term influences, primarily the bubble and its bursting, there are reasons to believe that long-term trends will stabilize or even reverse the shift of funds to institutional investors. One reason is that the baby boomer generation, which invested a large proportion of its retirement assets in stocks, is now starting to retire and withdrawals from this group will increase over time (Davis and Li 2002). A second is that trends in investment activity are very long term and an aversion to financial assets with higher levels of risk may last a very long time. In Germany the aversion to risky financial assets appears to be higher than in the USA, and the serious losses that many of the German

Company	Largest shareholding		
	% of shares	Shareholder	Type
Adidas-Salomon	<5		
Allianz	18.1	Münchener Rückversicherung	Insurance
Altana	50.1	Quandt Family	Founder/family
BASF	9.4	Allianz AG	Insurance
Bayer	5.9	Allianz AG	Insurance
Bayerische Hypo- und Vereinsbank	18.4	Münchener Rückversicherung	Insurance
BMW	48	Quandt Family	Insurance
Commerzbank	10	Assicurazioni Generali S.p.A.	Insurance
Continental	5.5	Barclays Global Investors	Institutional investor
DaimlerChrysler	12.5	Deutsche Bank	Bank
Deutsche Bank	<5		
Deutse Börse	5.1	The Capital Group	Institutional investor
Deutsche Post	68.8	Bundesrepublik	State
Deutsche Telekom	42.8	Bundesrepublik	State
E.ON	<5		
Fresenius Medical Care	50.8	Fresenius AG	Company
Henkel KGaA	57.8	Henkel Family	Founder/family
Infineon Technologies	12.5	Siemens AG	Company
Linde	12.6	Allianz AG	Insurance
Lufthansa	10.5	Allianz AG	Insurance
MAN	36.6	Allianz AG	Insurance
Metro	55.7	Beshaim/Haniel	Founder/family
Müncher Rückversicherung	10.0	Bayerische H + V	Bank
RWE	7.6	Allianz AG	Insurance
SAP	43.0	Tschira/Hasso/Hopp/Plattner	Family/founder
Schering	10.6	Allianz AG	Insurance
Siemens	<5		
ThyssenKrupp	16.9	Krupp Stiftung	Founder/family
TUI (formerly Preussag)	31.4	Westdeutsche Landesbank	State
Volkswagen	18.2	Land Niedersachsen	State
Median	12.6		

Source: Bundesanstalt für Finanzdienstleistungsaufsicht database.

Table 18.3 **Largest shareholdings in the DAX 30 companies (2003)**

'latecomers' to the game suffered may be reflected in very long-term aversion to stocks. One large-scale survey shows that the number of households with direct or indirect stock ownership has decreased continuously from 13.4 million in 2001 to 10.6 million in 2004. The percentage of shareholders in Germany, currently at 16.4 percent, is thus significantly below the figure of around 50 percent that one finds in countries like the USA and UK (DAI 2004). It appears that the Riester pension reform of 2001, which was designed to encourage more private savings, has also not done much to encourage the flow of funds to the stock market. The requirements imposed on personal and company pension plans by the Riester reform encourage the flow of funds into more conservative financial assets such as bonds and bank savings deposits (Vitols 2003).

Third, although the large private banks and Allianz, the largest insurance company, have announced that they wish to change their practice, it is not clear that this means that they – or other large shareholders – wish to reduce their holdings and role in governance down to US levels. The subsidiary that Deutsche Bank set up to manage its equity holdings, DB

	1991	1992	1993	1994	1995	1996	1997	1998	1999	2000	2001	2002
Direct shareholding	0.3	−0.5	3.4	6.1	−1.7	5.4	4.1	4.1	13.8	18.4	−28.7	−61.0
Equity mutual funds	0.8	1.3	5.7	7.5	0.6	1.3	15.1	19.5	33.2	65.8	8.3	4.0
Total equity inflows	1.0	0.8	9.1	13.6	−1.2	6.7	19.1	23.6	47.1	84.2	−20.4	−57.0

Source: Own calculations from Deutsche Bundesbank, Flow of Funds Accounts, and BVI, annual reports.

Table 18.4 **German household net investment in stocks (in billion €)**

Investor, has taken new large stakes in companies, for example in the battery manufacturer Varta.[3] Insurance companies, particularly Allianz, are accumulating more and more funds over time and, thus, will have to increase their overall stakes in companies. The percentage of shares in German companies held by insurance companies actually has increased from six percent in 1996 to 14.2 percent in 2002 (Deutsche Bundesbank 2003: 95). Many founders and families have also maintained their commitments to companies and have not reduced their equity stakes. Finally, spin-offs by firms have generally taken the form of partial stakes being sold on the stock exchanges (e.g. Siemens has retained stakes of 72 percent and 12.5 percent of the semiconductor manufactuer Infineon and components producer Epcos, respectively). Companies also remain eager to acquire new equity stakes in other companies that fit into their strategic portfolios. For example, at the end of 2002 the electronics company Robert Bosch bought up an eight percent stake in the mid-cap company Buderus from the Deutsche Bank. The federal state has also generally pursued partial rather than full privatization, retaining 71 percent of the Deutsche Post and 43 percent of Deutsche Telekom.

It thus appears that a mixed system of ownership involving large shareholders and institutional investors is a feature that will characterize Germany for the foreseeable future.

Stability in the role of labour

Many accounts of the declining role of labour in Germany have focused on the collective bargaining system, primarily on the decline in the level of trade union membership and the flight of some employers from employers' associations. Within firms, in contrast, works councils have, if anything, become a more important force for representing the interests of labour, both *vis-à-vis* management at the plant level and via the supervisory board at the company level (Thelen and Kume 2003).

Recent legislative changes have affected both company law and the works constitution act. Resisting proposals from some parties to reduce the influence of labour, the conservative–liberal coalition government's reform of company law in 1997 confirmed the dual board system and left the parameters of employee representation on company boards essentially unchanged (Ziegler 2000). A reform of the Works Constitution Act in 2001 under the red–green coalition government even strengthened the legal rights of works councils. For example, the minimum number of employees in a plant needed before a works councillor is released from normal duties to work full-time on works council business was reduced from 300 to 200. The ability of works councils to represent employees in companies with many small branches, which is typical of the service sector, was also strengthened (Behrens 2003).

Accounts of industrial relations claim that there is no tendency of works councils to lose influence, and in many companies influence even seems to have increased through a closer 'partnership' with management to solve problems (Jacobi *et al.* 1998; Höpner *et al.* forthcoming).

Summing up: changes in the role of the stakeholders

As reviewed above, the importance of the community and of suppliers and customers as stakeholders has probably been overestimated in many stylized accounts of the German model, with the exception of companies in which local or regional governments have a significant ownership role. Although some regional and local governments have announced the intention to privatize some companies, progress in this respect has been slow, and the tendency of local and regional governments has been to partially rather than to fully privatize.

The main change in the German stakeholder model has, therefore, been the integration of institutional investors into the coalition. Although the role of some large shareholders, particularly the large private banks, may have been reduced, other large shareholders remain committed to a strong corporate governance role. The influence of employees as stakeholders has also remained stable and, in some respects, even been strengthened by the reform of the works constitution act. Thus, it is possible to speak of the emergence of an augmented stakeholder coalition in German corporate governance.

CONSEQUENCES FOR PRACTICE: NEGOTIATED SHAREHOLDER VALUE

At the level of practice, a major consequence of the integration of institutional investors in the augmented stakeholder coalition is that their interest in shareholder value must be taken into account. However, due to the existence of this coalition, the practice of shareholder value in Germany differs in two important ways from the Anglo-American variant of shareholder value. First, the introduction of shareholder value concepts must be negotiated with other members of the coalition. Due to the reluctance of institutional investors to be linked too closely to firms, e.g. through representation on the supervisory board, this requires the establishment of new institutional mechanisms for mediating this relationship. Second, due to the different interests of the members of the stakeholder coalition, compromises need to be found which typically alter the nature of the demands made by institutional investors. This German variant can, thus, be characterized as negotiated shareholder value. This contrasts with Anglo-American shareholder value, which tends to be unilaterally imposed by management in the interests of shareholders.

What sort of evidence would support this thesis against the alternative theses of convergence or no essential change? First, one would expect evidence of a bargaining process, in which the original demands of a member of the coalition are confronted with objections or alternative proposals from other members of the coalition. Second, one would expect

that where opposition is strongest, the original proposals for shareholder value would be modified or even blocked. As a result of the dynamics of this augmented stakeholder coalition, one would expect a modification of the practices in German companies which takes into account some of the demands of institutional investors, without at the same time fully converging to the Anglo-American style of shareholder value.

An important change in large German companies has been the introduction of investor relations departments to institutionalize the dialogue with institutional investors. These departments are typically under the finance director and are responsible for providing institutional investors with timely and detailed information about the financial status of the company and other key information. Studies indicate that the introduction of investor relations units has been virtually universal within large German companies (Welskopp 2002).

Interviews conducted by the author with works councillors and managers in a number of large German companies indicate that demands for shareholder value are typically transmitted by the finance director into the management board and into negotiations with other stakeholders. This is not surprising given that the finance director is the nearest of the managing directors to investors.

One fairly rapid and universal change in the practice of large German companies was the introduction of international accounting standards (US–GAAP or IAS) at large German companies. German companies have traditionally used HGB (Handelsgesetzbuch) standards, which make comparison between companies difficult due to the numerous options for the accounting department to recognize income, or to even hide some of this income from investors ('hidden reserves'). The introduction of international accounting standards is one of the key demands of institutional investors, since they feel that they cannot truly measure the value of the firm in the absence of such transparency. Other members of the stakeholder coalition, in contrast, are relatively indifferent regarding the type of accounting standards used.[4] Thus, it is not surprising that adoption of these standards has been very rapid and practically universal.

One also finds that many companies have explicitly adopted shareholder value as one of their main corporate goals. Interestingly enough, however, many German companies have taken pains to avoid using either the English term or its direct translation into German, for example, with the phrase *wertorientierte*

Unternehmensführung.

More interesting are the cases where there are real concerns or differences of interest between large shareholders. There are numerous recent examples which show that large shareholders remain intimately involved in decision making in the firm, including in decisions about the implementation of corporate restructuring to achieve shareholder value. One interesting example is the introduction of shareholder value at Hoechst, one of the 'Big Three' diversified chemical–pharmaceutical companies in Germany (Vitols 2002). One of the key demands of institutional investors was that the company should 'de-diversify' by selling off either its chemicals or pharmaceuticals divisions. In fact, Jürgen Dormann, the CEO (and former finance director) of Hoechst, proposed that Hoechst should become a pure life sciences company by selling off its chemicals operations and building up critical mass in pharmaceuticals through merger. Dormann entered into merger negotiations with Rhone-Poulenc, a French company also involved in a variety of chemicals and pharmaceuticals operations. As part of the merger negotiations, however, Dormann had to fly to Kuwait to negotiate with the Kuwaiti government, which held a 25 percent stake in the company. Dormann could proceed with the merger of the two companies into a new company, Aventis, only after the Kuwaiti government was satisfied that its interests would not be harmed by the merger.

Another interesting example of the continued importance of large shareholders is the restructuring of the German financial services industry. German financial services firms, particularly banks, have come under increasing criticism from institutional investors, since their profitability is particularly low in comparison with Anglo-American banks. One of the demands of institutional investors is that German banks should merge in order to achieve economies of scale and reduce the degree of 'overbanking' in Germany. As a key shareholder in the large German banks, Allianz plays a key role in the restructuring of the German financial services industry. Allianz's consent had to be obtained in negotiations between Bayerische Hypobank and the Bayerische Vereinsbank, which merged to form the third largest private bank, Bayerische Hypo-und Vereinsbank. Allianz's permission was also needed in the merger proposal between Deutsche Bank and Dresdner Bank. When this merger failed due to internal management differences, Allianz stepped in and bought up the rest of Dresdner bank itself.

There are even more numerous examples of the involvement of works councils in negotiations over the introduction of shareholder value. One key demand of institutional investors is that employee and management remuneration should be tied more closely to performance, in the ideal case directly to share price. In Anglo-American companies, changes in incentive pay to base a greater proportion of pay on performance and profitability are generally imposed by top management. Furthermore, performance bonuses and pay increases are typically based on evaluations by immediate supervisors. In Germany, in contrast, changes in remuneration systems must be negotiated with the works council, which generally requires elements of collective regulation and limits on the extent of performance pay.

One typical example of how negotiated shareholder value works here is the response of the works council at Schering AG to demands from the finance director for more incentive pay.[5] The works council agreed in principle to introducing performance pay, but imposed a number of conditions for agreement. One was that performance pay only represent a small proportion of total remuneration. A second condition was that certain floors and ceilings be imposed on the amount of incentive pay received by each employee, to help maintain solidarity among the workforce. A third condition was that evaluations be based on standardized forms agreed between management and the works council, in order to improve transparency and fairness in the evaluation procedure.

A second example of involvement of works councils in negotiated shareholder value is the problem of under-performing business units. Anglo-American companies typically impose relatively short periods of time on business units which do not achieve important financial goals to improve their performance before they will be closed or sold off. In German companies, however, the involvement of works councils typically alters the way in which this problem is dealt with. First, the right of works councils to negotiate social plans for large-scale layoffs makes closure more difficult and expensive. Second, once the decision to sell has been made, works councils are typically involved in negotiations with potential buyers and can influence the decision in favour of buyers who will better take into account the interests of employees. VEBA's sale of AstaMedica (Zugehör 2001) and Bayer's sale of its pigments division to the US company Kerr-McGee are examples of this kind of involvement.[6] The works council at ThyssenKrupp has gone even further and negotiated a formal eight-point agreement with management regarding the sale of company units. A major point in this agreement is that the sale will be made to the 'best buyer' in terms of the future of the company unit and its employees, rather than to the highest bidder (Die Mitbestimmung 2004).

Many other types of examples of works council involvement in different kinds of restructuring can be found which alter the original demands to achieve shareholder value in the interests of shareholders. The works council at Mannesmann agreed with the takeover proposal of Vodafone when an arrangement was made to find a 'good German buyer' for the non-telecommunications parts of the company (steel and auto parts) (Höpner and Jackson 2003). Siemens, the large diversified electronics company, has also been seen as one of the most dramatic examples of an attempt to introduce shareholder value in Germany. Siemens has long been criticized by institutional investors for the 'cross-subsidization' of under-performing divisions by better-performing divisions. When the telecommunications equipment division made serious losses in 2001 and 2002, the division head demanded serious job cuts to try to attain profitability. The works council, however, opposed such drastic job cuts and, instead, a more moderate package of job cuts in the telecommunications equipment division was agreed.

Overall indicators of company practice and performance are also consistent with the picture that German company practice has, in fact, been modified, but remains far away from convergence to the Anglo-American model. One example of this is the use of stock options to align the interests of top company managers with shareholders. A change in company law in 1997 authorized German companies to introduce stock option plans, thus making it much easier for management remuneration to be tied to share performance. Since then, most large German companies have, in fact, established stock option plans.

However, German companies use stock options to a much lesser degree than Anglo-American companies.

One simple but useful indicator for comparing the degree to which stock options are used in a company is to divide the number of stock options granted and outstanding to the total number of shares outstanding. An analysis of stock option practices at the Dow Jones 30 Industrial companies shows that, in 2002, the average option/share ratio for was 7.7 percent. The ratio ranged from a low of 1.1 percent (at Wal-Mart) to a high of 17.3 percent (at Eastman Kodak). The average ratio in the DAX 30 companies is a much lower average of 0.9 percent. Only DaimlerChrysler has a level remotely approaching the US average (4.2 percent), which is not surprising given the attempt to increase German managerial compensation towards US levels within the merged firm.[7]

A second overall indicator is the distribution of value added between different constituencies of the firm (see Table 18.5). Earlier research noted that a much higher proportion of value added goes to shareholders in US and British companies than in German companies; De Jong (1997) finds that in the first half of the 1990s, shareholders (in the form of dividends) in Anglo-American companies received 15 percent of net value added versus three percent with 'Germanic' companies. Beyer and Hassel (2003) in a study of the distribution of value added in German firms find that the proportion of value added going to shareholders has increased somewhat (from 2 percent to 2.8 percent in the second half of the 1990s), but still remains far behind the level of 15 percent that de Jong reported for Anglo-American firms. The proportion of net value added received by labour in German firms has been reduced significantly over the 1990s, from 85 to 78 percent, but it seems that the greatest beneficiary has been the firm itself in the form of greater retained earnings.

Stakeholder	Anglo-American early 1990s	Germany early 1990s	Germany late 1990s
Labour	62.2	85.3	78.4
Creditors	23.5	5.4	4.3
Government	14.3	5.2	6.8
Retained earnings	3.2	2.2	7.8
Dividends	15	2.0	2.8

Sources: De Jong (1997), Beyer and Hassel (2003).

Table 18.5 **Distribution of net value added in Anglo-American and German firms**

CONCLUSIONS

This chapter has argued that current developments in Germany can be characterized as important, but essentially incremental modifications in the stakeholder system of corporate governance. In this respect it has disagreed with the theses of 'no essential changes' and of wholesale convergence to the Anglo-American shareholder model. The key issue for German corporate governance in the recent past has been how to change to deal with the demands for the implementation of shareholder value by institutional investors. These changes have been analysed on two levels.

On the institutional level, the major modification of the post-war stakeholder model has been the integration of institutional investors into an augmented stakeholder coalition. The greatest stability can be seen in the representation of labour, with the key role of the works council actually being strengthened through the reform of the Works Constitution Act in Germany in 2001. The power of the employees as a stakeholder group has, therefore, remained stable or even increased. The greatest changes have occurred in the sphere of ownership. In the post-war stakeholder coalition, large shareholders were the dominant owners. Small investors were generally passive and allowed their interests to be represented by banks. Rather than a wholesale shift toward dispersed ownership by institutional investors, which characterizes Anglo-American companies, however, the article has argued that a 'mixed' system of large shareholders and dispersed institutional investors is emerging. The post-war stakeholder coalition has, thus, been modified through the inclusion of institutional investors, rather than replaced by a shareholder system.

On the level of practice, a system of negotiated shareholder value is emerging. Negotiated shareholder value is a stable alternative that is distinct from Anglo-American shareholder value (1) in the processes by which decision-making takes place and (2) in the outcomes to which these negotiating processes lead. Evidence can be found for bargaining processes between the members of the augmented stakeholder coalition, leading to a modification of the original demands for shareholder value when other members of the stakeholder coalition object. Macro data, for example in the granting of stock options and the division of value added between different stakeholders, also supports this interpretation of a German variant of the Anglo-American form of shareholder value.

ACKNOWLEDGEMENTS

Many thanks to Lutz Engelhardt and Jana Meier for invaluable research assistance, to Pablo Beramendi for helpful comments, and to Martin Höpner and Gregory Jackson for useful clarifications.

NOTES

1 The typical definition of a large shareholding, or blockholding, is that at least five percent of the total outstanding shares of the company are held by the same owner.
2 Recent reforms in both the UK and USA have attempted to reduce the power of any single individual within the company board system, for example by seeing that the roles of CEO and chairperson are carried out by different persons.
3 Varta was in the MDAX, the midcap index for German stocks, but its management wished to take it private (i.e. de-list it from the stock exchange) since it felt that its stock was undervalued by small investors.
4 Höpner and Goyer emphasize the extent to which employees may have a positive interest in international accounting standards. However, the author's interviews with works councillors indicate that relative indifference is probably a more accurate characterization of their actual attitudes towards these changes.
5 Based on an interview with the chairman of the group works council, September 1999.
6 The case of Bayer is based on an interview in May 2001 with a works councillor at the subsidiary that was sold.
7 These data were based on an analysis of company annual reports.

REFERENCES

Bamberg, U., Bürger, M., Mahnkopf, B., Martens, H. and Tiemann, J. (1987) *Aber ob die Karten voll ausgereitzt sind. 10 Jahre Mitbestimmungsgesetz 1976 in der Bilanz* (Köln: Bund-Verlag).

Barca, F. and Becht, M. (Eds) (2001) *The Control of Corporate Europe* (Oxford: Oxford University Press).

Behrens, M. (2003) The new German works constitution act in practice. *WSI Mitteilungen*, 56 (Special Issue. Industrial Relations in Germany – An Empirical Survey), pp. 56–65.

Beyer, J. (2003) Deutschland AG a.D.: Deutsche Bank, Allianz und das Verflechtungszentrum des deutschen Kapitalismus, in: W. Streeck and M. Höpner (Eds) *Alle Macht dem Markt? Fallstudien zur Abwicklung der Deutschen AG*, pp. 118–46 (Frankfurt am Main: Campus Verlag).

Beyer, J. and Hassel, A. (2003) Die Folgen der Konvergenz. Der Einfluss der Internationalisierung auf die Wertschöpfungsverteilung in großen Unternehmen, in: J. B. Wiesbaden (Ed.) *Vom Zukunfts-zum Auslaufmodell?*

Die deutsche Wirtschaftsordnung im Wandel, pp. 155–84 (Wiesbaden: Westdeutscher Verlag).

Cioffi, J.W. (2000) Governing globalization? The state, law, and structural change in corporate governance, *Journal of Law and Society*, 27(4), pp. 572–600.

DAI (Deutsches Aktieninstitut) (2004) Stabilisierung der Aktiona·rszahlen setzt sich fort. *DAI Kurzstudie*, 1/2004 (Frankfurt am Main: DAI).

Davis, E.P. and Li, C. (2002) Demographics and Financial Asset Prices in the Major Industrial Economies. Unpublished manuscript (London: Brunel University).

De Jong, H. (1997) The governance structure and performance of large European corporations, *Journal of Management and Governance*, 1(1), pp. 5–27.

Deutsche Bundesbank (2003) *Finanzierungsrechnung 1991 bis 2002* (Frankfurt am Main: Deutsche Bundesbank).

Die Mitbestimmung (2004) Saying no is easy, *Mitbestimmung International Edition*, pp. 22–25.

Dore, R. (2000) *Stock Market Capitalism, Welfare Capitalism: Japan and Germany Versus the Anglo-Saxons* (Oxford: Oxford University Press).

Eckert, S. (2000) Konvergenz der nationalen Corporate Governance-Systeme?: Ursachen und Internationalisierungs-wirkungen der Denationalisierung der Corporate Governance großer deutscher Aktiengesellschaften am Beispiel der Hoechst AG, in: D. z. Knyphausen-Aufseß (Ed.) *Globalisierung als Herausforderung der Betriebswirtschaftslehre*, pp. 95–135 (Wiesbaden: Gabler).

Goyer, M. (2002) The Transformation of Corporate Governance in France and Germany: The Role of Workplace Institutions. Working Paper 2/10. (Cologne: MPIfG).

Hall, P. A. and Soskice, David (Eds) (2001) *Varieties of Capitalism: The Institutional Foundations of Comparative Advantage* (Oxford: Oxford University Press).

Hirschman, A. (1970) *Exit, Voice, and Loyalty: Responses to Decline in Firms, Organizations, and States* (Cambridge: Harvard University Press).

Höpner, M. (2000) Unternehmensverflechtung im Zwielicht. Hans Eichels Plan zur Auflösung der Deutschland AG, *WSI-Mitteilungen*, 53, pp. 655–63.

Höpner, M. (2003) *Wer beherrscht die Unternehmen? Shareholder Value, Managerherrschaft und Mitbestimmung in Deutschland* (Frankfurt am Main: Campus).

Höpner, M. and Jackson, G. (2003) Entsteht ein Markt für Unternehmenskontrolle? Der Fall Mannesmann, in: W. Streeck and M. Höpner (Eds) *Alle Macht dem Markt? Fallstudien zur Abwicklung der Deutschland AG*, pp. 147–68 (Frankfurt am Main: Campus Verlag).

Höpner, M., Jackson, G. and Kurdelbush, A. (forthcoming) Corporate governance and employees in Germany: changing linkages, complementarities and tensions, in: Gospel H. and Pendleton, A. (Eds) *Corporate Governance and Labour Management* (Oxford: Oxford University Press).

Hopt, K.J., Kanda, H. and Roe, M.J. (Eds) (1998) Comparative Corporate Governance: *The State of the Art and Emerging Research* (Oxford: Oxford University Press).

Hutton, W. (1995) *The State We're In* (London: Vintage).

Inagami, T. (2001) From industrial relations to investor relations? Persistence and change in Japanese corporate governance, employment practices and industrial relations, *Social Science Japan Journal*, 4(2), pp. 225–41.

Itami, H. (1999) Concept of the Firm and Corporate Governance in Japan. Paper presented at the 1st Humboldt Forum on Economics and Management on Corporate Governance, Berlin, 4–5 June.

Jackson, G. (2001a) Comparative corporate governance: sociological perspectives, in: Gamble, A. Kelly, G. and Parkinson, J. (Eds) *The Political Economy of the Company*, pp. 265–87 (Oxford: Oxford University Press).

Jackson, G. (2001b) Organizing the Firm: Corporate Governance in Germany and Japan, 1870–2000. Dissertation, Department of Sociology, Columbia University, New York.

Jackson, G. and Aguilera, R. (2003) The cross-national diversity of corporate governance: dimensions and determinants, *Academy of Management Review*, 28(3), pp. 447–65.

Jacobi, O., Keller, B. and Müller-Jentsch, W. (1998) Germany: facing new challenges, in: A. Ferner and R. Hyman (Eds) *Changing Industrial Relations in Europe*, pp. 190–238 (Oxford: Basil Blackwell).

Jürgens, U. (2002) Corporate Governance, Innovation, and Economic Performance – A Case Study on Volkswagen. Discussion Paper FS II 02-205 (Berlin: WZB).

Jürgens, U., Naumann, K. and Rupp, J. (2000) Shareholder value in an adverse environment: the German case, *Economy and Society*, 29(1), pp. 54–79.

Kädtler, J. and Sperling, H.J. (2002) The power of financial markets and the resilience of operations, arguments and evidence from the German car industry, *Competition and Change*, 6(1), pp. 81–94.

Kelly, G., Kelly, D. and Gamble, A. (Eds) (1997) *Stakeholder Capitalism* (London: Macmillan Press).

McCahery, J.A., Moreland, P., Raaijmakers, T. and Renneboog, L. (Eds) (2002) *Corporate Governance Regimes: Convergence and Divergence* (Oxford: Oxford University Press).

Pfeiffer, H. (1986) Großbanken und Finanzgruppen: Ausgewählte Ergebnissse einer Untersuchung der personellen Verflechtungen von Deutscher, Dresdner und Commerzbank, *WSI Mitteilungen*, 7(1), pp. 473–80.

Pfeiffer, H. (1993) *Die Macht der Banken. Die personellen Verflechtungen der Commerzbank, der Deutschen Bank und der Dresdner Bank mit Unternehmen* (Frankfurt: Campus Verlag).

Thelen, K. and Kume. I. (2003) The future of nationally embedded capitalism: industrial relations in Germany and Japan, in: Yamamura, K. and Streeck, W. (Eds) *The End of Diversity? Prospects for German and Japanese Capitalism*, pp. 183–211 (Ithaca, N.Y.: Cornell University Press).

Van Den Berghe, L., Van Der Elst, C., Carchon, S. and Levrau, A. (2002) *Corporate Governance in a Globalising World: Convergence or Divergence?: A European Perspective* (Dordrecht: Kluwer Academic Publishers).

Vitols, S. (1999) The Reconstruction of German Corporate Governance: Capital Market Pressures or Managerial Initiatives? Paper presented at the conference 'The Political Economy of Corporate Governance in Europe and Japan', European University, Florence, 10–11 June.

Vitols, S. (2002) Shareholder value, management culture and production regimes in the transformation of the German chemical–pharmaceutical industry, *Competition and Change*, 6(3), pp. 309–325.

Vitols, S. (2003) Varieties of capitalism and pension reform: will the Riester Rente transform the German coordinated market economy?, *Focus on Austria: Quarterly Bulletin of the Österreichische Nationalbank*, 2003(2), pp. 102–8.

Vitols, S., Casper, S., Soskice, D. and Woolcock, S. (1997) *Corporate Governance in Large British and German Companies: Comparative Institutional Advantage or Competing for Best Practice* (London: Anglo German Foundation).

Welskopp, T. (2002) *Corporate Governance: Herausforderungen und Losungsansatze* (Heidelberg: Physica-Verlag).

Wojcik, D. (2001) Change in the German Model of Corporate Governance: Evidence from Blockholdings, 1997–2001. Unpublished manuscript (Oxford: Oxford University).

Ziegler, N.J. (2000) Corporate governance and the politics of property rights in Germany, *Politics & Society*, 28(2), pp. 195–221.

Zugehör, R. (2001) Mitbestimmt ins Kapitalmarktzeitalter?, *Mitbestimmung*, 5/2000, pp. 38–42.

19 "Globalisation, Shareholder Value, Restructuring: The (Non)-Transformation of Siemens"

from New Political Economy (2004)

Alexander Börsch

Many observers agree that the German stakeholder system of corporate governance is under pressure to transform itself. Convergence theorists argue that its main features are inconsistent with the requirements of globalised financial and product markets. Therefore, it is predicted that German companies must change their behaviour significantly towards patterns prevalent in Anglo-Saxon corporate governance if they want to stay competitive. Above all, this means a shareholder value orientation in business policy. These claims are not undisputed. Theories of divergence, especially the 'varieties of capitalism' approach, argue that different institutional frameworks lead to different responses to globalisation, to distinct adjustment paths of firms and to a reinforcement of their strategies and structures.

This chapter takes a different approach in tackling these claims. Whereas convergence theory focuses on changes in the international economy and the 'varieties of capitalism' approach examines the incentive structures of national institutions, we focus here on the firm-level and the firm as an actor in its own right. In order to explore how globalisation affects firm behaviour and corporate governance, introducing the firm as a level of analysis seems a promising research strategy, which is largely neglected in the political economy literature.[1] Moreover, it can be expected that changes in corporate practices precede legal reform.[2] The case study deals with the adjustment path of Siemens. Besides being a 'flagship firm' whose behaviour is likely to affect the behaviour of other firms more generally through demonstration

effects,[3] Siemens offers an ideal setting for studying the effects of globalisation on German firms for four reasons.

First, it is one of the few German companies with dispersed ownership. Over 90 percent of Siemens' stock is dispersed and institutional investors own 45 percent of Siemens' capital stock. Thus it is exposed to an unusually high degree to capital market pressures compared to most German companies which have a controlling shareholder. Second, Siemens has a very broad business portfolio which financial markets tend to punish with the conglomerate discount. Furthermore, due to its broad portfolio it has lagged behind its competitors in terms of profits, which makes it a prime candidate for portfolio restructuring. Third, it became exposed to competitive pressures over the 1990s to a much higher degree. It lost its most profitable and protected markets due to privatisation of its main customers. Fourth, Siemens decided to list on the New York Stock Exchange (NYSE), which is seen by convergence theorists as a main mechanism for convergence towards the Anglo-American model of corporate governance.[4]

As a result of its unusually high exposure to globalisation pressures, Siemens can be regarded as a critical case for theories of divergence. If Siemens does not transform itself in the direction convergence theory expects, it can be argued that firms that are to a lesser degree affected by such pressures are not susceptible to a transformation of their strategies and structures. The chapter investigates the internationalisation of Siemens as well as its restructuring efforts. The main question regarding internationalisation is the extent to which Siemens has internationalised its operations over the 1990s and whether this has led to a disembedding from its home base, which would mean that it is not influenced by the German corporate governance system any longer.

In the area of restructuring, the research questions are whether the restructuring efforts have led to change in Siemens' governance structure in response to capital market pressures and to what extent Siemens has introduced shareholder value-related instruments and how they are designed. Restructuring is defined as a significant and rapid change in the assets, capital structure or organisational structure of a company. Financial restructuring involves changes in the debt equity mix, greater payments to shareholders or stock buy-backs, as well as changes in a firm's governance structure and in its relationships to shareholders and the capital market. Portfolio restructuring refers to asset divestment, diversification, acquisitions and downsizing. Lastly, organisational restructuring involves changes in the structure, systems and/or people of the company.[5] Following this definition, these dimensions will be investigated. A shareholder value strategy would imply at least the following:

- A firm should concentrate on its core markets, with other business units being sold;
- There should be minimum profits goals, with business units not meeting them sanctioned, sold or shut down;
- Firms should introduce stock options for management in order to align its interest with share price development; and
- Information policy should be transparent and investors equipped with all relevant information, including accounting according to international standards.[6]

The next section briefly describes the institutions of German corporate governance and analyses the possible impact of globalisation on this system from different angles. Afterwards the strategic behaviour of Siemens in the areas of internationalisation, as well as financial, organisational and portfolio restructuring, is dealt with, before the impact of restructuring on industrial relations and the theoretical implications of the case study are discussed.

GLOBALISATION AND GERMAN CORPORATE GOVERNANCE

National frameworks of corporate governance structure relations among owners, managers and employees. Institutions therefore influence how decisions are taken in a firm, how conflicts of interests between stakeholders are solved and which goals are pursued. The German corporate governance system is seen in the literature as the prototype of a stakeholder system. Decision making within the firm is of a corporatist nature and allows several stakeholders to exercise 'voice'. Neither the chief executive officer (CEO) nor the management board have unilateral control over the firm. Employees, through co-determination, banks and other companies, have a say in decision making—mostly through supervisory board representation. Management has to consider multiple interests and mobilise agreement, which results in rather slow decision making and incremental, rather than 'big leap', changes. Concentrated and cross ownership patterns shield firms from financial market pressures and prevent the emergence of a market for corporate control. They also mean that the large investors have strategic interests and a strong commitment to companies.[7] Share price and profitability are balanced with other strategic motives, such as product quality, market share and employment. The strategy of German firms has been production-oriented, that is, focused more on investment and sales growth than on profitability.[8] The institutions of corporate governance favour incremental innovation, enabled by a long-term employment policy and long strategic and investment horizons. German firms tend to compete in differentiated, technologically sophisticated markets and market niches, in which premium prices can be commanded.[9] In terms of internationalisation, German firms are said to pursue a comparatively low degree of active globalisation, coupled with a strong embeddedness in their home base.[10]

Rapid restructuring is hindered by consensual decision making. Employee representatives are committed to existing businesses and the preservation of jobs. The incentives and the scope for restructuring efforts that primarily benefit shareholders are limited.[11] Various and divergent stakeholder demands and weak shareholder power discriminate against massive divestments. Downsizing the corporation in times of financial hardship is rarely undertaken; the predominant reaction is expansion, enabled by retained earnings, coupled with a stabilisation of employment.[12] If a firm is downsized, management seeks to avoid large-scale involuntary lay-offs through socially cushioned measures, especially early retirements.[13] In this way, adjustment costs are externalised to the welfare state. Generally, adjustment patterns of German companies favour a strategy of small steps, since strategic decisions must be coordinated between several actors.[14]

This pattern of corporate governance differs in crucial dimensions from the Anglo-Saxon shareholder systems. These are centred on financial markets. Stakeholders are linked through contractual arm's length relations, shareholdings are dispersed, and the main actors on the financial markets are institutional investors, who are generally solely interested in a high return on their investments.[15] Therefore, firms are under high pressure to maximise profits and share price, and this is reinforced by an open market for corporate control and by the wide use of stock options for management compensation. Management has unilateral control over the firm. This institutional set-up results in a high flexibility in strategic terms and restructuring tends to be of the 'downsize and distribute' type. Corporations are downsized with an emphasis on cutting the workforce in order to increase return on equity and achieve rapid financial recovery.[16] The adjustment path of firms from outsider systems is therefore associated with far-reaching portfolio restructuring.

Convergence theory posits that the German pattern of corporate governance is no longer tenable under the conditions of integrated financial and product markets. It argues that globalisation forces the German corporate governance system to transform itself towards the pattern of shareholder systems. There are two reasons for this. First, the poor profit and shareholder value orientation of German firms will not be accepted by the financial markets. On globalised markets only those firms that satisfy investors' demands for high profits and share prices will get the necessary sums of capital. Thus companies must win the confidence of portfolio investors and surrender to the preferences of the capital markets.[17] Therefore stakeholder firms also have to prioritise shareholder value. This can be equated with a financialisation of strategy and a 'downsize and distribute' approach, which primarily means the distribution of free cash flow to shareholders.[18] Furthermore, investors expect management to simplify corporate structures, break up conglomerates and focus on the best performing businesses in which the company has a 'core competency', while getting rid of unrelated or underperforming lines of

business. Adopting a shareholder value orientation thus requires far-reaching strategic and institutional changes.

Second, convergence theory assumes that companies from shareholder systems produce more efficiently. Direct competition will wipe out firms from stakeholder-oriented corporate governance systems. Increased competition will force firms from stakeholder systems to adopt market-oriented corporate governance systems in order to achieve similar cost structures, which requires a similar organisation of firms and decision-making structures; otherwise they will be driven out of the market.[19] Generally, convergence theorists argue that the shareholder model has out-competed the stakeholder model.[20] On an ideological level, they see it as the only logically coherent system; on an economic level, they argue for its superiority in terms of economic outcomes, believing that, since international competition uncovers its superiority, it will replace the stakeholder model.[21] According to this reasoning, the 'triumph of the shareholder-oriented model of the corporation over its principal competitors is now assured'.[22]

A less sweeping view, though still partly related to convergence theory, is taken by an approach that could be called the 'hybridisation' perspective. Hybridisation basically means that the characteristics of the shareholder and stakeholder systems are mixed and create a new hybrid system, in which political economies move towards a middle ground between the two models.[23] The hybridisation approach has three variants. The first reaches similar conclusions as convergence theory, but investigates more closely the mechanisms that are supposed to lead to convergence. The argument is that each type of corporate governance system has its own distinctive logic, shaped by its own institutions, that are complementary to each other. This implies that a mixing of both systems will not increase economic efficiency, but may decrease it, because the system becomes incoherent.[24] In a dynamic perspective, it is argued that hybrid systems are not sustainable and will eventually converge. When elements from shareholder systems are imported to stakeholder systems, their underlying institutional logic becomes gradually undermined and the emerging system is temporary and unstable. Because of a strain for system coherence, the shareholder system is likely to ingrain itself in the long run.[25]

The second strand posits that the hybridisation process will have a positive outcome. It argues that stakeholder and shareholder systems mirror each other's strengths and weaknesses. Therefore, mutual learning, induced by globalisation, may lead to the emergence of hybrid best practices.[26] To this effect, the Organisation for Economic Cooperation and Development (OECD) writes: 'An overall trend towards a degree of convergence in governance and financing patterns may eventually emerge, with Anglo-American Systems accepting the best features of the German, and vice versa'.[27] Basically, this thesis implies that elements of corporate governance systems can be blended in order to increase efficiency. Zeitlin argues with regard to the organisation of production that borrowing and imitation of the dominant model is never complete, but only incremental. Therefore, selective adaptation takes place which requires innovative modification of the dominant model to domestic contexts, which can become 'sources of competitive advantage in their own right'.[28]

The last variant of the hybridisation thesis does not study the efficiency of corporate governance systems. Rather, it is primarily concerned with institutional change. Acknowledging that complementarities are of high importance for corporate governance systems, this variant argues that complementarities are not recognisable in advance, but only *ex post*. The fit between different practices is often unintended and becomes realised only *ex post* through organisational learning.[29] Thus it is unclear *a priori* whether hybrid models are unstable or not; it depends on adjustments in other institutions. It has been suggested, for example, that co-determination in Germany has been transformed from an institution that serves to solve class conflicts towards an institution that supports economic efficiency in order to re-establish complementarity with a higher shareholder value-orientation of management.[30] Thus functional conversion takes place; formal institutions survive; but they change their character and functions. However, wholesale convergence is not postulated, rather 'a decrease, not the disappearance of, the differences between the systems'.[31]

A third school of thought, the 'varieties of capitalism' approach, does not expect major changes in German corporate governance, but institutional reproduction and continued divergence in economic and corporate governance systems. The main argument is that national institutions with their different incentive structures shape the behaviour of firms and their possibilities to coordinate. Institutions provide certain opportunities and constraints for firms and firms can be expected to capitalise on these opportunities by specialising in markets and market segments for which there is institutional support. In these markets they possess a competitive advantage relative to firms from other countries, which translates into a comparative institutional advantage on the national level. The coordination problems of firms can be dealt with by market or non-market coordination. The type of coordination that will be prevalent is dependent upon national institutions, which are interdependent and complementary; hence each state develops institutions in different areas which all support the same type of coordination.[32] Depending on the mode of coordination, the approach distinguishes between liberal market economies, such as the UK or the USA, and coordinated market economies, with Germany being the prime example. Both frameworks generate competitive firms but in different industries and with a different organisation.

Because firms derive their competitive advantage from national institutions, they will try to preserve them even under conditions of globalisation. Furthermore, complementarities discriminate against radical change in corporate governance, because actors try to preserve complementary institutional arrangements in different spheres of the economy that are of value to them.[33] Hence globalisation will not transform economic and corporate governance systems, but reinforce their characteristics. Firms will try to sustain their institutional advantages by leveraging their traditional competitive advantages that are dependent on the institutional frameworks.[34] Therefore, adjustment paths and the strategic behaviour of firms will remain distinctive, depending on the national institutional context.[35] For the German corporate governance system this implies that we should not expect a major transformation, but a continuing or even increasing reliance on its traditional features.

All three approaches share a serious weakness, namely, that they fail to deal explicitly with the firm level. Even though firm behaviour is at the centre of their theoretical claims, they largely concentrate on the systemic level. Convergence theory concentrates on changes in the international environment and deduces, according to microeconomic reasoning, the consequences for firms. Institutional approaches and the 'hybridisation' thesis focus predominantly on the level of whole corporate governance systems and the effects of national institutions. However, actual firm behaviour under the constraints of globalisation has very rarely been subject to empirical investigation. This is unfortunate, since institutions cannot force firms to follow a certain pattern of behaviour; they can only provide incentives and constraints. Firms are not simple 'institution-takers'; firm strategies interact with the institutional framework, which can lead to institutional reconfigurations, especially in the process of adjustment.[36] Therefore, the remainder of this article explores the adjustment path of Siemens. Siemens is certainly not representative of the majority of German firms; however, because of its unusual exposure to globalisation pressures, it is an excellent case for studying the impact of globalisation on German corporate governance and its adjustment path.

SIEMENS' PROFILE AND THE CHANGING ECONOMIC ENVIRONMENT

Siemens is Germany's biggest electrical concern and Europe's largest private employer. It displays several features that in the theoretical literature are associated with the German model of corporate governance, such as long-term strategies, peaceful labour relations, diversified quality production, comparatively low profits and a sales growth orientation. Unusually for a German firm, its shares are widely dispersed, the biggest shareholder being the Siemens family with 5.3 percent of the equity share. Siemens' relationship with the banks was never as close as one would expect from well-known accounts of the bank–firm relationship in Germany. The *Hausbank* relationship has two components: long-term credits and supervisory board representation. In terms of financing, Siemens has not been dependent on external finance. It has accumulated enormous reserves that help to keep its independence from credit as well as from the capital markets. Banks have seats on the supervisory board, but very limited influence due to the absence of need to obtain credits. Moreover, Siemens has handled most of its financial transactions itself.[37] Traditionally, Siemens' business strategy was technology-centred and focused on high quality products.[38] Its broad product portfolio stems from the strategic goal, going back to its founding days, of covering as many areas of electronics as possible.

Siemens has had to cope with the changing structure of its product markets. Until the late 1980s almost 60 percent of Siemens' customers were public or semi-public institutions. It was the 'royal supplier' for most German public institutions, which sheltered Siemens to a certain degree from market volatility and price competition. But, owing to the privatisation of its main customers, formerly constant prices fell drastically and the public share of Siemens' orders was down to 20 percent by the mid 1990s.[39] Consequently, Siemens had to enter new markets and it internationalised vigorously throughout the 1990s. The main question for corporate governance in this context is whether internationalisation led to disembedding from the home base. If it did, it is likely that the corporate governance system of the home country will cease to exert an influence on the firm's behaviour.

INTERNATIONALISATION

Comparative research on the strategic behaviour of multinational companies (MNCs) has shown that the most distinguishing characteristic of German MNCs is their deep embeddedness in the German corporate governance system.[40] They tend to rely on their home base as the centre for economic activities and to pursue a multi-domestic strategy of internationalisation in which foreign direct investment is primarily undertaken to be close to customers and to adapt products to local needs. This is seen as a consequence of the high-quality strategies of German firms on the product markets, which require local adaptation of products and cooperation with customers.[41] Subsidiaries in this approach are appendages of a mainly domestic corporation; headquarters retain strategic and financial control. Hence organisational pressures from internationalisation are low and do not threaten the domestic corporate governance arrangements.

Siemens concentrated on the German home market until the mid 1980s, although it was already then a highly internationalised firm. In 1985 it made 53 percent of its sales in Germany, 21 percent in the rest of Europe and 10 percent in North America.[42] Since then Siemens has been pursuing a much more aggressive internationalisation strategy with a focus on the USA, which constitutes a third of the world electronics market, and to a lesser degree on Western Europe, especially the UK.[43] The motivation was the assumption that Siemens could only stay competitive if it was present in at least two of the three Triad regions. Sales in the USA doubled in the 1990s to 22 percent of total sales, with the number of employees increasing from 15,100 in 1985 to 76,000 in 2001.[44]

Nevertheless, Siemens' presence in the USA has been associated with high losses and the US business was still unprofitable in 2000.[45]

The strategic decision to grow internationally by acquisitions made Siemens the biggest German investor abroad. Expansion could only take place abroad as the German market was saturated. Moreover, the growing importance of electronics resulted in an explosion in R&D, whilst at the same time product life cycles and innovation cycles shortened dramatically. Whereas in the mid 1970s 39 percent of Siemens' products were younger than 5 years, the corresponding figure for the mid 1990s was 75 percent.[46] Economies of scale therefore became much more important; thus higher output was imperative to finance investment in R&D.

Consequently, in terms of sales, Siemens' home market has become relatively less important. Over the course of the 1990s Germany's share of total sales decreased from roughly 50 percent to 22 percent in 2001. The rest of Europe has increased its share from 20 to 30 percent and the Americas have increased their weight from 14 to 30 percent. Business in Asia has grown to 11 percent.[47] In absolute terms, Siemens' sales in Germany have remained by and large constant, with the growth coming from abroad. The sales pattern follows the distribution of electronics markets, whose growth takes place outside Europe.[48] There is a more balanced sales structure emerging, a key strategic goal since the mid 1990s.[49] However, profits have come mainly from German and European business. Hidden behind the relative distribution of sales, there is a pronounced absolute growth. Total sales grew, from DM63 billion to DM170 billion between 1990 and 2001.[50] Thus Siemens reacted to the changing international environment with an expansionist business policy.

In terms of employees, their number in Germany has decreased, from 230,000 in 1990 to 199,000 in 2001. By the mid 1990s Siemens for the first time had more foreign than domestic employees. The employment pattern is therefore following sales development. However, disproportionately many employees are still employed in Germany: 41 percent of the company's 484,000 employees. Even more important is the fact that two-thirds of value added is effected in Germany.[51] All central management functions are located in Germany; thus all important decisions are made in the home country. Top management is recruited almost exclusively from Germany. Among the 80 most senior middle managers, only two are non-Germans and foreigners account for only 20 percent in the senior middle management.[52] There have been no attempts to internationalise senior management because the recruitment of top management takes place internally and future top managers are selected very early in their careers. Non-German Siemens managers can reach the top positions in their respective countries, which are all headed by locals. Thus, in terms of socialisation of top management, foreign influence remains low.

Other indicators also point in the direction of a continuing embeddedness of Siemens in the German business system. Two-thirds of R&D employees are employed in Germany and 75 percent of all R&D expenses are spent domestically.[53] This is unlikely to change, because Germany is seen as the main location for R&D. Generally, Siemens had two-thirds of its capacity in Germany in 1996.[54] Furthermore, Siemens exports its production model to its foreign subsidiaries. It has introduced the dual education system in 20 countries in cooperation with local colleges. Also the distribution of assets is biased towards Germany; in 2001 42 percent of its long-term assets worth €17.8 billion were located in Germany, 22 percent in the rest of Europe and 25 percent in the USA.[55]

Overall, Siemens internationalised much more vigorously over the 1990s. However, its style and strategies of internationalisation followed its traditional trajectory. The strategic functions remain in Germany, the distribution of assets has a bias towards the home-base, top management is not at all internationalised, and R&D as well as value added activities are heavily concentrated in Germany. Therefore Siemens follows a multi-domestic strategy, which does not threaten domestic corporate governance arrangements. There are also no signs that Siemens is transforming itself into a network corporation without a clear centre, with strong influence by subsidiaries, and with no discernible nationality, as some management theorists have argued.[56] Thus Siemens' aggressive internationalisation, which has been supported by the works councils, has not resulted in a loosening of ties to the home base, and Siemens is still unquestionably embedded in the German system of corporate governance. However, it would be misleading to characterise Siemens as a slow globaliser, as German firms have sometimes been perceived to be in comparative perspective. It showed a high degree of active globalisation during the 1990s, but this catching-up process has not been hindered by the institutions of corporate governance.

RESTRUCTURING

Continuous restructuring efforts were the other main feature of Siemens' business policy in the course of the 1990s. The recession of the early part of the decade and the changing economic environment made restructuring efforts at Siemens unavoidable. The first significant move was the introduction of the *top* programme. *Top*, an abbreviation of 'time optimised process', started in 1993 and aimed at increasing productivity, growth and innovation. The goal was to reach a return on sales of 5 percent, after a figure of 2 percent in 1993. The programme achieved impressive improvements in productivity, but most of the increased productivity was eaten up by falling prices caused by increased competition.[57] Hence *top* allowed Siemens to hold its position, but it did not boost profits. *Top* led to a considerable number of dismissals. Between 1992 and 1996 40,000 people lost their jobs. Nevertheless, the programme has been fully supported by the works councils.[58] They accepted the necessity of cutting jobs and agreed to a socially cushioned programme of lay-offs. The dismissals were carried out by early retirement, transfers within the company, part-time work and severance payments; operational lay-offs were avoided. This approach brought high personnel costs, as expenses for restructuring-related personnel measures were roughly as high as the profits made in 1994.[59] Compared to similar, but much earlier, programmes at Siemens' main competitors, General Electric (GE) and ABB, *top* was much less radical and far-reaching.[60] It did not include portfolio restructuring and was focused on internal productivity gains. The profit goals were not met. Profits stayed more or less the same, while return on equity fluctuated between 9 and 10 percent, far behind its competitors: in 1998 Siemens had a return on equity of 9.9 percent, whereas ABB had 21 percent, and GE 23 percent.[61]

At the end of 1998 Siemens came under severe pressure. Share price and profits were falling sharply.[62] As a reaction, the CEO presented a 10-point programme that was supposed to get the company back on track. Some of the 10 points were intended to amend the capital structure in order to reach the desired financial figures; others were cost cutting or motivational measures. The main points included a focus on increasing the share price and setting clear goals for management, as well as the option of floating divisions and the decision to list on the NYSE. The following sections investigate these restructuring measures as well as others that were taken independently from the 10-point programme, namely, the introduction of stock options and a new system of financial performance measures in the areas of financial, organisational and portfolio restructuring.

Financial restructuring

Financial policy is above all about the question of how companies raise their capital. In the context of globalisation it is argued that firms become ever more dependent on the financial markets because their growing financing needs can only be covered by approaching them. The more dependent firms become upon financial markets, the more they have to behave according to the latters' preferences, so the argument goes. However, it does not apply to Siemens. It has been neither dependent on financial markets nor banks for finance and it has been trying to maintain this independence. It has, to a very great extent, been able to finance its investments from cash flow. Furthermore, its enormous reserves also sheltered it from external financial pressures. Liquidity has normally amounted to more than DM20 billion,[63] accumulated through a longstanding security-oriented financial policy and low dividends.

Also in dividend policies, no significant change occurred in the 1990s, despite the growing ownership of institutional investors who appreciate high dividends. From 1990 to 1995 Siemens paid a constant dividend of DM13 and from 1996 to 1998, after the introduction of the DM5 share, DM1.50. Considering that profits between 1996 and 1998 fluctuated between DM900 million and DM2.9 billion, dividend policy was not profit-dependent. By and large, 40 percent of profits have been paid as dividends.[64] However, financial restructuring encompasses more dimensions, especially changes in the relationship towards shareholders.

The most significant change took place in investor relations. In the 1990s Siemens disclosed much more information to the capital markets than it had done previously, and it abolished several traditions that might have deterred investors, such as multiple voting rights of family shares. Other capital market-related moves were the conversion of the DM50 shares into DM5 shares, which made them more appealing to investors, and the move to named shares in 1999 in order to communicate more directly with shareholders. These moves aimed at minimising transaction costs in acquiring Siemens shares and at adjusting to the standards of the international capital markets.

New standards have also been introduced for transparency. The most decisive move was that Siemens published divisional results, which has given analysts a better understanding of Siemens' individual divisions, but has made cross-subsidisation between divisions much more difficult, thereby putting more pressure on poorly performing businesses. The head of Siemens' investor relations department explained the shift this way:

> The financial landscape has internationalized through the globalization of financial markets; by this increase in transparency and the intensification of equity research, big companies have to adjust to a continuous dialogue with shareholders and financial analysts ... we have to formulate value creating strategies and communicate these to the financial markets. If this does not work, even big companies are in danger of falling behind in the global competition for equity and external capital ... investors have a natural interest in being informed exhaustively ... and we have an interest that our strategies are understood and valued by investors.[65]

Siemens also decided to get listed on the NYSE, which was seen as the jewel in the crown of the 10-point programme and a symbol for its more investor-friendly approach. This is a step with far-reaching consequences for corporate governance because—as convergence theorists argue—by doing so foreign firms become subject to US legal standards and encounter pressure to adopt American business practices. Therefore, for US-listed firms 'movement toward the American style appears almost inevitable'.[66] Several steps were necessary in order to get a listing, the most important being the introduction of accounting according to US-GAAP.[67] In terms of transparency, Siemens had introduced most of the transparency requirements before the listing and independently from it.

Apart from being a symbolic step in the framework of the 10-point programme, two factors were decisive for the listing. The USA had become Siemens' most important single market after Germany and Siemens had become the biggest foreign employer in the USA. Nevertheless, the company was not very well known

in the USA. Thus the listing aimed to increase its name recognition, especially at a time when Siemens was eager to enter the US mobile phone market. In this sense the step followed the logic of the listing in London in the early 1990s, when a significantly increased sales volume led to a listing in that country in order to support an expansionist product market strategy. Furthermore, Siemens could only introduce stock option schemes for its US employees if it was listed on the US stock exchange.

The second reason for seeking a US-listing had to do with the growing importance of stocks as an acquisition currency. Most mergers and acquisitions in the late 1990s had been financed by share swaps. According to its CEO, Siemens intended to secure the possibility of acquisitions with its own shares: 'since we are largely financed from our internal cash flow, listing in the worlds' biggest capital market wasn't absolutely necessary. The situation has changed now that stock has become an increasingly important acquisition currency in company take-overs and mergers. We also want to have this option available for dealings in the US.'[68] No capital was raised by the listing: the share was made tradeable by American Depository Rights. Therefore, it is unlikely that US shareholders will get a greater influence; their ownership base has remained constant. In 2001, US and Canadian investors held 8 percent of Siemens' shares, whereas German investors held 52 percent, continental European investors 29 percent, and UK investors 10 percent.[69] There is thus no direct causality linking a listing on NYSE with the outcome that convergence theorists expect, namely, a transformation of a firm's corporate governance system towards the preferences of investors.

Organisational restructuring

In order to meet the financial goals a new management and controlling instrument was introduced in 1998—the Economic-Value-Added (EVA) concept. EVA measures the success of each business group and of the whole company by incorporating the cost of internal and external capital. In this perspective businesses are only profitable if they earn at least their cost of capital. The expectations of the financial markets are thus incorporated into corporate decision making, because, in theory, the costs of capital can be equalised with the profit requirements of all investors, shareholders and creditors. The EVA emerges when more than the costs of capital are earned, which is then benchmarked against competitors.

EVA is the most far-reaching and systematic attempt to achieve the longstanding goal of a return on equity of 15 percent. However, the most important feature of the concept is how it is used. The logic of EVA decrees that business groups that underperform their capital costs should be fixed, closed or sold, in very much the same way as GE handles its business. However, Siemens seems not to be willing to follow the concept in this crucial regard, which would mean determined and fast disinvestments. When EVA was introduced, over half of the business groups earned less than their capital costs. In 2001 the biggest loss makers were Information and Communications, Automotive and Siemens Dematic, but their profit goals have been postponed and the CEO has declared that no division as a whole will be sold, only minor parts at most.[70] Siemens sees its broad portfolio as an asset: it makes it less vulnerable against downswings in certain markets, because the 'cash cows' and the loss-makers change and so the single divisions support each other over time. The prime example is medical equipment which had been run at a loss for a long time, but achieved a turnaround in the 1990s; it is now one of the most successful divisions. The 'fix-it' option enjoys primacy; despite EVA, Siemens is committed to its divisions and markets.

Furthermore, much depends on the definition of capital costs. On the whole, Siemens is operating with a figure of 9 percent, but the definition differs for each business group. This is significantly lower than the figure that Siemens competitors with a similar system try to achieve: for Ericsson, the figure is 16 percent, for GE 13 percent, Philips 12 percent and GEC 10 percent.[71] Hence Siemens has adjusted the concept to its own needs and its own environment, which ultimately means a soft version of the original concept. The works councils welcomed the introduction of EVA on the grounds that it provides higher transparency about goals and did not set uniform profit goals for the company as a whole; the latter had always been resisted by the works councils, but differentiated between the divisions.

In addition to EVA, a share option scheme has been introduced. The design of stock options is of crucial importance for a corporate governance system, because stock options can alter the managers' incentives and are the prime vehicle for a capital market orientation. Stock options are seen as the most important explanatory factor for the transformation of the US corporate governance system from a managerial to a capital market-oriented system: 'thanks to lucrative stock option plans, managers could share in the market returns from restructured companies. Shareholder value became an ally rather than an enemy.'[72] Thus, if management's compensation is closely tied to the share price, it can be expected that its primary focus will be on increasing that price. The crucial point is not the existence of incentive schemes *per se*. It is whether managerial incentives are directly tied to share price.

Siemens' incentive scheme was introduced in 1999 and affected 500 top managers; later it was extended to 1500 managers. The stock option plan is part of a broader incentive scheme. For the 200 top managers 40 percent of income is fixed, the rest is variable; for the next tier of 300 managers, the ratio is 60:40. Thirty percent of the variable part is an annual bonus and is based on yearly results: the remaining 70 percent is a long-term bonus and is based on three-year results, taking EVA and accounting figures as a baseline. The long-term bonus has the aim of preventing short-term incentives.[73] The stock options themselves are only a supplement to these incentives. In a best case scenario they can add up to 25 percent of the annual income of top management.[74] The whole incentive scheme shows a deliberate long-term orientation. The yearly bonus is not fully paid: two thirds of it is retained and paid only when the three-year goals are reached.[75]

Compared to US standards the programme does not provide high-powered incentives to tie strategic decisions to share price. Between 1980 and 1994 equity-based compensation in the US increased from less than 20 percent of total CEO compensation to almost 50.[76] It is obvious that Siemens' stock option plan is quite different. As indicated, the incentive scheme stresses long-term performance and in 1999 the market value of granted stock options for the management board was only 10 percent of total salary. Thus the design of the stock option programme can also be said to have been adjusted to Siemens' environment and provides comparatively low incentives to embrace the promotion of the share price as the main goal for management.

Portfolio restructuring

The most spectacular strategic decision of the 10-point programme was that the semi-conductor division should be spun off. Until then only marginal businesses had been sold, but listing semi-conductors meant giving up 60,000 jobs and DM17 billion in sales.[77] Siemens had invested huge sums in semi-conductors from the early 1980s onwards; they were seen as a technology that was crucial for all areas of Siemens' businesses and the company appeared willing to bear huge losses in this field (it lost at least DM10 billion on semi-conductors in the 1990s).[78] The division's losses were the main reason for the crisis in 1998, which led to the introduction of the 10-point programme.

Faced with the acute crisis in the semi-conductor industry,[79] Siemens was no longer willing to bear the cycles in this business and to finance the enormous capital requirement of the division. This capital would have been spent at the expense of the other businesses. Because of the extraordinarily capital intensive nature of the business, semi-conductors had absorbed a lion's share of Siemens' investment resources, thereby jeopardising the growth of other business groups.[80] Furthermore, semi-conductors should be able to engage in cooperations and acquisitions, which was seen to be easier for an independent firm.[81] The division was renamed Infineon Technologies and in 1999 listed on the New York and Frankfurt stock exchanges. Siemens gave Infineon a generous capital start-up and appointed the chairmen of the management and supervisory boards, both members of the Siemens management board.

However, the spin-off was not total. At the IPO only 29 percent of Infineon was floated, although Siemens wanted to float a further significant share soon afterwards. However, if Siemens had a share of less than 50 percent, it would lose important patent rights. Thus, it seems unlikely that Siemens is actively pushing to get rid of its stake. It recently decreased its stake to 51 percent; however, this stake was not floated, but instead transferred to Siemens' pension trust, leaving Siemens in control. Retaining a stake of more than 25 percent, Siemens would be able to control Infineon.[82] The works councils supported the spin-off. Crucial for the decision was the agreement of the divisional works councils whose main concern was Infineon's better future prospects as an independent firm.[83] Furthermore, Infineon adopted the employment conditions of Siemens wholesale, joined the employers' association and made sure that dismissals would be avoided. Although the spin-off marks a break in Siemens' traditions, it was nevertheless done in a very traditional way; jobs were not affected, the decision was taken in agreement with the works councils and Siemens is still in control of a majority stake.

From a shareholder value perspective it was not a far-reaching move. The core of the shareholder value approach is that firms should concentrate on one or only a few businesses with the highest profitability and growth perspectives. Conglomerates are punished by the conglomerate discount, which results from lower transparency. Siemens, with a portfolio that covers many more areas of electronics than all its competitors, is therefore under pressure.[84] Criticism by financial analysts thus centred on its missing core competencies and the broadness of its businesses. The suggestion has been to split and divest Siemens completely in order to unlock shareholder value; as a minimum it is said that it should concentrate on one or two core businesses, the then fashionable telecommunications business among them, and continue restructuring. The *Financial Times* suggested dividing it into a high-tech side comprising telecommunications, semi-conductors, computers and medical equipment, and a low-tech side with power plants, rail systems, capital goods and lighting.[85] J.P. Morgan urged Siemens to concentrate on a few core businesses and to get rid of all underperforming business groups.[86] M.M. Warburg thought that Siemens should sell or float businesses accounting for more than two-thirds of its turnover.[87] Thus a strict shareholder value orientation would mean a splitting up of the firm.

However, Siemens has remained firmly committed to its business groups. Even those that made heavy losses for a long time were kept and an attempt was made to repair them. The same strategy was initially followed in the semi-conductor business, although, after a severe crisis, a spin-off with continuing and controlling influence seemed the more promising alternative for a business in which Siemens never really succeeded. Moreover, there are no signs that Siemens is intending further to restructure its portfolio on a large scale. According to the CEO, the floating of Infineon and passive components was not intended to be the beginning of a broader restructuring, but the end of it.[88] Since then, there have been no other IPOs of divisions nor have significant parts of Siemens been sold. Siemens' broad portfolio is still seen by the management as one of the firm's key assets, enabling the company to weather economic crises and achieve long-term economic success for the benefit of customers, shareholders and employees.[89] Diversification means risk reduction for Siemens because it makes it more independent from the business cycles in different industries and helps to contribute to stability.[90] Thus it is unlikely that Siemens' structure and portfolio will change significantly in the foreseeable future.

RESTRUCTURING RESULTS, PROFIT DISTRIBUTION AND INDUSTRIAL RELATIONS

The restructuring measures managed to increase profits and share price significantly. In 1999 profits were €1.8 billion, although EVA was still negative to the tune of €650 million. In 2000 Siemens announced that profits had increased to €3.4 billion, with all business segments in the black, while EVA was positive to the tune of DM859 million. After the announcement of the 10-point programme Siemens' share price started to outperform the DAX-Index and has continued to do so quite significantly.[91] Siemens' market capitalisation increased, supported by the high-tech bubble on the stock markets, from €28 billion to €85 billion between 1998 and 2000.[92] However, it is still a long way behind its main competitor, GE, which has had a five to six times higher market capitalisation. Nonetheless, the restructuring programme with its target of boosting profits and share price accomplished its main goals.

The distribution of Siemens' all-time-high profits shows its continuing stakeholder orientation. The company significantly increased dividends, but also let the employees participate in the success of 'Germany's largest and most generous employee-share programme to date'.[93] The idea was to give an equivalent of the dividends to the employees in order to satisfy Siemens' two most important groups of stakeholders.[94] Siemens offered shares to its employees at a discount of 50 percent. This scheme involved costs of €600 million for Siemens. Comparing these payments with GE's shareholder orientation, the differences become obvious. Between 1994 and 1998 GE increased dividend payments by 84 percent and spent US$14.6 billion on share buy-backs, which together meant an outflow of 74.4 percent of cash from operations.[95]

The programme also led to an increase in employees' shareholdings of 1.2 percent. Before, the employees were estimated to hold somewhere between 9 and 17 percent of Siemens' equity.[96] Thus the employees are the most important group of shareholders, which increases their bargaining position. In this regard the plan also helps Siemens bolster its defences against potential take-over attempts. However, it also shows that Siemens is not only focused on its shareholders, but it is still investing in consensus with its employees.

Generally, restructuring did not negatively affect the cooperative and consensus-oriented character of industrial relations at Siemens.[97] Indeed, the full support of the works councils enabled the restructuring, which was carried out without major resistance and strikes. In exchange for their cooperation, employees were compensated by the avoidance of operational dismissals and a share in the financial success of the restructuring. The works councils were also successful in preventing uniform profit goals for the company as a whole, which would not differentiate between the divisions. They generally welcomed the higher transparency of the company, because it increased their access to information.[98] This confirms Hoepner's argument that co-determination is not an obstacle to an increasing capital market orientation, because a higher transparency is in the interest of the works councils and increases their capacities to monitor management.[99] Therefore, the change in Siemens' information policy and the introduction of EVA did not lead to resistance on the part of the works councils.

All in all, adjustment remains negotiated. The works councils have been included in the decision making from the beginning beyond the legal requirements, and a consensus was sought. Siemens has an extensive system of committees at which management and workers' representatives regularly meet and reconcile their positions to new developments, and where the works councils are informed about new management initiatives. Besides these committees, informal relationships between key players help to prevent serious conflicts.

CONCLUSIONS

Siemens' responses to globalisation show a complex mixture of change and continuity. Its adjustment path over the 1990s has been characterised by expansion through internationalisation and by internal restructuring. Siemens internationalised vigorously over the 1990s, but there was strong continuity in its means of internationalisation. Siemens followed a multi-domestic strategy with a strong bias towards the homebase in the distribution of activities and assets.

The restructuring measures show varying degrees of continuity. If we recall the four elements of a shareholder value strategy—concentration on core competencies, minimum profit goals for all divisions with the consequence of fast divestments, stock option programmes for management and a transparent information policy—the following picture emerges. The biggest change took place in information policy and transparency. In this area, Siemens has become much more investor-friendly and discloses much more information than it used to. Nevertheless, this greater capital market orientation did not affect other main features of financial policy, namely, financing and divided policy. In the realm of organisational restructuring, Siemens introduced stock options and profit goals. However, these are—compared to Anglo-Saxon practices—differently designed and provide much lower-powered incentives for management to prioritise shareholder value.

In terms of corporate strategy, the core concept of the shareholder value approach is the concentration on a few core businesses and the implied consequence of far-reaching portfolio restructuring, also resulting from minimum profit goals. Here, Siemens shows a high degree of resistance to divestments. According to all statements of its top management, the spin-off of Infineon was the last major divestment. Divisions that do not meet the profit goals, which are lower than the corresponding goals of Siemens' competitors anyway, are nevertheless kept. The broad diversification serves the goal of risk diversification and the survival of the company as a whole. In terms of consensual decision making, the stakeholder model is alive and corporate strategy builds on co-management with the works councils. The interests of shareholders and institutional investors have not become the only interests to be considered, even though profits and share prices have become more important aims in Siemens' strategy and have been more decidedly pursued.

Taking Anglo-Saxon practices as a benchmark, it can be argued that financial and product market globalisation have not pushed Siemens down a path leading to a pure shareholder value conception of the firm, even though it is highly exposed to these developments. Siemens imported several elements of the shareholder value approach, but neither are all features imported nor are the implemented features equivalent to Anglo-Saxon standards. The emerging corporate governance system at Siemens combines continuity in corporate strategy, financing policy and industrial relations with a transparent information policy and certain shareholder value instruments, such as stock options and profit goals. The shareholder value concept has been accommodated to Siemens' environment and governance style, rejecting short-term profit maximisation and stressing a long-term orientation.[100] All in all, there remain wide differences relative to Siemens' competitors from within shareholder systems of corporate governance. This implies that financial market pressures do not affect all elements of corporate governance and that partial adaptations, especially in the area of information policy, need not be damaging for other elements of corporate governance, such as industrial relations and corporate strategy. It appears that the pressure of financial markets prompts, above all, accurate information about the financial situation of enterprises, but does not extend to deeper strategic issues. Firms seem to have considerable degrees of freedom to respond to global financial markets. This is reinforced in the case of Siemens by its huge retained earnings, which give it a certain independence from the financial markets in terms of raising capital. This finding raises the wider question of whether financial markets really demand changes in corporate governance and strategy or whether they are satisfied if they are provided with adequate information. This question needs to be addressed by further research.

Since a wholesale transformation of Siemens' corporate governance system is not under way, but rather a selective adaptation of elements of the shareholder model that are adjusted to the German environment, the claims of convergence theory are misleading. As common in case-study research, there is a danger of overgeneralising from the case of Siemens. There may be other factors that force firms to adopt a strict shareholder value orientation, possibly of an internal nature, or factors that are ideological or rooted in firm or industry idiosyncrasies. However, if this is so, then it has not been adequately considered by convergence theory and a more complex approach is needed to account for the interplay between external and internal factors.

Whereas the continuing stakeholder orientation in decision making and the strategic stability is consistent with the predictions of the 'varieties of capitalism' approach, this approach has problems explaining the changes that are taking place. Its focus on processes of institutional reproduction and persistence and the methodological approach of comparative statics make the theory unable to distinguish between adaptation and fundamental institutional change and explain institutional development over time. This is reinforced by the assumption of strong complementarities in the German corporate governance system, leading to a tendency to see change as fundamentally damaging to the system. However, as the case of Siemens shows, a transparent information policy—the strongest change in its business policy—does not necessarily lead to a breakdown of other elements of corporate governance. The case study highlights the need for a better conception of complementarities and the need to determine the really crucial elements of corporate governance systems. Not all elements of corporate governance seem to be equally important for the emergence of a certain specialisation and certain product market strategies. Complementarities may be more loosely coupled than it is often assumed.

This seems to speak for the 'hybridisation' thesis. The pressure from financial markets has forced Siemens to change its information policy and introduce several elements of the shareholder value concept without leading to the breakdown of corporate governance institutions or their basic strategic orientations. However, it is not a simple hybrid form that is emerging, in which elements of both systems are transferred without modifications. It is an adjustment of certain instruments to the prevailing corporate governance system. In this sense, it is a path dependent process and discrete institutions do not change independently from the institutional framework, but are modified.

The long-run effects of the import of institutional features from shareholder systems, especially in terms of efficiency, are difficult to judge. Lane argues that the import of shareholder value elements destroys the institutional logic of the German corporate governance system and leads to an unstable system, which will sooner or later be replaced by the institutional logic of shareholder systems.[101] However, the import of several features of the US model in the immediate postwar years, including mass production and a set of new management techniques, did not unsettle the principles of the German corporate governance system; this import led instead to selective adaptation, piecemeal borrowing and the emergence of innovative hybrids.[102] Whether the negative or the positive view of hybridisation is correct in the present context can only be seen in the course of the future development of Siemens. The outcome is likely to be dependent on organisational learning and adjustment in other institutional features so that a fit between the imported and the old institutions can be created.[103]

The case of Siemens therefore suggests that there are important theoretical gaps to be filled by further research. The existing political economy approaches to the influence of globalisation on firms should be refined in order better to explain changes in firm behaviour. Convergence theory is too deterministic to explain firm behaviour, whereas the 'varieties of capitalism' approach in its present form cannot incorporate changes in firm strategy within its framework. It overlooks the agency of firms. The hybridisation thesis can explain some of the changes taking place, but cannot tell us why some features are imported and not others. It is also silent about differences in the design of imported institutions. Generally, the case study suggests that the most promising way is to complement institutional analysis with systematic firm-level analysis in order to model the interaction between institutional and enterprise change. After all, the adjustment paths of firms constitute an empirical question that needs to be answered by firm-level research. A stronger actor-centred approach focusing on firms as actors in their own right may be able to capture better the dynamics of corporate governance. Such a focus on firm behaviour can analyse how institutional and firm strategies interact and which features of corporate governance are most affected by the institutional environment and changes in the international economy.

NOTES

For constructive and very helpful comments I would like to thank Wyn Grant, Markus Lederer, Martin Rhodes, Justin Robertson and Jonathan Wheatley.

1   For studies that are exceptions to this tendency and deal with the level of firms, see Jeffrey N. Gordon, *Pathways to Corporate Convergence? Two Steps on the Road to Shareholder Capitalism in Germany: Deutsche Telekom and DaimlerChrysler*, Working Paper 2000/161, Columbia Law School, Center for Law and Economic Studies, New York; Mark Lehrer, 'Macro-varieties of capitalism and micro-varieties of strategic management in European airlines', in: Peter Hall and David Soskice (eds), *Varieties of Capitalism: The Institutional Foundations of Comparative Institutional Advantage* (Oxford University Press, 2001), pp. 361–86; and Wolfgang Streeck and Martin Höpner (eds), *Alle Macht dem Markt? Fallstudien zur Abwicklung der Deutschland AG* (Campus, 2003).

2   See Henry Hansmann and Reinier Kraakman, 'The End of History for Corporate Law', *Georgetown Law Journal*, Vol. 89, No. 1 (2001), p. 455.

3   See Christel Lane, 'Globalization and the German Model of Capitalism—Erosion or Survival?', *British Journal of Sociology*, Vol. 51, No. 2 (2000), p. 210.

4   See John C. Coffee, Jr., *The Future as History: The Prospects for Global Convergence in Corporate Governance and its Implications*, Working Paper 1999/14, Columbia Law School, Center for Law and Economic Studies, New York.

5   See Rolf Bühner, Abdul Rasheed and Joseph Rosenstein, 'Corporate Restructuring Patterns in the US and Germany: A Comparative Empirical Investigation', *Management International Review*, Vol. 37, No. 4 (1997), pp. 320–1.

6   See Sigurt Vitols, 'The reconstruction of German corporate governance: reassessing the role of capital market pressures', unpublished paper presented to the *1st Conference of the Research Network on Corporate Governance*, Wissenschaftszentrum Berlin für Sozialforschung, Berlin, June 2000, p. 3. See also Wolfgang Streeck, *The Transformation of Corporate Organization in Europe: An Overview*, Working Paper 2001/8, Max-Planck-Institute for the Study of Societies, Cologne, p. 11.

7   On the strategic interests of owners, see Ruth V. Aguilera & Gregory Jackson, 'The Cross-National Diversity of Corporate Governance: Dimensions and Determinants', *Academy of Management Review*, Vol. 12, No. 3 (2003), pp. 447–65; and Carl W. Kester, 'Industrial Groups as Systems of Contractual Governance', *Oxford Review of Economic Policy*, Vol. 8, No. 3 (1992), pp. 24–44.

8   See Sigurt Vitols, 'Viele Wege nach Rom? BASF, Bayer und Hoechst', in: Streeck & Höpner, *Alle Macht dem Markt*, p. 198.

9   See Michael Porter, *The Competitive Advantage of Nations* (Free Press, 1990), p. 356. For an analysis of the German production system and Diversified Quality Production, see Wolfgang Streeck, 'Productive constraints: on the institutional conditions of diversified quality production', in: Wolfgang Streeck, *Social Institutions and Economic Performance* (Sage, 1992), pp. 1–40.

10 See Lane, 'Globalization and the German Model', p. 208.

11 See Bühner *et al.*, 'Corporate Restructuring', p. 334.

12 See Henk De Jong, 'The Governance Structure and Performance of Large European Corporations', *Journal of Management and Governance*, Vol. 1, No. 1 (1997), p. 20.

13 See Mary O'Sullivan, 'The Political Economy of Comparative Corporate Governance', *Review of International Political Economy*, Vol. 10, No. 1 (2003), p. 63.

14 See Andreas Hackethal and Reinhard Schmidt, *Finanzsystem und Komplementarität*, Working Paper Series Finance and Accounting 2000/50, University of Frankfurt, Frankfurt, pp. 23–6.

15 See Sigurt Vitols. 'Varieties of corporate governance: comparing Germany and the UK', in: Hall and Soskice, *Varieties of Capitalism*, p. 341.

16 See De Jong, 'Governance Structure', p. 20.

17 See OECD, 'Shareholder Value and the Market in Corporate Control in OECD Countries', *Financial Market Trends*, No. 69 (1998), pp. 15–23.

18 See William Lazonick and Mary O'Sullivan, 'Maximising Shareholder Value: A New Ideology for Corporate Governance', *Economy and Society*, Vol. 29, No. 1 (2000), p. 28.

19 See William Bratton and Joseph McCahery, *Comparative Corporate Governance and the Theory of the Firm: The Case against Global Cross Reference*, Working Paper 2000/7, George Washington Law School, Public Law and Legal Theory, Washington DC, p. 18.

20 Another mechanism that might bring about convergence is that the financial industry is growing in importance and benefits from a shareholder value orientation of companies. Thus the interests of the financial industry as well as those of consultants and academics working in this field reinforce the trend towards greater shareholder power. For this argument, see Ronald Dore, *Stock Market Capitalism: Welfare Capitalism, Japan and Germany versus the Anglo-Saxons* (Oxford University Press, 2000), pp. 12–13.

21 See Hansmann and Kraakman, 'The End of History for Corporate Law', pp. 449–50.

22 *Ibid.*, p. 468.

23 See Mauro F. Guillen, 'Corporate Governance and Globalization: Is there Convergence Across Countries?', *Advances in International Comparative Management*, Vol. 13 (2000), p. 179.

24 See Reinhard Schmidt and Stefanie Grohs, *Angleichung der Wirtschaftsverfassung in Europa—ein Forschungsprogramm*, Working Paper Series Finance and Accounting, 1999/43, University of Frankfurt, Frankfurt, p. 41.

25 See Christel Lane, *Changes in Corporate Governance in German Corporations: Convergence to the Anglo-American Model?*, Working Paper 2003/259, University of Cambridge, ESRC Centre for Business Research, Cambridge, p. 6.

26 See Carl W. Kester, 'American and Japanese corporate governance: convergence to best practice?', in: Suzanne Berger and Ronald Dore (eds), *National Diversity and Global Capitalism* (Cornell University Press, 1996), pp. 107–37; as well as Bratton and McCahery, *Comparative Corporate Governance*.

27 OECD Economic Surveys, *Germany* (OECD, 1995), p. 119.

28 Jonathan Zeitlin, *Americanization and Its Limits: Reworking US Technology in Post-War Europe and Japan*, EUI Working Paper Series, RSC 1999/33, European University Institute, Florence, p. 3.

29 See Gregory Jackson, 'Corporate governance in Germany and Japan: liberalization pressures and responses during the 1990s', in: Kozo Yamamura and Wolfgang Streeck (eds), *The End of Diversity? Prospects for German and Japanese Capitalism* (Cornell University Press, 2003), p. 299.

30 See Martin Höpner, *Corporate Governance in Transition: Ten Empirical Findings on Shareholder Value and Industrial Relations in Germany*, Discussion Paper 2001/5, Max-

Planck-Institute for the Study of Societies, Cologne, p. 32.

31 *Ibid.*, p. 38.

32 See, for a general introduction, Peter Hall and David Soskice, 'Introduction', in: Hall & Soskice, *Varieties of Capitalism*, pp. 1–68.

33 *Ibid.*, p. 64.

34 See Guillen, 'Corporate Governance and Globalization', p. 200.

35 See Peter Hall, 'The political economy of Europe in an era of interdependence', in: Herbert Kitschelt *et al.* (eds), *Continuity and Change in Contemporary Capitalism* (Cambridge University Press, 1999), p. 161.

36 See Bob Hancké, *Large Firms and Institutional Change: Industrial Renewal and Economic Restructuring in France* (Oxford University Press, 2002), p. 2.

37 Siemens was also the first German industrial company to establish its own capital investment fund.

38 Frieder Naschold, *Die Siemens AG: Inkrementale Anpassung oder Unternehmenstransformation?*, Working Paper FS II 1997/201, Wissenschaftszentrum Berlin für Sozialforschung, Berlin, p. 5.

39 See 'Wie eine Lawine', *Wirtschaftswoche*, 26 October 1995.

40 See Lane, 'Globalization and the German Model', p. 208.

41 See Christel Lane, 'European Companies between Globalization and Localization—A Comparison of Internationalization Strategies of British and German MNCs', *Economy and Society*, Vol. 27, No. 4 (2000), pp. 477–8.

42 See Siemens, *Annual Report 1985*, p. 38.

43 The acquisition—in the first hostile takeover in Siemens' history—of the British telecommunications company Plessey, together with GEC, was the biggest investment in the company's history and one of the biggest foreign investments of a German firm until then. The price was about DM6 billion.

44 See 'Siemens will das US-Geschäft ausbauen', *Süddeutsche Zeitung*, 13 March 2001.

45 See 'Siemens baut das US-Geschäft um', *Financial Times Deutschland*, 13 March 2001.

46 See Günther Goth, 'Veränderungen in der unternehmerischen Personal-und Beschäftigungspolitik am Beispiel der Siemens AG', in: Winfried Schmähl and Herbert Rische (eds), *Wandel der Arbeitswelt— Folgerungen für die Sozialpolitik* (Nomos Verlagsgesellschaft, 1999), p. 97.

47 Siemens, *Annual Report*, various years.

48 Goth, *Veränderungen*, p. 85.

49 See Heinrich von Pierer, *Langfristige Ausrichtung des Unternehmens*, supervisory board presentation, 11 December 1996, internal Siemens document, p. 12.

50 See Siemens, *Annual Report*, various years.

51 See 'Von Pierer: Flächentarife müssen bleiben', *Handelsblatt*, 30 April 1996; and 'Der Riese in der Tretmühle der Globalisierung', *Süddeutsche Zeitung*, 9 October 1997.

52 See 'Unsere Leute brauchen Teamgeist', *Der Spiegel*, No. 20, 1998: interview with the head of human resource management, Peter Pribilla. See also 'Gehaltserhöhung

nicht mehr automatisch', *Süddeutsche Zeitung*, 15 June 1996.

53 See 'Jahresüberschuß soll um mehr als 20 percent steigen', *Handelsblatt*, 23 February 1996.

54 See 'Why there's still no payoff', *Business Week*, 30 December 1996.

55 Siemens, *Annual Report 2002* and author's own calculations.

56 See Gunnar Hedlund and Dag Rolander, 'Action in heterarchies—new approaches to managing the MNC', in: Christopher Bartlett *et al.* (eds), *Managing the Global Firm* (Routledge, 1990), pp. 22–6.

57 Siemens attained yearly productivity increases of 8.5 percent after 2–3 percent in the late 1980s. In 1995 these increases saved Siemens DM7 billion, but DM6.7 billion was lost by falling prices. See 'Rückenwind für Siemens', *Börsen-Zeitung*, 16 July 1996.

58 See 'Noch einmal mit Gefühl', *Manager Magazin*, No. 12, 1994: interview with the chairman of Siemens' works councils, Alfons Graf.

59 See 'Siemens auf der Suche nach höheren Renditen', *Neue Zürcher Zeitung*, 17 December 1994. Costs were DM2.3 billion.

60 See Naschold, 'Die Siemens AG', p. 20.

61 See 'Die letzte Reserve', *Manager Magazin*, No. 11, 1998.

62 Profits in 1998 were down to the all-time-low of DM0.92 billion. Overall, profits had fallen by two-thirds from 1996 to 1998. See 'Siemens climbs back', *Business Week*, 5 June 2000.

63 The exchange rate €/DM is 1.95.

64 See 'Siemens hält Kurs', *Börsen-Zeitung*, 15 December 1995; and 'Siemens-Konzernstruktur steht. Osram/BSH bleiben im Verbund', *Börsen-Zeitung*, 17 April 1999.

65 David Rothblum, 'IR: Zweigleisige Kommunikation entscheidend', *Börsen-Zeitung*, 7 November 1996 (translation by author).

66 Gerald Davis and Michael Useem, 'Top management, company directors and corporate control', in: Andrew Pettigrew *et al.* (eds), *Handbook of Strategy and Management* (Sage, 2002), p. 252.

67 Accounting according to US-GAAP had the pleasant side-effect that Siemens could separate out its pension requirements, which contribute to its enormous liquidity, but which it did not like to disclose. Pension funds were transferred to a newly founded pension trust.

68 Heinrich von Pierer, *Speech at the Annual General Meeting*, 18 February 1999.

69 See Siemens, *Annual Report 2001*, p. 20.

70 See 'Siemens verschiebt Renditeziele auf 2004', *Financial Times Deutschland*, 7 December 2001; and 'Bei Siemens rücken Sanierer an die Spitze', *Financial Times Deutschland*, 15 November 2001.

71 See 'Das neue "Win"-Dach auf dem Siemens-Haus', *Börsen-Zeitung*, 2 December 1997.

72 See Bengt Holmstrom and Steven Kaplan, *Corporate Governance and Merger Activity in the US: Making Sense of the 1980s and 1990s*, Working Paper 2001/8220, National Bureau of Economic Research, Cambridge MA, p. 3.

73 See Heinrich von Pierer, 'Stock Options für 500 Manager', *Börsen-Zeitung*, 4 December 1998.

74 See 'Ein Bonbon für die Top-Manager', *Süddeutsche Zeitung*, 15 February 1999.
75 See Siemens, *Annual Report 2000*.
76 Holmström & Kaplan, *Corporate Governance*, p. 16.
77 Also passive components, electron tubes and transistors were divested, because the division would have been too small without semi-conductors.
78 See 'Wegen Halbleitermalaise fliegt Siemens in Turbulenzen', *Computerwoche*, 31 July 1998.
79 The Southeast Asian economic crisis led to a general crisis in the industry. Because of the depreciation of those currencies, semi-conductor prices fell dramatically from US$50 to US$5 for a 16-bit chip between 1995 and 1998.
80 Yearly investments fluctuated between DM2 and 3 billion and R&D expenses were about DM1 billion each year.
81 See 'Siemens steckt Hagelschläge nicht ohne Spuren weg', *Börsen-Zeitung*, 5 November 1998.
82 Infineon Technologies, *Verkaufsprospekt*, 11 July 2001, p. 27.
83 Personal interview with a former Siemens manager.
84 In 1990 it covered 80 percent of the whole spectrum of electronics; the figures for its competitors were Hitachi: 71 percent, Toshiba: 64 percent, GEC: 52 percent, Philipps: 48 percent, General Electric: 28 percent. See 'Spotlight on Siemens' changing act', *Financial Times*, 24 December 1990.
85 See 'Splitting Siemens up', *Financial Times*, 6 November 1998.
86 See 'Siemens fehlt radikale Neurorientierung', *Börsen-Zeitung*, 21 January 1998.
87 See M.M. Warburg & Co. Investment Research, *Aktie im Blickpunkt Siemens*, August 1998, p. 7.
88 See 'New lean Siemens may still need toning up', *Financial Times*, 6 November 1998. Siemens has even excluded that business groups for which synergies with other divisions are hard to discover, such as the lightning group Osram or the joint venture with Bosch for household appliances, will be sold or floated. See 'Wir meinen es ernst mit dem Umbau', *Börsen-Zeitung*, 17 April 1999.
89 See Siemens, *Annual Report 2001*, p. 19.
90 See von Pierer, *Ausrichtung*,p. 4.
91 See http://aktien.onvista.de/charts.html?ID OSI = 82902
92 See Siemens, *Annual Report 2000*, p. 99.
93 See 'Siemens to spend €500m on employee shares', *Financial Times*, 20 October 2000.
94 See 'Bescherung für Mitarbeiter und Aktionäre von Siemens', *Financial Times Deutschland*, 20 October 2000.
95 Lazonick and O'Sullivan, 'Maximising Shareholder Value', p. 23.
96 See 'Bescherung für Mitarbeiter und Aktionäre von Siemens', *Financial Times Deutschland*, 20 October 2000.
97 Zugehör argues that Siemens has a particularly weak form of co-determination. However, his argument is focused on the influence of the unions in the supervisory board. The present article is more concerned with the cooperation between management and works councils. He also argues that the spin-off of Infineon is the beginning of a large-scale portfolio restructuring, in which the transportation, energy, medical equipment and lightning will be spun off. This, however, stands in stark contrast to the publicly stated plans of Siemens' top management and the observable developments of the last years. See Rainer Zugehör, 'Kapitalmarktorientierung und Mitbestimmung: Veba und Siemens', in: Streeck and Hoepner, *Alle Macht dem Markt?*, p. 257.
98 Personal interview with a former Siemens manager.
99 See Hoepner, *Corporate Governance in Transition*, p. 27.
100 Rothblum, 'Kommunikation'.
101 Lane, *Changes in Corporate Governance in German Corporations*, pp. 6–7.
102 See Zeitlin, *Americanization and Its Limits*,p. 3.
103 See Jackson, 'Corporate governance in Germany and Japan', p. 299.

F
I
V
E

PART SIX

CEO Power and Reward

INTRODUCTION TO PART SIX

One of the greatest contrasts between Anglo-American and European modes of corporate governance is the power and reward attributed to the Chief Executive Office. In Europe CEOs traditionally have enjoyed high status, with varying degrees of power and levels of reward, depending upon the region of Europe and the industry sector in which they worked. Almost invariably in Europe, however, there is a necessity for CEOs to work within an inclusive, and often social democratic normative order. The phenomenon of the Imperial CEO is largely recent and Anglo-American in origin. In the nineteenth and early twentieth century all of the industrial countries to some extent experienced the might of the early business entrepreneurs who enriched themselves exerting considerable monopoly power in unregulated economies. However, as Berle and Means examined in the *The Modern Corporation and Private Property* (1932), the development of the separation of ownership and control later in the twentieth century implied dispersed share ownership and professional managers. US CEOs certainly enjoyed significant influence in the corporations they controled in the middle decades of the century, for example in selecting their own board of directors (Mace 1971; Lorsch and MacIver 1989). But it was not until the widespread adoption of executive stock options in the United States in the early 1990s, intended to align executive motivations with shareholder interests, that paradoxically the remuneration of executives exploded. The cult of the US CEO, populating every airport bookshop, helped justify the astronomical remuneration packages that were now being demanded. It is interesting from a European perspective to study how US CEOs accumulated such power and wealth, since this explains the unbounded enthusiasm for the American way among some, particularly younger, European executives.

Englander and Kaufman graphically illustrate how in the 1980s and 1990s US managers succeeded in reformulating their fiduciary duties, the function of the board, and their own remuneration. The technocratic managers in the middle decades of the twentieth century professed neutrality in the distribution of wealth, and reduced risk by pursuing market share, diversification, and interlocking directorates. This comfortable managerial position was increasingly challenged in the 1980s by the growing demands of investors angered by the falling performance of US industry relative to overseas competitors, and even more threatened by the arrival of aggressive leveraged take-overs from marauding companies financed by junk-bonds. Managers responded to these threats by further entrenching themselves in control with an array of protective devices including poison pills, golden parachutes and staggered board elections. But it was the extensive application of executive stock options that really made the difference, opening up the possibility of CEOs becoming major shareholders in their own right, and entering the ranks of the very rich: managers transformed "their firm's technocratic hierarchies into CEO proprietary ones."

As the wealth accumulated by US CEOs expanded exponentially, the fiduciary obligations recognized towards wider stakeholders contracted. The data analysed by Englander and Kaufman shows how the trend towards egalitarian packages for senior executive teams was sharply reversed in the 1980s onwards to a position where US CEOs earn considerably more than other executives. In earlier decades, boards of companies were composed of firm managers, and managers from related companies. Responding to public criticism in the 1980s boards became smaller with a substantial majority of outside directors, often leaving the CEO as the only management member of the board in many companies. Englander and Kaufman ascribe the earlier technocratic views of managers to their defensive response to the regulatory battles of the New Deal, justifying their continued control over corporate assets. They see the later professional doctrines of managers as a response to the period of stagflation in the 1970s when productivity declined and managerial authority was again questioned. As a new conservatism was ushered into American society with the election of President Reagan, managers were free to pursue a narrower opportunism. At this point financial economists challenged the idea that managers acted as fiduciaries for firms, and portrayed them as self-interested agents "who used regulatory laws to sustain competitive advantage and conglomerate mergers to stabilize cash flows and secure managerial jobs." Tax reforms favored stock options over cash, and as the US stock-market rose at an unprecedented rate in the 1990s, CEOs incentive-based compensation packages delivered unprecedented wealth while the pay of other workers was held down. The balanced rhetoric of US CEOs about corporate social responsibility and meeting stakeholder claims was abandoned in this context in favor of the mantra of shareholder value maximization (without acknowledging that the CEOs themselves were becoming among the largest shareholders). While in general US CEO reward in the largest corporations remains vastly greater than that of European CEOs of similar-sized corporations, a few European CEOs are beginning to catch up with their US counterparts. The CEO of Porsche Wendelin Wiedeking is believed to have earned more than €60 million ($89 million) in 2007, ahead of Carlos Ghosn of Renault-Nissan, Alan Mullaly from Ford, Dieter Zetsche of Daimler and Sergio Marchionne of Fiat. In comparison, Ghosn's salary for 2007 was €34.49 million, according to *Automobilwoche*, and Zetsche's paycheck was €10.67 million. Mulally was paid the equivalent of €13.9 million last year and Marchionne earned just €6.91 million. Wiedeking has defended his salary, pointing to increased corporate profits and bonuses for workers and shareholders as justification for the excessive amount. Pre-tax profits for Porsche did rise nearly €4 billion from €2.1 billion to €5.9 billion over in 2007, and the car-maker took over the Volkswagen Group.

Boyer examines further the paradox of how the diffusion of stock options and financial market incentives, which are supposed to discipline managers, actually have allowed them to use their intrinsic power to massively increase their remuneration and wealth. He traces the conception of the corporation through historical stages beginning with the creation of the joint stock company in the nineteenth century, with the advent of professional management, and investors optimizing the return on their portfolios through financial markets. The managerial corporation was associated with dynamic efficiency (through eras punctuated with recession and world wars), until the 1970s, when oligopolistic conglomerates faced falling productivity. Financial liberalization and new financial markets and instruments created a new context in which corporations were pressured to concentrate on their core business, and executives were incentivized with stock options to increase their focus. This set the scene for the bubble economy of the 1990s, representing Enron as the result of the developing relations between corporate governance and financial markets. Boyer considers the discrepancy between the optimal contracting approach of agency theory which suggested that aligning executives with stock options would maximize shareholder value, when executive compensation continued to boom even when share price performance was falling. For a different explanation he turns to the analysis of entrenched managerial power of Bebchuk and Fried (2003).

Managers are able to exercise their power by leading alliances, and Boyer suggests that at different times accommodations have been reached with wage earners, and with consumers. The 1990s is typified as a time of a developing alliance between managers and a finance-led growth regime. Managers have redesigned their corporations to meet the demands of financial markets, and release windfalls for their own reward. During this period managers were under enormous pressure to deliver sustained return on equity, but when all else failed, given the discretionary power of US executives to inflate their profitability under the Generally Accepted Accounting Principles, creative accounting could provide the means to improve profits, increase the share price and exercise options. In this way US executives have allied themselves with financiers, and become detached from the wage earners they employ, in a way that would be unconscionable in Germany or Japan. The paradox of CEO performance and reward, together with the increasing involvement of CEOs of all industries with financial markets, are at the centre of the weaknesses of Anglo-American corporate governance, and yet it is precisely towards this mode of governance that European executives and corporations are increasingly drawn.

BIBLIOGRAPHY

Bebchuk, L.A. and Fried, J.M. (2003) Executive Compensation as an Agency Problem, *Journal of Economic Perspectives* 17(3): 71–92.

Bebchuk, L.A. and Fried, J.M. (2005) Pay Without Performance: Overview of the Issues, *Harvard Law School Discussion Paper* No. 528, Boston, MA: Harvard University.

Berle, A.A. and Means, G.C. (1932) *The Modern Corporation and Private Property*, New York Commerce Clearing House.

Lorsch, J.W. and MacIver, E. (1989) *Pawns or Potentates: The Reality of America's Corporate Boards*, Boston, MA: Harvard Business School Press.

Mace, M.L. (1971) *Directors: Myth and Reality*, Boston, MA: Harvard University Press.

Mizruchi, M.S. (1983) Who Controls Whom? An Examination of the Relation Between Management and Boards of Directors in Large American Corporations, *Academy of Management Review*, 8: 426–435.

Parkinson, J. (1994) *Corporate Power and Responsibility: Issues in the Theory of Company Law*, Oxford: Clarendon Press.

Pettigrew, A.M. (1992) On Studying Managerial Elites, *Strategic Management Journal*, 13: 163–182.

20 "Executive Compensation, Political Economy, and Managerial Control: The Transformation of Managerial Incentive Structures and Ideology, 1950–2000"

from SMPP Working Paper 03–01, Department of Strategic

Management and Public Policy, George Washington

University School of Business

Ernie Englander and Allen Kaufman

INTRODUCTION

Beginning in the late 1980s and the 1990s, the conflict between managers and institutional investors captured the attention of the business press.[1] These confrontations, whether over compensation, accounting and proxy rules, and board composition demonstrated the power that institutional investors had accumulated. But, by focusing on these contests, news reporters overlooked the fundamental changes that were occurring within the modern corporation's managerial hierarchies.

The same market forces (the declining dollar, international competition, deregulation, and new technologies) that undid the US manufacturing base and turned unions into enfeebled bargaining organizations aided institutional investors in their self-proclaimed campaign to discipline wayward managers.[2] In responding to the market's impersonal pressures and institutional investors' personal assaults, corporate CEOs found themselves leading a corporate bureaucratic reformation.

We say reform rather than restructure because the latter has become too connected with "downsizing."[3] Certainly, that form of restructuring did occur. However, popular press claims that managerial jobs were going to become scarce did not prove true. In 1991 and 1992 managers lost jobs at a rate higher than in other recessions (though at a rate lower than for blue collar workers).[4] As the recession receded, new white collar jobs quickly appeared, putting unemployed managers back to work. By 1994, displaced managers had the highest rate of re-employment among all occupational groups.[5]

Still, downsizing did have a lasting effect on the managerial labor market: managerial employment simply became riskier than it had been. Managers could no longer count on "life time employment" with a single firm.[6] They now had to anticipate periods of unemployment. And, those who actually got laid-off could expect substantial income loss that could not be regained once a new job came along.

Restructuring was only one part of a general transformation that occurred within the managerial community. During this period, a reformation took place in the way that managers' conceived: 1) of their fiduciary responsibilities;[7] 2) of the corporate boards' function and composition;[8] and 3) of their career path's grand payoff.[9] John Kenneth Galbraith's *The New Industrial State* and Joseph Schumpeter's *Capitalism, Socialism and Democracy* provide a vocabulary by which we can summarize the corporate changes that managers brought about in responding to market competition and institutional investor challenges: Managers transformed their technocratic norms and their firms' technocratic hierarchies into CEO proprietary ones.[10]

This concise chapter may be obscure for those unfamiliar with Galbraith's and Schumpeter's works. They are among the most important that appeared after World War Two describing the large corporation's operations and its uneasy place in U. S. democracy.[11] Galbraith and Schumpeter agreed that managers, in general, had replaced the firm's founding families as the corporate control group. But, while Galbraith argued that this power shift made for a system that could both provide jobs and stabilize democratic rule, Schumpeter had forebodings about the shift that left control in the hands of salaried employees. He feared that, without familial control, the firm would evolve into a steady-state machine, ushering in socialism and limiting human possibilities.

We borrow from Galbraith his idea of technocracy. It captures: 1) the managerial control group's bureaucratic nature; 2) its avowed neutrality in adjudicating contentious stakeholder claims; and 3) its alleged expertise in coalescing stakeholders into new-wealth creating teams.[12] Technocracy also points to the way that managers portrayed themselves as professionals who served a large social good. Their coordinating expertise, they proclaimed, ensured that the corporate sector would optimize its productive potential, generating surpluses that, when widely distributed, would ameliorate democracy's destabilizing distributional conflicts.[13]

To carry out this broad social good, managers adopted incentives that promised the most talented that they would receive large incomes and powerful positions, including corporate board membership. Top executive teams exerted control over their individual companies by claiming the right to a majority of the board seats. These executives, in turn, served on other boards to form an interlocking directorate through which managers gained a collective technocratic identity – that of a semi-public administrative

corps which oversaw the democracy's aggregated capital. Yet, neither their shared interest in sustaining corporate control nor their interlocking board network were sufficient to broach the competitive fractures. Top managers primarily considered themselves team members of a particular company and not of an intercorporate elite.[14]

Moreover, career paths, even the ones that led to the CEO, did not promise managers compensation sufficient to assemble an estate by which to found a proprietary family. Managers were, after all, corporate (estate) employees not owners. Nor, did the CEO payoff produce large compensation differentials between the CEO and senior management. If corporate boards had structured their managerial hierarchies as pyramids to proprietorship, managers would have lost their claim to neutrality among corporate stakeholders – particularly with labor.

This brings us to Schumpeter. Out of capitalism's many attributes, Schumpeter gave singular importance to the formation of a bourgeois community, comprised of families who owned substantial industrial enterprises. Schumpeter, rightly or wrongly, insisted that entrepreneurs dared all to amass an industrial fortune that would secure for him, his family and his heirs a place within this urbane society. Over time, Schumpeter tells us, family members calculated: 1) portfolio diversification a less risky affair than industrial enterprise; and 2) familial duties to be too great a constraint on individual expression. Consequently, family members sold off their shares, established liquid financial portfolios, and abdicated corporate control to salaried employees.

For Schumpeter, this transfer of power fundamentally undermined capitalism's dynamism. With no possibility of amassing a familial industrial estate, managers had little interest in risk-taking. To the contrary, they had an interest in reducing firm risk both by gaining market share and by diversifying into other industries. In the Schumpeterian imagination, managerial capitalism had divested entrepreneurial heroism from corporate culture, leaving bureaucratic meanness as the firm's motor force.[15]

Galbraith's and Schumpeter's ideological and behavioral descriptions fit corporate patterns from the1950s until the mid 1970s. As the 1970's stagflation lingered into the early 1980s and as deregulation and global competition proceeded, many had to reassess their old habits of thought and action. In seeking competitive efficiencies, managers sparked off the nation's fourth merger movement.[16] Although friendly bids accounted for nearly all of the decade's mergers, this wave was marked by the appearance of leveraged buyouts and more hostile tender offers than in previous merger waves.[17]

These came from takeover artists who scoured for firms that the market valued below replacement costs. Raiders were willing to pay shareholders a premium for control. Once in charge, raiders typically sold off the pieces at prices that, when added up, exceeded the firm's purchase price. Allied with investment bankers, institutional investors and outspoken academic theorists, these raiders squarely challenged the managerial firm as an efficient organizational form.[18] In these hostilities, institutional investors, in particular, public pension funds, had their first, but not their last, intoxicating experience in the whirlwind world of finance capital.[19]

During this fourth merger wave, managers' welfare fell relative to other high income earners. Managers' incomes rose, but not at the rate of other groups. This dislodged top corporate managers from the nation's top 1 percent of household wealth holders. Between 1983 and 1992, the number of self-employed household heads in the top wealth percentile nearly doubled, jumping from 38 to 69 percent. The increase was even greater in the top income percentile, climbing from 27 percent to 64 percent. As the self-employed gained positions within the top 1 percent of wealth holders, a shift occurred in the composition of this elite group's earnings. For these household heads, income from proprietary earnings, self-employment, partnerships and unincorporated businesses rose from 27 to 47 percent. And, the richest 1 percent of households readjusted their portfolios, substituting financial securities and pension accounts for stocks, mutual funds and trusts. Stock holdings fell from 17 to 12.1 percent, mutual funds from 6.9 to 4.6 percent; in contrast, financial securities rose from 5.7 to 9.9 percent and pensions from .9 to 3 percent.[20] While tax advantages undoubtedly explain the shift to pension funds, the buoyant buy out market most likely explains much of the increase in financial securities.

Taken together, these numbers indicate that a new group of individuals had entered Schumpeter's fabled proprietary class.[21] Who were these fortunate few? A partial answer comes when one looks at the new entrants into the top 1 percent by employment category. Among these various categories, individuals working in finance, business and business services showed the largest gain in the top 1 percent, increasing from 47 percent in 1983 to 58 percent in 1992.[22]

These numbers suggest that the new "proprietors" not only included traditional entrepreneurs but also those investment bankers and corporate attorneys who facilitated both friendly and unfriendly mergers. Moreover, proprietors' advances came at managers' expense. In 1983, professional, managerial, and administrative workers accounted for 62 percent of household heads in the top 1 percent of wealth holders. By 1992, this percentage had fallen to 29 percent.[23]

Managers, of course, refused to let their reversal of fortune continue, whether in terms of income or social standing. How, they wondered, could takeover marauders and their investors confiscate so much wealth without provoking a general public outcry? How could prominent academics, particularly in the field of corporate finance, portray managers as self-dealing bureaucrats which only takeover markets could keep in check? And, how could anyone accept the outrageous scholarly manifestos in which raiders were included among the nation's entrepreneurial assets?[24]

When we say managers, we have a particular group in mind – The Business Roundtable (BRT). Comprised of CEOs from among the nation's 200 or so largest firms, this business association speaks authoritatively for top executives within the nation's corporate sector.[25] Since its founding in 1972, the BRT has elaborated the corporate sector's collective view on broad trans-industrial issues, ranging from the budget to taxes, corporate governance to national security. Its strength derives both from its reliance on members' resources and from its lobbying status. It weakness lays in its volunteer character, in its lack of coercive power to direct membership action. Still, this qualification does not diminish the BRT's importance in identifying those salient public policy issues around which the nation's top executives mobilize corporate resources.

FROM TECHNOCRATS TO PROPRIETORS

We characterize the period from the end of World War Two to the early 1980s as technocratic and the period since as proprietary. During the technocratic period, compensation differences between CEOs and senior management were "marginal" in that they reflected their economic contributions to the firm.[26] This facilitated team cohesion among the senior managers, who, like the CEO, had membership "rights" to the board over which they, as a team, had control. Though constrained by antitrust regulations, managers shared knowhow across industries and built a corporate-wide identity through a system of interlocking directorates. While this network educated its participants in corporate-wide issues, those within it still identified first and foremost with their firm, where they spent most of their career. Finally, managers continued to conceive of their profession as one that served a larger social good. First, they accepted a legal duty of care to further the interests of the corporation as a whole. And second, they added a fiduciary duty to advance democracy.[27]

In contrast, the coalesced proprietary system has encouraged managers to think of themselves as a special class of shareholders. The extensive use of stock options to supplement their base salary has contributed heavily to this shareholder (as opposed to technocratic) managerial self-definition. This occurred as managers weighted their compensation packages with stock options to take advantage of an explosive equities market and alterations in the tax code. As "insider shareholders" who aimed merely to enhance their personal fortunes, managers turned their internal labor market into a contest for the prized CEO position. The compensation differential between the one who wins and those who lose has become substantial. Indeed, winners receive packages so large that they enter into the truly privileged sector of the very rich – the top 1 percent of the general population.[28]

Stated in this fashion, our argument falls within the well known tournament model that economists use to account for professional hierarchies and compensation schemes.[29] We merely observe that the tournament payoffs substantively changed after 1980 and continued for the next two decades. By the 1990s, payoffs were better aligned with the number of entrants, making managerial internal labor markets resemble "winner-take-all" markets.[30] In these markets, rewards are distributed by relative positions and concentrated among a few, even though marginal differences between those inside and those outside the chosen group are relatively small. Typically one thinks of sports and rock stars. However, entrepreneurs also fit into this category. Many set out to deploy a radical new innovation, but only a very few lucky ones reap the rewards. When managers modernized their firms *en masse* after the 1982 recession, they eventually imbued these bureaucratic organizations with this heroic ethos, by magnifying

the CEO payoff. In this way, managers attempted to regain economic ground and to sustain career paths that were competitive to "entrepreneurial" alternatives.

Moreover, the proprietary system placed board membership as a reward of the winner-take-all CEO package. Now the CEO alone has a guaranteed spot on the board and its accompanying wealth and prestige-enhancing intercorporate network.[31] This requires that corporate boards rely on outsiders to fill nearly all of the board positions. As this trend developed during the 1980s and 1990s, corporate boards shrank in size. Even with this decline, the demand for qualified members has not subsided, giving CEOs, both current and retired, an increasingly prominent position within the corporate board network. Among outside directors, CEOs form a substantial minority, one that shares common experiences and identity by which they can have a disproportionate effect on board deliberations. Consequently, the proprietary system has augmented the corporate-wide portion of the CEO functional portfolio. This augmentation has biased power from firm-level managerial teams to an inter-firm CEO "coterie".

Surprisingly, CEOs initially entered into this "fellowship" when they formed the Business Roundtable thirty years ago. There, they gathered as leaders of firm-level managerial teams to formulate opinions and take actions on pressing public policy issues – one of the most important being corporate governance. In these deliberations and confrontations over the decades with various corporate control challengers – federal regulators, public interest groups, investment bankers, and institutional investors – the BRT accommodated demands for board reform and implemented changes that turned managerial internal labor markets into CEO tournaments.

The newly constructed proprietary system has forced managers to discard their former professional identity. Managers' professional standard now falls under a narrow functional definition, perhaps, best captured by the business judgment rule. And, its social purpose simply imitates the one found in pre-corporate markets – namely, to make oneself rich. Gone are the managerial fiduciary obligations to the firm's contractual and noncontractual stakeholders and to the broad socio-economic goals of rising incomes for the many, of sustaining economic opportunity, and of stabilizing democratic rule. All these issues, the new managerial creed states, are better left with public policy makers than with managers.[32] Yet, even as managers have shed their commitment to serve a large social good, CEOs have constructed various organizations that allow them to effectively engage in public policy debates of this sort.

In all, four categories provide our standard for distinguishing between the technocratic and the proprietary managerial hierarchies: 1) the CEO compensation package relative to senior management; 2) the ratio of insider to outsider board directors 3) the ratio among outsider CEOs (current and retired) to non-CEOs, particularly on the board's audit, compensation and nomination committees; and 4) the substance of managers' professional creed. The first standard speaks of the payoff as compensation; the second speaks of the payoff as a guaranteed perk to be a member of the corporate interlocking directory; the third of CEO admission to a corporate-wide "oversight" group; and the fourth of the narrowing professional definition which senior managers have adopted – to serve shareholder rather than stakeholder interests.

In the remaining space of this paper, we summarize our research thus far. Because we consider the BRT the corporate sector's political "agent", its membership's compensation packages, its board composition and the interlocking links (particularly, CEO conduits) that connect these firms provide the relevant variables by which to quantitatively assess our "hypotheses". Currently, we are assembling these data. For this paper, we can only report on aggregate data that others have collected. These form the basis for conceptualizing the distinction between a technocratic and a proprietary managerial hierarchy.

Executive compensation

Two sets of studies on executive compensation, by Wilbur G. Lewellen and the Conference Board, provided the data from which we formulated our general thesis. Although these studies differ in many details, both depict a post-World War Two trend in which the ratio between CEO compensation and senior management narrows through the 1970s and then widens beginning with the economic recovery in 1983.

Over thirty years ago, Lewellen embarked on a multi-year research project in conjunction with the National Bureau of Economic Research[33] to trace the dimensions of executive pay. From this research, he published two NBER books and two follow-up articles in the *National Tax Journal*.[34] Lewellen selected the largest fifty manufacturing corporations from the *Fortune* annual survey[35] and used annual Securities Exchange Commission data. Although the 1934 securities legislation required public firms to report these data,[36] Lewellen found that full compliance did not begin until 1940. There he began his analysis which he extended until 1973.[37] From the proxy statements, he gathered compensation data – salaries and bonuses, pensions, stock options, deferred-pay agreements, and profit-sharing plans – on each firm's five highest paid executives.[38] To these data, he added his expert knowledge on tax legislation, which allowed him to compare: (a) the before-tax and after-tax total compensation for the executives in his data set; (b) the before-tax and after-tax returns for the individual components of the compensation packages; and (c) the returns between the top-paid executive and other managers.

The second data set on which we relied comes from the Conference Board, the leading not-for-profit business research organization.[39] In 1946, the Board began a series of studies on executive pay[40] that in 1983 became an annual report. For most of these studies, the Board, like Lewellen, used SEC proxy data.[41]

However, the Board's data set differs from Lewellen's in two important ways. Lewellen's data set has both before-tax and after-tax figures and a complete breakdown of the various components of the compensation packages. Until 1982, the Board's series only contains before-tax data on salaries and bonuses. (The reports do tell how many firms used non-salary and bonus compensation components). Only in 1982 did the Board include stock-based compensation in its reports.

The sampling procedure makes for the second difference. Lewellen selected the largest fifty manufacturers. The Board collected data on hundreds of companies across many industries. Instead of only following the same firms over the years of their studies, the Board reported the full results of their sample. For example, the 1946 study included 703 companies in 38 industries while the 1992 report included 644 companies in 23 industries. By including firms of various sizes and in across industries, the Board's average compensation numbers were lower than those in Lewellen's studies. For example, the 1946 Conference Board study reported that the average top executive[42] in the auto parts industry earned $54,400, while his counterpart in the steel industry earned $107,400. After combining all of these companies, the Board study reports that the average top executive earned $68,400 in 1946. The Lewellen study, which contains only the top 50 companies, reports an average before-tax salary and bonus of $136,900.[43]

Between 1956 and 1993, the Lewellen and Conference Board data sets differ in yet another way. In 1956, the Conference Board discontinued using SEC data. Instead, the Board compiled its own data through industry surveys. In 1994, the Board's annual studies once again used SEC proxy reports and reported compensation among the top five executives.[44]

For the years between 1946 and 1973, we compare Lewellen's findings on salaries and bonuses with the Board's data. After 1973, when Lewellen's studies end, we rely solely on the Conference Board reports. For consistency, we use only the Conference Board data on manufacturers. Despite their differences,[45] the two data sets provide comparable trend lines in which the difference between CEO and senior management compensation first narrows through the 1970s and then widens until today. Tables 20.5 and 20.7 provide the most recent data. In 1999, the number two manufacturing executive earned, on average, 62 percent of the CEO's pretax salary and bonus and only 57 percent of the CEO's total compensation. The next three executives earned progressively less. In other words, the average CEO earned $1.61 in salary and bonus for every $1 earned by the second-highest executive and $2.12 for every $1 earned by the third-highest paid executive.[46] Adding in the value of stock-related pay, the CEO earned $1.75 in total compensation for every $1 earned by the number two person and $2.32 for every $1 earned by the number three person. The difference between the fourth and fifth executives were proportionately lower.

Were these differences between CEOs and the next highest-paid executives in their firms consistent with the historical averages or were CEOs putting themselves apart from the rest of their management team? Table 20.1 presents Lewellen's figures. It shows that the ratios existing currently in corporate America were last seen during World War Two. But, from then on, the ratio between top executive and senior management compensation narrowed for more than quarter of a century. Although variations occurred during these years, the trend shows a clear rise in senior executive pay relative to the CEO. By 1973 (the last year in Lewellen's studies), the second highest paid executive averaged three-quarters of the top

Year	Second	Third	Fourth	Fifth
1940	61	51	44	40
1941	62	49	44	39
1942	63	51	46	39
1943	65	53	46	40
1944	64	51	46	40
1945	64	52	46	42
1946	69	57	49	46
1947	68	55	49	44
1948	68	54	49	47
1949	69	54	50	47
1950	72	56	51	47
1951	74	58	54	49
1952	74	61	54	50
1953	75	62	55	52
1954	76	62	55	52
1955	76	64	57	52
1956	75	63	56	53
1957	77	64	57	54
1958	73	61	54	51
1959	76	65	57	54
1960	75	65	57	51
1961	73	64	57	53
1962	76	67	57	52
1963	76	67	58	52
Average:				
1940–44	63	51	45	40
1945–49	68	54	49	45
1950–54	74	60	54	50
1955–59	75	63	56	53
1960–63	75	66	57	52
1964–69	77	62	56	51
1970–73	74	61	55	46

Sources: Lewellen, 1968, 1975

Table 20.1 **Executive ranking: average percentage of top executive's before-tax salary and bonus**

earner's before-tax income and the number three executive earned nearly two-thirds. Table 20.3 compares Lewellen's findings on the differences between the CEOs compensation and those of the second and third highest paid executives with the Conference Board data. Despite the differences in the sample sizes and compensation components, both data sets report comparable trends.

Table 20.2 presents the after-tax figures that Lewellen assembled. These numbers provide a more accurate picture of real purchasing power differences

Year	Second	Third	Fourth	Fifth
1940	59	49	44	40
1941	70	56	45	40
1942	72	61	55	48
1943	73	63	57	51
1944	72	59	51	47
1945	72	60	53	49
1946	76	62	57	52
1947	67	56	50	46
1948	73	60	54	51
1949	74	59	54	49
1950	69	57	50	46
1951	77	67	59	51
1952	74	63	55	49
1953	71	60	51	45
1954	71	58	51	45
1955	66	53	44	36
1956	67	53	44	38
1957	66	54	43	38
1958	68	55	42	38
1959	66	59	44	38
1960	69	57	45	40
1961	72	54	44	40
1962	65	57	46	39
1963	68	61	50	38
Average:				
1940–44	69	58	50	45
1945–49	72	59	54	49
1950–54	72	61	53	47
1955–59	67	67	43	38
1960–63	68	57	46	39
1964–69	69	54	46	40
1970–73	74	61	52	40

Sources: Lewellen, 1968, 1975

Table 20.2 **Executive ranking: average percentage of top executive's after-tax total compensation**

among top executives than before-tax figures.[47] Between the mid-1950s and late-1960s, average CEO compensation increased relative to senior management, falling as low as 65 percent in 1962. This fact seems to run contrary to our thesis that CEO and top executive salaries narrowed as the managerial thesis gained ideological weight. Lewellen himself warns against coming to this conclusion, for the after-tax differences have more to do with tax rules than with the structure of the managerial compensation structure. Table 20.10 shows that the largest portion of the next four executives' pay package, after-tax salary and bonus, increases relative to the top executives during this period. To account for these two trends – 1) an increase in CEO stock option compensation relative to senior managers, and 2) an increase in senior management after-tax salary and bonuses relative to the CEO – Lewellen argues convincingly that corporations attempted to correct for the progressive nature of marginal income tax rates by substituting non-cash pay. CEOs found themselves in higher income brackets than other managerial team members, forcing boards to award them options to ensure their after-tax earning power. This meant heavily weighing CEO pay packages with non-cash remuneration (particularly stock options) when compared with the second best paid executive.

Table 20.4 contains Lewellen's data on the average compensation components for the top three executives. This table clearly shows that the ratio between CEO and senior management compensation and the ratio between the stock option value of the CEO's total compensation package move in the same direction. Between 1955 and 1963, the number one executive received only 38 percent of his compensation from salary and bonus; but, between 1970 and 1973, his salary and bonus accounted for 55 percent. Over these two decades, the value of CEO stock options dropped by two-thirds. For the number two and three

Average (CB average sample size)	Second		Third	
	Lewellen	CB	Lewellen	CB
1960–63 (707)	75	74	66	64
1964–69 (688)	77	74	62	59
1970–73 (676)	74	74	61	58

* The Conference Board uses Median percentage
Sources: Lewellen, 1975; the Conference Board

Table 20.3 **Executive ranking: comparing Lewellen (50 firms) and the Conference Board [CB] on manufacturers' data only. Average* Percentage of top executives' before-tax salary and bonus**

	1955–63	1964–69	1970–73
Salary plus bonus as percentage of total pay			
Exec #1	38	41	55
Exec #2	50	50	57
Exec #3	56	57	59
Pension plan as percentage of total pay			
Exec #1	15	11	16
Exec #2	13	12	15
Exec #3	12	11	14
Deferred pay value as percentage of total			
Exec #1	11	14	17
Exec #2	9	11	17
Exec #3	8	9	17
Stock option value as percentage of total			
Exec #1	36	34	12
Exec #2	28	27	11
Exec #3	24	23	10

Source: Lewellen, 1975

Table 20.4 **Average composition of after-tax compensation**

executives, this change was much less dramatic. Salary and bonus for the number two executive went from a low of 50 percent between 1955 and 1963 to a high of 57 percent between 1970 and 1973. For the number three executive the percentage climbed from 56 to 59.

Lewellen offered a second, and also persuasive, reason for the increasing use of stock options during the period between 1955 and 1963. Adverse publicity on executive compensation stressed the largest and most easily understood numbers. This meant that salary and bonus, rather than stock options (which did not have to be valued) could be reduced and the other non-cash pay increased in order to deflect any negative criticisms of corporate pay.[48]

Although it would not be until the 1969 tax changes that there was a fundamental shift away from stock options, the value of the options as part of the pay packages decreased in the late 1960s. The equity markets (see Table 20.8) can help explain why this occurred. From 1955 to 1964, the Dow Jones average increased nearly 90 percent. From 1964 to 1969, it only increased by less than 10 percent. The comparable increases in the S&P were 200 percent versus 20 percent. In other words, the value of the options, themselves, rather than the number of options granted affected their after-tax value as a part of the overall

pay package. The Tax Reform Act of 1969 narrowed the differences between taxes on earned income and those on capital gains. This occurred as the stock markets continued their bearish performance begun in the mid-1960s. This gave top executives an incentive to shift the composition of their pay packages from options to salary and bonuses to see a much larger after-tax income gain.

Thus, by the end of Lewellen's study, each of these three executives roughly received the same percentage of their compensation in bonus and salary. And, over these decades, as the value of stock options fell as a portion of the CEO compensation package, the difference between CEO total compensation and the next two highest paid executives shrank. This narrowing of the CEO–senior executive compensation ratio conforms to our account of how managers built technocratic incentive systems during the first decades of the postwar period. And, the decreasing reliance on stock options for CEOs adds force to our

Year* (sample size)	Second	Third	Fourth	Fifth
1975 (712)	72	57	—	—
1977 (746)	70	56	—	—
1979 (470)	71	55	49	44
1981 (531)	70	54	47	43
1982 (510)	71	56	48	44
1983 (478)	69	54	47	42
1984 (475)	68	53	47	42
1985 (404)	68	54	48	42
1987 (254)	66	52	45	40
1988 (321)	66	50	43	39
1989 (291)	64	50	43	38
1990 (300)	64	50	43	38
1991 (284)	62	50	44	39
1992 (301)	62	50	42	38
1993 (231)	63	48	41	38
1994 (427)	62	48	43	38
1995 (418)	62	47	40	36
1996 (646)	65	49	41	36
1997 (730)	61	47	40	35
1998 (801)	63	49	41	35
1999 (821)	62	47	41	36
2000 (803)	61	47	41	36

* no 1986 data

Source: The Conference Board

Table 20.5 **Executive ranking of manufacturers. Median percentage of top executives' before-tax salary and bonus**

interpretation. For, as the management compensation took on an "egalitarian-like" character, the CEOs lost their status as a "special class" of shareholders.

However, by the early 1980s, the trends of egalitarian pay packages and the retreat from stock had both reversed. Table 20.5 presents the Conference Board figures on the before-tax ratio of CEO to senior management compensation. Beginning in 1975, the gap between CEO and senior management compensation steadily widened. In 1975, on average, the second highest paid executive received 72 percent of the top paid executive. By 2000 the percentage fell to 61. For the third highest paid executive, the percentage went from 57 to 47 between 1982 and 2000. As the absolute value of CEO compensation increased over these decades, so did the differential between the CEO and the other top executives. By 2000, the second highest paid executive dropped to 55 percent of the CEO's after-tax compensation and the number three dropped to 40 percent (Table 20.7).

Year	CEO	Second	Third
1982	85	83	79
1983	104	100	89
1984	98	91	86
1985	99	99	89

	Top five executives as a group
1987	141
1988	117
1989	123
1990	130
1991	149
1992	168
1993	173

	CEO	Top four (excluding CEO) as a group
1994	189	125
1995	254	162
1996	292	192
1997	369	249
1998	400	268
1999	646	376
2000	636	390

* Value is defined in this table as the number of shares multiplied by the market price at the time of grant

Source: The Conference Board

Table 20.6 **Median value of stock option grants***
As a percentage of salary

Year (sample size)	Second	Third	Fourth	Fifth
1997 (730)	58	46	40	35
1998 (801)	58	45	39	35
1999 (821)	57	43	37	32
2000 (803)	55	40	35	29

Source: The Conference Board

Table 20.7 **Executive ranking of manufacturers. Median percentage of CEO's total compensation: salary, bonus, stock option grants, restricted stock, and long-term performance plans**

Table 20.6 presents these figures from 1982 until 2000 – in the less than ideal format by which the Conference Board collected the data. Still, they clearly show that firms increasingly used stock options to compensate top managers.[49] Beginning in 1982, top executives received stock options worth 80 percent of their salaries.[50] By 1987 that percentage had increased to 141 percent, by 1993 to 173 percent and by 1999 to 292 percent. And, during these years, Table 20.6 shows that CEO stock options as a percentage of salary rose at a greater rate than for other senior executives. In 1983 the average CEO and the second highest paid executive both had stock options worth 99 percent of their salary. By 2000, the average CEOs had options worth 636 percent of their salary and the top four executives less than 400 percent of their salaries. Table 20.7 recounts that, on average, CEOs have earned considerably more than the other top managers. By 2000, the second highest paid executive (on average) dropped below 60 percent of the average CEO's after-tax compensation and the number three dropped to 40 percent. In short, the 1980s and 1990s witnessed a transformation in the senior executive compensation system, a transformation that turned managers into a special class of shareholders and the CEO position into a proprietary payoff.

BOARDS OF DIRECTORS

The challenge to managerial control of corporate boards predates institutional investor activism[51] and effectively began in the early 1970s.[52] This followed a series of corporate misdeeds that led public officials, public interest groups, academics, and even some corporate leaders to question the adequacy of board oversight of corporate activities. The precipitating

Year	Dow Jones industrial average	Standard & Poor's composite index	Year	Dow Jones industrial average	Standard & Poor's composite index
1949	179.48	15.23	1976	974.92	102.01
1950	216.31	18.40	1977	894.63	98.20
1951	257.64	22.34	1978	820.23	96.02
1952	270.76	24.50	1979	844.40	103.01
1953	275.97	24.73	1980	891.41	118.78
1954	333.94	29.69	1981	932.92	128.05
1955	442.72	40.49	1982	884.36	119.71
1956	493.01	46.62	1983	1,190.34	160.41
1957	475.71	44.38	1984	1,178.48	160.46
1958	491.66	46.24	1985	1,328.23	186.84
1959	632.12	57.38	1986	1,792.76	236.34
1960	618.04	55.85	1987	2,275.99	286.83
1961	691.55	66.27	1988	2,060.82	265.79
1962	639.76	62.38	1989	2,508.91	322.84
1963	714.81	69.87	1990	2,678.94	334.59
1964	834.05	81.37	1991	2,929.33	376.18
1965	910.88	88.17	1992	3,284.29	415.74
1966	783.60	85.26	1993	3,522.06	451.41
1967	879.12	91.93	1994	3,793.77	460.42
1968	906.00	98.70	1995	4,493.76	541.72
1969	876.72	97.84	1996	5,742.89	670.50
1970	753.19	83.22	1997	7,441.15	873.43
1971	884.76	98.29	1998	8,625.52	1,085.50
1972	950.71	109.20	1999	10,464.88	1,327.33
1973	923.88	107.43	2000	10,734.90	1,427.22
1974	759.37	82.85	2001	10,189.13	1,194.18
1975	802.49	86.16			

* Averages of daily closing prices

Source: *Economic Report of the President*, 2002

Table 20.8 **Common stock prices***

events included the collapse and bankruptcy of the Penn Central Railroad in 1970, the illegal campaign contributions to the 1972 Nixon re-election campaign, and overseas payoffs scandals eventually leading to passage of the 1977 Foreign Corrupt Practices Act.

During the technocratic period, corporate boards, particularly in manufacturing industries, were dominated by management. Even though there were nominal "outsiders" on these boards, many of them represented firms which had "business connections" with the corporations on whose boards they sat.[53] Boards ranged in size from a handful of directors at small companies to well into the twenties in others,

particularly in banks. The size of the corporation (as measured by sales) influenced the size of the board with larger firms averaging nearly one-third more members (see Table 20.11). In the 1970s, boards of larger firms were averaging 15 members with six or seven managers serving on the board.[54]

Conference Board surveys during this time indicated the predominance of outsiders on boards (Table 20.14). However, the surveys did not take into consideration the former insiders still on the board and "grey" directors who had business dealings with the companies on which they served. One important trend in the make-up of boards first appeared in the 1970s when a large number of corporate presidents

Year	Both ISOs and Only Incentive		Only Nonqualified
	Nonqualified	Stock Options (ISOs)	
1981	45	26	29
1982	67	16	17
1983	57	26	17
1984	58	24	19
1985	58	21	21
1987	33	8	59
1988	26	14	61
1989	24	10	66
1990	28	3	69
1991	28	7	65

Source: The Conference Board

Table 20.9 **Stock option grants by type. Percentage of manufacturers**

Year Average	Second	Third	Fourth	Fifth
1940–44	73	63	59	53
1945–49	77	67	62	59
1950–54	81	70	64	61
1955–59	83	73	67	64
1960–63	83	75	67	63

Source: Lewellen, 1968

Table 20.10 **Executive ranking. Average percentage of top executives' after-tax salary and bonus**

Year	Sample size	All firms	Largest firms (number)
1958	638	11	14 (105)
1961	592	11	14 (130)
1966	456	11	14 (153)
1973	511	11	15 (137)

Source: The Conference Board

Table 20.11 **Average board size in manufacturing companies**

and board chairmen took their place on boards as the largest class of outside directors (see Table 20.13).

In response to the scandals and to the challenges, the Business Roundtable initiated discussions on corporate governance.[55] By 1978, the Roundtable issued a statement on its view of the role and composition of the corporate board.[56] While rejecting most of the criticisms and the calls for wholesale changes, it gave a qualified endorsement to the proposition that the majority of board members should be non-management directors.

By 1980, a majority of large corporate boards were made up of directors who were independent of management, i.e., without any past or current business ties, directors.[57] A report sponsored by the Business Roundtable in 1982 stressed that business leaders still advocated that top corporate officers should not only attend board meetings, but "serve as full members and acquire board experience as potential candidates for promotion to the office of chief executive."[58] As seen in Tables 20.15a and b and 20.16, during the 1980s, the large corporate boards and the number of insiders were shrinking among big firms.[59] By the early 1990s, the boards were averaging 14 members with only three insiders.[60] (Although another study of *Fortune* 1000 firms placed the average at 12 with three insiders.)

These trends continued through the end of the 1990s and were endorsed by the Business Roundtable. In a 1997 "Statement," the Roundtable concluded that smaller boards are "more cohesive and work more effectively" than larger ones. The Roundtable also called for a "substantial majority" of directors to be independent of management.[61] In 1998, Spencer Stuart found an average of 12 board members with three insiders from proxy data of the S&P 500. Korn/Ferry found an average of 11 directors with two outsiders. In their 2001–2002 survey, the National Association of Corporate Directors found an average of eight directors and three insiders.

The CEO has become the only management member of the board in many companies,[62] particularly in manufacturing. In many others, particularly in

Year	Sample size	All firms		Largest firms	
		Insiders	Outsiders	Insiders	Outsiders
1958	638	46	54	50	50
1961	592	44	56	48	52
1966	456	42	58	42	58
1973	505	49	51	—	—

Source: The Conference Board

Table 20.12 **Average board composition in manufacturing companies**

Year	Number companies	Number directors	Bankers	Attorneys	Corporate presidents	Corporate chairmen
1958	431	2466	17%	13%	13%	5%
1961[reported same data as 1958]						
1966	436	2859	15%	11%	12%	7%
1973	508	2692	[not listed]	3%	28%	22%

Source: The Conference Board

Table 20.13 **Principal occupations of outside directors in manufacturing companies**

Year	Sample size	Percentage
1953	—	54
1958	431	57
1961	592	61
1966	456	63
1973	511	71
1989	268	86

Source: The Conference Board

Table 20.14 **Percentage of manufacturing companies with majority of outside directors (former employees counted as insiders)**

Year	Outsider/ insider ratio	Firms with CEO as only insider	Firms with two insiders
1982	2/1	—	—
1987	2.5/1	3	—
1988	2/1	5	—
1991	—	9	—
1992	3/1	11	—
1993	3.5/1	14	—
1995	—	15	32

Source: Spencer Stuart

Table 20.16 **Outsider/insider ratio in 100 large corporations**

Total board membership	1982	1987	1992
more than 20	12	6	2
16-19	39	32	22
13-15	32	38	44
less than 12	17	24	32

Table 20.15a **Size of corporate boards in 100 large corporations**

Total board membership	1983	1988	1993	1998
more than 19	—	12	4	—
15–18	—	37	31	—
12–14	—	43	42	—
less than 11	—	8	22	—
Average	16	15	14	13

Source: Spencer Stuart

Table 20.15b **Size of corporate boards in 100 large corporations**

the service industry, the CEO is only accompanied by one other manager[63] (see Table 20.16).

Although most all large companies have created official nominating committees on their boards, the anecdotal and available empirical evidence suggests that CEOs still dominate the process of identifying, nominating, and choosing new members as they did in the technocratic era.[64] In this proprietorship era in which fewer and fewer directors are chosen, the CEO can wield even more influence in bringing a selected manager to the board with him and a selected group of CEOs to serve with him.

CONCLUDING REMARKS

These data on executive compensation and corporate board composition certainly make a case for our general thesis. But, what of managers themselves? Did they first fashion a technocratic creed and then adopt a proprietary one? Yes, they did. A brief summary of this transfiguration brings this paper to its conclusion.

During the regulatory battles that the New Deal provoked, managers honed a fiduciary argument to justify their collective control over corporate assets. These ideas gained credence through business magazines, in particular, Fortune, and educational institutions, the most important being the Harvard Business School.[65] In the early post-WWII period, scholars surveying business attitudes found a divergence between those who managed the large firm and those who managed small and medium size companies.[66] Where the former saw imperfect markets and fiduciary responsibilities to corporate dependants, the latter repeated free market rhetoric, which denied differential bargaining power.

Managers did not formally explicate their "professional doctrine" until the 1970s when social regulatory battles and stagflation had put managerial authority into doubt.[67] As productivity rates declined and incomes stagnated, critics argued that managers had proven themselves incompetent stewards of the nation's productive capabilities. Managers retorted by blaming excess government spending and onerous regulations for the economic malaise.

To reverse these circumstances, the corporate sector took overt political action that rivaled its mobilization against the Second New Deal. Corporate boards began to write firm-specific ethical codes designed to internalize negative externalities and minimize social regulation. And, corporations rapidly assembled political action committees that, in the 1980 election, played an important role in bringing President Reagan to the White House, a Republican majority in the Senate, and Republican gains in the House. In this electoral earthquake, liberal fiscal policy crumbled. The polity replaced it with a conservative policy that emphasized tax cuts over social welfare spending.

First, through the Committee for Economic Development (CED) and, then, through the Business Roundtable (BRT), managers collectively crafted a professional standard that addressed their responsibilities to corporate stakeholders and their pivotal place in preserving democracy in the United States.[68]

The BRT played a vanguard role in the corporate sector's political revival. Unlike the CED, the BRT acted as a lobbying organization. Comprised of CEOs from, eventually, the nation's 200 largest firms, the BRT's political clout was first felt under the Carter administration, when the Roundtable made important contributions in stopping consumer protection and labor reform.[69]

The CED and the BRT began their justification for managerial corporate control by specifying the corporate control group's fiduciary obligations. While some maintained that the control group acted solely as the shareholder's agent, these business associations dissented, arguing that the control group acted on behalf of corporate stakeholders. Unlike other control groups, the CED and the BRT asserted that managers possessed special expertise in facilitating and negotiating contracts among the firm's stakeholders. By aligning these various constituents' interests with the firm's new wealth creation objective, managers could build the teams needed to develop and introduce new wealth-enhancing practices and technologies. By raising productivity, managers improved the income for their immediate constituents and for society as a whole. By acting in accordance with these professional standards, managers effectively served as corporate fiduciaries in administering the nation's productive resources.

Managers extended these economic arguments into political ones. As corporate trustees, managers asserted that they preserved decentralized, private negotiations even in concentrated industries. These negotiations might occur within a regulatory setting, but managers emphasized that the corporate bargaining process still remained a private one among the firm's stakeholders. Managers admitted that they jealously guarded their position and the process's private character by sustaining goodwill among corporate contractual stakeholders and by engaging in political activities. For managers, these actions limited the federal government's oppressive reach and redrew the bright line between private and public authorities that the modern corporation had erased.

At the same time, managers calmed fears about their ability to undermine majoritarian rule. Critics warned that managers' control over concentrated assets and their small numbers made it likely that managers would cooperate to set political agendas. Managers responded by noting that market competition incessantly splintered them into competing factions on specific economic issues. Moreover, managers' professional responsibilities forced them to sustain a pragmatic as opposed to partisan or ideological political outlook. This pragmatism kept managers focused narrowly on public policies that affected market conditions.[70] On the rare occasions that managers rallied together – as when they acted in 1980 to stymie excessive government spending – their action would trigger labor and its allies as a counterbalancing force.

As they enhanced productivity and living standards, managers mitigated the distributional conflicts that endanger democracy's stability. Such promises put managers under public scrutiny. If managers failed to improve productivity and their firms' values, the financial (takeover) markets would respond appropriately. If these productivity gains did not improve general living conditions, then, managers' broken promises would incite public action to limit managerial prerogatives and to readjust income disparities.

In all, managers reasoned that they politically coalesced on those infrequent occasions when public authority directly challenged their control position. In doing so, managers helped sustain the public–private distinction so important to a liberal polity. At the same time, managers contended that they fragmented on most economic issues, rendering their political advantages ineffectual in a bid to set the political agenda. For these reasons, managers proclaimed themselves liberty's steward.[71]

Even as managers fully articulated their professional doctrine during the 1970s and 1980s, economists and financial agency theorists honed arguments that markets had matured sufficiently to make regulatory agencies and managers' stakeholder fiduciary duty obsolete. These scholars: 1) portrayed the relationship between managers and corporate stakeholders as mutually "dependent;" 2) found that managerial professional norms did not sufficiently restrain managerial "opportunism;" and 3) developed market-based regulatory procedures to address negative externalities and managerial opportunism.[72]

These arguments gained ground as the US economy fell into stagflation doldrums. The de-regulatory movement that gained credibility during the 1970s and the takeover movement of the 1980s challenged the notion that managers acted as fiduciaries both for their firms' stakeholders and society as a whole.73 Instead, these literatures portrayed managers as self-serving agents who used regulatory laws to sustain competitive advantage and conglomerate mergers to stabilize cash flows and secure managerial jobs.

During this period, financial institutions, in particular, public pension funds, re-aggregated shares and improved shareholders' bargaining position.[74] As the funds' managers gained negotiating savvy with corporate managers – first through corporate takeovers and then through corporate governance procedures – a few even asserted that shareholders have regained effective control over the large firm, weakening the need for fiduciary standards.[75]

Financial agency theorists found these developments socially beneficial for they reduced shareholder costs in overseeing managers.[76] Together, these structural changes and analytic refinements provided evidence that managers have no extraordinary market power and no need for a professional creed to temper their discretionary authority. But, managers still needed strong boards to monitor them.

During the 1980s, managers actively lobbied for anti-takeover legislation. Although they were successful among state governments, managers encountered well-organized resistance in Congress. Legislatures interpreted managers' continued poor performance in increasing productivity and reviving stagnant wages as evidence of their misuse of corporate resources. Battered from this experience, managers regrouped over the next several years. As they deliberated, tax reform that favored stock options over salary spurred managers to reconfigure their compensation packages. Fortune favored managers by pushing the stock market up at an unprecedented rate and with it their incentive-based compensation packages.[77]

These circumstances persuaded managers to revise their fiduciary doctrine of corporate social responsibility.[78] Where managers once spoke about their discretionary powers, they now speak of market constraints; where they once spoke about balancing stakeholder claims, they now speak about shareholder wealth maximization; where they once spoke about their responsibility to enhance productivity and improve living standards, they now only consider productivity to be their responsibility, leaving issues of income disparity to others. And, where managers once considered themselves members of a profession that served a large social good, they now think of themselves as technocrats employed to maximize shareholder wealth. These changes put corporate ethical codes into doubt, for they rested on stakeholder presuppositions.

S
I
X

OUR IMMEDIATE RESEARCH AGENDA

For presentation purposes, we focused on a quantitative review of data to support our chapter on the new proprietary class. As we noted, we are in the process of collecting data from proxy materials on many of the companies and their executives who are in policy-making positions on the Business Roundtable. Instead, for this paper we used published, aggregate data. As a second part of this paper, which we are not presenting here, we are including an abridged narrative which summarizes applicable parts to the current story of a much broader work we are undertaking.

The condensed narrative consists of four discrete parts. The first recounts the national debates over corporate takeovers, for managers there restated their stakeholder ideology and warned of the coming battle against institutional investors. The second concerns engagements to alter SEC shareholder communication rules. Its importance becomes obvious when one understands that these had prevented institutional investors from communicating with one another over proxy matters and, so, in acting collectively during governance disputes. Here conventional wisdom has portrayed institutional investors as the winners. But, close analysis shows this not completely to be the case, that the regulatory system still favors managers as the corporate control group and that the BRT had some influence in bringing about this "favorable" outcome. The third tells of how tax policies and market circumstances have shaped managerial compensation decisions. When these factors are considered, the shift from cash compensation to stock option looks less like a mechanism for aligning managers' interests to shareholders' and more like an managerial maneuver to maximize personal wealth. Finally, we trace out the debates over corporate governance reform that, for our purposes, actually began after the Penn Central and Watergate crises. These sparked concerted and enduring discussions on the board's responsibilities and the structure that would best ensure these ends. Here, the BRT played an important role in meeting criticisms, in outlining alternatives and in instituting changes – long before activist institutional investors garnered wide publicity.

NOTES

1   See, e.g., *Business Week*, "The Battle for Corporate Control," May 18, 1987, pp. 102–109; *Directors & Boards*, "Corporate Control in the 1990s: Institutional Ownership, Activism, and Design on the Board," Fall 1988, pp. 43–45; Nancy J. Perry, "Who Runs Your Company Anyway?," *Fortune*, September 12, 1988, pp. 140–146; Alan Farnham, "The Trust Gap," *Fortune*, December 4, 1989, pp. 56–75; Thomas A. Stewart, "The King is Dead: Why more boards are waking up and pushing out the CEO," *Fortune*, January 1, 1993, pp. 34–40.

2   See, Frank Levy, *The New Dollars and Dreams: American Incomes and Economic Change* (New York: The Russell Sage Foundation, 1998); Gordon L. Clark, *Pensions and Corporate Restructuring in American Industry* (Baltimore: Johns Hopkins Press,1993); Jefferson Cowie, *Capital Moves: RCA's 70-Year Quest for Cheap Labor* (Ithaca, NY: Cornell University Press, 1999); Margaret M. Blair and Thomas A. Kochan, editors, *The New Relationship: Human Capital in the American Corporation* (Washington, DC: Brookings Institution Press, 2000); Margaret M. Blair and Mark J. Roe, *Employees and Corporate Governance* (Washington, DC: Brookings Institution Press, 1999); and Mary A. O'Sullivan, *Contests for Corporate Control: Corporate Governance and Economic Performance in the United States and Germany* (Oxford: Oxford University Press, 2000).

3   See, Gordon Donaldson, *Corporate Restructuring: Managing the Change Process from Within* (Boston: Harvard Business School Press, 1994); Robert M. Tomasko, *DOWNSIZING: Reshaping the Corporation for the Future*, (New York: American Management Association, 1987); "Special Issue on 'Corporate Restructuring'," *Strategic Management Journal*, Summer 1993; Jeffrey K. Liker, ed., *Becoming Lean: Inside Stories of U. S. Manufacturers* (Oregon: Productivity Press, 1998); Robin Cooper and Regine Slagmulder, *Supply Chain Development for the Lean Enterprise: Interorganizational Cost Management* (Oregon: Productivity Press, 1999); Bennett Harrison, *Lean and Mean: The Changing Industrial Landscape of Corporate Power in the Age of Flexibility* (New York: Basic Books, 1994).

4   *The New York Times* published a series of articles on downsizing's effect on the managerial labor market in March 1996 and then published as a book. See, The New York Times, *The Downsizing of America*, (New York: Times Books, 1996).

5   David M. Gordon, *Fat and Mean: The Corporate Squeeze of Working Americans and the Myth of "Managerial Downsizing"* (New York: Free Press, 1996), pp. 56–58. And, see Sanford M. Jacoby, "Kenneth M. Piper Lectures: Melting Into Air? Downsizing, Job Stability and the Future of Work," *Chicago-Kent Law Review* (2000) 76:1195–1234. The classification of managers in the Bureau of Labor Statistics is "Managerial and Professional Speciality Occupations," so there is no firm fix of data for managers only. But the numbers and percentage changes are still revealing. From 1987–1989, the number of jobs in this category increased by an average of 4.6 percent per year. From 1990 to 1992, they increased by an average of 0.75 percent per year. From 1993 to 1995, they increased by an average of 4.3 percent per year. In real numbers, there were 27,742 managers in 1987, 30,398 in 1989, and 31,085 in 1992. By 1995 there were

35,318, by 1998 there were 38, 937, and by January 2002 there were 41,564. Bureau of Labor Statistics Data, Series ID #LFU1125 at http://stats.bls.gov.

6 Paul Osterman, editor, *Broker Ladders: Managerial Careers in the New Economy* (New York: Oxford University Press, 1996); Charles Heckscher, *White-Collar Blues: Management Loyalties in an Age of Corporate Restructuring* (New York: Basic Books, 1995); Jacoby, "Melting Into Air?"

7 The Business Roundtable, "Statement on Corporate Governance," September 1997.

8 See, e.g., John Pound," Beyond Takeovers: Politics Comes to Corporate Control," *Harvard Business Review* (March/April 1992) 70: 83–95.

9 See, Lucian Arye Bebchuk, Jesse M. Fried, and David I. Walker, "Executive Compensation in America: Optimal Contracting or Extraction of Rents?," Harvard Olin Center for Law, Economics, and Business, Discussion Paper No. 339, 2001.

10 John Kenneth Galbraith, *The New Industrial State* (Boston: Houghton Mifflin, 1967), and Joseph A. Schumpeter, *Capitalism, Socialism and Democracy*, 3d ed. (New York: Harper & Row, 1950) at pp. 111–165.

11 The debate over the managerial firm first took on its modern shape during the 1920s. In the post-war period, many had reconciled the managerial firm with democracy's need. Those, like Galbraith, who advocated the "managerial thesis" viewed managers' interest to secure their positions by passing up risky ventures, by obtaining market share through mergers and by reducing market risk through conglomeration served the nation's interest in steady job creation and in business cycle moderation. See for example, Robin Marris, *The Economic Theory of Managerial Capitalism* (Great Britain: The Free Press of Glencoe, 1964); Marris, "Galbraith, Solow and the Truth About Corporations," *Public Interest* (1968) 11:37–46. Williamson. For a contrary position see James Burnham, *The Managerial Revolution: What is Happening in the World* (New York: John Day, 1941). For an overview see Allen Kaufman, Lawrence Zacharias and Marvin Karson, *Owners vs. Managers: The Struggle for Corporate Control in American Democracy* (New York: Oxford University Press, 1995), pp. 63–68; and Loren J. Okroi, Galbraith, *Harrington, Heilbroner: Economics and Dissent in an Age of Optimism* (Princeton, NJ: Princeton University Press, 1988).

12 See, John Kenneth Galbraith, *The New Industrial State* (Boston, MA: Houghton-Mifflin, 1971).

13 See, Francis X. Sutton, *The American Business Creed* (Cambridge: Harvard University Press, 1956); Committee for Economic Development, *Business and Social Progress: Views of Two Generations of Executives* (New York: Praeger, 1970); Committee for Economic Responsibility, *Social Responsibilities of Business Corporations: A Statement on National Policy by the Research and Policy Committee of the Committee of Economic Development* (New York: Committee for Economic Development, 1971); Francis W. Steckman, *Corporate Performance: The Key to Public Trust* (New York: McGraw-Hill, 1982); Allen Kaufman and Lawrence Zacharias, "From Trust to Contract: The

Legal Language of Managerial Ideology, 1920–1980," *Business History Review* (1992) 66: 547–549.

14 See, Edward, Herman, *Corporate Control, Corporate Power* (Cambridge: Cambridge University Press, 1981).

15 Schumpeter, *Capitalism*, pp. 111–165.

16 Jonathon Barron Baskin and Paul J. Miranti, Jr. *A History of Corporate Finance* (Cambridge: Cambridge University Press, 1997), pp. 285–302.

17 From 1982 to 1989 there was a yearly average of 2423 merger and acquisition (M&A) announcements and an average of 37 contested tender offers among those. In other words, a yearly average of one and half percent of the M&A announcements were hostile. George P. Baker and George David Smith, *The New Financial Capitalists: Kohlberg Kravis Roberts and the Creation of Corporate Value*, (Cambridge: Cambridge University Press, 1998), pp. 21–25.

18 See, Allen Kaufman and Ernie Englander, "Kohlberg Kravis Roberts & Co. and the Restructuring of American Capitalism," *Business History Review* (1993) 67: 52–97; Baker and Smith, *New Financial Capitalists*.

19 For a historical explanation for the absence of institutional investor activism prior to this period see, Mark J. Roe, *Strong Managers, Weak Owners: The Political Roots of American Corporate Finance*, (Princeton, NJ: Princeton University Press, 1994).

20 Edward N. Wolff, "Who Are the Rich? A Demographic Profile of High-Income and High-Wealth Americans, in Joel B. Slemrod, ed. *Does Atlas Shrug? The Economic Consequences of Taxing the Rich* (Cambridge, MA: Harvard University Press, 2000), p. 86.

21 Our argument on how managers refashioned their "culture" from a technocratic to a proprietary one could easily put us into that tired debate over whether a small number of families, based in property (equity) holdings and social connections, can exert control over a significant portion of the corporate sector. Certainly, the aggregation of corporation wealth has allowed a few families to become extraordinarily rich, to have the means for transmitting this wealth from one generation to the next, and to develop intricate social organizations both within the corporate sector and outside of it. And, the market's dynamic character (as the 1980s indicate) has supplied entrepreneurs the opportunities for deploying new technologies that establish new industrial estates and familial wealth. Whether this group constitutes a ruling class or faction within the power elite is irrelevant for our argument. So, too, is uncovering the mechanism by which one gets admitted to this class or elite faction – presuming that such a cohesive group even exists. We are not concerned with how much wealth it requires for inclusion. What manners does one need to master for social acceptance? Who sets the initiation fee? Or, who controls the social register?

22 Wolff, "Who Are the Rich?" pp. 109–110.

23 Wolff, "Who Are the Rich?" p. 86.

24 See the testimony of Andrew Sigler, CEO of Champion International and chair of the Business Roundtable Task Force on Corporate Governance US Senate, Committee on Banking, Housing, and Urban Affairs, Subcommittee on Securities, *The Impact of Institutional Investors on*

Corporate Governance, Takeovers, and the Capital Markets, 101st Cong., 1st Sess., October 3, 1989.

25 For a description of the BRT's formation and its activities see, Sar A. Levitan and Martha R. Cooper, *Business Lobbies: The Public Good and the Bottom Line* (Baltimore: Johns Hopkins University Press, 1984), particularly, pp. 34–40; Kaufman, Zacharias, and Karson, *Managers vs. Owners*, pp. 133–135; Michael Useem, *The Inner Circle: Large Corporations and The Rise of Business Political Activity in the US and UK* (New York: Oxford University Press, 1984); Kim McQuaid, *Big Business and Presidential Power: From FDR to Reagan*, (NY: William Morrow and Co., 1982), pp. 284–326; Mark Green and Andrew Buchsbaum, *Corporate Lobbies: Political Profiles of the Business Roundtable and the Chamber of Commerce* (Washington, D.C.: Public Citizen, 1980); Tim Smart, "Knights of the Roundtable: Tracking Big Business' Agenda in Washington," *Business Week*, October 21, 1988, pp.39–44; Kenneth R. Andrews, "The Roundtable statement on boards of directors," *Harvard Business Review* (September/October 1978) 56: 24–38.

26 We use marginal to indicate that the firm administered an internal labor market. Where managers received a "marginal wage" comparable to one that they would receive on a managerial spot market. Here education, years of service, age all affected pay differentials among managers. See, Michael L. Bognanno, "Corporate Tournaments", *Journal of Labor Economics (2001)* 19:290–315.

27 See, Sutton, *The American Business Creed*.

28 See, Edward N. Wolff, *Top Heavy: A Study of Increasing Inequality of Wealth in America* (New York: Twentieth Century Fund, 1995); Wolff, "Recent Trends in Wealth Ownership, 1983-1998," Working Paper No. 300, Jerome Levy Economics Institute, April 2000; Lisa A. Keister, *Wealth in America: Trends in Wealth Inequality* (Cambridge: Cambridge University Press, 2000); and Joel B. Slemrod, editor, *Does Atlas Shrug? The Economic Consequences of Taxing the Rich* (New York: Russell Sage Foundation and Cambridge: Harvard University Press, 2000).

29 See, Bognanno, "Corporate Tournaments;" Richard A. Lambert, David Larcker, and Keith Weigelt, "The Structure of Organizational Incentives," *Administrative Science Quarterly* (1993) 38: 438–461; Martin Conyon, Simon I. Peck, and Graham V. Sadler, Corporate Tournaments and Executive Compensation: Evidence from the UK," *Strategic Management Journal*, (2001) 22: 805–815; Tor Eriksson, "Executive Compensation and Tournament Theory: Empirical Tests on Danish Data," *Journal of Labor Economics* (1999) 17: 262–280; and Canice Prendergast, "The Provision of Incentives in Firms," *Journal of Economic Literature* (March 1999) 37: 7–63. For an application to another profession, see Marc Galanter and Thomas Palay, *Tournament of Lawyers: The Transformation of the Big Law Firm* (Chicago: Chicago University Press, 1991.

30 Bognanno, "Corporate Tournaments" found that his sample of 600 firms between 1981 and 1988 did not offer prizes predicated by a tournament model, even though the process closely resembled the model in other

ways. Our figures suggest that had Bognanno's study extended into the 90s, his results might approximate the model. On "winner take all" markets see, Robert H. Frank and Phillip J. Cook, *The Winner-Take-All Society: Why Few at the Top Get So Much More Than the Rest of Us* (New York: Penguin, 1996). For one of the few studies that applied the tournament model to CEOs, see J. Benjamin Forbes and James E. Piercy, *Corporate Mobility and Paths to the Top* (New York: Quorum Books, 1991).

31 Interlocking directorates has long been a subject of controversy, dating back to the Pujo Hearings in 1912. From the 1970s on, scholars debated whether these networks shaped a control group that spanned the corporate sector. Some banks filled this role because they were hubs for the interlocking directorate, and they allegedly provided much needed commercial financing. The most recent work shows that banks' centrality has diminished and that banks formerly served as a disciplinary force when firms went into distress. See, Gerald F. Davis and Mark S. Mizruchi, "The Money Center Cannot Hold: Commercial Banks in the U. S. System of Corporate Governance", *Administrative Science Quarterly* (1999) 44: 215–239. Also, see Beth Mintz and Michael Schwartz, *The Power of American Business* (Chicago: University of Chicago Press, 1985) and Herman, *Corporate Control*.

32 See, Michael C. Jensen, "Value Maximization, Stakeholder Theory, and the Corporate Objective Function, *Business Ethics Quarterly*, forthcoming and Allen Kaufman, "Managers' Double Fiduciary Duty: to Stakeholders and to Freedom," *Business Ethics Quarterly*, forthcoming.

33 NBER sponsored this work as part of its study on the relationship between federal tax structure and economic growth and, in particular for this study, on the relationship between tax policies on personal income and individual work effort.

34 *Executive Compensation in Large Industrial Corporations*, New York: Columbia University Press, 1968; *The Ownership Income of Management*, New York: Columbia University Press, 1971; "Managerial Pay and the Tax Changes of the 1960s, *National Tax Journal* (June 1972) 35: and "Recent Evidence on Senior Executive Pay," *National Tax Journal* (1975) 37: 159–172.

35 The companies' rankings would change over time and there were mergers, as well, so he went below the actual top 50 to keep the same companies in his profile. For his 1971 work, he supplemented the manufacturing sample with a selection of fifteen of the largest retail stores and sixteen small manufacturers. The retail sample of firms represented about six percent of retail sales in 1963 compared to the manufacturing sample which represented nearly one-fourth of industry sales. In his later articles covering the period from 1963 to 1973, he only presented data on the large manufacturers.

36 Congress directed the Federal Trade Commission, empowered to regulate the stock market under the 1933 Securities Act, to conduct the study on executive pay in 1934. See, United States Federal Trade Commission, *Report of the Federal Trade Commission on Compensation of Officers and Directors of Certain Corporations*, 15

volumes, Washington, D.C., mimeographed, 1934. Upon its release, *The New York Times* front page, all-caps headline read, "PAY AND BONUSES OF BUSINESS HEADS LISTED FOR SENATE," February 27, 1934. On the legislative debates regarding the reporting requirements specified under the 1934 Act, see Joel Seligman, *The Transformation of Wall Street: A History of the Securities and Exchange Commission and Modern Corporate Finance*, Boston: Houghton Mifflin, 1982, pp. 86–100.

37 His original work covered the period until 1969. His 1975 article extended the data set to include compensation through 1973.

38 See Lewellen, *Executive Compensation*, p. 7–8.

39 It was named The National Industrial Conference Board, Inc. when it started publishing its reports on executive pay.

40 Their initial report was, The National Industrial Conference Board, Inc., *Studies in Business Policy, No. 13*, "Compensation of Executives," New York, 1946. Motivating this work were the continuing controversies over executive pay since the 1930s. The intent of the research was to provide:

facts in hand [to] those responsible for determining executive compensation [in order to] have at least rough guides [to] comparability and "reasonableness," even though they will obviously not have the answer to the question of the exact amount that should be paid any single executive. p.3.

The first study on executive pay to be completed after the securities legislation mandated corporations to report information to the government was done under the aegis of the Harvard Business School. See John Calhoun Baker, *Executive Salaries and Bonus Plans*, New York: McGraw-Hill, 1938. Baker opened his book with a similar reference to the, then, current debate on the size of executive compensation:

How much are executives paid and how do these payments vary among companies and industries? Does executive compensation fluctuate with sales and earnings? Does the distribution of stock ownership affect executive compensation and earnings? Should data on payments to executives be published? Can current payments to executives be justified?

To summarize, this disclosure of compensation data, properly analyzed, should not only reveal answers to the above questions but should also (a) cast light on the theory of profits, (b) permit an explanation of the practices followed by corporations in paying executives, (c) allow an appraisal of the fairness of such policies, and (d) furnish information of importance to the courts and other public bodies. p.3

41 It supplemented proxy data with other reports filed with the SEC and with income tax returns released by the Treasury Department. Lewellen also used supplemental government data in his work.

42 In the early years covered in this paper, the highest-paid executive generally held the title of "president." It would be many years before "CEO" became the regular title. This is why we use "highest-paid" executive in most instances until the modern era.

43 The studies show that the wealthiest executives have the ability to alter the make-up of their compensation packages to best maximize their long-term returns and increase the differential between their and their immediate subordinates' income. Including the lower paid top executives will most likely reduce the variation among packages and the differentials.

44 Although for three years they reported compensation for the four executives (not including the CEO) as a group rather than individually.

45 For the difficulties in gathering compensation data and then testing hypotheses about managerial behavior relating to compensation, see David H. Ciscel and Thomas M. Carroll, "The Determinants of Executive Salaries: An Econometric Survey," *The Review of Economics and Statistics*, (1980) 62: 7–13.

46 In 1999, CEOs in the United States earned more than twice as much as CEOs in all industrialized countries and one hundred times what the average US worker earned. Lawrence Mishel, Jared Bernstein, and John Schmitt, *The State of Working America 2000–2001* (Ithaca: Cornell University Press, 2001), pp. 208–212.

47 Yet the Conference Board always reported before-tax compensation and was doing so to provide "guidelines" for companies to compare their compensation patterns with others of like size and industry. In fact, most all of the public reporting of executive compensation is done using before-tax figures.

48 Lewellen, *Executive Compensation*, pp. 211–226.

49 This was also supplemented by other forms of stock-related pay such as stock appreciation rights (SARs) and restricted stock. SARs allowed executives to receive the increased value of share prices without having to purchase the stock as they must with stock option grants. Restricted stock is awarded to an executive at no cost to the executive. The shares earn dividends, but cannot be sold until the restriction lapses at which time they become common shares.

50 We did see evidence that stock options were returning to compensation packages even while the equities market was languishing. See "The Year Stock Options Came Back," *Business Week*, May 19, 1976, p. 117; "Executive Stock Options on the Comeback Trail," *Business Week*, May 17, 1976, p. 133; "A Year for Stock Options and Bonuses," *Business Week*, May 23, 1977, p. 48.

51 See, Michael Useem, *Investor Capitalism: How Money Managers Are Changing the Face of Corporate America* (New York: Basic Books, 1996), pp. 218–223.

52 In fact, when William O. Douglas was the chairman of the Securities and Exchange Commission in 1939, he called for directors to be outsiders. See, Judge George Thomas Washington and V. Henry Rothschild, *Compensating the Corporate Executive*, Third Edition (New York: The Ronald Press Company, 1962, p. 260.

53 National Industrial Conference Board, *Corporate Directorship Practices*, Business Policy Study No. 125, pp.7, 14. As an indicator of how directors were classified, the Conference Board studies on corporate boards considered former employees to be "outsiders" until 1973. The Conference Board, *Corporate Directorship Practices: Membership and Committees on the Board* (New York: The Conference Board., 1973), p. v.

54 Most of the studies on boards have been conducted by executive search firms. The first Korn/Ferry International study, "Boards of Directors Annual Study," November 1973 found that more than half of the 327 firms they surveyed had between 10 and 15 board members and, of those, four to six were insiders. p.5.

55 In 1977, the New York Stock Exchange required its listed firms to create board audit committees made up only of independent directors. See Joel Seligman. *The Transformation of Wall Street: A History of the Securities and Exchange Commission and Modern Corporate Finance* (Boston: Houghton Mifflin, 1982), p. 547. In 1977, the American Law Institute (ALI) initiated its Corporate Governance Project in response to the "ferment of corporate governance discussion." See, Roswell B. Perkins, "Thanks, Myth, and Reality," *The Business Lawyer* (April 1993) 48: 1313–1317 at 1313.

56 See, The Business Roundtable, "The Role and Composition of the Board of Directors of the Large Publicly Owned Corporation," reprinted in *The Business Lawyer* (July 1978) 33: 2083–2113.

57 Based on a study of the executive search firm, Heidrick and Struggles, "The Changing Board." See, Francis W. Steckmest, *Corporate Performance: The Key to Public Trust* (New York: McGraw-Hill), p.186.

58 *Ibid*, p. 187.

59 See, Stuart Spencer company, "Stuart Spencer Board Index, annual proxy reports, Board Trends & Practices at 100 Major Companies."

60 In 1993, the tax laws were amended to require that corporations must have outsiders control the board compensation committee in order for the firm to qualify for certain executive pay expenses.

61 The Business Roundtable, "Statement on Corporate Governance," September 1997, p. 10.

62 See, Directorship, "Significant Data for Directors: Board Policies and Governance Trends," 1999, which is a study of *Fortune* 1000 proxy statements; James Kristie, Editor, Directors & Boards, "Board Trends 1970s to the 1990s: 'The More Things Change…',", presentation to the Institutional Shareholder Services, Washington, D.C., February 1999.

63 The Conference Board, *Directors' Compensation and Board Practices in 2000*, 2000, p. 34.

64 See, Lorsch, *Pawns*, pp. 20–31; Robert A.G. Monks and Nell Minow, *Watching the Watchers: Corporate Governance for the 21st Century* (Cambridge, MA: Blackwell, 1996) pp.182–187; Ralph D. Ward, *21st Century Board* (New York: John Wiley & Sons, 1997), pp. 226–233; Anil Shivdasni and David Yermack, "CEO Involvement in the Selection of New Board members: An Empirical Analysis," *The Journal of Finance*, vol. 54, no. 5, October 1999: 1829–1853; Benjamin E. Hermalin and Michael S.

Weisbach, "Boards of Directors as an Endogenously Determined Institution: A Survey of the Economic Literature," Working Paper 8161, Cambridge, MA: National Bureau of Economic Research, March 2001; James D. Westphal, "Board Games: How CEOs adapt to increases in structural board independence from management," *Administrative Science Quarterly* (September 1998): 43:11–537; Eliezer M. Fich and Lawrence J. White, "Why do CEOs Reciprocally Sit On Each Other's Boards?," Working Paper No. 01002, New York University Center for Law and Research, December 2000.

65 See, William Benton, *The Economics of a Free Society: A Declaration of American Business Policy* (New York: Committee for Economic Development, 1944); Fortune, special issue, "U.S.A. The Permanent Revolution," February 1951; Robert T. Elson, *Time, Inc.: The Intimate History of a Publishing Enterprise, 1923-1941* (New York: Atheneum, 1968); Jeffery L. Cruikshank, *A Delicate Experiment: The Harvard Business School, 1908–1945* (Boston: Harvard Business School), 1987).

66 Sutton, *American Business Creed*.

67 See, David Vogel, *Fluctuating Fortunes: The Political Power of Business in America* (New York: Basic Books 1989).

68 See, Alfred C. Neal, *Business Power and Public Policy: Experiences of the Committee for Economic Development* (New York: Praeger, 1981) Committee for Economic Development, *Social Responsibilities of Business Corporations* (Washington, D.C.: Committee for Economic Development, 1971); The Business Roundtable, "Statement on Corporate Responsibility," October 1981.

69 McQuaid, *Big Business*.

70 See Edwin M. Epstein, *The Corporation in American Politics* (Englewood Cliffs, NJ: Prentice-Hall, 1969 ; E.E. Schattschneider, *Semisovereign People: A Realist's View of Democracy in America* (New York: Holt, Rinehart and Winston, 1960).

71 See, Kaufman, Zacharias, and Karson, *Managers vs. Owners*; and David Vogel and Leonard Silk, *Ethics and Profits: The Crisis of Confidence in American Business* (New York: Simon and Schuster, 1996).

72 See, Erik G. Furubotn and Svetozar Pejovich, "Property Rights and Economic Theory: A Survey of Recent Literature," *Journal of Economic Literature*, 1972, vol. 10: 1137–1162; Stephen Ross, "The Economic Theory of Agency: The Principal's Problem," *American Economic Review* (1973) 63: 134–139; Michael C. Jensen and William H. Meckling, "Theory of the Firm: Managerial Behavior, Agency Costs and Ownership Structure," *Journal of Financial Economics* (1976) 3: 305–360; Eugene F. Fama, "Agency Problems and the Theory of the Firm," *Journal of Political Economy* (1980) 88: 288–307; and Eugene F. Fama and Michael C. Jensen, "Agency Problems and Residual /Claims," *Journal of Law and Economics* (1983) 26: 327–349.

73 See, Allen Kaufman and Ernest J. Englander, "Kohlberg Kravis Roberts & Co. and the Restructuring of American Capitalism," *Business History Review* (Spring 1993) 67: 52–97; Henry Manne, "The 'Higher Criticism' of the

Modern Corporation," *Columbia Law Review* (1962) 62: 401–432; Henry Manne, "Mergers and the Market for Corporate Control," *Journal of Political Economy* (1965) 73: 110–120; and Baskin and Maranti, *Corporate Finance.*

74 See, John C. Coffee, Jr., "Liquidity Versus Control: the Institutional Investor as Corporate Monitor," *Columbia Law Review* (October 1991) 91: 1277–1368; and Thomas A. Smith, "Institutions and Entrepreneurs in American Corporate Finance," *California Law Review* (January 1997) 85: 1–78.

75 See, Useem, *Investor Capitalism*; and a critical review by John C. Coffee, Jr., "The Folklore of Investor Capitalism," *Michigan Law Review* (May 1997) 95:1970–1989.

76 See, John Pound, "The Promise of the Governed Corporation," *Harvard Business Review* (March 1995) 73: 89–99.

77 See, Kevin J. Murphy, "Executive Compensation," in Orley Ashenfelter and David Card, editors, *Handbook of Labor Economics, volume 3B*, (Amsterdam: Elsevier, 1999): 2485–2563.

78 The Business Roundtable, "Statement on Corporate Governance," September 1, 1997.

21 "From Shareholder Value to CEO Power: the Paradox of the 1990s"

from Competition and Change (2005)

Robert Boyer

SUMMARY

Why did CEO remuneration explode during the 1990s and persist at high levels, even after the internet bubble burst? This chapter surveys the alternative explanations that have been given of this paradox, mainly by various economic theories with some extension to political science, business administration, social psychology, moral philosophy and network analysis. It is argued that the diffusion of stock options and financial market-related incentives, supposed to discipline managers, have entitled them to convert their intrinsic power into remuneration and wealth, both at micro and macro level. This is the outcome of a *de facto* alliance of executives with financiers, who have exploited the long-run erosion of wage earners' bargaining power. The chapter also discusses the possible reforms that could reduce the probability and the adverse consequences of CEO and top-manager opportunism: reputation, business ethic, legal sanctions, public auditing of companies, or a shift from a shareholder to a stakeholder conception.

INTRODUCTION: A PUZZLING PARADOX

In the era of shareholder value, how should we explain the boom in managers', especially CEOs', remuneration, which persisted even after the bursting of the internet bubble? This chapter tries to disentangle alternative explanations of this paradox. It suggests a likely interpretation: the diffusion of stock options and financial market-related incentive mechanisms, that were supposed to discipline managers, has entitled them to express their *power*, not least in terms of the remuneration and wealth. This is the outcome of a *de facto* alliance of executives with financiers, who have exploited the long-run erosion of wage earners' bargaining power.

Why did such acute concern about managers' remuneration arise at the end of the 1990s and not before? Both corporate-related factors and the macroeconomic context seem to have played a major role in the emergence of the paradox of managers' compensation (section 2). The complexity of the forces that shape the performance of corporations and the incentives that govern managers' behaviour address challenging questions for economic as well as managerial theories of the firm. In a sense, the search for an optimal principal/agent contract is bound to fail precisely because the objectives of the managers and shareholders can never be totally reconciled. This article develops an unconventional interpretation of the seminal analysis by Jensen and Meckling (1976). Given the near impossibility of convergence towards a first-best pay system for managers, there is some room for an alternative approach, taking into account the existence of a significant managerial power within the modern large corporation (section 3).

The analysis is extended to a political economy approach. During the last half-century the relationships between executives, employees, consumers, finance and the State have been transformed. Taking into account the shifting alliance between these stakeholders casts some light upon the issue under scrutiny: how can we explain the unprecedented boom in executive remuneration, which runs far ahead of corporate performance in terms of value creation and shareholders' wealth? The answer is simple, if not trivial: managers have used the pressures of institutional investors and diverted them for their own benefit. This gives *ex post* the impression of a *de facto* alliance of managers with institutional investors. The shift has contributed to the process that had already curbed the bargaining power of employees; furthermore the financialization of the wage/labour nexus has imposed/induced labour to accept a larger share of risk (section 4).

The bulk of the chapter surveys the empirical evidence from the abundant literature about managers' compensation. Numerous converging statistical analyses confirm the rather large autonomy and significant power of managers at the firm level (section 5). Similarly, it is argued that the highly specific social and macroeconomic context of the 1990s has given managers renewed power in the political arena. Even economic policy and the tax system have been redesigned according to this new distribution of power between corporations, institutional investors and wage earners (section 6).

A short conclusion summarizes the core arguments and findings. It is argued that history does not stop there. Public opinion is infuriated by the persistent rise of some chief executive officers' (CEO) remuneration in spite of poor corporate performance and sharp stock market decline. This puts two other actors at the forefront: the lawyers and more generally the judiciary. Finally, the State, even though basically pro-market and pro-business, is compelled to intervene: the Sarbanes–Oxley legislation, passed in the United States under the pressure of recurring scandals, probably opens a new epoch for corporate governance with uncertain long-term consequences.

AT THE ORIGIN OF THE CONTEMPORARY CONCERN ABOUT MANAGERS' REMUNERATION

The history of intellectual representation of the corporation and its various legal conceptions in a sense mirrors the actual long-term historical process of transformation of business. Each of these conceptions tries to capture a specific feature that has been dominant at some epoch. Thus the complexity of the issue of controlling and rewarding managers cannot be understood without a brief history of the factors that have shaped the present position. For simplicity's sake, a contemporary query about executive

compensation may be seen as the most recent act in a drama that began more than a century and half ago.

The crisis of the previously successful managerial corporation

The first act takes place in the last third of the nineteenth century. In most industrialized countries, and especially in the United States, family-founded and owned firms encounter limits in capturing the advantage derived from the new technologies that required more capital and closer links with scientific advances. A wave of mergers makes clear the merits of the joint-stock corporation as a method of mobilizing dispersed savings. This is so for the railroad industry and then the chemical industry. The invention of a limited liability for shareholders plays a crucial role: individuals can diversify risk by investing in a portfolio of various traded companies. Thus the stock market and the bond market become highly liquid via the activity of buying and selling shares, quite independently of the irreversibility of productive capital and the everyday management of the company.

Consequently, there are two sources to the separation of ownership and control. On one side, family managers are replaced by salaried ones to whom the management of the firm is delegated. Incidentally, the division of labour that had taken place at the shop-floor level is also observed in the management of large companies. In a sense, managers tend to become bureaucrats in charge of taking rational decisions, informed by the advance of science, technology and management. On the other hand, individuals, as investors, enjoy the freedom to optimize the rate of return on their wealth by transacting in more and more developed financial markets in London and New York. By the way, except when scandals erupt, individual investors do not ask for close monitoring of the managers, provided they deliver a reasonable rate of return. It is the epoch of the triumph of the managerial corporation '*à la* Berle & Means': the *de facto* complementarity between the liquidity of saving and the specialization of management delivers an unprecedented dynamic efficiency, and therefore few criticisms are voiced by experts and public opinion on behalf of discontented shareholders. The only concern is about the risk of monopolization of product markets and concentration of capital, but these are mainly the complaints of the labour and socialist movements (Figure 21.1).

But the heyday of the managerial corporation does not survive into the 1970s. *Act II* begins when the previous favourable trends are reversed. The very diffusion of this canonical model to many activities finally triggers adverse trends. First, managers embark on excessive diversification with no clear synergy with their 'core competences', to use the term that will be proposed during the 1980s to promote the splitting of the large conglomerates. Second, this excessive diversification and the strains associated with the impact of near full employment upon labour discipline and work intensity trigger a significant productivity slowdown. Third, the oligopolistic nature of competition in product market erodes the innovativeness of the maturing large corporation, at the very moment when newcomers in Europe and Asia challenge the American way of doing business. These strains on the managerial corporation are correlated at the macro-level with the demise of the post-World War II growth regime: the productivity slowdown generates pressures on costs that are turned into price increases due to a rather accommodating monetary policy (Aglietta 1982). The stage is ready for Act III.

Value creation and shareholder value as disciplinary devices

The first reversal takes place in the conduct of monetary and budgetary policy. Conservative central bankers replace the Keynesian principles with a monetarist credo according to which inflation has to be curbed in order to move towards monetary and financial stability, at the possible cost of a growth slowdown due to high and unprecedented real interest rates. Since the real interest rate on bonds becomes superior to the dividend/price ratio on stocks, corporations accordingly have to adjust wages, employment and their investment decisions (Lazonick 1992). The bargaining power of wage earners is therefore eroded and this opens a new epoch for the evolution of the distributive shares between wages, profit and the revenue from finance. Financial liberalization defines the second structural transformation of the 1980s and 1990s: new financial instruments are created and diffused, especially in the United States and to a minor extent in the United Kingdom. Derivatives and stock options are good examples of the success of financial innovations. Consequently, financial instruments are more and more diversified and therefore attract new customers in response to an unprecedented specialization of

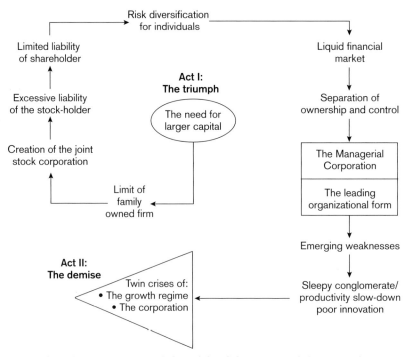

Figure 21.1 **Acts I and II: the emergence and the crisis of the managerial corporation**

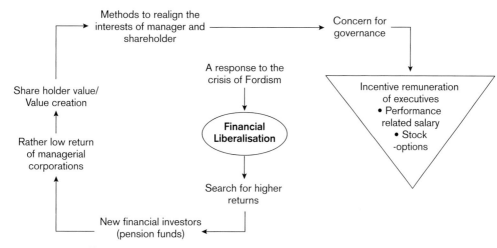

Figure 21.2 **Act III: disciplining the managers by shareholder value**

financial institutions and investors. A final shift, in the United States, concerns the transformation of pay-as-you-go pension systems into pension funds: the large and permanent influx of savings into financial markets improves their liquidity and depth and simultaneously increases the probability of financial bubbles (Orléan 1999). Furthermore, the concentration of the management of these savings brings a counter-tendency to the extreme dispersion of ownership: some pension funds may use not only exit (selling the shares of a badly managed corporation) but also voice (by stipulating conditions for approval of board decisions).

It is the epoch of *value creation*, and then *shareholder value* (Figure 21.2). In this context, the divergence of the interests of managers and owners emerges as a crucial issue. Why not try to align the strategy of top managers with the objectives of stock market value maximization on behalf of shareholders? The use of stock options is therefore widely diffused, not only to the traditional corporation operating in a mature industry but also to start-ups in the information and communications technology industry. In the former (traditional) industries, stock options are conceived as an incentive to good management and shift the strategy of CEOs from extreme diversification to concentration on their core business, and economizing on the use of capital. In the latter industries, a large proportion of personnel receive a modest wage but a significant number of stock options that can be cashed if or when the expected profits materialize. Incidentally, this reduces production costs and increases profits, since US accounting principles in the 1990s did not require stock options to be expensed in the income statement. The search for radical innovations and stock options as

a form of remuneration are closely associated in the vision of the 'new economy'.

Stock options are therefore central to American business in the 1990s: they are supposed to *control* the managers of mature corporations and *reward* the professionals and managers of the sunrise sectors. Act III seemed to promise a happy ending, but such was not the case.

Financial bubble and infectious greed: executive compensation under scrutiny

In fact the very optimistic views about higher and higher rates of return on equities drove the boom of the mid-1990s in American stock markets. What was supposed to be a rational method of generating value and wealth has become 'a casino economy' whereby everybody tries to get rich as quickly as possible, with little concern for the long-run viability of their strategy. The implicit rate of return of most of the start-ups of the new economy was implausible but nevertheless attracted investment from well established investment banks and institutions. The public were convinced by the financial and popular press that the boom in the stock markets was not a bubble but evidence of an unprecedented area for investment featuring totally new economic regularities. This was an illusion, since the divorce between the actual and the expected rate of return was bound to be recognized and hence reduced, if not by a progressive reappraisal, then by a brusque downturn in the financial markets. This took place in March 2001, when the internet bubble burst, generating an impressive series of bankruptcies: in a sense, the trajectory of Enron is typical of these new relations between corporate governance and financial markets (Figure 21.3).

In this context, the divorce between the supposedly rational goals of incentive pay and the effective use of financial, performance-related compensation is made clear by the multiplication of financial scandals and some spectacular bankruptcies. In retrospect, the surge of stock options appears as a method of fast wealth accumulation by top executives rather than a method of rewarding the quality of their management. The previous methods of controlling and rewarding managers are therefore under public scrutiny. Should this come as a surprise to the proponents of the indexation of top managers' compensation to shareholder value?

A MAJOR CHALLENGE TO ECONOMIC THEORY

Actually this issue is not so new. Since Berle & Means, economists have deployed two contrasting strategies. The first takes into account the transformation of the joint-stock corporation and finally adopts the *stakeholder* conception, with no primacy of shareholders' interests. A second considers that the discrepancy between the optimal profit-maximizing strategy and the actual strategies of managers should as far as possible be removed, in order to restore the primacy of shareholders. In periods of patient capital and a leading role for the banks in financial intermediation the first conception may prosper. When finance is liberalized, many new financial instruments are created and diffused around the world, and when professional

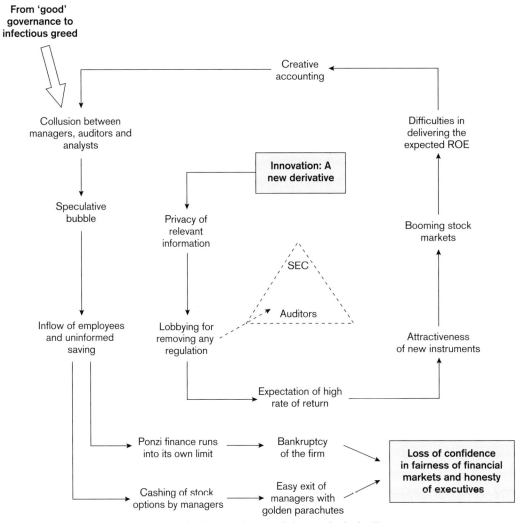

Figure 21.3 **How an alleged virtuous circle turns into a vicious spiral: the Enron story**

investors manage a large proportion of savings – especially pension funds – the issue of control and reward of CEOs becomes central and triggers a boom in academic research (Murphy 1999).

Back to Michael Jensen and William Meckling's seminal article

Within the patrimonial conception of the joint-stock corporation the problem is simple: the top executives are the agents of the shareholders, since they are hired by them in order to defend and promote their interests, namely their income and wealth. Generally speaking, principal/agent relations were already being used in the Roman empire within the rural economy, but the innovation of the manager/shareholder principal/agent relation is to mobilize specific economic incentives. What type of contract, including pay systems, dismissal conditions and fringe benefits, would realign the objectives of the CEOs with the interests of shareholders?

The literature offers a hint: in order to limit the distortion of CEO decisions in such a way as to benefit the CEO but reduce the value of the firm, a proportion of the capital should be given to the CEO in order to fill the gap between the patrimonial firm run by the owner and a joint-stock corporation under the supervision of a manager (Jensen and Meckling 1976: 221). This result has frequently been interpreted somewhat optimistically: adequate incentive mechanisms (profit sharing, stock options, linking CEO compensation to a performance index) could overcome the discrepancy between a first-best solution and organization, i.e. profit maximization, and the actual decisions of managers that may distort the strategy of the firm in favour of their own interests.

A closer look at the argument shows that the cost of agency cannot be reduced to zero, because the manager has to be compensated at the expense of shareholders, unless they are given all the capital and thus become an entrepreneur without shareholders. From a purely theoretical point of view, the dichotomy between management and ownership cannot be overcome. Whatever the pure economic and financial incentive mechanism, *there is a cost of agency* associated with the joint-stock corporation. A second wave of the literature has progressively recognized the limits of these incentives. For instance, Michael Jensen and Kevin Murphy (1990) are surprised by the low sensitivity of CEO compensation with respect to shareholder wealth (approximately $3 for each $1,000 change in stock market value). They hypothesize that public and private political forces explain this departure from what theory would suggest. This probably explains why other mechanisms have been proposed: the strength of a *corporate culture* may reduce the opportunism of the executives, or a form of *business ethic* may play the same role. But this overestimates the degree of conformity to social norms and their effectiveness, at odds with the principle of individualism that is at the centre of modern societies. This is the reason why alternative methods of dealing with the agency problem have been proposed and, indeed, implemented.

A whole spectrum of incentives and constraints

Many CEO pay systems coexist and deliver different outcomes in terms of free cash flow, investment, diversification, risk, innovation policy and the choice between internal growth and expansion via merger and acquisition. *A priori*, a compensation scheme could be tailored to any precise objective articulated by the board that would transmit the will of shareholders (and other stakeholders if they are represented). Within the conventional patrimonial conception of the corporation, many devices have been proposed in order to control and reward managers (Table 21.1).

The value of the stock of the corporation is only one possible reference index, since *a bonus payment* can be indexed to profits, measured according to various definitions. If financial markets are imperfect, inefficient, and if stochastic shocks affect the firm's results and its stock market value, then profit-related pay systems and stock options are far from equivalent. Furthermore, stock options are different from the attribution of stock to the managers. A basic divergence relates to accounting rules: until recently, stock options were not taken into account as costs, whereas a profit-sharing mechanism would explicitly affect the financial situation of the corporation. The various components of CEO compensation – wage, bonus, stock options, fees for sitting on boards, special credit terms, severance payment, contribution to retirement – do not attract the same rate of tax. Thus, indirectly, government may influence the form of CEO compensation.

Incentive pay is not the only mechanism: shareholders' access to information about CEO remuneration may trigger their demands for control of those payments, on top of the activities of any remuneration committee. Simple *transparency* may have a disciplinary role when CEO compensation explodes at a time when their corporation is near bankruptcy. But such a mechanism can affect only major discrepancies between executive compensation and the firm's performance, it does not deliver the fine tuning that would be required for good governance on an everyday basis. Another avenue explores the role of the *independence* of the members of the remuneration committee: *a priori*, at each period they could adjust managers' compensation to actual achievement. The issue is the choice between an automatic rule and pure discretion.

But, for most economists, only competition can govern this complex process. If CEOs divert too many resources from an efficient allocation the undervaluation of the firm on the stock market will trigger a hostile take-over. In order to prevent such a take-over, the board should *ex ante* limit the opportunistic behaviour of top managers. The last-resort threat is, of course, bankruptcy. Back in the 1960s and 1970s large corporations were supposed to be 'too big to fail' but such is no longer the case. But, if bankruptcy is the last-resort deterrent against excessive CEO remuneration and bad managers, there is a more common mechanism, i.e. the creation of *a market for corporate governance*. Actually, the firing of CEOs has become more frequent and the duration of

Device	Rationale	Limits
Incentive pay		
Indexing wage on performance	Aligning managers' and rank-and-file workers' interests	Possible manipulation of performance by managers
Bonus linked to profit	Aligning managers' interests and firm strategy	
Stock options	Aligning CEO interest with shareholders' wealth	Still a major gap between CEO and shareholders' interests
Attribution of stock of the company	Aligning CEO interest with shareholders' wealth	Loosely correlated with CEO strategy and large benefits during financial bubble
Transparency		
Public disclosure of CEO's remuneration	Trigger *outrage* from shareholders and institutional investors	*Camouflage* tactic by managers in spite of statements in favour of transparency
Remuneration setting		
Creation of an independent remuneration committee	Prevent self-determination of remuneration by CEOs	The CEO may largely control the committee
Large number of independent members of the board	Prevent excessive remuneration to the detriment of shareholders	The income of members may depend on their generosity to the manager
Survey by consultant firms of CEO remuneration	Set an objective benchmark	The reference to average or median remuneration induces spill-over and excessive pay increases
Market for corporate governance		
Firing of CEOs	Incentive to committment	Exceptional configuration in the past
Threat of take-over	Puts a limit on CEO opportunism	Golden parachute for losers CEO income may increase even if shareholders suffer value destruction

Source: Inspired by Bebchuk and Fried (2003).

Table 21.1 How efficient are the various methods of controlling managers?

employment of CEOs has been reduced, especially in the United States. For instance, the period of notice for executive directors was drastically reduced between 1994 and 2001 (PIRC 2003: 8). This is an interesting development, since it could work as a Smithian solution to CEO remuneration: the creation of a fully fledged market for managers could provide an objective basis for determining their value. But this is to assume that complete recognition and assessment of the quality of managers is possible, and it is not at all evident, given the idiosyncratic nature of managerial talents. After all, the net profit of a corporation is the outcome of the mix of complementary and specific assets, including executive talents (Biondi *et al.* 2004). Therefore, generally speaking, the market is unable to fix a price for managers.

Clearly, all these devices are far from implementing shareholder value, since they are all constrained (see Table 21.1, column 3). Managers can manipulate the index of performance, not least by means of dubious if not illegal accounting practices. During financial bubbles the tide of speculation enriches those CEOs who benefit from stock options, but only a small fraction of the extra compensation is related to the quality of their management. Even when the bubble burst, it is quite surprising to note, some CEOs renegotiated their stock options in order to maintain their total remuneration. In 2001 the value of stock options granted to the CEOs of S&P companies, America's largest, rose by 43.6 percent in a year when the total return of those companies fell by almost 12 percent (*Economist* 2003). Similarly, in 2002 the median pay of the 365 CEOs covered by *Business Week* increased by 5.9 percent but the total returns of the S&P 500 companies were down by 22 percent (Johnson 2003).

Transparency is quite difficult to achieve, since part of the profitability of corporations derives from proprietary information, knowledge and technology. The public disclosure of CEO remuneration may trigger outrage from shareholders and institutional investors, but the more complex and diverse the compensation mechanisms the more easily managers can adapt their tactics and adopt camouflage. Similarly, independent directors and members of the board and remuneration committee are *a priori* desirable but do not necessarily overcome the large asymmetry of information and power between CEOs and those directors. Another mechanism may hinder the efficiency of the remuneration committee: the directors and CEOs may belong to the same web of boards,

so forming a network of mutual exchange of high remuneration (*Economist* 2003). Furthermore, the reference to the current remuneration of CEOs via surveys undertaken by remuneration consultants may have perverse effects: the reference to average or median remuneration generally triggers a spill-over of excessive increases. Last but not least, the frequent negotiation of golden parachutes even for the least successful CEOs drastically reduces the incentive for managers to be efficient and fulfil shareholder value and wealth creation.

From optimal contracting to a managerial power approach

Both the historical retrospective study of US corporations and the conclusions derived from transaction costs and principal/agent theory confirm that it is quite difficult to monitor executives in order to comply with the objective of profit maximization of shareholder value promotion. Therefore it is not surprising to observe during the 2000s a disparity between still booming executive compensation and poor stock market performance. This suggests that the normative theory of CEO compensation should be completed by another approach. One of the best candidate stresses *entrenched managerial power* (Bebchuk and Fried 2003) and it enlightens the apparent paradox that optimal contracting recurrently faces.

Here the diagnosis is quite different (Table 21.2). For optimal contracting, the opportunistic behaviour of managers should be controlled by the strengthening of competition on product, labour and corporate governance markets. More precisely, the recognition of value creation and shareholder value should be imposed on managers as a core if not a unique incentive mechanism. The managerial power theory develops a more Machiavellian vision: in order to minimize the outrage of shareholder and public opinion, managers adopt camouflage strategies. Similarly, the enthusiasm of investors for equity-based compensation is adopted and used by CEOs who thereby find a justification for large increases in their incomes. Whereas in the 1960s and 1970s executive wages were defined as a multiple of median workers' income, during the 1990s the larger part of their income was related to the flow of profit or the appreciation of their shares. Hence a device that was supposed to discipline managers has actually been distorted in order to extend their wealth to unprecedented levels (see Figure 21.10).

Optimal contracting	Managerial power
Diagnosis	
1 Opportunistic behaviour of managers	Minimize outrage, via camouflage
2 Market for capital, labour and corporate control are not sufficient	Enthusiasm about equity-based compensation benefits to managers'[a]
Solution	
3 Design incentive pay systems. Managers' behaviour optimizes value creation and/or shareholder wealth	Compensation consultants justify *executive* pay CEOs control the board in charge of the remuneration
Adverse effects	
4 Managers reap windfall income via stock price increase independent of their actions	Option plans that filter out windfalls are not in the interests of managers. Therefore they are not used[b]
5 The threat of take-over should discipline CEOs	Mergers and acquisitions justify higher compensation of managers but do not always increase shareholder value

Notes:
[a] 2000: CEO compensation was an average 7.89 percent of corporate profits in firms making up the 1500 company exe comp data set (Balsam 2002).
[b] 2001: 5 percent of 250 largest US public firms used some form of reduced windfall options (Levinston 2001).

Source: Inspired by Bebchuk and Fried (2003).

Table 21.2 **Two approaches to the control of managers**

Any reference to market benchmarking for CEO compensation may have the effect not of disciplining the remuneration committee but of triggering spill-over and escalation, whereby less well paid managers ask for median or average pay, which in turn raises average pay and thus initiates a vicious circle. Similarly, the shift from indexation of pay related to profit or cash flows to stock options is not without risk. First, the stock market valuation takes into account the macroeconomic situation, the level of short-term interest rate and sectoral effects, and does not exclusively gauge the contribution of the managers to the prosperity of the joint-stock corporation. Furthermore, there are a lot of stochastic elements and mimetism in the valuation of a firm. It is therefore risky not to filter stock market value by these macro and sectoral determinants. Second, and still more important, the net profit of any firm does not result from the optimal mix of substitutable standardized factors valued on the market. Almost by definition, higher than average profit rates derive from the complementarity of firm-specific assets: among these, the talents of the manager cannot be measured by a typical competitive market. Third, today's decisions of top executives lead to tomorrow's investments and the product/profits of the day after tomorrow. Stock options that can be used over a short period of time cannot capture the necessary long-term orientation of an efficient pay system.

This confirms the *merit of the managerial power approach* in explaining these features that are at odds with the predictions of *optimal contracting*. Option plans that filter out windfalls are not in the interest of CEOs. Mergers and acquisitions frequently destroy value instead of creating it, but the executives nearly always increase their compensation along with the size of the corporation. More fundamentally, CEOs by definition have access to insider information[1] and they are generally better informed of the specific sources of competitiveness in their firm than financial analysts working outside the firm. Even the most highly specialized analysts, who are experts in crunching financial data and gleaning *ad hoc* information during roadshows, are rarely able to capture the intrinsic assets and liabilities of a firm.

Controlling and rewarding managers: an issue of political economy

If the managerial joint-stock corporation is not more efficient and does not increase its share via the selective mechanisms of competition – both in product and financial markets – how should we explain the boom in CEO remuneration during the 1990s? Nearly all countries are affected, and the trend persists in spite of suspicion from minority shareholders and in the face of hostile public opinion. For instance, in France one still observes diverging trends of CEO remuneration and financial results for a significant number of corporations (see appendix, p.392). This article proposes a twofold explanation.

1 First, history suggests that managers have always been part of the leading alliance, reaching an accommodation successively with various groups. The novelty of the present period is an alliance with finance, at odds with the Golden Age of Fordism, when a compromise was struck with wage earners.

2 Second, there is a more theoretical and structural reason for this hegemonic role of managers. Where does the profit of any firm come from? Basically, from the idiosyncratic mix of firm-specific assets, and it is precisely the role of managers to organize the related complementarity such that they have significant autonomy in deploying their strategies and still more in informing outsiders about the financial situation of the firm.

Managers are the centre of shifting alliances, most recently with financiers

The current bargaining position of executives is the outcome of a series of long-run transformations in the relations between wage earners, consumers, financial markets, the international economy and the nation State. Three quite distinct periods can be distinguished.

The 1960s: an alliance between wage earners and managers in the Fordist growth regime

This period has already been mentioned by the brief history of the concept and the forces that shape the modern corporation. Actually the 1960s experienced a quite atypical accommodation between wage earners and managers. Given the strong bargaining power of trade unions, the pro-labour orientation of many governments and the high control over finance via a series of national regulations, a Sloanist corporation was built upon three premises. First, workers accept modern production methods and productivity increases in exchange for indexation of real wages to productivity (Aglietta 1982; Boyer and Juillard 2002). This creates a large market for mass production and sustains the multidivisional and large conglomerates (Boyer and Freyssnet 2002). Second, professional managers see themselves as wage earners and express their income as a multiple of the average wage. Third, financial markets are not in a position to exert a strong influence on the strategic choices of corporations. This *de facto* alliance of managers with wage earners triggers an unprecedented growth regime. Its economic benefits easily sustain the related social compromise (Figure 21.4). Paradoxically, this period was perceived by contemporary analysts as highly prone to conflict between labour and capital, whereas in retrospect the demand for higher wages and better welfare was highly functional for the growth regime.

The 1980s: internationalization erodes the old alliance

But such a regime was not to last for ever: its very success triggered adverse trends such as accelerating inflation, rising unemployment and more basically a degree of internationalization that progressively eroded the alliance between managers and wage

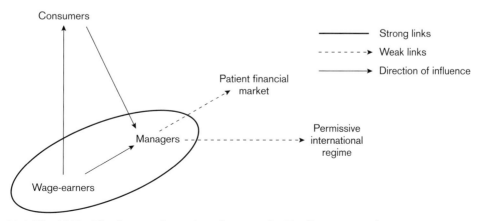

Figure 21.4 **The 1960s. The first configuration of actors: the Fordist compromise**

earners. Whereas the international regime was highly permissive in the 1960s, recurring external trade deficits put the question of competitiveness of firms at the centre of the political and economic agenda. Corporations had to restructure their organization and frequently slim down their work force, and this was quite a drastic reversal with respect to the previous Fordist compromise. During this period competition in product markets put consumers at the forefront, who are seen as gaining from external competition via moderation of the prices of imported manufactured goods. The competitiveness motive is invoked by managers in order to rewrite labour contracts and internationalization becomes the main preoccupation of governments. In a sense, the sovereignty of *consumers* plays the role of an enforcement mechanism in order to discipline workers, and managers cleverly used this device (Figure 5). Implicitly at least, managers invoked the role of consumer demand in the context of more acute international competition, in order to impose or negotiate a new configuration of the wage/labour nexus. During this period the adjustments required by a rather turbulent international

economy involved greater risk sharing by workers via flexibility of hours, the revision of the laws protecting employment and, of course, greater flexibility of wages and the slimming down of welfare.

The 1990s: under the rubric of shareholder value, a hidden alliance of managers with financiers

The internationalization of production has not been the only feature of the last two decades. Since the mid-1980s financial liberalization, the multiplicity of financial innovations and their diffusion from the United States to the rest of the world have drastically changed the conception of corporate governance as well as the conduct of economic policy. The conventional view is that joint-stock corporations in the manufacturing and service sectors have been submitted to the strong requirements of institutional investors. The power of these new players precisely derives from financial deregulation, and the high mobility of capital entitles them to demand changes in the rules of the game: higher rates of return on invested capital, profits that meet forecasts and financial analysts' expectations, and a steady flow of profits generated

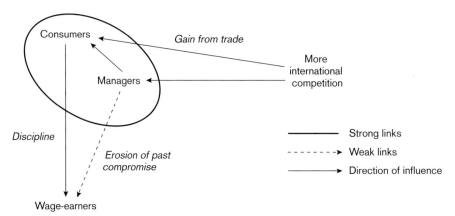

Figure 21.5 **The 1980s. The second configuration of actors: an international competition-led regime**

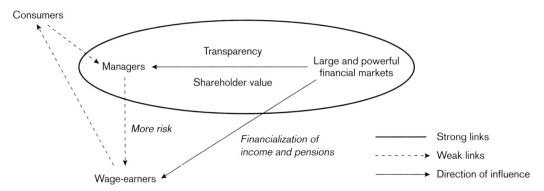

Figure 21.6 **The 1990s. The third configuration of actors: the alliance of investors and managers**

by the corporations. In the United States, and to a lesser extent in the United Kingdom, a finance-led growth regime has replaced the Fordist one, but the relevance of this model was not warranted in countries such as Germany or Japan (Boyer 2000). In spite of this divergence in national growth regimes, the ideal of shareholder value, or at least its rhetoric, has been diffused all over the globe.

Nevertheless, closer investigation suggests a more nuanced appraisal. Given the fad promoted by financial investors around the promotion of stock options, and the support of many experts in corporate finance, the objective of realigning the interests of shareholders and managers has been widely diffused, first in the United States, then in many other OECD countries. Cleverly, without necessarily admitting it openly, managers have used the demands of institutional investors to redesign their own compensation. On top of their salary, many forms of remuneration related to profit and stock market valuation have therefore been evolving, and they have drastically increased the total income of CEOs (see Figure 21.11). Top executives have been practising the art of judoka: converting the pressure of the financial community into a counter-move that benefits them and continues to erode the bargaining power of wage earners.

Thus, beneath the tyranny of investors, an implicit alliance between *managers* and *investors* takes place, and wage earners have to submit to a new wave of labour market deregulation (Figure 21.6). For instance, they have to bear a greater share of risk, so as to stabilize corporate rates of return, and to avoid the elimination of their jobs. The wage/labour nexus itself is transformed accordingly. First of all, the shift from pay-as-you-go pension schemes to pension funds generates a huge inflow of savings into the stock market (Montagne 2003), and this propels a finance-led growth regime in the United States. Second, in order to try to compensate for very modest wage increases, permanent workers accept various forms of profit sharing, and even gain access to shares in their company via special schemes. Managers have been reorienting their alliances, and this has definite consequences for macroeconomic patterns, *régulation* modes, income inequality and even economic policy formation.

The power and informational asymmetry in favour of executives

How can we explain this pivotal role of managers? A political economy approach suggests one inter-pretation: given their position in the firm, structurally managers are able to exert power within the economic sphere. Power relations are not limited to the political sphere: they exist in other guises in the economy (Lordon 2002). Many factors may explain a clear asymmetry both with respect to labour and to finance:

1 First, a mundane observation: executives make decisions on an *everyday basis* and directly affect the strategy of the firm. By contrast, boards exercise control at a *low frequency*, the control exerted by financial analysts is only *indirect* and in most OECD countries wage earners have *no say* in the management of the firm they work for.

2 Therefore managers built up *special knowledge* and competences that are not revealed to financial markets, competitors or representatives of labour. External financial analysts may gather statistical information about the firm and its competitors, but the real sources of profitability may still be hard to pin down from lack of familiarity with the details of particular corporate success and its determinants.

3 By definition, no *insider information* should be revealed or divulged to outsiders, since it might well be the source of extra profits. There is therefore a clear incentive to use such information strategically and opportunistically. Of course, insider trading on the stock market is illegal, but the everyday use of insider information and knowledge is not.

4 There is *a strong asymmetry of power and information* between the top managers and the various boards and committees. Members of the latter are appointed by the executives, the information they are given is assembled by the staff of the corporation, and, finally, the members of the board tend to belong to the same social network. Thus the probability of the agenda and the proposals put forward by the CEO being accepted is quite high. Similarly, during the general meeting of shareholders, minorities do not have the resources to put forward alternative nominations and proposals (Bebchuk 2004). Therefore the control of managers by auditors, financial analysts and shareholder organizations is exercised *ex post* and generally when the situation has become dramatic. Fine tuning the control of managers is difficult indeed.

All these arguments derive from the same central feature of profit generation. The *patrimonial conception of the corporation* assumes that profit derives from the mix of substitutable and generic factors of production, according to the prevailing system of prices. The basic hypothesis is that each factor is paid according to its marginal productivity. This model breaks down as soon as an organic conception is adopted: the corporation is defined by a set of complementary competences that are difficult to replicate. This is the source of the net profit of the firm (after interest payments). In effect, the entrenched power of executives is the mirror image of the ability of the firm to generate profits. It is therefore illusory to think that traders on the financial markets can know better than the managers the origin and causes of the success of a given corporation. Their informational advantage derives from statistical analysis of the macro and sectoral determinants of a sample of firms belonging to the same sector.

When the financial crises and scandals erupt, two new players: the lawyer and the activist
The bursting of the internet bubble in the United States and the financial scandals that affected the United States and many other OECD countries again shifted the previous alliances. Paradoxically, the instability of the finance-led growth regime could have been predicted, and the history of financial crises reveals that the situation in the 2000s is not totally new. Two new actors then enter into the plot.

Whatever the conflict of interest, the lawyers always win
Given the role of lawyers and the judiciary in the United States, it is no surprise to observe that the excess of greed of some managers has entailed the multiplication of lawsuits whereby disappointed shareholders or wage earners made redundant demand compensation from top executives. But since, the responsibility for problems is shared among a whole spectrum of professionals (institutional investors, financial analysts, auditors, rating agencies and fund managers and, of course, corporate managers), this is a wonderful opportunity for lawyers to extract a quasi-secure income: whoever wins the case, lawyers benefit from a positive and substantial fee. The key role of these players probably means the

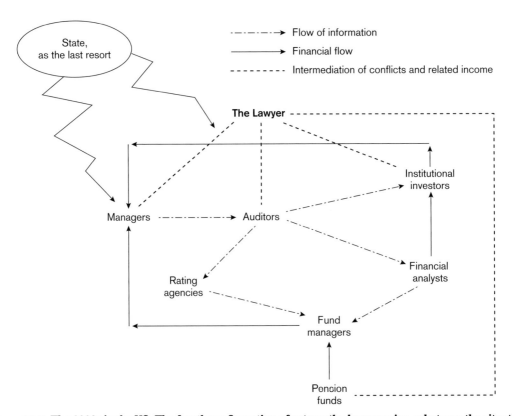

Figure 21.7 **The 2000s in the US. The fourth configuration of actors: the lawyer wins, whatever the situation**

disruption of the previous alliance between managers and financiers (Figure 21.7).

Public concern about financial regulation: domestic and international activists

Two final actors have to be brought into the picture. First, households that have lost a significant part of their capital do complain and may sue joint-stock corporations, pension funds, financial analysts and institutional investors. Second, activists make their voices heard demanding reform of the law on the responsibility of managers and financial intermediaries. Both domestic and international activists focus their criticisms and demands for reform on finance: the latter complain about the social cost of globalization, including financial globalization (Figure 21.8). The only way of converting these voices into action is by pressing the State to pass laws to try and curb the power of corporations and institutional investors. This is essentially a matter of domestic policy. Where the financial scandals have been most acute, new Bills have been passed, such as the Sarbanes–Oxley Act in the United States.

THE POWER OF MANAGERS AT THE FIRM LEVEL: MUCH CONVERGING EMPIRICAL EVIDENCE

In many of the previous configurations, top managers have a pivotal role, since they develop alliances with other social groups and these alliances vary according to the institutional, political and economic context. The previous hypothesis about the intrinsic power of managers, at both the micro and the macro level, is difficult to test fully and directly, but much scattered evidence suggests the existence and permanence of such a power.

Insider trading: a manifest use of strategic information

Top managers and members of the board of directors of publicly traded corporations possess more information about their company than the individual shareholder or even professional analysts. Given this asymmetry, insider trading conveys some information to outsiders, and this may contribute to the efficiency of the stock market. Generally the literature

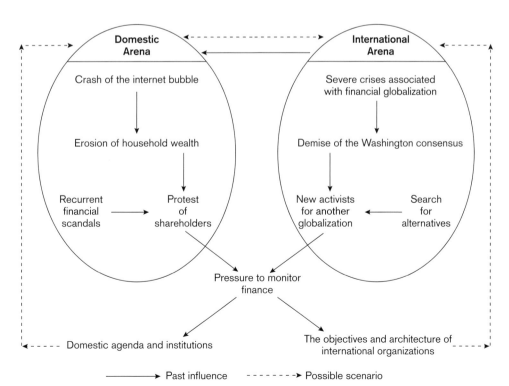

Figure 21.8 **The 2000s. The fifth configuration of actors: the threat of State intervention in order to discipline global finance**

finds that stock prices increase after publicly announced grants of stock options to executives (Yermack 1997). Two opposing interpretations might be given to this phenomenon. Either the incentive mechanisms of stock options trigger better management that is afterwards translated into more profits and higher stock market prices. Or executives time their option grants in anticipation of news which may be likely to boost stock prices.

A recent study of UK listed companies (Fidrmuc *et al.* 2003) does confirm that market reaction to the announcement of directors' purchases is positive and, conversely, that the announcement of directors' sales induces a decline in the stock market. The mere observation of the sequence of announcements and returns suggests that the second hypothesis is likely. In fact, insider purchases are associated with a prior decline in the rate of return and, conversely, insider sales are observed after a period of abnormal positive returns. This could be a sign of strategic behaviour by managers and directors.

The diffusion of stock option plans: a response to shareholder value

If, in theory, stock options are supposed to discipline managers according to the interests of shareholders, the idea cannot be excluded that managers use this pressure in order to increase their total compensation. Such a hypothesis comes out from a comparison of CEO pay in the United States and the United Kingdom (Conyon and Murphy 2000).

First, *the timing of the diffusion of stock option plans* is quite different in the two countries. In the United States the top executives of the S&P 500 have regularly benefited from stock option plans since the 1980s and they experienced a new increase in this frequency during the 1990s. What was new in the 1990s was the diffusion to small and medium-capitalization firms of this type of remuneration for executives (Figure 21.9). In the United Kingdom the pattern of diffusion is U-shaped, with stock options almost non-existent in the early 1980s, followed by widespread diffusion until they reach a plateau, followed by decline since 1993. These contrasting trajectories could sustain the hypothesis that the unequal maturation of financial markets, including the diffusion of pension funds, may explain the differences observed in the structure of the remuneration of top executives in both countries.

Actually, *the structure of CEO compensation* is quite different in each country. In the United Kingdom, base salary is the largest element of total compensation, annual bonus is a secondary source of remuneration, whereas option grants represent only 10 percent of total CEO compensation. By contrast, in the United States, base salary is less than a third of

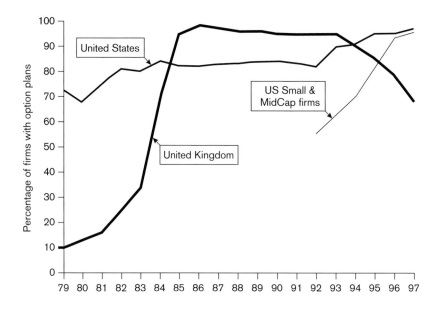

Source: Conyon, Murphy, 2000: 650. Reprinted with permission of Blackwell Publishing, Oxford.

Figure 21.9 **The contrasted patterns of stock option diffusion in the US and UK**

Group	Total pay (£000)		Average composition of total pay (%)				
	Sample firms	Average	Median	Base salary	Annual bonus	Option grant	LTIP shares	Other pay
United Kingdom								
All companies	510	589	414	59	18	10	9	5
By firm sales (£ million)								
Less than 200	152	452	287	64	17	10	4	5
200–500	119	403	335	61	19	8	6	6
500–1,000	116	601	507	54	20	10	12	4
Above 1,500	123	927	811	55	16	10	15	4
By industry								
Mining/manufacturing	217	564	436	59	17	9	9	5
Financial services	84	559	411	60	22	6	7	4
Utilities	19	448	382	58	15	6	14	8
Other	190	645	397	58	17	11	8	5
United States								
All companies	1,666	3,565	1,508	29	17	42	4	8
By firm sales (£ million)								
Less than 200	339	1,166	686	38	14	43	1	4
200–500	379	1,833	926	36	18	36	3	7
500–1,000	458	3,038	1,604	28	18	40	5	9
Above 1,500	490	7,056	3,552	20	17	48	5	10
By industry								
Mining/manufacturing	842	3,388	1,540	28	17	43	3	8
Financial services	198	6,277	2,787	19	20	47	5	8
Utilities	120	1,333	707	43	15	23	6	13
Other	506	3,326	1,438	32	16	43	3	6

Source: Conyon and Murphy (2000: 646).

Table 21.3 **Differing structures of CEO compensation in the UK and the US, 1997**

CEO compensation, while stock options represent the largest source of income for top executives (Table 21.3). Total pay doubles in the United Kingdom only when the size of the firm goes from less than £200 million to more than £1.5 billion, but in the United States this remuneration is multiplied by more than six times for the same range of size. Lastly, the United States displays an interesting feature: CEO remuneration is far higher in financial services, nearly double average remuneration, and option grants in this sector are the major source of total compensation. This is further evidence of the financialization of corporate remuneration that starts in the financial sector and then diffuses to other sectors.

The divergence of CEOs' remuneration between the United Kingdom and the United States is confirmed by the most recent studies that provide data for the early 2000s (Erturk *et al.* 2005). The CEOs of the FTSE 100 receive 74.5 percent of their compensation by way of basic pay, whereas the share of base salary is only 11.5 percent for CEOs running S&P 500 companies. Conversely, cashed options are more than 71.2 percent of total compensation of the largest quoted American companies. These findings are congruent with the general hypothesis that shareholder value has permeated American corporations more easily than British ones. Thus American managers have been able to capture a larger remuneration via the adoption of stock option plans.

The larger the corporation the less the CEO pay/performance sensitivity

If the hypothesis that stock options were designed as an incentive mechanism in order to control the opportunistic behaviour of those CEOs in charge of the large quoted corporations, we should observe greater responsiveness of CEOs' compensation as the size of the company increases. Quasi-unanimously the econometric literature finds the opposite result. For instance, Conyon and Murphy (2000) find that the pay/performance sensitivity is about 0.07 for small companies but only 0.02 for the largest ones in the United States. Similar results emerge from the British data: pay/performance sensitivity is around 0.05 for small companies and decreases relentlessly along with size (only 0.003 for the largest companies; Table 21.4). Of course, this is not necessarily evidence of the immunization of large corporations' CEOs from the market's evaluation of their performance. Rather, the estimated coefficient combines the impact of the size and the elasticity of CEO remuneration.

There is more evidence of significant autonomy in the determination of CEO remuneration: the mechanism of stock options itself gives them room for manoeuvre. If the options are under water, CEOs suffer no downward adjustment of their actual remuneration, since the only loss is unseen, thanks to the gap between the actual performance of the company on the stock market and that which was expected when the stock options were granted. Conversely, exceptional performance by the company is rarely rewarded with an increase of the volume of stock options (Stathopoulos *et al.* 2005).

The surge in mergers and acquisitions: a benefit for the managers, less often for shareholders

Additional evidence of the power of CEOs can be found by considering the merger mania of the 1990s and previous episodes. On the one hand, most studies find no correlation between financial performance and the size of quoted companies (Main *et al.* 1995). On the other, total CEO remuneration clearly increases with size, especially in the United States (Erturk *et al.* 2005). Consequently, although shareholders would be likely to be interested in a cautious approach to external growth, CEOs usually have a different vision: big is beautiful, especially for their remuneration. Therefore if the financial markets are highly liquid, and if a financial bubble distorts the valuation of the company, it is very tempting for CEOs to use mergers and acquisitions in order to expand their turnover and the capital they control.

These conditions were precisely fulfilled in the US stock market during the 1990s: once again, a merger mania was rife in spite of the robust evidence that previous episodes have generally been quite detrimental to the rate of return of the companies that embarked on mergers and acquisitions (Kaplan 2000). The internet bubble was no exception: *ex post* it is clear that the start-ups of the new economy have globally been destroying stock market value, whilst the

Group	Share holdings (£ million)		Share holdings (% of common)		Option holdings (% of common)		Pay/performance sensitivity (%)	
	Average	Median	Average	Median	Average	Median	Average	Median
United Kingdom								
All companies	7.01	0.46	2.13	0.05	0.24	0.11	2.33	0.25
By firm sales (£million):								
Less than 200	9.86	1.41	4.38	0.63	0.38	0.21	4.72	1.09
200 to 500	9.50	0.70	2.55	0.14	0.24	0.14	2.75	0.42
500 to 1,500	4.55	0.13	0.76	0.02	0.19	0.12	0.91	0.16
Above 1,500	3.40	0.33	0.21	0.01	0.10	0.04	0.31	0.05
United States								
All companies	60.37	3.26	3.10	0.29	1.18	0.72	4.18	1.48
By firm sales (£million):								
Less than 200	16.63	2.07	5.32	0.96	1.84	1.37	6.98	3.65
200 to 500	23.84	2.93	3.94	0.58	1.39	0.94	5.20	2.05
500 to 1,500	32.25	2.64	2.36	0.25	1.12	0.70	3.43	1.26
Above 1,500	145.26	4.96	1.61	0.09	0.62	0.40	2.17	0.56

Source: Conyon and Murphy (2000: 655).

Table 21.4 **Statistics for stock-based CEO incentives by size**

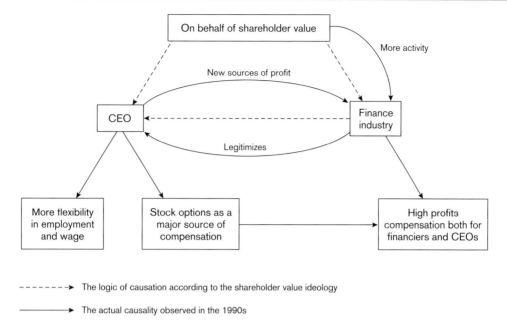

Figure 21.10 **From the rhetoric to the reality of shareholder value**

so-called mature industries have been more profitable than the sunrise industries. Nevertheless, the compensation of CEOs has rocketed, largely owing to the fact that the speculative wave lifted nearly all stock market prices, regardless of the company.

This is fresh evidence of the implicit alliance between CEOs and top executives, on the one hand, and between investment banks and high-level financiers on the other. The former group enjoyed rapid rises in their total remuneration, while the latter group were able to generate larger and larger profits, by the multiplication of the fees associated with merger and acquisition operations and active portfolio management, for example on behalf of pension funds. The average shareholder saw only a fraction of the total financial gains, precisely because operational costs have been increasing with the sophistication of financial methods. Thus, beneath the shareholder value rhetoric, an implicit alliance between the financial industry and top corporate management seems to have been at work during the 1990s (Figure 21.10).

Clear windfall profits for managers benefiting from stock options

The intensive use of stock options in the United States was supposed to align the strategies of CEOs with the interests of shareholders. It has already been argued

that, at the *micro* level, such an alignment of interests can never be perfect. New sources of discrepancies also emerge when the firm is considered in the *macroeconomic* context (Figure 21.11):

1 First, the contemporary financial performance of a firm is largely shaped by the decisions taken by previous CEOs, given the large time lag between an investment (particularly research and development expenditure) and its impact on the competitiveness of the firm. Actually the *time horizon of financial valuation* by stock markets is far shorter than the *time of maturation of innovation* and productive investment. The car industry and even more so the biotech sector are good examples where such time lags may cover one or two decades.

2 There is a second source of discrepancy between stock options and the actual merits of CEOs. During the second half of the 1990s fast and stable growth with little inflation resulted in very *low interest rates*, thus generating and diffusing *a speculative bubble* that had no direct correlation with the quality of management (Boyer 2004). Bad and good managers benefited equally from the common belief that a new growth regime had emerged, and that profit could only grow and thus sustain unprecedented rates of return on capital invested.

3 A third limit of stock options derives from the fact that financial markets are generally *micro-efficient* (i.e. in valuing the relative price of stocks) but *macro-efficient* in the sense that they are not immune to poor intertemporal allocation of capital: over-confidence and mimetism are the response to the typical uncertainty of highly liquid financial markets, thus generating speculative bubbles (Orléan 1999). During such speculative periods the compensation of CEOs bears no clear relation to their contribution to the performance of the company they run.

These three mechanisms (path dependence and chance, the impact of the macroeconomic context and the imperfection of financial markets) totally distort the core virtuous circle envisaged by the proponents of stock options (Figure 21.11.)

These divergences between the incentive mechanism of stock options at the micro-level and their macro-determinants have had a major impact in the skyrocketing of CEO remuneration from 1995 for shareholders and CEOs benefiting from stock options.

In reality, since the early 1980s, the increase in the share price has represented between two-thirds and three-quarters of the total return to shareholders. This is a rough approximation of the overvaluation of CEO compensation during this period.

CEOs have asymmetrical power on the remuneration committee

In large US corporations the compensation level of chief executives is set by a remuneration committee. The conventional wisdom states that the independent board of directors safeguards shareholders' interests and reduces opportunism on the part of management. But neither social science theory nor empirical studies confirm this optimistic view (Main *et al.* 1995). From a theoretical standpoint, CEOs have at least three trump cards compared with the members of the remuneration committee:

1 The first bias in favour of top management may be termed *cognitive*: insiders such as CEOs have a

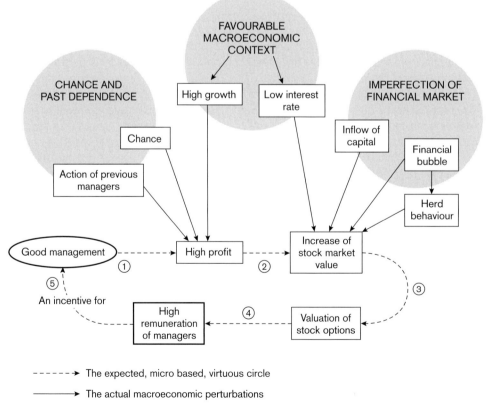

Figure 21.11 **Why stock options do not sort out the contribution of managers to the performance of the corporation**

better knowledge of the company's activities, strengths and weaknesses than outsiders. Furthermore, the executives and financial officers control the information issued to the various boards as well as to the financial markets. This first asymmetry is obvious when one considers the average time spent by independent directors in controlling corporate management as compared with the full-time activity of top executives.

2 *Social psychology* points out a series of other small-group mechanisms that come into play on the board of directors or/and remuneration committee. The principle of reciprocity plays a role in the escalation of remuneration, since the members of the board and CEOs tend to belong to the same closely knit social group. The respect due to the authority of the CEO is a second factor that may explain why top executives are overpaid with respect to an accurate assessment of their contribution to the performance of the firm. A third mechanism relates to similarity and potential liking for members of the same 'small world' (Temin 1999).

3 The issue of *power* introduces a third asymmetry between CEOs and members of the various boards. Who nominates whom? If the CEO is nominated before the remuneration committee, econometric studies show this has a positive impact upon the level of the CEO's remuneration, particularly when they can nominate economic

variables that capture the performance of the corporation in a way that is likely to be advantageous in determining pay.

In fact some econometric studies based on *Business Week* compensation surveys (as far back as 1985) confirm the prevalence of these asymmetries in favour of top executives (Main *et al.* 1995: 317–18). One interesting and one surprising result emerge. On one hand the ability of the board to monitor CEO performance and set pay appears greater in owner-controlled firms. On the other, CEO compensation is higher when the directors are independent! This is the exact opposite of the prognosis put forward by the advocates of transparent corporate governance.

After 1997, a favourite corporate strategy: distorting the profit statements

The relative autonomy of top executives, including CEOs and CFOs, is significant in relation to the information provided to capital markets. In this respect, the American system permits significant freedom in the interpretation of the general principles of accounting. In fact, during the Internet bubble, many firms used and abused this opportunity (Himmelberg & Mahoney 2004). In retrospect, the overestimation of corporate profit is so large that the *ex post* accurate

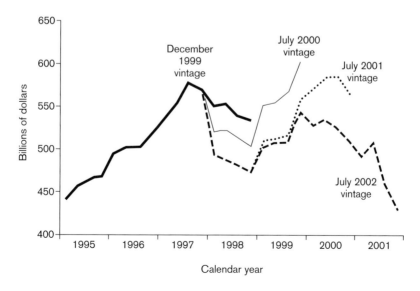

Source: Himmelberg and Mahoney (2004), p. 10.

Reproduced with permission of the Federal Reserve Board.

Figure 12 **The systematic overstatements of profits after 1997: as slow process of adjustment in the US.**

figures show a *reduction* of corporate profit after 1997, whereas *ex ante*, until July 2001, corporations had persistently announced an ongoing *rise* in their profits (Figure 21.12).

Such a discrepancy between real-time private information and *ex post* public evaluation in the American national accounts might have many sources. First of all, the accounting rules are not the same for corporate and national accounts, although this cannot explain the discrepancy shown in Figure 21.12, where the Bureau of Economic Analysis estimates have been elaborated using the same set of rules. A second and quite important source of discrepancy relates to an *unexpected surge in employee stock options exercised* during the second half of the 1990s. During this period, stock options were not regarded as a cost by corporations and were thus not expensed in the income statement. This contributed to the upward spiralling of stock markets: the shift of employee remuneration from basic wage to stock options increases corporate profit, leading to higher valuation of the corporation's shares and, finally, new incentives to award stock options to a broader category of personnel. Of course, CEOs and CFOs have been the key beneficiaries of this trend.

From the mid-1990s to the early 2000s two independent surveys show that the share of stock options exercised in total corporate profit has steadily increased. For the Bureau of Economic Analysis they represented 12.4 percent in 1997 and grew continuously until the 2000s, when they represented nearly 39 percent of corporate profits. According to a survey by *Business Week* (2003: 38), option expenses as a percentage of net earnings of S&P companies

represented only 2 percent in 1996, 8 percent in 2000 and finally 23 percent in 2003 (Table 21.5).

Nevertheless, a third and more problematic strategy has to be brought into the picture in order to explain the diverging evaluations in Figure 21.12: quoted corporations have intentionally inflated their profit statements, largely using the flexibility of Generally Accepted Accounting Principles (GAAP), playing the game of *creative accounting* and in some extreme cases using lies in order to bolster the rise in their share prices (Enron, Worldcom, Ahold). This is the unintended fall-out of the conjunction of shareholder value and the convention of a required return on equity (ROE) of 15 percent. Such a target cannot be reached on a permanent basis by the majority of firms and sectors, so it is not really surprising if creative accounting has become one of the favourite disciplines taught in prestigious business schools and practised by CFOs. During this process CEOs, CFOs and top executives became rich, potentially or actually when they had the opportunity to exercise their stock options before the stock market nosedived. Again, this is further evidence of the discretionary power that benefits top management in modern corporations.

A last-resort weapon of CEOs: the shift from the transparent to the hidden

Corporate misbehaviour is a recurrent pattern in the history of financial systems. Lawmakers then pass new Bills in order to prevent the repetition of financial scandals that are detrimental to the transparency

	Stock options exercised as a percentage of after corporate profit			
	1997	1998	1999	2000
Stock options exercised	68.61	100.08	139.29	197.37
Profit estimated by Bureau of Economic analysis	552.10	470.00	517.20	508.20
Stock options exercised compared with profit	12.40	21.30	26.90	38.80

Source: Himmelberg and Mahoney (2004: 10).

	Options expenses as a percentage of net earnings for S&P companies			
	1996	1998	2000	2002
	2	5	8	23

Source: The analyst's accounting observer in *Business Week*, 20 July 2003, p. 38.

Table 21.5 **Two evaluations of the impact of stock options on corporate profits in the US**

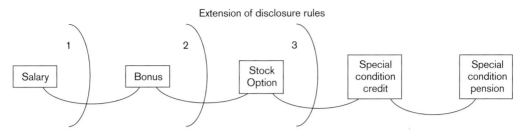

Figure 21.13 **From the transparent to the non apparent: the trickle down strategy of CEOs about their compensation**

required in order to foster and sustain the confidence of savers in the fairness of financial markets. The Sarbanes–Oxley legislation is no exception, but will it overcome the divergence in the interests of top executives and shareholders? Not necessarily, given the structural power exerted by CEOs at the corporate level. A brief retrospective analysis of the evolution of disclosure rules suggests a cautious approach to the issue of how managers are rewarded and controlled (Figure 21.13).

First the salaries of top management had to be made public, then disclosure was extended to bonuses and more recently to stock options, but none of it has prevented the use and abuse of this quite specific and not very efficient form of remuneration. The financial press has pointed out that even after implementing quite unsuccessful strategies some CEOs have left their corporations not only with golden parachutes but also with access to special personal credit facilities and, in some instances, special pension provision. Significantly, financial markets were oblivious to such conditions. This means that, even if legislation brings control over an extended share of CEO remuneration, such executives will still be able to devise new and innovative methods of gaining access to other and hidden (at least transitorily) forms of compensation.

The financialization of CEO compensation: the consequence of the internal restructuring of the divisions of the quoted corporation

The transformation of the structure of CEO compensation suggests another interpretation derived from the history of the internal organization of large American corporations. In the early days of the so-called American mass-production system stands the emblematic figure of an *engineer* who conceives new production methods and products: Henry Ford is a

good example of such a view of the corporation. But the implementation of mass production triggered many problems with the work force (high turnover, strikes, absenteeism, poor product quality). Thus *Personnel Management* becomes an important division of the large corporation. During the inter-war period, one of the issues was the discrepancy between the explosion of mass production with a still limited market, due to an income distribution distorted in favour of the wealthiest stratum of the population. Such an imbalance meant that *Marketing and Design* became increasingly important corporate departments. Together these elements helped to deliver the configuration of the American corporation that emerged during the Golden Age of Sloanism.

But progressive financial liberalization triggered a series of innovations that called for the specialization of top management in *financial asset management*. Since the mid-1980s the chief financial officer (CFO) has become a central figure in the American corporation. Whereas the expertise of the engineer, like that of the production system specialist, was largely specific to a sector, a product, a method of production or a certain type of equipment, financial management is much more homogeneous across corporations. Furthermore, in the era of global finance, the ability to generate financial profits by clever portfolio management has contributed to the performance of corporations that used to be focused on manufacturing and marketing. Last, but not least, the rise of the CFO fits quite well with the growing role of direct finance, since the CFO is in a good position to deal with institutional investors, analysts, trusts and pension funds and to convince them to buy shares in his/her company (Figure 21.14).

This shift in the distribution of power within quoted corporations may help explain at one and the same time the increasing share of stock options in the compensation of CEOs (Table 21.5) and the rapid increase in CEOs' total compensation: has the financial sector

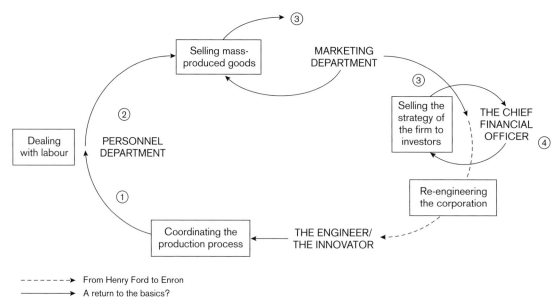

Figure 21.14 **The shift of internal control within the corporation: the rise of CFO as CEO**

been the promoter of higher compensation (see Table 21.3)? If one believes in the cyclical pattern of managerial strategies and fads, the bursting of the internet bubble and the rediscovery that mature sectors can provide a significant and stable rate of return could imply a comeback for the production manager, and by extension the R&D manager, as the key competitive assets of the large corporation.

THE POWER OF MANAGERS IN THE POLITICAL ARENA

It is now time to look beyond the inner *micro-structure* and functioning of the large corporation that give rise to the significant autonomy and power of top executives and explore how the insertion of the large quoted corporation into the social and political system has changed since the mid-1980s. The rise of CEO compensation and, in particular, the surge in stock options may find a series of relevant explanations at the *macro-level*.

Financial liberalization has been a prerequisite for the CEO compensation explosion

The internal shift in the hierarchy of the departments of the large firm shown by Figure 21.16 is closely

related to the transformation in the American growth regime. Clearly, the explosion of CEO compensation and the rise of the CFOs could not have happened under the Fordist regime, since finance was strictly regulated and the major issue was about the mutual adjustment of production along with (largely domestic) demand, in accordance with the then overwhelming reference to the Keynesian style of monetary and budgetary policies. But the crisis of Fordism back in the late 1960s opens a period of major structural change, including import penetration, labour market deregulation, and financial innovation and liberalization. Wage earners' bargaining power is therefore eroded and, correspondingly, managers have to respond more to the demands of financial markets and less to those of labour. The reform of pensions plays a crucial role, since it links the evolution of the wage/labour nexus with the transformation of the financial regime (Montagne 2003). On one hand, the influx of pension funds into the stock market increases its *liquidity* and thus makes the market prone to financial bubbles. On the other, financial intermediaries and institutions put forward the idea that *shareholder value* should be the only concern of quoted corporations. The financialization and explosion of CEO compensation are the logical outcome of the interaction of these two mechanisms (Figure 15).

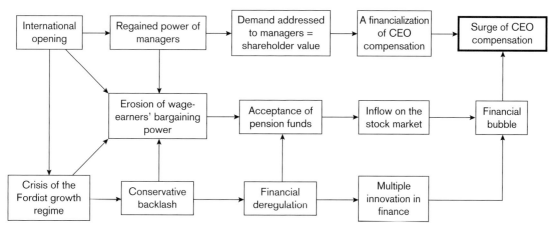

Figure 21.15 **The main episodes and factors in the financialization of executive remuneration**

When economic power is converted into political power

This explanation in terms of political economy usefully complements a typically micro-grounded analysis of the power of managers within the corporation. It is an invitation to explore how they convert their economic power into the ability partially to shape economic policy according to their interests. Over the last two decades, large corporations have used both *exit* and *voice* in order to be influential in the political arena. First, with the great opening up of national economies and the free movement of capital, the managers of multinational corporations have been able to redraw domestic labour contracts according to the requirements of the competitiveness of their domestic sites of production (see Figure 21.5). Second, they have sought lower taxation of profits, on the implication that they might otherwise take up the preferential treatment on offer abroad. Thus managers have been combining the threat of delocalization, i.e. *exit*, along with *voice* via lobbying in the direction of lawmakers.

During the post-war Golden Age there was an implicit alliance between a fraction of the managers and wage earners, and this compromise was also embedded in the style of economic policy: the search for full employment, the constitution of welfare, as well as high and redistributive taxation. Nowadays, implicitly or explicitly, governments are adopting pro-business policies: deregulation of labour markets, slimming down of welfare benefits, lower taxation of high incomes, and an accommodating concept of fair competition. This is the context that has encouraged the profound transformation in the economic and social position of top managers. The purpose of the next section is to offer some evidence in order to sustain the hypothesis put forward by Figures 21.6 and 21.10: the transformation of core economic institutions during the last two decades has consolidated and legitimized the power of top managers at the society-wide level.

Year	Effective federal tax rate	
	Median family	Millionaire or top 1%
1948	5.30	76.9
1955	9.60	85.5
1960	12.35	66.9
1965	11.35	68.6
1970	16.06	—
1975	20.03	35.5
1977	—	31.7
1980	23.68	—
1981	25.09	—
1982	24.46	—
1983	23.76	—
1984	24.25	—
1985	24.44	24.9
1986	24.77	—
1987	23.21	—
1988	24.30	26.9
1989	24.37	26.7
1990	24.63	—

Source: Phillips (2002: 96).

Table 21.6 **Contrasted evolutions of US tax rates for middle-class and wealthy families**

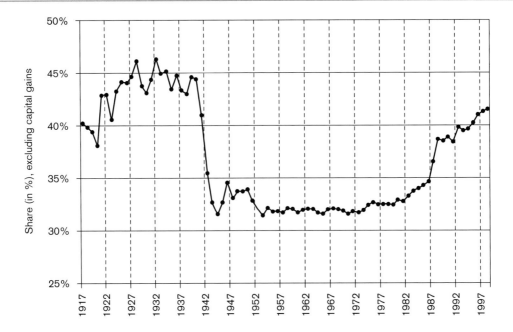

Source: Piketty, Saez (2003), figure 1, p. 11.

Reproduced with permission of MIT Press .

Figure 21.16 **The US: the top decile's income share. 1917–1998**

Year	share of total receipts (%)	
	Corporate taxes	Payroll taxes[a]
1950	26.5	6.9
1960	23.2	11.8
1970	17.0	18.2
1980	12.5	24.5
1990	9.1	35.5
2000	10.2	31.1

Note:

[a] Social security and Medicare

Source: Phillips (2002: 149).

Table 21.7 **The declining share of the US federal tax burden paid by corporations and the rising share of payroll taxes**

The general context of rising inequality

In retrospect, it is clear that the period 1950–70 saw a quite unprecedented reduction of inequality. The top decile's income share (representing nearly 45 percent in the 1930s) was drastically reduced to 32 percent after the Second World War. This proportion rose slowly from 1973 to 1987, before rising rapidly during the 1990s (Figure 21.16). This upward trend coincided first with the stiffening of foreign competition and labour market deregulation (1973–87) and then with the evolution of the American economy towards a finance-led regime (1988–97).

This rising inequality within households assumed a specific form in the United States, where the redistributive role of taxation (see Tables 21.6–21.7) and a limited universal welfare could not counteract the trends generated by labour markets. For nearly three decades – more precisely, from 1971 to 1995 – the poorest 20 percent of households experienced near stagnation of their real income after taxation. By contrast, the most affluent households became still more affluent, especially after 1987 and after 1995 (Figure 21.17). These shifts coincide with the dates of international pressure on American competitiveness (the mid-1980s) and the boom in financialization (1995).

The compensation of CEOs has been evolving within this general context. In the United States, over the last two decades, attitudes to the dividing line between legitimate and exorbitant inequality have been shifting. The question is then: how have capital and entrepreneurial incomes contributed to such a rise in the income of the richest 1 percent of the population?

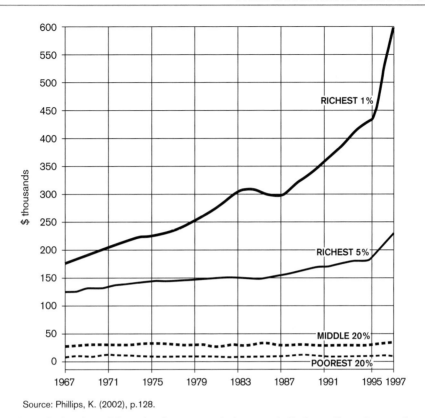

Source: Phillips, K. (2002), p.128.

Figure 21.17 **The polarization of America (1967–1997). Average inflation-adjusted annual tax income of poor, middle-class, and rich households**

The surge of entrepreneurial incomes contributes to the growing number of super-rich

A recent study compares the distribution of total income between wages, capital income and entrepreneurial income among the wealthiest 10 percent of the population at two periods, in 1988 and 1929 (Piketty and Saez 2003). Whereas in 1929 capital income represented 70 percent of the income of the wealthiest 1 percent of households, in 1998 this source of income represented only 10 percent, since the largest proportion of income is related to wages. Nevertheless, a quite interesting feature is that the share of entrepreneurial income is increasing steadily as we shift from the wealthiest 5 percent to the wealthiest 1 percent (Figure 21.18). Interestingly, the share of capital income is also increasing, but at most it represents 20 percent of total income for the wealthiest 1 percent. In comparison with the inter-war period, these data suggest two conclusions:

1 First, the wealthiest part of the population nowadays belongs to *the elite of wage earners* and they combine the two other sources of income, which complement rather than substitute for wages.

2 Second, the fact that income of entrepreneurial origin is increasing among the top percentiles faster than income derived from capital suggests that the *power of managers* has been more significant *than the power of financiers*.

Top executives have divorced from labour

More direct evidence of the power of CEOs can be found in the same research (Figure 21.19). Back in the early 1970s, the average compensation of the top ten CEOs was around $1.3 million (at 1999 prices), whereas the average salary was around $40,000. Since 1975 the trends of these two variables have been diverging: over a quarter of a century there has been quasi-stagnation of the average salary, while

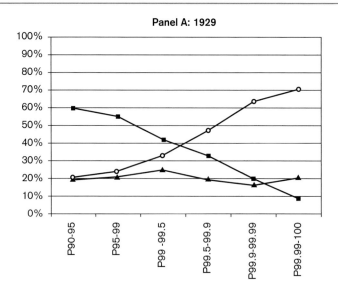

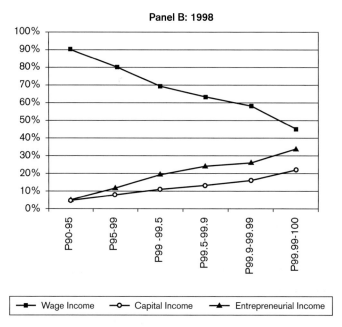

Souce: Piketty and Saez (2003), figure 4, p. 16.

Reproduced with permission of MIT Press

Figure 21.18 **The US: Income composition of top groups within the top deciles in 1929 and 1998**

rapid and quasi-continuous increases in the average compensation of the top 100 CEOs allowed pay to reach the level of $40 million in 1999. Again, an acceleration of CEO total compensation after 1995, i.e. the beginning of the financial bubble in the United States, can be noted.

These figures seem to confirm the core hypothesis of this article: benefiting from the competitive threat exerted by foreign competition, and even more so as a consequence of corporate governance of financialization, American CEOs no longer consider themselves as the elite of the permanent wage earners.

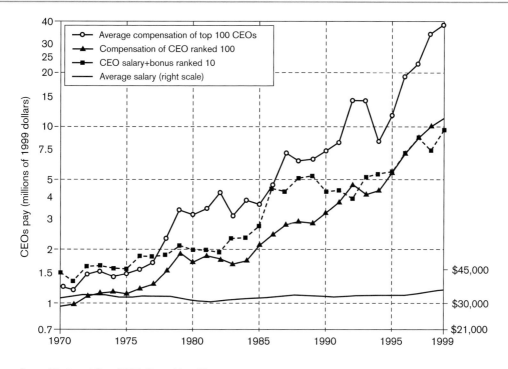

Figure 21.19 **The US: CEO pay versus average wage, 1970–1999**

Nevertheless, in Germany or Japan CEOs continue to see themselves as the upper stratum of wage earners. Not any more in the United States, where they are part of an implicit alliance with financiers.

The concentration of wealth goes along with stock market bubbles

In historical retrospect, the surge of inequality in terms of income, and even more so wealth, is closely associated with the waves of financial speculation, at least in economies such as that of the United States, where tax and welfare systems do not have significant redistributive effects (Figure 21.20). The previous developments suggest that top executives benefit more than the typical *rentier*, even though finance seems to play the leading role in shaping the objectives and organization of the corporate world. If financial markets constrain corporate strategies in the short run by their rapid changes in the value of stocks, in the long run executives of service and manufacturing firms do control the sources of profit.

The tax system is redesigned in favour of the wealthiest

In European countries, such a pattern is less marked and can be mitigated by intensive redistribution via progressive income tax, heavy inheritance tax and of course the role of universal welfare. Such is not the case in the United States, since rich individuals do participate in political debates and polls. Consequently, they are more efficient at lobbying in order to deliver reductions in the high-bracket income marginal tax than the underprivileged are at mobilizing in favour of redistributive measures.

Whereas the effective federal tax rate for the median American family has been nearly constant since 1980, after a significant increase since the 1960s, the shift has been in the opposite direction for millionaires and the top 1 percent wealthiest households (Table 21.6). Similarly, corporate taxes have been declining to very modest levels (10 percent), but payroll tax and welfare contributions are at 31 percent in 2000, up from 6.9 percent in 1950 (Table 21.7). This is new evidence in favour of *a political economy*

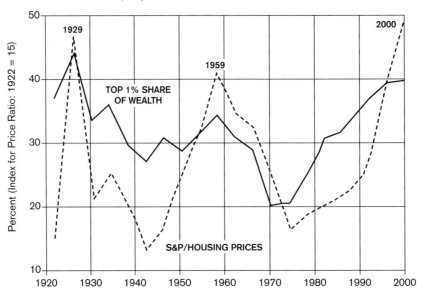

Wealth Inequality and the Ratio of Stock to House Prices, 1922–2000

Source: Edward Wolff, *Top Heavy* (New York, 1995), p. 30. Data from Appendix, Table A–1; US Bureau of the Census, *Historical Statistics of the United States*, Part 1 (1975); US Council of Economic Advisors (1992). Data and estimates for 1990s added by author.

Figure 21.20 **The US: wealth inequality and stock market peaks**

interpretation that links the political and economic spheres.

Considering all the previous evidence, it becomes clear that the power of managers is not restricted to the information and power asymmetry typical of any firm, and which is exacerbated in the large corporation. At the *society-wide level*, the rise of entrepreneurial income, the evolution of the conception of social justice (market allocations are fair), the revision of income tax, and finally the reduction in the share of corporations in total tax receipts confirm the hypothesis of a *renewed political power on the part of large corporations*, and especially of their top executives.

CONCLUSION: MANAGERS, FINANCIERS AND POLITICIANS

The main objective of this article has been to propose an explanation for one of the biggest contemporary paradoxes, i.e. the explosion of CEOs' compensation far ahead and frequently quite independently of the actual performance of their corporations.

The contemporary situation in historical perspective

The issue of the control and reward of managers is an integral part of the wider question about the nature of corporate governance in a world of largely open national economies and global finance. Contemporary concerns about the legitimacy and efficacy of stock option grants as an incentive for controlling managers have their origins in the crisis of the Sloanist corporation and the related domestic growth regime. The progressive opening-up to world competition, labour market deregulation and then financial deregulation, the rise of pension funds and the evolution of the bargaining power of unions have induced a dual shift. At the company level, restructuring has affected production organization but also shifted priorities to financial management. At the macroeconomic level, the previous model based on mass production and consumption has undergone a crisis, and after a long period of trials and errors the engine of growth has been the outcome of the synergy between financial innovations and the creation and diffusion of information and communication technologies.

The plea for stock options has no theoretical rationale

The arguments that have been used to justify the introduction of preferred stocks or stock options have proven to be erroneous by contemporary theories as well as by many empirical evidences. The interests of professional managers and owners can never be fully reconciled, and the diffusion of ownership makes the control of managers still more difficult. Incidentally, optimal contract theory would advise the use of indexed stock options that would reward only relative performance with respect to peers, filtering out the perverse effects associated with past dependence, lax monetary policy, macroeconomic and sectoral booms and last but not least the macro-inefficiency of financial markets. The fact that only a minority of stock options are indexed means that they are not at all endorsed by contemporary micro-analyses of principal/agent literature and the theory of contracts. The idea that stock options were the required complements to shareholder value and value creation has been invalidated by the evolution of the rate of return on equity of large corporations during the 1990s. Almost no empirical study finds a positive correlation between option grants and the economic performance of the firm. Repeated financial scandals have made clear the difference in the interests of and the returns for top managers and the average stockholders respectively.

The intrinsic power of managers at the firm level and its extension at the society-wide level

The observed asymmetry between top managers and stockholders finds its origins at the core of the objective of the firm: how to generate profits? The old conventional neoclassical theory states that profit results from the optimal combination of totally substitutable factors of production: labour, equipment and managerial talents, in response to their market prices. On the contrary, modern theorizing on the firm stresses that a positive net profit is the outcome of the combination of complementary assets and firm-specific competences: none of these factors can be bought or mimicked by the market, still less by financial markets. Who is in charge of generating these profits? Precisely, the top executives. The very reason that makes the firm efficient confers on CEOs and CFOs significant economic power. First, they have access to the relevant and private information that has not necessarily to be made public (for instance, about the real sources – and even the amount – of profit generated by the firm). Second, they have a better knowledge than shareholders, analysts or fund managers of the strengths and weaknesses of the firm, since they know the routines and the synergies that make the firm profitable. (Outsiders are best equipped to analyse the impact of macroeconomic/sectoral variables upon the evolution of the profit, not its internal determinants.) Third, CEOs and directors have the power to make decisions about the strategy as well as the day-to-day management of the firm. (Shareholders have only *ex post* control, mainly by exit, i.e. selling their shares, and annually they have a chance to voice their opinion and cast their vote on an agenda set by the corporation.) Managers' control over their remuneration largely results from this intrinsic asymmetry. In the era of financialization this superiority took the form of remuneration by stock options. In the past it had another form (salaries, bonuses), and in the future it will evolve toward new forms.

In the 1990s, in defence of shareholders, managers have converted this internal power into financial wealth, thus benefiting from the liquidity and the speculative bubble associated with the internet. Given the long-lasting erosion of wage earners' bargaining power and the shift of governments towards a pro-business stance, the business community has lobbied for reform of labour laws and the welfare and the tax systems. In a sense, the economic power of managers has been extended to include a significant dose of political power. For instance, the fact that stock options enjoyed privileged taxation status, and were not regarded as a cost to be taken into account in the evaluation of profits, created a virtuous circle of seemingly impressive company performance and the rise of stock market valuations.

This is why the optimal contract approach to the control and rewarding of managers is bound to fail, given the intrinsic power of top managers, the origin of which is related to the very sources of profit in contemporary capitalism. By contrast, combining a managerial power approach with a typical political economy analysis conveys a simple and rather convincing interpretation of the paradox under review. *Under the motto of shareholder value, managers implicitly allied with financiers in order to extend their power and remuneration.*

The search for a new form of corporation?

The limits of the current organization of quoted corporations have become clear since the early 2000s, and almost all countries are trying to cope with the issue of managerial control. This chapter has argued that there is no panacea but it has pointed to two possible items on the agenda of corporate reform. First, any move from a purely shareholder vision towards *a stakeholder conception of the corporation* would reduce the probability of managerial greed and erroneous strategic decisions. Second, no contract is self-enforcing and therefore some *other form of public control* of the accounting practices of quoted corporations is required in order to prevent an alliance between CEOs and auditors, at the expense of rank-and-file shareholders. Lastly, some macroeconomic contexts are more likely to generate speculative bubbles and allow excessive power to CEOs: when inflation and consequently interest rates are low, *de facto* the central bankers may be at the origin of financial speculation, and indirectly trigger quite detrimental strategies on the part of top executives. During the 1980s in Japan and subsequently during the 1990s in the US, *monetary policy* has been at the heart of erroneous business strategies and unjustified wealth from CEOs. All policy makers should learn from this episode.

ACKNOWLEDGEMENT

This chapter develops the ideas presented at the conference on 'Controlling and Rewarding Managers' held at the University of Manchester, 14 May 2004.

NOTE

1   For instance, Chauvin and Shenoy (2001) show that on average stock prices usually decrease prior to executive stock options grants.

REFERENCES

Aglietta, M. (1982) *Regulation and Crisis of Capitalism* (New York, Monthly Review Press).

Bebchuk, Lucian A. (2004) The Case for Shareholder Access: A Response to the Business Roundtable, SEC Round Table, 10 March.

Bebchuk, Lucian A., and Fried, Jesse M. (2003) Executive compensation as an agency problem, *Journal of Economic Perspectives* 17 (3), pp. 71–92.

Berle, A., and Means, G. (1932) *The Modern Corporation and Private Property* (2nd edn 1991, New Brunswick NJ, Transaction Publishers).

Biondi, Y., Bignon, V., and Ragot, X. (2004) Une analyse économique de l'évolution des normes comptables européennes: le principe de « juste valeur » (mimeo), Centre de recherche en économie, Saint-Goban, 24 March.

Boyer, R. (2000) Is a finance-led growth regime a viable alternative to Fordism ? A preliminary analysis, *Economy and Society* 29 (1), pp. 111–45.

Boyer, R. (2004) *The Future of Economic Growth as New becomes Old* (Cheltenham, Elgar).

Boyer, R., and Freyssenet, M. (2002) *The Productive Models* (Chippenham, Palgrave Gerpisa).

Boyer, R., and Juillard, M. (2002) The United States: goodbye, Fordism! in R. Boyer and Y. Saillard (eds) *Régulation Theory. The State of the Art* (London, Routledge), pp. 238–56.

Business Week (2003) Beyond options, European edn, 28 July, pp. 38–9.

Business Week (2004a) The best and worst managers of the year, European edn, 12 January, pp. 35–63.

Business Week (2004b) Corporate governance: investors fight back, special report, European edn, 17 May, pp. 53–67.

Chauvin Keith, W., and Shenoy, C. (2001) Stock price decreases prior to executive stock option grants, *Journal of Corporate Finance* 7 (1), pp. 53–76.

Conyon, Martin J., and Murphy, Kevin J. (2000) The prince and the pauper? CEO pay in the United States and United Kingdom, *Economic Journal* 110 (November), F640–71.

Economist (2003) Executive pay: fat cats feeding, 9 October, p. 37.

Erturk, I., Froud, J., Johal, S., and Williams, K. (2005) Pay for corporate performance or pay as social division? Rethinking the problem of top management pay in giant corporations, *Competition & Change* 9 (1) pp. 49–74.

Fidrmuc, Jana P., Goergen, M., and Renneboog, M. (2003) Directors' Share Dealing and Corporate Control (mimeo), University of Manchester.

Himmelberg, Charles P., and Mahoney, James M. (2004) Recent revisions to corporate profits: what we know and when we knew it, *Federal Reserve Bank of New York* 10 (3).

Jensen, M., and Meckling, W. (1976) Theory of the firm: managerial behavior, agency costs and ownership structure, *Journal of Financial Economics* 3, pp. 305–60.

Jensen, M., and Murphy, K. (1990) Performance pay and top-management incentives, *Journal of Political Economy* 98 (2), pp. 225–64.

Johnson, J. (2003) US: CEO pay continued upward spiral in 2002, www.wsws.org/articles/2003/ceo-j03_prn.shtml.

Kaplan, Steven N., ed. (2000) *Mergers and Productivity*, NBER Conference Report series (Chicago and London, University of Chicago Press).

Lazonick, W. (1992) Controlling the market for corporate control: the historical significance of managerial capitalism, *Industrial and Corporate Change* 1 (3), pp. 445–88.

Lordon, F. (2002) *La Politique du capital* (Paris, Odile Jacob).

Main, Brian C., O'Reilly III, Charles A., and Wade, J. (1995) the CEO, the board of directors and executive compensation: economic and psychological perspective, *Industrial and Corporate Change* 4 (2), pp. 293–332.

Montagne, S. (2003) Les Métamorphoses du trust: les fonds de pension américains entre protection et spéculation (thesis, University of Paris 10 – Nanterre).

Murphy, Kevin J. (1999) Executive compensation, in C. Orley and David, C. Ashenfelter (eds), *Handbook of Labor Economics* IIIb, pp. 2485–563.

Orléan, A. (1999) *Le Pouvoir de la finance* (Paris, Odile Jacob).

Phillips, K. (2002) *Wealth and Democracy* (New York, Broadway Books).

Piketty, T. and Saez, E. (2003) Income inequality in the United States, 1913–1998, *Quarterly Journal of Economics*, February, pp. 1–39.

PIRC (Pensions & Investment Research Consultants Ltd) (2003) Directors' Remuneration: Evidence to the Trade and Industry Committee (mimeo), London, PIRC.

Stathopoulos, K., Espenlaub, S., and Walker, M. (2005) The compensation of UK executive directors: lots of carrots but are there any sticks? *Competition & Change*, 9 (1), pp. 89–106.

Temin, P. (1999) The stability of the American business elite, *Industrial and Corporate Change* 8, pp. 189–209.

Yermack, (1997) Good timing: CEO stock option awards and company news announcements, *Journal of Finance*, June, 52, 449–76.

S
I
X

Appendix

The remuneration of French CEOs in 2003: discrepancies persist in respect of stock market evaluation and profitability

CEO	Company	Total salary, 2003 (€ million)	% change, 2002–03	Stock options allocated, 2003 (No.)	Income from directorships of other CAC 40 companies (€)	Change in stock price, 2003 (%)	Financial results, 2003 (€ million)
Lindsay Owen-Jones	L'Oréal	6.57	+4.6	1,000,000	95,720	-10.41	1,653
Edouard Michelin	Michelin	4.26	146	15,000	—	10.71	280
Antoine Zacharias	Vinci	3.03	n.a.	150,000	—	22.25	541
Daniel Bernard	Carrefour	2.96	11.6	Not disclosed	64,169	2.57	1,625
Daniel Bouton	Société générale	2.80	55.0	109,000	136,500	26.13	2,497
Igor Landau	Aventis	2.77	38.4	300,000	—	1.16	1,901
Patrick Le Lay	TF1	2.63	42.0	300,000	—	8.72	192
Thierry Demarest	Total	2.52	5.0	60,000	80,000	8.30	7,025
Martin Bouygues	Bouygues	2.49	19.8	200,000	—	4.13	450
Franck Ribaud	Danone	2.49	4.7	50,000	104,830	0.94	835
Jean-René Fourtou	Vivendi Universal	2.25	n.s.	1,500,000	349,680	22.21	-1,143
Jean-François Dehecq	Sanofi Synthélabo	2.20	10.7	150,000	—	2.49	2,076
Henri de Castries	Axa	2.09	34.7	904,496	—	34.60	1,005
Phillipe Camus	EADS	2.03	n.a.	135,000	—	91.37	152
Louis Schweitzer	Renault	1.97	20.0	100,000	74,210	22.15	2,480
Jean-Martin Folz	Peugeot	1.89	n.a.	60,000	32,460	3.96	1,497
Patrick Ricard	Pernod Ricard	1.88	-19.1	15,840	19,900	19.38	464
Serge Weinberg	PPR	1.87	6.90	60,000	30,490	9.34	645
Henri Lachmann	Schneider Electric	1.82	43.20	150,000	154,320	15.1	433
Gérard Mestrallet	Suez	1.77	-22.0	350,000	104,340	-3.69	-2,165
Michel Pébereau	BNP Paribas	1.72	-13.6	225,000	159,950	28.56	3,761
Thierry Breton	France Télécom	1.70	n.s.	No plan	66,580	56.87	3,206
Jean-Louis Beffa	Saint-Goban	1.66	1.2	240,000	20,960	38.80	990
Betrand Collomb	Lafarge	1.63	-9.1	100,000	108,920	3.39	728
Henri Proglio	Veolia environn	1.61	22.1	220,000	—	-4.14	-2,055
Jean-Marc Espalloux	Accor	1.53	-4.6	No distribution	80,083	24.39	270
Serge Tchuruk	Alcatel	1.53	n.a.	500,000	46,500	144.26	-1,944

Appendix

Continued

CEO	Company	Total salary, 2003 (€ million)	% change, 2002–03	Stock options allocated, 2003 (No.)	Income from directorships of other CAC 40 companies (€)	Change in stock price, 2003 (%)	Financial results, 2003 (€ million)
Pierre Richard	Dexia	1.41	17.0	120,000	—	16.80	1,431
Arnaud Lagardère	Lagardère	1.41	n.s.	Not disclosed	142,000	18.24	334
Benoît Potier	Air Liquide	1.34	28.8	No distribution	11,000	11.38	726
Paul Hermelin	Cap Gemini	1.21	32.3	135,000	—	61.66	−197
Jean Laurent	Crédit agricole	1.05	n.s.	Not disclosed	—	32.65	1,026
Jean-Philippe Thierry	AGF	0.92	−7.0	100,000	—	34.98	808
Charles Dehelly	Thomson	0.90	n.s.	No distribution	—	3.75	26
Guy Dollé	Arcelor	0.78	n.a.	50,000	—	17.92	257

Source: *Le Monde*, 11 May 2004, p.16.

Index